COMMENTARY ON THE LAW OF PRIZE AND BOOTY

NATURAL LAW AND
ENLIGHTENMENT CLASSICS

Knud Haakonssen
General Editor

Hugo Grotius

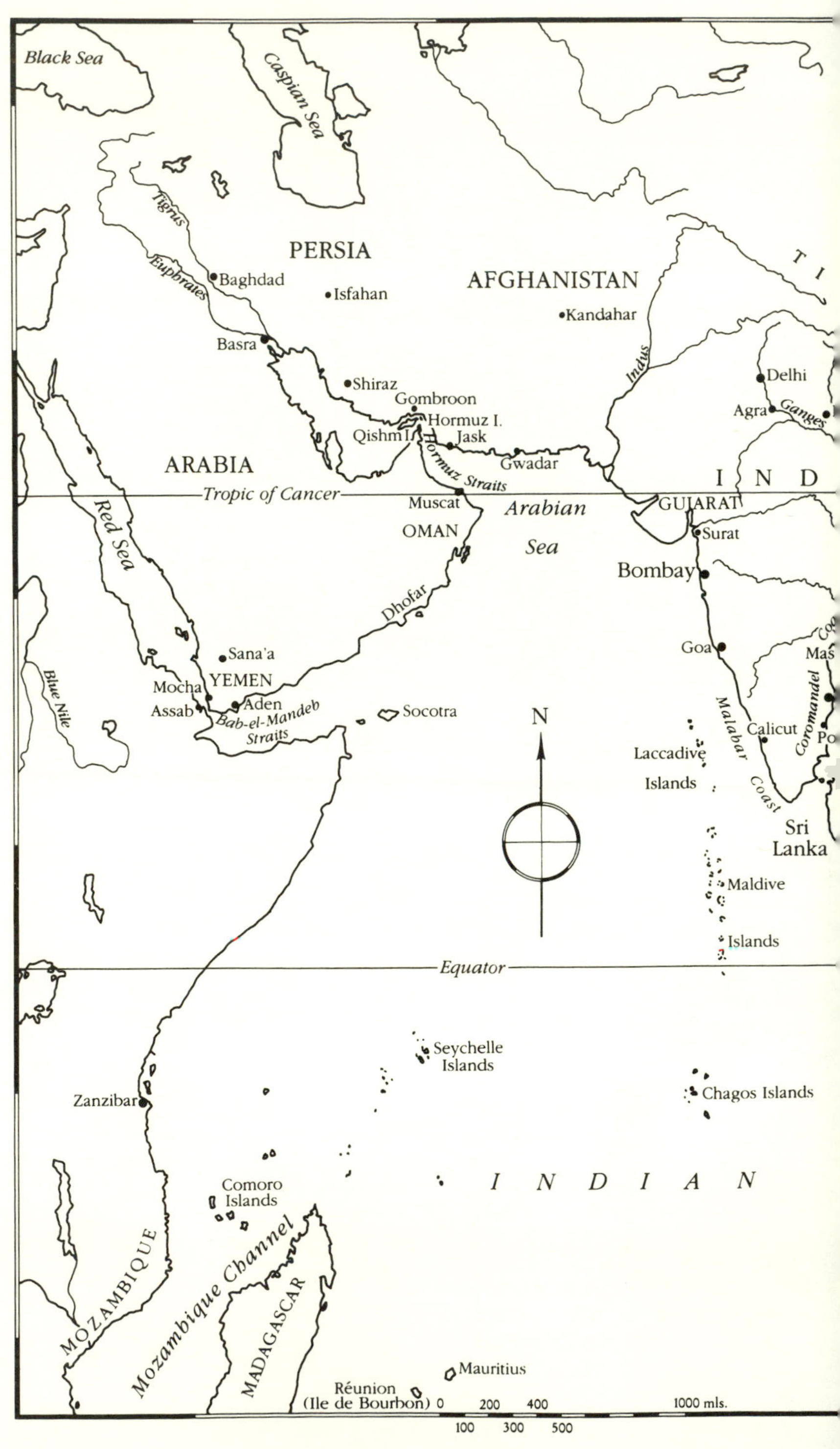
Black Sea
Caspian Sea
Tigrus
Euphrates
PERSIA
AFGHANISTAN
Baghdad
Isfahan
Kandahar
Basra
Indus
Delhi
Shiraz
Gombroon
Agra
Ganges
Hormuz I.
Qishm I.
Jask
Hormuz Straits
Gwadar
ARABIA
I N D
Tropic of Cancer
Muscat
Arabian
Sea
GUJARAT
OMAN
Surat
Bombay
Red Sea
Dhofar
Goa
Sana'a
YEMEN
Blue Nile
Mocha
Aden
Assab
Bab-el-Mandeb
Straits
Socotra
N
Malabar Coast
Calicut
Coromandel
Laccadive
Islands
Sri
Lanka
Maldive
Islands
Equator
Seychelle
Islands
Zanzibar
Chagos Islands
Comoro
Islands
I N D I A N
MOZAMBIQUE
Mozambique Channel
MADAGASCAR
Mauritius
Réunion
(Ile de Bourbon)
0
200
400
1000 mls.
100
300
500

100 300 500
0 200 400 1000 mls.
Peking
Tientsin
CHINA
Yellow River
Yangtze Kiang
Pearl River
Canton
Hong Kong
Hainan
KOREA
JAPAN
Hokkaido
Honshu
Osaka
Tokyo
Fukuoka
Hirado
Nagasaki
Kyushu
Okinawa
Formosa (Taiwan)
Tropic of Cancer
Salween
Mandalay
BURMA
Chieng Mai
Rangoon
TONGKING
Mekong
ANNAM
SIAM (THAILAND)
Ayuthia
CAMBODIA
COCHIN CHINA
Mergui
Nicobar Is.
Aceh
Luzon
PHILIPPINES
Manila
Marianas Islands
Pelew Is. (Palau)
Mindanao
South China Sea
Balambangan Island
Malacca
Singapore
Equator
BORNEO
Sulawesi
Molucca Is. (Spice Islands)
Ambon
Banda Is.
New Guinea
SUMATRA
Benkulen
Bantam
Krakatoa
Batavia
JAVA
Makassar
INDONESIA
Timor
N
Cocos Islands
NEW HOLLAND (AUSTRALIA)

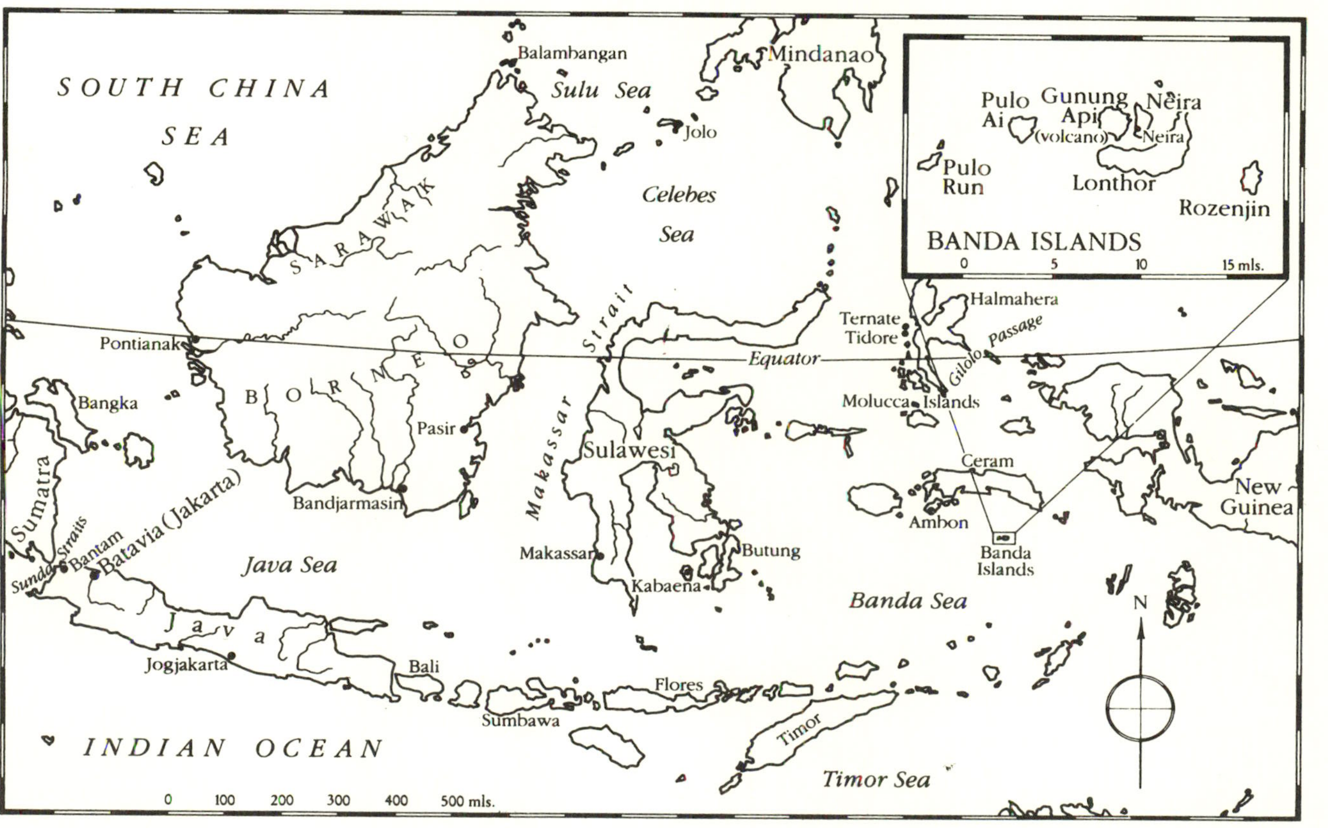

The Spice Islands

NATURAL LAW AND
ENLIGHTENMENT CLASSICS

Commentary on the Law of Prize and Booty

Hugo Grotius

Edited and with an Introduction by
Martine Julia van Ittersum

Major Legal and Political Works of Hugo Grotius

LIBERTY FUND
Indianapolis

This book is published by Liberty Fund, Inc., a foundation established to encourage study of the ideal of a society of free and responsible individuals.

The cuneiform inscription that serves as our logo and as the design motif for our endpapers is the earliest-known written appearance of the word "freedom" (*amagi*), or "liberty." It is taken from a clay document written about 2300 B.C. in the Sumerian city-state of Lagash.

The text of this edition is a reprint of the translation of *De Jure Praedae* by Gwladys L. Williams published in 1950 by the Carnegie Endowment for International Peace.

Frontispiece: Portrait of Hugo de Groot by Michiel van Mierevelt, 1608; oil on panel; collection of Historical Museum Rotterdam, on loan from the Van der Mandele Stichting. Reproduced by permission.

Map of the Far East on pp. iv–v and map of the Spice Islands on p. vii are reproduced from John Keay, *The Honourable Company: A History of the East India Company,* published by Harper Collins, London: 1990. Used by permission.

Printed in the United States of America

10 09 08 07 06 C 5 4 3 2 1
10 09 08 07 06 P 5 4 3 2 1

Library of Congress Cataloging-in-Publication Data

Grotius, Hugo, 1583–1645.
[De jure praedae commentarius. English]
Commentary on the law of prize and booty/Hugo Grotius;
edited and with an introduction by Martine Julia van Ittersum.
p. cm.—(Natural law and enlightenment classics)
"Major legal and political works of Hugo Grotius." Originally published:
Oxford: Clarendon Press, 1950. (The classics of international law; no. 22)
(Publications of the Carnegie Endowment for International Peace)
Includes bibliographical references and index.
ISBN-13: 978-0-86597-474-6 (alk. paper) ISBN-10: 0-86597-474-8 (alk. paper)
ISBN-13: 978-0-86597-475-3 (pbk.: alk. paper) ISBN-10: 0-86597-475-6 (pbk.: alk. paper)
1. Prize law. 2. Booty (International law) 3. War, Maritime (International law)
I. van Ittersum, Martine Julia, 1968–. II. Title. III. Series.
KZ2093.A3D413 2006
343.09′6—dc22 2005026380

LIBERTY FUND, INC.
8335 Allison Pointe Trail, Suite 300
Indianapolis, Indiana 46250-1684

CONTENTS

INTRODUCTION

In the early morning hours of February 25, 1603, the Dutch captain Jacob van Heemskerck attacked the Portuguese merchantman *Santa Catarina* in the Strait of Singapore and obtained its peaceful surrender by nightfall. His prize was a rich one indeed. When the carrack and its cargo were auctioned in Amsterdam in the autumn of 1604, the gross proceeds amounted to more than three million Dutch guilders—approximately three hundred thousand pounds sterling.

Piracy was nothing new in Asian waters, of course. For centuries it had been the occupation of choice of the inhabitants of the Riau Archipelago, south of the Strait of Singapore. Nor was Van Heemskerck the first European interloper to seize a carrack in the Portuguese East Indies. The English captain Sir James Lancaster had taken a richly laden carrack in the Strait of Malacca in October 1602, for example. Yet Lancaster had possessed a privateering commission from the Lord High Admiral of England. Van Heemskerck, on the other hand, lacked any such authorization to prey on the Portuguese merchant marine. His voyage to the East Indies was supposed to be a peaceful trading venture. The directors of the United Amsterdam Company had explicitly prohibited the use of force, except in cases of self-defense or for the reparation of any damages sustained. None of this seemed applicable to Van Heemskerck's premeditated seizure of the *Santa Catarina.* Even if the Dutch Admiralty Board had authorized him to attack Portuguese shipping, the validity of such a privateering commission would have been highly questionable in international law. The northern Netherlands were in a state of rebellion against their rightful overlord, the king of Spain and Portugal, and achieved de jure independence only in 1648. It was up to a young and ambitious Dutch lawyer, Hugo Grotius (1583–1645), to sort out these problems in his first major work on natural law and natural rights theory, *De Jure Praedae Commentarius* (*Commentary on the Law of Prize and Booty*).

Grotius did not produce any significant legal scholarship prior to the writing of *De Jure Praedae.* He had been trained in the liberal arts at the University of Leiden, where he was tutored in classical rhetoric, philology, and philosophy by the likes of Joseph Justus Scaliger, the greatest Protestant intellectual of his generation. Born into a patrician family in the town of Delft, Grotius could not pursue the *studia humanitatis* to the exclusion of more practical considerations. He obtained a doctorate in civil and canon law from the University of Orléans in 1598, which served as a stepping-stone to a brilliant political career in his country of birth. At the instigation of Johan van Oldenbarnevelt, the political leader of the Dutch Republic, Grotius was appointed public prosecutor of the province of Holland in 1607 and Pensionary of Rotterdam ("legal officer") in 1613. In the latter capacity, he became a member of the provincial government, the Estates of Holland, and, in 1617, of the Estates General, the federal government of the Dutch Republic. However, a coup d'état by Maurice of Nassau, the Dutch Stadtholder ("governor") and army leader, cut short Grotius's meteoric rise in Dutch politics. He was put on trial for sedition in 1619 and banned to the castle of Loevestein. Two years of reflection and study at Loevestein turned Grotius into the finest legal scholar of his age. After escaping to Paris in a book trunk, he published major works like *De Jure Belli ac Pacis* (On the Law of War and Peace) in 1625 and *Inleidinghe tot de Hollandsche Rechtsgeleerdheid* (Introduction to Dutch Jurisprudence) in 1631. He died in the German port of Rostock at the age of sixty-two, an embittered exile and, like so many of his countrymen, the hapless victim of a shipwreck.

Grotius was still a relatively unknown solicitor in The Hague when his friend Jan ten Grootenhuys asked him in September 1604 to write an apology for the United Dutch East India Company, or VOC (Verenigde Oostindische Compagnie). The Holland and Zeeland overseas trading companies, including the United Amsterdam Company, had merged in March 1602 to form the VOC, which enjoyed a government-sanctioned monopoly of Dutch trade with the East Indies. Jan ten Grootenhuys was the younger brother of VOC director Arent ten Grootenhuys and the liaison between Grotius and the Amsterdam merchants. Judging by Grootenhuys's correspondence, a bulky volume like *De Jure Praedae* was not what the merchants had in mind when they commissioned a formal defense of Van Heemskerck's seizure of the *Santa Catarina.* In his letter of October 15, 1604, Grootenhuys expressed the hope that "your apology, begun so felicitously, will be completed in a short while thanks to your attentiveness."[1] As far as the VOC directors were concerned, the verdict of the Amsterdam Admiralty Court of September 9, 1604, settled the legal aspects of the case quite satisfactorily. The Admiralty Court had confiscated the carrack and assigned it jointly to the VOC directors and Van Heemskerck and his crew. The directors realized, however, that it would take more than a verdict to win widespread support for their cause, both in domestic and international politics. It was imperative to placate Henry IV of France and James I of England, for example, who had recently made peace with the king of Spain and Portugal but who might be induced to back the Dutch diplomatically over their attacks on the Iberian colonial empire. In addition, Grotius should subtly remind the Estates General that it had virtually ordered the directors in November 1603 to go on the offensive against the *Estado da India,* and that it could not, therefore, disavow the company's privateering campaign in good conscience. In sum, directors expected him to write a short, inflammatory pamphlet detailing the iniquity of the Portuguese in the East Indies, who deserved condign punishment for the ceaseless harassment and intimidation to which they had subjected Dutch merchants ever since Cornelis de Houtman's voyage to Java in 1595–97. In order to supply Grotius with the right information, the directors put together a "book treating of the cruel, treasonous and hostile procedures of the Portuguese in the East Indies" and sent him various other materials that served to justify Van Heemskerck's capture of the *Santa Catarina.*[2]

1. Document V in appendix II.

2. W. Ph. Coolhaas, "Een bron van het historische gedeelte van Hugo de Groot's *De Jure Praedae,*" *Bijdragen en Mededelingen van het Historisch Genootschap* 79 (1965): 415–26.

Grotius took the directors' documentation very seriously indeed and faithfully incorporated it in *De Jure Praedae.* The volume of "Indian reports" survives in his personal papers at the Dutch National Archives. It consists of twelve sworn statements of Dutch merchants and mariners, along with three diary extracts, which describe, in Grootenhuys's words, "what the Portuguese have attempted against each of the voyages for the purpose of destroying our men." At the behest of the Amsterdam VOC directors, these attestations and diary extracts were collected from the former employees of the regional overseas trading companies. There is every reason to believe that Grotius understood the "Indian reports" in the manner intended by Grootenhuys, as "countless proofs of [Portuguese] perfidy, tyranny and hostility."[3] They form the basis of the eleventh chapter of *De Jure Praedae,* a long narrative of the early Dutch voyages to the East Indies.

Grotius had no intention of producing an objective historical account. Instead, he was eager to comply with the criteria of forensic rhetoric as defined by the orators of ancient Rome. Like Cicero and Quintilian, he considered it sufficient to present some, but not all, of the facts of the case. Yet he carefully refrained from any kind of willful distortion of the evidence at hand. In lawyerlike fashion, he decided to furnish material proof of Portuguese culpability in order to win his case in the court of public opinion. Thus he indicated on the manuscript's last folio that the integral text of eight documents should be appended in Latin translation:

the edict of the Estates General of April 2, 1599

the verdict of the Admiralty Court of September 9, 1604

the decree of the Estates of Holland of September 1, 1604

the letter of the bishop of Malacca to the king of Spain and Portugal of April 30, 1600

Van Heemskerck's correspondence with the captain of the *Santa Catarina,* and with the town councillors and governor of Malacca in March 1604

3. Document V in appendix II.

Grotius considered these documents conclusive evidence of (1) a systematic Portuguese campaign to oust Dutch merchants from the East Indies, (2) the *Santa Catarina*'s capture in a just war, and (3) its rightful possession by the VOC. English translations are included in appendix I below.

His painstaking reconstruction of the early Dutch voyages to the East Indies notwithstanding, Grotius must soon have realized that he could never satisfactorily relate the "facts" of the case to its underlying legal principles in a pamphlet written on the spur of the moment. He probably finished chapter eleven of *De Jure Praedae* in the winter of 1604–5 and pointedly ignored Grootenhuys's request for a quick publication. He opted instead for an in-depth study of the "universal law of war," revolutionizing natural law and natural rights theories in the process. He admitted as much in his letter to the Heidelberg town councillor George Lingelsheim of November 1, 1606, wherein he announced the completion of his "little treatise on Indian affairs." He confidently declared that, although "the universal law of war" was a tried and tested subject, he had thrown new light on it by means of "a fixed order of teaching, [viz.] the right proportion of divine and human law mixed together with the dictates of philosophy."[4]

Grotius's decision to investigate "the universal law of war" resulted in a significant expansion of the manuscript—it consists of 163 closely written folios—and a somewhat lopsided organization. The first half of the manuscript contains the introduction, followed by nine chapters of legal principles, the so-called *Dogmatica de Jure Praedae.* The second half consists of Grotius's account of the early Dutch voyages to the East Indies in chapter eleven and a Ciceronian-style closing argument that covers chapters twelve through fifteen and presents VOC privateering as just, honorable, and beneficial.

The second chapter of *De Jure Praedae,* also known as the *Prolegomena,* contains an elaborate system of nine rules and thirteen laws (reproduced in appendix A), which Grotius deduced from an individual's right to self-defense and the law of inoffensiveness. The sovereign, free

4. Document VIII in appendix II.

individual was indeed the starting point of his political and legal philosophy. Yet Grotius should not be considered a proponent of democratic government and inalienable individual rights in a twenty-first-century sense of the word. He argued, for example, that human beings could become slaves of their own volition, in which case their total subjection to the will of others constituted a valid contract. In addition, he strenuously denied that the Dutch war of independence (1568–1648) had originated in a popular revolt against Philip II of Spain and Portugal. Instead, he reserved the right of resistance for the traditional governing elite, the Dutch magistrates who were bearers of the "marks of sovereignty." In Grotius's view, it was the king's unconstitutional behavior that had forced the provincial Estates, assembled in the Estates General, to take up arms to defend themselves, acquiring full sovereignty and independence in the process.

Although Grotius does not qualify as a democrat or human rights activist, his justification of Van Heemskerck's capture of the *Santa Catarina* was unprecedented in early modern political and legal philosophy. He was the first to introduce the notion of subjective rights—man was born a sovereign and free individual who could execute his own right—and used it to defend the establishment of a Dutch empire of trade in the East and West Indies. He boldly argued in chapter thirteen of *De Jure Praedae* that Van Heemskerck had acted as the agent of a sovereign and independent Dutch state, which could order indiscriminate attacks on Iberian shipping as part of its public war against Philip III of Spain and Portugal. Few of Grotius's contemporaries would have agreed with this analysis. When he learned of the Twelve Years' Truce between Spain and the United Provinces in April 1609, Henry IV of France famously declared that his Dutch allies might be free but were certainly not sovereign and independent. Grotius would have had a hard time convincing the statesmen and lawyers of his age that Van Heemskerck's capture of the *Santa Catarina* was a legitimate act of public war. Yet his argument in chapter twelve of *De Jure Praedae* was more radical still: a trading company might legitimately engage in a private war against other merchants, or even against the agents of a sovereign state, in order to enforce the natural law, which mandated freedom of trade and navigation.

Granted that the United Provinces had an ambiguous status in international politics, its inhabitants were nonetheless entitled to freedom of trade and navigation, a right innate to all free peoples, which they could enforce themselves in the absence of an independent and effective judge. Since the right to self-defense made private individuals judges and executioners in their own cause, a company of merchants like the VOC must, under certain circumstances, also qualify as a full-fledged actor in international politics. When confronted by Portuguese harassment and intimidation, the VOC had every right to take up arms in order to safeguard its trade with Asian princes and peoples. Civil magistrates could not be expected to call the Portuguese to account on the high seas, or in countries where judicial systems were either weak or nonexistent. Hence it fell to the VOC to enforce freedom of trade and navigation in the East Indies and to punish Portuguese transgressions of the natural law by means of a just war.

Once it was established that Van Heemskerck had engaged in a just war, Grotius could simply cite the law of war to show that he was entitled to reparations for injuries sustained by himself, his employers, and the Dutch Republic. Grotius admitted that the Portuguese had never harmed Van Heemskerck in his own person or made any attempts on his crew, cargo, and fleet. Yet chapter eleven of *De Jure Praedae* was proof that Portuguese harassment and intimidation of the natives had materially damaged Dutch prospects for trade in Monsoon Asia. Van Heemskerck himself had not been able to return to the Spice Islands, for example, which were laid waste by the armada of André Furtado de Mendonça in the summer of 1602. If the dismal fate of Ambon and Ternate was not sufficient reason to engage the *Estado da India,* the execution of seventeen Dutch sailors in the Portuguese port of Macao in November 1602 should certainly qualify as a casus belli. The sailors belonged to the crew of Jacob van Neck, who, like Van Heemskerck, was employed by the United Amsterdam Company. They had committed no crime except to unwittingly enter the harbor of Macao. Their execution was a blatant injustice, which Van Heemskerck could not ignore in his capacity as agent of the Dutch government and servant of the United Amsterdam Company. Predictably, Grotius concluded that his capture of the *Santa Catarina* had been justified in order to obtain damages on behalf of his employer and the Estates General.

Grotius's demonstration had been adumbrated in the verdict of the Amsterdam Admiralty Court, which, in turn, had derived part of its argument from Van Heemskerck's correspondence with the directors of the United Amsterdam Company and the minutes of his council of naval officers (see appendixes I and II below). They show that Van Heemskerck had already interpreted his commission as authorizing the use of force for the purpose of safeguarding Dutch trade in the East Indies and obtaining damages for the United Amsterdam Company. The Amsterdam Admiralty Court had not just endorsed Van Heemskerck's reading of his commission, but also cited the edict of the Estates General of April 2, 1599, commanding its subjects to attack Iberian shipping indiscriminately, and added some inchoate references to natural law and the law of nations. Clearly, the distinct elements of Grotius's argument in *De Jure Praedae* were already present in the mode of reasoning adopted by Van Heemskerck, the VOC directors, and the Amsterdam Admiralty Court. Yet it was Grotius who turned this hotchpotch of legal grounds into a seamless whole by means of a radical redefinition of natural law and natural rights.

In his letter to George Lingelsheim of November 1606, Grotius did not just announce the completion of *De Jure Praedae,* but also wondered whether it should appear in print "as it was written, or only those parts which pertain to the universal law of war."[5] With the exception of its twelfth chapter, *De Jure Praedae* did indeed remain in manuscript until the nineteenth century. Grotius must have realized that it was not opportune to publish a defense of Dutch privateering in the East Indies on the eve of peace and truce negotiations between the United Provinces and Philip III of Spain and Portugal. Yet he continued to feel a strong commitment to the VOC. In March 1606, he drafted a petition for the VOC directors, for example, wherein he asked the Estates General to forgo its legal share of all booty taken in the East Indies (20 percent) out of consideration for the great expenses incurred by the company in fight-

5. Ibid.

ing the Portuguese. After he had finished *De Jure Praedae,* he wrote several draft letters for the VOC directors, addressed to various Asian rulers, all allies of the VOC. Grotius assured them of the company's continuous military and naval support but requested that they sell spices exclusively to the Dutch as a quid pro quo.[6] When the Dutch East Indies trade became a topic of discussion at the Ibero-Dutch peace conference in The Hague in February 1608, Grotius provided the VOC directors with a road map for the negotiations and correctly predicted that the privateering war would continue in the East Indies, regardless of whether a treaty should be concluded in Europe. At the request of the Zeeland VOC directors, he published the twelfth chapter of *De Jure Praedae* as *Mare Liberum* (*The Free Sea*) in March 1609. Although the pamphlet appeared too late to influence the negotiations for the Twelve Years' Truce—the treaty was signed on April 9, 1609—it had clearly been conceived by the VOC directors as a means to thwart Iberian demands for a Dutch withdrawal from the East Indies and "persuade both our government and neighboring princes to staunchly defend our, as well as the nation's, rights."[7] The publication of *Mare Liberum* hardly marked the end of Grotius's involvement in the company's affairs. He served as the VOC's chief negotiator at the Anglo-Dutch colonial conferences in London in 1613 and The Hague in 1615, for example, which induced Richard Hakluyt the Younger to produce the first English translation of *Mare Liberum.*[8] When living in exile in Paris in 1628, he could justifiably claim in a letter to his brother-in-law, Nicolaas van Reigersberch, that "he merited thus much of this company that, even if all others sleep, they ought to keep watch over me."[9]

6. Document IX of appendix II.

7. Document X of appendix II.

8. Hugo Grotius, *The Free Sea,* trans. Richard Hakluyt, with William Welwod's Critique and Grotius's Reply, ed. David Armitage (Indianapolis: Liberty Fund, 2004).

9. Hugo Grotius to N. van Reigersberch, June 12, 1628, in *Briefwisseling van Hugo Grotius,* ed. P. C. Molhuysen, B. L. Meulenbroek, and H. J. M. Nellen, vol. 3 (The Hague: Martinus Nijhoff, 1961), 323.

NOTE ON THE TEXT

Upon Hugo Grotius's death in 1645, the manuscript of *De Jure Praedae* remained in the possession of his descendants, the Cornet de Groot family, for over two centuries. In fact, legal scholars did not know of its existence until the Dutch bookseller and printer Martinus Nijhoff auctioned off Grotius's personal papers in 1864. The manuscript was purchased by Leiden University Library. One of its humanities graduates, H. G. Hamaker (1819–92), published the first Latin edition of *De Jure Praedae* in 1868. His text was the basis for the English translation that Gwladys L. Williams prepared for the Carnegie Endowment for International Peace in the middle of the twentieth century.

The Liberty Fund edition of *De Jure Praedae* reproduces her translation, which first appeared as part of the Classics of International Law series. In addition to Williams's translation, we reissue appendix A of the Carnegie edition, along with the superb author and subject indexes by Walter H. Zeydel. With two exceptions we have left unchanged the editorial conventions that govern Williams's translation of *De Jure Praedae.* These editorial conventions are explained in full in the Translator's Note to the Carnegie edition[1] but may be summarized as follows.

The words and phrases that Grotius wrote in capital letters for purposes of emphasis are printed in italic type in the body of the text. Bold type is used for words that are similarly emphasized in Grotius's marginal

1. Hugo Grotius, *Commentary on the Law of Prize and Booty* (*De Jure Praedae Commentarius*), eds. Gwladys L. Williams and W. H. Zeydel (Oxford: Clarendon Press, 1950), vol. 1: *A Translation of the Original Manuscript of 1604* by Gwladys L. Williams, with the collaboration of Walter H. Zeydel, xxvii–xxx.

headings and subheadings. Williams used brackets when she felt she had amplified Grotius's thought in translating his concise Latin phrases.

The manuscript's folio numbers appear at the end of the relevant text line, which is a change from the Carnegie edition, where they appear in the margin. The position of the folio numbers in the text approximates that of the folios in the manuscript. They should not be considered the equivalent of modern page breaks, however. Williams was frequently obliged to reverse the Latin word order of the manuscript in order to produce a flowing English translation. A comparison with the collotype reproduction of the manuscript reveals that, in a few instances, she either forgot to include the manuscript's folio divisions or made a mistake in doing so.[2] Although Williams did make some mistakes, the sometimes erratic numbering also reflects the fact that Grotius revised the theoretical chapters numerous times.

Footnotes identified by arabic numerals have a threefold function in Williams's translation: (1) to indicate gaps in the manuscript that may cause doubt regarding the original text, (2) to clear up questions that may arise from Grotius's own correction of the manuscript, and (3) to comment on Grotius's use of sources. Since Grotius's quotations often are loose paraphrases of the originals, Williams translated these quotations on the basis of the manuscript text, not the text quoted. Any unavoidable departure from this rule is marked with a numbered footnote. If Grotius's deviation from his source was "too striking to pass without comment," Williams inserted a numbered footnote there as well.[3] Page numbers listed in the footnotes of the Carnegie edition have been replaced with page numbers from the Liberty Fund edition. Oddly enough, Williams referred to the page numbers, instead of the folio numbers, of the collotype reproduction of the manuscript, which she consulted for her translation. This has been left unchanged.

Footnotes that start with lowercase letters (a, b, c, etc.) denote Grotius's references to his alleged sources, both in the running text of the manuscript and in the marginalia. Unlike the Carnegie edition, where

2. Grotius, *Commentary on the Law of Prize and Booty,* 1:258, 389.
3. Ibid., 1:xxix.

they appear in the left and right margins, these references are placed at the bottom of the page in the current edition. Square brackets signal Zeydel's extensions or corrections of Grotius's references to other authors. Lettered footnotes are also used for Grotius's cross-references to other parts of the manuscript. Many of these cross-references are of a general nature: they relate not so much to a particular article or conclusion cited by Grotius as to the argument that follows or precedes the passage indicated in his marginal annotation. Although his cross-references do not rely on the manuscript's folio numbering, the relevant page numbers of the English translation, as identified by Zeydel, are added for the benefit of the reader.

Walter H. Zeydel undertook the difficult task of verifying Grotius's direct and indirect references to other authors. The editions consulted by Zeydel used in checking Grotius's quotations are specified after each entry in the Index of Authors Cited. Where no edition is mentioned, the work in question was not available in the United States at the time that Walter Zeydel compiled his index. The titles of the more familiar works are given in English; others retain their Latin form.

Four modest changes have been made in the author and subject indexes as compared with the Carnegie edition. Zeydel indicated in his author index whether a particular work had been mentioned more than once on a particular page, using Latin terms like "bis," "ter," etc. The present publication omits these notations because changes in pagination make them no longer accurate. Zeydel put multiple works by one author in alphabetical order on the basis of the first letter of the first noun of the (Latin) book titles. This order has been adjusted to conform with the standard letter-by-letter alphabetization of the indexes in the Natural Law and Enlightenment Classics series. In addition, the author and subject indexes have been silently corrected to reflect the most recent historical scholarship, and, where possible, *floruit* or birth and death dates have been provided for important authors and historical figures. The material from the introduction and from appendixes I and II has been integrated into both indexes: existing entries have been amplified for this purpose, and new ones have been created when necessary. All of the original page references given in the Carnegie indexes have been preserved and translated into the corresponding page numbers for the Liberty Fund edition. However, the reader should be aware that the Carnegie references are sometimes more oblique than what the modern reader might expect.

The present publication improves upon the Carnegie edition of *De Jure Praedae* in various ways. It comprises two sets of appendixes of important archival and printed documents, all in English translation, which place *De Jure Praedae* in its historical context. The most up-to-date studies of Grotius's natural rights and natural law theories are listed as suggestions for further reading. There is a detailed bibliography for the new introduction and appendixes I and II. Since the present volume does *not* reproduce the introduction and note on the text of the Carnegie edition, footnotes and index entries that refer to these matters have been omitted as well.

Appendix I reproduces eight documents that Grotius himself wished to affix to *De Jure Praedae.* It contains a wide variety of texts, which range from the verdict of the Amsterdam Admiralty Court, declaring the *Santa Catarina* good prize, to an intercepted letter of the Bishop of Malacca, urging Philip II of Spain and Portugal to take drastic action against Dutch interlopers in *Asia Portuguesa.* Grotius considered these documents conclusive evidence of (a) a systematic Portuguese campaign to oust Dutch merchants from the East Indies, (b) the *Santa Catarina*'s capture in a just war, and (c) its rightful possession by the United Dutch East India Company, or VOC. The present text is partly based on a new transcription of the original sources.

Appendix II is a mixture of archival and printed documents, some of which were discovered only a few years ago in the Dutch national archives in The Hague. Documents I–IV consist of an intercepted Portuguese letter, addressed to Admiral André Furtado de Mendonça; Jacob van Heemskerck's correspondence with the directors of the United Amsterdam Company; and the minutes of his council of naval officers. These sources reveal the motives behind Van Heemskerck's privateering campaign in Malayan waters, give a detailed description of his capture of the *Santa Catarina,* and outline his ambitious plans for Dutch trade in Southeast Asia. Van Heemskerck urged his employers, for example, to establish a rendezvous near the Strait of Singapore and oust the Portuguese from the lucrative trade between the Indian subcontinent and the Far East. Two letters by Jan ten Grootenhuys (documents V and VI) prove that the VOC commissioned *De Jure Praedae* and provided Grotius with important information about the early Dutch voyages to the East Indies and his country's official war policy, which endorsed indiscriminate attacks on Iberian shipping by private merchants. Document VIII is a brief selection from Grotius's letter to George Lingelsheim in November 1606, announcing the completion of *De Jure Praedae.* Documents VII and IX testify to Grotius's close collaboration with the VOC directors, both before and after he finished *De Jure Praedae.* He petitioned the Estates General in the spring of 1606, demanding that it alleviate the VOC's heavy financial burdens, caused by the war against the Portuguese, and wrote to the company's indigenous allies the following winter, offering military support in exchange for a monopoly of the spice trade. Finally, document X is the famous request for the publication of *Mare Liberum,* which Grotius received from the Zeeland VOC directors in November 1608.

ACKNOWLEDGMENTS

I would like to thank Knud Haakonssen for his invitation to contribute this volume to the series Natural Law and Enlightenment Classics and for his invaluable advice and support at every stage of the editorial process. David Armitage encouraged me to make my doctoral research on *De Jure Praedae* available to a wider audience. He assisted my editorial efforts in various ways and put his own edition of *Mare Liberum* at my disposal even before it appeared in print. My greatest debt is to Peter Borschberg, who has generously shared with me his extensive knowledge of Asian history in the early modern era. His erudition and unfailing good humor were indispensable to me in my work on the translation and annotation of the source materials in appendixes I and II. Fernando Arenas and Paulo Pinto helped me identify Portuguese terms and names. Wil Dijk enlightened me about the coins and measures that were common in Southeast Asia in the seventeenth century. International scholarly collaboration is clearly a sine qua non for the study of any aspect—be it military, political, socioeconomic, or cultural—of the long and fascinating history of the Dutch East India Company. I am very grateful for the assistance that I have received from so many wonderful colleagues around the globe.

COMMENTARY ON THE LAW OF PRIZE AND BOOTY

CONTENTS

CHAPTER I [2]

Introductory Remarks—Outline [of the Case]—Divisions [of the Discussion]—Method—Order

Introductory remarks

A situation has arisen that is truly novel, and scarcely credible to foreign observers, namely: that those men who have been so long at war with the Spaniards and who have furthermore suffered the most grievous personal injuries, are debating as to whether or not, in a just war and with public authorization, they can rightfully despoil an exceedingly cruel enemy who has already violated the rules of international commerce. Thus we find that a considerable number of Hollanders (a people surpassed by none in their eagerness for honourable gain) are apparently ashamed to lay claim to the spoils of war, being moved forsooth, by compassion for those who in their own relations with the Dutch have failed to observe even the legal rights of enemies!

Since this state of affairs is due partly to the malicious falsehoods of certain persons insufficiently devoted to the commonwealth, partly to the scruples and somewhat superstitious self-restraint of other individuals, it has seemed expedient that we should undertake to enlighten the artless innocence of the latter while combating the malice of the former. For no discerning person can be unaware of the consequences toward which these debates are tending, nor of the hostile wiles intermingled with them. That is to say, if the Dutch cease to harass the Spanish [and Portuguese][1] blockaders of the sea (which will certainly be the outcome

1. *Hispanos:* Grotius sometimes uses the terms "Spaniards," "Spanish," "Spain," &c., in the strict sense (as in the immediately preceding paragraph, where he refers

if their efforts result only in profitless peril), the savage insolence of the Iberian peoples will swell to immeasurable proportions, the shores of the whole world will soon be blocked off, and all commerce with Asia will collapse—that commerce by which (as the Dutch know, nor is the enemy ignorant of the fact) the wealth of our state is chiefly if not entirely sustained. On the other hand, if the Dutch choose to avail themselves of their good fortune, God has provided a weapon against the inmost heart of the enemy's power, nor is there any weapon that offers a surer hope of liberty.

Yet there is some reason to congratulate the fatherland on these erroneous scruples, since it is a rather strong indication of Dutch innocence that Hollanders should hesitate even before committing acts sanctioned by the moral law of nations and by the precepts of public law. Justice can never be found wanting, nor can there be a lack of good faith, in those who proceed so carefully and with hesitant tread (so to speak) in exercising this right which is most certainly possessed by all peoples and which would seem questionable to no one save the Dutch themselves.

It is, however, indubitably true that virtue, at both extremes, [2′] borders upon vice.[a] While this fact is fairly obvious in some cases, in others it more easily escapes notice, owing to the magnitude of the evil opposed to the particular virtue involved. For example, because of our aversion to a wrathful disposition, we so disregard the stolidity which

---

to a war that did not officially involve the Portuguese); but in many instances the historical facts or the trend of Grotius's own argument point to the necessity or advisability of interpreting the same terms to include the Portuguese, who were ruled by the King of Spain at the time of the events described. In this particular instance, the reference to a blockade affecting commerce with Asia (a Portuguese rather than a Spanish sphere of interest), as well as the indirect allusion to the reward due the representatives of the East India Company for their defiance of Portuguese threats, necessitate the insertion of the bracketed phrase.

In order to avoid overloading the English text with brackets and footnotes, attention will not be called again to these broad interpretations of *Hispani* and related terms, unless there is doubt as to the author's true meaning.

a. Aristotle, *Nicomachean Ethics,* II. vii [II. vi. 13–17].

constitutes the opposite extreme of vice, and which the Greeks[a] called ἀοργησίαν [lack of rancour], that this quality has not even found a Latin name. Assuredly, too, the consuming greed for gain denoted by the Greek term αἰσχροκερδεία [sordid covetousness], is a vile disease of the spirit, characterized by complete disrespect for law and morality; yet it is possible to sin in contrary fashion, neglecting opportunities to promote one's own interests, through an anxious and overnice avoidance of things not essentially dishonourable. For the Socratists show that the wise and good man is φῐλοκερδής, that is to say, by no means disregardful of his own advantage. The philosophers likewise deny that justice is οἰκοφθόρον and πτωχοποιόν, "a destroyer of domestic property" and "the author of indigence."[b] As Lucilius[c] has correctly observed, it is indeed

> A virtue to be mindful of restraints
> And moderation, in the search for gain,

but it is also

> A virtue to be able with one's wealth
> To pay one's debt in full. . . .

Even in this [abstention from greed], we should guard against excess. In other words, let us not imagine that to be vicious which is devoid of vice; and let us not be unjust to ourselves while shunning injustice toward others. The weapon that flies far past the target, misses the mark no less than the weapon that falls short of its aim. Both extremes are blameworthy; both are tainted by error. The fault of those persons whose hearts have grown hardened to every evil deed is perhaps the more shocking and execrable (though one can also conceive of a disposition to [3] take offence at entirely inoffensive things, which may be described as excessively delicate and scrupulous); but impious irreverence for justice and equity is sufficiently revealed through its own infamy because it is repugnant to human nature, whereas there is more need to guard against that other form of vice, the form rooted in a sense of superiority, for the

a. Gellius, I. xxvi [10]; Arist., *Nic. Ethics,* IV. xi [IV. v. 5].
b. Plutarch, *Cato* [*Comparison of Aristides and Cato,* iii. 3].
c. [Lactantius, *Divine Institutes,* VI. v.]

reason that it bears no distinctive mark and therefore easily assumes the aspect of virtue, under which guise it creeps into our hearts. Such is the vice epitomized in the old saying as "hunting for knots in a bulrush" [i.e. seeking for trouble where it does not exist].

Justice consists in taking a middle course.[a] It is wrong to inflict injury, but it is also wrong to endure injury. The former is, of course, the graver misdeed, but the latter is also to be avoided.

Owing, however, to the fact that we are more frequently impelled toward the first extreme, the precept of regard for others is usually held up to us with excessive zeal, the implication being that we are by nature sufficiently inclined to care for ourselves. Nevertheless, the wise man does not belittle himself, nor does he neglect to avail himself of his own advantages, since no other person will use them more properly.[b] By the same token, he will repel every injury to himself in so far as law and justice permit him to do so.[c] Thus the truly good man will be free from *μειονεξία*, that is to say, from the disposition to accord himself less than his due.

To be sure, such a disposition, as long as the loss resulting from it affects no one save the individual in error, customarily excites more ridicule than reproach and is called folly rather than injustice. But if at any time private loss brings common peril in its train, then indeed, we must combat it with all our force, lest the public welfare be harmfully affected by the mistaken convictions of individual citizens. Under this head should be placed the weakness of those persons who betrayed their own possessions to the enemy because some conscientious scruple prevented them from fighting. We know about the Jewish Sabbaths[d] and the Greek Moons.[e, 2] If there be other men who have not borne sufficiently in mind the famous epic passage, let them remember that:

a. Arist., *Nic. Ethics,* V. ix [V. v. 17] and xv [V. xi. 7–8].
b. *Ibid.* IX. iv [3] and *ibid.* viii [8] and Arist., *Politics,* II. v [II. ii. 6].
c. Arist., *Nic. Ethics,* V. xii [V. ix. 6].
d. Josephus [*Jewish Antiquities*] XIV. viii [XIV. 63].
e. Herodotus, VIII [VI. 106]; Lucian, *Astrology* [25].

2. That is to say, certain periods of certain months devoted to religious festivals, during which it was considered unlawful to undertake a military expedition.

Εἷς οἰωνὸς ἄριστος, ἀμύνεσθαι περὶ πάτρης.

There is no act more noble than defence
Of one's own land upon the battlefield.[a]

I could cite numerous examples of persons who have sinned in this way, but what need is there of such citations? For who doubts but that the Hebrews thought themselves pious and humane because they did not savagely massacre the Midianites and Canaanites?[b] Who does not know of Saul's mistaken pity for the conquered king?[c] Yet on this very score both Saul and the Hebrews were severely rebuked and punished. Moreover, the case with which we are dealing does not even involve this question of slaughter, but turns merely upon the issue of not leaving in the enemy's possession resources which may be used to destroy the innocent.

Saint Augustine,[d] that supreme authority on piety and morals, [3′] spoke truly indeed when he declared that it was *characteristic of timid men,*[3] not *of the pious,* to condemn war because of the ills—such as slaughter and plunder—which follow in its train.

Thus it is needful that these *clouds of fear*
Be vanquished, not by any solar shaft
Nor by the day's bright spear, but by the mien
And *ordered plan of nature. . . .*[e]

For unless I am mistaken, we may appropriately borrow here the words of the poet Lucretius, since it is solely from that very "mien of nature" and from no other source that one should seek to ascertain how much

a. Homer, *Iliad,* XII [243].

b. *Numbers,* xxxi [1–19]; *Deuteronomy,* vii. 2.

c. *1 Samuel,* xv; Ambrose, *On Duties* [*On Psalms,* CXVIII. lviii. 25], cited in *Decretum,* II. xxiii. 4. 33.

d. Augustine, *Against Faustus,* XXII. lxxiv, cited in *Decretum,* II. xxiii. 1. 4.

e. Lucretius [*De Rerum Natura*], II [59–61].

3. Words written entirely in capital letters in Grotius's manuscript are italicized in the English translation. In the case of quoted passages this does not necessarily indicate that the words thus italicized were stressed by either device in the original work.

is owed to others and how much to oneself. Accordingly, after a careful study of the law of war, in which special attention will be given to the precepts governing captured property, we shall find that this whole question has become clear to any person not devoid of ordinary intelligence.

Outline [of the case]

The particular case underlying this discussion is summarized in the following paragraph.

Ships dispatched by the merchants of Holland and Zeeland to the various islands of the Indian Ocean not subject to Portuguese rule had been sailing forth on commercial ventures from as far back as 1595, when our sailors at last prepared to seek vengeance for the slaughter of many of their comrades, as well as for the losses suffered both by themselves and by their allies either in consequence of Portuguese calumnies or at the hands of Portuguese emissaries, through the perfidy of the latter and finally through the open armed violence of that people and their allies. In the year 1602, after several manifestations of hostility on both sides, it so happened that Jacob Heemskerck (Commander of the Amsterdam fleet of eight ships lying in the Strait of Singapore, one of the two straits by which Sumatra[4] is separated from the Malay Peninsula) forced a Portuguese vessel to surrender and, disbanding its crew, sailed it home. This vessel, the *Catharine* by name, a ship of the class known as "caracks," was laden with merchandise. Quite similar acts had of course been committed by other persons prior to that time, and have also been committed since then; but inasmuch as this particular instance is for many reasons the most widely celebrated, we have chosen it for examination as the [4]

4. *Taprobane* in the Latin, a term generally interpreted as the ancient and medieval name of Ceylon. Nevertheless, the geographical data presented here and elsewhere in the *Commentary,* taken in conjunction with the categorical assertion that Taprobane is "an island . . . which is now called Sumatra" (*infra,* p. 263), prove beyond any possibility of doubt that Grotius himself was speaking of Sumatra. Accordingly, wherever Grotius is not citing another author on the subject of Taprobane, the rendering "Sumatra" is adopted throughout the translation. On the other hand, in those passages where Classical Latin descriptions of Taprobane are quoted or paraphrased, the Latin term is retained and footnotes call attention to the fact that most authorities interpret such descriptions as references to Ceylon.

Cf. notes, *infra,* pp. 263, 307–8, and 335; and notes 8 and 9 on p. 472.

episode representative of all such captures, so that on the basis of this investigation judgement may readily be passed in regard to the other cases.

Divisions [of the discussion]

Upon approaching the task indicated, however, I find myself involved in an extremely complex debate: not because our thesis is at all difficult in itself, but because of the differing views of the very persons who dispute it. Some of these critics, guided in a sense by punctilious motives, hesitate to approve of the prize, apparently regarding it as something wrongfully acquired and illegitimate. Others, though they entertain no doubt from the standpoint of legitimacy, seem fearful of bringing some stain upon their reputations by such an act of approval. Again, there may be individuals who have no misgivings regarding the justice of the cause in question and who do not believe that their good name can be impaired thereby, but who nevertheless imagine that this very proposition which at the moment appears to be beneficial and profitable, may eventually result in some still latent loss and harm.

Thus our undertaking requires a combination of all the various forms of discourse customarily employed by orators.[a] It calls not only for debate as to whether the aforesaid act was right or wrong, to be conducted as if the point were being argued in court, but also for the assumption of the censor's functions of praise and blame; and furthermore, since the circumstances that gave rise to the act remain unchanged, advice must be given as to whether or not the course of action already adopted is expedient for the future.

First of all, then, we must examine the matter from the standpoint of law, thus establishing a basis, so to speak, for the treatment of the other questions to be considered.

Method

The ordered plan of nature to which I referred above has a very important bearing upon this phase of the discussion. For, in my opinion, it would be a waste of effort to pass judgement regarding acts whose scope is international rather than domestic—acts committed, more-

a. Quintilian [*Institutes of Oratory*], III. iv.

over, under conditions not of peace but of war—solely on the basis of written laws. That Dio[a] who is called "the golden-tongued" by [4′] virtue of his eloquence, puts the point very neatly, when he says: *τῶν μὲν ἐγγράφων οὐδὲν ἐν τοῖς πολεμίοις ἰσχύει· τά τε ἔθη φυλάττεται παρὰ πᾶσι, κἂν εἰς ἐσχάτην ἔχθραν προέλθωσι.* "To be sure, nothing written is valid between enemies; but customs are observed by all, even when the extreme of hatred has been reached." In the passage just quoted, the term "customs" is equivalent to Cicero's[b] concept in the phrase, "not written law, but the law sprung from Nature," and to that expressed in the words of Sophocles,[c] *ἄγραπτα κἀσφαλῆ θεῶν νόμιμα,* "not those written laws, indeed, but the immutable laws of Heaven." Yet again, Lactantius[d] goes so far as to censure the philosophers because in their discussion of military duties they take as their criterion, not true justice, but civic life and custom. If those persons [who base their judgement on written laws] do not read the works of the authors above cited, they ought at least to pay heed to their own Baldus,[e] who has wisely ruled that in any controversy arising between claimants of sovereign power the sole judge is natural reason, the arbiter of good and evil. Other quite learned authorities[f] uphold this same doctrine. Nor does it differ greatly from the popular maxim that he who seeks for a statutory law where natural reason suffices, is lacking in intelligence. Therefore, it is from some source other than the Corpus of Roman laws that one must seek to derive that pre-eminent science which is embodied, according to Cicero,[g] in the treaties, pacts, and agreements of peoples, kings, and foreign tribes, or—to put it briefly—in every law of war and peace.

Considerably better and more dependable is the method chosen by those who prefer to have such questions decided on the basis of Holy Writ, except that the persons employing this method frequently cite

a. In oration *On Custom* [*Orations,* lxxvi, pp. 269–70].
b. *For Milo* [iv. 10].
c. *Antigone* [454–5].
d. *Divine Institutes,* VI. vi.
e. In Preface *On Code.*
f. Vázquez, *Illustrium Controversiarum,* li. 29.
g. *For Balbus* [vi. 15].

simple historical accounts or the civil law of the Hebrews in the place of divine law. For the materials collected indiscriminately from the annals of all nations, while they are extremely valuable in elucidating the question, have little or no value in providing a solution, since as a general rule the wrong course is the one more often followed [in the instances recorded in those annals] [5].

The true way, then, has been prepared for us by those jurists[a] of antiquity whose names we revere, and who repeatedly refer the art of civil government back to the very fount of nature. This is the course indicated also in the works of Cicero.[b] For he declares that the science of law must be derived, not from the Praetor's edict (the method adopted by the majority in Cicero's day), nor yet from the Twelve Tables (the method of his predecessors), but from the inmost heart of philosophy.

Accordingly, we must concern ourselves primarily with the establishment of this natural derivation. Nevertheless, it will be of no slight value as a confirmation of our belief, if the conviction already formed by us on the basis of natural reason is sanctioned by divine authority, or if we find that this same conviction was approved in earlier times by men of wisdom and by nations of the highest repute.

Order

For the rest, it is expedient for our purposes to order the discussion as follows: first, let us see what is true universally and as a general proposition; then, let us gradually narrow this generalization, adapting it to the special nature of the case under consideration. Just as the mathematicians customarily prefix to any concrete demonstration a preliminary statement of certain broad axioms on which all persons are easily agreed, in order that there may be some fixed point from which to trace the proof of what follows, so shall we point out certain rules and laws of the most general nature, presenting them as preliminary assumptions which need to be recalled rather than learned for the first time, with the

a. *On Dig.* I. i, XLI. i, XLI. ii and elsewhere *passim;* also *On Dig.* V. i. 76 and XLI. iii. 30.

b. *On Laws,* I [v. 17].

purpose of laying a foundation upon which our other conclusions may safely rest.

In this connexion I must crave indulgence for the novelty and also, perhaps, for the prolixity of my work. Accordingly, I ask the reader to be patient and to accept on faith for the moment my assurance as to what the event will later confirm, namely: that the accuracy of the arguments to be derived from our premisses will compensate for any tedium caused by this preliminary matter, which will be regarded by many critics as already sufficiently familiar and by everyone as too repetitious in its presentation. Moreover, I can quite truthfully assert that certain problems bound up with the law of war and hitherto exceedingly confused, are susceptible of explanation and solution (even though they will not all be expressly mentioned in this treatise) on the basis of the said premisses and by the very method of demonstration herein employed.

Here follow the dogmas relating to the law of prize and booty.

CHAPTER II

Prolegomena, Including Nine Rules and Thirteen Laws[1]

Where should we begin, if not at the very beginning? Accordingly, let us give first place and pre-eminent authority to the following rule: *What God has shown to be His Will, that is law.* This axiom points directly [5′] to the cause of law, and is rightly laid down as a primary principle.[a] **Rule I**

It would seem, indeed, that the very term *ius* [law] is derived from *Iovis* [Jove] and that the same process of derivation holds good for *iurare* [to swear] and *iusiurandum* [an oath] or *Iovisiurandum* [an oath in the name of Jove]. Alternatively, one might trace the development of these terms to the fact that the ancients designated as *iusa*[b]—that is to say *iussa* [things commanded]—those precepts which we designate as *iura* [laws]. In any case, the act of commanding is a function of power, and primary power over all things pertains to God, in the sense that power over his own handiwork pertains to the artificer and power over inferiors, to their superiors.

Ausonius[c] has declared that, "Law is the unerring mind of God." This was the sentiment that inspired Orpheus—and after him, all the old

a. Thomas Aquinas, I–II, qu. 93, art. 1.

b. Festus [*De Verborum Significatu,* 92].

c. *Monosyllables* [in *The Technopaegnion,* iii. 13].

1. Throughout the *Commentary* Grotius refers repeatedly to these numbered rules and laws, without restating their content. In order that the reader may follow the argument more readily at such points, a complete table of the precepts in question is appended to the translation (*infra,* pp. 499 f.).

poets[a]—to say that Themis and Diké [Right and Justice] were the judicial assessors of Jove; whence Anarchus has correctly inferred (even though he does put the conclusion to an improper use) that a given thing is just because God wills it, rather than that God wills the thing because it is just. According to the somewhat more subtle contention of Plutarch,[b] however, the goddesses Right and Justice are not so much the assessors of Jove, as Jove himself is Right and Justice, and the most ancient and perfect of all laws. It is the latter view that Chrysippus also adopts[c] when he asserts that Jove is the name given to "that force inherent in the constant and eternal law, which guides our lives, so to speak, and instructs us in our duties."

The law of nature The Will of God is revealed, not only through oracles and supernatural portents, but above all in the very design of the Creator; for it is from this last source that the law of nature is derived.[d] Thus Cicero[e] very wisely maintains that the study of celestial phenomena is beneficial in relation to justice, as well as in other ways, because the student "becomes acquainted with the will, plan and purpose of the Supreme Ruler and Lord, to whose nature (so say the philosophers) that true rational principle and sovereign law conform." The following assertion made by Lucan,[f] is also pertinent to this point: "And *the Creator* revealed to us once and for all, *at our birth,* whatever we are permitted to know." According to Chrysippus,[g] too (whom we quoted above), *οὐ γάρ ἐστιν εὑρεῖν τῆς δικαιοσύνης ἄλλην ἀρχὴν οὐδὲ ἄλλην γένεσιν, ἢ τὴν ἐκ τοῦ Διὸς καὶ τὴν ἐκ τῆς κοινῆς φύσεως*; "No beginning, no origin, can be assigned to

a. Hesiod, *Theogony* [901 ff.]; Plato, *Laws,* IV [p. 716 A]; Demosthenes, *Against Aristogeiton* [*Orations,* XXV. 11 = p. 772]; Themistius, *Orations,* VI [p. 79 C]; Ammianus Marcellinus, XXI [i. 8]; Pindar, *Olympian Odes,*VIII [21–2]; Plutarch, *Alexander* [lii = p. 695 A].

b. *To an Uneducated Ruler* [p. 781 A, B].

c. Cicero, *On the Nature of the Gods,* I [xv. 40].

d. *Institutes,* I. ii. 11.

e. *On Ends,* IV [v. 11].

f. Lucan [*The Civil War*], IX [575–6].

g. [Plutarch, *On the Contradiction of the Stoics,* ix, p. 1035 C.]

justice other than its derivation from God and from the universal aspect of nature."

Therefore, since God fashioned creation and willed its existence, every individual part thereof has received from Him certain natural properties whereby that existence may be preserved and each part may be guided for its own good, in conformity, one might say, with the fundamental law inherent in its origin.[a] From this fact the old poets and philosophers[b] have rightly deduced that love, whose primary force and action are directed to self-interest, is the first principle of the whole natural order. Consequently, Horace[c] should not be censured for [5′a] saying, in imitation of the Academics, that expediency might perhaps be called the mother of justice and equity. For all things in nature, as Cicero repeatedly insists, are tenderly regardful of self, and seek their own happiness and security. This phenomenon can be observed not only in the human race, but among the beasts also and even in connexion with inanimate objects, being a manifestation of that true and divinely inspired self-love[d] which is laudable in every phase of creation. As for the *φιλαυτία*, which is classified as a vice—in other words, immoderate self-interest—it is an excess of such love. Thus Socrates (as quoted by Xenophon[e] and Plato[f]) and Diogenes,[g] too, have correctly maintained that justice is a virtue which makes us useful to ourselves as well as to others, so that the just man will in no way inflict injury upon himself or upon any of his members, nor will he bring pain or distress upon himself. Plutarch[h] expounds this doctrine admirably, illustrating it by means of a negative simile when he declares that justice is not like oil, which doctors describe as beneficial to the body externally but injurious

a. Cicero, *Academics,* I [vi. 22–3]; *id., On Ends,* IV [x. 25].

b. Plato, *Symposium,* quoting Hesiod and Parmenides [p. 178 B].

c. *Satires,* I. iii [98].

d. Arist., *Nic. Ethics,* IX. iv [3] and IX. viii [8]; *id., Politics,* II. v [II. ii. 6]; Castrensis, *On Dig.,* I. i. 1, § 4.

e. *Memorabilia,* IV [iv].

f. *Republic,* I. iv [I. xxiv = p. 353 E].

g. Stobaeus, *Sermones* [in *Florilegium*], IX [n. 49].

h. [*Comparison of Aristides and*] *Cato* [iii. 5].

internally, since the just man's highest concern is for himself. Other authorities,[a] distinguishing more subtly between terms, maintain that such concern is the function not so much of justice as of that love [for self] to which we are impelled by nature; but at the same time, they admit that in human affairs the first principle of a man's duty relates to himself.

In fact, all duty (according to the philosophers) consists in *περὶ τά πως ἔχοντα πρὸς ἡμᾶς*, that is to say, in those things which in some way pertain to self. Such things, to be sure, fall under a twofold classification. For some concern us from the standpoint of good, others from the standpoint of evil, as is indicated, indeed, by the two mental attitudes of aversion and desire, attitudes implanted by nature not in man [5′a′] alone, but in all living creatures.

The particular aspect of duty that we are about to discuss, however, is bound up not with all goods and ills, but solely with those which men can either bestow upon or take from other men, including not only concrete goods and ills but also their external effects. For only these [transferable] things can enter into any comparison that seeks to establish how much a person owes to himself, and how much to his fellow man.

Generally speaking, these good and evil things are likewise divided into two classes. The first and more important group consists of those which directly concern the body itself: for example, among the ills, death, mutilation of the members (which is akin to death) and disease; among the blessings, life with the body whole and healthy. The second group has to do with things existing outside of ourselves but nevertheless beneficial or injurious, painful or pleasing, to us—such as, on the one hand, honour, riches, pleasure; and on the other hand, infamy, poverty, pain. Thus, when Plato[b] says that justice is concerned with *περὶ σώματος θεραπείαν, ἢ περὶ χρημάτων κτῆσιν*, that is to say, with the care of the body and the possession of property, he includes under the head of "property" the results consequent upon its possession.

a. Th. Aq., I–II, qu. 77, art. 4, in reply; Seneca, *On Benefits,* V. ix.
b. *Republic,* III [I. v = p. 331 A, B].

Accordingly, from this combination of concepts, two precepts of the [6] law of nature emerge:[2] first, that *It shall be permissible to defend* [*one's own*] life and to shun that which threatens to prove injurious; [a] secondly, that *It shall be permissible to acquire for oneself, and to retain, those things which are useful for life.* The latter precept, indeed, we shall interpret with Cicero[b] as an admission that each individual may, without violating the precepts of nature, prefer to see acquired for himself rather than for another, that which is important for the conduct of life. Moreover, no member of any sect of philosophers, when embarking upon a discussion of the ends [of good and evil],[3] has ever failed to lay down these two laws first of all as indisputable axioms.[c] For on this point the Stoics, the Epicureans, and the Peripatetics are in complete agreement, and apparently even the Academics have entertained no doubt.

Law I

Law II

Since we ourselves are corporeal entities, other bodies are naturally able to benefit or injure us. Thus the first law is put into practice through the repulsion of one body from another, and the second law, through the attachment of one body to another. To this end, the lower animals were given their corporeal members and we, our hands and feet, as instruments for the two functions of repelling and attaching. This function of attachment is a gift from God. For He who bestowed upon living creatures their very existence, bestowed also the things necessary for existence. Some of these things, indeed, are necessary to being, while others are necessary only to well-being; or, one might say that they relate respectively to safety and to comfort. In a universal sense, moreover, in-

a. Cicero, *On Duties,* I [iv. 11]; *id., Academics,* IV [II. xlii. 131]; *id., On Ends,* IV [vii. 16] and V [ix. 24]; *id., For Milo* [iv. 10].

b. *On Duties,* III [v. 22].

c. Cicero, *On Ends,* II and III [vi. 20] and *passim.*

2. The first four words of collotype p. 6, *similiter iuris naturalis duae* (likewise [there are] two precepts of the law of nature), are omitted from the translation at this point. Obviously, they represent a continuation of the passage deleted at the bottom of collotype p. 5′, and should have been deleted also, when pp. 5′*a* and 5′*a*′ were inserted.

3. *Finibus* is written with a capital letter in the Latin, and Grotius evidently had in mind the title of the Ciceronian work *De Finibus Bonorum et Malorum,* cited by him immediately below.

ferior things were given for use by their superiors. Plants and herbs, for example, were given to the beasts, and beasts—as well as all things in general—to man,[a] inasmuch as man excels in worth all other created things. However, since God bestowed these gifts upon the human race, not upon individual men,[b] and since such gifts could be turned to use only through acquisition of possession by individuals, it necessarily followed that *τὸ ἐσφετερισμένον*, "what had been seized as his own" by each person should become the property of that person. Such seizure is called *possessio* [the act of taking possession], the forerunner of *usus* [6′] [use], and subsequently of *dominium* [ownership].[c]

The act of taking possession, and ownership

But God judged that there would be insufficient provision for the preservation of His works, if He commended to each individual's care only the safety of that particular individual, without also willing that one created being should have regard for the welfare of his fellow beings,[d] in such a way that all might be linked in mutual harmony as if by an everlasting covenant. Seneca[e] has said: "You must needs live for others, if you would live for yourself."

Love, then, is twofold: love for oneself, and love for others. In the former aspect, it is known as "desire"; in the latter, as "friendliness."[f] While a certain form of friendliness is discernible even within inanimate objects, and more clearly so in the lower animals, this manifestation of love burns most brightly in man, as in one who is peculiarly endowed not only with the affections shared in common with other creatures but also with the sovereign attribute of reason: that is to say, as in a being derived from God Himself, who imprinted upon man the image of His own mind. Epicharmus calls attention to this point in the following verse:[g]

a. *Genesis,* i, at end; Cicero, *On Duties,* I [iv. 11]; *Dig.,* XXII. i. 28; Arist., *Politics,* I. viii [I. iii. 7–8].

b. Cicero, *On Laws,* I [viii. 25].

c. *Dig.* XLI. ii. 1, § 1. See Thesis III, chap. xii, *infra,* pp. 314ff.

d. Plato, *Lysis* [p. 207 c].

e. [*Epistles,* xlviii. 2–3.]

f. Th. Aq. I–II, qu. 26, art. 4.

g. [Clement of Alexandria, *Stromata,* V. xiv.]

ὁ δέ γε τἀνθρώπου λόγος πέφυκ᾽ ἀπὸ τοῦ θείου λόγου.

Man's reason from God's reason takes its being.

To be sure, this rational faculty has been darkly beclouded by human vice; yet not to such a degree but that rays of the divine light are still clearly visible, manifesting themselves especially in the mutual accord of nations. For evil and falsehood are, in a sense and by their very nature, of infinite extent[a] and at the same time internally discordant, whereas universal concord can exist only in relation to that which is good and true.[b] Many persons, indeed, have chosen to call that very accord the secondary law of nature, or primary law of nations;[4] and Cicero[c] has said that the principle informing this law is nothing more nor less than right reason derived from the will of the gods. In another passage, the same author[d] declares that, "on any matter, the consensus of all nations should be regarded as a precept of the natural law." Heraclitus[e] perceives this truth; for though he postulates the existence of two kinds of reason—*λόγους, τὸν ξυνὸν καὶ τὸν ἴδιον*, that is to say, a universal form of reason or understanding, and an individual form—he maintains that universal reason is the *κριτήριον* [criterion] and judge, so to speak, of truth, *τὰ γὰρ κοινῇ φαινόμενα πιστά*, "on the ground that those things are worthy of faith which are commonly so regarded." To this assertion he adds the following comment: *τρέφονται πάντες οἱ ἀνθρώπινοι νόμοι ὑπὸ ἑνὸς τοῦ θείου*; "All the laws of mortals rest upon one divine law."[f] Thus a second rule is derived from the first, namely: *What the common consent of mankind has shown to be the will of all, that is law.*

The primary law of nations

Rule II

a. Arist., *Nic. Ethics,* II. v [II. vi. 14].

b. [Arist., *Nic. Ethics*] IX. iv; *ibid.* IX. vi; Cicero, *On the Nature of the Gods,* I [xliv]; Th. Aq., I–II, qu. 93, art. 3.

c. *Philippics,* XI [xii. 28].

d. *Tusculan Disputations,* I [xiii. 30].

e. In Sextus Empiricus [*Against the Logicians,* I. 131–4].

f. Cicero, *On Laws,* I [vii. 22–3].

4. *Ius gentium primarium,* the body of moral precepts imposed by natural reason upon all peoples, as opposed to *ius gentium secundarium,* the positive and consensual law of nations compounded of rules commonly accepted by the members of the international community for the good of all (*infra,* p. 45).

Now, men agree most emphatically upon the proposition that it behoves us to have a care for the welfare of others; for the acceptance of this obligation might almost be termed a distinguishing characteristic of man. It is for this reason that the wise philosophy[5] of Seneca[a] ascribes to the concept of good the quality of pertaining both to oneself and to others. Here we have the starting-point of that justice, properly so called, which Aristotle[b] and various writers have described as being concerned with the good of others, and which Cicero[c] and Apuleius[d] depict as "looking outwards." Hesiod[e] offers the following admirable comment on the same subject: [7]

> *Τόνδε γὰρ ἀνθρωποῖσι νόμον διέταξε Κρονίων,*
> *Ἰχθύσι γὰρ καὶ θηρσὶ καὶ οἰωνοῖς πετεηνοῖς*
> *Ἐσθέμεν ἀλλήλους· ἐπεὶ οὐ δίκη ἐστὶ μετ᾽ αὐτῶν·*
> *Ἀνθρωποῖσι δ᾽ ἔδωκε δίκην, ἣ πολλὸν ἀρίστη.*
>
> *For laws were giv'n to man by highest Jove.*
> *The beasts, forsooth, the fish, the birds that soar*
> *Feed on each other, ignorant of right;*
> *On us, however, justice—best of gifts—*
> *Hath been conferred. . . .*

Seneca[f] has said: "Just as all the bodily members function in mutual harmony because it is to the advantage of the whole that the individual parts be preserved, even so mankind will show forbearance toward individuals because we are born for a life of fellowship. Society, too, can be kept safe from harm only by love and watchful care for its component

a. *Epistles,* lxxxvi [lxxxv. 36].
b. *Nic. Ethics,* V. iii [V. i. 13].
c. *Republic,* II [III. vii. 11].
d. *On Plato* [p. 1099].
e. *Works and Days* [276–9].
f. *On Anger,* II. xxxi [7–8].

5. The collotype clearly has *sapientia,* but it should be noted that a more accurate paraphrase of Seneca's statement would result from altering the word very slightly to read *sapientis.* The phrase could then be translated: ". . . the good of Seneca's wise man pertains both to himself and to others."

parts." Elsewhere, he[a] declares that, "Security must be obtained by offering security in exchange." Herein lies that brotherhood of man, that world state, commended to us so frequently and so enthusiastically by the ancient philosophers and particularly by the Stoics, whose view Cicero[b] adopts. This view is also the basis of the statement made by Florentinus,[c] namely, that because of a certain kinship established among us by nature, it is sinful that man should lie in ambush for his fellow man, a precept which Cicero[d] very properly ascribes to the law of nations.

The foregoing observations show how erroneously the Academics—those masters of ignorance—have argued in refutation of justice, that the kind derived from nature looks solely to personal advantage, while civil justice is based not upon nature but merely upon opinion; for they have overlooked that intermediate aspect of justice which is characteristic of humankind.[e]

Accordingly, from the First and Second Rules two laws arise, relating to the good of others, whereby the preceding laws, which relate to one's own good, are complemented and confined within just limits.[f] One of the two laws in question runs as follows: *Let no one inflict injury upon* **Law III** *his fellow.* The other is the precept: *Let no one seize possession of that which* **Law IV** *has been taken into the possession of another.* The former is the law of inoffensiveness; the latter is the law of abstinence. As a result of the Third Law, life is rendered secure; as a result of the Fourth Law, distinctions of ownership arise, together with the well-known concept of Mine and Thine.[g]

It was this concept that the ancients[h] had in mind when they called

a. *On Mercy,* I. xix [5–6].

b. *On Laws,* I [vii. 23].

c. *Dig.* I. i. 3.

d. Cicero, *Republic,* III [xix and xx]; Lactantius, *Divine Institutes,* V. xv, xvii, xviii.

e. Lactantius, *ibid.* xviii.

f. Cicero, *On Duties,* I [vii. 20 ff.]; *Institutes,* I. i. 3.

g. *Dig.* I. i. 5.

h. Macrobius, *Saturnalia,* III. xii [10].

Ceres "the Lawgiver" and spoke of her sacred rites as "the Lawgiver's festival," intimating that the establishment of laws grew out of the division of lands. The principle underlying the Fourth Law is expounded by Quintilian[a] in the following terms: "If we accept the proposition that anything whatsoever that has fallen to man's lot for his use, is the property of the person who has possession thereof, then assuredly it is a wrongful act to take away anything rightfully possessed." In this principle of confidence, so to speak, lies the origin of human society, a way of living towards which, by the design of the Creator, man was more strongly impelled than any other living creature.[b] That social impulse was the source of *τὰ ξυμβόλαια*, that is to say, of reciprocal acts and sentiments, and of the intermingling of one's own goods and ills with the goods and ills of others. From the same source arose the saying that man is a god or a wolf to his fellow man.

Consequently, we feel the need of that form of justice properly [8][6] known as *ἀρετὴ κοινωνική*, or "social virtue."[c] Now, the good to which this social justice has reference is called "equality," or *ἰσονομία*; the evil, "inequality," or *πλεονεξία*. For just as in nature, so also in every society, that is good which is reduced in the greatest possible degree to unity; and unity connotes primarily identity, but also, in a secondary sense, equivalence, so that wherever the former quality cannot exist, the latter takes its place.

But there are two kinds of equivalence, based respectively on number and on proportion. For example, twenty exceeds fifteen, and ten exceeds five, by an equal numerical difference, that is to say, by five; whereas twenty exceeds ten, and ten exceeds five, in an equal proportional measure, or in other words, each by a half of itself. Number merely orders the parts in their relations with one another; proportion relates the parts to the whole.

Accordingly, those persons who are charged with the management of

a. *Declamations,* xiii [8].

b. Arist., *Politics,* I. ii [I. i. 12].

c. *Ibid.* III. xiii [III. vii. 8].

6. Collotype p. 7′ contains only deleted matter and is therefore omitted from the translation.

some whole, exercise proportional justice,[a] which may also be called "Justice the Allotter" [i.e. distributive justice]. In conformity with this phase of justice, the head of a household allots to its various members, shares measured and weighed in proportion to their different ages and conditions. The Universe is ordered in consonance with this same justice by God Himself, called by Plato "the Geometer," precisely because He administers law and equity according to a certain principle of proportion, as the above-mentioned author explains in the *Gorgias;*[b] for the end sought by the geometrician is the reduction of all things to equality.

The other kind of justice, which we now choose to designate as the Compensator [i.e. compensatory justice], is concerned not with communal affairs but with those peculiar to the individual. Thus compensatory justice does not relate the parts to the whole; that is to say, it weighs things and acts without regard for persons. The function of such justice is twofold, namely: in regard to good, the preservation thereof; in regard to evil, its correction. Hence these two laws arise: first, *Evil deeds must* Law V
be corrected; secondly, *Good deeds must be recompensed* (or, to use the Law VI
Greek term, ἀντευποιητέον).

For this process of relating the component elements to one another may be described as made up in part of the refluent action of the laws of the first order [Laws I and II], and in part of the outward-flowing action of the laws of the second order [Laws III and IV].[7] In itself, the process is mutual and alternating. Here we have the origin of τὸ ἀντιπεπονθός, "retaliation"—or, in the language of the Scholastics, "restitution"—the task of compensatory justice. In accordance with this form of justice, he who has derived gain from another's good deed repays that exact amount to the benefactor whose possessions have been diminished, while he who has suffered loss through the evil deed of an-

a. See Plutarch, *Symposiacs,* VIII. ii [in *Moralia,* p. 719 B, C].

b. [p. 508 A, B.]

7. That is to say, the acts coming under the laws relative to defence of one's own life and possessions are acts whose effect falls back upon the agent himself, while the laws against infliction of injury or property loss upon others, are concerned with effects external to the agent.

other receives the exact equivalent of that loss from the malefactor whose possessions have been increased. Hence it follows that there are two kinds of obligation: in the terminology of the philosophers[a] ἑκούσιον καὶ ἀκούσιον, "voluntary and involuntary"; in that of the jurists,[b] obligation *ex contractu* [i.e. arising from a contract] and obligation *ex delicto* [8′] [i.e. arising from wrongdoing]. In both cases, the person who has gained is regarded as the debtor and he who has lost as the creditor, the former having been enriched by the precise amount of the latter's impoverishment; and if the amount thus lost is taken from the debtor and given to the creditor,[c] that is true justice. Such justice requires that the thing taken shall be returned in the case of a theft just as in the case of a loan, and that, even as payment is made of a purchase price or of revenue from a contract, so also reparation for loss inflicted and satisfaction for injuries should be provided.

It sometimes happens, however, that things properly pertaining to the parts tend to affect the whole, even though they are not directed toward the whole as such. In these circumstances, one must weigh, not the merits of persons, but the value of the things or the force of the actions involved. This is the basis of rewards and punishments. For the whole world should be grateful to him who has bestowed a universal benefit. The devisers of useful inventions, for example, have received praise and honour from all mankind. Conversely, those persons who have inflicted universal injury, no less than those who have injured a single individual, ought to give proportionate satisfaction. In a sense, however, an injury inflicted even upon one individual is the concern of all, and this is true primarily because of the example set; just as it is the concern of the whole body that its various members should be sound, particularly as a guard against contagion.

Now it may seem strange, inasmuch as punishment is hurtful to the person on whom it is inflicted, that justice, which is motivated by solicitude for all, should be directed to the harm of any individual. In order

a. Arist., *Nic. Ethics,* V. v [V. ii. 13].
b. *Dig.* XLIV. vii. 1.
c. Arist., *Nic. Ethics,* V. vi and vii [V. ii. 1–5].

to throw light on this point, it may be observed that no art ever sets up evil as its ultimate goal, and that nevertheless there are times when an art makes use of evil—though only in cases of necessity—as an intermediate measure without which good cannot be attained. Doctors will never inflict pain upon the sick, unless considerations of health demand that they do so; nor will they amputate any part of the body, save in the interest of the body as a whole. Thus pain and mutilation, originally evil in themselves, may assume the quality of goodness because they lead to a good greater than the one to which as evils they were diametrically opposed.

With a view to clarifying the foregoing simile (which is frequently employed in this connexion by the philosophers), we must draw a distinction between different kinds of punishment. Gellius[a] has observed that there are three kinds according to Taurus, and two, according to Plato.[b] Taurus, however, included *τιμωρίαν* "vengeance,"[8] which pertains properly to relations between individuals; so that only two kinds pertinent to the whole remain to be considered. Of these two, the first is chastisement, referred to by Taurus as *νουθεσία* [admonition], *κόλασις* [correction, punishment], or *παραίνεσις* [exhortation], and also, by Plato,[c] as *εὐθύνη* [a setting straight, correction]. Chastisement involves an attempt to correct the particular individual punished and also to [9] render him more useful to humanity. It is a form of *θεραπευτικὸς τρόπος*, or "curative procedure," which operates (as Aristotle[d] explains) through the application of opposites [e.g. by applying pain to remedy a condition arising from an excess of pleasure; or loss, to remedy the effect of excessive gain]. The second type of punishment is *παράδειγμα*, that is to say, exemplary punishment, which by arousing the fear of a like

a. *Attic Nights,* VI. xiv [VII. xiv. 5–6].

b. *Gorgias* [p. 525 A, B].

c. *Protagoras* [p. 326 E].

d. *Nic. Ethics,* II. ii [II. iii].

8. In the translation of this term, the Greek is followed rather than the Latin, which has *satisfactionem* ("satisfaction," "amends," "reparation"). The context clearly indicates that Grotius was referring specifically to satisfaction attained through the infliction of punishment, i.e. vengeance.

penalty deters others from sinning. This type is, so to speak, *προφυλακτικὸς τρόπος*, "a preventive procedure." The first kind of punishment has as its aim the correction of one individual; the second kind is aimed at the correction of all other persons, in addition to that one. The attainment of these two objectives leads to a third: universal security. For if all persons conduct themselves aright, it necessarily follows that no one will suffer wrongfully.

These are the three ends sought by the law (so Seneca[a] says) in the punishment of wrongdoing: ends which coincide for the most part, and to such an extent, indeed, that even capital punishment, according to the Platonists,[b] is in a sense beneficial to the guilty parties, whenever there is no other remedy for their incurably diseased spirits. It is clear, then, that the following assertion made by Plato[c] is entirely true: *οὐ γὰρ ἐπὶ κακῷ δίκη γίγνεται οὐδεμία*; "No legal punishment has evil as its aim." As the Scholastics[d] have maintained, it is not proper for the spirit of the avenger to dwell with pleasure upon any person's ill fortune. According to the teachings of Seneca,[e] he who inflicts vengeance in the right way exacts punishment not eagerly and for its own sake, but because it behoves him to do so; not as if vengeance were sweet, but on the ground that it serves a useful purpose; not in anger, but in the exercise of caution. Such a person is intent upon future acts that can be averted, rather than upon acts that are past and irrevocable; and, as Plato[f] observes, he imposes punishment not because sin has been committed but in order that its commission may be prevented. A part of these precepts regarding punishment is so necessary, indeed, that some persons[g] have described justice itself as *τιμωρίας ἀπαίτησιν παρὰ τῶν προηδικηκότων*, "the exaction of a penalty from those who have pre-

a. *On Mercy,* I. xxii.

b. Plato, *Republic,* III [p. 410 A]; Apuleius, *On Plato* [II, p. 1122] and Seneca, *On Anger,* I. v. [I. vi].

c. *Laws,* IX [p. 854 D].

d. Th. Aq. II–II, qu. 108; Sylvester, on word *vindicta.*

e. *On Anger,* I. ix [4], II. xxxii [II. xxxiii. 1], II. xxxi [8], I. xvi [I. xix. 7].

f. *Protagoras* [p. 324 B; also in Plato, *Laws,* XI, p. 934 A].

g. Hierax in Stobaeus [*Florilegium,* IX, n. 58].

viously committed a wrongful act." Such is the purport of the legal maxims, "Evil deeds ought not to go unpunished," "Indulgence should not be shown to human wickedness," and various similar sayings.

But that other law, [the Sixth,] regarding repayment for good deeds, is characterized by an equity no less manifest. We find this passage in Xenophon:[a] *τί δέ τοὺς εὖ ποιοῦντας, ἀντευεργετεῖν οὐ πανταχοῦ νόμιμόν ἐστι; νόμιμον ἔφη;* "'Again, is it not the universal law, that we should repay with benefactions those persons who have deserved well of us?' 'To be sure, it is,' said he." The jurists,[b] too, hold that *πρὸς* [9′] *ἀντίδωρα*, "the obligation to repay," is a natural obligation, and that it is unjust in the eyes of nature for one individual to be enriched at the expense of another, or for any person to suffer loss in consequence of his own good deed. Seneca[c] declares that, "The maxim, 'Repay what you owe,' is just in the highest degree, and constitutes a pronouncement of the law of nations." [10]

However, since the exchange of good things is voluntary (as we have already pointed out), the extent of the credit involved is measured by the will of the creditor. For there is one kind of good that is so called in an absolute sense, and there is another kind that is good from the standpoint of a particular individual. Indeed, to borrow Aristotle's[d] admirable explanation, *ὅσα περὶ ἕκαστον νοῦς ἀποδίδωσιν ἑκάστῳ τοῦτ' ἐστιν ἑκάστῳ ἀγαθόν;* "Whatever each person's understanding has ruled for him regarding a given matter, that to him is good." For God created man *αὐτεξούσιον*, "free and *sui iuris*," so that the actions of each individual and the use of his possessions were made subject not to another's will but to his own. Moreover, this view is sanctioned by the common consent of all nations. For what is that well-known concept, "natural liberty," other than the power of the individual to act in accordance with

a. *Commentaries* [or *Memorabilia*], IV [iv. 24].

b. *Dig.* V. iii. 25, § 11.

c. *On Benefits,* III. xiv.

d. *The Art of Rhetoric,* I. vi [2] and *Nic. Ethics,* III. vi [III. iii. 17]. Add Apuleius, *On Plato* [II, p. 1099].

Liberty and ownership

his own will?[a] And liberty in regard to actions is equivalent to ownership in regard to property.[b] Hence the saying: "Every man is the governor and arbiter of affairs relative to his own property."[c] To be sure, one's will may undergo change, but not to the extent of deceiving others;[d] that is to say, not to the extent of winning another person over to a state of credulous confidence advantageous or pleasurable to oneself[e] but for the most part harmful to that other individual. For even if no additional injury is involved, it is in any case an evil to be deceived in one's belief. Plato[f] put this thought in the form of a question: *τὸ ἐψεῦσθαι τῆς ἀληθείας κακόν;* [Or is it not an evil to be deceived concerning the truth?] Assuredly, no just man will be the cause of such an evil to his fellow man.

Rule III

From the foregoing considerations the rule of good faith is derived: *What each individual has indicated to be his will, that is law with respect to him.*[g] With this rule the old saying agrees, that no injury[h] is committed against a person who is willing; as does also the traditional maxim that nothing else is so congruous with natural equity and the good faith of mankind, as is the observance of agreements which have been accepted among the various parties.[i] Thus Cicero,[j] too, declares that good faith is the foundation of justice.

But there is a difference between tacit indication of will and express indication thereof. Tacit indication is effected by giving any kind of sign; express indication, by the means which God granted to man alone for this very purpose, namely, the medium of speech.[k] This gift is [10′]

a. *Institutes,* I. i. 3; Arist., *Politics,* VI. ii [VI. i. 7].
b. See Vázquez, *Ill. Cont.* I. xvii [5]; Arist., *The Art of Rhetoric,* I. v [7].
c. *Code,* IV. xxxv. 21.
d. See *Dig.* XLVII. ii. 55 (54).
e. Plato, *Republic,* II [p. 382 B].
f. *Ibid.* III [p. 413 A].
g. Plato, *Laws,* XI [IX, pp. 863 E, 864 A]; *Psalms,* xii.
h. Arist., *Nic. Ethics,* V. xi [10]; *Dig.* XXXIX. iii. 9.
i. *Dig.* II. xiv. 1; *Institutes,* II. i. 40; *Dig.* XIII. v. 1.
j. *On Duties,* I [vii. 23].
k. Arist., *Politics,* I. ii [10]; *Dig.* XXXIII. x. 7, § 2; *ibid.* XLIV. vii. 38; Th. Aq. II–II, qu. 109, art. 3.

regarded as so sacred and inviolable an instrument for the interchange of blessings and the reciprocal intimation of human will that, in the eyes of all men, there is no more grievous disgrace than that attached to lying.[a] Herein lies the origin of pacts, which is necessarily bound up with the Sixth Law, as has been indicated above. It was this law that Simonides had in mind when he proposed the following definition of justice: "To speak the truth, and to pay back what has been received."[b] The Platonists, moreover, frequently refer to justice as ἀλήθειαν, a term translated by Apuleius[c] as "trustworthiness" [*fidelitas*]. **Pacts**

When it came to pass, after these principles had been established, that many persons (such is the evil growing out of the corrupt nature of some men!) either failed to meet their obligations or even assailed the fortunes and the very lives of others, for the most part without suffering punishment—since the unforeseeing were attacked by those who were prepared, or single individuals by large groups—there arose the need for a new remedy, lest the laws of human society be cast aside as invalid.[d] This need was especially urgent in view of the increasing number of human beings, swollen to such a multitude that men were scattered about with vast distances separating them and were being deprived of opportunities for mutual benefaction. Therefore, the lesser social units began to gather individuals together into one locality, not with the intention of abolishing the society which links all men as a whole, but rather in order to fortify that universal society by a more dependable means of protection, and at the same time, with the purpose of bringing together under a more convenient arrangement the numerous different products of many persons' labour which are required for the uses of human life. For it is a fact (as Pliny[e] so graphically points out) that when universal goods are separately distributed, each man's ills pertain to him individually, whereas, when those goods are brought together and intermingled, in-

a. *Romans,* i. 31.
b. See Plato, *Republic,* I [p. 331 D, E].
c. *On Plato* [II, p. 1099].
d. See Plato, *Politicus* [*passim*] and *Republic,* II [p. 369 B, C].
e. *Panegyric* [xxxii, p. 57].

dividual ills cease to be the concern of any one person and the goods of all pertain to all. In this matter, too, as in every other, human diligence has imitated nature, which has ensured the preservation of the universe by a species of covenant binding upon all of its parts. Accordingly, this smaller social unit, formed by a general agreement for the sake of the common good[a]—in other words, this considerable group sufficing for self-protection through mutual aid, and for equal acquisition of the necessities of life—is called a commonwealth [*Respublica*]; and the individuals making up the commonwealth are called citizens [*cives*].

The commonwealth and citizens

This system of organization has its origin in God the King, who rules the whole universe and to whom, indeed (so the philosophers[b] declare) nothing achieved on earth is more acceptable than those associations and assemblies of men which are known as states [*civitates*]. According to Cicero,[c] Jupiter himself sanctioned the following precept, or law: All things salutary to the commonwealth are to be regarded as legitimate and just.

There is agreement on this point, moreover, among almost all peoples, for in every part of the world we find a division into just such united groups, with the result that persons who hold themselves aloof from this established practice seem hardly worthy to be called human beings. Thus one might almost say that the ultimate infamy is the condition described in the words[d] ἀφρήτωρ, ἀθέμιστος, ἀνέστιος, "a lawless man, without tribe or hearth."

In addition to the common opinion of mankind, another factor has played a part: the will of individuals, manifested either in the formal acceptance of pacts, as was originally the case, or in tacit indication of consent, as in later times, when each individual attached himself to the body of a commonwealth that had already been established.[e] For a commonwealth, even though it is composed of different parts, [11]

a. See Apuleius, *On Plato* [II, p. 1147]; Cicero, *Republic,* III [I. xxv. 39–40].
b. Cicero, *Scipio's Dream* [*The Republic,* VI. xiii. 13].
c. *Philippics,* XI [xii. 28].
d. Homer [*Iliad,* IX. 63].
e. Th. Aq. II–II, qu. 98, art. 4; Vázquez, *Ill. Cont.* xxviii. 18.

constitutes by virtue of its underlying purpose a unified and permanent body, and therefore the commonwealth as a whole should be regarded as subject to a single law.[a] [11 a]

Now, within this corporate whole, which is in a sense a condensed version of that larger entity, [the universal society established by nature,] the functions of the two forms of justice above mentioned, [i.e. distributive and compensatory justice,] are revealed in a much clearer light. For distributive justice allots public possessions to various owners on a comparative basis of individual merit, and assigns duties and burdens to the various citizens in accordance with the strength of each. Compensatory justice, on the other hand, is concerned not only with the preservation of equality among individuals, but also with the bestowal of appropriate honours and rewards upon deserving patriots, and with the punishment of persons who are injuring the community. Furthermore, this same form of justice shows us how acts directed to individuals are of interest to the whole, for it confers civic crowns as well as triumphal honours, and does not confine its public judgements to cases of high treason, but on the contrary demands punishment also for homicides, forgers, and similar malefactors. Such functions, of course, are in quite close accord with the law of the society founded by nature.

It seems, however, that there are laws peculiar to the civil covenant, which are derived from the three rules above stated and which extend beyond the laws already set forth, as follows: first, *Individual citizens* [11] Law VII *should not only refrain from injuring other citizens, but should furthermore protect them, both as a whole and as individuals;*[b] secondly, *Citizens should* Law VIII *not only refrain from seizing one another's possessions, whether these be held privately or in common, but should furthermore contribute individually both that which is necessary to other individuals and that which is necessary to the whole.* In relation to the former precept, Plato[c] calls citizens *βοηθούς*, and in relation to the latter, he calls them *κοινωνούς*, that is to say, "auxiliaries" of one another, and "partners."

a. *Dig.*, V. i. 76; *ibid.* XLI. iii. 30.
b. Arist., *Politics,* III. ix [III. v. 13].
c. *Republic,* II [p. 369 c].

These two laws, then, are directed in a certain sense to the common good, though not to that phase of the concept with which the laws of the third order [Laws V and VI] are concerned, namely, the good of the different individuals composing the community. Laws VII and VIII relate rather to the common good interpreted as the good of the unit and therefore [in a subordinate sense] as one's own. Accordingly, although the order of presentation of the first set of laws and of those following immediately thereafter has indicated that one's own good takes precedence over the good of another person[a]—or, let us say, it indicates that by nature's ordinance each individual should be desirous of his own good fortune in preference to that of another, which is the purport of the proverbs, "I myself am my own closest neighbour," *γόνυ κνήμης ἔγγιον* [My knee is closer than my shin], "My tunic is closer than my cloak"—nevertheless, in questions involving a comparison between the good of single individuals and the good of all (both of which can correctly be described as "one's own,"[b] since the term "all" does in fact refer to a species of unit), the more general concept should take precedence on the ground that it includes the good of individuals as well.[c] In other words, the cargo cannot be saved unless the ship is preserved. Hierocles[d] says: *χρὴ τὸ κοινὸν τοῦ κατ' ἰδίαν μὴ χωρίζειν, ἀλλ' ἓν ἡγεῖσθαι καὶ ταὐτόν, τό τε γὰρ τῇ πατρίδι συμφέρον κοινόν ἐστι καὶ τῶν κατὰ μέρος ἑκάστῳ.* "That which is public should not be separated from that which is private [. . .].[9] For whatever is beneficial for one's country [as a whole] is likewise of common [advantage] to the various parts thereof." The speech of Pericles, as recorded by Thucydides,[e] clarifies this very prob-

a. Arist., *Nic. Ethics,* IX. viii [2].

b. *Dig.* L. xvi. 239, § 9.

c. Th. Aq. II–II, qu. 26, art. 4, ad 3; *Authentica to Code,* VI. xliii. 3 [= *Novels,* XXXIX. i].

d. [In Stobaeus, *Florilegium,* XXXIX, n. 35.]

e. II [lx. 2–4].

9. At this point Grotius omits from his Latin text a phrase that is included in the Greek quotation. This phrase, which lends added emphasis to the statement made by Hierocles, reads in English as follows: "but [the two concepts] should be thought of as one and the same."

lem of why and to what extent private well-being is subordinate to public well-being. Pericles is represented as speaking thus:

ἐγὼ γὰρ ἡγοῦμαι πόλιν πλείω ξύμπασαν ὀρθουμένην ὠφελεῖν τοὺς ἰδιώτας, ἢ καθ' ἕκαστον τῶν πολιτῶν εὐπραγοῦσαν, ἀθρόαν δὲ σφαλλομένην· καλῶς μὲν γὰρ φερόμενος ἀνὴρ τὸ καθ' ἑαυτὸν, διαφθειρομένης τῆς πατρίδος, οὐδὲν ἧσσον ξυναπόλλυται· κακοτυχῶν δὲ ἐν εὐτυχούσῃ, πολλῷ μᾶλλον διασώζεται. ὁπότε οὖν πόλις μὲν τὰς ἰδίας ξυμφορὰς οἵα τε φέρειν, εἷς δὲ ἕκαστος τὰς ἐκείνης ἀδύνατος, πῶς οὐ χρὴ πάντας ἀμύνειν αὐτῇ; καὶ μὴ, ὃ νῦν ὑμεῖς δρᾶτε, ταῖς κατ' οἶκον κακοπραγίαις ἐκπεπληγμένοι τοῦ κοινοῦ τῆς σωτηρίας ἀφίεσθε. [11 b]

For it is my belief that private citizens, too, derive more benefit from a state which is successful as a whole, than from one where individual interests flourish but where the state itself, as an entity, is falling into ruin. For even he whose personal fortunes are well invested, must nevertheless perish if his country is destroyed; while on the other hand, if some individual within a prosperous state is not particularly fortunate, he is still far more likely to be preserved unharmed through the latter. Accordingly, since the state is undoubtedly able to endure the misfortunes of private citizens, whereas the citizen cannot in like manner endure public misfortune, how can it be otherwise than fitting that all persons take counsel together for the state and for its defence, instead of adopting the course which you now follow in betraying the commonwealth because you are stunned, so to speak, by your private losses?

Livy[a] summed up this view in the following concise statement: "While the state remains unharmed, it will easily answer for the safety of private property, too. In nowise will you be able to protect your own interests by betraying the public interest." [11]

Moreover, since it is the will involved that constitutes the measure of a good, as we have already pointed out, it follows that the will of the whole group prevails in regard to the common good, and even in regard to the good of individuals, in so far as the latter is subordinate to the former. For the individual members of the group have themselves con-

a. [XXVI. xxxvi.]

sented to this arrangement, and one of the various attributes of free will is the power to accommodate one's own will to that of another.[a] The will of all, when applied to all, is called *lex* [statutory law]. This law proceeds from God, wherefore it is proclaimed to be[b] εὕρημα καὶ δῶρον θεοῦ, "the invention and gift of God." It is approved by the common consent of all mankind, a point borne out by the words of Chrysippus: νόμος γὰρ τῶν φύσει πολιτικῶν ζώων προστατικός; "for *lex* is the guardian of those living beings who are by their natures adapted to civil life."[c] In short, *lex* rests upon the mutual agreement and the will of [11′] individuals, and with this fact in mind, Demosthenes and Plato sometimes refer to it as κοινὴ πόλεως συνθήκη, "the common pact of the state."[d]

Lex, properly so called

Rule IV

Thus, on the basis of the earlier rules, the following additional rule has developed: *Whatever the commonwealth has indicated to be its will, that is law* [ius] *in regard to the whole body of citizens.* This principle is the source of that branch of law described by the philosophers as θετικόν [positive], or νομικόν [conventional], or even ἴδιον [particular, domestic],[10] and by the jurists as "municipal law." It is law not in an absolute but in a relative sense.[e] The distinction may be illustrated by means of the following analogy: if an ox is exchanged for a sheep, the objects exchanged are certainly not equal in themselves, but equal merely in that the contracting parties have been pleased to make them so. Thus it is quite understandable that what would not otherwise be illicit should become so in this relative sense.[f] Nor is it strange that laws of the kind

Municipal law

a. *Dig.* III. iv. 6; Th. Aq. I–II, qu. 95, art. 1.

b. *Dig.*, I. iii. 2.

c. *Ibid.*

d. *Ibid.* 2 and 1; Arist., *Politics,* I. vi [I. ii. 16] and *The Art of Rhetoric,* I. xv [21]; see also Vázquez, *Ill. Cont.* xliv. 5 and xxviii. 12.

e. Arist., *Nic. Ethics,* V. x [V. vii. 1]; *id., The Art of Rhetoric,* I. xiii [2]; Th. Aq. II–II, qu. 57, art. 2, in reply.

f. *Dig.* XXXIX. i. 20; *ibid.* XXVII. vi. 1, § 5.

10. The term "private," by which this Greek word is commonly rendered in English, would be misleading here. Obviously, Grotius is not referring to the "private law" that governs relations between individuals, as opposed to "public law." More-

in question should change with their cause[a]—that is to say, in accordance with the human will—while natural precepts, based as they are upon a constant cause, remain constant in themselves; or that the former should vary in different localities, since the various communities differ, of course, in their conception of what is good.

A Judgement [or Judicial Pronouncement]

The will of the whole, when applied to particular individuals with the public good in view, becomes a "judgement." For, owing to the fact that men (repeatedly carried away not by true self-love but by a false and inordinate form of that sentiment, the root of every evil) were mistaking for equality that which was in point of fact disproportionate ownership, and because this false conception was giving rise to dissension and tumult, evils which it was important to avoid for the sake of concord and public tranquillity, the state intervened in the role of arbiter among the contending parties, and divided the various portions equitably. [11′a] This is the point made by Democritus[b] when he says: *οὐκ ἂν ἐκώλυον οἱ νόμοι τὴν ἕκαστον κατ' ἰδίην ἐξουσίαν, εἰ μὴ ἕτερος ἕτερον ἐλυμαίνετο. φθόνος γὰρ στάσιος ἀρχὴν ἀπεργάζεται.* "Assuredly, the laws would not have prohibited that each person should live in accordance with his own free will, had there been no tendency on the part of any man to injure his fellow. For it is ill will that paves the way for civil discord." The origin of judgements, then, is the same as the origin of laws. For those persons are called "princes,"[c]

> *δικάσπολοι οἵ κε θέμιστας*
> *ἐκ Διὸς εἰρύαται.*
>
> *Who to the nations of the world hand down*
> *The sacred laws of Jove. . . .*

---

over, in the passage which he cites from Aristotle's *Art of Rhetoric,* the adjective *ἴδιον* is specifically applied to the "particular laws" established by each nation "with reference to itself," as opposed to the "general laws" established by nature.

a. *Institutes,* I. ii. 11 and Theophilus, *Institutes,* I. ii. 11; Arist., *Politics,* III. ix [III. v. 11].

b. [In Stobaeus, *Florilegium,* XXXVIII, n. 57.]

c. [Homer, *Iliad,* I. 238 f.]

In like vein, the poet above quoted wrote:[a]

> *εἷς βασιλεὺς ᾧ ἔδωκε Κρόνου παῖς ἀγκυλομήτεω*
> *σκῆπτρόν τ' ἠδὲ θέμιστας.*
>
> *Let one king rule, he to whom Saturn gives*
> *The golden sceptre and the judge's robe!*

Yet another author has said:[b]

> *μεσταὶ δὲ Διὸς πᾶσαι μὲν ἀγυῖαι,*
> *πᾶσαι δ' ἀνθρώπων ἀγοραί.*
>
> *For Jove's divinity fills all the towns*
> *And forums of mankind.* [11]

Accordingly, even though the precepts of nature permitted every individual to pronounce judgement for himself and of himself, it is clear that all nations deemed it necessary to institute some orderly judicial system, and that individual citizens gave general consent to this project. For the latter, moved by the realization that otherwise their own weakness would prevent them from obtaining their due, bound themselves to abide by the verdict of the state. Indeed, as is quite commonly acknowledged, the very nature of jurisdiction renders it absolutely impossible for any jurisdiction to be established save by general consent.[c]
Rule V This fact is brought out by the following rule: *Whatever the commonwealth has indicated to be its will, that is law for the individual citizens in their mutual relations.*

A Judgement The Fifth Rule differs from the Fourth, in that a judicial pronouncement differs from a precept of municipal law. For such a pronouncement is law made applicable to a particular case. Therefore, in so far as municipal law is concerned, the precept of prime importance for the preservation of human society is the one that makes judicial procedure a [12]

a. [*Ibid.* II. 205 f.]
b. [Aratus, *Phaenomena,* 2 f.]
c. Argument of *Dig.* IV. viii. 27, § 2.

requisite. This precept runs as follows: *No citizen shall seek to enforce his own right against a fellow citizen, save by judicial procedure.* [a] Law IX

Now, the Ninth Law is applicable even to the state itself; for the state is obliged to proceed in accordance with judicial usage when involved in any contention with individuals.[b] Nevertheless, since the state has no superior, it is necessarily the judge even of its own cause. Thus the assertion made by Tacitus[c] was true, namely, that by a provision emanating from the Divine Will, the people were to brook no other judge than themselves.

In the light of the foregoing observations, it is clear that the civil power which manifests itself in laws and judgements[d] resides primarily and essentially within the state itself; for just as power over individuals and their possessions pertains in the nature of things to those individuals, even so there can be no power over all persons and over their goods unless it be a power pertaining to all. On the other hand, just as in private matters we contract obligations or acquire benefits not through our own actions alone but also through the agency of those whom we have placed in charge of our affairs (for it makes no difference whether we perform directly or by proxy[e] any act that we are permitted to perform), so by a similar process it came to pass, as customarily occurs even now in the case of the larger social units, that society, exercising its lawful power over individuals, delegated these functions in whole or in part to specific persons from among its own members. For not every individual in the various nations was free to devote his time to the administration of civil affairs; and furthermore, certain situations were wont to arise which were more satisfactorily handled by a few representatives. Those who are entrusted with such a commission are called, in Greek, ἄρχοντες [archons]; in Latin, *magistratus* [magistrates]. Magistrates

At this point, it is opportune to note that some contracts look to the

a. *Dig.* IV. ii. 13; *Code,* I. ix. 14.

b. See Panormitanus, *On Decretals,* II. ii. 4, n. 21; Innocent, *On Decretals,* V. xl. 23.

c. *Annals,* XIII [lvi].

d. Victoria, *De Potestate Civili,* 7; Covarruvias, *Practicae Quaestiones,* i [2].

e. *Dig.* XXXI. 77, § 20.

advantage of both contracting parties in an equal degree, whereas others are drawn up for the benefit of one party only, with the implication that the omission in regard to the party not specifically benefited will be repaired by the supplementary factor of his willingness, inasmuch as this factor connotes a disposition to be content with simple esteem in exchange for the costs or labour involved. Thus a lease differs from a commodate, barter from donation and a partnership from a mandate gratuitously undertaken. Both of the latter two items are included in the above-mentioned concept of magistracies, each from a different standpoint. For magistrates, in so far as they themselves are citizens, reap on their own behalf the harvest of their administrative labours, namely, the public good;[a] on the other hand, in so far as they are stewards of the state, they have been appointed to their posts not for their own but for the public welfare,[b] very much as if they were the pilots of a ship.

Consequently, in this connexion also two laws exist, laws inherent in
Law X the contract of [magisterial] mandate by its very nature: first, *The mag-*
Law XI *istrate shall act in all matters for the good of the state;* secondly, *The* [12′] *state shall uphold as valid every act of the magistrate.* Seneca[c] rightly maintains, with reference to the prince and the state, that we cannot dispense with either one, save to the destruction of both: "for just as the former needs supporting strength, so does the latter need a head." If we turn back here in order to trace the foregoing assertions to the basic principles on which they rest, it will readily become apparent, in the light of the general consent given by the state and the sanctity with which all peoples invest the title of magistrate, that the author of this arrangement, [i.e. this relationship between prince and state,] is none other than God Himself. Such is the purport of the saying,[d] *ἐκ δὲ Διὸς βασιλῆες*, "Kings are from Jove."

The power thus inherent in the [magisterial] mandate is the basis, moreover, of two rules which are connected with the Fourth and Fifth

a. Plato, *Republic,* III [p. 412 D, E]; Arist., *Politics,* II. v [II. i. 6].
b. Arist., *Nic. Ethics,* V. x [V. vi. 5]; Plato, *Republic,* I [p. 341 C, D].
c. *On Mercy,* I. iv [3].
d. Hesiod, *Theogony* [96].

Rules, and which serve to confirm, in the first instance, the authority of legislators, and in the second instance, the authority of judges. I refer to the following precepts: first, *What the magistrate has indicated to be his will, that is law in regard to the whole body of citizens;* and secondly, *What the magistrate has indicated to be his will, that is law in regard to the citizens as individuals.* [a]

Rule VI

Rule VII

A supplementary observation should be introduced at this point, namely: that there exists a species of mixed law, compounded of the [primary] law of nations and municipal law, and designated in correct and precise terminology as "the secondary law of nations."[b] For just as the common good of private persons gave rise to the precepts above set forth, so also, owing to the existence of a common good of an international nature, the various peoples who had established states for themselves entered into agreements concerning that international good. From this circumstance another rule arose, a rule modelled on the fourth, which in turn had derived its basic principle from the second and third and, consequently, from the first. According to this Eighth Rule, *Whatever all states have indicated to be their will, that is law in regard to all of them.*

The Secondary law of nations

Rule VIII

As illustrations of this precept, one might mention the inviolability of ambassadors[c] (to whom all peoples organized in the form of a state accord equal sanctity), various matters relating to the burial of the dead[d] and other institutions of a similar kind. [12′a]

Such institutions, indeed, are divided into two classes. For some have the force of an international pact, as in the cases just mentioned; others lack that force, and these I should prefer to classify under the head of accepted custom rather than under the head of law.

New explanation

a. *Institutes,* I. ii. 6.

b. Peter Faber, *Semestria,* II. i, near middle; Vázquez, *Ill. Cont.* lxxxix. 25.

c. *Dig.,* L. vii. 17.

d. Sophocles, *Ajax* [1356]; *id., Antigone* [*passim*]; Dio Chrysostom, *De Consuetudine* [*Orations,* lxxvi]; Isocrates, *Helen* [p. 214] and *id., Panegyricus* [55–6].

Nevertheless, even these consuetudinary institutions are frequently described as forming a part of the [secondary] law of nations. This occurs, for example, in connexion with the provisions relative to servitude, to certain kinds of contract, and to order of succession, provisions which have been adopted in identical form—either imitatively or as a coincidence—by all or at least by a majority of nations, in accordance with their separate and individual interests. It is permissible for individual states to renounce such institutions, because of the very fact that the latter were established not by common [international] agreement but by the respective states, acting singly; just as, in the case of a given political community, not everything customary among the majority of persons will forthwith constitute law, but only that which concerns the mutual relations of the citizens. For there are many customary practices of a private rather than a public character (such as the vast number of customs recorded in the compilations of antiquarians, connected with clothing, banquets, or funerals) which the head of any household is free to discard at will even though they have been generally accepted.

Among the other precepts of the law of nations—those binding upon the various peoples as if by force of contract—the most important [12′] is the one which resembles the first precept of municipal law [Law IX], Law XII and which may be worded thus: *Neither the state nor any citizen thereof shall seek to enforce his own right against another state or its citizen,* [13] *save by judicial procedure.* The necessity for this precept is indeed self-evident, and can be deduced from the observations already set forth.

But a new difficulty presents itself at this point, one which did not appear in connexion with municipal law. For citizens ὑποτάσσονται [are subject] to their respective states, and therefore, both in disputes with one another and in disputes with the state, they rightly submit to the judgement of the latter; whereas one state [οὐχ] ὑποτάσσεται, but rather, ἀντιτάσσεται—that is to say, it is not in subjection but in contraposition—to another state, and citizens of the one are likewise contraposed to citizens of the other. New explanation While it was readily agreed, of course, that the judicial function should be exercised by a state, there was a possibility of disagreement as to which of two states should be the one to discharge this function; for each of them, indeed, could refer to those famous lines:[a]

> δίκαιοι δ' ἐσμὲν οἰκοῦντες πόλιν
> αὐτοὶ καθ' αὑτοὺς κυρίας κραίνειν δίκας.
>
> *All we who dwell within these city walls,*
> *Have power to execute our courts' decrees.*

Truly, there is no greater sovereign power set over the power of the state and superior to it, since the state is a self-sufficient aggregation. Nor was it possible for all of the nations not involved in a dispute to reach an agreement providing for an inquiry by them into the case of each disputant.

Thus it was necessary to settle any controversy of this kind by resorting to some distinction, such as that incorporated in the following rule: *In regard to judicial procedure, precedence shall be given to the state which is the defendant, or whose citizen is the defendant; but if the said state proves remiss in the discharge of its judicial duty, then that state shall be the judge, which is itself the plaintiff, or whose citizen is the plaintiff.* As a matter of fact, such disputes could not have been settled in any other way. For two parties—the plaintiff and the defendant—are involved in every lawsuit, and in the situation which we are discussing it was absolutely necessary that the state representing one of the parties should be given the role of judge; so that the most suitable procedure consisted in bringing the case first of all before the state which could most easily execute the judgement, in other words, the state said to be in possession of the surplus whose seizure would result in an equitable distribution of the whole. Treaties between friendly nations, too, are usually drawn up in accordance with this principle. For example, in the treaty between the Gauls and Hannibal, it was provided that, if the Gauls accused a Carthaginian, the case should be tried by the Carthaginians; whereas, if [13′] the latter accused a Gaul, then Gallic women[b] (for in Gaul the female

Rule IX

a. Euripides, *The Children of Hercules* [142 f.].
b. Plutarch, *Bravery of Women* [in *Moralia,* vi, p. 246 C].

sex enjoyed great authority, even in public affairs) should adjudicate the dispute. Reasoning in the same manner, Demophoon replied to Eurystheus, King Tatius to the Laurentines, the Athenian people to Alexander, and others on a great many occasions to yet other parties, when they were ordered to hand over certain fellow countrymen for punishment, that they themselves would administer the punishment in accordance with justice and the laws, if anyone should bring forward an accusation.

On the other hand, if a state stubbornly defends an injury inflicted by its citizens or (as more frequently happens) by itself,[a] and if it neither confesses that the injury has been committed nor makes amends therefor, then, to be sure, the conduct of the trial passes by the aforesaid natural law to the other party, namely, the state that has complained of injury suffered either by itself or by one of its citizens. Accordingly, in cases of this kind, the mere passing of judgement in any form whatsoever will not suffice, as it does when a judge lays down the law within a single state. For it is not as the result of a compact that one state has power over another, but rather by the force of nature, which allows every individual to seek his own right. Therefore, the existence of such a right is a preliminary requisite. This is the significance of the universally accepted doctrine[b] that one state is made subject to another by transgressing. For whosoever wages war justly must become to that extent the judge of his adversary, or (as Plato[c] has said), *σωφρονιστής*, "censor and chastiser" of the latter, turning back of necessity to the system in force under the law of nature, which permitted each individual to be the judge of his own cause.

Up to this point, we have been discussing laws that accord with established usage.

All of these precepts are of a general and necessary character, save that they are naturally and implicitly subject to one exception:[d] that is to say,

a. Sylvester, on word *repressalia,* iii. 2, 3, 4.

b. Innocent, *On Decretals,* II. ii. 14; Cajetan, *On Thomas Aquinas,* II–II, qu. 40, art. 1 and Th. Aq., II–II, qu. 67, art. 1, ad 3; Baldus, *On Feuds* [p. 18 verso]; Victoria, *De Jure Belli,* 17, 19, 46, and 56.

c. *Republic,* V [p. 471 A].

d. Sylvester, on word *lex,* viii: *Hoc tamen.*

whenever a case arises in which the laws appear to conflict with one another—a situation described by the rhetoricians as *τὴν κατὰ περίστασιν μάχην*, "a conflict produced by circumstances"—the principle embodied in the superior law is upheld, and the inferior law is set aside. Accordingly, the law of all laws, so to speak, may be stated as follows: *In cases where* [*the laws*] *can be observed simultaneously, let them* [*all*] *be observed; when this is impossible, the law of superior rank shall prevail.*[a] Law XIII

Now, this very point as to which law is of superior rank, may be determined on the dual basis of the origin and the purpose of the precepts involved. For, from the standpoint of origin, the divine law is superior to human law, and the latter to civil law.[b] From the standpoint of purpose, that which concerns one's own good is preferred to that which concerns another's good; the greater good, to the lesser, and the removal of a major evil, to the promotion of a minor good. If, for example, your life is imperilled in the wilderness as the result of an attack from some individual, under circumstances of time and place that do not permit of recourse to a judge, you will rightly defend yourself, disregarding the Ninth Law, relative to judicial procedure.[c] For that matter, not even the Third Law, which forbids you to injure another, will be an obstacle to such righteous self-defence; for otherwise you would not be able to exercise your right under the First Law, which commends your own [14] life to your care.[d] Similarly, if any person holds property of mine in his possession without reimbursing me for it, and if that person is preparing for flight so that there is no hope of recalling him for trial, then I must have recourse to the Sixth Law, which requires that good be done to the doers of good, or in other words, that the loss [suffered by the benefactor] be compensated by gain,[e] since the above-mentioned precept regarding judicial procedure ceases to apply. Nor will the Fourth Law, for-

a. Scotus, 21, dist. 41 [in *Scriptum Oxoniense,* IV, dist. 21, qu. 4, n. 24]; Cicero, *On Invention,* II [xlix].

b. See *Decretum,* II. xi. 3. 97.

c. *Dig.* IX. ii. 4 and 5; *ibid.* 45; Cicero, *On Behalf of Milo* [iv. 10 f.].

d. Sylvester, on word *furtum,* x. 4; *id.* on word *homicidium* [Pt. I], ix.

e. *Dig.* XLIII. xvi. 3, § 9; *ibid.* XLII. viii. 10, § 16; Sylvester, on word *bellum,* [Pt.] II, at beginning.

bidding the seizure of another's property, serve as an obstacle to my recovery of compensation contributory to my livelihood in accordance with the Second Law. For no one should be compelled to throw away his own property. But as soon as that imminent peril of death or loss shall cease, it will be obligatory to observe the different laws, no longer in mutual conflict, at one and the same time.

We have seen what constitutes a "right" (*ius*); and from this concept we derive also the definition of a "wrong" or "injury" (*iniuria*), guided by the basic belief that this term refers to whatever is done in opposition to right.[a] Accordingly, that action is just whereby a right is awarded to the party to whom it is conceded by the various rules and laws, whereas actions of a contrary nature are unjust.

Now, even as actions have their inception in our minds, so do they culminate in our bodies, a process which may be called "execution." But man has been given a body that is weak and infirm, wherefore extra-corporeal instruments have also been provided for its service. We call these instruments "arms." They are used by the just man for defence and [lawful] acquisition, by the unjust man, for attack and seizure. Armed execution against an armed adversary is designated by the term "war." A war is said to be "just" if it consists in the execution of a right, and "unjust" if it consists in the execution of an injury. It is called "public" when waged by the will of the state, and in this latter concept the will of magistrates (e.g. princes) is included. Moreover, public war may be either "civil" (when waged against a part of the same state) or "foreign" (when waged against other states). What is known as a "war of allies" is a form of foreign war. Those which are waged otherwise [than by the public will], are "private" wars, although some authorities[b] have preferred to describe such conflicts as "quarrels" rather than as "wars." These conflicts, too, may be either civil or foreign. In the present work, the terms "seizure of prize," "seizure of booty,"[11] are used to refer to the acquisition of enemy property through war.

War

Just war

Unjust war

Public war

Civil war

Foreign war

Private war

Seizure of prize or booty

a. *Dig.* XLVII. x. 1.

b. Th. Aq. II–II, qu. 40, art. 1; Seneca, *On Anger,* III. v [6].

11. These two English expressions are used here to translate the single Latin word, *praeda.*

CHAPTER III

Question I

Article I. Is any war just?

Article II. Is any war just for Christians?

Article III. Is any war just for Christians, against Christians?

Article IV. Is any war just for Christians, against Christians, from the standpoint of all law?

Accordingly, before we enter into a discussion of prize and booty, we must dispose of a certain question regarding war, namely: Can any war be just? [14′]

To be sure, no one has ever succeeded in representing this as a doubtful issue without also rejecting a large part of Holy Writ, together with the supreme benefactions conferred by the Divine and Eternal Spirit, that is to say, civil order and the lawful authority of magistrates. In earlier times the Manichees were included in this subversive group, and even now there are persons who revive many errors of the Manichees, under a new name. The ignorant teachings of the Manichaean sect, however, both in regard to the question propounded above and on other matters, were refuted long ago by Augustine;[a] nor has our own age lacked authorities to beat back with unanswerable arguments the recrudescent tide of superstition released by fanatics.

In our opinion there is less need to refute the doctrines of such fanatics than there is to strengthen the stand taken by other persons, who do not profess the said doctrines but who nevertheless lack an adequate under-

a. Particularly, in *Against Faustus* [XXII. lxxiv].

standing of the reason for adopting a different belief. Therefore, we shall elucidate this point, as follows.

Formal Exposition of Article I

He who wills the attainment of a given end, wills also the things that are necessary to that end.[a] God wills that we should protect ourselves, retain our hold on the necessities of life, obtain that which is our due, punish transgressors, and at the same time defend the state, executing its orders as well as the commands of its magistrates. All this is plainly revealed in the laws set forth in the preceding chapter.[b] But these divine objectives sometimes constitute causes for undertaking and carrying on war. In fact, they are of such a nature that it is very often impossible for us to attain them without recourse to warfare, as is indicated in the definition of war already formulated.[c] Just as a certain natural conflict is waged, so to speak, between dryness and moisture, or between heat and cold, so there is a similar conflict between justice and injustice. Indeed, factual evidence clearly shows that there are in existence many men of a bloodthirsty, rapacious, unjust, and nefarious disposition, traitors to their native lands and disparagers of sovereign power—men who are strong, too, and equipped with weapons—who must be conquered in battle (as Tacitus puts it) in order that they may be brought to book as criminals. Thus it is God's Will that certain wars should be waged; that is to say (in the phraseology of the theologians),[d] certain wars are waged in accordance with God's good pleasure. Yet no one will deny that whatsoever God wills, is just.[e] Therefore, some wars are just; or, in other words, it is permissible to wage war.

Nor is there even any pretext for objecting to these just wars. For the persons who hate war, base their hatred either upon its causes or upon its effects. The theologians and the philosophers have levelled many severe criticisms at such causes as ambition, avarice, and dissension;

a. Scotus, 41, dist. 1, only qu. [in *Scriptum Oxoniense,* I, dist. 41, n. 11].
b. In Chap. ii.
c. At end of Chap. ii, *supra,* p. 50.
d. Rainerius of Pisa, *Pantheologia,* word *bellum,* ii.
e. See Rule I.

yet the same authorities, despite their censorious attitude towards unjust wars, do not by any means deny that certain wars are just. As for the critics whose condemnation of war is based upon its effects, such persons fall into the all-too-frequent error of failure to distinguish between *τὸ καθ᾿ αὑτὸ καὶ τὸ κατὰ συμβεβηκός*, "the essential and the [15] incidental." For, granting that damage and destruction frequently occur in the course of a war even when it is justly waged, nevertheless, we cannot raise any objection on this ground, when those who are fighting for a righteous reason have as their purpose the conservation of their own lives and property. Every act should be judged by its essential nature, not on the basis of additional and extraneous factors. "Virtue is never increased by its consequences";[a] neither, therefore, can it be impaired by its consequences. In other words, as the Stoics[b] quite rightly taught, acts that spring from virtue should be deemed righteous in the light of their very inception and not because of their perfect execution. In so far as concerns the actual outcome in the majority of cases, however, it is permissible to assert that God customarily interposes His judgement in the fortunes of war in such a way that success falls not infrequently on the side where right also lies.

First Formal Exposition of Articles II and III

As for a certain fanciful belief entertained by some persons—namely, that warfare was formerly permissible but has become illicit since Christ propounded His teachings, or at least that this is the case as regards wars among Christians—that supposition might be viewed with tolerance if it were interpreted as meaning that there always exists in any war, on one side or the other, some guilt unworthy of the name of Christian; but in the present instance, when the said persons maintain that both sides are necessarily committing a sin, their contention is the height of absurdity.

For the law of nature—that is to say, the law instilled by God into the heart of created things, from the first moment of their creation, for

a. Lucan [*The Civil War,* IX. 571].
b. Cicero, *On Ends,* IV [III. ix. 32].

their own conservation—is law for all times and all places,[a] inasmuch as the Divine Will is immutable and eternal. This is the conclusion reached by Socrates, as quoted in Plato's *Minos.*[b] The validity of such law for all times is proclaimed by Sophocles,[c] when he says:

> οὐ γάρ τι νῦν τε κἀχθές, ἀλλ' ἀεί ποτε
> ζῇ ταῦτα.
>
> *Not of to-day, nor yet of yesterday,*
> *Are these,* [the laws of Heav'n,] *but for all time.*

Its validity for all places is recognized by Empedocles[d] in these lines:

> ἀλλὰ τὸ μὲν πάντων νόμιμον, διά τ' εὐρυμέδοντος
> αἰθέρος ἠνεκέως τέταται, διά τ' ἀπλέτου αἴης.
>
> *That law has common force and is upheld*
> *Throughout the far-flung heav'ns and earth's vast realms.*

But the law of war is a phase of the law of nature, a point supported by the foregoing discussion and correctly explained by Josephus[e] in the following statement: φύσεως γὰρ νόμος ἰσχυρὸς ἐν ἅπασι τὸ ζῆν ἐθέλειν, διὰ τοῦτο καὶ τοὺς φανερῶς ἀφαιρουμένους ἡμᾶς τούτου πολεμίους ἡγούμεθα. "For the law of nature is the law in force among all beings, which imposes upon them the will to live; and precisely herein lies our reason for regarding as enemies those persons who manifestly desire to deprive us of life." Moreover, we see other living creatures similarly engaged in strife, impelled by a certain natural instinct and acting not [15′] only in defence of their lives but also for the sake of their conjugal companions (so to speak), their offspring, their homes, and their sustenance. Therefore, if this law is valid for all times, it is valid even for times after

a. See Arist., *The Art of Rhetoric,* I. xiii [13] and *ibid.* xv [6–7]; *id., Nic. Ethics,* V. x [V. vii. 1–2]; Cicero, *On Invention,* II [liii]; *Institutes,* I. ii. 11; Th. Aq. I–II, qu. 94, art. 5.

b. [p. 316 B.]

c. *Antigone* [456–7].

d. [*Nature and Principles of Things* in *Fragments,* lines 426–7.]

e. *Jewish War,* III. xxv [III. 370].

the advent of Christ; if it is valid for all places, it is valid even among Christians.[a]

Second Formal Exposition of Articles II and III

Let us demonstrate the same point in another way. That which is approved by the universal consent of all peoples is law for all and in regard to all. But war falls under this head; for any precept of the law of nature must necessarily be a precept of the law of nations, since it clearly enjoys the support of reason. Thus Hermogenianus[b] ascribes the authorization of wars to the law of nations; and Florentinus[c] derives from the same source authorization for the protection of one's body and for the repulsion of all injuries. Baldus,[d] the finest philosopher among the jurists, adopts an identical view when he says that reason has recourse to arms whenever justice cannot be secure without arms. Furthermore, throughout the world, explored by now almost in its entirety, no nation has been found that does not regard as lawful the prosecution of its rights, even by armed force. What, indeed, is the nature of the threat to adversaries implicit in the ramparts of walled cities (so lofty even in times of peace!), in boundary fortifications, in the guards posted at city gates, if it be not the threat of war? But if the law in question exists for all and in regard to all, then it must surely exist even for Christians against Christians, since we certainly do not deny that the latter form a part of mankind, and since the logical principle involved is, moreover, the same, inasmuch as Christians both suffer and inflict injury—even, at times, armed injury. For the term "Christians" is employed here with reference to the profession of that name, rather than to the imitation of Christ's life which proves that we are truly Christians.[e] Let us grant that we are brothers; but, unless I am mistaken, it is right that I should repulse with arms a brother who is eager to slay me and who is already brandishing his weapons!

a. Th. Aq. I–II, qu. 93, art. 6 and qu. 94, art. 3.
b. *Dig.* I. i. 5.
c. *Ibid.* 3.
d. *On Code,* III. xxxiv. 2, n. 69.
e. See Th. Aq. II–II, qu. 108, art. 1, ad 3.

Formal Exposition of Article IV

Therefore, according to every kind of law, it is permissible to wage war. For we have already made it sufficiently clear that warfare is compatible with divine law, that is to say, with the law of nature and the law of nations; and the precepts of these two bodies of law certainly cannot be invalidated by civil law.[a] As Cicero[b] observed, civil precepts do not necessarily form a part of the law of nations, but the precepts of the latter ought to be recognized as a part of civil law. For even citizens, since they are also human beings, should desire what all humanity desires; and as human beings, representing the handiwork of God, they are obliged to obey the dictates imposed by Him through nature. Furthermore, wars have a bearing not only upon the safety of individuals, but also upon the defence of the state and its magistrates. It is for this reason that there is no state which has refrained entirely from establishing some provision relative to the law of war. As a matter of fact, the most illustrious legislators have devoted a chief part of their labours to the task of decreeing rewards for the brave and punishments for the cowardly. Roman law, indeed, is justly regarded as having attained to the highest degree of perfection in the magnitude and long duration of its sway; and if we search this field for the authoritative opinions of jurists and the imperial regulations of the Caesars, we shall find whole chapters [16] "Concerning Captives and *Postliminium,*" "Concerning Military Matters," and "Concerning Veterans," as well as others dealing with the privileges accorded to soldiers.[c] Again, if we turn to the papal Decrees,[d] many of these will be found—whether issued by the pontiffs themselves or assembled from the statements of ancient writers—which quite clearly proclaim the justice of wars.

First Informal Exposition of Article I

Now let us consider the testimony of Holy Writ. Although this method of proof is ἄτεχνον, "not derived from the art [of logic]," it is indeed by far the most certain method. For just as the Will of God—consti-

a. *Dig.* I. i. 9; Th. Aq. I–II, qu. 95, art. 2; Plato, *Minos* [p. 316 A–C].

b. *On Duties,* III [xvii. 69].

c. *Institutes,* II. xi and *Dig.* XLIX. xvii, and in many places in the last book of the *Code.*

d. *Decretum,* II. xxiii; *ibid.* I. i. 7.

tuting the norm of justice, as we have already indicated—is revealed to us through nature, so also is it revealed through the Scriptures.

But God has commanded that wars be waged, as undertakings congruous with His Will,[a] and has furthermore declared Himself to be their Author and Aid.[b] He has even accepted the appellation "a man of war" as appropriate to His own majesty.[c] This same point is borne out by the divinely inspired pronouncement of the high priest who assured Abraham that God had delivered Abraham's enemies into his hands;[d] and also by the words of the wise woman Abigail,[e] addressed to King David: ". . . my lord fighteth the battles of the Lord." Indeed, the very fact that God endowed the state established by Himself with this institution of war,[f] as a form of defence, alone affords sufficient proof that the said institution is just and should be adopted by other nations whenever a like reason exists. Moreover, I believe all sane men will agree that he who lays down laws to regulate a given act does not disapprove of the act itself, and that this is especially true as applied to God, who does nothing without purpose or erroneously. Yet God prescribed regulations for warfare, through Moses,[g] and again, through the forerunner of Christ, as recorded in the New Testament.[h] With reference to the latter passage, Augustine[i] says: ". . . if Christian doctrine condemned all wars, [the soldiers] who sought [John's advice], according to the Gospel [of Luke], would have received, instead [of the advice they did receive], the following counsel of salvation: that they should cast away their arms and withdraw completely from military service. The counsel given them, however, was this: 'Do violence to no man . . . ; and be content with your wages.' Surely [John] was not prohibiting military service for those

a. *Judges,* xx. 18; *1 Samuel,* xxiii. 2 and 38 [xxiii. 8]; *2 Samuel,* v. 19; see also Legnano, *De Bello,* xi.

b. *Psalms,* xviii. 35 [34]; *ibid.* cxliv, at beginning.

c. *Exodus,* xv. 3.

d. *Genesis,* xiv. 20.

e. *1 Samuel,* xxv. 28.

f. Sacred history, *passim.*

g. *Deuteronomy,* xx. 10.

h. *Luke,* iii. 14.

i. *Letters,* iv [v. 15], *To Marcellus,* cited in *Decretum,* II. xxiii. 1. 2.

to whom he addressed the precept that their due wage [as soldiers] should suffice."

Second Informal Exposition of Article I

The principle stated above[1]—namely, that he to whom a given end [16′] is pleasing, cannot be displeased by what is necessary to that end—may be deduced from authoritative passages no less than by a logical process, since all of the laws thus far propounded are also inscribed in Holy Writ. For He who bids us love our neighbour as ourselves,[a] gives first place to the true love of self, regarded as the πρωτότυπον, or prototype, whose ἔκτυπος, or image, is love for others.[b] If we combine this maxim with the precept laid down by the Creator for mankind,[c] we shall arrive not only at the conclusions incorporated in the First and Third Laws, but also at those expressed in the Second and Fourth.[2] Indeed, since we are admonished by God to deliver them that are drawn unto death,[d] we are under a particularly solemn obligation to deliver ourselves. Yet again, we are bidden to "give to him that needeth,"[e] and therefore we are bidden to avert need from ourselves. The Fifth and Sixth Laws, too, are implicit in these passages: "Divers weights, and divers measures, both of them are alike abomination to the Lord";[f] ". . . with what measure ye mete, it shall be measured to you again";[g] "And as ye would that men should do to you, do ye also to them likewise"[h] (what ye would not have done unto you, do ye not unto others).[i, 3] Christ does indeed show us that the law

a. *Leviticus,* xix. 18; *Matthew,* xix. 19.

b. See Scotus, 29, dist. 1, only qu. [*Scriptum Oxoniense,* III, dist. 28, n. 2]; Th. Aq. II–II, qu. 26, art. 4.

c. *Genesis,* i. 28 and 29.

d. *Proverbs,* xxiv. 11.

e. *2 Corinthians,* viii, whole chap.; *Ephesians,* iv. 28.

f. *Proverbs,* xx. 10.

g. *Matthew,* vii. 2.

h. *Luke,* vi. 31.

i. *Matthew,* vi. 46 [vii. 12].

1. *Supra,* p. 52, "Formal Exposition of Article I."

2. For the content of the numbered laws and rules mentioned by Grotius here and in many other chapters of the *Commentary,* see appendix A.

3. *quae nolis, ne feceris:* these four words are underscored in the Latin manuscript, indicating that Grotius regarded them as part of the quoted matter; but the phrase

of nations requires that good be done to the doers of good; yet He also says: ". . . all they that take the sword shall perish with the sword."[a] This same doctrine was expressed in the Old Law,[b] which goes so far as to prohibit us strictly from showing compassion to evildoers. But it often happens that, owing to the power of our adversaries, we are unable to defend ourselves and our possessions, exact that which is due us, or enforce punishment, save by resorting to armed force. Therefore, it is permissible to wage war.

Other laws, too, are found to have a firm foundation in the Sacred Scriptures. For example, when the advantages of social organization are pointed out to us [in the Book of *Ecclesiastes*],[c] we acquire an understanding of the origin of the state; just as we come to understand the sanctity of magistrates, when Paul[d] asserts in no uncertain terms that magistrates "are ordained of God." From this same source the force of civil laws is derived, as is the power of judgement, given from above by Jesus Himself,[e] the Author thereof. Thus Divine Wisdom—of which all human wisdom is but ἀπορρώξ, "a fragment," or offshoot, as it were—is represented as saying:[f] "Counsel is mine, and sound [17] wisdom: I am understanding; I have strength. By me kings reign, and princes decree justice. By me princes rule, and nobles, even all the judges of the earth." Again, what could be clearer than the exhortation of Paul?[g] "Let every soul be subject unto the higher powers. For there is no power but of God: the powers that be are ordained *of God.* Whosoever there-

---

is evidently his own, introduced to emphasize the relationship between the Golden Rule and the laws in question. The marginal citation in the Latin manuscript corresponding in its position to this negative paraphrase of the Golden Rule, is *Matthew,* vi. 46. Since the chapter cited contains only 34 verses in the King James version, the reference has been altered to read *Matthew,* vii. 12, where the Golden Rule appears in substantially the same form as in the passage cited immediately above from the *Gospel According to St. Luke* (vi. 31).

a. *Matthew,* xxvi. 52.

b. *Deuteronomy,* xiii [xii] at end. See also Ambrose, *On Duties,* I [xxx].

c. iv. 9.

d. *Romans,* xiii. 1.

e. *John,* xix. 11.

f. *Proverbs,* viii. 14 ff. [11–16].

g. *Romans,* xiii. 1 ff.

fore resisteth the power, resisteth the ordinance of God: and they that resist shall receive to themselves damnation. For rulers are not a terror to good works, but to the evil. Wilt thou then not be afraid of the power? do that which is good, and thou shalt have praise of the same: For he is the minister of God to thee *for good.* But if thou do that which is evil, be afraid; for he beareth not *the sword* in vain: for he is the minister of God, *a revenger to execute wrath* upon him that doeth evil. Wherefore ye must needs be subject, not only for wrath, but also for conscience sake." In all the works of the philosophers—howsoever numerous and wheresoever found—there is no finer passage regarding the justice of magistrates. Do you ask who is the [true] author of this exhortation? The Author is God. For what purpose is it formulated? For your own good. And since God wills that the authority of magistrates shall be sacrosanct, does He not also approve of arms, whereby at times that authority must be defended? But will God extend to magistrates an avenging sword for use against unarmed culprits while refusing to give them a weapon against culprits who are armed, thus affording grounds for that incitement to all wickedness, the belief that "Whatever sin is committed by the many, goes unpunished"?[a] By no means! For the individual who sins alone ought not to be in a worse position than those persons who add to their own direct transgressions another evil—namely, the exposure of many people to the contagion of crime, and attack by open violence upon the laws and the public peace—and who are not therefore more in the right than other sinners, but rather, less susceptible to fear and shame.

From the foregoing observations it follows that some public wars are just. This same conclusion may be confirmed in yet another way.

Third Informal Exposition of Article I

For anyone who approves of the institutions established for the attainment of an end, can scarcely fail to approve of the end itself even much more emphatically; and no one is ignorant of the fact that tribute is an institution established primarily for purposes of war. Tacitus[b] spoke

a. Lucan [*The Civil War,* V. 260].

b. *Histories,* IV [lxxiv].

truly when he said: "there can be no tranquillity among nations unless there are armies, there can be no armies without pay, and pay cannot be provided without the exaction of tribute." But God Himself, [17′] speaking both through Christ and through the Apostle Paul, ordains the payment of tribute.[a] Therefore, from this argument, too, it follows that some wars are approved by God as just.

First Informal Exposition of Article II

To the preceding assertion, I shall add the phrase, "even wars on the part of Christians." For everything permitted prior to the establishment of the Law of Christ and not expressly prohibited by Him, is permissible for Christians;[b] we have already shown, and it is universally admitted, that there were just wars before the time of Christ; and He prohibited none of the things that were just according to the law of nature, among which (as we have observed) wars were included. Furthermore, Christ changed no part of the Old Law[c] that pertained in any way to justice and moral usage in human activities, under which head we place warfare. The contention that warfare was clearly approved, is quite convincingly supported, moreover, by the above-cited[d] opinions of both John the Baptist and Paul.

Second Informal Exposition of Article II

Third Informal Exposition of Article II

First Informal Exposition of Article III

Some wars, then, are just for Christians. This conclusion is applicable even to some wars against Christians, that is to say, against persons who profess Christianity. For, by definition and in accordance with the very nature of opposites,[e] war is just when waged against those who commit injustice; but some Christians commit evil and unjust deeds, a fact to which Christ bears witness;[f] and therefore, it is lawful to proceed against such Christians with armed force.

a. *Matthew,* xxii. 21; *Romans,* xiii. 7.
b. *St. James,* i. 21 and 25; Th. Aq. I–II, qu. 107, last art.
c. *Matthew,* v. 17; see also *Decretum,* I. vi. 3.
d. In First and Second Informal Expositions of Art. I, *supra,* pp. 56 ff.
e. See at end of Chap. ii, *supra,* p. 50.
f. *Matthew,* vii. 22.

Second Informal Exposition of Article III

Again, Christians are subject to punishment; for it is to them that Paul[a] speaks, in the passage above quoted. Indeed, those persons whom reverence for the most sacred of names has been unable to restrain from injurious conduct, are perhaps deserving of punishment by no means less severe than that merited by others. But certain penalties cannot be exacted without warfare. Consequently, even as it is unquestionably true that just wars were waged among the Hebrews,[b] despite the fact that they were bound to one another by ties not only of religion but also of government and blood relationship, so it cannot properly be doubted that similar conflicts may arise among Christians.

At the same time, one must admit that persons who furnish grounds for war by their injurious acts, are certainly not complying with the duties imposed upon Christians, since the followers of Christ are subject to a special and solemn obligation of love and concord, surpassing the common bond that unites all mankind. On the other hand, the [18] arguments above set forth are in no sense incompatible with the prohibition laid down by Christ Himself and also by the philosophers (particularly the Platonists), against *τὸ ἀνταδικεῖν*, "the requital of injury." For, in the light of the fairly extensive consideration we have already given[c] to the subject of punishments, we are able to perceive just what it is that these authorities condemn.

In the first place, it is quite obvious that the precepts in question were addressed to private individuals, or to servants of the Church whom Christ chose to regard in this connexion as private individuals; and it is equally obvious that those acts [of individual vengeance] are rightly prohibited, which would disturb the whole order of the state, shattering the public peace, if they were permitted. This point has been brought out in our discussion of the Ninth Law. Thus a rule of ancient law[d] declares that action which may be taken publicly through a magistrate is prohibited for private persons, lest occasion be given for graver disturbances.

a. *Romans,* xiii. 4. See also Th. Aq. II–II, qu. 104, art. 6.
b. *Judges,* xx.
c. Chap. ii, *supra,* pp. 29–33.
d. *Dig.* L. xvii. 176.

In another context, we shall see how far the application of this rule should be extended. Meanwhile, suffice it to say that the precepts which we are discussing, clearly do not refer to the public use of arms. If we took the contrary view, we should be subscribing to the accusation brought by Celsus and Julian, enemies of our faith, who falsely declared that the Christians, in abolishing revenge, were abolishing all laws, together with magistracies and the punishment of malefactors. This is so far from being the truth that, on the contrary, our theologians[a] place Punishment in the category of the virtues, regarding her as the handmaiden of Justice. A second fault susceptible of condemnation in connexion with vengeance, stands out so plainly that it could be left unmentioned. This is the fault involved when the cause of the avenger is unjust. A third fault consists in exceeding the limits of vengeance appropriate to the transgression. Seneca[b] has said that the second fault is incompatible with justice, and the third, with clemency. A fourth fault arises when vengeance is inflicted in a spirit of injustice, or in other words, when neither the good of the person punished nor the common good is kept in view. The two faults last named are mentioned by that same Seneca[c] in a single passage, [the description of an occasion on which Plato refrained from inflicting punishment and explained his self-restraint in these words: "I am angry;] I should be apt to do more than I ought, and with too much pleasure."

For punishment, according to our preceding analysis of terms, consists properly in the repayment of that which is owed by the part to the whole as a result of wrongdoing; and therefore, it ought to be directed to the public interest. Together with this observation, one should take into account the fact (already brought out in the aforesaid analysis) that it is frequently better for the sinner himself, that wickedness should not be allowed to go unpunished. Herein lies the purport

a. Th. Aq. II–II, qu. 72, art. 3; *ibid.* qq. 108 and 158 [art. 1, ad 3]; Sylvester, on word *ira,* ii and iii, and on word *vindicta.*

b. *On Mercy,* I. xx and II. iv.

c. *On Anger,* III. xii.

of Augustine's[a] declaration that nothing is more infelicitous than the felicity of sinners.

Surely, then, if it is not always our duty to remit punishments, far less can it be our duty to remit that which is owed us on the basis of reciprocal justice. For even the precepts that apparently favour remission do [18′] not command us to renounce indiscriminately and to fling away,[b] as it were, that which belongs to us. In fact, men of saintly character have never scrupled to obtain what was their due, either through judicial procedure or, when other means were lacking, through the just application of force. What those precepts do command, is that we should yield in preference to involving ourselves in sin or becoming an impediment to the public welfare. In many cases, however, it is advantageous not only for our own sake but also because of the example set before the public, that we should possess that which is rightfully ours.

Informal Exposition of Article IV

Therefore, according to the opinions which we have cited, divine law is not opposed to all wars. Furthermore, since law as a whole is rightly [19] divided into the divine branch and the human branch, and since we have already shown that some wars have a basis in divine law, it follows from the doctrine[c] which denies the validity of human law whenever the latter branch comes into conflict with the divine, that those same wars are just from the standpoint of all law.

So far our citations have been drawn from divine testimony.[d] From this same source many additional arguments could be derived, if [19′] we combined that testimony with the logical considerations expounded in preceding passages and based upon nature itself.

We turn next to that human authority which is of course more open to question, but which nevertheless carries considerable weight. Now, such authority is divided into two kinds: that derived from facts, and that derived from words.

a. *On the Sermon of Our Lord on the Mount* [II. xxiv. 79].

b. Augustine, *Letters,* iv, *To Marcellus,* cited in *Decretum,* II. xxiii. 1. 2. Add *Letters,* I, *To Boniface,* cited in *Decretum,* II. xxiii. 4. 42, 51, and 52.

c. *Acts,* v. 29.

d. See Exposition of Arts. [I,] II, III, and IV, *supra,* this chapter.

For, assuming that the actions of just men are properly regarded as just—in other words, assuming that example is of paramount importance in the decision of all questions—I shall cite the following sources: the age when men lived under the guidance of nature,[a] which supplies the example of the warring Abraham; the [Old] Law itself,[b] which gives us Moses and David as examples; New Testament history,[c] including more than one reference to centurions as well as the request made by Paul himself for a military guard against the snares of his enemies; and the centuries following thereafter,[d] with their record of numerous exceedingly pious emperors and most Christian kings who waged wars even against men bearing the name of Christians. And what of the written accounts which relate that wars were carried on by those illustrious ancients, Gideon, Barak, Samson, Jephthah, Samuel, and various prophets who were quickened by the same true faith in Christ that quickens us?[e] From these examples, it follows that some wars are just for the faithful.

Informal proofs relative to whole question, based on examples

Again, since it is rightly maintained that those things are just and pious which have been so adjudged by just and pious men (not to mention the entire number of the philosophers, or the jurisconsults, none of whom has expressed any doubt on this point), I shall quote a very few of the opinions formulated by persons highly esteemed for their piety and erudition. The following assertion was made by Augustine:[f] *"The functions of vengeance* may be discharged by virtuous men acting with virtuous intent, just as they may be discharged by *a judge,* or by *the law."* The same author wrote:[g] "Not for nothing have these institutions been established: kingly *power,* and the lawful authority of *judicial inquisitors;* the clawlike instruments of the torturer; *the arms of the sol-*

Informal proofs relative to whole question, based on recorded opinion

a. *Genesis,* xiv. 15.

b. *Exodus,* xvii. 9; *Numbers,* xxxi. 7; *1 Samuel,* xvii. 48.

c. *Matthew,* viii. 8; *ibid.* xxvii. 54; *Mark,* xv. 39; *Luke,* vii. 6 [viii. 8]; *Acts,* x. 1 [x. 5]; *ibid.* xxix. 17, 23 [xxiii. 17, 23].

d. See accounts in histories of France, Germany, and other nations.

e. *Hebrews,* xi. 32; add *1 Chronicles,* v. 20.

f. *Evangelical Questions,* I. x, cited in *Decretum,* II. xxiii. 5. 15 [16].

g. *Letters,* liv [vi], *To Macedonius,* cited in *Decretum,* II. xxiii. 5. 17 [18].

dier; the discipline of the absolute master, and even the severity of the good father. All of the things above mentioned have their methods, *causes, reasons, uses.* When they are feared, the wicked are held in check, and the good dwell in tranquillity among the wicked." This passage, too, is taken from Augustine:[a] "The greedy urge to inflict harm, [20] *cruel vengefulness,* an unappeased and unappeasable spirit, savage rebellion, lust for dominion and any similar trait that may appear—these are the things that law finds blameworthy in warfare. Frequently, in order that such things may also be punished in accordance with law, war itself—of the kind necessarily waged against the violence of opponents, whether by *divine* command or at the instance of some *lawfully constituted sovereign power*—is undertaken by good men, who find themselves involved in an order of human events that constrains them, as a matter of *justice,* either to issue or to obey commands to this effect. Wherefore, John does not instruct the soldiers to abandon their arms, and Christ directs that *tribute* be paid to Caesar; for, *on account of wars,* it is necessary that *pay* be provided for the soldiery." Augustine[b] also supplies us with this correct and extremely concise statement: "Among the *true worshippers of God,* even wars themselves have a pacific character, being waged not because of cupidity or *cruelty,* but because of an earnest desire for peace, with the purpose of restraining the wicked and giving support to the virtuous." He[c] takes into account not only divine law, but human law as well, saying: "When a soldier slays a man in obedience to the power under which that soldier has been legitimately enrolled, he is not charged with homicide by any *law* of his own *state."* One among many observations made by Jerome[d] runs as follows: "He who smites the wicked because of their wickedness, and holds the implements of destruction for the purpose of putting to death the vilest sinners, is a minister of *God."* It was Jerome,[e] too, who said: "He is not *cruel,* who slays

a. *Against Faustus,* XXII. lxxiv, cited in *Decretum,* II. xxiii. 1. 4.
b. *De Diversis Ecclesiae Observationibus* cited in *Decretum,* II. xxiii. 1. 6.
c. Augustine, *On the City of God,* I. xxvi, cited in *Decretum,* II. xxiii. 5. 12 [13].
d. *On Ezekiel,* IV [III. ix], cited in *Decretum,* II. xxiii. 5. 28 [29].
e. *On Isaiah* [V] xiii, cited in *Decretum,* II. xxiii. 5. 27 [28].

the *cruel.*" The words of Ambrose[a] may also be cited: "The courage which by warlike means protects the fatherland from alien enemies, or defends the weak at home, or guards one's comrades against bandits, is *just* in the *fullest* sense of the term."

Accordingly, whether we obey the guidance of nature (which we must obey, even though it be unwillingly), whether we heed the teachings of Holy Writ (from which it is sinful to dissent), whether or not we are also influenced in some degree either by the example or by the pronouncements of famous men—in short, whatsoever line of reasoning, whatsoever authority, we embrace—we must conclude that: *Some wars are just for Christians, against Christians, from the standpoint of all law.* [b] **Conclusion I**

a. *On Duties,* I. xxvii [129], cited in *Decretum,* II. xxiii. 3. 5.

b. Agrees with Th. Aq. II–II, qu. 40, art. 1; Martinus Laudensis, *De Bello,* Qq. 9, 32, and 45.

CHAPTER IV

Question II

Article I. Is the seizure of prize or booty[1] *ever just?* [20′]

Article II. Is it ever just for Christians?

Article III. Is such seizure ever just for Christians, from Christians?

Article IV. Is such seizure ever just for Christians, from Christians, and from the standpoint of all law?

Having completed our discussion of the question [of justice] in relation to war, let us pass to another phase of the subject, [justice in relation to] the seizure of prize or booty. The problems arising under this second head are not unlike those previously included under the head of war, and may be dealt with on the basis of the arguments already set forth.

General Exposition Based on Concl. I and preceding proofs. See also Chap. ix, *infra*, discussion of aims [of war].

For, when a particular thing is just in so far as it tends toward the attainment of a given end, that end itself is just in a much higher degree. But war is just for the very reason that it tends toward the attainment of rights; and in seizing prize or booty, we are attaining through war that which is rightfully ours. Consequently, I believe those authorities to be entirely correct who hold that the essential characteristic of just wars consists above all in the fact that the things captured in such wars become the property of the captors:[a] a conclusion borne out both by the German word for war,[b] [*krieg* from Middle High German *kriec*(*g*), which means

a. Panormitanus, *On Decretals,* II. xxiv. 29, n. 2.

b. Krijgh.

1. These three English words are a translation of the single Latin term, *praedam.*

"exertion," "endeavour to *obtain* something,"[2]] and by the Greek word for Mars, since Ἄρης, ["Ares," i.e. "Mars,"] is apparently ἀπὸ τοῦ αἴρειν, "derived from ἀείρειν," [which means "to take away," "to seize"]. Therefore, the seizure of spoils of war is necessarily just on some occasions;[a] and furthermore, it must be just in regard to the same persons and by that same criterion of all law, embraced in our demonstration of the justice of war.

However, since it is especially important that this part of our discussion should be understood, and since the matter has not been thoroughly dealt with by other writers on the law of war, it seems expedient to re-examine in this connexion the divisions of subject-matter already considered in answering the preceding question.

Formal Exposition of Article I
Cf. 1st Form. Exp. of Art. I, Concl. I

Accordingly, in order to understand how seizure of spoils is agreeable to the Divine Will as revealed through laws, one must realize that such seizure is made up of two elements, namely, deprivation of previous possession, and acquisition of new ownership. For, just as it is impossible that a given thing should appear at one and the same time in two different forms, so there cannot exist simultaneously two full possessors, or owners, of one and the same thing;[b] and therefore, just as removal of the old form must precede the introduction of any new form, so deprivation must precede the establishment of [new] possession and ownership.

The concept of deprivation, too, has a dual character. It may be absolute, [i.e. a total negation of ownership,] as the naturalists hold that it is by natural disposition in the case of primal matter, and as we [jurists] find it to be in the case of all things that have not yet come into anyone's possession, a situation which we call ἀδεσποτεία, "absence of ownership." Thus we say, "Nature has granted freedom even to dumb animals," meaning by this assertion that such animals, as long as they have

a. See Expositions which follow.

b. *Dig.* XIII. vi. 5, § 15.

2. Grotius may have meant to give the term *Germanica* (German) its broadest meaning, thus basing his argument on the Germanic group of languages in general, and on his native tongue, Dutch, in particular. The etymology of the Dutch word for war, *krijg,* is similar to that of the German *krieg.*

not been captured, are not subject to anyone's ownership.[a] Again, deprivation may be specific, as the naturalists describe it in connexion with secondary matter, and as we use the term when ownership has been taken away in actual fact.

The latter process assumes various guises, but the simplest is that in which loss of ownership follows upon loss of possession, precisely as acquisition of ownership follows upon acquisition of possession.[b] For this is a natural train of events, and one which would always find [21] acceptance if the Fourth Law did not stand in the way. Under the said law, disregard of [existing] possession gives rise to legal claims;[c] that is to say, seizures made contrary to law are held to be invalid.

But the Fourth Law cannot operate in defiance of the laws of the first order [Laws I and II];[d] and since the latter allow us to commit any act necessary for the protection of our lives and property, it cannot be doubted that they allow us to take away the instruments with which we are attacked. Now riches, whether in private life or in affairs of state, are rightly defined as constituting a vast stock of instruments.[e] Thus all enemy possessions are so many instruments prepared for our destruction; that is to say, through them weapons are provided, armies are maintained, the innocent are stricken down. It is no less necessary to take away these possessions, wresting them from the enemy, than it is to wrest the sword from a madman, if we wish to protect our property or even our personal security. Onasander[f] supports this view, when he says: *ζημία γὰρ χρημάτων καὶ καρπῶν ἔνδεια μειοῖ πόλεμον, ὥσπερ ἡ οὐσία τρέφει*; "For the infliction of property losses and scarcity of revenue weaken the sinews of war, which feeds upon riches." In such circumstances, indeed, we shall not be deterred by the precept that bids us refrain from seizing another man's possessions, since even the prohibition against infliction of injury upon others will have no force. For the dif-

a. Tacitus, *Histories,* IV [xvii]; *Dig.* XLI. i. 5; *Decretum,* I. i. 7.
b. *Dig.* XLI. i. 3, last sect.
c. *Ibid.* VI. i. 23.
d. See discussion of Law XIII, *supra,* p. 49.
e. Arist., *Politics,* I. viii [I. iii. 9].
f. [*The General,* vi. 11.]

ferent laws must be observed in the order of their importance. Moreover, the rule[a] which decrees that "The lesser ought not to be impermissible for him to whom the greater is permitted," rests upon precisely the same basis of certainty as the rule of the mathematicians to the effect that "The greater always includes the lesser"—a principle also adopted by the jurists,[b] and quite rightly, since regard for proportion is as important in the legal realm as it is in the measurement of numbers and magnitudes. But killing exceeds plundering in gravity to the same extent that life takes precedence over property in the computation of our blessings;[c] and therefore, since one is not charged with homicide for having slain a man in a just war, far less is one convicted of theft for having borne away an enemy possession. Cicero's[d] statement, "Nor is it contrary *to nature, to despoil* (if one can) any person whom it is right *to slay,*" has been repeated by the jurists[e] in various passages. [21′]

Surely the reason why an enemy ought to be deprived of his property is by now sufficiently apparent; but there is still room for doubt as to whether or not an impartial examination of the laws already cited will result in assigning irrevocable ownership to the party who seizes the property.

New explanation

For some persons will be of the opinion[f] that the thing seized is *res nullius,* inasmuch as the former owner has been lawfully deprived of it, and that consequently it becomes (like other things so classified) the property of the first party to take possession. Such would seem to have been the view adopted by Nerva the Younger and, after him, by Paulus,[g] when these authorities included property taken in war among the things nat-

a. *Dig.* L. xvii. 21.
b. *Ibid.* 110; *Sext,* V. xii, ult., rule 53.
c. *Code,* I. ii. 21.
d. *On Duties,* III [vi. 32].
e. Glossators, *On Feuds,* II. xxii; Baldus, *On Code,* VIII. iv. 1, n. 58 [n. 35]; Jason, *On Dig.* I. i. 3, n. 17 and *passim* in arguments of those cited, in connexion with property.
f. See Law II, Chap. ii, *supra,* p. 23.
g. *Dig.* XLI. ii. 1, § 1, and Bartolus thereon, in substance.

urally acquired (in virtue of the fact that they were previously *res nullius*) by the person first taking possession. This contention will be strengthened, moreover, by the argument which we ourselves adduced just above, namely: that the laws of the superior order, relative to our own good, do not give way for the sake of another's good when they come into conflict with lesser laws. A thoughtful reading of the passage in question indicates that Cicero[a] had precisely this principle in mind when he observed that Cassius had set out "for a province which, if men obeyed written laws, would be regarded as *belonging to another,* but which, when such precepts had been overthrown, was *his own by the law of nature,"* that is to say, by that precept which we have listed as Law II.[b]

Nevertheless, anyone who pauses to reflect, more carefully, that all laws are equally to be observed as soon as such general observance becomes possible, will readily perceive that a just distinction should be drawn in this connexion. For he will understand clearly enough that, for the duration of the war and in view of the continued danger, it will not be permissible, for captured possessions to be reclaimed by the one who lost them;[c] but he will fail to see any reason why, after peace has been restored, you should not give back those things which you have seized solely for the sake of your own security,[d] since the Fourth Law does not conflict with any other law under these circumstances, and should therefore come into force again. Thus there is a vast difference between acquisition of that which was truly *res nullius,* and acquisition of property formerly belonging to another. Mere possession suffices for acquiring those things which had no owner, whereas the appropriation for oneself of another person's property requires not only possession but also cause, that is to say, some reason on the basis of which the original owner of the property should, willingly or unwillingly, be deprived of it. Therefore, that general title which we invoke for the seizure of previously ownerless property, does not suffice for the establishment of full legal rights

a. *Philippics,* XI [xii. 28–9].

b. As was said in connexion with Law XIII, Chap. ii, *supra,* p. 49.

c. Vict., *De Jure Belli,* 18, 44, 55.

d. See Sylvester, on word *bellum* [Pt. I.] xi. 3.

over enemy possessions. On the contrary, some other title is needed. In time of war, however, this title is never lacking,[a] a fact which may be deduced in the following manner.

In the first place, with reference to those cases in which we take [22] up arms for the purpose of recovering our own property, there is no question but that we may rightly employ military force to divert unjust possession from an armed possessor.[b] For who can fail to perceive that, when we are granted the right to acquire for ourselves those things which are useful,[c] the further right to guard such things after they have been acquired and to recover them if they are taken from us, is implicitly conceded at the same time? But if I am not able to regain the actual piece of property involved, then that unjust possessor is nevertheless my debtor to the extent of the value of the said property.[d] Therefore, I should be permitted to obtain from among his goods, the equivalent of his debt to me. Moreover, the same argument will apply if from the very beginning I was not laying claim to my own property, but was attempting to collect a debt.[e] For, since the excess possessed by that other person corresponds exactly to the deficit in my own possessions, that excess should be taken from him and given to me. Similarly, in cases involving the execution of a judicial decree,[f] we see creditors put in possession of debtors' goods, in order that the former may obtain satisfaction therefrom. To be sure, the rule that such goods should be put up for public auction and the proceeds applied solely for the benefit of the creditors, arises not from the law of nations but from civil law,[g] which has been accepted as a model even in the case of reprisals.[h] Nature herself, however, grants me permission to acquire in any way whatsoever, from him through whom I suffer the loss of property belonging to me, the exact

a. See *infra,* Chap. vii, see also Law II.
b. *Dig.* VI. l. 68; *ibid.* XLIII. iv. 3.
c. See Law II, *supra,* p. 23.
d. *Dig.* VI. i. 68 ff.
e. See Law VI, *supra,* p. 29.
f. *Dig.* XLII. v, whole title.
g. *Code,* VIII. xxxiii, whole title.
h. Bartolus, *On Reprisals,* Qu. 9, ad 3.

equivalent of that lost property; and the thing so acquired becomes my own. This principle is also accepted by the theologians.[a] Indeed, in the natural order, it is impossible for one who is not himself the owner of a thing, to transfer a valid title to ownership;[b] and this rule has, moreover, been incorporated in [man-made] law.

In the second place, if it is also our purpose in warfare to inflict punishment for offences,[c] then such punishment will surely be directed not only against the person of the offender but also against his property, which is ordinarily awarded to the injured party in forensic judgements, too.[d] The reason underlying this method of punishment is explained by Tryphoninus,[e] as follows: "For he who has deserved ill of the state ought also to suffer extreme poverty, in order that he may serve as an example to deter others from wrongdoing." The words of Cicero[f] are pertinent in the same connexion: "[Even the confiscation of goods is prescribed, in addition,] to the end that every torment of mind and body, including want and beggary, may follow." Again, this passage regarding Lepidus[g] is peculiarly appropriate: "And if, after laying down his arms, he should be condemned for violence (a judgement against which he certainly could not offer any defence), his children would share in the same disaster through the confiscation of [his] goods." Yet again, we find this query, which also refers to Lepidus:[h] "And if that very penalty is applied to citizens condemned in court, how could we have been more lenient toward public enemies?"

Furthermore, the right to acquire enemy property—whether for the sake of [recovering] the property itself, or in the process of collecting a simple debt, or in cases where such collection is combined with a penal

a. Sylvester, on word *furtum,* xix from [the beginning].

b. [Margin of MS. torn. Fragment of note remaining, as well as text proper, indicates *Dig.* XLI. i. 20, intended.]

c. See Law V; Vict., *De Jure Belli,* 19 and 56.

d. Sylvester, on word *poena,* ii: *tertium genus. Institutes,* IV. vi. 23; *ibid.* xviii. 8; *Dig.* XLVIII. xx. 1.

e. *Dig.* XVI. iii. 31.

f. *Against Catiline,* IV [v. 10].

g. Cicero, *Letters to Brutus,* xi [I. xii. 2].

h. *Ibid.* xiv [I. xv. 11].

purpose—does not necessarily exist prior to war, but may sometimes be a concomitant thereof.[a]

For, in the first place, who among the enemy seeks only our lives and not our property, also? Or rather, what enemy does not seek our lives because of our property? We shall be acting justly, then, if we recover through war whatever is taken from us day by day, or the equivalent of what is taken.[b] On this basis, it has been widely held that wars carry with them a tacit agreement of exchange,[c] so to speak, an agreement to the effect that each belligerent, acquiescing in the turn of the die as the contest proceeds, shall take the other's property or lose his own, thus [22′] bearing out Menander's[d] assertion that,

> *οἱ γὰρ θέλοντες προσλαβεῖν τὰ τῶν πέλας*
> *ἀποτυγχάνουσι πολλάκις νικώμενοι,*
> *τὰ δ' ἴδια προστιθέασι τοῖς ἀλλοτρίοις.*
>
> *They who desire to snatch a neighbour's wealth,*
> *Fall oft from hope to ruinous defeat,*
> *Adding their own goods to that alien store.*

Aristotle,[e] too, makes much the same point when he says: *ὁ γὰρ νόμος ὁμολογία τίς ἐστιν, ἐν ᾧ τὰ κατὰ πόλεμον κρατούμενα τῶν κρατούντων εἶναι φασιν*; "For this law is a species of common agreement under which things captured in war are said to be the property of the captors."

A second consideration, to which I now turn, has constant force and can never be absent from war. For what war is waged without expense and loss? Assuming that all else prospers according to one's desire (although this is never the case), he who is forced to engage in warfare is nevertheless diverted meanwhile from the management of his private affairs. Yet any person who justly takes up arms has a right to collect indemnity for all losses and expenses, regarding them as debts due to

a. See *infra,* Chap. vii.
b. *Dig.* II. ii, whole title; Cicero, *On Invention,* II [xlii]; Sylvester, on word *bellum* [Pt.] I. i. 1.
c. See Vázquez, *Ill. Cont.* ix. 17.
d. [In Stobaeus, *Florilegium,* X, n. 3.]
e. *Politics,* I. vi [I. ii. 16].

him,[a] just as it is right, in forensic disputes,[b] that the person who has deliberately failed to obey the law should make reparation not only for the costs and expenses connected with the suit itself, but also for those involved in the execution of the sentence. This is the principle underlying the formula,[c] "bound to pay the expenses of war, in accordance with the law governing the conquered."

Finally, it is an indisputable fact that he who knowingly resists a just war, commits a grave offence.[d] Even if such a belligerent is to some extent successful, he is a thief, an armed robber, an assassin. Now, these crimes are of such a nature as to bring upon the defendant a fine depriving him of all, or at least a large portion[e] of, his goods; and the goods thus forfeited should be allotted to the injured party, whether the latter be an individual or a state. Moreover, the theologians[f] lay down the following doctrine: if, at the beginning of a war, the enemy offers full reparation, not only for the injury done and the damage to property but also for losses and expenses, he should be given a hearing; but it is a different matter if the war is already raging, for the culpable belligerent will no longer be in a position to make amends; on the contrary, it will be[3] [entirely just for him] to suffer [penalties graver than the original

a. Vict., *De Jure Belli,* 17, 50, 54; Bartolus, *On Reprisals,* Qu. 9, ad 3; Martinus Laudensis, *De Bello,* Qu. 1.

b. *Institutes,* IV. xvi. 1; *Code,* VII. li, whole title.

c. Justin [*Histories*], XXXIII [1].

d. Martinus Laudensis, Qq. 14, 16.

e. See statements made *supra.*

f. Cajetan, *Summula Peccatorum,* words *belli revocatio.*

3. A portion of MS. p. 22′ is missing at this point, and had already been destroyed when Hamaker published his Latin edition of the *Commentary,* in 1868. The English interpretation given above is based substantially upon Hamaker's conjectural reconstruction of the mutilated text, which reads as follows: *sed* [*illatis graviora haud injustum*] *est pati, altero videlicet judice jam constituto, qui* [*de poena pro libitu statuere*] *possit.* The suggested phrase *pro libitu* (as one pleases) is perhaps not quite satisfactory, since it implies that no moral restriction at all is to be placed upon the judgement of the injured belligerent. The present translator therefore assumes that Grotius used some milder phrase, such as *ex sua sententia* (according to one's own decision).

It should also be noted that the word *sed,* before *illatis,* is only partially visible in the collotype, and that the system of spelling followed by Hamaker differs from that

injuries], with the opposing side constituted, of course, as the judge empowered [to impose such penalties according to its own decision].

In the light of the foregoing discussion, it is quite evident that even the peace of the state and the authority of magistrates cannot always be preserved without the seizure of enemy spoils.[a] This is true above all because of the vast expenditures necessary for the preservation of such peace and such authority, as well as because of the fact that those persons who rashly offer resistance ought not to go unpunished. Accordingly, since we have clearly shown[b] that it is just, inasmuch as it is pleasing to God Himself, that we should safeguard our own welfare, defend or recover our own property, and collect the debts due to us (including those whose payment involves punishment), all of these acts being based upon rights that God does not compel us to remit in behalf of any other person,[c] owing primarily to the fact that it is to the common advantage that evil deeds should not remain unpunished and that the state and its magistrates should be actively defended; since none of these ends can be attained unless the enemy is stripped of his resources; since, moreover, there are many things which we ourselves cannot obtain save by acquiring through war that which was formerly enemy property; and finally, since this procedure constitutes what is known as the seizure of prize or booty,[d] it follows, as an absolutely certain conclusion, that such seizure is sometimes just.

First Formal Exposition of Articles II and III

We have already demonstrated[e] that the institutions of prize and booty spring from the law of nature. This origin is clearly apparent [not only among human beings, but] also in the case of other animate creatures, including even those that feed in flocks and those that fly; for though,

adopted in the Grotian MS. (e.g., Hamaker has *injustum* for *iniustum, poena* for *paena,* &c.).

a. Cf. Laws VII ff., see *supra,* pp. 37 ff. See also Vict. [*De Jure Belli*], 15; Sylvester, on word *repressalia,* in beginning: *Qui autem* [*Igitur repraesalia . . . Qui autem?*].

b. In whole of Chap. ii, *supra.*

c. Wilhelm Matthaei, *De Bello Justo et Licito,* in Req. 3.

d. Cf. definition of prize and booty at end of Chap. ii, *supra,* p. 50.

e. Cf. First Formal Exposition of Arts. II and III, Conclusion I, *supra,* p. 53.

at times, creatures of this kind cede to the possessor those things which have been taken into the possession of the latter, yet they act otherwise when enraged by combat. The following passage from Plutarch[a] may be quoted in this connexion: *οὐδὲν αὐτοὺς δεινὸν οὐδ' ἄδικον ποιοῦντας, ἀλλὰ τῷ πρεσβυτάτῳ τῶν νόμων ἀκολουθοῦντας, ὃς τῷ κρείττονι* [23] *τὰ τῶν ἡττόνων δίδωσιν, ἀρχόμενος ἀπό τοῦ θεοῦ, καὶ τελευτῶν εἰς τὰ θηρία.* "You are doing nothing that is harsh or unjust; rather, you are following the most ancient of laws, which bestows upon superiors the goods of their inferiors: a law that has its beginning *in God* and its final effect in the beasts." Similar statements are found in the *Gorgias* of Plato, and also elsewhere, in the works of various authors. Josephus,[b] too, and Aristides,[c] in more than one passage, have assigned this same precept to the law of nature, on the ground that it has force even among wild animals. And Aristotle[d] declares that, *ἡ πολεμικὴ φύσει κτητική πως*; "in the natural order, the art of war is, in a sense, an art of acquisition." Theophilus[e] calls such acquisition *φυσικὴν κτῆσιν*, that is to say, "natural possession." Whence it follows that even among Christians there is a place for the laws of prize and booty.

Second Formal Exposition of Articles II and III

The institutions of prize and booty have also been traced, quite correctly, to the law of nations,[f] or (in the language of Theophilus) to *ἐθνικῷ νόμῳ*. Thus Demosthenes[g] says: *εἶτ' οὐ δεινὸν ὦ γῆ καὶ θεοί, καὶ φανερῶς παράνομον, οὐ μόνον παρὰ τὸν γεγραμμένον νόμον, ἀλλὰ καὶ παρὰ τὸν κοινὸν ἁπάντων ἀνθρώπων νόμον, τὸν ἄγοντα καὶ φέροντα βίᾳ τἄμα ἐν πολεμίου μοίρᾳ μὴ ἐξεῖναι μοι ἀμύνασθαι*; "Then is it not grievous—O, Heaven and Earth!—is it not manifestly unjust, and contrary not only to written statutes but also to the universal law of mankind, that I should be prohibited from repaying like for like

a. *Camillus* [xvii. 3–4].
b. *Jewish War,* V. xxvi [V. 367–8].
c. Cited in Faber, *Semestria,* II. ii [p. 24].
d. *Politics,* I. viii [I. iii. 8].
e. *Institutes,* II. [17].
f. Cf. Second Formal Exposition of Arts. II and III, Concl. I, *supra,* p. 55.
g. *Against Aristocrates* [p. 639].

when my possessions are taken from me by violence and borne away in hostile fashion?" In the opinion of Cyrus,[a] too, *νόμος ἐν πᾶσιν ἀνθρώποις ἀΐδιός ἐστιν ὅταν πολεμούντων πόλις ἁλῷ τῶν ἑλόντων εἶναι τὰ χρήματα*; "It is an *enduring* law of *mankind* that, when a city belonging to the enemy has been captured, the goods and the wealth of that enemy shall be ceded to the victor." (I am speaking of that same Cyrus to whom God Himself[b] awarded the eastern kingdoms sought by force of arms.)

The law of war is a part of the law of nations. Accordingly, Aeschines[c] says: *εἰ μὲν πρὸς ἡμᾶς πολεμήσας δορυάλωτον τὴν πόλιν εἷλες, κυρίως ἔχεις τῷ τοῦ πολέμου νόμῳ κτησάμενος*; "But if, in a war undertaken against us, you have occupied a city that was captured by armed force, you rightly retain possession of that city, under the law of war." Others[d] have called this same law "the law of victory." Moreover, all the philosophers[e] hold that there is a certain special kind of acquisition from enemies, which they variously designate as acquisition *πολεμικήν* [by war], *λῃστικήν* [by piracy], *ἀγωνιστικήν* [in combat], or *χειρωτικήν* [by conquest]. Xenophon[f] also tells us how Socrates, in accordance with his habitual practice of drawing out the truth (by obstetrical skill, as it were) from the seeds already implanted in human minds, leads Euthydemus through a process of interrogation to an admission of the fact that, despite the latter's classification of despoliation under the head of injustice, nevertheless this very act of despoiling is consonant with justice, when committed against an enemy. Plato,[g] too, makes the following statement: *πάντα τῶν νικωμένων ἀγαθὰ τῶν νικώντων γίγνεσθαι*; "all those goods which were the property of the vanquished, become the property of the victor."

a. Xenophon, *Training of Cyrus,* VII [v. 73].

b. *Isaiah,* xlv, whole chap.

c. *On the Embassy* [33]; Faber, *Semestria,* II. iii.

d. Tacitus, *Histories,* IV [lxxiv].

e. Plato, *Sophist* [p. 219 D, E]; Arist., *Politics,* I. v, vi, viii [I. ii. 14, 16; I. iii. 8]; Cicero, *On Duties,* I [vii. 21].

f. *Memorabilia,* IV [ii. 15].

g. [Partly obscured.] *Laws.* [p. 626 B].

Thus we clearly perceive the absurdity of the belief[a] that seizure of spoils should be excluded from wars among Christians; unless, perchance, all such wars are held to be unjust. But other authorities[b] have laid bare the ignorance underlying this contention on the part of men who are otherwise learned. We ourselves, on the basis of the [23′] principles already expounded, believe the matter to be so clear that it requires no more protracted discussion; and we furthermore consider it permissible to observe that the proponents of a different opinion have lacked even an adequate understanding of what constitutes prize and booty.

As for the argument derived by our opponents from civil war, it is doubly absurd. For, in the first place, who will acquiesce in their assumption that the wars of Christians are civil wars, as if to say, forsooth, that the whole of Christendom constitutes a single state?[c] Again, they are mistaken even in their contention that seizure of spoils has no proper place in civil warfare. For, aside from the testimony of history, which teaches us that the very abundance of spoils taken in civil wars is such that men have on numerous occasions been impelled to revolution by their greed for plunder,[d] what logical argument can be advanced to show that a magistrate ought not to collect by armed force[e] the debt that is owed to the state, even when that debt consists solely in the penalty for rebellion, if he cannot collect it by any other means? Plato,[f] in fact, even while maintaining that in cases of civil dissension war should be conducted as temperately as possible, nevertheless concedes that, *τὸν ἐπέτειον καρπὸν ἀφαιρεῖσθαι* [. . .] *τοῖς κρατοῦσι τῶν κρατουμένων*, "the annual harvest may be taken from the vanquished by the victors."

a. Alciati, *On Digest,* L. xvi. 118.

b. Ayala, *De Iure Belli* [*De Iure et Officiis Bellicis*], I. v. 2; Belli, *De Re Militari,* II. xviii. 1.

c. See Vázquez, *Ill. Cont.* xxii ff.

d. See thereon Tacitus, *Histories,* III [xxxiii], concerning Cremona.

e. Add limitations of Sylvester, on word *bellum* [Pt. I.] xi. 8.

f. *Republic,* V [xvi].

Besides, what could be more inconsistent than prohibiting the seizure of prize or booty in a situation where slaughter is permitted?[a]

Formal Exposition of Article IV

Surely, since the despoliation of enemies is accepted under the law of nations, it must necessarily be sanctioned by civil law, too. This inference is clearly confirmed by the laws and customs of individual nations relative to the distribution of spoils; and in every part of the world, such laws and customs abound. Again, the Roman *Corpus Iuris*[b] repeatedly states that things captured in war become the property of the captors; and the same rule is approved by canon law.[c] The facts just stated, considered as a whole, make it impossible for us to doubt that seizure of enemy spoils is permitted by every branch of law.

First Informal Exposition of Article I

The same view is explicitly supported in Holy Writ. Is anything more truly one's will, than that which one commands through an express legal precept? Yet we find among the precepts of military law, this divine pronouncement[d] concerning captured cities: "[. . .] *all the spoil thereof, shalt thou take unto thyself; and thou shalt eat the spoil of thine enemies, which the Lord thy God hath given thee.*" Accordingly, just as victory flows from God, so also do the institutions of prize and booty. It is recorded, moreover, that a part of the spoils was consecrated to God and claimed [24] by Him.[e] Not even the profane nations of the Gentiles were altogetherunacquainted with this practice;[f] for they offered sacrifices taken from the goods captured in war, to Jove the Plunderer and Minerva the Dispenser of Spoils, and also, indeed, to Mars or Hercules or Vulcan. The sanctity of trophies was derived from this same origin. To take another instance, among the precepts laid down for Joshua[g] when he set out

a. *Supra,* this chapter, p. 71.

b. *Dig.* XLI. i. 5, § 7; *ibid.* 6; *ibid.* XLIX. xv. 28; *Institutes,* II. i. 17.

c. *Decretum,* I. i. 10; *ibid.* II. xxiii. 5. 25; see also Glossators, *On Decretum,* I. i. 10 and 2.

d. *Deuteronomy,* xx. 14.

e. *Numbers,* xxxi, and elsewhere in this book.

f. Diodorus Siculus, in many places, also Virgil and Livy; Faber, *Semestria,* II. iii, at end.

g. *Joshua,* viii. 2.

against Ai, we find the following injunction: "[. . .] the spoil thereof, and the cattle thereof, shall ye take for a prey unto yourselves [. . .]."[4] And who can deny that the following command, though it was pronounced by that same Joshua,[a] was θεόπνευστον [divinely inspired], and dictated by the Will of God? "Return with much riches unto your tents, and with very much cattle, with silver, and with gold, and with brass, and with iron, and with very much raiment: divide the spoil of your enemies with your brethren." Or we may quote the words of David:[b] "Behold a present for you of the spoil of the enemies of the Lord." Sufficient proof was afforded, however, in the sole fact that it was God's Will that the Israelites, a nation formed by God Himself, should defend their rights in this fashion;[c] or again, in the fact that He prescribed limits for the seizure of spoil,[d] and indicated the manner in which it should be divided.

Second Informal Exposition of Article I

Cf. 1st Inf. Exp. of Art. I, Concl. I, together with Gen. Exp. at beg. of this chap.

Nor is it inappropriate to cite in this connexion the authoritative passages which demonstrate that war is just, either in an absolute sense or on the basis of [a just] origin, since the very passages that show the permissibility of war for Christians and against Christians, are likewise pertinent to the question of booty. For certainly that which was by its nature immutable could not have suffered change, nor was any innovation introduced into matters of moral conduct by the doctrines laid down in the Gospels.

a. *Ibid.* xxii. 11 [8].

b. *1 Samuel,* xxx. 26.

c. See First Informal Exposition of Art. I, Concl. I, at end, *supra,* p. 57.

d. *Numbers,* xxxi. 26; *Deuteronomy,* xx. 19, [*1*] *Samuel,* xxx. 22.

4. This sentence appears in the Latin as an insertion at the top of MS. p. 24. No corresponding insertion symbol is visible in the collotype, but the context indicates that the passage should occupy the position given to it in the English translation. It should be noted, perhaps, that the inserted sentence and the one that follows it in the English, might equally well have been placed in reverse order (as was done in Hamaker's Latin edition), were it not for the fact that the word *ipsius* (that same), modifying *Josuae* in the second sentence (according to the English order) would thereby be deprived of its force. Our reading is also supported by the fact that *ipsius* itself was apparently inserted as an afterthought, since the word appears in unusually small and cramped handwriting at the end of the MS. line (l. 4).

Neither is it possible to believe that the precept formulated by John the Baptist,[a] ["Do violence to no man, neither accuse any falsely; and be content with your wages,"] was in conflict with the unequivocal oracles of God. In regard to this point, we should note that John was being consulted, not by soldiers girded for battle and prepared to march against the enemy, but by those stationed in the garrisons of Judea. Now, the writers of that time bear witness to the many injuries inflicted by Roman soldiers upon the unfortunate provincials, and to the extensive desolation wrought in the vicinity of the Romans' winter quarters. Thus John prohibited such vexatious conduct—which he described as "violence" (*concussiones*), the word that is used even to-day—as well as all false accusations, and told the soldiers to be content with their wages (for that is the usual meaning of the term employed [in the Gospels]).[5] Nor does his admonition require forbearance in regard to any person other than the peasants and the hosts of the soldiers, against whom the latter too frequently commit offences. This is the universally recognized interpretation[b] of the passage in question. For it is an act of the gravest injustice to despoil innocent rustics who are bearing, for their own [24′] protection and for the maintenance of the soldiers, burdens that have been imposed in the name of the state. In no sense, however, does the said passage refer to enemy property; nor does its purport differ from that of the dictum laid down already by John in reply to the publicans, namely, that they should exact no more than that which was stipulated for them by law. Therefore, if those in command have so decreed, spoil will justly be transferred from the enemy to the soldiers; and it will even be considered a part of the soldier's pay, that is to say, a part of the profits

Third Informal Exposition of Article I

Cf. 2d Inf. Exp. of Art. I, Concl. I, together with Gen. Exp. in this chap.

First, Second, and Third Informal Expositions of Article II; First and Second of Article III

Cf. 1st, 2d & 3d Inf. Exps.

ὀψωνίοις of Art. II, Concl. [I], & also 1st & 2d Exps. of Art. III, same Concl., together with Gen. Exp. in this chap.; or Inf. Exp. of Art. I of Qu. II, together with 1st & 2d Form. Exps. of Arts. II & III, Concl. I.

a. *Luke,* iii. 14.

b. See Cajetan, *Summula Peccatorum,* words *belli damna;* Fulgentius Ferrandus (Diaconus), Epist. vii, *Ad Reginum Comitem,* Rule 2.

5. ὀψωνίοις (provision-money), in the Greek New Testament. The Vulgate has *stipendiis,* rendered in the King James version of the Bible as "wages," and in the Douay version as "pay," though there are several other connotations attached to the Latin word (taxes, tributes, income, periods of military service, duties, &c.). Grotius uses the more specific term *salariis* ("salt-money" given to soldiers, and hence "salaries" or "allowances").

of war rightfully awarded to them according to the testimony of Paul.[a] Thus the rule formulated by John for the soldiers serving in Judea, was in effect the same as that decreed by Aurelian[b] for his armies: "Let each man be content with his own ration; let him live by spoil taken from the enemy, not by the tears of the provincials."

Informal Exposition of Article IV

Similarly, the authoritative statements already cited to prove that war is just from the standpoint of all law, suffice also to prove that seizure of prize and booty is just from the standpoint of all law.

Exposition of whole question by examples

The examples set by holy men remain for our consideration. Abraham[c] easily leads them all in supplying us with a wealth of arguments. For, in the first place, when Abraham[d] forcibly bears away goods that were previously in the possession of the enemy, he makes it sufficiently clear that one ought not to relinquish, on the ground that it is another's property, that which the enemy are seeking to retain; and therefore, we shall act rightly in imitating his conduct on this point. Secondly, he grants recognition to the institution of spoil when he gives a tithe thereof to the priest,[e] a fact expressly brought out in the *Epistle to the Hebrews.*[f] Moreover, this same practice relative to a tenth part of the spoils is found to exist among other peoples.[g] Finally, Abraham could not have offered clearer confirmation of the right to take spoil than he did in assigning certain portions of it for the maintenance of his attendants and in willing that other portions be allotted to his allies.[h] For Abraham was not one to bestow a gift that could not honourably be accepted.

a. *1 Corinthians,* ix. 7.
b. Vopiscus, *Aurelian* [in the *Scriptores Historiae Augustae* (Vol. III), VII. 5–6].
c. The account is in *Genesis,* xiv.
d. *Ibid.* 15, 16.
e. *Ibid.* 20.
f. vii. 4.
g. Livy, V [xxv].
h. *Genesis,* xiv. 24.

On the other hand, he rejected the remainder of the captured goods, not on the ground that it had been unlawfully acquired (for he had openly declared himself to the contrary on this very point, nor, for that matter, has such a construction been placed upon his behaviour by any interpreter),[a] but rather for a far different reason. Some persons, indeed, explain the passage in question by asserting that Abraham had already bound himself, before setting out on the expedition, by a vow to the effect that he would take no part of the spoil for himself. Now, it cannot be denied that we make vows for undertakings other than those which constitute [in themselves] inescapable obligations; and in any case, [25] whether or not Abraham was bound by a vow in this matter, the reason that impelled him to repudiate any share in the spoils is indicated in the words:[b] "lest thou shouldest say, I have made Abram rich." Thus he ceded his right freely and because of a certain nobility of spirit. For this guiltless man quite justifiably feared that impious persons who were hostile to the true faith might heedlessly calumniate him, giving the impression that he had meddled, solely through greed for plunder, in a war that did not properly concern him.

The case of Abraham, then, is based upon a special motive, and his conduct does not differ greatly from that of Pericles and Fabius, who brought private loss upon themselves lest unjust suspicion be excited against them. Fabricius, too (according to Dionysius'[c] account), offers a somewhat similar explanation of the fact that he made no part of the spoils his own, although he could have done so: *καὶ τὸν ἐκ δικαίου πλοῦτον ὑπεριδὼν ἕνεκα δόξης*; "spurning riches, even those justly gained, in comparison with glory." Fabricius furthermore asserts that, in taking this step, he was following the example set by Valerius Publicola and others. Marcus Cato conducted himself in much the same fashion after the victory in Spain, saying[d] (almost in the very words employed

a. See Ambrose, *De Patriarchis,* III. ii [*On Abraham,* I. iii]; Nicholas of Lyra, *On Genesis,* xiv. 24; Wilh. Matthaei, *De Bello Justo,* Req. 2, p. 5.

b. [*Genesis,* xiv.] 23.

c. *Fragments* [43, p. 747].

d. Plutarch, *Marcus Cato* [x. 4].

by Abraham) that no part of the spoils of war would be acquired by him, save only those things which he had eaten or drunk. He added that, in taking this stand, he was not casting reproach upon those other leaders who would accept the profits assigned to them from the said spoils, but merely preferred for his own part to vie in virtue with the most virtuous rather than in wealth with the wealthiest.

Abraham may also have been influenced by the fact that many of the things found in the possession of the conquered kings had not belonged to them in olden days, having been snatched away recently from the citizens of Sodom, who were the allies of Abraham himself at the time in question.[a] Consequently, there was some reason for him to return these possessions to their former owners or to the ruler of the latter, in accordance (so to speak) with the principle of *postliminium.* The Roman juridical principle of equity,[b] too, has given rise to a similar procedure in regard to certain things. Furthermore, we read of occasional instances in which such a procedure has been adopted out of benevolence, even though the law makes no provision to that effect. Thus the behaviour of Abraham in the case under consideration, was the same as that of the Romans on another occasion, when the latter, after the camp of the Volscians had been captured, and the Latin and Hernician allies had been summoned by edict to identify their property, gave back the possessions so identified.[c] In connexion with the conquest of the Samnites, Volumnius and subsequently Atilius followed the same course of action. Gracchus and Lucius Aemilius customarily did likewise. Scipio, too, gave similar orders after the Lusitanians were vanquished, and again, after the capture of Carthage, with reference to the standards and votive offerings that had belonged to the Siculians.

For the rest, if there is anyone to whom the above-mentioned examples are displeasing, let him pause to consider what men he is condemning, and of what sort. For we read that the seizure of spoils was

a. [*Genesis,* xiv.] 11 and 16.

b. *Code,* VIII. li. 12, at end; see also Angelus [de Ubaldis], *On Code, ibid.* and Jason, *On Dig.* XLI. ii. 1, nn. 11 and 12.

c. Livy [IV. xxix, X. xx. 15, and XXIV. xvi] and Polybius [II. xxxi].

practised by Moses[a] (a far more reliable model of justice than was either Lycurgus or Aristides); by that exceedingly saintly leader, Joshua;[b] by David,[c] the King who was most pleasing to God; by the sons of Reuben, too, in company with the children of Gad and the half tribe of Manasseh, of whom it is written[d] that they were enriched with the spoil of their enemies because they had placed their trust in God, and also by Asa,[e] a prince most highly commended for his piety. Again, if [25′] we turn our attention to Christian princes, we shall find not a single one who failed to follow those same examples. For although slavery has fallen into disuse in Christian practice[f] (at a late date, to be sure, and owing to a reason distinct [from condemnation of spoils], as we could easily demonstrate save that in so doing we should be straying from the plan of our discussion), nevertheless, all authorities on law[g] have come to the conclusion that the following principle still stands: "Things captured in war shall be acquired by the captors."

Exposition of whole question on basis of authoritative opinions

There is no need, however, to amass a great heap of additional testimony on this point. Do we seek the opinion of the theologians? Then let Augustine[h] speak alone for all of them, as follows: "If you have been deprived of anything originally possessed by you, for the reason that the Lord God hath given to us goods that were taken from you, we are not on that account [to be regarded as] covetous of property belonging to others; for those goods have become ours and are justly held as our own, by the command of Him who owns all things." Is it our pleasure to consult the doctors of pontifical law? Pope Innocent[i] himself declares

a. *Numbers,* xxxi. 9.

b. *Joshua,* viii. 27; *ibid.* xxii. 8.

c. *1 Samuel,* xxx. 20; *2 Samuel,* viii; *1 Chronicles,* xviii.

d. *1 Chronicles,* v. 18 ff.

e. *2 Chronicles,* xiv.

f. See *Dig.* XXII. i. 28.

g. Innocent, *On Decretals,* II. xiii. 12; Panormitanus, *On Decretals,* II. xxiv. 29, n. 8; Bartolus, *On Dig.* XLIX. xv. 24, at end; Baldus, *On Code,* VII. xiv. 4; Laudensis, *De Bello,* Qu. 19.

h. *Against Petilianus,* II. xliii and it is also in *Decretum,* II. xxiii. 7. 2.

i. *On Decretals,* III. xlix. 8.

that, "Things acquired in legitimate warfare are legitimately retained." Moreover, this assertion is repeatedly confirmed by Hostiensis,[a] by Panormitanus,[b] and by Archidiaconus.[c] And what do we find among the interpreters of Roman law? Bartolus[d] says: "In cases of licit warfare, those who have taken spoil are not bound by civil law to make restitution." Baldus[e] goes still further, asserting that, "Even before the inner tribunal of the conscience, it is licit to retain things captured in a just war." The opinion of Baldus is cited by Jason,[f] and is universally approved not only by the jurists but also by those commentators on Holy Writ who have devoted special attention to this question; for example, Sylvester,[g] Adrian,[h] Angelus [de Ubaldis],[i] Lupus,[j] and (among the Spaniards) Victoria[k] and Covarruvias.[l] Indeed, if we examine the pronouncements of all the authorities, we shall find that not one of them condemns the seizure of spoils, although many do condemn manifestations of greed in connexion with that practice, that is to say, τὸ πλεονέκτημα, "the acquisition of more than one's due"; just as it was not war itself that we found to be blameworthy, but rather cruelty in warfare.

Conclusion II Therefore, *from the standpoint of all law, it is sometimes just for Christians to take prize or booty from Christians.* [m]

a. *Ibid.* V. xxxviii.
b. *Ibid.* II. xxiv. 29 and *ibid.* xiii. 12.
c. *On Decretum,* II. xxiii. 2. 2.
d. *On Dig.* XLI. i. 5, § 7.
e. *On Feuds* [p. 52].
f. *On Dig.* XLI. ii. 1, n. 8.
g. On word *bellum* [Pt. I.] i and ix [x].
h. In Qu. *De Rest. in Part.* and Qu. *De Bello.*
i. *In Disputations,* words: *Renovata guerra.*
j. *De Bello,* last sect.
k. *De Jure Belli,* 51 ff.
l. *On Sext,* rule *peccatum,* Pt. II, § 11.
m. Laudensis, Qu. 11.

CHAPTER V

Question III. What seizures of prize or booty are just?

Question IV. What wars are just? [26]

Granting, then, that there are certain cases in which the seizure of prize or booty should be characterized as just, we have still to ascertain what cases come under that head. This problem does not call for prolonged consideration, since the foregoing discussion clearly shows that *all seizures of prize or booty are just, which result from a just war.* [a] That is the universally accepted conclusion.

Conclusion III. Based upon Gen. Exp. of Qu. II

The entire argument now turns upon the question, "What wars are just?" [b]

First of all, we must clear away the ambiguity attached to the term *iustus* [just, proper, perfect, &c.]. For when I use this term I do not have in mind the sense in which it is sometimes employed, connoting full attainment of inherent potentialities (as in the expressions *iusta aetas* [a proper age], *iustum navigium* [a perfect boat], *iustum opus* [a perfect work]), nor do I refer to the acquisition of certain formal external attributes (the concept underlying the phrase *iusta materfamilias* [a perfect *materfamilias*]). To be sure, these connotations do enter into the question under consideration, since the expression *iustum bellum* [a just *or* proper war] is used in both of the above-mentioned senses by writers on the subject. Nevertheless, I am employing the word *iustus* exclusively to

a. Agrees with Th. Aq., II–II, qu. 66, art. 8, ad 1.

b. See Budaeus, *On Dig.* XVII. ii. 3; Ayala, *De Iure Belli* [*De Iure et Officiis Bellicis*], I. xxxiv [I. ii. 34].

denote that which lacks none of the qualifications required by any law, human or divine.

Now, these qualifications have been discussed by the different authorities in varying and rather disorderly fashion. Certain writers[a] have listed seven names, rather than seven kinds, of war. Moreover, their list is not complete, nor are the items included therein sufficiently distinct from one another. Other writers have maintained that a just war must be directed by a [competent] judge and in accordance with law. Still others,[b] dealing with this same point, inquire into the authority behind the war, its cause (their term for its origin) and the accompanying intention (or rather, the purpose of the various participants). There are some whose inquiries relate to "cause," "mode," and "necessity." Yet another group[c] contributing to this discussion, contend that the war should be necessary to such a degree as to be avoidable only at the cost of imperilling the state, and that it should be waged by command of the supreme magistrate, for a just cause, after formal declaration and notice to the enemy. There are some authorities,[d] too, who discuss the problem under these heads: "subject-matter of the dispute," "cause," "intent," "authority," and "persons engaged."

New explanation The defects or superfluous aspects of each of the classifications mentioned will become apparent, however, if we analyse war on the basis of four types of cause.[e] For actions, no less than other matters, are customarily explained on this fourfold basis. Indeed, the faultiness of any of the causes underlying an action will suffice to render that action faulty;[f] whereas, in order that the action may be righteous, it is necessary [26′] that all of those causes should exist concurrently in the proper form,

a. Geminianus, *On Sext,* V. iv. 1, and others on war.

b. Th. Aq. II–II, qu. 40; Bartolus, *On Reprisals* [qu. 1, ad 1]; Castrensis, *On Dig.* I. i. 5; Rainerius of Pisa, *Pantheologia,* i.

c. Wilhelm Matthaei, *De Bello Justo,* at beginning.

d. Lupus, *De Bello* [*passim*], citing Hostiensis, *On Decretals* [p. 323].

e. Arist., *Metaphysics,* IV. ii [V. ii]; see also Sylvester, on word *lex,* v.

f. Dionysius [the Pseudo-Areopagite], *De Divinis Nominibus* [iv]; Th. Aq. II–II, qu. 110, art. 3.

since righteousness, of course, must conform to a single standard. This distinction is pointed out in the Greek saying,[a]

> ἐσθλοὶ μὲν γὰρ ἁπλῶς παντοδαπῶς δὲ κακοί.
>
> *Goodness wears a single form, but evil is multiform.*

We conclude, therefore, that *every war derived entirely from just causes, is a just war.* **Conclusion IV**

Consequently, it is necessary to investigate the subject of causes. We must ascertain, first, what persons justly wage war; secondly, on what grounds and against whom they do so; thirdly, in what manner—that is to say, within what limits—war is so waged, and fourthly, to what end and with what intent this is done.

It should be observed, moreover, that we have not undertaken this task because we disapprove of the work done in connexion with the law of war by other investigators, whose authority, as a matter of fact, will prove very helpful to us. We are motivated rather by the belief that, with the aid of the additional material so far gathered by us, we shall be able to make some further contribution to the accuracy, or at least to the clear and orderly arrangement, of the doctrines handed down by those earlier investigators.

a. Arist., *Nic. Ethics,* II. v [II. vi. 14].

CHAPTER VI

Concerning the Efficient Cause of War

Question V

Article I. What is a just efficient cause of private war?

Article II. What is a just efficient cause of public war?

We are told that some of the causes effecting a given result are principal causes, while others are contributory and still others are to be classified as instrumental. Certainly all three kinds of cause are discernible in connexion with voluntary human actions (among which war is included), just as they are in regard to most other things.

In the natural order, as we have already pointed out, every individual is charged with the execution of his own rights. For we have been compounded of mind and body with precisely this purpose in view, namely, that the body may be the servant of the mind.[a] This very point is borne out by the uses of our bodily members, and particularly by the uses assigned to the hands,[b] since we defend ourselves by thrusting the hands forward, and claim a thing as our own by laying our hands upon it. [27]

It is also natural for us to do good to one another, and to lend each other aid.[c] For it is right that we should accord to others the same treatment that we wish to receive when we ourselves are in distress.[d] It has

a. See Rule V and end of Chap. ii, *supra,* pp. 42 and 50.

b. See discussion of Law II, *supra,* p. 23.

c. See part before Laws V and VI, *supra,* p. 28, and compare Rule III.

d. See Second Informal Exposition of Art. I, Concl. I, *supra,* p. 58; *Dig.* XVIII. vii. 7.

been well said by those writers[a] who discuss the subject of duties that, in accordance with God's Will, nothing—save God Himself—should be more useful to man than his fellow man. Moreover, human beings employ certain terms denoting fellowship; and in obedience to the implications thereof, kinsmen unite for mutual aid, neighbours are called upon in time of need[b] and all the citizens of a given community are likewise invoked as a whole,[c] whence there has arisen that well-known line employed on the stage, "Forward, Roman citizens!"[d] Thus Solon (so we are told) laid down the doctrine that the state wherein each individual regards injuries to others as injuries to himself, will be a happy state. Democritus[e] has said: *ἀδικουμένοισι τιμωρεῖν κατὰ δύναμιν χρὴ καὶ μὴ παριέναι· τὸ μὲν γὰρ τοιοῦτο δίκαιον καὶ ἀγαθόν, τὸ δὲ μὴ τοιοῦτον ἄδικον καὶ κακόν·* "It behoves us to defend with all our might the victims of unjust oppression, and not to leave them neglected; for the former course is just and good, whereas the latter is unjust and wicked." In the works of Aristotle,[f] too, we find this excellent passage: *δεῖ τοὺς ἀδικουμένους ὑπὲρ ἑαυτῶν πολεμεῖν, ἢ ὑπὲρ συγγενῶν, ἢ ὑπὲρ εὐεργετῶν, ἢ συμμάχοις ἀδικουμένοις βοηθεῖν.* "If injury has been inflicted upon any person, it is fitting that we should take up arms, whether in self-defence or for the sake of kindred or benefactors; or again, if our allies have been wronged, it is fitting that we go to their aid." For that matter, even if other bonds are lacking, the universal fellowship of mankind and the communion established by nature, will still cause us to be affected in our turn by ills inflicted upon others. For human beings should not hold themselves aloof from anything that is of human import. Indeed, this maxim holds good to such an extent that great nations, as well as theologians and jurists[g] of no slight authority,

a. Cicero, following Panaetius, *On Duties,* II [iii. 11]; *ibid.* III [vi. 26–7].

b. Doctors, *On Dig.* XLVII. ii. 7; *Code,* X. i. 5.

c. See Law VII, Chap. ii, *supra,* p. 37.

d. [Laberius in Macrobius, *Saturnalia,* II. vii. 4.]

e. [In Stobaeus, *Florilegium,* XLVI. n. 43.]

f. *Rhetoric to Alexander,* iii [ii, p. 1425 A].

g. See discussion of Rule II; Bartolus, *On Dig.* I. i. 3, nn. 7, 8; Jason, *On Dig.* I. i. 3, n. 29; Castrensis, *On Dig.* I. i. 1, § 4, nn. 10, 11, 12; Bartolus, *On Dig.* XLIX. xv.

in many cases regard as punishable the negligence of those who have allowed some person to be injured when they could have prevented such injury.

The authors of a deed, however, and their allies, act of their own force (the former, to be sure, on their own behalf, and the latter on behalf of another); instruments, on the other hand, act by the force of him who wields them, not by their own force. For in a certain sense, instruments fall into the category of parts, and a part is naturally the servant of the whole.[a] Thus the hand is, so to speak, *ὄργανον ὀργάνων*, "the instrument of all instruments"; and in this connexion the poet Lucretius[b] observes:

The weapons of old were hands, teeth, and nails.

Conversely, weapons are the hands of the soldier. Nevertheless, when we speak of the instruments of war, we do not wish to be understood as referring to projectile engines, swords, and spears, since these things are scarcely pertinent to the question of justice; we refer rather to the men themselves whose deeds are performed subject to the commands of others. Take sons as an example:[c] for a son is from the standpoint of nature a part of his father, inasmuch as the former has derived his very existence from the latter. The slave also provides us with an illustration,[d] because he is in a sense, like any other possession, a part of his owner. For just as a given part does not merely pertain to its whole by virtue of the same relationship in which the latter is the whole corresponding to the said part, but furthermore depends upon that constituent whole for the very fact of existence, even so a possession is essentially a thing

24, n. 9; Innocent, *On Decretals,* II. xxiv. 29 and *ibid.* xiii. 12; Panormitanus, *On Decretals, ibid.* n. 18; Sylvester, on word *bellum,* [Pt.] II. viii; Th. Aq. I–II, qu. 47, art. 1. See also *Genesis,* xiv, whole chap.; *Proverbs,* xxiv. 11; *Psalms,* lxxxii. 4; Dynus, *On Sext,* V. xii, rule 19; Sylvester, on word *homicidium,* [Pt.] I. x; Seneca, *Epistles,* xcv [49].

a. Arist., *Politics,* I. iv [I. ii. 4–5].

b. V [1283].

c. *Code,* XI. xlviii (xlvii). 22, § 1; Arist., *Nic. Ethics,* V. x [V. vi. 8–9]; add *Code,* IX. ix. 4; Seneca, *Controversies,* I. iv.

d. Add *Dig.* XXIX. v. 19.

pertaining to the possessor himself. Democritus[a] gives us this advice: *οἰκέτῃσιν ὡς μέρεσι τοῦ σκηνέος χρῶ ἄλλῳ πρὸς ἄλλο*; "Use your servants as you use the parts of your body: different ones for different purposes." Nor is Aristotle[b] mistaken when he says that certain persons are by nature slaves, not because God did not create man as a free being, but because there are some individuals whose character is such that it is expedient for them to be governed by another's sovereign will [27′] rather than by their own.[c] Thus a household consists, as it were, in a multitude of bodies directed by one mind; and absolutely every person who serves another is an instrument, wherefore we refer to those whose labour we utilize, as our "hands." Let us apply the designation "subjects," then, to all such persons.

Subjects

Conclusion V, Article I

Therefore, on the basis of the foregoing observations, we conclude that *private wars* (for these should be dealt with first) *are justly waged by any person whatsoever, including cases in which they are waged in conjunction with allies or through the agency of subjects.* In this connexion, one may quote the words of Baldus:[d] "Some persons make war directly, and not through the agency of another; some make war directly in conjunction with another; some do so through another's agency, without intervening directly, and some do so both directly and through another's agency." The three kinds of warfare in question, [warfare by direct personal intervention, with the aid of allies, and through the agency of subjects,] are all clearly exemplified in a single instance drawn from the story of Abraham,[e] wherein war is waged not only by Abraham himself, but also by his allies (Aner, Eshcol, and Mamre) and, furthermore, by his household slaves, who are called in that story, "the young men."

Moreover, I except no one from the conclusion set forth in the preceding paragraph. For if a given individual is prohibited from waging

a. [In Stobaeus, *Florilegium,* LXII. 45.]
b. *Politics,* I. v [I. ii. 13].
c. Plato, *Republic,* IX [xiii, p. 590 D].
d. *On Code,* III. xxxiv. 2 [n. 77].
e. *Genesis,* xiv. 13, 14, 24.

war, that prohibition is based not upon a defect in personal qualifications but upon a procedural defect,[a] or in other words, upon the Ninth Law, the force of which we shall have occasion to discuss elsewhere. It is in the light of this distinction that we should interpret the admonition of Augustine:[b] "In such circumstances, the chief thought of the just man shall be for this consideration alone, namely: that the war be undertaken by one who may lawfully wage war. For not all persons may lawfully do so."

To be sure, in the majority of cases where writers employ the term "war," they are referring not to private but to public war, which is more frequently the subject of discussion.[c] Let us now turn our attention to this public aspect of war.

Just as the power to wage war privately resides in the individual, so the power to wage war publicly resides primarily in the state,[d] regardless of whether the subject-matter of the dispute was public from the beginning or whether it has been changed from a private into a public

The State

matter through a judicial process.[e] Now, a state must be conceived of as something αὐταρκής, "self-sufficient," which in itself constitutes a whole entity: something αὐτόνομος, αὐτόδικος, αὐτοτελής, as Thucydides would express it, that is to say, possessed of its own laws, courts, revenue, and magistrates; something endowed with its own council and its own authority, as is explained by Cajetan,[f] and also by Victoria[g] in the passage where the latter lays down the doctrine that there is nothing to prevent several sovereign and perfect states from being subject to one prince, or otherwise very closely bound together, by treaty.[h] But if a given state lacked power to wage war, it would not be self-sufficient for

a. See example in exposition of Law XIII, *supra*, pp. 49–50.

b. *Questions on Heptateuch*, VI, qu. x, *On Joshua*, cited in *Decretum*, II. xxiii. 2. 2.

c. See Laws VII and VIII, *supra*, p. 37.

d. Agrees with Vict. [*De Jure Belli*], 5; Cajetan, *On II–II*, qu. 40, art. 1 and *id.*, *Summula Peccatorum*, words *bellum iniustum*.

e. Baldus, *Consilia*, IV. cvi; Bartolus, *On Reprisals*, at beginning, n. 6 [qu. 1, ad 2, n. 6].

f. *On II–II*, qu. 40, art. 1, and *Summula Peccatorum*, words: *bellum iniustum*.

g. *De Jure Belli*, 5 and 7; Henry of Gorkum, *De Bello Justo*, in Pref.

h. Arist., *Politics*, II. ii [II. i. 4–5] and *ibid.* III. ix [III. v. 10].

purposes of defence.[a] Consequently, it was permissible for the Roman people to decree war, as it was also for the Latins, the Etruscans, the Samnites, the Tarentines, and numerous other peoples of Italy who (so we are told) fought against the Romans;[b] not to mention for the [28] moment the Carthaginians in Africa, the Spartans and Athenians in Greece, and many other nations. The same may be said of the ancient Hebrews, and of all the peoples who have lived *sui iuris.* Accordingly, Bartolus[c] (following Cuneo) declares that war is just when waged between two free states, and that possessions captured in such a war become the property of the captors.

The authority to undertake public wars also resides in magistrates.[d] For when the state has once transferred its will into the keeping of the magisterial will, whatever is permissible for the state on its own behalf is likewise permissible for the magistrates on behalf of the state.[e] The term "magistrate" should here be understood, of course, as referring to one who has been entrusted with a mandate for the waging of war. In a sense, however, all magistrates have been invested with this attribute, save in those cases that are specifically excepted, since the rendering of judgements and the defence of one's jurisdiction, the issuance and the execution of decrees, pertain to one and the same office,[f] and since such functions sometimes cannot be discharged without resort to war. Furthermore, punishment of domestic enemies and punishment of external enemies naturally pertain to one and the same power.[g] Nevertheless, regard must be had for rank. Thus, in view of the fact that there is nothing which more gravely imperils the welfare of the state than war, there can be no doubt but that the state has willed that the power of making war

a. See definition following Rule III, Chap. ii, *supra,* p. 36. Arist., *Politics,* VII. iv [3].

b. See *Dig.* XLIX. xv. 24.

c. *On Dig.* I. i. 5 and *ibid.* XLIX. xv. 24.

d. See discussion of Laws X and XI, Chap. ii, *supra,* p. 44.

e. See definition, Chap. ii, *supra,* p. 43.

f. See *Dig.* VI. i. 68; Bartolus, *On Dig.* XLIX. xv. 24, n. 11.

g. Cajetan, *Summula Peccatorum,* word *bellum;* Fulgosius, *On Dig.* I. i. 5; Oldradus, *Consilium* lxx.

shall be given into the hands of him in whom it has placed the greatest trust; and since the state has established various grades of magistracies, the clearest possible indication has been given of its will that, in a matter so grave, recourse shall first be had to the supreme magistrate, to the one second in rank if the supreme magistrate is not accessible or fails to discharge his functions, and so on, successively. For at all times the state desires both to be defended and to see justice administered; and care for the common welfare is the function of all magistrates.[a]

Therefore, in localities where it is not the custom for the people themselves to assemble as a whole, and where they have not decided that such an assemblage would be to their advantage, authority to undertake a war is invested primarily in those persons, or in that person, to whom [28′] all civil power, or the greater part thereof, has been committed. For in some states this power is entrusted to a number of individuals, for example, to a specific portion of the people, or to the aristocrats; while in other states it is entrusted to a single individual who is called the prince. Thus Augustine[b] says: "The natural order, the order adapted to the maintenance of peace among mortals, demands that authority and discretion for the undertaking of wars should reside in princes."[c] In my opinion, however, when the prince is absent or negligent, and when no law exists expressly prohibiting this alternative course, the magistrate next in rank will undoubtedly have power not only to defend the state, but also to make war, to punish enemies, and even to put malefactors to death.[d]

A paradoxical contention

On the other hand, there is a dispute as to whether or not, if a case of this kind should arise, the term "public war" would be applicable. I myself see no objection to this application of the term. For such wars are supported by the will of the state; and the state's will, whether expressly

a. See Law X, Chap. ii, *supra,* p. 44.

b. *Against Faustus,* XXII. lxxiv [lxxv], cited in *Decretum,* II. xxiii. 1. 4.

c. See *1 Samuel,* viii. 20.

d. Vict. [*De Jure Belli*], 9, at end; Bartolus, *On Dig.* I. i. 5 [n. 3]; *id., On Reprisals,* Qu. 3, at beg., ad 2, n. 6; Laudensis, *De Bello,* Qu. 2.

or tacitly indicated, ought assuredly to be regarded as authority for the waging of war, as has been argued not only by Cicero[a] but also (among the theologians) by Cajetan,[b] who bases his contention on what is undoubtedly an ancient formula: "Let the welfare of the people be the supreme law." Indeed, this very question has been weighed on various occasions, both in Rome and elsewhere. For by the law of the Quirites, it was impossible (generally speaking, at least) for war to be undertaken otherwise than through a decree of the People or of the Senate. Nevertheless, when Gnaeus Manlius made war upon the Galatians, for cause but without any previous declaration of hostilities, he was not only acquitted after being accused; he was even rewarded with triumphal honours. Again, Cato's opinion was repudiated when he characterized as "private" the war undertaken by Julius Caesar (who had been sent into Gaul with supreme power) against Ariovistus and the Germans, and the war of that same Caesar against the Britons. I, for my part, do not doubt that both Manlius and Caesar could have been defended on this ground, namely, that whenever war has been publicly declared upon any nation, all persons of potential aid to that nation would seem to be tacitly included under the declaration. In fact, it is my belief that even the war waged against Antony by Decimus Brutus, as Governor of Gaul, was a public war. Accordingly, in the light of the foregoing arguments and examples, I am moved to reject the authority of Innocent[c] and that [29] of Bartolus,[d] who follows him. Certainly their authority should carry little weight in cases relating to public law or to the law of nations; especially in view of the fact that the opposite opinion does not lack adherents, even among the Spaniards,[e] a race by no means to be despised in the field of jurisprudence. In particular, it may be noted that there is

a. *Letters to His Friends, To Brutus,* vii [XI. vii. 2].

b. *On II–II,* qu. 64, art. 3, at end.

c. *On Decretals,* II. xiii. 12, n. 8; *ibid.* xxiv. 24, 29, n. 5 and Panormitanus on same chaps.

d. *On Dig.* XLIX. xv. 24, nn. 11, 12.

e. Vict. *De Jure Belli,* 9; Ayala, *De Iure et Officiis Bellicis,* I. ii. 9; add Sylvester, on word *bellum* [Pt. I.] ii: *Sufficit etiam.*

no one who does not concede the truth of this very opinion in relation to reprisals,[a] which may be regarded as a form of war.

Now, just as private individuals are rightly drawn into war by other private individuals, so also a given state or magistrate may be joined in warfare not only by such individuals but even by another state or magistrate.[b] Here we have the origin of allied forces. In regard to this institution, the Greeks[c] drew a neat distinction, employing the terms *ξυμμαχίαν* and *ἐπιμαχίαν*, which refer respectively to alliances established with a view to any cause of war whatsoever, and to those formed for defensive purposes only, in accordance with the First Law.

Subjects (that is to say, those persons who are bound by the laws of a state) likewise serve as instruments of public warfare. This is the sense, in part, of the Seventh and Eighth Laws, and also of the Fourth Rule. Consequently, no subject should be excepted from this category, save perchance on the basis of a special law or because of the customs of the particular state concerned: as slaves, for example, were excepted under Roman law and clerics under pontifical law, though for diverse reasons. But the extent to which subjects participate in public warfare is a matter which will be discussed in another context.[d]

For the present, our inquiry is concerned solely with the rights of [different classes of] persons [viewed as potential participants in public warfare], and those rights may be summarized as follows: *Public wars are justly waged by a state or by a magistrate in accordance with his rank, both in conjunction with an allied state or allied magistrate, and through the agency of subjects.*

Conclusion V, Article II

a. See Sylvester, on word *repressalia,* ii.

b. Cicero, *On Duties,* I [xli. 149]; Ambrose, *On Duties,* I. xxxvi, cited in *Decretum,* II. xxiii. 3. 7; Baldus, *On Code,* VIII. iv. 1, nn. 46, 47 [nn. 35, 36]; Cajetan, *On II–II,* qu. 40, art. 1, ad 2; Laudensis, Qu. 15; Vázquez, *Ill. Cont.* xxii. 6.

c. Thucydides, I [xliv. 2], and the Scholiast thereon.

d. On subject-matter and form.

ꕤ CHAPTER VII ꕤ

Concerning the Subject-Matter of War for What Cause and in What Circumstances Is War Justly Waged?

Question VI

Article I. What constitutes just subject-matter of war, in a causal sense, for voluntary efficient agents?

Article II. What constitutes just subject-matter of war, from the standpoint of attendant circumstances, for voluntary efficient agents?

Article III. What constitutes just subject-matter of war, in a causal sense, for subjects?

Article IV. What constitutes just subject-matter of war, from the standpoint of attendant circumstances, for subjects? [29′]

Corollary to Question VI. Can there be a war that is just for both parties?

Article I. With respect to voluntary agents?

Article II. With respect to subjects?

Let us consider next the following question: For what cause, and against whom, are wars waged? And let us devote the first part of our inquiry to what is properly termed the "cause of war," although Aristotle[a] refers

a. *Politics,* I. vi [I. ii. 18].

to the same concept as the "origin of war" and others, more specifically, as its πρόφασις [pretext *or* occasion].[a]

In view of the fact, then, that a just war consists in the execution of a right,[b] the matter regarding which a just war is waged must of necessity be a right.[c]

In this connexion, however, it should be noted that, although two types of belligerents have been mentioned above—the one type, voluntary, and the other (to which we applied the term "subjects"), instrumental, so to speak—the concept of "right" is not to be interpreted in the same way for the two cases. For subjects as such enjoy a right not absolutely, but in a relative sense, as the Scholastics have maintained. Indeed, in the strict sense of the term, a right pertains only to those who act voluntarily.[d] Furthermore, in order that a right may exist, it is necessary for volition to spring from an intellectual act of understanding, and that understanding must in turn be derived from truth itself. For the ancients were not unjustified in defining law as "right reason." Those persons, moreover, who give the command for war, are properly admonished not to employ this last weapon of necessity unless such a course of action is based upon just cause.[e] Cicero[f] has said: "Those wars are unjust which have been undertaken without cause."

Now, every right that we possess may be referred to one of four laws: the First, the Second, the Fifth, and the Sixth. For the Third and Fourth Laws, when interpreted from the standpoint of personal welfare, differ not at all from the First and Second, save only in the fact that the terms are reversed; while the Seventh, and all of the laws following thereafter, may be traced back to the Sixth (with the support, that is to say, of the Third Rule). Therefore, every [just] war must have its origin in one of four causes.

The first of these is self-defence, which is based upon the First Law.

a. Polybius, *Histories,* III [vi].

b. Chap. ii, at end, *supra,* p. 50.

c. Beginning of Chap. vi, *supra,* pp. 92–94.

d. Arist., *Nic. Ethics,* V. x [V. viii. 1]; *Institutes,* I. i, at beginning.

e. Panormitanus, *On Decretals,* II. xxiv. 29, n. 12; Vict., *De Jure Belli,* 21.

f. *The Republic,* III [xxiii. 35]. Also in Isidore [*Etymologies,* XVIII. i. 2–3].

For, as Cicero[a] observes, ". . . the act [of homicide] is not only just but even necessary, when it represents the repulsion of violence by means of violence." Many statements to the same effect are to be found in the works of various authors.

A second cause is defence of one's property, based upon the Second Law,[b] which makes it permissible not only to offer resistance but also to dispossess others. Moreover, the term "property" is to be understood not exclusively in a material sense, but as referring to every right, including that right to a good name which is justly the possession of virtuous persons and of which they ought by no means to be deprived.

A third cause—one that a great many authorities neglect to mention—turns upon debts arising from a contract or from some similar source. To be sure, I presume that this third group of causes has been passed over in silence by some persons for the reason that what is owed us is also said to be our property.[c] Nevertheless, it has seemed more satisfactory to mention this group specifically, as the only means of interpreting that well-known formula of fetial law:[d] "And these things, which ought to have been given, done or paid, they have not given, paid or done." Plato, too, in the *Alcibiades,*[e] has said that wars are waged not only when one suffers oppression by violence, or despoliation, but also when one has been deceived. Yet again, the statement made by Seneca[f] may be cited: "Even cities bring charges against cities on the basis of services rendered." Moreover, Baldus[g] expresses a similar view regarding pecuniary debt. [30]

The fourth cause arises from wrongdoing, and from every injury—whether of word or deed—inflicted with unjust intent. Augustine[h] wrote: "Just wars, indeed, are wont to be defined as those which avenge

a. [*For Milo,* iv. 9.]
b. *Dig.* XLIII. xvi. 3, § 9; *Decretum,* II. xxiii. 2. 1.
c. *Dig.* L. xvi. 91.
d. Livy, I [xxxii. 5]. Add *Institutes,* IV. vi. 1.
e. [p. 109 A, B.]
f. *On Benefits,* III. vi.
g. *On Dig.* I. i. 1.
h. *Qu. on Heptateuch: On Joshua,* VI, qu. 10, cited in *Decretum,* II. xxiii. 2. 2.

injuries. Accordingly, that people or state should be attacked, which has neglected to punish evil conduct on the part of its citizens, or to restore what was unjustly taken away." [30a]

Now, I wish to have it understood that these four causes listed as suitable subject-matter for war, are of the same character whether the war be private or public. In the case of public wars, however, the rights as well as the examples involved are more clear-cut; and private wars furthermore differ from public wars with respect to their efficient agents and their form. Nevertheless, they are not different in their subject-matter. The examples afforded by all living creatures show that force privately exercised for the defence and safeguarding of one's own body is justly employed.[a] Furthermore, such force is also just when the purpose is defence or recovery of one's property;[b] nor is it less so when employed for the collection of a debt.[c] Even private exaction of a penalty for crime is sometimes permitted: for example, when the penalty is imposed upon adulterers (in certain cases), robbers, rebels, or deserters.[d] It was for this reason that Tertullian[e] said: "Every man is a soldier against persons guilty of high treason, and against public enemies." Nor is it by mere chance that the very laws[f] expressly apply the term *ultio* [meaning primarily "vengeance"] to an "indulgence" that has been granted. [30a′]

On the other hand, even as certain private wars are just by virtue of their cause, so public wars are unjust in the absence of due cause.[g] Thus Seneca[h] complained: "We put a check on homicide and *isolated* cases of murder. But what of wars and the boasted crime of slaughter

a. *Dig.* I. i. 3; *Code,* IX. xvi. 2; *Dig.* XLVIII. vi. 11; *Decretals,* V. xii. 18; *Constitutions of Clement,* V. iv.

b. Sylvester, on word *duellum,* iii and on word *bellum,* Pt. II. x, xi, xii; *Dig.* XLIII. xvi. 1, § 27; *Decretals,* II. xiii. 12; *Code,* VIII. iv. 1; *Dig.* XLIII. xxiv. 7, § 3; and *ibid.* 22, § 2; *Exodus,* xxii. 2; *Decretals,* V. xii. 3.

c. *Dig.* XLII. viii. 10, § 16; Innocent, *On Decretals,* II. xiii. 12, n. 8.

d. *Code,* IX. ix. 4; see especially Vázquez, *Cont. Post.* IV. viii [*Ill. Cont.* Pt. II, bk. I, chap. viii]; *Code,* I. iii. 54; *ibid.* III. xxvii, whole title.

e. *Apology* [ii. 8].

f. *Code,* III. xxvii. 1, § 1; *ibid.* XII. xl. 5 [§ 1a].

g. Sylvester, on word *bellum* [Pt.] I. iv.

h. *Epistles,* xcvi [xcv. 30].

inflicted upon whole nations? Neither *avarice* nor *cruelty* recognize any bounds. [. . .] savage acts are committed in accordance with decrees of the Senate and the popular assembly, and the performance of deeds forbidden to private individuals is commanded by public authority." Cyprian[a] follows Seneca, saying: "When *single individuals* indulge in homicide, that is a crime. When homicide is committed by public authority, it is termed a virtuous act." Herein lies the origin of the saying, "And law was given for [the service of] crime." Accordingly, King Alexander was rightly included by the pirate among the latter's partners in crime, if that ruler had no just cause for war against Asia; and in this same sense Lucan[b] called Alexander the "plunderer" of the world, while Seneca[c] described him as a "robber." A similar view may be taken of Crassus' war against the Parthians.

Therefore, in both kinds of warfare, [public and private,] one must consider the causes involved. Of these there are four kinds, as we have pointed out: for the authorities who hold that there are three just [30] causes of war[d] (defence, recovery, and punishment, according to their classification), fail to mention the not uncommon cause that arises whenever obligations are not duly discharged. Indeed, in so far as we are concerned with subject-matter, which is the same in warfare and in judicial trials,[e] we may say that there should be precisely as many kinds of execution as there are kinds of legal action. To be sure, legal judgements are rarely rendered in consequence of causes of the first class, since the necessity for defending oneself does not admit of such delay; but interdicts against attack properly fall under this head. The actions relating to property which we call civil claims, arise from the second kind of cause, as do also injunctions obtained in behalf of possession. The

New explanation

a. *Epistles,* II. ii [I. vi].
b. [*The Civil War,* X. 21.]
c. See Seneca, *On Benefits,* I. xiii.
d. Baldus, *On Code,* III. xxxiv. 2, n. 71 [n. 77], and the theologians; also Matthaei, *De Bello Justo.*
e. See *infra,* on forms [in war, Chap. viii].

third and fourth classes give rise to personal actions, namely, claims to restitution, founded upon contract or upon injury.

Even as in the case of a lawsuit, however, so also in war, those causes which would justify the action taken by the plaintiff if they were genuine, serve instead to place the accused, or defendant, in the right if they do not have that just character which is claimed for them. For example, if a claim is presented against us for property that is our own, or if we are pressed to do something that we are under no obligation to do, or if it is demanded that we be given up for punishment when we are innocent, then, since the action against us is unjust, the defence must necessarily be just, in accordance with the First Law.

Furthermore, in these disputes involving war just as in the courts of law, not every rightful claim comes into existence before the process of execution. For the execution of one's right in itself constitutes a right, a point already touched upon in our discussion of prize and booty.[a]

Accordingly, it is apparent from the foregoing comments that arms are not justly taken up for the sake of undue dominion or liberty,[b] whereas, for the purpose of rightfully retaining dominion and liberty already acquired, not even war should be shunned. Nevertheless, we should see to it (although this is a matter not so much of right as of discretion) that we do not rashly allow ourselves to be aroused by comparatively trifling injuries; for it is frequently less of a hardship to tolerate these, than it would be to endure the conditions that inevitably accompany war. We must steer clear of Charybdis without falling upon [30′] Scylla. Of a similar character is the forensic principle that it is not necessarily expedient to enter into litigation on every occasion when it is just to do so.

Our remarks on the subject of rights are applicable no less to allies than to the principal authors of a war,[c] since allies, too, should take care lest they involve themselves in a war that is not just. For they are not

a. See Exposition of Art. I, Concl. II, *supra,* pp. 68 ff.

b. Vict. [*De Jure Belli*], 11, 12; Arist., *Politics,* VII. iii [VII. ii. 10].

c. [Trovamala], *Summa Rosella,* word *bellum,* n. 10; Sylvester [on word *bellum,* Pt. I.] ix [x]. 4.

compelled to do so, inasmuch as unconditional contracts of alliance for war are invalid even from the legal standpoint.[a] It is for this reason that Abraham[b] instructs his allies in regard to the justice of his cause; and Achilles, too, when he is about to aid the Greeks, is represented by the Latin poet Statius[c] as first inquiring into the causes of the war, in these words:

> What was *the source,* for Greece, of war so grave?
> Tell me! It is my wish straightway to build
> *Just* wrath upon this knowledge. . . .

Therefore, *in so far as concerns the persons who wage war voluntarily, that war has a just cause, wherein the said persons defend their lives or their property, or seek to recover the latter, or attempt to exact either payment of that which is due or punishment for wrongdoing.* Conclusion VI, Article I

Having settled this point, we shall have no difficulty in solving the second problem. For whatever is subject to a given action or suffers the effects thereof, is also customarily regarded as subject-matter of that action. An example of such subject-matter, pertinent to the discussion of war, is to be found in the party against whom war is waged, or in other words, the enemy, although the latter term has an active as well as a passive connotation. For, in the natural order, when the agent acts with calorific force, it follows that the passive recipient of the act is [relatively] cold;[d] and in precisely the same way, when it is evident that the belligerent waging a just war is acting with rightful force, it follows that the enemy against whom the just war is waged must necessarily be disposed in the opposite fashion. But we have already shown[e] that the opposite of a right is a wrong. Therefore, in short, that party rightly becomes the passive subject of the said war, who is in his turn the perpetrator of a

a. Innocent, *On Decretals,* II. xxiv. 29; Matthaei, *De Bello Justo,* in Req. 1.
b. *Genesis,* xiv. 14.
c. *Achilleid,* II [47–8].
d. Arist., *On Generation and Decay,* I. vii.
e. At end of Chap. ii, *supra,* p. 50.

wrong.[a] Augustine[b] maintains that, "The injustice of the opposing party brings just wars upon him"; and the following pronouncement of the Emperor Leo[c] is in accord with the statement formulated by Augustine: ὁ γὰρ τοῖς ἀδικήσασιν ἀνταμυνόμενος οὗτος δίκαιος ἐστίν; "For he is just who inflicts vengeance upon those who have done an injury."[1] The theologians,[d] too, expressing themselves in their own manner, declare that, "A party properly disposed to be the passive subject of war, is a party unwilling to give satisfaction."

New explanation

In order to expound this portion of our argument more accurately, however, we must explain the concept of "wrongs."

The expression "a wrong," when opposed to "a right," has three meanings, differentiated among the Greeks by the use of three separate terms, as we learn not only from the philosophers[e] but also from Ulpian[f] and Theophilus.[g] Again, the same distinction is clearly revealed in Themistius' speech to Valens and in the words of Gylippus as quoted by Diodorus.[h] The Greek terms in question are, first, τὸ ἄδικον [wrong in the generic sense, that which is unrighteous *or* unjust]; secondly, [31] ἀδίκημα [intentional wrongdoing] which manifests itself in either of two aspects, ὕβρις καὶ ζημία [wanton violence, and damage], and thirdly, ἀδικία [habitual and characteristic wrongdoing, injustice]. Hierax[i] the philosopher, in his book on Justice, draws a neat distinction

a. Vict. [*De Jure Belli*], 13.
b. *On the City of God,* IV [xv].
c. [Constitution lxi.]
d. Cajetan, *On II–II,* qu. 40, art. 1.
e. Arist., *Nic. Ethics,* V. x, xi [V. vii. 7] and *Rhetoric,* I. xiii.
f. *Dig.* XLVII. x. 1.
g. *Institutes,* IV. iv, at beginning.
h. *Library of History,* XIII [xxix].
i. [In Stobaeus, *Florilegium,* IX. 58.]

1. Grotius's Latin translation of Leo's pronouncement is perhaps a little stronger than the Greek text warrants. The latter refers to self-defence rather than to vengeance, and literally translated into English would run as follows: "For he who defends himself against those who have done him injury, is a just man." But here, as in other cases not specifically noted where there is a discrepancy between the Greek and Latin texts, the present translation of the *Commentary* is based upon the Latin.

in regard to these three terms, observing that the first represents ἀποτέλεσμα [completion *or* result], the second πρᾶξις [action], and the third ἕξις [a habit *or* state of mind]; or in other words, an accomplished act or result,[2] the performance of an act and the disposition to act, concepts which differ from one another just as a completed picture, the act of painting and the art of painting differ. On the basis of the first concept, the term ἄδικόν τι πράσσοντες [persons through whom wrong is effected], is applied; on the basis of the second, ἀδικοῦντες [intentional wrongdoers], and on the basis of the third ἄδικοι [unrighteous persons]. Now every instance of ἀδικία [or habitual and characteristic wrongdoing] carries with it an element of ἀδίκημα [intentional wrongdoing], and the latter always involves τὸ ἄδικον [generic wrong]; but the reverse need not be true. For although these concepts differ not at all in so far as concerns the person upon whom the injury is inflicted, nevertheless they do differ with respect to the person who is committing the injury. Thus ἀδικία [habitual and characteristic wrongdoing] cannot occur otherwise than ἐκ προαιρέσεως, "by premeditated choice," whereas ἀδίκημα [intentional wrongdoing] sometimes occurs apart from premeditation, though always with antecedent knowledge and volition, or ἑκοντί [voluntarily], that is to say, in circumstances indicating that the agent understands against whom, in what way, and for what reason he is acting, so that his own volition is indeed involved in the act. On the other hand, τὸ ἄδικον [generic wrong]—which the Scholastics[a] call "material injustice," as opposed to formal injustice, while Baldus[b] describes it as "a factual fault," distinguishing it thus from a conscious fault—can exist even in cases where the performance is not voluntary. "Mischances and mistakes" (ἀτυχήματα καὶ ἁμαρτήματα) both fall under this one head. To be sure, the latter type of wrong occurs when an act has its origin in the mind of the agent, though in such a way that he is somehow

a. Th. Aq. II–II, qu. 59, art. 2.

b. *On Code,* VIII. iv. 1.

2. Simply *opus* (a work performed) in the Latin, interpreted by this expanded English phrase on the basis of the context.

deceived; whereas mischances have some other origin, such as the fact that a weapon has slipped from one's hand in crowded surroundings.

The ancient authorities on Roman law[a] placed every instance of τὸ ἄδικον [generic wrong] under the general head of *noxa* [harm, injury, offence], and to those particular cases which were free of τὸ ἀδίκημα [intentional wrongdoing], they applied the term *pauperies* [loss *or* damage inflicted without volition]. An animal, in that it lacks the rational faculty, does not act with wrongful intent.[3] In other words, neither ἀδίκημα [intentional wrongdoing] nor ἀδικία [habitual and characteristic wrongdoing] can be ascribed to animals; for animals are not endowed with volition, and far less do they possess the power of premeditated choice. Nevertheless, they can bring about a wrong. For "wrong" is a general term, applicable even in cases where the agent has not willed to do harm, as is indicated by the Aquilian Law.[b]

Perhaps, then, we shall not err if we say that the Greek phrases τὸν ἄδικόν τι πράττοντα, τὸν ἀδικοῦντα, τὸν ἄδικον, refer respectively to the man who brings about a wrong, the man who acts with wrongful intent (*facere iniuria*) and the man who acts as an unrighteous person. In direct contrast with these phrases, we have the following expressions: δίκαιόν τι πράττειν, δικαιοπραγεῖν καὶ δικαίως πράττειν, "to bring about [31′] what is right," "to act with righteous intent" (*facere iure*), and "to act as a righteous person." The above-mentioned concepts can also be adapted to conform with the phraseology of Marcianus[c] in his discussion of public prosecutions, so that the expression ἄδικόν τι πράττειν may be applied to one who brings about a wrong by chance, ἀδικεῖν to one who does a wrong upon a sudden impulse, and ἀδικῶς πράττειν to one who acts habitually as a wrongdoer.

Accordingly I maintain that in treating of wrongs, or injuries,[4] per-

a. *Dig.* IX. i. 1.

b. *Dig.* IX. ii. 5, § 1.

c. *Dig.* XLVIII. xix. 11, § 2.

3. *facere iniuria* (to act by way of wrong); Grotius's argument in the immediately following paragraph and in subsequent passages of this chapter clearly calls for some such interpretation of the phrases *facere iniuria* and *facere iure* (to act by way of right, i.e., to act with righteous intent).

petrated by the enemy, we include under this head even injuries that are not voluntarily inflicted. This point may be clarified as follows.

Just as right has been shown to consist in that which accords with the First and Second Laws and also in that which accords with the Fifth and Sixth Laws, even so it may be shown that a wrong, or injury, is that which conflicts with the Second [Third][5] or Fourth Law, or with the Fifth or Sixth. For the laws of the first and second orders [Laws I and II, and Laws III and IV, respectively] are of an unmixed character, whereas those of the third order [Laws V and VI] have a mixed character and are therefore taken into consideration from two points of view [i.e. in connexion with both rights and injuries]. Thus, if any person threatens me with danger while he is dreaming (a supposition based upon actual occurrences, according to certain learned authorities[a]) or, for that matter, while he is insane (as may happen at any time), there is no doubt but that I may rightly repel force with force, even to the point of slaying that person if no other way of ensuring my own safety is left open.[b] Yet such an assailant is not "acting with wrongful intent," since at the time in question he is *non compos mentis.* It suffices that his act is in conflict with the Third Law. For, on the basis of the First Law, which charges me to have a care for myself even in preference to others, I have the right to ward off an act of that kind by any means whatsoever. As Seneca[c] says, "Necessity, the great defence of human weakness, breaks down every law." Indeed, as we observed at the outset,[d] necessity is the first law of nature. Similarly, a claim may be made upon property that is being held in good faith; that is to say, although the possessor is not voluntarily transgressing the Fourth Law, nevertheless the Second Law may properly

a. Bartolus, *On Dig.* I. i. 3, n. 1 [n. 5]; Baldus, *On Code,* VIII. iv. 1, n. 50 [n. 38].

b. *Constitutions of Clement,* V. iv.

c. *Declamations,* IX [*Controversies,* IX. iv. 5].

d. Laws I and II, *supra,* p. 23.

4. These three English words are a translation of the single Latin word *iniuriam,* sometimes best translated as "a wrong" (e.g., in the immediately preceding discussion of right as contrasted with wrong), but commonly rendered as "injury" (the translation usually adopted for Grotius's more general statements).

5. *Secunda* was obviously written by a slip of the pen for *tertia.* Cf. appendix A.

be applied against him. Furthermore, it is possible that, owing to any one of several causes, the possessor of certain property may owe me a debt of which he himself is unaware. This situation may arise, for example, if he is an heir. In such circumstances, he is violating the Sixth Law by failing to pay the debt, and despite the fact that the violation is not voluntary, the benefit of that law should not be denied to me. For what could be more unjust than the loss of one person's right because of another person's error? Moreover, the foregoing observations are applicable in warfare just as they are in legal disputes. [32]

Volition is taken into account only in connexion with the Fifth Law. Thus offences against this precept are not punished unless they were voluntarily committed. The reason for the exception lies in the fact that evil is repaid to the guilty person in proportion to the good seized by him in an unrighteous manner,[a] that is to say, through another's ill; but no person can be judged to have enriched himself by means of another's loss unless he was voluntarily the author of that loss; and therefore, not every instance of *ἄδικον* [generic wrong], but only *ἀδίκημα* or *ἀδικία* [intentional or habitual wrongdoing], can appropriately be viewed in this light. Later on, we shall see how these different forms of injury give rise to different modes of execution.[b]

For the present, it is clear that those persons who bring about injury in any way whatsoever are liable to prosecution in war, if they are liable to legal prosecution. For the law, according to Demosthenes,[c] is *ἐπανόρθωμα τῶν ἑκουσίων καὶ ἀκουσίων ἁμαρτημάτων*; that is to say, law corrects not only voluntary but also involuntary sins. Hence it follows that not merely persons who act with free-will, namely, principals and allies, but instruments, too, or in other words, subjects, are included under the head of "enemies." For the subject, in the course of obeying commands, even if he does not "act with wrongful intent" (*ἀδικεῖ*), at least "brings about a wrong" (*ποιεῖ τὰ ἄδικα*).[d] It is to [enemy] subjects

a. See Law V in Chap. ii, *supra,* p. 29.
b. In forms [on war, Chap. viii].
c. Cited in *Dig.* I. iii. 2.
d. Arist., *Nic. Ethics,* V. xii [V. ix. 11].

that the following ritualistic phrases of the Romans[a] refer: (in the declaration of war) "I declare and make war upon the nations of the ancient Latins, *and the men* of the ancient Latins"; (in the inquiry[b] addressed to the people) "Whether they wished and ordered that war be declared upon King Philip and upon the Macedonians *under his rule";* (and in the actual decree[c] mentioned by Cincius in his discussion of military affairs) "The Roman people have declared war against the Hermandulan nation and against *the men* of that nation." Allies, too, are included in the formula,[d] "Let the enemy be that one, *and whatsoever persons are within his garrisons."*

Another point that should be brought out, is this: the same principle that we laid down in connexion with rights holds good in regard to injuries, by a reverse process of reasoning; that is to say, a certain form of injury may be suffered during the very execution of a right. For he who resists a just execution, whether knowingly or ignorantly, causes an injury, since he either keeps back that which belongs to another or fails to do that which he is under an obligation to do, and since, moreover, he is also offending one whom he ought not to offend. Therefore, it is proper to proceed against a state in war, not only when that state itself commits the original injury, or when its magistrates do so on its behalf and by its authority[e] (for we commit those acts, too, which we perform through another), but also when the said state protects citizens who have committed an injury; and it is proper to proceed in like manner against the citizens, in their turn, when they fight in defence of a state or magistrate that is the author of an injury.[f] In other words, inferior laws such as the Seventh and Eleventh (being derived, as they are, from the Third and Fourth Rules), when preferred to any of the first six [32′] laws, which are precepts of nature and of the law of nations (precepts

a. Livy, I [xxxii. 13].
b. Livy, XXXI [vi. 1].
c. Gellius, XVI. iv [1].
d. Livy, XXXVIII [xlviii. 10] and *passim.*
e. See *infra,* in forms [on war, Chap. viii].
f. Th. Aq. II–II, qu. 104, art. 5; Vázquez, ii and xxvi. 29.

based, that is to say, on the First and Second Rules), result not in the execution of rights but rather in the perpetration of injuries.[a]

Conclusion VI, Article II

In the light of the facts above established, *war is just for those who wage it voluntarily against individuals, or against a state, by whom, or by which, or by whose magistrate, an injury has been brought about;*[b] *and it is also just when waged against a state that protects a citizen who is the author of an injury, or against the allies and subjects, in their capacity as such, of any opponent who brings about an injury.*

Strictly speaking, as was noted above, the question of right does not arise where the actions of subjects are concerned; at least, it does not arise in so far as the source of these actions lies outside of the subjects themselves. For we have already intimated that the fundamental factor involved in this question is that of volition, which is directed by rational understanding, a point confirmed by the theologians; and instruments act in accordance with another's volition. On the other hand, account must be taken of the fact that subjects, although they are instruments, are nevertheless human beings; but human beings—save of course for certain actions imposed by nature—do not act otherwise than of their own volition. How, then, shall we reconcile these statements?

New explanation

We may do so by arguing as follows: the will of subjects is ruled by the will of those who are in command, as is proper wherever instruments are concerned, but with the proviso that reason must not rebel, a proviso which in itself constitutes a phase of justice. Let us illustrate this argument by considering the character of slaves, a subject discussed at length by Aristotle.[c] Although some persons maintain that the slave is completely devoid of any capacity for virtue or even for justice, while others concede to him the same capacity for virtue as that which resides in a free man, the above-mentioned philosopher draws an admirable distinction, explaining that the virtue desirable in a slave is not the perfect

a. See Law XIII, *supra,* pp. 49–50.

b. See Plato, *Alcibiades,* I [p. 109].

c. *Politics,* I, last chap. [I. ii. 13–23]; *id., Nic. Ethics,* VIII. xii [VIII. x. 4].

form required of one who commands but rather the form necessary for servile purposes, and that this virtue is, moreover, very limited in extent. Inasmuch as slaves partake of the rational faculty, they may not be deprived of all claim to virtue; yet they cannot be placed on a level with free men, since they do not possess τὸ βουλευτικόν, "the deliberative faculty." Accordingly, the point I set out to make is this: the slave does exercise reason in a partial degree, and in part he does not. The [33] well-known verses of Homer[a] are remarkably appropriate in this connexion:

> Ἥμισυ γάρ τε νόου ἀπαμείρεται εὐρύοπα Ζεὺς
> Ἀνδρῶν, οὓς ἂν δὴ κατὰ δούλιον ἦμαρ ἕλησι.
>
> *Jove from this class of men takes half the mind,*
> *Willing that they should lead the life of slaves.*

Similarly, the slave is in a partial sense capable of virtue, and partially incapable thereof.

> ἥμισυ τῆς ἀρετῆς ἀποαιρεῖ δούλιον ἦμαρ
>
> *Forced into bondage he doth lack the half*
> *Of virtue. . . .*[6]

Furthermore, this same principle that is applicable to slaves, may be applied to other subject persons. For, as the author first cited [Aristotle][b] asserts, the virtue of a child, οὐκ αὐτοῦ πρὸς αὐτόν ἐστιν, ἀλλὰ πρὸς τὸν τέλειον καὶ ἡγούμενον; "is not personal and relative to the child himself,

a. [*Odyssey,* XVII. 322 f.]

b. [*Politics,* I. v. 9.]

6. The two passages ascribed here to Homer appear to be an unduly expanded paraphrase of a single passage from the *Odyssey* (XVII. 322–3). Evidently Grotius was not only quoting from memory at this point, but was also confused by variant readings of the two lines in question. The Loeb edition of the *Odyssey* has adopted the reading ἀρετῆς (worth) instead of νόου (mind) in the first line, and translates the entire passage as follows: "for Zeus, whose voice is borne afar, takes away half his worth from a man, when the day of slavery comes upon him." On the other hand, Plato, in quoting the same passage (*On Laws,* VI, p. 777A), uses νόου, not ἀρετῆς. Grotius expands Homer's statement by making it refer to both the worth (or virtue) and the mind of slaves.

but relative rather to the individual who is set in authority over him as a more fully developed being." The distinction in question also has a universal application, namely, between *τοῦ ἄρχοντος καὶ ἀρχομένου*,[a] "the one who commands and the one who obeys"; and in this latter class, citizens, even when they are considered as individuals, are included. For citizens, according to Cicero,[b] are servants of the law. Furthermore, as Aristotle[c] explains, all that commands is a cause of virtue to that which obeys.[d] Tacitus[e] has in mind the same distinction when he says: "The gods have assigned to the prince the supreme power of judgement; to the subjects, the glory of obedience has been left." Thus, with respect to subjects, that contention is true which Carneades and the Academic philosophers have mistakenly applied to all persons, namely, that justice is a matter of opinion, *οὐ φύσει ἀλλὰ νόμῳ*, "based not upon nature but upon law," inasmuch as it consists in compliance with the established institutions of the various nations. By the [33a] Peripatetics, this justice [characteristic of subjects] is described sometimes as "legal" and sometimes as "general," because it can be ascribed to the same underlying principle as all the virtues, in so far as these are in conformity with some precept. The Scholastics add that, even as the phase of justice which relates to exchange takes its course between different parts of the whole, while distributive justice proceeds from the whole to the parts, so the phase to which we now refer consists in a process flowing from the parts to the whole. [33]

Thus my original assertion—namely, that a war is not just even for subjects if it is repugnant to their reason[f]—is equivalent to the opinion proclaimed by the theologians[g] in the following terms: "Whatever does not have its origin in good faith, is sinful." For, as the Scholastics[h] ob-

a. [*Ibid.* I. v. 6.]
b. *For Cluentius* [liii. 146].
c. [*Politics,* I. v. 5–6.]
d. *Colossians,* iii. 20, 22; *Titus,* vi. 1 [iii. 1]; *Ephesians,* vi. 1; *Romans,* xiii. 1.
e. *Annals,* IV [VI. viii].
f. Angelus, [de Clavasio], *Summa,* on word *bellum,* n. 8.
g. *Romans,* xiv. 23; *Vict.* [*De Jure Belli*], 23.
h. Th. Aq. I–II, qu. 19, art. 4. See also Arist., *Nic. Ethics,* VI. ii [2].

serve, that act of volition is evil which is at variance with reason, even though reason be in error; and reason is indeed rebellious whenever it declares that the command of some state or magistrate, and consequently, the laws of the inferior orders, are in conflict with the laws of the superior orders and therefore unjust according to the Thirteenth Law. This point is convincingly confirmed by the rules from which the various laws are respectively derived. We are familiar with the saying, "It is better to obey God than to obey men,"[a] a maxim which Ambrose[b] adapts to our argument by offering this concrete example: "The Emperor Julian, although he was an apostate, nevertheless had Christian soldiers under him. When he said to those soldiers, 'Advance your battle line for the defence of the state,' they would obey him; but when he addressed them thus, 'Advance your arms against the Christians,' then they would recognize [only] the divine Commander." For that matter, all of the jurists,[c] too, declare that one ought not to obey a prince who is manifestly issuing an unjust command. Furthermore, they maintain that, in cases of wrongdoing, no one is excused on the ground that he is acting under command,[d] since even a slave who obeys the order of a master engaged in piracy or in any like pursuit of a wrongful nature, is not immune from punishment.[e] Again, Seneca[f] has said: "For we may not command all things [from slaves]; nor are slaves compelled to obey in all things. They shall not execute commands adverse to the state, nor shall they lend a hand in any criminal act." In a preceding passage, Seneca[g] also points out that the relationship of a soldier to his general and that of a subject to his king, are the same as that of a slave to his master. Jerome[h] [33 a′] adopts a similar view, saying, with reference to slaves and children: "They ought to be subject to their masters and parents only in those ways

a. *Acts,* v. 29; *Decretum,* II. xi. 3. 93; *Ecclesiastes,* viii. 1.
b. In *Decretum,* II. xi. 3. 94.
c. Vázquez, *Ill. Cont.* ii. 12.
d. *Dig.* XLVII. x. 11, §§ 3 and 5.
e. *Dig.* XLIV. vii. 20; *ibid.* L. xvii. 157 and Peter Faber thereon.
f. *On Benefits* III. xx.
g. *Ibid.* viii [xviii].
h. *On Ephesians* [*On Titus,* ii], cited in *Decretum,* II. xi. 3. 93.

which are not contrary to the commands of God." By the same [33] token, those persons are not free from guilt who allege as an excuse the fear either of death or of property losses, while they lend themselves as accomplices to some act known or suspected to be unjust. For [33′] fortitude, the companion of justice, decrees that it is better to endure evils of any kind rather than to concur in evil, as Augustine[a] has observed in a similar connexion.

On the other hand, when reason is not opposed, even a war which in itself involves an injury is not unjust from the standpoint of subjects.[b] This principle (as Victoria[c] maintains in his refutation of Adrian's opinion) is applicable even in the case of subjects who are doubtful as to the justice [of a war]. For we have laid down a rule[d] to the effect that "The authorities must be obeyed"; and no one may depart therefrom[e] save through an application of the Thirteenth Law, whereas a person in doubt makes no such application. Neither is any obstacle presented by the precept, "Commit no act concerning which you are doubtful"; for he who is in doubt as to the justice or injustice of a war proclaimed by command, does not forthwith conceive an additional doubt as to whether or not obedience is due in doubtful cases. Moreover, while the foregoing argument is valid even in cases where reason fails in the sense that no definite decision is reached, the same argument will have far greater force when the reason of the subject favours the war, as it does quite properly in a great many instances.

New explanation

For right is based upon fact. And facts—that is to say, specific facts—are learned neither through art nor through science, which are of a purely universal nature. Again, very few facts are discernible through the senses, since we cannot be in more than one place at one particular time, and since the senses perceive only those things which are very close at hand.

a. *On the City of God,* II [I. xviii], cited in *Decretum,* II. xxxii. 5. 3.

b. Ayala, *De Iure et Officiis Bellicis,* I. ii. 33.

c. [*De Jure Belli*] 31.

d. See Rules IV and VI, in Chap. ii, *supra,* pp. 40, 45. Add Second Informal Exposition of Art. I, Concl. I, in Chap. iii, *supra,* pp. 58–60.

e. Th. Aq. II–II, qu. 64, art. 3 [art. 6], ad 3.

Yet there is no other way of attaining to true knowledge. Impelled thus by necessity, human reason has fashioned for itself certain rules of probability, or τῶν εἰκότων, for passing judgement in regard to facts. These rules consist of various προλήψεις, or (to use the Latin term) *praesumtiones* [preliminary assumptions], which are not fixed and unchangeable like scientific rules but rather of a character considered concordant in the greatest possible degree with nature; that is to say, on the basis of what commonly occurs, conclusions of a similar trend may be drawn.[a] In this sense, a question of fact may be called conjectural. For, among the proofs which we accept in forming judgements, there is not one that is necessarily conclusive; on the contrary, all of them are derived from the aforesaid preliminary assumptions ὡς ἐπὶ τὸ πολύ, "based on what commonly occurs."[b] [34]

Now, the primary principle among these assumptions of fact would seem to be our supposition that those inclinations which are in the highest degree natural (such as the inclinations toward the True and toward the Good), as well as the others derived therefrom, exist inherently in some measure within all things. Here we have the source of such concepts as assured belief in posterity, the beneficial nature of property ownership, the credibility of witnesses or documents, and the gravity of oaths. Moreover, not only does the rule of charity instruct us to think well of private individuals,[c] but also (and this is a particularly important point) both reason and Holy Writ[d] forbid disparagement of magistrates. For magistrates have the support of the weightiest preliminary assumptions, partly because of the oath they customarily take, partly as a result of the general consent expressed by the state and the testimonial of confidence given by the citizens, considerations of such a nature that anyone holding a different opinion in regard to these officials would not only be charging the magistrates themselves with treachery but would also

a. See Th. Aq. I–II, qu. 105, art. 2, ad 8; *id.* II–II, qu. 70, art. 2; Vázquez, *Ill. Cont.* xiv. 2; Doctors, *On Decretals,* II. xxiii. 2.

b. Arist., *Nic. Ethics,* I. i. [I. iii. 4]; *Dig.* I. iii. 3.

c. *Dig.* XVII. ii. 51.

d. *Ecclesiastes,* x. 17; *Exodus,* xxii. 28; *1 Peter,* ii. 17.

condemn a vast multitude of persons on a charge of folly. For all such charges would be contrary to those natural impulses which I have called "inclinations." Furthermore, if anyone who practises a particular profession or art is properly regarded as expert and painstaking in his special field,[a] why, pray, should not magistrates be considered to have judged wisely (inasmuch as they are the Priests of Justice) concerning the cause of a war? For it is the function of a good magistrate to formulate such judgements. And when the magistrates hold that things justifying entry into war have befallen the citizens, why should not faith be placed in those authorities, as in persons who speak *the truth?*[b] Yet again, why should it not be right to believe that the laws of an inferior order are in agreement with the higher laws, and that the commands of the magistrate are identical with the commands of God,[c] whenever no obstacle exists to preclude such a belief? In short, subjects subordinate to a given state or magistrate occupy a position analogous to that occupied by children and slaves, who are subject respectively to the solemn *patria potestas* and to the power of the master.

Nevertheless, when we append the condition that reason must not rebel, it should be understood that we are referring to reason guided by the weighing of probabilities. For neither crass ignorance (for example, ignorance of the natural law) nor lack of knowledge regarding a fact which anyone ought to have known, constitutes an excuse for sinning.[d] There are certain things, indeed, of which one cannot be blamelessly ignorant; and, according to the teachings of both the jurists and the philosophers,[e] this very condition of blameworthy ignorance merits punishment.

But we have demonstrated the validity of the opinion which tends

a. Bartolus, *De Testibus,* 86 [85].

b. *Dig.* I. iii. 20, and Baldus and Doctors thereon.

c. *Code,* I. xiv. 12; Panormitanus, *On Decretals,* I. iii. 5; Felinus, *On Decretals,* I. iii. 8.

d. Th. Aq., II–II [I–II], qu. 76, arts. 1, 2, 3, 4.

e. Arist., *Nic. Ethics,* II. vii [III. v. 2–3]; *Dig.* XXII. vi. 6.

not a little to placate the consciences of many persons. Augustine[a] has expounded this opinion in the following terms: "Therefore, the just man, if he should by chance be serving as a soldier even under an impious king, may righteously wage war at the latter's command, provided that, while he observes the dispositions of rank established to maintain peace within the state,[7] it is certain either that the order issued to him is [34′] not contrary to the law of God, or, at least, uncertain that the order does conflict with God's law; so that the king may perhaps be held responsible for an unjust command while the soldier is shown to be innocent because of his rank as one who serves."

We ourselves shall state our conclusion thus: *For subjects, that war has a just cause which is ordered by a superior, provided that the reason of the subjects is not opposed thereto after weighing the probabilities.* [b] Conclusion VI, Article III

Through this same process of reasoning, we arrive at the answer to another question, namely: what persons may justly be attacked in war by subjects? In the [Civil] Law,[c] the enemies of the Romans are defined as those against whom the Roman People have decreed war. Indeed, in all parts of the world, subjects justly wage war upon those against whom war is ordained by the state or magistrate of the said subjects, save in

a. *Against Faustus,* XXII. lxxiv [lxxv], cited in *Decretum,* II. xxiii. 1. 4. Agrees with Innocent, *On Decretals,* II. xxiv. 29, n. 1.

b. Sylvester, on word *bellum* [Pt. I.] ix [x]. 3.

c. *Dig.* XLIX. xv. 24.

7. Reading *si civicae pacis ordinem servans,* the correct wording of the passage cited from Augustine, and not *si vice pacis ordinem servans* (. . . provided that, while he observes the claims of rank rather than those of peace . . .), the phrase actually employed here by Grotius. Since the same passage is correctly quoted in Grotius's own treatise *On the Law of War and Peace* (II. xxvi. 4. 3), and since the similarity in sound between the two phrases suggests that the alteration in the *Commentary* may have been the unintentional result of an aural misunderstanding (such as could have occurred in the process of dictating the quotation from Augustine), the wording of the *Contra Faustum* has been followed in the English translation.

Other very slight discrepancies between the quoted passage and the original do not affect the meaning, and need not be noted here.

cases conflicting with the limitation explained above[a] [i.e. cases in which reason rebels after the probabilities have been weighed].

At this point, however, we are confronted with a difficult problem. For we have already said that in an essentially unjust war the subjects, though acting in ignorance, are nevertheless "bringing about a wrong"[8] and are therefore rightly attacked in war; yet in the present connexion we say that those same subjects, when ignorant, "act as righteous persons" when they wage war; but he who "acts as a righteous person" is at the same time "acting with righteous intent" and "bringing about what is right"; now, a single act cannot be both right and wrong, since these two concepts are diametrically opposed to each other, and on the other hand, it is certain that a given individual cannot be acting both "as a righteous person" and "as an unrighteous person," since both these forms of conduct relate to the disposition of the agent, in which contrary feelings regarding a given matter cannot be entertained simultaneously. Nevertheless, it is possible for the same person to bring about a wrong and a right effect at one and the same time, though not with respect to a single object. For actions which proceed from an identical source can have an opposite effect upon different objects. For example, clay is hardened by the action of the selfsame fire that softens wax. Similarly, when a subject is waging by lawful authority a war that is in itself unjust, the effect constitutes a wrong in relation to the party against whom the war is directed; yet it represents a right from the standpoint of the party who gives the order, and not merely a right, but justice itself. For (as we indicated above) virtue in the subject must bear a relation to the authority in command. The following argument will clarify this point: any act whose omission would be characteristic of an unrighteous person, is characteristic of a righteous person when it is not omitted; and a subject would be "acting as an unrighteous person" if, when his magistrate gave

a. See discussion of Art. II of Concl. VI, *supra,* pp. 114 ff.

8. Grotius's argument here must be read in the light of his general discussion of certain concepts relating to right and wrong; cf. collotype pp. 30′–31′.

orders for a war not known by the subject to be unjust, the latter should refuse to carry on that war; moreover, he would be sinning not only in a civic capacity but also against his conscience.[a] For, as Augustine[b] [35] explains, "when a soldier, acting in obedience to the power lawfully set over him, slays a man, that soldier is not guilty of homicide by any law of his own state; on the contrary, if he has failed to act thus, he is guilty of betrayal and contempt of sovereign authority. If, however, he had committed this same act of his own accord and by his own authority, he would have become liable to the charge of shedding human blood. Thus he will be punished for failing to perform, when bidden to do so, the very act that he is punished for performing unbidden." Hence it follows that a subject "acts as a righteous person" when waging a war that he does not regard as unjust, even if wrong is thereby inflicted upon another.[c]

Nor is there any reason to be surprised at this conclusion. For the judge who sentences an innocent prisoner when the latter has been convicted by legal proofs, is also "acting as a righteous person," since he is doing that which it would be sinful for him not to do; yet the wrong done to the innocent person is not lessened by these circumstances. A similar statement could be made in regard to the person executing a death sentence, inasmuch as he is bound to execute that sentence unless he is convinced that the command to do so is unjust. Despite the fact that such cases admit of an occasional error in reasoning, this possibility of error does not vitiate the justice of the act involved, since (as the Scholastics[d] have taught) the volition attached to erring reason is wicked only in those instances where knowledge is obligatory. Furthermore, there are many just causes of war whose public disclosure is inexpedient,[e] nor is it fitting that a private individual should be curious in such a situation; for if a delay were permitted for each person's examination of

a. Th. Aq. I–II, qu. 96, art. 4; Soto, *De Iustitia et Iure,* I, qu. 6, art. 4.

b. *On the City of God,* I. xxvi, cited in *Decretum,* II. xxiii. 5. 13.

c. Sylvester, on word *bellum* [Pt.] I. ix [x]. 4.

d. Th. Aq. I–II, qu. 19, art. 6.

e. Vict., *De Jure Belli,* 31; Cajetan, in *Summula Peccatorum,* words *bellum dubium.*

the cause in question, opportunities to build up resistance would be afforded to the enemy.

In the foregoing observations, we have an explanation of the ruling, "He inflicts harm who commands that it be inflicted, but he is guiltless who must necessarily obey";[a] and of this other ruling, too: "If a free man has inflicted a wrong with his own hand by order of another, [35′] action may be brought against the party who gave the command, provided that the latter had the right of command; but if he did not have this right, the action must be brought against the party who committed the act."[b] The same principle may be applied to explain the words of Augustine:[c] "the just man shall give no special thought to any consideration other than this, that the person undertaking the war is one who has a lawful right to wage war." Thus Panormitanus[d] appends a shrewd restriction to Hostiensis'[e] pronouncement against war, in stating that a war is presumed to be just when it has been declared by a superior power. Not only in the opinion of Panormitanus, but also by unanimous agreement among all of the theologians and teachers of canon and civil law,[f] in every case of this kind, subjects fight justly and are exempt from any charge of murder.

Conclusion VI, Article IV

In short, the contention of these authorities is equivalent to the conclusion which we shall formulate in the following terms: *For subjects, that war is just which is waged against an opponent whom their superior has ordered them to attack in war, provided that the reason of the subjects is not opposed thereto after weighing the probabilities.*

The difficult and much-mooted question of whether or not it is possible for a war to be just on both sides,[g] is susceptible of clarification on

a. *Dig.* L. xvii. 169.

b. *Dig.* IX. ii. 37; add Glossators, *On Dig.* L. xvii. 167, § 1.

c. [*Questions on Heptateuch,*] VI. x, *On Joshua,* cited in *Decretum,* II. xxiii. 2. 2.

d. *On Decretals,* II. xxiv. 29, n. 13.

e. *On Decretals,* V. xxxiv. 1; add Sylvester, on word *bellum* [Pt.] I. iv and v.

f. Vict. [*De Jure Belli*], 25, 31; Innocent, *On Decretals,* III. xxxiv. 8; Castrensis, *On Dig.* I. i. 5, n. 9; Ayala, I. ii. 31.

g. See Piccolomini, *Philosophia Civilis* [*Della Filosofia Naturale*], VI. xxi.

the basis of the comments already made. For there is no doubt but that the remaining requisites of justice—for instance, those relative to authority, mode of warfare, or intent—can be present in both belligerents, so that the whole of the difficulty lies in the matter with which we have just dealt. Indeed, it does not seem possible that one might justly resist a person seeking to obtain his rights, in the same manner as if one were resisting the perpetrator of a wrong. Thus it becomes necessary to draw a distinction between subjects and persons in command.

For if we are referring to the state or magistrate authorizing a war, we are more likely to find both belligerent parties in the wrong than we are to find right on both sides. Take for example a case in which a debt of five is owed, and one party seeks to collect ten while the other offers no payment whatsoever. For we have here a situation identical with that created by two mutually contradictory statements, which may both be false at one and the same time whereas they cannot both be true simultaneously. Of course, it is possible for princes to fall into error either of law or of fact,[a] and the error may be excusable; but if such an inadvertent mistake should occur during a judicial trial, that would not enable us to say any more truly that the suit was justly litigated. For in the case [36] of voluntary agents it is necessary, if they are to be regarded as acting justly, that their action shall in itself be in conformity with the laws. Therefore, *in so far as voluntary agents are concerned, there can be no war that is just for both parties.* Article I of Corollary

On the other hand, if we refer exclusively to those persons who serve in warfare, there is nothing to preclude the possibility of a war that is just on both sides. For the issue of justice as a whole turns not upon a single fact, but rather upon the conflicting orders and opinions of the various persons in command; and furthermore, the conflicting acts of different commanders do not necessarily invalidate each other, just as it is not impossible that contrary opinions, both of a credible nature, may occur to different men in regard to one and the same matter.

a. Vict., *De Jure Belli,* 59.

'Tis not permitted us to know which one
More justly wars; for each supports his cause
With high authority. . . .[a]

The same theme is touched upon in the following quotation from Cicero:[b] "Indeed, a certain confusion prevailed: generals of the greatest renown were pitted against each other. Many persons were in doubt as to what would be the best course: many, as to what would be expedient for themselves; many others, as to what would be seemly; and some were doubtful even as to what would be lawful." Such, then, are the persons referred to in various passages as "just enemies," namely, those who do what they do at the command of a superior power. Consequently, within a state tyrants and rebels are not classified as just enemies, and outside the bounds of any state brigands and pirates are excluded from this classification, although the reason for excluding these groups has not hitherto been given sufficient consideration.

Just enemies

Article II of Corollary

All of the theologians and jurists[c] agree, however, in accepting this principle: *In so far as subjects are concerned, a war can be just for both parties: always provided, of course, that the war be preceded by a command against which reason does not rebel after the probabilities have been weighed.* [36′]

a. Lucan [*The Civil War,* I. 126f.].

b. *For Marcellus* [x. 30].

c. Vict. [*De Jure Belli*], 32; Covarr., *On Sext,* rule *peccatum,* Pt. II, §§ 9 and 10; Soto, *De Iustitia et Iure,* V. qu. 1, art. 7; Vázquez, ix. 16 [15].

CHAPTER VIII

Concerning the Forms to Be Followed in Undertaking and Waging War

Question VII

Article I. What constitutes just form in undertaking a private war?

Article II. What constitutes just form in undertaking a public war?

Article III. What constitutes just form in waging a war, in so far as voluntary agents are concerned?

Article IV. What constitutes just form in waging a war, in so far as subjects are concerned?

Corollary I. To what extent is aggressive action permissible against enemy subjects?

Corollary II. Can seizure of prize or booty be just for both parties, in so far as subjects are concerned; and if so, to what extent is this possible?

Corollary III. Can [*permanent*] *acquisition of prize or booty be just for both parties; and if so, to what extent is this possible?*

The forms and modes of warfare, too, must be considered in one light with reference to voluntary agents, and in a different light with reference to subjects. Furthermore, just as in most matters there is one form for an inchoate stage, and another form for a permanent condition, even so there is one mode of voluntarily undertaking a war while there is another mode of carrying it on voluntarily.

Now, form (according to the ancient philosophers)[a] consists in what may be described as a certain orderly arrangement; and therefore, a just form is an orderly arrangement concordant with law, or in other words, a kind of internal harmony among the various laws. This harmonious blend (so to speak) is governed by the Thirteenth Law, [which requires the observance of the different laws in the order of their importance]. As we have already stated, however, war is a process of execution, and only the Ninth and Twelfth Laws, [relative to respect for judicial procedure in the private and public execution of rights,] are pertinent to the proper initiation of this process.

First of all, let us consider those wars which are undertaken by private individuals. Here we are at once confronted with a rather grave difficulty. For a private war cannot possibly be preceded by a judicial process, since the power of judgement resides in the state and the war would cease to be private as soon as the state interposed its authority.[b] How, then, can a private war be just in its external form, when the Ninth and Twelfth Laws call for judicial procedure as a preliminary requisite?

Even with respect to private individuals, this requirement is confirmed by the authority of sages and of civil law. For no one is [37] given power to set armed forces in motion when the ruler has not been consulted.[c] Such conduct, indeed, would constitute not a just war but private robbery.[d] Consequently, he who wages war or holds a levy or makes ready an army independently of any command to that effect from the people or the prince, is punishable under the Julian law of high treason.[e] Moreover, why are guards stationed in public places, why have prohibitions and warnings against offensive action been incorporated in the laws, if not with the purpose of precluding any excuse for private defence?[f] In so far as [unauthorized] defence of one's own property is

a. See Arist., *Metaphysics,* VIII. iii [8].

b. See Concl. V, Art. I, *supra,* pp. 95 ff. Sylvester, on word *bellum,* [Pt. I.] iii: *primo.*

c. *Decretum,* II. xxiii. 1. 4; *Code,* XI. xlvii (xlvi).

d. Livy, XXXVIII [xlv].

e. *Dig.* XLVIII. iv. 3.

f. See Bartolus, *On Dig.* XXXIX. ii. 13, § 11.

concerned, we know that a precept has been established to the following effect: if the owner of a piece of property shall have forcibly seized possession thereof prior to the rendering of a judicial decision, possession shall be restored [to the party from whom the property was seized] and the [original] title to ownership shall be lost.[a] Similarly, with reference to debts, violence is said to be employed whenever any person reclaims otherwise than through a judge that which he believes to be his due; and it is also maintained that the legal right of the creditor is lost when the latter has declared the law for himself.[b] In the case of crimes, the matter is even clearer: *μὴ ἑαυτοὺς ἐκδικοῦντες*, "avenge not yourselves," says the Apostle Paul.[c] And Seneca[d] observes: "'Vengeance' is an inhuman word, yet it is accepted as having a just connotation; nor does it differ greatly from 'violence,'[1] save in degree. He who returns an injury merely sins more pardonably." This same point is borne out in the other pronouncements against violence, made by the philosophers[e] and by Christian writers.[f] Thus Quintilian[g] says: "Requital of injury is inimical not only to law but also to peace. For laws, courts, judges, are all available, save perchance for those who are ashamed to vindicate themselves by legal means." Quintilian's assertion is clearly equivalent to these words from the decree of the Roman Emperor [Theodosius]:[h] "even if one of them [the Jews] be implicated in crime, the authority of judgements and the protective force of public law have been established in our midst for this very purpose, namely, to preclude the possibility that any individual should be in a position to indulge in direct personal vengeance." Theodoric[i] supports the same view when he tells us that, "Pious reverence for

a. *Code,* VIII. iv. 7.
b. *Dig.* XLVII. viii. 2, § 18; *ibid.* IV. ii. 13; *ibid.* XLVIII. vii. 7–8.
c. *Romans,* xii. 19.
d. *On Anger,* II. xxxii.
e. Plato, *Crito* [p. 49 B]; Arrian, *Epictetus,* II. x.
f. Lactantius, *Divine Institutes,* VI. xviii.
g. *Declamations* xiii [11].
h. *Code,* I. ix. 14. Add *Dig.* IX. ii. 5; *Code,* IX. xviii. 9.
i. Cassiodorus, *Variae,* IV. x.

1. Grotius has *contumelia* (violence, abuse, injury), whereas the word actually employed by Seneca is *talio* (retaliation).

the laws is found to have its origin in this very principle: that nothing shall be done by violence, nothing on individual impulse."

On the other hand, we have shown in a preceding passage[a] that just wars which are nevertheless private, do spring from the four causes already mentioned; whence it follows that the Ninth and Twelfth Laws must sometimes become invalid, or rather, dormant. Now, they become dormant in obedience to the principle laid down in the Thirteenth [37′] Law, that is to say, as a result of necessity based upon the superior laws; and it is understood that this necessity arises when judicial means for the attainment of our rights are defective. For in so far as such a defect exists, to that extent recourse to force—or, in other words, private execution in accordance with the natural order—is just.[b] But as soon as judicial means can be employed, then, as we stated in our discussion of the thirteen laws, all of the said laws must be observed simultaneously. It should be noted, moreover, that the defect in judicial recourse is sometimes of brief duration, sometimes of a more or less continuous nature.[c]

Force

New explanation

The defect is of brief duration whenever our rights have not yet been violated but the matter does not permit of the delay necessary for judicial procedure.[d] In the first place, then, as Baldus[e] has said, whatever is expedient for self-defence in such cases, is likewise permissible; for a crisis that threatens our lives permits of no delay. The jurists,[f] indeed, approve of everything done to ward off danger, or through fear of death, or for the protection of our persons, or in order to repel violence, in so far as it is impossible for us to defend ourselves becomingly or effectively in any other way. This contention is equivalent to that rule of blameless self-defence which is so frequently reiterated.[g] Similarly, it is permissible

a. Art. I, qu. 6 [Concl. VI, Art. I], *supra*, pp. 92–95.

b. Bartolus, *On Reprisals*, Ad 2, n. 6 [Qu. 9, ad 5]; Cajetan, *On II–II*, qu. 66, art. 8: *Ex dictis autem patet.* And it is also evident from what is said above. *Dig.* IX. ii. 29, § 1.

c. Baldus, *On Code*, VIII. iv. 1, nn. 38, 40 [nn. 22, 23].

d. Sylvester, on word *bellum* [Pt. I.] iii: *Unde dico.*

e. *On Code*, VIII. iv. 1.

f. *Dig.* IX. ii. 4, 5; *ibid.* I. i. 3; *ibid.* IV. ii. 12; *ibid.* IX. ii. 45.

g. Sylvester, on word *bellum* [Pt.] II, at beg.; Th. Aq. II–II, qu. 64, art. 7; Glossators and Baldus, *On Code*, VIII. iv. 1; Panormitanus, *On Decretals*, II. xxiv. 29,

for us to defend or recover our own property, even with the assistance of groups of men assembled for that purpose, but only if such action is taken at once. For after an interval during which there has been time to appear before a judge, force should no longer be used. In regard to the collection of debts, it is my belief that no concession has been made other than that relative to the seizure of pledges, or "the laying on of hands" (as the legal phrase goes), in cases where we are in danger of forfeiting our rights because the debtor has fled;[a] so that, as soon as the matter can be laid before a judge, the latter, rather than the creditor acting for himself, will award the debtor's possession to the creditor in payment of the debt. Thus we find that among the Athenians, ἀνδρολῃψίας,[b] that is to say, seizure of human beings as pledges, was permitted to private individuals; but the question of whether the pledges had been rightfully or wrongfully given was a matter for public judgement. A similar concession is made in the case of crimes, when it seems that the transgressor is on the verge of escaping punishment; for by commonly accepted law[c] (special laws being at times more indulgent) it is permissible to seize and detain the guilty person, though only on condition that he be handed over at once to a judge, since the laws forbid the maintenance of private prisons.[d] [38]

As regards continuous lack of means for judicial settlement, the authorities[e] maintain that there are two ways in which such a defect may occur: it may be either a defect in law or a defect in fact. It is a defect in law when in a given place there is no one possessing jurisdiction, a state

---

n. 15; Bartolus, *On Dig.* I. i. 3, nn. 9, 10; Jason, *On Dig.* I. i. 3. n. 7; Angelus, *Summa,* on word *bellum,* § 6; Sylvester, *loc. cit.* xiii; *Dig.* XLVII. ii. 7; Bartolus, *On Dig.* I. i. 3, n. 7 and *On Dig.* XLIX. xv. 24, n. 9; *Code,* VIII. iv. 1 and Baldus thereon; *Decretals,* II. xiii. 12; *Dig.* XLIII. xvi. 3, § 9 and *ibid.* xvii; Gabriel, *On the IV Sentences,* IV, dist. 15, qu. 4.

a. Festus, on word *struit* [p. 38]; *Code,* X. xxxi. 54; *ibid.* I. iii. 12; Doctors, *On Dig.* IX. ii. 39; and also *On Dig., ibid.,* § 1; Bartolus, *On Reprisals,* Qu. 9 [ad 4].

b. Julius Pollux [VIII. l and li].

c. *Dig.* XLVIII. v. 25; Jason, *On Dig.* I. i. 3, n. 25; Baldus, *On Code,* VIII. iv. 1, n. 33 [n. 12].

d. *Code,* IX. v, whole tit. and Bartolus thereon.

e. Bartolus, *On Reprisals,* Qu. 2, ad 5, near beg.; Sylvester, on word *repressalia,* iii.

of affairs which may exist in desert lands, on islands, on the ocean or in any region where the people have no government. The defect is one of fact whenever the person to whom jurisdiction properly pertains, is disregarded by those subject to him, or when he is not at leisure to conduct a judicial inquiry.[a] In such cases, as Castrensis[b] rightly observes, the situation becomes very much what it was before states and courts of justice were established.[c] But in those days human beings were governed in their mutual relations solely by the six laws which we laid down first of all. Those six precepts were the source of all law, and also of the principle that each individual was the executor of his own right, a principle consonant with the natural order, as we have already remarked, and as is indicated by the conduct of other living creatures.[d] Accordingly, from this point of view, it will be permissible not only to defend oneself and one's own possessions, but also to recover such possessions after any interval, howsoever long, and to pay oneself from the property of debtors. [39][2]

A paradoxical contention

Thus I find that there is universal agreement as to the fact that just private wars may arise from three of the four causes enumerated above.[3]

There remains for consideration the fourth cause, wrongdoing; and,

a. Baldus, *On Code,* VIII. iv. 1, n. 45 [n. 22].

b. *On Dig.* I. i. 5 and *Consilium* 399, words: *Priusquam iura fierent.*

c. Discussion of Law II, *supra,* pp. 23–24. *Dig.* I. ii. 2, § 13.

d. *Dig.* IX. i. 1, § 11; Laudensis, *De Bello,* Qu. 5, at end; Bartolus, *On Dig.* I. i. 5 and Jason thereon, n. 38; Gloss, *On Dig.* XLIII. xxiv. 7, § 3; Bartolus, *On Dig.* XLIX. xv. 24; Innocent, *On Decretals,* II. ii. 14 and *ibid.* [II. xiii. 12], n. 9; Cajetan, *On II–II,* qu. 66, art. 5, ad 3; Panormitanus, *On Decretals,* II. xiii. 12, n. 23; Sylvester, on word *furtum,* xvii, and on word *bellum* [Pt.] II. xiii; see also Menochio, *De Arbitrariis Judicum Quaest.* [II. ii], case 516, where many theologians and jurisconsults are mentioned.

2. A long deleted passage begins at this point, covering approximately the lower half of collotype p. 38 and all of p. 38′, so that the text in its corrected state is continued on p. 39, to which we now pass in the English translation. This rejected material is continued on pp. 43, 43′, and 44, which were also deleted in the course of revision, with the exception of the lower portion of p. 44. Cf. note 7, p. 122, *infra.* The substance of the passages thus excluded from Grotius's corrected text is restored, for the most part, on other pages of the collotype.

3. Chapter VII, *in princ.*

unless I am mistaken, no one will doubt that this cause, too, in so far as it leads only to the exaction of restitution for the injured party, can justly give rise to private wars. For it is no less truly my right to exact whatever amount is involved because of injury inflicted, than it is to seek possession either of my own property or of property due me on some other basis.

It is not so easy to decide the question of whether or not a private individual may under any circumstances seek to impose punishment for a crime. Indeed, since a great many persons maintain that the power to punish has been granted to the state alone (wherefore judgements, too, are [habitually] termed "public"), it might seem that private application of force is ruled out entirely. The best method we can adopt for the discussion of this point will be found, however, in the consideration of what was permissible for individuals prior to the establishment of states.

When the Emperor Theodosius asserts (in the decree quoted in part just above)[a] that the judicial system was established precisely for the purpose of preventing any individual from indulging in private vengeance, he certainly implies that in his opinion vengeance was permissible for private individuals before the said system was adopted. But a change was introduced in regard to that privilege, owing to the fact that the bounds of moderation were easily overstepped either through love of self or through hatred of another. Nor is there any great difference between this development in the matter of vengeance and the developments relative to defence of property and collection of debts; for, although each individual formerly conducted these latter transactions personally, the establishment of courts of justice was undertaken in order to avert the perils arising from this earlier practice. Lucretius[b] expresses the same idea very clearly indeed, in the following lines:

> Since each man, moved by wrath, was wont to plan
> Vengeance more harsh than just laws now allow,
> Men wearied of a life of violence. . . .

a. *Code,* I. ix. 14.
b. V [1148 ff.].

Cicero[a] himself, after observing that the law of nature is the principle implanted in us not by opinion but by innate force, places vengeance, which he describes as the opposite of gratitude, among the manifestations of the natural law; and I note that the most eminent theologians[b] do not condemn him on this score. Moreover, in order that there [39′] may be no doubt as to the exact scope of the concept included under the term "vengeance," Cicero defines it as "that act by which, defensively or punitively, we repel violence and abuse from ourselves and from those close to us whom we should hold dear," and also as "that act whereby we inflict punishment for wrongdoing." Civilis is quoted by Tacitus[c] as saying: "In accordance with the law of nations, I demand the infliction of punishment." In Scriptural history,[d] too, Samson declares that he has incurred no guilt by inflicting injury in his turn upon the Philistines who injured him when they carried off his wife; and afterwards, when he has completed the act of vengeance, he once more excuses that act on the same grounds, asserting that he has done unto them as they themselves first did unto him. To be sure, the fact that Samson was moved by the Spirit of God [to seek an occasion for conflict with the Philistines][4] exonerates him, in that he had no need of public authorization; but in any case, his conduct in defending himself against the nations of the Gentiles was righteous by the law of nations. Accordingly, that precept of law which demands the punishment of evildoers is older than civil society and civil law, since it is derived from the law of nature, or law of nations. This assertion would seem to be supported by the Sacred Scriptures. For I find in them no reference to the existence of any civil state in the period following the Flood, during which the survivors of the human race were included in a single household, yet I do find reference

a. *On Invention,* II [xxii].

b. Th. Aq. II–II, qu. 108, art. 2; *ibid.* qu. 158, art. 1, ad 3.

c. *Histories,* IV [xxxii].

d. *Judges,* xv. 3 and 11.

4. Grotius's reference to *Judges,* xv, does not cover every part of the story of Samson necessary for an understanding of this passage. See also *Judges,* xiii, xiv, and especially, xiv. 4.

to a law of that period which commands that evil deeds be punished: "Whoso sheddeth man's blood, by man shall his blood be shed."[a]

Perhaps mention should also be made of the fact that this law is subordinate to another, [laid down on the same occasion],[5] which delivers the beasts into man's service. For when the theologians[b] inquire into the origin of punishments, they avail themselves of an argument based upon comparison, as follows: all less worthy creatures are destined for the use of the more worthy; thus, despite the fact that the beasts were indeed created by God, it is nevertheless right that man should slay them, either in order to convert them to use as his own property, or in order to destroy them as harmful, both of these purposes being mentioned in the Scriptural passage to which I have referred; similarly, so the theologians contend, men of deplorable wickedness, for the very reason that they are of such a character—stripped, as it were, of all likeness to God or humanity—are thrust down into a lower order and assigned to the service of the virtuous, changing in a sense from persons into things, a process which constitutes the origin of slavery in the natural order, too; and therefore, it is permissible to destroy such men, either in order that they may be prevented from doing harm or in order that they may be useful as examples. Seneca[c] made this very point, when he wrote: "so that they shall serve as a warning to all, and so that the state may at least derive profit from the death of those who were unwilling to be of use when alive." For we shall presently show that Seneca's remark concerning the state is applicable to the whole body of mankind. Democritus, too, in his discussion of natural law, draws an example from the beasts to justify the punishment of the guilty. Thus he[d] says: *κατὰ δὲ ζῴων φόνου* [40] *καὶ μὴ φόνου ὧδε ἔχει· τὰ ἀδικέοντα καὶ θέλοντα ἀδικεῖν, ἀθῶος ὅ κτείνων· καὶ πρὸς εὖ ἐς οὖν τοῦτο ἔρδειν μᾶλλον ἢ μή.* "As to the question of whether or not animals should be slain, the matter stands as

a. *Genesis,* ix. 6.

b. Th. Aq. II–II, qu. 64, art. 1 and Cajetan thereon.

c. *On Anger,* I. vi.

d. In Stobaeus [*Florilegium,* XLIV. 16].

5. See *Genesis,* ix. 2 and 3.

follows: whosoever shall slay animals that are doing harm or desiring to do harm, is free from guilt; indeed, it is even more righteous to have committed such an act of slaughter than to have abstained therefrom." Farther on, the same writer[a] declares: *κτείνειν χρὴ τὰ πημαίνοντα παρὰ δίκην πάντα περὶ παντός*; "It is proper in every way and for all persons, that those creatures whose harmfulness exceeds the bounds of law, should be slain." Yet again, he makes the following observation:[b] *ὅκως περὶ κιναδέων γε καὶ ἑρπετέων γεγράφαται τῶν πολεμίων οὕτω καὶ κατὰ ἀνθρώπων δοκεῖ μοι χρεὼν εἶναι ποιεῖν*; "Furthermore, it would seem that the very acts which we have mentioned in connexion with foxes and harmful serpents are proper in connexion with human beings, also." And to this he adds:[c] *κιξάλλην καὶ ληστὴν πάντα κτείνων τις ἀθῷος ἂν εἴη καὶ αὐτοχειρίᾳ, καὶ κελεύων, καὶ ψήφῳ*; "That person is innocent who slays a thief and robber in any manner whatsoever, whether *by his own hand,* by his command, or by his vote of condemnation." One might suppose that the comments of Democritus were read by Seneca,[d] who says: "when I give the order for a criminal to be beheaded [. . .], I shall look and feel exactly as I do when killing a snake or any poisonous creature." In another passage, Seneca[e] observes: "We would not destroy even vipers and water-snakes, or any creature that does harm by biting or stinging, if we were able (as we are in the case of other animals) to tame them, or to arrange that they should not be a source of danger to ourselves or to our fellow men; neither, then, will we inflict harm upon a human being because he has sinned, but rather in order to prevent him from sinning. . . ."

In the light of the foregoing discussion, it is clear that the causes for the infliction of punishment are natural, and derived from that precept which we have called the First Law. Even so, is not the power to punish essentially a power that pertains to the state? Not at all! On the contrary,

a. [*Ibid.* 17.] [*Florilegium,* XLIV. 16]
b. [*Ibid.* 18.]
c. [*Ibid.* 19.]
d. *On Anger,* I. xvi.
e. *Ibid.* II. xxxi.

just as every right of the magistrate comes to him from the state, so has the same right come to the state from private individuals; and similarly, the power of the state is the result of collective agreement, as we demonstrated in our discussion of the Third Rule.[a] Therefore, since no one is able to transfer a thing that he never possessed, it is evident that the right of chastisement was held by private persons before it was held [40′] by the state. The following argument, too, has great force in this connexion: the state inflicts punishment for wrongs against itself, not only upon its own subjects but also upon foreigners; yet it derives no power over the latter from civil law, which is binding upon citizens only because they have given their consent; and therefore, the law of nature, or law of nations, is the source from which the state receives the power in question.

It will be argued, however, that punishments are ordained solely for the good of the state. But this assertion may be repudiated. For the cause of punishments is a natural cause, whereas the state is the result, not of natural disposition, but of an agreement. Human society does indeed have its origin in nature, but civil society as such is derived from deliberate design. Aristotle[b] himself, the author chiefly relied upon by those who hold the contrary view, writes as follows: *ἄνθρωπος γὰρ τῇ φύσει συνδυαστικὸν μᾶλλον ἢ πολιτικόν· καὶ ὅσῳ πρότερον καὶ ἀναγκαιότερον οἰκία πόλεως, καὶ τεκνοποιία κοινότερον ζῴοις*; "For man is by nature a conjugal creature to a greater extent than he is a political creature, in that the family is in truth an earlier and more necessary institution than the state, and the procreation of children a more general characteristic of the animal kingdom [than the gregarious instinct]." This conclusion is also borne out by sacred history. For God, who created all things in the image of His own perfection, created not a state but two human beings. Thus human society already existed at that time, but the state did not exist. Accordingly, as the numbers of mankind steadily in-

a. See Chap. ii, *supra*, pp. 34 ff.
b. *Nic. Ethics*, VIII. xiv [VIII. xii. 7].

creased, natural power was vested (so Homer[a] tells us) in the heads of households.

> *θεμιστεύει δὲ ἕκαστος*
> *παίδων ἠδ' ἀλόχων.*
>
> *For wives and children, each man made the laws.*

Therefore, it is reasonable to assume that these household heads had external as well as internal jurisdiction for their own protection and that of their families; and Seneca,[b] referring to this attribute, has called them "domestic magistrates." Now, whatever there was of law at the world's beginning, prior to the establishment of states, must necessarily have continued to exist afterwards among those human beings who did not set up courts for themselves, and for whom (in Seneca's[c] phrase) "might is the measure of right." Quintilian[d] also makes this very point. Similarly, Nicholas of Damascus[e] informs us that among the Umbrians it was the custom for each individual to avenge himself by his own hand. Moreover, the same custom persists to a certain extent among the [41] Sarmatians of the present day. Indeed, we may regard those single combats to which recourse is had even now in many localities, as relics of the said custom and as exceptions (in a manner of speaking) to the Ninth Law. The ancient Romans, too, granted powers of life and death to masters, fathers, husbands, and blood relations.

The power of execution conferred upon private individuals by a special law springs, of course, from a different cause. For the wars that result when arms are taken up in such circumstances, should perhaps be called public rather than private, since the state undertakes those wars, in a sense, and gives the command for them to be waged by the said individuals. Yet it is true that, in the majority of cases, the rational origin of such conflicts is the same as that of private wars. To take one example,

a. [*Odyssey,* IX. 114–15.]
b. *On Benefits* [III.] 11.
c. *On Anger,* III. ii.
d. *Declamations,* xiii.
e. Stobaeus, *De Legib.* [*Florilegium,* X. 70].

certain laws[a] grant the power of direct self-defence and vengeance[6] to private individuals, precisely on the ground that it is not easy to resist soldiers and collectors of public revenue through the medium of the courts; and these particular precepts accordingly represent what we retain of natural law—the vestiges of that law, so to speak—in regard to punishments.

One point, however, still remains to be clarified. If the state is not involved, what just end can be sought by the private avenger? The answer to this question is readily found in the teachings of Seneca,[b] the philosopher who maintains that there are two kinds of commonwealth, the world state and the municipal state. In other words, the private avenger has in view the good of the whole human race, just as he has when he slays a serpent; and this goal corresponds exactly to that common good toward which, as we have said, all punishments are directed in nature's plan. The same point is expounded by Plutarch[c] in this admirable statement: *τῷ δὲ (θεῷ) ἕπεται δίκη τῶν ἀπολειπομένων τοῦ θείου νόμου τιμωρός· ᾗ χρώμεθα πάντες ἄνθρωποι φύσει πρὸς πάντας ἀνθρώπους ὥσπερ πολίτας.* "Justice walks with God, bringing vengeance upon those who trespass against the divine law; and *in the natural order, all* of us, as human beings, avail ourselves of that justice, as against *all* men in their *civic* character." The explanation offered by Plutarch does not differ greatly from the contention of the Scholastics,[d] that we ought to seek vengeance even for our own injuries if they are of such a nature as to redound to the detriment of the Church, that is to say, to the detriment of all good men.

It would seem, indeed, that this care for the common good is in equal degree the proper function of every person, whether the injury in ques-

a. *Code,* III. xxvii; *ibid.* X. i. 5; *ibid.* XII. lxi. 5; *ibid.* XII. xli. 5; Jason, *On Dig.* I. i. 3, n. 15.

b. *On the Happy Life,* xxxi [*On Leisure,* iv].

c. *On Exile* [v = p. 601 B].

d. Th. Aq. II–II, qu. 108; Sylvester, on word *vindicata* [*immo melius*].

6. *se vindicandi potestas:* the Latin verb may refer either to punishment or to vengeance, and the passages cited from the *Code* involve both concepts; hence the dual interpretation in the English translation.

tion has been inflicted upon that person himself or upon another, save for one difference, namely, that it may be more hazardous to execute vengeance for one's own injuries, because the observance of a just moderation and a just purpose is difficult in such a case. For as a general [41′] rule that person does not move toward a goal but is driven (to borrow the phrase of Seneca),[a] who, instead of entrusting his revenge toanother, rages alike in thought and in deed while exacting vengeance personally. It is for this reason that princes—the only persons under the established judicial system who cannot be avenged otherwise than by their personal intervention—are wont to be admonished that they should weigh out vengeance not with a view to inflicting pain but for the purpose of setting an example.[b]

Natural reason persuades us, however, that the faculty now vested in princes in consequence of the fact that civil power must have lapsed in some other possessor, formerly resided in private individuals. Moreover, whatever existed before the establishment of courts, will also exist when the courts have been set aside under any circumstances whatsoever, whether of place or of time. In my opinion, this very argument has served as the basis for the belief that it is right for private persons to slay a tyrant, or in other words, a destroyer of law and the courts. The opinion of the Stoics may be interpreted thus when they maintain that the wise man is never [merely] a private citizen, an assertion supported by Cicero,[c] who points to Scipio as an example. Horace,[d] in the lines, "And not consul of a single year," &c. (from the *Ode to Lollius*), has the same principle in mind. Even Plutarch,[e] despite the fact that he represents a different school of thought, does not disagree on this point. On the contrary, he declares that it is nature herself who designs the statesman (in a permanent sense, moreover) to serve as a magistrate; and he adds that the law always confers princely power upon the person who does what

a. *On Anger,* III. iii.
b. Seneca, *On Mercy,* I. xx.
c. *Tusculan Disputations,* IV [xxiii. 51].
d. *Odes,* IV. ix [39].
e. *Precepts of Statecraft* [pp. 813 C and 817 D, E].

is just and knows what is advantageous, although that person will use the power so conferred only when the perfidy or negligence of the men elected to public office has brought matters to a perilous pass. When Caesar[a] (he who afterwards became Dictator) was still a private citizen, he pursued with a hastily raised fleet the pirates by whom he had been captured on an earlier occasion. Some of their boats he put to flight, some he sank; and when the Proconsul neglected to punish the guilty captives, Caesar himself put out to sea again and crucified the culprits, influenced undoubtedly by the knowledge that the judge to whom he had appealed was not fulfilling the functions of the judicial office, as well as by the consideration that it was apparently possible to take such action guiltlessly upon the seas, where one is governed not by written precepts but by the law of nations.

Reflection along the lines just indicated, gave rise to the view that circumstances could exist (though rarely, perhaps, owing to the weaknesses of human nature) in which it would be possible under the natural law for a private person to inflict punishment upon another person without sinning, and likewise possible for one private individual to serve in a sense as magistrate over another, but always on condition that the former should observe the scrupulousness of a judge even in the act [42] of chastisement. I see that Castrensis[b] lends support to this theory with a wealth of arguments. For the laws, [according to Castrensis,] were devised to promote man's welfare, not to injure him; and ordinary remedies do not serve in an extraordinary situation, nor is it forbidden that a person in peril shall take heed for himself and for others, just as one might when abandoned by the sailors in a shipwreck or by the physicians in illness. In cases of necessity and for the purpose of preventing the loss of our rights, many things are permitted which otherwise would not be permitted; and when one recourse fails, we turn to another. Such would seem to have been the opinion of the most learned men of all lands: for example, Connan, Vázquez, and Peter Faber. In the same list, one

a. Velleius Paterculus, II [xlii. 2 ff.]; Plutarch *Caesar* [ii, p. 708 A–C].
b. *Consilium* 399.

might include the name of Ayala, who cites Socinus Nepos[a] in this connexion. [44][7]

Conclusion VII, Article I

Accordingly, we conclude that *a private war is undertaken justly in so far as judicial recourse is lacking.*

Public wars, on the other hand, arise sometimes from a defect of judicial recourse, and sometimes out of a judicial process.[b]

They originate in a defect of judicial recourse in the same way that private wars spring from that origin. Now, as Cicero[c] explains, this [justification for extra-legal warfare] exists whenever he who chooses to wait [for legal authorization] will be obliged to pay an unjust penalty before he can exact a just penalty; and, in a general sense, it exists whenever matters do not admit of delay. Thus it is obvious that a just war can be waged in return, without recourse to judicial procedure,[d] against an opponent who has begun an unjust war; nor will any declaration of that just war be required, a contention confirmed by the decision of the Roman college of fetials in regard to the Aetolians,[e] [who had already committed warlike acts against the Roman people]. For—as Aelian[f] says, citing Plato as his authority—any war undertaken for the necessary repulsion of injury, is proclaimed not by a crier nor by a herald but by the voice of Nature herself. The same view may be adopted with respect to cases in which the sanctity of ambassadors is violated or any other act disruptive to international intercourse is committed. For judicial pro-

a. Connan, *Commentaries,* I. vi; Vázquez, *Ill. Post.* IV. viii [*Ill. Cont.* Pt. II, bk. I, chap. viii]; Faber, *Semestria* II. ii, at end; Ayala, I. ii. 9 and *ibid.* v. 1; Socinus, *Consilia,* III. 68.

b. See Gentili, *De Iure Belli,* II. i and ii.

c. *On Behalf of Milo* [iv. 11].

d. See Baldus, *Consilia,* III. lviii; Gabriel, *On the IV Sentences,* IV, Dist. 15, qu. 4, case 2.

e. Livy, XXXVI [iii].

f. [*Tactica,* i.]

7. MS. p. 42 is evidently one of the pages inserted in the course of the revision mentioned in note 2, p. 132, *supra.* MS. p. 42′ (i.e., the reverse of p. 42) was left entirely blank, and the pages now numbered 43 and 43′, as well as the upper portion of p. 44, contain only deleted matter. Consequently, the English translation passes at this point from p. 42 of the Latin to the line on p. 44 where the revised text is continued.

cedure cannot be expected of those peoples who grant no one safe passage to and from their respective countries.

We must bear in mind, however, a certain point already mentioned, namely the obligation to return to observance of the laws as soon as the peril subsides. For example, if any citizen of a foreign state manages to seize someone's property, it will be permissible not only to recover that property but also to seize other goods by way of security before a judicial decision is rendered, subject to the condition that the goods are to be returned when the judgement has been executed.[a] Nevertheless, whenever considerations of time so permit, all persons whatsoever who undertake to wage war, and all those against whom war is waged, ought to submit to a judicial settlement. [44′]

Thus civil wars are justly undertaken in conformity with the Fifth or Seventh Rule and the Ninth Law; foreign wars, in conformity with the Twelfth Law and the Ninth Rule.[b] Accordingly, in cases of civil warfare, a magisterial or state pronouncement against one citizen and in favour of another citizen or in defence of the state, is a desideratum, nor is there any further requirement;[c] whereas, in the case of foreign wars, the situation is different. Cicero[d] rightly drew this distinction in connexion with his remark that envoys should not be sent to Antony, since the latter ought rather to be compelled to abandon the siege of Mutina, an assertion which Cicero defended on the ground that the quarrel was not with an enemy of the [Roman] state, such as Hannibal, but with a fellow citizen. Seneca[e] subtly indicated the existence of the same distinction, when he spoke of "wars declared upon neighbouring nations, or wars carried on with fellow citizens." For it is not customary, nor is it necessary, to declare a civil war; and this statement is also applicable to warfare against tyrants, robbers, pirates, and all persons who do not form part of a foreign state. In so far as foreign wars are concerned,[f] the

a. *Dig.* XLIII. xvi. 17; Arias, *De Bello,* n. 25 [n. 24], particularly during war.
b. See Chap. ii.
c. Baldus, *On Code,* VI. vi. 4.
d. *Philippics,* V [x. 26 ff.].
e. *On Anger,* III. ii [3].
f. Laudensis, *De Bello,* Qq. 9, 37, 38.

Twelfth Law and the Ninth Rule above mentioned do provide for that declaration of hostilities which plays such an outstanding part in the law of war, and with respect to which the ancients held varying opinions.

As for our own opinions, this whole problem will be resolved on the basis of the preliminary material which we have already presented.

Quite properly did the soldier Thraso keep matters under his own management, [instead of allowing his companions to employ force,] in the episode described by that ἠθικώτατον [highly moral] author, Terence,[a] whose work teems, so to speak, with pithy sayings. I refer to Thraso's admonition:

> The wise man first tries every verbal[8] means,
> Before he takes up arms. How do you know
> She will not yield without the use of force?

Euripides,[b] too, had already written:

> λόγοισι πείθων, εἰ δὲ μὴ βίᾳ δορός.
>
> *I shall achieve my aim through words; or else,*
> *Should words fail, force will serve my ends. . . .*

Cicero[c] expressed the same thought in fuller form when he said: "Since there are two ways of settling a contested question—first, by *discussion,* and secondly, by violence—[and since the former method is characteristic of human beings, the latter characteristic of brutes,][9] we should resort to violence [only] if we are not permitted to avail ourselves of discussion." The following statement from the works of Thucydides[d] may also be cited: ἐπὶ τὸν δίκας δίδοντα οὐ νόμιμον ὡς ἐπ᾽ ἀδικοῦντα ἰέναι; "It is not lawful to proceed against him who is prepared to accede

a. *The Eunuch* [789 f.].

b. [*Suppliants,* 347.]

c. *On Duties,* I [xi. 34]; add *2 Samuel,* xx. 19.

d. I [lxxxv].

8. The word *verbis* (verbal) does not appear in the text of Terence.

9. This bracketed clause was not quoted by Grotius; but it does form part of the passage cited from Cicero's work *On Duties,* and it is needed to round out the argument.

to a judicial settlement, as one would proceed against an unjust person." The words of Theodoric[a] have a similar import: "The time for taking up arms arrives when justice cannot find admittance on the opposing side." This principle constitutes in part the basis of the above-mentioned doctrine of the Scholastics,[b] namely, that he who is unwilling to give satisfaction is justly attacked in war. We see that this was the order of events accepted by the Israelites,[c] who desired that the tribe of Benjamin should inflict punishment upon the men of Gibeah, and declared war upon that tribe only when their request was not granted.[10] In like manner, Diodorus[d] described the war of Minos against the Athenians as "just," because the request of Minos for justice against the slayers of his son had not been granted.

Certainly resort to arbitration is an honourable procedure, but arbitration is a voluntary, not a necessary measure; for it is common agreement that gives the arbiter his authority, and no one is compelled to entrust his rights to this or that person. We are dealing, however, with necessary measures. It is clear, then, on the basis of the Ninth Rule, that a twofold obligation must necessarily be met by him who is about to undertake a war.

New explanation

For, in the first place, an opportunity to apply judicial procedure must be offered to that state which is the defendant, or whose citizen is the defendant, in a given case; and furthermore, if the said state fails to discharge this duty, the state which has itself been injured, or whose citizen has been injured, must pass judgement. Formerly, in the fetial law of the Romans (a people who certainly have never been surpassed in scrupulous

a. Cassiodorus, *Variae,* III. i, xvii [III. i].
b. At beginning of Chap. vii, *supra.*
c. *Judges,* xx.
d. [IV. 61.]

10. Owing to the fact that an insertion symbol is missing here in the collotype (either because Grotius omitted to write it, or because the margin of the MS. has been worn away), a question could be raised as to the proper position of the foregoing sentence, in the Latin text. But a careful study of the collotype (which shows that an insertion was made within an insertion at this point), and above all, attention to the context, should satisfy the reader that the order followed in the English translation is correct.

attention to that phase of law), this preliminary procedure was called *clarigatio* [a demand for redress and, at the same time, a declaration of war to be waged if redress was not received within thirty-three days], or *rerum repetitio* [reclamation of goods or rights].[a] This latter expression (as Servius[b] well says) covers every possible case of injury, inasmuch as both *res* [things, goods] and *repetitio* [reclamation] are general terms. Now, that which is claimed is threefold: *restitution, satisfaction, surrender;* and the third item is not of an unmixed character, since it may consist in simple surrender, or it may involve punishment. In other words, these three claims are founded respectively upon the Second Law as opposed to the Fourth, upon the Sixth Law and upon the Fifth. As for cases in which the First Law conflicts with the Third, we have already observed that in such circumstances there is no necessity for [45] judicial measures.

Clarigatio or Rerum repetitio

The second necessary step is the order for war, or decree condemning the opposing side, issued by the state which has been injured or whose citizen has been injured, or by a magistrate of that state.[c] From this practice certain formulas arose. The first ran as follows: "I bear witness that the said nation is unjust and does not make just reparation." Another formula was couched in the following terms:[d] " '[What is your opinion[11]] regarding the things, the suits, the causes, concerning which formal claims have been presented by the *pater patratus*[12] of the Roman People of the Quirites to the *pater patratus* of the Nation of the Ancient

a. Pliny, XII. i [*Natural History,* XXII. ii].

b. *On the Aeneid,* IX [53]; *ibid.* X [14]; see Brisson, *De Formulis,* IV; *Dig.* XII. i. 1; and Festus, on word *recipere* [p. 228]; *Dig.* L. xvi. 35.

c. Sylvester, on word *repressalia,* iii. 4.

d. From Livy, I [xxxii].

11. Livy wrote this passage in dialogue form, but Grotius presents it as the statement of a single person. In order to preserve the spirit of the formula more faithfully, and also because Grotius's abbreviated paraphrase results in a rather awkward construction of the Latin, bracketed phrases have been introduced into the English translation, representing certain portions of the original passage which do not appear in the *Commentary.* In accordance with the general rule adopted for the translation, however, other inaccuracies of little or no importance have not been corrected by the translator.

12. I.e., the fetial priest, who ratified treaties with religious rites.

Latins and to the men of the Ancient Latins, which things the latter nation has not paid, delivered nor acted upon, and which should have been delivered, acted upon and paid?' 'I hold that these things should be sought in a blameless and righteous war, and to that course I lend my vote and approval.'" A third formula was worded thus: "Because the tribes of the Ancient Latins have committed acts and offences adverse to the Roman People of the Quirites, and because the Roman People of the Quirites has commanded that war be made on the Ancient Latins and furthermore the Roman Senate of the Quirites has voted, agreed upon, and decreed the waging of war against the Ancient Latins, I, therefore, together with the Roman People, *declare* and make war upon the Nation of the Ancient Latins."

To be sure, these two steps (*rerum repetitio* and the declaration of war) may be taken either separately or as a combined action: separately, if (in the manner above indicated) they are executed singly and with an interval of time between; as a combined action, if the injured state, on the occasion when it offers the other party an opportunity to employ judicial measures, appends a declaration of the judgement to be pronounced by the injured party itself in the event that the other does not judge justly. In the latter case, the formula used runs more or less as follows:[a] "That they themselves will repel the injury with might and main, unless the said injury is wiped out by its own authors." Or it may take this form:[b] "Unless they forestall him by inflicting the death penalty upon the wrongdoers, he will resort to indiscriminate slaughter." Theseus, too (according to Euripides),[c] followed just such a procedure when he instructed the herald to transmit these demands to Creon:

> *Θησεύς σ' ἀπαιτεῖ πρὸς χάριν θάψαι νεκρούς,*
> *συγγείτον' οἰκῶν γαῖαν, ἀξιῶν τυχεῖν,*
> *φίλον τε θέσθαι πάντ' Ἐρεχθειδῶν λεών·*
> *κἂν μὲν θέλωσιν αἰνέσαι, παλίσσυτος*

a. Livy, VIII [xxiii].
b. Tacitus, *Annals,* I [xlviii].
c. *Suppliants* [385 ff.].

> στεῖχ'· ἢν δ' ἀπιστῶσ', οἵδε δεύτεροι λόγοι·
> κῶμον δέχεσθαι τὸν ἐμὸν ἀσπιδηφόρον.
>
> *Theseus, ruler of a neighbouring land,*
> *Asks for the dead that he may bury them.*
> *To win Athenian friendship, grant this plea.*
> *If it be granted, herald, turn thou back;*
> *If disobeyed, speak then these other words:*
> *"Look soon to see my men arrayed in arms."* [45′]

Moreover, similar messages were brought to Theseus from Creon, so that we find the Greek custom clearly portrayed in tragedy. An analogous custom is depicted in many passages of Roman history.

Denuntiatio or Indictio

Now, when the two steps in question are combined in this manner, the procedure involved is properly called *denuntiatio* [notification by way of warning], or *indictio* [declaration]; and he who has already employed the device of *rerum repetitio* is under no obligation [from the standpoint of the law of nations] to issue a second notification. On the contrary, just as those edicts which appear after sentence has been pronounced are derived not from the law of nations but from the established practices of individual states, so the customary formalities attendant upon the undertaking of wars, whenever they constitute an addition to those above mentioned[a] (as they do, for example, when the warning notification is reiterated), originate in no other source than the customs of individual nations. Maecenas, so Dio tells us, apparently supports this view. The Romans adopted many such customs, borrowed from the Aequi: among others, the symbolic use of the bloody spear, and similar practices. Again, just as an interval of exactly thirty days after the pronouncement of a sentence was conceded to the party condemned in a legal trial, so, for a like reason, the same interval was granted to the party against whom war had been decreed. This practice need not be regarded as particularly strange, since other nations have frequently gone so far as to announce in advance the locality and time when a battle would take place, a procedure which is sometimes nobly magnanimous but by the

a. Bodin, *De Republica,* I. vii; Faber, *Semestria,* II. ii, at end.

same token always unnecessary. Thus we find that even the Romans, during the most scrupulous period of their history, never presented the demands classified under the head of *rerum repetitio* to any persons other than the actual perpetrators of an injury or the magistrates of the latter. To be sure, after war was decreed, the Romans were wont to issue a declaration of that fact not only to the parties just mentioned, but also—for form's sake, as it were—to neighbouring regions; yet they omitted even this step in certain cases, when the reclamation had been lawfully presented and the law had not been obeyed [by the defendant]. Furthermore, Varro[a] and Arnobius[b] testify that the custom of formally announcing entry into war was eventually abolished among the Romans, as were other practices pertaining to civil law.

The foregoing observations indicate to us the proper construction to be put upon the assertion made by learned authorities,[c] that no war is just unless it has been legally declared, an opinion which cannot be better interpreted than it is in the words of Cicero:[d] "No war is just unless it is waged either after the procedure of *rerum repetitio* has been followed, or after notification and warning thereof have been given and a formal declaration made." Cicero requires that one of these conditions, not both, shall be fulfilled.

Even this statement of the case must be taken in a limited sense, with the understanding that there is no need of a warning announcement (as we have already pointed out) when the person against whom action is to be taken has previously begun the war. A certain well-known [46] fragment from the works of Isidore[e] is pertinent in this connexion: "That war is just which is waged by command on matters already brought to attention through the process of *rerum repetitio*, or which is

a. *On the Latin Language,* IV [V. 86].

b. *Against the Heathen,* II [lxvii].

c. Giovanni Andrea, *On Sext,* V. iv. 1; Baldus, *On Code,* III. xxxiv. 2, n. 71 [n. 76]; *ibid.* VI. vi. 4; *ibid.* VII. liii. 8.

d. *On Duties,* I [xi. 36] and *Republic,* II [xvii. 31].

e. [*Etymologies,*] XVIII. i, cited in *Decretum,* II. xxiii. 2. 1.

waged in order to repel public enemies."[13] For the term *hostes* [public enemies], in its legal connotation,[a] comprises not only those persons against whom we publicly decree war, but also those who publicly decree war against us. Therefore, no warning notification is necessary for war against persons who are already conducting themselves as enemies of our state. This principle is commonly accepted by the doctors of law,[b] who maintain that those persons who are openly harmful and troublesome to us are *ipso iure* proclaimed liable to confiscation of goods on the ground of bad faith;[14] for, according to the said doctors, such a proclamation is equivalent to a formal declaration of war. A notable example is found in the history of the Israelites,[c] who had been commanded by God to refrain from making an armed attack against any people without first inviting that people, by formal notification, to establish peaceful

a. *Dig.* XLIX. xv. 24; *ibid.* L. xvi. 118.

b. Bellarmine [*De Controversiis*], V, cont. iii, chap. xv; add *Dig.* XIX. i. 1, at end; Vázquez, *Ill. Cont.* xxiv. 5.

c. *Deuteronomy,* xx. 10.

13. The text of the *Commentary* at this point does not follow exactly either that of Isidore himself (*Etymologiarum sive Originum Libri XX,* XVIII. i; Oxford edition), or that of the quotation cited above from the *Decretum,* although Grotius was evidently influenced by the latter when he employed *edicto* (edict *or* command) for *praedicto* ("command," the term used by Isidore) and *hominum* (men) for *hostium* ("public enemies," Isidore's term). Since *hostium* is obviously the reading required for Grotius's own argument, and since the other variations are of slight importance, the English translation of the entire quotation is based upon the Oxford text of Isidore's statement, which reads as follows: *Iustum bellum est quod ex praedicto geritur de rebus repetitis aut propulsandorum hostium causa.*

14. The phrase "proclaimed liable . . . bad faith" is a translation of the single Latin word *diffidatos.* Primarily, this term connotes a lack of good faith, the quality mentioned in the passage from the *Digest* cited here, although the passage itself does not contain any form of *diffido.* On the other hand, Grotius was familiar with Sylvester's definition of *diffidare* as equivalent to *bannire,* "to confiscate" (in passage cited *infra,* note *f,* p. 174), and is dealing in the present paragraph with the preliminaries necessary to justify seizure (i.e. "confiscation") of enemy property. Thirdly, certain medieval documents employ various forms of *diffido* and *diffidatus* in the sense of "to challenge to combat," and "challenged" or "quarrelsome, belligerent," respectively; and Grotius's quotation from Baldus a few lines below clearly indicates that the former had these connotations in mind, too. In order to carry over into the English all three of the concepts implied (bad faith, confiscation, and proclamation of hostility), the Latin term must be rendered by a rather lengthy phrase.

relations; for the Israelites thought that this prohibition was inapplicable to many of the Canaanite tribes, inasmuch as they themselves had previously been attacked in war by the Canaanites. Hence we arrive at the following deduction: once the formality of *rerum repetitio* has been observed and a decree on the case in question has been issued, no further proclamation or sentence is required for the establishment of that right which arises in the actual process of execution. For, in such circumstances, one is not undertaking a new war but merely carrying forward a war already undertaken. Thus the fact that justice has once been demanded and not obtained, suffices to justify a return to natural law, that is to say, a return to the precept which permits us to obtain by force that which is properly ours. Nevertheless, even when formal notification is unnecessary, it is not inappropriate to issue a general statement, for example, a statement relative to the collection of debts, and particularly punitive debts, so that enemy property may be seized as if by judicial authorization.

For the rest, when formal notification has been given by the principal author of a war, there is no need for such notification on the part of his ally, who is merely assisting in the attainment of another's right without presenting any separate demand for himself. Similarly, when a war has been begun with the proper formalities against a given state or magistrate, no formal declaration of that war need be issued to the allies and subjects of the said state or magistrate. Our commentators[a] word this conclusion in their own fashion, as follows: When a prince has been challenged to combat,[15] all of his subjects, confederates and assistants have been challenged.[15] Moreover, this very conclusion formed one of the basic points for Gnaeus Manlius' defence of his own conduct, when he was reproached by his legates because of the Galatian war.

But, to return to the statement quoted above from Isidore, we find that its meaning is clearly the same as if one should say: *A public war is undertaken justly in so far as judicial recourse is lacking, or if the formality* **Conclusion VII, Article II**

a. Baldus, *On Code,* III. xxxiv. 2, n. 70 [n. 76].

15. *Diffidato* and *diffidatos.* Cf. footnote 14.

of rerum repetitio *has been observed, and a decree has been passed by the state undertaking the war.* [46′]

We come now to another question, namely: What qualifications should be sought in voluntary agents who are participating in a war, and what is permissible for them? This question is of course extremely broad, but we shall discuss it summarily under several main heads.

Just form, as we have already observed,[a] consists in conformity with the laws. Now, even as the laws relative to judicial procedure appeared to be incompatible with the act of undertaking a war (though we have demonstrated that these laws are partially invalidated by others of a superior order, while we have been able in part to reconcile the seemingly incompatible factors), just so the Third and Fourth Laws apparently conflict with the act of carrying on a war. For if the words of Virgil[b] are not deceptive,—

When that time comes, [the lawful time for strife,]
It shall be licit to contend in hate,
And play the plunderer's part. . . .

—if, I say, slaughter and plunder are the concomitants of war, how shall we deal with those laws which forbid us to injure another, or to lay hands upon another's property? In many cases, too, the Third Rule would seem to constitute an obstacle, since any interchange based on human law is apparently swept away, so to speak, once a war has begun.

Who, of a foe, would ask: "Is this deceit
Or valor?" . . .[c]

For we seek to do harm to our foes,

ἢ δόλῳ ἠὲ βίῃ, ἢ ἀμφαδὸν ἠὲ κρυφηδόν;[d]

Whether by fraud or unmasked violence,
By stealth or openly. . . .

a. At beginning of this Chap.
b. *Aeneid,* X [14].
c. *Ibid.* II. 390.
d. [Cf. Homer, *Odyssey,* I. 296; Stobaeus, *Florilegium,* LIV. 46.]

First, however, let us consider the problem presented by the laws of the second order, that is to say, the Third and Fourth Laws. These are invalidated (as we have pointed out elsewhere) by the force of the Thirteenth Law, not only when they come into conflict with the First or Second Law, but even when there is occasion to apply the Fifth or Sixth, inasmuch as the Fifth and Sixth inherently embrace the First and Second, as well as the Third and Fourth Laws themselves. But, by the same token, if any act is committed in excess of what is commanded by the laws of the first and third orders [Laws I, II, V, and VI], or against any person at whom the said laws are not aimed, that act will exceed the limits defining a just mode of warfare.

Enemies attack us, and are attacked in turn, in a twofold manner: corporeally, and by attack upon property. Consequently, four [47] *συζυγίαι*, or "reciprocal combinations," are to be considered.[a] That is to say, either we attack in our turn the body of him who has attacked our bodies; or we despoil the despoiler; or we inflict damage upon the property of the person who imperils our lives, or we unsheathe our swords in defence of our own property. It has been shown above that none of these procedures is essentially unjust. Now let us see to what extent they are permissible.

Granting, then, that we are permitted to wound or even to despoil another in defence of our lives or property (I put the assumption in these terms so that it may refer to the First and Second Laws, and not to the commission of a crime), nevertheless, we ought to desist from violent action against him as soon as the danger is past: for example, when victory has been achieved. If we are laying claim to property of our own or to something which is owed us, it will not be permissible, after we obtain the thing thus claimed, to arrogate to ourselves any additional object. If we seek vengeance for a wrong inflicted, that vengeance, too, should be tempered to accord with the measure of the wrong, in observance of

a. Doctors, *On Dig.* I. i. 3 and *On Code,* VIII. iv. 1.

The rule whereby the punishment befits
The crime. . . .[a]

The question at present under discussion differs, of course, from that treated in the preceding chapter; for we were concerned there with the necessity for an underlying cause, whereas in the present chapter we are adding to the causal considerations the requisite of moderation. Seneca[b] holds that those persons are properly called cruel, who have cause to inflict punishment but observe no moderation in so doing.

New explanation

In this connexion it must be noted, moreover, lest one person should suffer in another's stead from the ills of war, that an obligation is sometimes incurred in consequence of one's own act or an act committed in common with others, whereas sometimes it is incurred in consequence of another's conduct but through one's own previous or subsequent act. In regard to the laws of the first order, this distinction has no force; for those laws are concerned only with the act itself and take no account of intent. It frequently happens, however, that the distinction does have a bearing upon cases involving contract, as may also occur in the case of a delict, in so far as the punishment for the delict is pecuniary or pertains to property.[c] The institution of bail rests upon this principle. But the laws refuse to recognize the vicarious acceptance of corporal punishment,[d] for the reason that no one can place under liability that which he does not own.[e] God has given us ownership over things; ownership over ourselves, He has retained for Himself. Therefore, we may transfer our goods when it pleases us to do so, but we may not lay down our lives;[f] just as private property, but not power over himself, is given to a slave. [47a]

Accordingly, in the first place, the obligation incurred by one ally in

a. Horace, *Satires,* I. iii [118].

b. *On Mercy,* II. iv.

c. *Dig.* XLVIII. iii. 4; Sylvester, on word *fideiussor,* vii and viii.

d. Bartolus, *On Dig.* XLVIII. xix. 6; Doctors, *On Dig.* XLVIII. xix [XLVI. i. 70].

e. *Dig.* IX. ii. 13; *Decretum,* II. xxiii. 5. 9.

f. This opinion finds support by [Trovamala,] *Summa Rosella,* Qu. *De Iudice;* Sylvester, on word *iudex,* Pt. II, v: *Ex his duabus.*

consequence of an act committed by another ally, arises from an act of the former, that is to say, from an actual deed and not merely as a result of the contract of alliance. For, with respect to the debt incurred, the theologians[a] have declared, most admirably and on the basis of natural equity, that all persons who have in any way contributed to the causes of inequality, are under an obligation to contribute to the causes of equality; moreover, it is maintained that a contribution to inequality has been made, not only by the individuals who personally perform the act of violent seizure or detention, but also by those other individuals who furnish the command, advice, consent, or labour for the act of deprivation, or who subsequently obstruct the making of restitution. But all allies do one or the other of these two things; and therefore, it is necessary to regard the joint obligation thus created,[b] as binding upon every person by whose aid the unjust party is rendered bolder or the opposing party, more fearful. This is an unchanging principle applicable to all warfare. With respect to punishments,[c] on the other hand, it is likewise unquestionably true that those individuals who fail to give material aid but who nevertheless lend encouragement by their advice, are liable to punishment, also, and even to the very same punishment as that incurred by the principal actors in the case; for such individuals are themselves offenders. [47]

As for the state, it is bound by the act of its magistrate[d] as if by the force of a contract, just as he who has set up a director or agent in [47′] some matter is bound;[e] and at times this binding obligation embraces

a. Covarr., *On Sext,* rule *peccatum,* Pt. II, § 12, n. 2; see Sylvester, on word *restitutio,* Pt. III, vi. 4 and on word *bellum,* Pt. I, xi. 1 and 7.

b. *Dig.* II. x. 1, § 4; Scotus, *On the IV Sentences* [in *Scriptum Oxoniense*], IV, dist. 15, qu. 2, n. 4 and Gabriel thereon. Richard Middleton, *On the IV Sentences,* IV, dist. 15, art. 5, qu. [n.] 4 and Th. Aq. [*On the IV Sentences,* IV, dist. 15], art. 5, qu. 3; Matthaei, *De Bello,* in Req. 1.

c. *Decretum,* II. xi. 3. 100; *Institutes,* IV. i, § 11; *Dig.* XLVII. viii. 2, § 12; Sylvester, on word *homicidium,* Pt. I. xiii [xii], xv–xvii. Add Baldus, *On Code,* IX. ii. 5; *ibid.* III. xxxiv. 2, n. 70 [n. 76]; *ibid.* VIII. iv. 1, n. 24.

d. Vict., *De Potestate Civili,* 12; *Dig.* XIV. i.

e. Sylvester, on word *restitutio,* [Pt.] III, v. 5 and xi. 10 and on word *obligatio,* vi [*Idem dic.*]; *Dig.* XIV. iii; *ibid.* IV. ix.

even liability to punishment. For those persons are liable, who have transferred authority over themselves to such representatives as might prove to be the source of injury to others, since he who has put his trust in an unworthy individual would seem to be involved,[a] so to speak, in the fraudulence [of the latter]. Thus it is by no means undeservedly that,

> For every folly of their kings, the Greeks
> Pay penalties. . . .[b]

Nor was that situation unreasonable which caused Hesiod[c] to lament as follows:

> ὄφρ᾽ ἀποτίσῃ
> δῆμος ἀτασθαλίας βασιλέων,
>
> *So that the impious sins which stem from kings,*
> *The people expiate. . . .*

This same principle is put into practice by God Himself, who not infrequently has punished the people for the sins of princes, a point that could be illustrated with many notable examples.[d] In the words of the blessed Justin:[e] *πικροτάτη τιμωρία τῶν ἡμαρτηκότων βασιλέων τιμωρία τοῦ λαοῦ*; "The most bitter punishment imposed on erring princes, is the punishment exacted of the people." Ambrose,[f] too, has said: "The delinquency of kings results in the punishment of peoples; for, just as we are protected by the virtue of kings, so also are we endangered by their transgressions."

Furthermore, a state is bound by the act of its citizen:[g] not in an absolute sense, of course, but in cases where the state itself fails to render justice, thereby making the cause of the offender its own. For liability

a. *Dig.* XI. vi. 2; *ibid.* XVII. ii. 23; *ibid.* IV. ix. 7, § 4; *ibid.* X. ii. 45, § 1.
b. Horace [*Epistles,* I. ii. 14].
c. [*Works and Days,* 260 f.]
d. *Genesis,* xx. 4 and 9; see also Faber, *Semestria,* III. xix.
e. [Pseudo-Justin Martyr, *Quaestiones ad Orthodoxos,* cxxxviii.]
f. *Defence of David* [xi. 56].
g. See Bartolus, *On Reprisals,* Qu. 4 [ad 6], n. 13.

is incurred by the act of approval no less than by the act of command.[a] It was on this very ground (so we read) that the Amphictyons in ancient times condemned the Scyrians,[b] some of whom had practised piracy with impunity. In this sense, the state is not bound entirely by another's act; for its own action is also involved, not only because the state [by failing to render justice] impedes another in the attainment of his right, but also because it sins in contravention of its duty under the Ninth Rule, which indicates that just judicial recourse should be provided for foreigners as well as for citizens. Moreover, it cannot be doubted that he who fails to prohibit that which he can and should prohibit, is liable for the consequences of the act in question, a principle applicable to debts involving punishment as well as to other debts. Hesiod[c] has this fact in mind when he says: [48]

> πολλάκι καὶ ξύμπασα πόλις κακοῦ ἀνδρὸς ἐπαυρεῖ.
>
> *Often a nation pays the penalty*
> *For one man's wickedness. . . .*

To Hesiod's observation, Proclus[d] appends the following admirable explanatory comment: ὡς ἐξὸν κωλύειν μὴ κωλύουσα τὴν τοῦ ἑνὸς πονηρίαν; "because the state does not prohibit that wickedness, although it is able to do so." Proclus also adds two examples: one (which Horace likewise notes) is taken from the opening passage of the *Iliad* and concerns Agamemnon; the other has to do with the Greek fleet that was burned,

> Solely because of one man's frenzied guilt,
> The guilt of Ajax, son of Oileus,[e]

a. *Decretum,* II. xxiii. 2. 2; Covarr., *On Sext,* rule *peccatum,* Pt. II, § 10; Th. Aq. II.–II, qu. 62, art. 7, in reply; Sylvester, on word *restitutio,* Pt. III, vi. 2 and 8 therein; Laudensis, Qu. 18.

b. Plutarch, *Cimon* [p. 483 B, C].

c. [*Works and Days,* 240.]

d. [*On Hesiod's Works and Days.*]

e. Virgil, *Aeneid,* I [41].

that is to say, because the Greek nation had not shown indignation at the shameful deeds of Ajax. Herein the institution of expiations has its source. For that matter, we find in Holy Writ[a] outstanding proofs of the fact that expiation by whole nations for unpunished sins committed by individuals is a practice pleasing to God. Agapetus,[b] in his *Paraeneticus* addressed to Justinian, explains this point as follows: *ἴσον τῷ πλημμελεῖν τὸ μὴ κωλύειν τοὺς πλημμελοῦντας λογίζου. κἂν γάρ τις πολιτεύηται μέν ἐνθέσμως, ἀνέχεται δὲ βιούντων ἀθέσμως, σύνεργος τῶν κακῶν παρὰ θεῷ κρίνεται.* "Consider the failure to restrain transgressors as equivalent to the transgression. For a person who administers the state justly in other respects but shows tolerance toward those whose lives are unjust, is in God's judgement an abettor of the wicked."

On the other hand, individual citizens are also bound by the act of the state. Indeed, it is in keeping with natural equity, since we derive advantages from civil society, that we should likewise suffer its disadvantages.[c] The interpreters of the civil law[d] have expressed varying opinions in regard to this point, but always on the basis of that law; for even though people grouped as a whole and people as private individuals do not differ in the natural order, a distinction has arisen from a man-made fiction and from the consent of citizens.[e] The law of nations, however, does not recognize such distinctions; it places public bodies and private companies in the same category. Now, it is generally agreed that private societies are subject to the rule that whatever is owed by the companies themselves may be exacted from their individual partners. Furthermore, it is obvious that the state is constituted by individuals[f] just as truly as the magistrate is constituted by the state,[g] and that therefore the said

a. *Numbers,* xxxv. 33–4.

b. [N. 28, p. 367 c.]

c. Joannes Cephalus, *Consilium* 58.

d. [Glossators,] *On Dig.* III. iv. 2 and 7; *ibid.* XII. i. 27; *ibid.* XLII. i. 4; Baldus, *On Code,* IV. xiii. 1; *ibid.* VII. liii. 8; *Code,* XI. lvii; *Novels,* xii; Seneca, *On Benefits,* VI. xix.

e. *Dig.* III. iv. 1, § 1.

f. In Chap. ii, *supra,* pp. 35–36.

g. Sylvester, on word *repressalia,* at beginning, and add statement of Th. Aq. II.–II, qu. 40.

individuals are liable in the same fashion as the state in so far as concerns reparation for losses, even when the claim in question is founded on wrongdoing. Far be it from us to say, however, that the lives of innocent citizens are ἀντίψυχα, forfeited, or liable to punishment,[a] for offences committed by the state; especially since the state itself can be punished as such. For the life of a state can be weakened (as in cases where the state becomes a tributary, a practice sanctioned by divine law)[b] and, in a sense, annihilated. πόλεως γὰρ ἐστι θάνατος ἀνάστατον γενέσθαι;[c] "A city dies when it is completely laid waste." Such was the fate of Carthage and of other cities which were razed by the enemy's plough[d] and which suffered dissolution of the body politic. But it is evident that pecuniary penalties owed by the state may be exacted from the [48′] subject, since there would be no state if there were no subjects. St. Thomas[e] [16] declares that those persons who are essentially possessions and parts, so to speak, of another entity—a description which ought to cover subjects no less than children and slaves—may be penalized in the place of that other entity for losses suffered. Yet subjects are frequently free from guilt, as we have already observed. This is indeed true; but the very Scholastics[f] above cited [St. Thomas and Sylvester] teach us that punishment, while it is never imposed unless guilt exists, often is imposed where there is no guilt on the part of the person punished, though never without cause. In the case under discussion the cause is obvious. Here we have the sole argument supporting that custom of reprisals, practised not only in the modern world but also by nations of ancient times, known as *pigneratio* [seizure of pledges], or as ἀνδροληψιῶν [seizure of hostages for vicarious punishment]. For what is owed to me by

a. *Dig.* IV. ii. 9, § 1.
b. *Deuteronomy,* xx. 11.
c. Lycurgus, *Against Leocrates* [lxi, p. 156].
d. *Dig.* VII. iv. 21; see also Faber, *Semestria,* I. i.
e. II.–II, qu. 108, art. 4; add Sylvester, on word *bellum* [, Pt. I.] xi. 6–7.
f. *Sext,* V. ult., rule 23 and Dynus thereon; Sylvester, on word *poena,* at beg.

16. Grotius's marginal note is misplaced in the collotype. In the passage cited, St. Thomas mentions children and slaves as examples of those persons who are the "temporal goods" of other persons.

the citizen of a state is owed by the state, too, when the latter does not enforce the claims of justice; and what is owed by a state, is owed by its individual citizens. This is a point which has not escaped the observation of Bartolus.[a] An additional consideration is that of convenience, since it is not easy for creditors to obtain their rights in any other manner, whereas it is less difficult for citizens themselves to resort to suits at law against one another, exacting reparation for their respective losses from the individual at fault.[b]

Conclusion VII, Article III, Part I

In short, we may summarize the restrictions of form in this matter by saying that, *A war is justly waged by voluntary agents in so far as it remains within the sphere of the right contested and is waged among the persons obligated with respect to that right.*

New explanation

The discussion of certain special cases will enable us to clarify this conclusion, particularly in regard to the subjects of public enemies, who constitute, as a rule, the chief cause for dispute among writers[c] on the law of war. Accordingly, we should ascertain the extent to which this famous passage from Euripides[d] is true:

> καθαρὸς ἅπας τοι πολεμίους ὃς ἂν κτάνῃ.
>
> *That man is undefiled and dutiful*
> *Who slays a public enemy. . . .*

We must decide, too, whether or not Tacitus[e] was right when he wrote: "In time of peace, causes and merits are taken into consideration; when war breaks out, the innocent and the guilty fall side by side." For if we apply this generalization specifically to the subject of the laws of prize and booty, the said laws will become more readily understandable.

In so far as bodily attack is concerned, it is permissible—in accordance

a. *On Reprisals,* at beg. add *Dig.* XIV. i. 1; Laudensis, *De Bello,* Qu. 38.
b. *Code,* XI. xxxvii. 1.
c. Vict. [*De Jure Belli*], 37 and 45.
d. [*Ion,* 1334.]
e. [*Annals,* I. xlviii.]

with the laws of the first order [Laws I and II], which do not take into account the intent of one's adversary—to make an attack upon all enemy subjects who resist, whether knowingly or in ignorance, the execution of our rights.[a] For such subjects, without exception, are "bringing about" an injury, even though that injury may not be "voluntary."[17] This assertion is expressly confirmed by divine law,[b] which decrees the slaughter of the whole adult population of certain cities taken by storm, although many of the adults in question must be innocent. Conversely, the same rule will be applicable in justifying the defence of a city. Thus Augustine[c] has said: "Nor does that man incur guilt for another's death, who has surrounded his property with walls which have been utilized in causing someone to be wounded and to perish."

Nevertheless, if there are some individuals who can be separated from the whole body of the enemy and who do not impede the execution of our rights,[d] such individuals should of course be spared altogether from attack upon their persons. Cicero[e] offers the following admonition: "Furthermore, we ought to accord a favourable reception to those who, having laid down their arms, take refuge in the good faith of our generals, even though the battering-ram has struck through their walls." Moreover, scholarly authorities have expressed the opinion that this is precisely the interpretation which must be given to the pronouncement of Celsus,[f] namely, that by the law of war we "receive"[18] deserters, that is to

a. See Concl. VI, Art. II, *supra,* p. 114.

b. *Deuteronomy,* xx. 13; add *Joshua,* vi [21]; *1 Samuel,* xv.

c. *Letters,* cliv [5], *To Publicola,* cited in *Decretum,* II. xxiii. 5. 8; and *Dig.* IX. ii. 9.

d. Vict. [*De Jure Belli*], 49; Gentili, *De Iure Belli,* II. xvi, xvii, xviii, xx, xxi; Matthaei, *De Bello,* in Req. 2, p. 3.

e. *On Duties,* I [xi. 35].

f. *Dig.* XLI. i. 51; Cujas, *Observationes,* IV. ix.

17. The interpretation of the phrases *faciunt . . . iniuriam* and [*faciant*] *non iniuria* in this Latin sentence, is based upon the discussion of such terms contained in Chapter VII (*supra,* pp. 108 ff.).

18. *Recipimus,* the term used also in the passage cited immediately above from Cicero, where it connotes a favourable, or protective, reception. We should note, however, that this verb may also be translated "we seize," the interpretation adopted by Scott in his English rendering of the *Digest* passage in question (see S. P. Scott, *The Civil Law,* vol. ix, p. 173).

say, those persons who have abandoned the enemy ranks. Yet again, [49] just as the precepts of equity and those of divine law,[a] that infallible guide of equity, direct us to spare all persons in a surrendered city, so also they direct that in the case of a city taken by assault, all those whose lives do not impede the execution of our rights shall be spared in so far as is possible. Thus Seneca, in his tragedy *Octavia,*[b] suggests that the title "foe" cannot be applied to a woman. Similarly, Camillus[c] asserts that he bears no weapons against persons of that tender age which is spared even when cities are captured. Alexander,[d] too, declares: "I am not wont to wage war against captives and women; he whom I hate must bear arms." The inclusion of a reference to "captives" is commendable; for that other [war-like ruler, Pyrrhus,] speaks falsely and in the excessively ferocious fashion characteristic of Aeacus' descendants, when he says:[e]

> There is no law to spare the captive foe,
> Or bar his punishment. . . .

Nor is the answer given him,

> That act which law forbids not, shame forbids,

sufficiently forceful. For such conduct as that of Pyrrhus is forbidden by law, too—in fact, by that most sacred of natural precepts which declares that man must not be prodigally misused by his fellow man. Seneca[f] maintains that "the essential principles of equity and virtue demand that mercy be shown even to captives." The theologian Augustine[g] admonishes us as follows: "Let it be by necessity, not by choice, that we lay low the enemy who battles against us. Just as he who offers warlike resistance is repaid with violence, so mercy is owed to him who has been

a. *Deuteronomy,* xx. 14; Plato, *Republic,* V [p. 471 A, B].
b. [Line 864.]
c. In Livy, V [xxvii].
d. Quintus Curtius, V [*History of Alexander,* IV. xi. 17–18].
e. Seneca, *Trojan Women* [333 f.].
f. *On Mercy,* I. xviii.
g. *Letters,* i [clxxxix. 6], *To Boniface,* cited in *Decretum,* II. xxiii. I. 3.

captured through our victory, and especially to him from whom no disturbance of the peace is feared." Wherefore Eurystheus also, according to Euripides,[a] declared that those hands would never be washed clean, which should fail to spare him whom the fortunes of war had spared. Farmers—that is to say, unarmed men who dwell amid the open fields and who readily yield to armed force—are properly included in more or less the same category. For what purpose is served by raging against these men, since they are not an obstacle to the conduct of the war, but rather, as Pollio was wont to say, a prize for the victor? In accordance with this very argument, however, a different criterion will prevail if the enemy is rendered stronger by the fact that agricultural activities have not been hampered.[b]

These same observations may be applied, moreover, to those subjects who act in good faith, or in other words, to those who have incurred no guilt. As Seneca[c] says, the wise man "will let his enemies go unharmed, sometimes even with praise, if they have girded themselves for war *with honourable motives,* [for example,] in order to keep faith, in observance of a treaty, or in defence of freedom."

But the guilty must by all means be punished,[d] in conformity with the Fifth Law. The right underlying this law does not cease to exist once victory has been attained, as does that other right [for which the war is prosecuted], a distinction which will be obvious to anyone who considers the matter at all carefully. Therefore, culpable persons ought to be subjected even to corporal punishment, provided only that the offence involved calls for such a penalty. When this is the case, the same judgement should be rendered in warfare as in legal trials.[e] Plato[f] expresses admirably his approval of the discord attendant upon war, *μέχρις οὗ ἂν οἱ αἴτιοι ἀναγκασθῶσιν ὑπὸ τῶν ἀναιτίων ἀλγούντων δοῦναι δίκην,* "up to the point where those who have incurred guilt, are forced by the in-

a. *Madness of Hercules* [1009 ff.].
b. Matthaei, *De Bello,* in Req. 2, p. 2.
c. *On Mercy,* II. vii.
d. Vict. [*De Jure Belli*], 46.
e. Vict., *ibid.* 47.
f. *Republic,* VII [V, p. 471 B].

nocent victims of the original injury, to pay the penalty." According to Diodorus Siculus,[a] Gylippus, in his oration against the Athenian captives, maintains that the said captives, overtaken by disaster because of their own wickedness and cupidity, are striving in vain to lay the [49′] blame on their ill fortune and to acquire the status of suppliants, since this defence is reserved for men of pure hearts which have been led astray solely by circumstances. For it was the intention of the authors of the law regarding suppliants, that mercy should be granted to the unfortunate, but that punishment should be inflicted on those who had transgressed with unjust intent. Gylippus then comes to the following conclusion: *διόπερ ἑκουσίως ἑλόμενοι πόλεμον ἄδικον εὐψύχως ὑπομενόντων τὰ τούτου δεινά*; "Wherefore, since they have begun *an unjust war of their own free will,* let them bear with fortitude the misfortunes attending that war." Themistius[b] follows a like trend of thought when he says that pardon should be extended to misfortune, correction to error, and punishment to iniquity. Under the third head he places those individuals who have been the instigators of rebellion; under the second, those who have been carried away, so to speak, by the impetus of war; and under the first, those who have succumbed to the party which at the time happened to be the stronger. Similarly, Velleius[c] observes that the Athenians in the time of Mithridates were overwhelmed by their enemies and besieged by their friends, so that their hearts were outside the city walls while, in obedience to necessity, their bodies remained within the walls. This example may be used to confirm the distinction implicit in the saying that, "Some men are of the enemy, while others are with the enemy." Accordingly, the victor, having attained judicial authority, will temper in the manner above indicated the punishments to be decreed.

So much, then, for the question of bodily attack.

Turning now to the matter of attack upon property, we shall have no difficulty in reaching the conclusion to be drawn in this connexion with

a. XIII [xxix].

b. *Orations, On Valens* [15, p. 111]; *ibid., On Valentinian* [3, p. 148].

c. [*History of Rome,* II. xxiii. 5.]

respect to subjects. For we have explained elsewhere[a] that property may be seized in order to ward off peril that menaces one's own life or possessions, and that it may also be acquired on the ground of debt, the former right being derived from the laws of the first order [Laws I and II], and the latter from the laws of the third order [Laws V and VI]; but we have also stated[b] that subjects, even when innocent, are liable to attack in war in so far as they impede the attainment of our rights; now, all subjects, even those who do not themselves serve as soldiers,[c] impede our efforts by means of their resources, when they supply the revenue used in the procurement of those things which imperil our lives and which do not only hinder the recovery of our possessions but also compel us to submit to fresh losses;[d] and therefore, subjects must be deprived of such resources, unless it be considered just that we ourselves should pay the penalties attendant upon the pursuit of our rights. Nor is any distinction to be made here on the basis of varying circumstances among the different subjects, since the laws in question, as we have repeatedly pointed out, have regard not to the intent of one's adversary but to his deed. [50]

Hence it is permissible to infer, not only that possessions maybe forcibly taken from the said subjects, but also that these possessions may be added to our own. For if, on the one hand, they were snatched away from us by these very subjects, whom we regard as personally under obligation to us because of their injurious conduct or for whatsoever reason, nothing could be more just than that we should take back by armed force that which could not be reclaimed in any different way; or if, on the other hand, it is a state that has wronged us[e] or otherwise incurred a debt to us, there is even then nothing to prevent the seizure of the subjects' goods in payment, since it has been demonstrated[f] above that such goods are liable to seizure for the debt of the state. This one re-

a. Formal Exposition of Art. I, Chap. iii, *supra,* p. 52. Vict. [*De Jure Belli*], 39, 55.
b. Concl. VI, Art. II, *supra,* p. 114.
c. See Chap. ii [iv, *supra,* pp. 70 ff.? See also pp. 154–63].
d. Sylvester, on word *restitutio* [, Pt.] III, at end [xii].
e. See Vict., *ibid.* 56.
f. A little above, pp. 158–60.

striction is imposed, however: that nothing shall be taken in excess of the debt due us, which is reckoned in such a way as to include reparation for both losses and costs. Moreover, the claim to reparations continues to operate as a cause even after victory has been achieved[a] and after the first-named cause, the need to ward off danger, has been dispelled. For our object in waging wars is nothing more nor less than attainment of our rights through victory. In the words of Livy,[b] "When all things have been surrendered to him who is the mightier in arms, it is the latter's right and privilege to decide which of those things he shall choose to retain as victor,[19] and exact from the conquered[20] as a penalty."

Therefore, we conclude that all subjects, at all times, are liable to despoliation, but not necessarily to forfeiture of their lives. For, as far as the question of our own peril is concerned, there are many persons who oppose us not at all by bodily violence, so that nothing is to be gained by inflicting violence of any kind upon their bodies; but there is no individual among the enemy who does not harm us with his possessions, even though he may be most unwilling to do so. Or, if we choose to view the question from the standpoint of the rights of creditors, we shall find that the goods of subjects, but not their persons, are liable to seizure for the debt of the state;[c] and consequently, in the case of reprisals, too, seizure of property is permitted but corporeal attack is prohibited.[d]

a. Vict., *ibid.* 50, 57.

b. [XXXIV. lvii. 7.]

c. See Ayala, I. iv. 6.

d. Bartolus, *On Reprisals,* Qu. 8, beg. of n. 1; Sylvester, on word *repressalia,* in beg. [i.] 6; Covarr., *On Sext,* rule *peccatum,* Pt. II, § 9, n. 4, at end.

19. By substituting *victor* (the conqueror) for *victos* (the conquered), Grotius has weakened the force of Livy's statement, which in its original form might be translated as follows: "When all things have been surrendered to him who is the mightier in arms, it is the latter's right and privilege to decide which of those things he chooses to have the conquered retain, and which he wishes to exact from them as a penalty." The alteration in question also impairs the syntax of the sentence; cf. the immediately following footnote.

20. Simply *eos* (them), which in Livy's text referred back to the preceding *victos.* The above-mentioned substitution of *victor* for *victos* has left *eos* without a grammatical antecedent, although the context indicates that some term referring to the conquered must be understood as the antecedent.

Therefore, the argument relative to things is not valid when applied to persons. For he to whom something of lesser importance is permitted does not forthwith receive permission also for that which is of greater importance.

Moreover, although other writers have gone less thoroughly into the reasons underlying this opinion, it is supported by all of the theologians and experts in law.[a] For they maintain that what is known as "prize," or "booty," becomes the property of him who seizes it in a just war, and that it should be understood that such prize or booty is taken not only from the goods of him who fights unjustly, but also from those of all his subjects (women and children not excepted) until complete satisfaction has been given to the just belligerent for that which is due him, whether because of an injury or offence inflicted, or because of a [50′] loss occasioned to him or his and the factors attendant upon that loss; or else until the enemy shall be prepared to give satisfaction, or shall make known his readiness to comply with the law. For the rest, Cajetan[b] and (among the Spaniards) Covarruvias[c] declare that the question of whether or not a given individual is innocent, is not taken into account in this connexion. Yet another Spaniard, Victoria,[d] holds that if the enemy refuses to make restitution of the goods wrongfully taken away, and if the injured party cannot very well secure reparation from some other source, he may obtain satisfaction from any source whatsoever, whether from the guilty or from the innocent, so that neither *merchants* nor farmers are excepted. That is the view adopted by Victoria. As for the opinion of other authorities[e] who hold that even in this matter forbearance should be shown to sailors and merchants, these very authorities explain that they are referring to sailors cast upon a foreign shore by the force

a. Th. Aq. II.–II, qu. 66, art. 8, ad 1; Ant. de Butrio, *On Decretals,* II. xiii. 12; Hostiensis, *Summa on Decretals,* V. xxxviii, and comments on this by Lupus, *De Bello,* § *Si bene advertas;* Innocent, *On Decretals,* II. xiii. 12; Joh. Faber, *On Institutes,* II. i.

b. *Summula Peccatorum,* words *belli damna.*

c. *On Sext,* rule *peccatum,* Pt. II, § 11.

d. [*De Jure Belli,*] 39, 41.

e. Bartolus, *On Reprisals,* Qu. 7, beg. of n. 15 [n. 16]; Bellarmine, *De Controversiis,* V, cont. iii, chap. xv; Sylvester, on word *repressalia,* viii.

of a tempest, and to foreign merchants only or those who are on their way to public fairs. Merchants who are subjects, however, are not spared even in the case of reprisals.

Now, the views above set forth are valid, save in cases where security has been promised to certain individuals[a] or classes of persons or localities, either through pacts or through a tacit usage prevailing on both sides: that is to say, on a basis of good faith, a matter with which we shall deal presently. Thus we read that the Indians spared the farming class. Again, the Lateran Council[b] decreed that a suitable security should be enjoyed by priests, monks, converts, pilgrims, merchants, and rustics who were journeying to or fro or else engaged in agricultural labours, and that the same security should be extended to the animals used by rustics in ploughing or in transporting seed to the fields. With respect to this order, too, the proper interpretation of the term "merchants" includes foreigners only. Cajetan[c] says: "I interpret the word 'merchants' as referring, not to traders who reside within the place in question, but to those who are guests or transients there. For it does not seem to me that *resident merchants* are in any better position than artisans." As a matter of fact, the canonists[d] deny the acceptance in present-day practice of the entire edict of pontifical law (known to them as the "Canonical Truce") which we have just cited; and certainly that edict is not based upon a permanent cause. Nevertheless, it is obviously true that the property of others, when it does not belong to the foe (that is to say, property belonging neither to allies nor to subjects of the foe), even if it be located in enemy territory, may no more be acquired by those who seize it, than loaned or stolen property found among the goods of a debtor may be acquired by the creditor. [50′a]

New explanation

At this point, we may consider in passing a question frequently raised and extensively discussed by other writers,[e] namely: What conduct is

a. Matthaei, in Req. 2, p. 4; Cajetan, *Sum. Pecc.* words *belli damna.*

b. *Decretals,* I. xxxiv. 2.

c. *Summula Peccatorum,* on words *belli damna.*

d. Panormitanus, *On Decretals,* I. xxxiv. 2; Matthaei, in Req. 2, p. 2.

e. Gentili, *De Iure Belli,* II. xxii.

permissible for an enemy in regard to foreigners found among that enemy's adversaries, and in regard to those [foreigners] who are lending aid to the said adversaries in the form of commodities? In the first place, it is quite evident that the locality where a person happens to be found is a consideration of no weight in this connexion; for the factor of locality does not in itself constitute a source of liability, whereas those individuals whom it is permissible to despoil, must indeed be persons who are liable [to local obligations].[a] Therefore, sojourners are proper objects of warfare only if they form a part of the opposing state in the same sense as other subjects. The term "part" should be interpreted, moreover, as referring (in so far as the present question is concerned) to individuals whose legal status is such that they can be compelled to defend the said state and to pay tribute to it. For, as Agathias[b] rightly explains, a given person is to be regarded as an enemy, not because of fortuitous circumstances pertaining to his origin, but on the basis of his zeal and with reference to whether or not he does those things which are pleasing or helpful to the foe. As for the conveyors of commodities, it has been established by the theologians and jurists that no individual is responsible for damage following upon his acts, unless that individual is the one who caused the damage; and also that no one is responsible for damage preceding his acts, unless he himself served to impede restitution. Nor does it necessarily suffice that such a person shall have furnished cause in any way whatsoever; on the contrary, either evil intent or, at least, guilt must be involved. Thus he who has conveyed arms to the enemy, or any other article at all that is appropriate for use in warfare, is responsible to the party waging a just war,[c] in so far as it is evident that the said conveyor furnished cause for the damage following his act, or that he hindered the process of reparation for damage previously done. For, inasmuch as his act is adapted to the purposes of war, he is not guiltless after aiding the unjust belligerent, however thoughtlessly he may have done so. In other words, his conduct is similar to that of a

a. See Sylvester, on word *repressalia,* v.

b. III [*Histories,* IV. xix].

c. See *Decretals,* V. vi. 6; *ibid.* 17; *Code,* IV. xli. 2.

man who, moved by pity,[a] has delivered a debtor from prison, or pointed out means of flight to a criminal, [or caused unjust losses to the side he opposes when acting as][21] advocate in a lawsuit;[b] for, according [50′a′] to the opinion invariably expressed by learned authorities, the perpetrator of any of these acts is in every case bound by an obligation to make reparation. This is the purport of the reply given by Amalasuntha to Justinian, to the effect that they who aid the enemy by supplying him with the necessities of war, are to be regarded as enemies.[c][22] Again, if the commodities supplied should be of a nature not essentially directed to the purposes of war, but nevertheless such as to furnish the unjust party with a means of prolonging the conflict, then the same conclusion will hold true, always provided that the conveyor was in a position where he ought to have been aware of that fact. If he was not in such a position, he should not be held culpable unless the state waging a just war has formally notified him of this very circumstance, appending proof of the justice [of its cause].[d] An outstanding argument in support of this distinction can be drawn from the words of Seneca,[e] who holds that in the repayment of benefits received from a tyrant moderation should be observed, in accordance with the following rule: "If the benefit bestowed upon the tyrant by me [in return for benefits received], is likely neither

a. Sylvester, on word *restitutio,* Pt. III, xii. 6 and 7.

b. Sylvester, on word *advocatus,* xvi.

c. Procopius, *Gothic War,* I [in *History of the Wars,* V. iii. 23].

d. See *Decretals,* V. vi. 11, 12; *Extravagantes,* VIII. i; *Code,* IV. xl, xli, lxiii; Matthaei, in Req. 2, p. 2.

e. *On Benefits,* VII. xx [1–3].

21. MS. p. 50′a is badly mutilated at this point. The bracketed phrase in the English translation is based solely on the fact that the words *litis patrono* (advocate in a lawsuit) appear at the top of p. 50′a′, immediately after the missing portion, and evidently bear some relation to the passage cited here from Sylvester (on word *advocatus,* § 16), in which it is asserted that an advocate is under an obligation to furnish reparation for all unjust losses suffered by the opposing party in consequence of his advocacy.

22. Strictly speaking, the statement ascribed to Amalasuntha by Procopius is the obverse of Grotius's statement; that is to say, Amalasuntha apparently declared that, "the man actually found assisting another in war with respect to his every need" could justly be called the ally and friend of the person thus assisted.

to increase his power to do general harm, nor to strengthen the power already possessed by him; and if the benefit in question be one that enables me to repay him without causing public disaster, I shall render that payment." A little further on, Seneca adds: "I shall not provide money which will serve him as wages to maintain a bodyguard." And again: "I shall not furnish him with soldiers and arms." The same author declares that he would send the tyrant pleasure-boats, but would refuse to send him triremes [i.e. warships]. In short, the greater the estimate of the loss, or of the impediment to the process of compelling the enemy to obey the law, that has resulted from such services, the further one may proceed in seizing spoils by way of reparation without resorting to additional judicial measures; for that very attempt to obtain reparations is in a sense one of the consequences of the war.

Returning from this digression to our discussion of just forms of warfare against subjects, we find that the observations already assembled on this point, constitute in their entirety an opinion which may be [50′] impressed upon our memory in the following terms: *Bodily hurt is justly inflicted upon subjects in so far as they either deserve it because of wrongdoing,*[a] *or impede* (*albeit in ignorance*) *the execution* [*of justice*]*; but prize or booty is justly taken from all subjects, at any time, up to the full amount of the debt owed.* [51] **Corollary I**

Now that we have seen how the laws of the second order [Laws III and IV] may be reconciled with the waging of wars, let us turn our attention to the Third Rule.

In accordance with this rule, it is our duty to fulfil, regardless of possible harmful consequences to ourselves, whatever promises we have made, in relation of course to matters under our control. This admonition is not incompatible with the Second Law;[b] for our own possessions are subject to our own will, and they are dispensed in conformity with that precept which I have called the Third Rule, an assertion that

a. See Th. Aq. II.–II, qu. 40, art. 1; Baldus, *Consilia,* IV. 329; Vict. [*De Jure Belli*], 50, 52, 54; Sylvester, on word *bellum,* Pt. I, x [xi]. 7.

b. See Chap. ii, *supra,* pp. 23 and 34 f.

will be more readily intelligible if viewed in the light of the observations made by us at the outset.

Accordingly, if the law of nations is taken as a criterion rather than some civil precept, faith must be kept with the enemy in every way (as Cicero[a] maintains), and even (so Ambrose[b] specifies) when one is dealing with a treacherous enemy. It should be understood, however, that the foregoing doctrine is dependent upon the supposition that the enemy has not previously departed from the particular contract[c] that is the basis of the required good faith;[d] for in such cases it will be evident, inasmuch as the obligation is mutual, that the terms of the promise have lapsed, so to speak. Apart from this one exception, it may be said that,

> He is the best of soldiers who aims first
> And last, 'mid wars, to keep good faith intact.[e]

Neither, then, can fear be accepted as an excuse, since even he who has made a promise in order to escape misfortune cannot deny that he himself chose this course of action in preference to the alternative course. In short, will that is thus coerced nevertheless retains its voluntary character and, once it has been expressed (albeit to an adversary), has binding force. With respect to this point, we should abide by the opinion of the theologians[f] rather than by that of the jurists. For the former follow the guidance of natural reason, whereas the latter are guided by civil precepts, which frequently, for the sake of some advantage, permit an act that would not otherwise be permitted.

New explanation

Moreover, the will is bound not only by treaties and pacts, but also by agreements tacitly indicated. For example, any person who has placed

a. *On Duties,* I [xiii. 39]; *ibid.* III [xxix. 10].
b. *On Duties,* II [I. xxix].
c. Matthaei, in Req. 2, p. 1.
d. Rule III, previously cited.
e. Silius [*Punica*], XIV [169 f.].
f. [Fulgentius] Ferrandus [Diaconus], *Ad Ducem Regini,* Rule 5; Sylvester, on rd *bellum,* Pt. I. ix [1]; Rainerius of Pisa, *Pantheologia,* word *bellum,* v; Laudensis, Qu. 24.

himself under the protection of another in such a way as to be in the possession and under the power of that protector, makes himself for the time being a part, as it were, of the latter, and by his silence promises clearly enough that he will devise nothing prejudicial to the welfare and sovereign status of the said protector. Thus we abhor traitors and [51′] suborned assassins and—far more intensely—poisoners.[a] [23] This abhorrence is accompanied, too, by the sentiment that wrongdoing lies in the giving of commands no less than in their execution, so that precisely the same guilt is incurred by the buyers and by the sellers of evil deeds. Furthermore, we see that such practices [as the suborning of poisoners and other assassins] were never accepted by the men of early Rome.

For the rest, all those stratagems of war are just which a prudent enemy has reason to fear, and in which no pretence of friendship is involved. When one "has undertaken a just war, it matters not at all from the standpoint of justice whether the fight be waged openly or by artifice."[b] To this extent we agree with Ulpian[c] and the Socratics[d] that the guile which is of use against an enemy is good.

In short, the conclusion set forth in an earlier part of this chapter—namely, that a war is justly waged by voluntary agents in so far as it remains within the sphere of the right contested and is waged among the persons obligated with respect to that right—should be interpreted, or supplemented, by the following phrase: *and in so far as it is permitted by good faith.* **Conclusion VII, Article III, Part II**

We must consider next the question of what constitutes, for subjects, just form in the waging of wars. For it is not clearly established that war is actually undertaken by subjects.[e]

a. See Gentili, *De Iure Belli,* II. iii–v.

b. Augustine, *Questions on Heptateuch,* VI, qu. 10, *On Joshua,* cited in *Decretum,* II. xxiii. 2. 2.

c. *Dig.* IV. iii. 1. 3.

d. Plato, *Republic,* II [xxi]; *ibid.* III [iv]; Xenophon, *Memorabilia,* IV [ii. 15]; Laudensis, Qu. 44.

e. At beg. of this Chap.

23. That is to say, poisoning is a particularly guileful and treacherous device. Cf. the passages above cited from Gentili's treatise *On the Law of War.*

The substantial factor underlying a war is, for voluntary agents, the right involved; but for subjects, it is the command of a superior. Accordingly, just as the former may not safely exceed the limits implicit in the said right,[a] so the latter may not safely exceed those implicit in the command. For conformity of the laws with the reason of subjects, as we have pointed out in another context,[b] lies in the belief that the commands of superiors are concordant with justice; and this principle cannot serve as a defence for the subjects when they fail to observe the limits attached to the command. Thus they will be waging war justly in so far as they have received an order to do so. For they are not all ordered to follow the same course of action. It is indeed the common lot to contribute property for the uses of war; but the command to give one's body for service in warfare (the act described as "military service") is not imposed upon all persons.[c] Nor, to be sure, would such a general [52] command be expedient; on the contrary, a certain orderly method and principle of selection must be observed, just as, in connexion with judicial decisions, the function of execution pertains not to every individual but solely to those who have been specifically charged with that function.[d] Moreover, selection for military service is effected either through express designation, or on a group basis (so to speak), that is to say, by means of a summons such as that issued in cases of insurrection. An example of this type of summons is the famous proclamation of the consuls:[e] "Let those who desire to preserve the state, follow me." In just proscriptions, [which authorize the slaying of the persons outlawed,] we have another example.[f] Furthermore, selections for service are made not only *ἀμέσως*, or directly, but also *ἐμμέσως*, or through the interposition of another party. For we find that the state or prince chooses a leader for the war, that the leader—after he has been invested with that status—creates tribunes and centurions, and that these officers select the sol-

a. In Concl. VI [Chap. vii], *supra,* pp. 107 and 114.
b. Concl. VI, Art. III, *supra,* p. 121.
c. *Decretum,* II. xxiii. 5. 8.
d. *Code,* III. i. 18; *Dig.* XLII. i. 6, § 2.
e. Servius, *On the Aeneid* [VIII. 1].
f. Sylvester, on word *assasinus,* iii.

diers.[a] Cato, indeed, perceives clearly enough that military service is justly rendered only in obedience to a command; for he admonishes his son, after the latter's discharge, to beware of engaging in battle without taking the military oath again, since it is unlawful for one who is not a soldier to fight against the foe.[b]

This force attaching to commands has a bearing also upon individual acts. Thus soldiers sin when they proceed to plunder and burn without authorization from their leaders.[c] In fact, we know that in earlier times punishment was actually inflicted upon those individuals who had conducted any transaction against the enemy, howsoever successfully, when they had not been ordered by their commanders to do so;[d] and conversely, praise is rightly bestowed upon a certain soldier of Cyrus who sheathed the sword already drawn in battle as soon as the signals for retreat were sounded.

We therefore conclude that: *A war is justly waged by subjects, in so far as such warfare is ordered by a superior.* **Conclusion VII, Article IV**

If this conclusion is valid in regard to individual acts, it must necessarily hold good even when applied to seizure of prize or booty.[e] For seizures of this kind, arising as they do from the institution of war, are governed by the law of war. Therefore, since we have shown[f] that wars are just for the subjects of both contending parties when waged by a command from superiors that is acceptable on the basis of probabilities, the following inferences must likewise be accepted: first, spoils are justly taken on both sides, in the course of such wars; and secondly, these [52′] spoils are licitly retained.[g] For why should the consciousness of despoliation rest more heavily upon a person who accepts enemy property

a. *Dig.* XIV. i. 1, § 1.

b. Cicero, *On Duties,* I [xi. 37].

c. Vict. [*De Jure Belli*], 53; Sylvester, on word *bellum,* [Pt.] I. xi. 4.

d. Sylvester, *ibid.* vii. 8; Laudensis, Qu. 22, citing *Dig.* XLIX. xvi. 3, § 15, and Qu. 47.

e. See Concl. III, *supra,* p. 89.

f. Corollary [Art. II], Chap. vii, *supra,* p. 126.

g. Sylvester, on word *restitutio,* Pt. III, vii. 3.

given him by a state or magistrate, when he believes that the said state or magistrate has the right to make this grant, than does the consciousness of slaughter upon a person who kills another at the bidding of those same authorities? Again, if I buy from the public treasury certain property that has been confiscated by a judicial decree, it will not be necessary for me to inquire into the justice of the said decree; and shall the same principle not be applied in cases based upon war? Rightly, then, do the theologians[a] assert that he who has fought in good faith may with a clear conscience keep the things captured in warfare; and rightly do they add that such a person, even though he be advised subsequently of the injustice of the war, will be under no obligation to make reparation for those things which he has consumed, save in so far as he has been rendered richer thereby.

In fact, this privilege [of retention without giving redress] is always accorded to possessors in good faith; and since we include under that head all persons who have accepted any piece of property from one who was not the owner but whom they sincerely regarded as such,[b] we cannot bar the subjects in question from the title whereby ownership actually is transferred from true owners.[c] For spoils are bestowed upon subjects (as we shall note in another context)[d] by public grant and as a gift, a procedure which establishes a true title. Moreover, any person who believes that a state or magistrate is waging war justly, will also believe that the said state or magistrate possesses a right over things captured in the war,[e] so that this circumstance, too, constitutes a mode of acquiring ownership, a mode not at all dissimilar to the procedure involved in a legal judgement:[f] that is to say, the state justly engaged in warfare would be set up as a judge even over a foreign foe.[g] Accordingly, we find a fitting

a. Sylvester, on word *bellum* [Pt. I] x. 3; Vict. [*De Jure Belli*], 33; Cajetan, *Summula Peccatorum,* on words *belli damna.*

b. *Institutes,* II. i. 35.

c. *Dig.* L. xvi. 109.

d. Chap. X, *infra,* p. 226.

e. On the basis of Concl. III, *supra,* p. 89.

f. *Dig.* XLI. i. 5, § 7.

g. See discussion of Rule IX, *supra,* p. 48.

application here for the common saying that he is a just possessor, who acquires or holds possession by authority of the praetor[a] [i.e. the magistrate charged with the administration of justice].

Hence we infer that, even as war is just under similar circumstances, so also *the seizure and detention of captured goods is conceded to be just for subjects of both belligerent parties, always provided that a command has first been given which is not repugnant to reason after the probabilities have been weighed.* [53] **Corollary II**

But the question of whether or not ownership in the sense of an irrevocable right may also be acquired on both sides, is one that calls for some deliberation.

Viewing the matter from the standpoint of that primary law of nations which is derived from nature, I should certainly not hesitate to assert that such acquisition is impossible. For no one's opinion carries sufficient weight to take away ownership [irrevocably] from an owner who is unwilling;[b] and furthermore, according to the precepts of nature, we are under an obligation to furnish repayment not only for the unjust acceptance of another's property, but also for the fact of possession in whatsoever form. This is the basis of the undeniably true opinion that, under the said primary law, not even titles acquired by prescription are admissible.[c] **New explanation**

In reply to the foregoing contention, however, it may be alleged that this right [of irrevocable acquisition] is derived from the secondary law of nations, which we have described as civil in its origin.[d] In fact, the various nations appear to have agreed that things captured in war become the property of the captors of either belligerent party;[e] and there is no lack of reasons in favour of this view.

a. *Dig.* XLI. ii. 11; *ibid.* L. xvii. 137.
b. *Dig.* I. vi. 2; *ibid.* III. v. 39; *Code,* VIII. xiv. 14–15; *ibid.* III. xxxii. 3.
c. Vázquez, *Ill. Cont.* li. 23.
d. See Rule VIII, *supra,* p. 45.
e. See Vict. [*De Jure Belli*], 49 [50].

For citizens defend their state more zealously and bear the burdens of war more willingly under the influence of personal interest,[a] when the hope of recovering their property, if it is once lost, has in a sense been cut off. Nor does the state lose anything in consequence of the said agreement. For the vanquished state will possess merely an empty right devoid of force, and the victorious state will acquire, among other possessions found under the ownership of the enemy, those very things which were taken from it in war. Another weighty argument in support of this theory lies in the fact that, when peace has been made, those things whose return has not been expressly agreed upon remain with the possessor as prizes of war.[b] Thus, even though provision ought to be made by pact for their recovery, it would seem that common law prevails to the contrary; and this form of law cannot be derived from any source other than the tacit consent of the citizens. Yet another proof of the same theory may be deduced from the fact that all things seized in war fall either into, or outside of, the sphere of postliminium. In the case of those things to which the right of postliminium is not attached, it is certain (since they do not return to their original owners even after being recaptured) that the right of ownership has been lost and that the enemy did in very truth become the owner. On the other hand, the things to which the said right is attached should be regarded as restored to one's ownership, not as having continued therein, since "postliminium" is defined as the right of recovering a thing that has been lost and alienated,[c] in such a way that the thing thus recovered is accorded the same status as if it had never been in the power of the enemy. Moreover, we have been clearly told that where ownership is retained, there is no need of postliminium. The same inference can be drawn from the fact that things redeemed from the enemy are said to become forthwith the property of the one who redeems them, whereas the right of postliminium is conceded to someone who offers a prize.

The right of postliminium

a. *Dig.* XLIX. xv. 12, beg.

b. *Dig.* XLIX. xv. 28; Cujas, *On Dig.* II. xiv. 5 and Cujas, *Observationes,* XIX. 7.

c. *Dig.* XLIX. xv. 19; Cicero, *Topics* [viii. 36]; *Dig., ibid.* 12, § 6; *ibid.* 7 and 24; *ibid.* 12, § 7.

Now, the law very plainly provides that all of these principles are valid for one belligerent as much as for another;[a] and certainly I am not aware that any nation holds the opposite view. For even in the Sacred [53a] Scriptures,[b] the expression "David's spoil" is applied to that which David took from the Amalekites and which the latter had formerly taken from their own enemies, so that it is evident that the ownership of the said spoil was twice transferred. The opinion of the exceedingly learned [53] jurist, Fulgosius,[c] with whom Jason agrees, is of a similar nature. For that matter, the Romans, a people characterized by the greatest regard for the principles of equity, had left this point so clearly established that no room for doubt remained;[d] and indeed, not even the interpreters of pontifical law[e] dissent thereon.

Hence it would seem to follow that a subject who has waged war in good faith is in nowise bound to restore those things which he has obtained from the spoils, even if he learns afterwards that the war was [53′] unjust. For what I have once rightfully acquired cannot possibly cease to be mine, save by my own act.[f] Similarly, a possessor in good faith takes as his own the fruits of the possession in question;[g] and these naturally belong to the true owner. Again, if any person, acting in good faith, has acquired another's property by usucapion, he becomes the rightful owner of that property; and this is true, not because the passage of time has in itself any power to confer ownership, but because civil law creates a right[h] of such sort that he who avails himself thereof cannot be described as unjust or unscrupulous. In my opinion, indeed, it has been correctly taught by many authorities[i] that the force inherent in this

a. Festus, on word *postliminium* [on word *receptum,* p. 244]; *Dig.* XLIX. xv. 12, § 9.

b. *1 Samuel,* xxx. 20.

c. *On Dig.* I. i. 5.

d. *Institutes,* I. xii. 5; *Dig.* XLIX. xv.

e. Glossators, *On Decretum,* I. i. 4. 9; Panormitanus, *On Decretals,* II. xxiv. 29.

f. *Dig.* L. xvii. 11.

g. *Dig.* VI. i. 44.

h. *Decretum,* II. xxiii. 4. 40.

i. Vázquez, *Ill. Cont.* lxxiv; Scotus in 4, dist. 15 [in *Scriptum Oxoniense,* IV, dist. 15, qu. 4, n. 14]; Sylvester, on word *praescriptio,* Pt. I, xiii.

right is so extensive, that he who has completed the period of prescription in good faith is not bound even in conscience to make restitution because of subsequent bad faith; for he now possesses ownership in law.[a]

On the other hand, I am altogether unable to approve the contention of the Spaniard Ayala[b] concerning cases in which the injustice of a war is clearly evident, namely, the contention that the things captured in that war are nevertheless [permanently] acquired. For I do not believe that there is in existence any law from which such a principle could be derived.[c] Furthermore, judging from the precedents established under other laws favourable to plunderers, I do not think that a precept of this kind could properly be tolerated even if it did exist, since it would not only lack a rational basis but would also incite men to wrongdoing. [53′a]

In short, the rights to which we refer, are valid in the case of *legitimate* enemies, as the Imperial Regulations of Severus[d][24] declare; and we have said[e] that those enemies are legitimate, or just, who are acting in obedience to magisterial authority that is acceptable in the light of probabilities, whereas other enemies are in no sense different from robbers,[f] so that things seized by them do not undergo a change of ownership, nor is there any need to apply the rule of postliminium in reclaiming such things.[g]

Consequently, the statements made above are applicable only to foreign and not to civil wars, for these two reasons: because it is scarcely possible in a civil war that both belligerent parties should be invested with equal authority; and because individual citizens have not agreed to this transfer of property [within their respective states] as the states themselves have agreed thereto [in the international realm], nor does the

a. See Vázquez, *Ill. Cont.* xxviii. 21.
b. I. ii. 34.
c. *Decretals,* II. xxvi. 20.
d. *Code* [*Dig.* XLIX. xv. 24].
e. Art. II of Corollary in Chap. vii, *supra,* p. 126.
f. Chap. vii, beg.
g. *Dig.* XLIX. xv. 24.

24. This is not found in the Regulations of Severus. It appears in Ulpian, *Institutes,* I, and is incorporated in the *Digest,* but not in the *Code,* as cited by Grotius.

same motive for such an agreement exist among citizens, since it is comparatively easy for them to settle disputes with one another in court when peace has been established.[a]

Accordingly, [permanent] acquisition does result from seizure in so far as foreign wars are concerned—on the basis, that is to say, of the aforementioned universal agreement among states—with the proviso that the attendant claim to possession shall be sound and secure in a specified degree, rather than open to question. For it seems that we, [as the original owners,] do not lose ownership[b] until the attempt to follow up our possessions has begun to be so difficult that there is little hope of recovery. Now, it is assumed under military law that this point is reached when the property in question has been brought within the fortifications and boundaries of the enemy. Other authorities[c] have [53′a′] held that the exact point should be determined by considerations not of place but of time: for example, ownership might expire after an interval of twenty-four hours, which constitutes a civil day. To be sure, I am inclined to consider the latter criterion as less correct, apart from my recognition of the fact that it is evidently accepted, not without reason, in regard to ships captured at sea.

Therefore, by the law of nations,[d] not in its natural but in its positive phase, and in consequence of a pact, so to speak, agreed upon at least by a large number of nations, *the [permanent] acquisition of goods* [53′] *captured in foreign public wars is conceded to be just for subjects of both belligerent parties, always provided that a command has first been given which is not repugnant to reason after the probabilities have been weighed.*[e] Corollary III

a. *Ibid.* 21, § 1. [*Dig.* XLIX. xv. 24.]

b. *Dig.* X. ii. 8; *ibid.* XLI. i. 44; *ibid.* 5, § 4; *ibid.* XLIX. xv. 5, § 1.

c. Argument of *Dig.* XLIII. xvi. 3, § 9; see also Duaren, *On Dig.* XLI. ii. 1.

d. Constitutions of France [in *Code de Henry III*], XX. xiii. 24.

e. Vázquez, ix. 17; Covarr., *On Sext,* rule *peccatum,* Pt. II, § 11, words: *Hinc mirum est.*

CHAPTER IX

Concerning the Aims of War

Question VIII

Article I. What constitutes a just purpose in war, for voluntary agents?

Article II. What constitutes a just purpose in war, for subjects? [54]

War is waged by the virtuous in order that justice may be enjoyed; and justice, as Polus Lucanus[a] so admirably explains, is the very same quality that is called "peace" with reference to the community, whereas with reference to subjects in their relation to rulers it is called "ready obedience."

Let us deal first with Article I of this question, which pertains to voluntary agents.

Peace, then, is the fruit of justice. Plato[b] expresses the same idea when he says that laws were established for the sake of true justice, and therefore for the sake of peace. Cicero[c] maintains that war ought to be undertaken in such a way "as to make it evident that peace is the only end sought." In another work,[d] moreover, he points out that the term "peace" should be applied, not to "a pact of slavery" but to a state of tranquil freedom. Yet again, he[e] unites the two concepts in the following statement: "Wars should be undertaken *for this purpose,* that we may live

a. In Stobaeus [*Florilegium,* IX. 54].

b. *Laws,* I [p. 628 c]; add Arist., *Politics,* VII. xv [VII. xiii. 15].

c. *On Duties,* I [xxiii, 80].

d. *Philippics,* XII [vi. 14].

e. *On Duties,* I [xi. 35].

in *peace* and *free from injury.*" According to Crispus,[a] wise men "wage war for the sake of peace, and endure toil in the hope of leisure," an observation interpreted by Crispus himself in another work,[b] where he asserts that, "Our forebears, the most scrupulous of mortals, snatched away nothing from the conquered save the latter's licence to inflict injury." Among the theologians, we may cite Augustine,[c] who says: "Peace is not sought in order that warfare may be practised; on the contrary, war is waged in order that peace may be attained"; and the same author[d] defines peace as "a well-ordered concord." The ancient theologians,[e] too, explain in connexion with the story of Melchisedec that peace and justice differ not in fact but merely in name.

Accordingly, the peace set up as an objective for belligerents is not any kind of peace whatsoever, but solely and exclusively the kind that is just and honourable. For otherwise, those wars would be vainly undertaken which we are almost compelled to wage as a matter of necessity, at times when (to borrow the phrase of Florus)[f] laws more savage than arms are imposed. Thus Cicero[g] warns us to beware of the peace wherein snares are concealed. Again, according to the admonitions of Tacitus,[h] war itself is less perilous than a peace that is either vile or entangled with suspicion.[1] Yet again, it was Demosthenes[i] who formulated that excellent maxim, *πόλεμος ἔνδοξος εἰρήνης αἰσχρᾶς αἱρετώτερος*; "a glorious war

a. [Pseudo-Sallust] *Speech to Caesar* [vi. 2].

b. In *Jugurtha* [Sallust, *The War with Catiline,* xii. 3–5].

c. *Letters,* i [clxxxix. 6], *To Boniface,* cited in *Decretum,* II. xxiii. 1. 3.

d. *On the City of God,* XV [v].

e. *Hebrews,* vii. 2; Clement of Alexandria, *Stromata,* IV [p. 231].

f. [*Epitome,* II. xxx. 32.]

g. [*On Duties,* I. xi. 35.]

h. *Annals,* III [xliv] and *Histories,* IV [xlix].

i. Demosthenes [*De Corona,* 201].

1. The phrase employed by Grotius, *pace . . . suspecta,* might be translated more faithfully as "open to suspicion"; but the passage cited from Tacitus as pertinent to this point refers not to a peace that invites suspicion, but to a person who is suspected in time of peace and who therefore finds that war is the safer course. Here, as in many other cases throughout the *Commentary,* words presented by Grotius in the form of a quotation (i.e., words underscored in the MS.) represent in reality a paraphrase.

should be preferred to an inglorious peace." Thucydides[a] likewise observes: "Peace is strengthened by war; moreover, he who shuns war because he loves peace will not thereby place himself beyond the reach of danger." This thought is clarified by Thucydides himself in the following words: "To be sure, it is characteristic of men of moderation to remain at peace when they have not been provoked by injury; but it is also characteristic of the brave to exchange peace for war if injury is [54′] done them and then to resume friendly relations, laying aside their arms, when the opportunity presents itself and the affair has been carried to a successful conclusion." To this he adds: "It is not fitting that any man should be extolled because of success in war; but neither is it fitting that any man should endure contumely while wallowing in peaceful ease. For he who shrinks from war for the sake of the pleasures of peace will (if he remains idle) right speedily be despoiled of that delightful tranquillity which so captivated him that he was too slothful to take up arms." These are the beliefs expressed by Thucydides. Similarly, Thomas Aquinas[b] says: "Assuredly, war is waged for the sake of peace, but for the sake of a good peace, not for one that is evil. For there is also a kind of peace which Christ declares that He came not to send upon earth." Apart from Saint Thomas, there are other theologians[c] who hold that the purpose of war is the removal of those things which are a menace to peace; and, according to these same theologians, peace is menaced when any one is unjustly attacked or deprived of his property or subjected to injury, while justice, or righteous punishment, is nevertheless withheld. Certainly each of these points is in exact conformity with the statements already made by us[d] regarding the causes that give rise to war.

New explanation

Thus the kind of peace suggested as the proper aim of belligerents is nothing more nor less than the repulsion of injury, or (and this, in the

a. I [xxxvi].
b. II.–II, qu. 40, art. 1, ad 3.
c. Matthaei, in Req. 2, p. 7.
d. Concl. VI, Art. I, *supra,* p. 107.

end, amounts to the same thing) the attainment of rights, not only one's own, but also, at times, the rights of others.[a]

This last objective clearly exists in the case of allies; and for that matter, it can equally well be the objective sought by the very instigators of a war, as may occur, for example, when the injured parties have been so thoroughly crushed that they themselves lack the power to offer resistance. So it was that Abraham undertook to wage war in behalf of Lot and the citizens of Sodom. Constantius did likewise in behalf of the Romans against Maxentius, as did Theodosius for the cause of the Christians against Chosroes the Persian. "The courage which [. . .] defends the weak" is called "justice," by Ambrose.[b] According to Seneca,[c] "He who does not attack my country but nevertheless oppresses his own, harassing his people though he keeps aloof from mine, has destroyed by the depravity of his spirit that fellowship based upon human rights which he shared with me, so that my duty to the whole of mankind is a consideration more fundamental and more powerful than my duty to that one man." Cicero[d] asks: "Who that does nothing save for his own sake, is a good man?" To be sure, in striving thus for the good of others, we strive for our own good, also. For it is important to the security of all that injuries [to any person] shall be warded off, lest the perpetrators of the injurious acts, rendered more powerful thereby, should at some future time rise up against us, too, and also in order that others may not be encouraged to wrongdoing by a multitude of instances in which injurious conduct has gone unpunished. Furthermore, it is a fact worth noting that, just as a state often undertakes a public war for the personal benefit of citizens (a point already mentioned by us[e]), so also citizens take up arms privately for the benefit of the state. This sometimes happens when the state has been crushed and is unable to act as a whole [55] in its own defence. [Scipio] Nasica [Serapio] adopted this course of

a. See Chap. vi, *supra,* pp. 92 f.

b. See at end of Chap. iii, *supra,* p. 67 [and Ambrose, *On Duties* I. xxvii. 129].

c. *On Benefits,* VII. xix.

d. *Letters to his Friends,* VII. xii.

e. In Chap. vi, *supra,* pp. 93 f.

action against [Tiberius] Gracchus, and certainly his deed is praised by all good men. Octavian did likewise against Antony. The same may be said of all tyrannicides. Yet it is obvious that these persons acted partly in their own interest; for, just as it is to the advantage of the state that its citizens should be safe and prosperous in their private lives, even so, and in a far greater measure, it is to the advantage of the citizens that the state should be preserved.

Furthermore, whosoever engages in war in behalf of another's right, necessarily regards his own right as bound up therewith in the collection of damages and costs.[a] Accordingly, we find all those persons blameworthy who wage wars, even with just cause, if they do so *ἐκ πλεονεξίας* [out of greed] and in a spirit of injustice. Therefore, let the state, magistrate, or private citizen who undertakes a war, and the ally of any such belligerent as well, remain wholly free from "deep-seated lust for empire and riches,"[b] and from the sentiments described by Seneca[c] in the following lines:

> Unholy thirst for gain, and headlong wrath,
> Broke through this covenant. . . .

These are the very sentiments to which Augustine[d] refers in the passage already quoted[e] from that author: "The greedy urge to inflict harm, cruel vengefulness," and so on. For, as this same Father of the Church[f] declares, "Among the true worshippers of God, even wars themselves have a pacific character, being waged not because of cupidity or cruelty, but because of an earnest desire for peace, with the purpose of restraining the wicked and giving support to the virtuous."

Conclusion VIII, Article I

In short, *Voluntary agents wage with a just purpose whatever war they wage in order to attain a right.*

a. In Chap. iv, *supra,* pp. 75 f.
b. Sallust, *Frag.* [*Letter of Mithridates,* 5].
c. *Hippolytus* [540–1].
d. [*Against Faustus,* XXII. lxxiv] cited in *Decretum,* II. xxiii. 1. 4.
e. At end of Chap. iii, *supra,* p. 66.
f. *De Diversis Ecclesiae Observationibus* cited in *Decretum,* II. xxiii. 1. 6.

Now, in the case of subjects (as we indicated at the outset of this chapter),[a] the factor of obedience is stressed, a point brought out in pontifical law by the words of Pope Gregory:[b] "Among other good and meritorious attributes of military service, the most praiseworthy is this: *obedience* to the needs of the state." Wherefore subjects, too, must necessarily be free from those failings which we forbade in the case of voluntary agents.

Mercenaries, however, are for the most part apt to display such failings, as Plato[c] shows by quoting Tyrtaeus to that effect; for it is evident that mercenaries defy danger solely in the hope of gain.[d] [55′] Antiphanes[e] gives us a rather neat phrase describing the soldier who,

> ὃς ἕνεκα τοῦ ζῆν ἔρχετ' ἀποθανούμενος.
>
> *In quest of a living, forsooth, rushes*
> *Forth headlong to death!* . . .

Paul[f] bears witness to the fact that soldiers are not forbidden to accept payment; and under the head of such payment (as we have noted before and shall note again[g]) spoils are included, when they are bestowed by a state or magistrate. On the other hand, it is a vicious practice to aim at gain through spoils as one's principal goal. To take an analogous case, we know that it is right for persons in public office to accept fees, including upon occasion the fines paid by citizens, since it would be unjust if the common interest were served at the expense of one individual; but the magistrate should nevertheless have in view a different objective, to wit, the public weal. Augustine[h] sought to make this very point when he said: "It is not a crime to serve as a soldier, but it is a sin to do so *for*

a. Beg. of chap.

b. [*Letters,* XII. xxiv, cited in] *Decretum,* II. xxiii. 1. 7.

c. *Laws,* I [p. 630 B].

d. Sylvester, on word *bellum* [Pt. I] x. 4; Cajetan, *Summula Peccatorum,* words: *bellum dubium.*

e. [In Stobaeus, *Florilegium,* LIII. 9.]

f. *1 Corinthians,* ix. 7.

g. Chap. iv, *supra,* pp. 83–84, and Chap. x, *infra,* pp. 217 ff.

h. *De Verbis Domini* cited in *Decretum,* II. xxiii. 1. 5.

the sake of spoils; neither is it a blameworthy act to rule a state, but to rule it *for the purpose* of augmenting one's wealth, is an act that clearly calls for condemnation." Those individuals, however, who have themselves suffered loss, quite properly fight even for the sake of spoils—in other words, for the attainment of their rights, a process bound up with the process of despoliation—until they have obtained reparation for that loss.

Now, what we have said regarding the rectitude of one's purpose falls exclusively into the realm where one's innermost thoughts are examined,[a] that is to say, the realm wherein God passes judgement on a man or the latter passes judgement on himself. Yet whenever a matter of this kind is brought before a court—for example, when some judge, in peaceful surroundings, passes upon a question relative to spoils of war—all points not susceptible of proof must be disregarded. Furthermore, even in the court of conscience, he who wages war for an unjust purpose is indeed convicted of sin, but he rightfully retains the spoils. Thus the Scholastics[b] wisely maintain that, "Righteous intent is not a prerequisite for the licit retention of those things which have fallen to one's lot in war, any more than the process of execution resulting from the order of a judge is to be evaluated on the basis of the executing agent's intent." For wrongful intent on the part of the person who seizes something, never of itself creates an obligation to make restitution.[c]

From the standpoint of those tribunals established outside the realm of one's own conscience, the same principle holds true with respect to the good faith, or belief in the justice of one's cause, which we require of subjects [in the waging of wars]: that is to say, this factor is not even taken into account, unless perchance the injustice of the cause is entirely obvious. Hence it follows that only those matters susceptible of certain

a. Scotus, 15, dist. 41, qu. 4 [in *Reportata Parisiensia,* II, dist. 39, qu. 2, n. 6].

b. Cajetan, *On II.–II,* qu. 40, art. 1, ad 2; and in same art.; Arias, *De Bello,* n. 58; Covarr., *On Sext,* rule *peccatum,* § 9, n. 2; *Angelus, Summa,* n. 5; [Trovamala] *Summa Rosella* [word *bellum*], nn. 3 and 8; Sylvester, n. 2: *tertium* [on word *bellum,* Pt. I. ii, *Sed istud tertium*].

c. Th. Aq. II.–II, qu. 66, art. 8; Cajetan, *Summula Peccatorum,* words: *bellum iniustum.*

proof are submitted to the judgement of the said tribunals: for [56] example, such matters as the authority of a superior. This is the doctrine laid down by all the jurists.[a]

Conclusion VIII, Article II

If, on the other hand, we do wish to take into account the criterion of conscience, we may say that, *Subjects wage with a just purpose whatever war they wage in order to render obedience to a superior.*

a. Adrian [*Quaestiones Quodlibeticae*], in c. *aggredior;* Cajetan, *On II.–II,* qu. 40, art. 1, at end; Covarr., *On Sext,* rule *peccatum,* Pt. II, §§ 10, 11.

CHAPTER X

Question IX. By whom may prize or booty be acquired?

Article I. By whom may it be acquired in private wars?

Article II. By whom may it be acquired in public wars?

Corollary. To what extent is the acquisition of prize or booty permissible for those who are waging a public war at their own expense, to their own loss and [*at the*] *risk* [*of damage to their personal interests*],[1] *through the efforts of their own agents, and in the absence of any agreement regarding recompense?*

We have satisfactorily demonstrated,[a] so I believe, the truth of the proposition that enemy property can be rightfully seized and acquired.

There still remains one controversial point that is pertinent to our inquiry, namely: Who should become the owner of property seized in war? In considering this question, too, we shall adopt the natural order of discussion, dealing first with private wars and afterwards with public wars,[b] a method of approach which will contribute not a little toward clarifying the matter.

a. Concl. II and Arts. III and IV; Corolls. II, and III to Concl. VII, *supra,* pp. 68–88, 177, and 181.

b. Cf. Chap. vi, *supra,* pp. 92–100.

1. The single Latin word *periculo* would seem to call for a more general interpretation, e.g., "and at peril to themselves." Near the close of the present chapter, however, Grotius presents this corollary in a slightly fuller form, employing the phrase *suarum rerum periculo* (literally: "and at the risk of one's own interests"); hence the expanded English interpretation. Cf. notes 32 and 33, p. 242, *infra.*

As regards the question in its entirety, moreover, it should be evident from the observations already made[a] that things seized in war and things seized on the basis of a judicial award fall into the same class. For war, if it is supported by public authority, differs from execution of a judicial sentence[b] only in the fact that it must be carried out by armed force, owing to the power possessed by the opponent; or, if the conflict is waged because of a private need, the case clearly reverts to that early law which made each individual the judge of his own affairs. Accordingly, no one will properly become the owner of booty unless he has a rightful claim, that is to say, grounds for claiming something as his due. Therefore, the minds of men should be completely cleared of the false belief that an enemy possession becomes public property destined for the one who seizes it, in accordance with the practice established for *τῶν ἀδεσπότων*, or "ownerless property," just as if every bond of human fellowship had been abolished between enemies. For, despite the many statements made by ancient authorities[c] which seem to favour this belief by comparing such a process of acquisition with the chase, despite the apparent confirmation of the same belief to be drawn from the pronouncements of the orators and philosophers whom we cited at the outset[d] in order to establish the right to acquire spoils, and despite the fact that, even among the authorities on law, we find Paulus[e] evidently placing things seized in war under the head of goods which have no owner and which, [56′] furthermore, may be acquired by the first person to take possession—I repeat, regardless of all these indications to the contrary—it cannot be denied that there is a notable difference between those things which have never been subject to anyone's ownership and those which have admittedly belonged to the enemy: a difference not unobserved even by our

a. Concl. II and Art. III, Concl. VII, *supra,* pp. 68–88 and 152 ff.

b. See Concl. VII, Arts. I and II, *supra,* pp. 127–152.

c. Xenophon, *Training of Cyrus,* II [iii. 2]; Plato, *Sophist* [p. 219 D, E]; *id., Laws,* I [p. 626 B]; Arist., *Politics,* I. viii. [I. iii. 8].

d. Chap. iv, *passim, supra.*

e. *Dig.* XLI. ii. 1, § 1; and *ibid.* i. 5, at end; and *ibid.* 7, at beg.

own jurists.[a] For if we concede so much more force to the demands of hatred than to those of nature, that we are led to abrogate between enemies the law that bids us refrain[2] from seizing the property of others, then there is nothing to prevent us from abolishing also the principle of good faith in the observance of pacts and, indeed, the entire body of precepts known as the law of arms. But we accept the opinion of Socrates, who argues (in Book I of Plato's *Republic*)[b] that any of these acts [repudiating justice between enemies] is unjust. Nor did Pindar[c] escape reproach from the philosophers for his assertion that,

χρὴ δὲ πᾶν ἔρδοντ' ἀμαυρῶσαι τὸν ἐχθρόν.

'Tis right to do whatever deed you will,
Whereby you bring destruction on the foe.

I recall the words of Cicero,[d] also: "Moreover, there are certain duties to be observed even in regard to those persons by whom one has been injured. For limits are imposed upon vengeance and punishment." Your words, too, come back to me, O second Romulus![3] For when you sent the tutor back to Falerii, you said:[e] "Between us and the Faliscans there is no fellowship founded upon man-made covenants; but the fellowship implanted by nature assuredly[4] does exist and will continue to exist.

a. Jason, *On Dig.* XLI. ii. 1, n. 8; Duaren, *On Dig. ibid.;* Doneau, *Commentaries,* IV. xxi.

b. [p. 335 D, E.]

c. [*Isthmian Odes* IV. 48.]

d. *On Duties,* I [xi. 33].

e. Livy, V [xxvii].

2. Reading *abstinere iubet* (bids us refrain), or possibly, *capere vetat* (forbids us to seize) for the phrase actually written by Grotius, *abstinere vetat* (forbids us to refrain). The context clearly indicates that Grotius was referring to the principle laid down in Law IV, and that he distorted his own thought by a slip of the pen.

3. I.e. Camillus, as quoted by Livy in the anecdote concerning Camillus' refusal to take advantage of a Faliscan tutor's treacherous offer to deliver his charges into the hands of the Romans.

4. *utique,* in Grotius's text; *utrisque* (on both sides, in both peoples) in Livy's text. While such slight variations from the language of the authors quoted are the rule rather than the exception in the *Commentary,* this particular inaccuracy calls for comment, partly because it is so slight that it could be interpreted as an inadvertent mis-

There are laws of war just as there are laws of peace." Nor does Seneca[a] praise Fabricius more highly on any other ground [than on that of justice toward enemies, in the passage where he describes Fabricius thus]: "tenaciously faithful to a noble ideal, and—a most difficult feat!—guiltless even in warfare; for he believed that there was such a thing as sinful conduct even against enemies." War does away with political fellowship, but not with the fellowship of humanity. Thus even the Fourth Law remains operative, save in so far as it may be outweighed by the Second Law; and the force of the Second, as we have observed, is contained also in the Fifth and Sixth Laws. Hence it follows that one may not acquire enemy property save on account of a debt. That is to say, in addition to the fact of possession, cause also is required, a principle which we expounded in an earlier chapter[b] but which is not inappropriately repeated at this point.

Let us turn our attention now to the question, "By whom may prize or booty be acquired in private wars?"

To be sure, any person who asks this question evidently presupposes the existence of a body of law governing prize and booty, and derived from private warfare, whereas a great many interpreters of canon or civil law and writers on the laws of war[c] appear to repudiate that supposition. But we have already remarked on several occasions that there is no reason why we should invariably accept the opinion of those who, content with the knowledge they have acquired concerning civil law, have neglected to acquaint themselves with the precepts based upon the fundamental truths of the law of nations.[d]

A paradoxical contention

In this connexion it is worth while to note the determining principle

---

spelling of the word Grotius actually intended to write, and partly because stress upon the factor of *mutual* obligation would make the quotation still more forceful for his purposes.

a. *Epistles,* cxx [6].

b. Beg. of Chap. iv.

c. Innocent and Panormitanus, *On Decretals,* II. xiii. 12 and II. xxiv. 29; Bartolus, *On Dig.* XLIX. xv. 24 [nn. 9–11]; Jason, *On Dig.* I. i. 5, n. 30; Arias, *De Bello,* 24 ff.

d. *Institutes,* II. i. 17.

introduced by Faber.[a] For he rejects the belief that the institutions of prize and booty have a place in private warfare, on the ground that no statement to this effect is written in the laws: an argument which is equivalent to denying that the contents of the *Corpus* of Roman laws pertain primarily to civil law, and thus leave unmentioned many matters which might better be decided by the common criterion of reason, rather than on the basis of any [civil] authority. In any case, it is easy to explain [57] why no treatment of the question engaging our attention is found [in Roman law]. For the majesty and power of the Roman Empire were such that Rome was hardly ever troubled by a lack of judicial recourse (that is to say, by any continuous lack), which is an especially weighty factor in the development of private wars, as we have pointed out.[b]

Nevertheless, if we are seeking sound arguments on which to base our solution of the question, what is more certain than the fact that in warfare—whether public or private—everything necessary for the execution of one's right is permissible?[c] It is indeed necessary, if we wish to obtain that which is our due, that we should acquire enemy property [*rem hostilem*]; and the acquisition of such property is nothing more nor less than that very practice which we call "acquisition of prize or booty,"[d] except that some objection may possibly be advanced against designating the person who attacks us privately as an enemy [*hostem*][5] and the property seized in such circumstances as "prize or booty." Although I have no wish to engage in a stubborn dispute on this matter of definition, provided that the substance of our contention is accepted, nevertheless I regard it as extremely important for the clarification of the whole question, that different terms should not be employed in the discussion of a single right.

Now, if we examine with care the opinions formulated by the above-

a. [*On Institutes,* II. i. 17.]

b. Concl. VII, Art. I, *supra,* pp. 130–42.

c. See beg. of Chap. iv, *supra,* p. 68 and Concl. VII, Art. I, *supra,* pp. 130–42.

d. At end of Chap. ii, *supra,* p. 50.

5. *Hostis* usually refers to a public enemy, whereas an individual who bears us ill will in a private capacity is called in Latin *inimicus.*

mentioned jurists,[a] we shall find that their statements seem almost identical with ours in substance, though the terminology differs. For their doctrine runs as follows: in private warfare, if no judge is available, and if our purpose is the recovery of our own property and the collection of the debt due us, we may seize the possessions of our adversaries, even after an interval of time has elapsed, up to the point where we shall have obtained value comparable to that debt. But if this is permissible with respect to all debts owed us, then surely it is permissible with respect to damages and costs incurred in the attainment of our rights; and the same inference applies even to the dangers and cessation of profit involved, or in other words, to extrinsic losses and all attendant factors. That is the opinion laid down by the theologians,[b] and based by them upon the following argument: the judge himself, if there were one available, would award the said items to the innocent party, since it is right that all of the losses mentioned should be charged against him who caused them.[c] Indeed, one may go so far as to say that such seizures are permissible even for the collection of what is owed on the basis of sinful conduct. For in judicial decisions, too, a thief is sentenced to pay the party who has been despoiled twice or four times the value of the goods stolen, and a robber must pay the victim three times the value. The injury done is also estimated and weighed; and the laws decree in favour of injured parties [as such], penalties similar to those decreed in favour of plaintiffs in a lawsuit. Thus when Boethius[d] was asked upon whom punishment would properly be inflicted according to his judgement, if he were sitting as judge—whether upon the party who had committed the injurious act or upon the party who had suffered the injury—he replied that undoubtedly he would order satisfaction given to the victim at the expense of the perpetrator of the injury. That is to say (as a certain author[e] has rightly pointed out in his treatise on war, and as Aristotle[f]

a. See Arias, *De Bello,* 24 ff.
b. Matthaei, in Req. 1, also *Dig.* IX. ii. 25–6.
c. *Decretals,* II. xxiv. 29; *Code,* IX. xii. 6.
d. *On the Consolation of Philosophy,* IV [120–1].
e. Henry of Gorkum, *De Bello Iusto,* Prop. 10.
f. *Nic. Ethics,* V. vii [V. iv].

maintains) everything that has the character of an ill, including injury received, is embraced in the term "loss"; and therefore, the opposing factor of gain, which has the character of a good (for example, just vengeance) is naturally the proper due of the injured party. This point has already been discussed by us in another passage.[a] [57′]

Accordingly, we arrive at one and the same conclusion in regard to both public and private wars. But, if this is the universally accepted conclusion, wherein lies the distinction between the two kinds of warfare?

Perhaps the said distinction turns partly upon the contention apparently supported by a considerable number of authorities,[b] that things taken in private warfare should be subjected to a strict accounting, whereas things acquired in public warfare need not be balanced against the principal debt and may remain in the possession of the person who seized them even when they exceed in value the loss that was suffered. The persons who argue thus, however, fail to realize that all spoil seized over and above the amount required to cover losses and the cost of prosecuting a case, may be retained [after a public war] in so far as they represent the punishment owed by the offending state to the offended state, but must not be retained in excess of that penalty; nor do they take into account the fact that whatever does remain in excess of the amount due for just punishment should be returned, as Sylvester[c] quite correctly rules and as we ourselves have agreed. Now, I see no reason why one should not make that same concession [regarding retention of spoil by way of punishment] in the case of private wars, in accordance with the considerations pointed out just above and more fully discussed in earlier passages of the present work. Of course, spoils seized in private warfare (even when the war is just) are much more apt to exceed in value the debt, losses, and penalty involved than spoils seized in public warfare.

a. In Chap. iv, *supra,* pp. 72 ff.; see also Chap. ii, Law V, *supra,* pp. 29 f., and Chap. viii, Concl. I [Concl. VII, Art. I], *supra,* pp. 130 ff.

b. Archidiaconus, *On Decretum,* II. xxiii. 2. 2; Sylvester, on word *bellum* [Pt. I] x; Vict., *De Jure Belli,* 51.

c. *Ibid.* and on word *repressalia,* at beg. [i.] 4; Laudensis, *De Bello,* Qu. 5.

For in the latter case (owing undoubtedly to the lengthy duration and vast scope of public wars) the amount taken from the enemy rarely balances even the expenses incurred. Consequently, those jurists[a] who more or less make a practice of *τὸ ἅπαξ ἢ δὶς παραβαίνειν*, "omitting to mention that which has occurred only once or twice," have asserted that things taken in public wars are acquired without restriction, while they hold that in private warfare such acquisitions may not exceed the amount of compensation due to the private individuals concerned.

Up to the point indicated, then, the public and private laws governing prize and booty are in mutual agreement. Yet we cannot overlook the fact that there is a subtle difference between them. For a certain assertion made by us[b] with reference to public wars—namely, that for subjects waging war in good faith, things captured by either belligerent party fall properly under the head of acquisitions—is in my opinion not easily applicable to private warfare. Private individuals have adopted no common agreement to this effect, as states have done; and in this lack of a specific agreement lies the most satisfactory explanation of the opinion ascribed above to certain learned authorities, which rules that things seized in a private war do not become the property of those who seize them. In other words, the war does not in itself suffice to produce this effect, without the additional factor of a truly just cause.

There is another distinction which will become clear if we first reflect upon the question, "How do private individuals differ from a state?" For I do not believe that the answer to this question can be limited to numerical considerations, since a collection of individuals sufficient in number to set up a state but gathered together in a chance assemblage would have no more legal standing than one or two individuals. Besides, what numerical requisite can be specified for that sufficiently large group, which will preclude the possibility of any objection that a smaller number suffices? What, then, is the basic factor underlying the difference? Undoubtedly, that factor is civil power, which is established by

a. *Dig.* I. iii. 4–6; *Dig.* V. iv. 3, at end.
b. Chap. viii, Coroll. III, *supra,* p. 181.

common consent; and common consent (as we have already pointed out)[a] is the source of legal judgements.

Now, this difference in judicial attributes creates a distinction [58] that concerns the acquisition of spoil. For states are inherently endowed with judicial authority,[b] whereas private individuals are not so endowed save in so far as public power is found to be defective. We have made a rather convenient division of these instances of defective power into two classes: cases in which the defect appears to be of brief duration, and cases in which it appears to be continuous.

When the defect is of brief duration, the laws must be restored to force as soon as possible. Accordingly, the assertions made by the authorities[c] above cited, to the effect that in private warfare vengeance is not permissible, seizure is not [properly] practised, and so on, are to be interpreted as referring to private wars derived from a momentary lack of judicial recourse, an interpretation supported by logic itself, by a careful examination of the passages in question and by the observations which we ourselves have made. Additional confirmation of this point is found in another statement laid down by those same authorities,[d] namely, that any person whose property has been snatched from him by stealth or violence may take by way of compensation the equivalent thereof, subject to the subsequent award of his superior. For even though the law of vengeance is properly applicable to the original despoiler,[e] nevertheless, a restriction must be imposed upon the second despoiler, [i.e. the avenger,] limiting the compensation he receives to the exact extent of the spoliation or injury inflicted by the other party. Thus it would seem that the right originally possessed by the avenger with respect to the property seized, was a right to hold it as security [*pignus*], whereas later he acquired the right of ownership in virtue of a judicial decision.

a. In Chap. ii, *supra,* pp. 40 f.

b. Cf. Laws IX and XIII [XII?], *supra,* pp. 43, 46; see discussion of Concl. VII, Art. I, *supra,* pp. 127 ff.

c. Arias and others cited above.

d. Innocent, *On Decretals,* II. xiii. 12, n. 8; *ibid.* II. xxiv. 29, n. 6 and Panormitanus, on the same passages of the *Decretals;* Sylvester, on word *bellum* [Pt. I] iii.

e. See also Sylvester, *ibid.* x: *prima.*

Here we have the origin of the very term *pigneratio* [seizure of pledges];[6] and the same order of events is observed in connexion with reprisals.[a] But I hold that even in such cases, where a thing privately seized is publicly awarded in settlement of a debt,[b] an attempt should be made to combat the rejection of the terms "prize" or "booty," since this very property which we acquire through a civil judgement (so the learned men of law tell us), would seem to be received not from the hands of a judge but from an adversary.

If, however, the lack of judicial recourse is of an enduring nature (as it would be, for example, in a locality subject to no one's jurisdiction), the case clearly comes under that law of nature which existed everywhere prior to the establishment of courts of justice, so that one belligerent, acting for himself in the capacity of judge, acquires forthwith the goods seized as a pledge from the other belligerent. Nor will the former incur, at some later date when recourse to a judge becomes possible, any obligation to make restitution. The reason for this immunity is the same as that repeatedly adduced by the Scholastics[c] in connexion with a similar thesis. For the Scholastics say that a case which is complete in itself and not bound up with any additional act, is not reopened even though its underlying cause may later cease to exist. Moreover, if the need should arise, even in a case of this kind, for a subsequent judgement based upon civil law rather than upon the law of nations, nevertheless, that judgement ought to be interpreted not as bestowing the right of ownership but merely as a declaration[d] that the said right has been acquired. It is evident that this procedure was introduced partly in order to search out the frauds perpetrated by dishonest persons, and partly with a view to ensuring a greater degree of security for rightful captors by means of a proclamation imposing silence upon all persons [who might wish to

a. See Bartolus, *On Reprisals,* IX, qu. 1, ad 2 and 3.

b. See Sylvester, on word *repressalia,* at end [ix].

c. Sylvester, on word *furtum,* x [3]; and discussion of *Sext,* V, ult. reg. 73.

d. Cf. *Dig.* VIII. v. 8, § 3.

6. *Pignerationes* was evidently employed in both civil and canon law as equivalent to *represaliae.* Cf. Bartolus, *On Reprisals,* Qu. 1, ad 1, and Sylvester, word *bellum,* Pt. I. x: *prima.*

question the right of those captors]. There are many other causes, [58′] however, that may result in the adoption of the same procedure. For we often hear of a summons addressed by the true owners of property to all persons of any kind who may possibly wish to enter into a controversy regarding that property,[a] the purpose of the summons being the increased future security of the owners.

It is a fact, then, that seizure of spoil is not impermissible in private warfare. For it would indeed be difficult to prove that the celebrated war waged by Abraham against King Chedorlaomer and his allies was not a private war;[b] yet Abraham certainly did not hesitate to take away spoil from that conflict. The same may be said of Gaius Julius Caesar,[c] who as a youth pursued with a private fleet the pirates by whom he had previously been captured, and apportioned their goods as prize. It is equally indisputable that a similar course of action was followed in Octavius' war against Antony. The view taken by Socinus Nepos[d] clearly bears out our own statements; and his opinion appears to have been adopted by Ayala,[e] the Spaniard, primarily on the ground that, when a war of this kind is just, the rights and consequences attaching to war [in general] should be recognized for the particular case in point.

Thus the fact of acquisition is established. But we have yet to consider the question, "By whom are such acquisitions made in private warfare?"

New explanation

Now, since any principal agent must be regarded as acting chiefly in his own behalf, I hold that he who is the principal author of a private war becomes the owner of the goods taken in that war in so far as he has been attempting to obtain his rights; and I intend that this statement shall furthermore be interpreted to mean that, even if the enemy also owes debts to other parties, the aforesaid principal agent will nevertheless hold a privileged position in regard to the spoil.[f] For, in the first place,

a. *Code,* VII. xiv. 5.
b. *Genesis,* xiv.
c. Plutarch, *Caesar* [p. 708 A–C].
d. *Consilia,* III, cons. 68.
e. *De Iure Belli,* I. ii.
f. See discussion of Corollary, this chap., *infra,* pp. 227–42.

all of the losses and expenses involved are the concern of the party who undertook the war, since he is of course obligated under the law of nations to his allies and subjects for the sum of the expenditures and costs [on his side]; and it is certain that everything reckoned under the head of costs of execution is deducted before all else from whatever is collected out of the property of a debtor,[a] a principle established by the very force of necessity, since otherwise (that is to say, unless such costs are met) one person cannot even prosecute another. Furthermore, if the initiator of a war has possessed, prior to the execution of his undertaking, any claim as a creditor of the party despoiled, I do not doubt but that preference should be given him in this matter, too, in accordance with the established precedent relative to the particular creditor who has been more vigilant than the rest.[b] For he who has in good faith collected his due from a debtor obligated to a number of creditors, is not bound, even by the judgement of his conscience, to make restitution.

Afterwards, however, if any goods remain in the possession of the adversary, [i.e. the debtor,] the other creditors to whom he is obligated shall be granted access to this remaining portion. Finally, whatever is left after their claims have been settled shall be preserved for the despoiled combatant himself and restored to him at the close of the war, [59] when the danger has disappeared.[c] For the authorities on law agree that this is the prevailing practice even in the case of reprisals; and the same practice is always followed in connexion with the seizure of debtors' goods on the basis of a judicial decree.

But if the spoil is acquired by the party who undertakes a private war, then it is not acquired by the individuals who seize it; that is to say, it is not acquired by them in a primary and direct sense, or in other words, in the natural course of events and independently of any additional act. Nor can any objection be made to this inference on the ground that the initiator of the war does not himself seize possession in his own person;

a. See Bartolus, *On Reprisals,* IX, qu. 1, ad 3.

b. *Dig.* XLII. viii. 6, § 6; *ibid.* 24.

c. See *supra,* Chap. iv, p. 72, and Concl. VII, Art. III, *supra,* pp. 153, 164–65; Sylvester, on word *bellum,* [Pt.] I. vii. 5 [xi. 3].

for he does take possession through other individuals, who are either subjects or assistants. In so far as subjects are concerned, this point has already been explained. For, [to take an analogous case,] acquisition is effected in every sense of the term through children and through slaves, just as if they were parts of one's own body, as the jurists[a] readily agree. The question of how acquisition is effected through assistants, however—that is to say, through persons who are *sui iuris*—appears to be more difficult of solution. But this problem, too, will be solved with sufficient ease if it is understood that we define as "assistants," or "allies in war," those persons who attach themselves to the principal agent but who do not assume for themselves an equal status as principals; for if they did assume that status, they would enjoy the same right as the aforesaid principal party. We are speaking, then, of persons who have received their orders from the initiator of the war; and therefore, we may say that, just as we gain possession even through a free agent who has received his orders from us, so also we acquire ownership through that same act of possession.[b]

New explanation The foregoing statement merits special consideration. For if it is rejected, we shall be acquiring, not ownership over the property in question, but merely a right of personal action, which is a very different matter. To be sure, in the dissertations of the jurists[c] the following assertions have become exceedingly familiar: that by my agency I place another person in possession, since the person in whose name possession is held is himself the possessor; and again, that agents lend their services solely in order that others may gain possession.

A question might be raised, however, as to whether these precepts are derived from natural reason, or from the law of the Quirites and the Imperial Regulations of Severus,[d] especially since acceptance of the said

a. See Chap. vi, *supra,* pp. 94 f.; *Institutes,* II. ix, at beg.; *Dig.* I. vi. 1, § 1; *ibid.* XLI. i. 10, § 1; *ibid.* ii. 1, § 5.

b. *Dig.* XLI. i. 20, § 2; *Institutes,* II. ix. 5.

c. *Dig.* XLI. i. 54; *ibid.* ii. 1, § 22; *Code,* IV. xxvii. 2; *ibid.* II. xix. 23; *Dig.* XLI. ii. 18.

d. *Code,* VII. xxxii. 1.

precepts is apparently classified as a matter of expediency.[a] Nevertheless, in my opinion, they undoubtedly proceed from the law of nations. [59′] This conclusion is supported by the very weighty argument that the situation is different in the case of civil acquisitions, such as those effected through *stipulationes* [verbal contracts], which cannot be made in another person's name.[b] Moreover, Modestinus[c] subtly calls attention to this difference, saying: "That which is acquired *by a natural process*—possession, for instance—may be acquired through the agency of any person, *provided that we wish* to obtain it."

But there are also other questions which were subjects of dispute among the ancient writers on law,[d] for example: "To what extent is such possession acquired when we ourselves are ignorant of the transaction?" "To what extent will usucapion take place with knowledge as an added factor?" Severus[e] propounded a rule to cover these points, too, and based his ruling (as he himself explains) not upon [public] expediency alone but also upon jurisprudence. As we intimated at the outset,[f] possession is derived from a twofold source, mental and physical: it should have its origin in the mind of the agent, and therefore it is not acquired under the rules of nature by an infant of tender age, by an insane person, or by any person who does not will to acquire it;[g] but the body must serve the mind, if possession is to be taken by a natural process, although this service is not necessarily rendered by one's own body. Paulus,[h] in his collection of accepted opinions, makes the following statement: "We acquire possession by means of the mind and the body: through our own minds, in every case, and through our own bodies or those of others." But another person's body will adapt itself to the service of our

a. *Code,* VII. xxxii. 8; *Dig.* XIII. vii. 11, § 1; Paulus, *Sententiarum Receptarum,* V. ii, at beg.

b. *Dig.* XLIV. vii. 11; *ibid.* XLV. i. 38, § 17; *Code,* IV. xxvii. 1.

c. *Dig.* XLI. i. 53.

d. *Dig.* XLI. ii. 1; *ibid.* 34, § 1.

e. *Code,* IV. xxvii. 1 [VII. xxxii. 1].

f. See discussion of Law II, Chap. ii, *supra,* pp. 23–25; add *Dig.* XLI. ii. 8.

g. *Dig.* XLI. ii. 1, §§ 3 and 20.

h. *Sententiarum Receptarum,* V. ii.

minds only if the mind of that other person assents; that is to say, his mind must have accepted our command.[a] This is the interpretation which should be given to the assertions that one can do through another that which one has power to do directly, and that he who has acted through another is regarded as occupying exactly the same position as if he had acted in his own person.[b] For Nature, who has bound men together in such close fellowship, undoubtedly permits the adoption of a procedure which is even necessary at times because of infirmity or absence, namely, the procedure whereby one man acts through another, although the latter may be a free individual. Accordingly, in order that another person may acquire possession for us, this one requirement must be met: that he shall be directing his efforts solely to our service. In fact, these are the very words used by Paulus.[c]

Furthermore, in cases where we have all the other attributes necessary to constitute ownership and where only possession is lacking, we [60] acquire the status of owners simultaneously with that indirect acquisition of possession. This fact is stated in the laws,[d] and is confirmed by examples based upon the sale or donation of property [through an agent of the new owner].[e] Hence it follows that whenever possession alone is needed to produce ownership, one becomes an owner through the agency of others far more easily than would otherwise be possible. Thus in the Olympic Games, those persons who had sent the victors to the contest found their own names recorded in the inscriptions and became the owners of the prizes. So it is, too, that whatever is taken by fowlers, fishermen, hunters, and pearl-fishers straightway becomes our own, if the said persons have been hired or induced in any other way to devote their labours solely to our interest;[f] for this is a different matter from a

a. Chap. v, *supra,* pp. 89 f., and in discussion of Concl. VI, Art. III, *supra,* pp. 114–21.

b. *Sext,* V, ult., reg. 68, 72; see also discussion of Law X, Chap. ii, *supra,* p. 44.

c. *Dig.* XLI. ii. 1, § 20.

d. *Code,* VII. xxxii. 8.

e. *Dig.* XLI. ii. 42, § 1; *ibid.* i. 20, § 2; *ibid.* XXXIX. v. 13.

f. *Dig.* XIX. i. 11–12.

sale based upon a future contingency, inasmuch as contracts do not in themselves suffice to transfer ownership.

The same inference follows even more certainly in the case of deeds of war, since things seized by means of such deeds are seized either on behalf of the captors or on behalf of the person who undertook the war. If the seizure is made for the initiator of the war, the captors lack that intent without which one cannot have possession.[a] On the other hand, if it is made on behalf of the captors themselves, the latter have no personal cause for action against the adversary, so that the result will be, not acquisition, but rapine or theft. For we have already concluded that seizure of spoil is not permissible without cause based upon a debt. Moreover, the story of Abraham,[b] handed down from that age in which the law of nature prevailed in all its purity, supplies a noteworthy argument in support of our inference, namely, the statement made by that holy man acknowledging as his own both the portion of the spoil given by him to his attendants and the portion he might choose to distribute among his allies; for Abraham declared that, with the exception of those portions, nothing would be acquired *by him.*

Conclusion IX, Article I, Part I

Therefore, in so far as primary rights are concerned, *in a private war, the spoils are acquired* neither by subjects nor by allies, but *by the principal author of the war himself, up to the point where his rightful claim has been satisfied.*

New explanation

On the other hand, every individual is invested with power over his own property,[c] so that it is proper for any person to transfer a right of ownership already possessed by him, or even one that he is destined to possess in the future. For I may licitly transfer something that is not yet mine, with reference to that future contingency which will make it mine. Furthermore, the party to whom such property has been transferred may take possession in my name, as a deputy; and this very act of possession,

a. *Dig.* XLI. ii. 1, § 20.
b. *Genesis,* xiv, at end.
c. See discussion of Rule III, Chap. ii, *supra,* p. 34; *Institutes,* II. i. 40.

supported by my assent, will acquire the force of a delivery of property, just as it does when one person delivers to another, either as a gift or as a purchase,[7] something already freely loaned for the use of that other person.[a] Thus the said deputy will at first possess the property in my name; but later, he will come to possess it through me, for himself. It is in this way that we pay creditors through our own debtors; and when such a transaction takes place, two processes of acquisition are involved in actual fact, although one of them (as Ulpian[b] explained) is concealed by the rapidity with which the two acts merge into each other. This is the method to which we refer, in connexion with Roman law, as *brevi manu*[c] [immediate or fictitious delivery]. Therefore, just as it is permissible, after the spoil has become my property, that I should transfer that property to another as a gift or pay a debt with it or alienate it in any way whatsoever, so also it is permissible for me to give another person spoil that is to be acquired in my name. When this happens, the order of events is such that the spoil comes to me through the efforts of that other individual, but is not destined to remain in my possession [60′] for a single moment, since it will pass instantly to him as to one who has present possession and still earlier grounds for ownership.

For these reasons, we have said that the person undertaking the war becomes primarily and directly owner of the spoil, unless he has previously made an agreement to the contrary. For either he himself becomes the owner, *or else that person does so, to whom he assigned in advance the spoil that was to be acquired.*

Conclusion IX, Article I, Part II

a. *Institutes,* II. i. 44.
b. *Dig.* XXIV. i. 3, § 12.
c. *Dig.* XXIII. iii. 43.

7. *Mutuo,* which refers properly to a loan for purposes of consumption, made subject to an agreement providing for equivalent compensation. The passage cited here from the *Institutes,* however, clearly refers to cases in which "anyone has *sold* or given to you, something already freely loaned . . . to you"; and even in Grotius's statement, the translation of *mutuo* as "loan" would be somewhat confusing. Hence the translator assumes that Grotius meant to stress the idea of payment implicit in this term.

New explanation

The next division of our discussion relates to acquisition of spoil in public warfare. In this connexion, indeed, it behoves us to exercise all the more care for our own part, because the jurists of a comparatively recent date, following the interpreters of canon law, classify items derived from custom (and from a form of custom, too, that is by no means universal) under the head of the primary law of nations. Moreover, these jurists develop their argument in so distorted a fashion that, even after repeatedly reading (in the Roman *Corpus* of civil law) that captured goods become the property of the captors and (in canon law) that spoil is distributed according to the will of the state, they arrive, one after another, at the same conclusion,[a] namely: captured goods become first the property of the individuals who seize them, but must nevertheless be given over to the leader, who shall distribute them among the soldiers.

Certainly this view is founded upon no rational basis. For we have already explained that those individual captors have no [personal] case [against the enemy], and are therefore unable to make acquisitions in public warfare just as they are unable to do so in private warfare, since the same considerations hold good in both cases. In the first place, inasmuch as the losses and expenses sustained by subjects and allies are the concern of the state that undertakes the war (a point which we have made elsewhere and which will presently be more fully elucidated), the equivalent of these losses and expenses must be deducted from the spoil as a claim of fundamental importance. Furthermore, the state should be given preference over other claimants in regard to every right that it possesses against the enemy, both because the state has exercised vigilance, and because it is a universal rule, accepted not without reason, that the public treasury shall possess *πρωτοπραξίαν*, "the right to be first in exacting repayment," above all in connexion with the crime of high treason. For the iniquitous conduct of a state that disturbs the peace and public order of another and innocent state may be likened to treason.

a. Bartolus, *On Dig.* XLIX. xv. 28; Alexander of Imola, and Jason, *On Dig.* XLI. ii. 1; Angelus de Ubaldis, *On Institutes,* II. i. 17; Panormitanus, *On Decretals,* II. xxiv. 29, n. 7; Thomas Grammaticus, *Decisiones Neapolitani,* lxxi. 17; Laudensis, Qu. 4.

A paradoxical contention

On the basis of the foregoing observations we shall formulate a new opinion, as follows: things captured in a public war become the property of the state undertaking the war, up to the point where the [61] said state shall have received satisfaction. But why should I describe this opinion as "new"? In the writings of Isidore,[a] among other fragments handed down by him from a more learned age, we find a statement to the effect that these two items fall under military law:[8] the disposition of spoils in accordance with the qualifications and exertions of the persons involved, and also the matter of the prince's portion. If we pause to examine this statement, we shall see clearly that the right herein described is not τὸ τῶν συναλλαγμάτων διορθωτικόν, that is to say, not the right underlying transactions governed by a regard for quantitative equality,[9] but τὸ διανεμητικόν,[b] [a distributive concept,] which underlies distribution governed by a proportional rather than by a quantitative principle, or in other words, by the principle of geometric equality.[c] We have described[d] the latter of these two concepts as the work of distributive justice, and the former as the work of compensatory justice. Now, this distributive right, as it is called, has no existence founded upon the interrelationship of the individual parts to one another, nor does it flow from the parts to the whole; on the contrary, it flows from the whole to the parts, which differ in their worth and in their relation to the whole.[e] Consequently, the right in question has a bearing only upon those matters which are general, or public. From this explanation, we may infer that in the natural order spoil seized in public warfare is public property,

a. *Etymologies,* V. vii, cited in *Decretum,* I. i. 10, and see Gloss thereon.

b. See Arist., *Nic. Ethics,* V. v–vii [V. ii. 12–13, V. iv. 2].

c. Th. Aq. II-II, qu. 61, arts. 1 ff.

d. Chap. i [ii], before Law V, *supra,* pp. 28 f.

e. See Glossators, *On Decretum,* II. xii. 2. 25 ff.

8. Various items not mentioned here by Grotius are included in Isidore's definition of *ius militare,* which is considerably broader than the modern definition of "military law." On the other hand, Isidore's interpretation of the term in question does not cover the entire field included in Grotius's *ius belli* (law of war), so that it has seemed best to translate *ius militare* literally, rather than as the equivalent of *ius belli.*

9. In the Greek, "corrective [i.e. compensatory] transactions."

prior to its distribution. Ambrose[a] takes the same view when he declares it to be a rule of military science "that everything shall be preserved for the king." For when Ambrose uses the term "king," he has reference to the person who represents the state. He adds, however, that part of the acquisitions may justly be given to those who have been of assistance to the community, as a reward for their labours. At the moment, indeed, the reward is not yet ours; but it is a debt owed to us, and it may be paid from any source whatsoever. This is the thought that Scipio had in mind when he said, in the speech addressed to Masinissa, an ally of the Romans:[b] "Syphax has been conquered and captured under the auspices of the Roman People. Therefore, he himself, his wife, his kingdom, his lands and towns, the inhabitants thereof and, in short, everything that formerly belonged to Syphax, are now spoils belonging to the Roman People." Lucius Aemilius, too, as quoted by Livy, clearly declares that, when a city has been captured, the right of decision regarding the spoils rests not with the soldiery but with the commander: that is to say, with the person who has received this right from the state, a point which we shall clarify presently by citing examples.

Nor is there any incompatibility between the theory just [61′] expounded and the well-known maxim[c] that things captured in war become forthwith the property of the captors. For that maxim is quite reconcilable with our opinion that things so captured cease to be enemy property, although the term "captor" should be interpreted as referring to the state, which effects the captures through the agency of others. Certainly, if this last assumption is not acceptable, nothing at all can be acquired for the state through the process of seizing possession,[d] since the whole must rely for that purpose upon the services of the individual parts.

Accordingly, in our discussion of public wars, we shall apply to citizens the same assertions that we applied to children and slaves in dis-

a. *On Abraham,* I. iii [17], cited in *Decretum,* II. xxiii. 5. 25; Gloss thereon; Baldus, *On Code,* VIII. liv. 36.

b. Livy, XXX [xiv. 8–10].

c. *Dig.* XLI. i. 5, § 7; *ibid.* 7; *Institutes,* II. i. 17; *Dig.* XLI. ii. 1, § 1.

d. *Dig.* XLI. ii. 2.

cussing private warfare.[a] For citizens are just as truly subject persons, and in that capacity they are part of the state itself; nor does the fact that they may also be considered as individuals capable of gaining acquisitions for themselves, have any bearing on this point, since the activities involved in a public war proceed from the citizens as such. Moreover, just as a distinction is made between the case of a son who possesses in his own name[b] property acquired with his father's consent through military service,[10] and, on the other hand, the case of a slave owned in common by two or more individuals or in whom some person other than the owner possesses a usufructuary right, or that of a person serving another in good faith,[c, 11] so also in the present connexion we shall be justified in saying that whatever is acquired through the citizens by the command and in the interests of the state is acquired for the state.

As for allies who make acquisitions by command [of the principal belligerent], the statements already applied to them in our analysis of private warfare are equally applicable at this point.

For the rest, there is a single argument that suffices to refute the contentions of those persons who would interpret the maxim concerning things captured in war to mean that, by the primary law of nations, such things become the property of the individual captors. I refer to the fact that this primary law, which may also be called the law of nature, involves no need for a distinction between movable and immovable possessions, in relation to acquisitions. Thus an island rising from the sea becomes the property of him who takes possession, in the same way that pearls

a. See Chap. vi, at end [at beginning], *supra;* Arist., *Politics,* I. ii.

b. *Institutes,* II. ix. 1.

c. *Code,* IV. xxvii. 3; *Dig.* XLI. i. 23, § 3; *ibid.* 10.

10. The passage cited here from the *Institutes* merely brings out the fact that ordinarily, under the old Roman law, property acquired by children still under the control of their ascendants, was acquired for the latter; but the phrase *castrense peculium,* in its primary acceptation, refers to property owned by the child himself under special conditions, as indicated above in the expanded English interpretation of that phrase.

11. That is, property acquired by such slaves or individuals serving in good faith was acquired for the person or persons under whose control the former were acting.

become the property of him who takes them from the ocean.[a] Nevertheless, the fact that lands and cities captured from the enemy are public property and not that of the individuals who seize them, is so clearly established by all historical records and by the categorical [62] pronouncement of Pomponius,[b] that no one has ever ventured to deny it. Therefore, the same conclusion should hold true in regard to other captured goods, save in so far as distinctions have been expressly introduced by a later law,[c] as we shall presently explain.

The assent of all nations and the tradition of all ages serve, too, as additional confirmation of this principle whose truth we have already demonstrated by logic, namely: that rights over spoil reside, not in the individuals who seize it, but in the state; or else in the prince who rules the state, or in the leader who directs the war, to the extent that such rights have been transmitted to the said prince or leader by the state. We know that, among the Hebrews,[d] spoil was brought to the leaders, and was not given over to the individuals who had seized it with their own hands, nor even exclusively to those who had engaged in actual combat; on the contrary, a part was assigned to the army as a whole, a part was given to the people, and yet another part was consecrated in accordance with divine command and accepted custom. Again, has it not been observed that the same practice was followed among the Greeks? Thus Homer[e] wrote:

> ἀλλὰ τὰ μὲν πολίων ἐξεπράθομεν, τὰ δέδασται.
>
> *All things have been apportioned that we seized*
> *In pillaging the towns. . . .*

a. *Institutes,* II. i. 18, 22.

b. *Dig.* XLIX. xv. 20, § 1.

c. See Glossators, *On Dig.* XLIX. xiv. 31; Bartolus, *On Dig.* XLIX. xv. 28; Alexander of Imola and Jason, *On Dig.* XLI. ii. 1; Covarr., *On Sext,* rule *peccatum,* Pt. II, § 11.

d. *Numbers,* xxxi. 27, 31, 47; *Joshua,* vi. 27 [24]; *ibid.* xxii. 7–8; *1 Samuel,* xxx. 22 f.

e. [*Iliad,* I. 125.]

According to the same poet,[a] Achilles spoke as follows of the cities he had captured:

τάων ἐκ πάσεων κειμήλια πολλὰ καὶ ἐσθλὰ
ἐξελόμην, καὶ πάντα φέρων Ἀγαμέμνονι δόσκον
Ἀτρεΐδῃ· ὁ δ' ὄπισθε μένων παρὰ νηυσὶ θοῇσι
δεξάμενος διὰ παῦρα δασάσκετο, πολλὰ δ' ἔχεσκε.

From all of these, much precious spoil we took
With our own hands; but I as victor brought
All things to Atreus' royal son, who stayed
By his swift ships and gave a scanty share
To others, keeping for himself the most.

It was Achilles, too, who addressed these words to Agamemnon:[b]

οὐ γὰρ σοί ποτε ἶσον ἔχω γέρας, ὁππότ' Ἀχαιοί
Τρώων ἐκπέρσωσ' εὖ ναιόμενον πτολίεθρον·

For, if Greek valor sacks a Trojan hold,
My share of spoils will not be like to thine.

And it was likewise on behalf of the state that,

Phoenix and dread Ulysses, chosen guards,
Watched o'er the spoil: treasures from all of Troy,
Brought here from blazing shrines; altars of gods;
Vessels of solid gold, and raiment snatched
From vanquished foes—all these together heaped![c] [62′]

Nor was this custom abandoned in later times: a point which I shall prove by citing only a few celebrated examples. Aristides[d] guarded the spoils from Marathon. After the battle of Plataeae, the Greeks issued a proclamation prohibiting removal by private individuals[e] of any part of the captured goods, which were distributed instead in accordance with

a. [*Ibid.* IX. 330 ff.]
b. [*Iliad,* I. 163 f.]
c. Virgil, *Aeneid,* II. 762 ff.
d. Plutarch, *Aristides* [v. 5].
e. Herodotus, IX [80 ff.].

the deserts of each national group. When Athens had been subdued, Lysander[a] handed over as public property everything that he had taken. If an example from Asiatic practice is sought, you will find that the Trojans were accustomed (so Virgil[b] observes) "to draw lots for the spoils." The power of decision in such matters was vested in the commander. Otherwise Dolon would not have asked Hector for the horses of Achilles, nor would Hector have promised to comply with the request, an incident recorded by both Homer[c] and Euripides.[d] Furthermore, how much fell to the lot of Cyrus, when Asia was conquered, and how much to Alexander?[e] Shall we extend our inquiries to the customs of Africa and the Carthaginians? We know what was acquired by Carthage from the battle of Cannae, after Agrigentum and the other cities were captured.[f]

But the Romans are the most worthy of our attention, among all those peoples whose opinions are heeded in relation to the various branches of law and, most especially, in matters pertaining to the law of war. Nor am I by any means the first[g] to declare that, among the Romans, every kind of spoil, including even movable possessions, was acquired not for the soldier who seized it, and not even for the commander in his own right, but for the Roman People.

This assertion apparently meets with opposition in the statement made by Celsus:[h] "And those enemy possessions which are found among us become, not public property, but the property of the persons who seize them." However, aside from the fact that the entire law of which this statement forms a part, has been so wrenched from its context that one can scarcely ascertain its intended field of application, the words

a. Plutarch, *Lysander* [xvi. 1].

b. [*Aeneid,* IX. 268.]

c. *Iliad,* X [319 ff.].

d. *Rhesus* [181 ff.].

e. Pliny [*Nat. Hist.*], XXXIII. iii; Plutarch, *Alexander* [xxxvi. 1] and Curtius Rufus [*History of Alexander,* V. vi. 20]; Diodorus Siculus, XVII [66 and 71]; Strabo, XV [iii. 6–9].

f. Diodorus Siculus, XIII [90]; Livy, XXIII [xii].

g. See Faber, *Semestria,* II. iii–iv.

h. *Dig.* XLI. i. 51.

themselves certainly indicate that Celsus is speaking, not of enemy goods captured by force, such as we are discussing here, but rather of enemy goods (movables, I believe) which are caught in our own possession at the time when war breaks out. Things of this kind, since they were not acquired at public expense, evidently fall to the lot of the individuals who seize them, after the fashion of ownerless property, though not so much in accordance with the law of nations, as by Roman civil law. That is to say, although the actual title under which Celsus is cited ("Concerning the Acquisition of Property Ownership")[a] pertains [63] properly to the law of nations, nevertheless, a great many items are included under this head which represent a departure from the universal law and which are based on statutes, or on custom, or on accepted opinion. For the title in question embraces both the varying pronouncements of the jurists and the collections of imperial ordinances.

As for that other maxim which has misled the legal commentators—namely, the doctrine that captured goods become the property of the captors[b]—we have already made it quite clear that the said maxim should be understood as referring to the state.[c] Moreover (in my opinion, at least), no interpreter of Roman law could be superior to Dionysius of Halicarnassus;[d] and this most painstaking of writers on Roman history makes the following statement in regard to the laws governing prize and booty: *τὰ ἐκ τῶν πολεμίων λάφυρα, ὅσον ἂν ἡμῖν ὑπάρχῃ τυχεῖν δι᾽ ἀρετὴν, δημόσια εἶναι κελεύει ὁ νόμος, καὶ τοῦτο οὐχ ὅπως τις ἰδιώτης γίνεται κυρίος, ἀλλ᾽ οὔδε αὐτὸς ὁ τῆς δυνάμεως ἡγεμών· ὁ δὲ ταμίας αὐτὰ παραλαβὼν ἀπεμπολεῖ καὶ εἰς δημόσιον ἀναφέρει.* "The law ordains that all spoils whatsoever obtained from the enemy as a result of valor, shall be *public* property, in the sense that neither private individuals nor even the commander of the army himself may become the owners thereof. On the contrary, the quaestor receives

a. *Dig.* XLI. i. 50; *ibid.* 7, § 7; *ibid.* 19; *ibid.* 27, § 1; *ibid.* 16; *Institutes,* II. i. 39.
b. *Dig.* XLI. ii. 18.
c. *Ibid.* i. 7.
d. *Roman Antiquities,* IV [VII. lxiii. 2].

such spoils, and returns to the public purse the proceeds derived [64][12] from their sale." According to Dionysius, these were the words employed by the accusers of Coriolanus. In part, they are true; and in part, swollen into an expression of envy, they exceed the truth. It is true that the owner of the spoil is not the soldier nor the commander, but the Roman People; on the other hand, it is no less true that by Roman law the commander is the steward of the spoil and holds the supreme power of decision in regard to it. Lucius Aemilius is quoted by Livy[a] as saying: "Captured, not surrendered, cities are plundered; and even in the case of captured cities, *the power of decision* rests with *the commander,* not with the soldiers." Thus the commanders occasionally transferred this power, delegating it to others in order that envy might not be aroused (as Camillus,[b] for example, delegated it to the Senate), while on other occasions they retained it for themselves.

We find, moreover, that those who adopted the latter course used their power in diverse ways, according to the varying temper of the times, or their own devotion to fair fame, piety, or ambition.

Those who wished to be regarded as exceedingly virtuous did not touch the spoils, but ordered instead that the quaestor of the Roman People should take possession of that part in which money was included, while the rest should be sold at auction through the quaestor. The money received from such sales constituted what some writers[c] designate as *manubiae.* This money was subsequently transferred by the quaestor to the state treasury, although a public display preceded the transference in cases involving a triumphal celebration. Such was the course followed by Pompey, as described in this statement taken from the works of Vel-

a. XXXVII [xxxii. 12].

b. V [xx].

c. Gellius, XIII. xxiii [xxv].

12. Collotype p. 63′ contains only deleted material which is apparently part of a long deleted passage extending from the bottom of p. 63 through pp. 63′ and 67. In confirmation of this supposition, it may be noted that pp. 63 and 63′ make up the sheet originally numbered "56," while p. 67 was once numbered "57."

The material stricken out by Grotius at this point reappears in substance on other pages of the collotype.

leius Paterculus:[a] "In accordance with Pompey's custom, the money paid by Tigranes was delivered into the hands of the quaestor, and recorded in the public accounts." Similar measures were adopted in connexion with the Parthian war by Marcus Tullius Cicero,[b] who says, in a letter addressed to Sallust: "As for my booty, no one except the city quaestors—in other words, the Roman People—has touched or shall touch a farthing from it." This was the most usual practice under the old Republic, too, whose customs Plautus[c] had in mind, when he wrote:

> Now to the quaestor all this spoil I'll bear
> Without delay. . . .

Again, Plautus[d] describes the captives thus:

> Whom I bought of the quaestors from the spoils.

Moreover, the phrase, "sold under the slave's chaplet," refers to captives of this kind. [64′]

Some other commanders, however, were not in the habit of delivering the spoils to the quaestor. It was their custom to conduct the sales themselves and pay the proceeds into the public treasury, as Dionysius of Halicarnassus clearly implies in the passage following immediately after the one above cited from the accusation against Coriolanus.[13] [64′a] Similarly, we [read][14] that even in very ancient times King Tarquin [sent] booty and captives to Rome after routing the Sabines;[e] and also that,

a. II [xxxvii. 5].

b. *Letters to his Friends,* II. xvii [4].

c. *The Two Bacchises* [1075].

d. *Captives* [34 and 111].

e. Livy, I [xxxvii. 5].

13. It was charged that Coriolanus "neither reported to the quaestor" the prisoners and booty captured from the Antiates, "nor sold them himself and turned over the proceeds to the state treasury," but distributed everything instead among his own friends (*Antiquities,* VII. lxiii. 3).

14. One corner of MS. p. 64′a has been torn away. The bracketed words in this English sentence represent a conjectural restoration of the missing Latin text, based primarily on Grotius's own wording in an almost identical passage deleted by him at the top of p. 64′, and confirmed by the text of the two citations from Livy. Thus *misisse legi*[*mus*] is supplied at the end of line 1, and *propter* at the end of line 2.

[because of] the impoverished condition of the treasury, the Consuls Romilius and Veturius sold the spoils taken from the Aequians, an action viewed with displeasure by the army.[a]

A special inquiry into the subject would be needed, however, before one could ascertain how much each general delivered to the treasury directly and how much through the quaestors, first, as a result of the victories in Italy, and subsequently, as a result of the African, Asiatic, Gallic, and Spanish triumphs; for there is no point that recurs more frequently in the pages of Roman history. Furthermore, it is evident [64′] from those same historical records that the said generals were not necessarily obliged to follow either of the courses mentioned, as their accusers would seem to intimate. For spoil was sometimes offered to the gods, sometimes to persons who had fought in the war, and at other times to other recipients.

Spoil was offered to the gods either in its original form, as in the case of that dedicated by Romulus[b] to Jupiter Feretrius,[15] or else through the money received from its sale, as when Tarquinius Superbus decided to build a temple consecrated to Jupiter on the Capitoline Hill, with the money obtained from the sale of the Pometian booty.[c]

The bestowal of captured goods upon soldiers was, in the eyes of the ancient Romans, an act of ambitious ostentation. For example, Sextus, the son of Tarquinius Superbus, was said to have lavished spoil upon the soldiery (not in Rome, to be sure, but while he was a fugitive in Gabii) in order that he might thus gain power for himself.[d] Appius Claudius,[e] speaking before the Senate, declared that largess of this kind was unusual, prodigal, unfair, and ill-advised.

Now, the spoils that fall to the soldiery are either given by a process of apportionment, or snatched up as plunder. Apportionment may take

a. *Ibid.* III [xxxi. 4]. [Livy]

b. Dionysius of Halicarnassus [*Roman Antiquities*], II [xxxiv].

c. Livy, I [liii. 3].

d. *Ibid.* [liv. 4].

e. *Ibid.* V [xx. 5].

15. "Jupiter the Subduer of Enemies," to whom the arms taken in battle from vanquished generals were frequently offered.

the form of payment of wages, or of reward for merit. Appius Claudius[a] urged that the distribution should be made as payment of wages, if the money received from the spoils could not be allowed to lie in the treasury. The entire procedure involved in such apportionment has been explained by Polybius,[b] as follows: it was customary to send half the army, or less, during each day or each watch period, to collect the booty; and whatever the various individuals found would be gathered together and conveyed to the camp for equitable distribution by the tribunes, those persons also being summoned to receive their share who had stayed to guard the camp, or who had been absent because of ill health or [65 a][16] special duties assigned to them. On some occasions, it was not the actual spoil, but money in the place of spoil, that was given to the soldiers. This latter procedure was usually adopted in the case of triumphal celebrations. I find that the following proportionate system of distribution was in use:[c] a single share for the foot-soldier, a double share for the centurion, a triple share for the cavalryman; or, in some instances, a single share for the foot-soldier, and double for the cavalryman;[d] or again, in other instances, a single share for the foot-soldier, double for the centurion, and four shares for the tribune as well as for the cavalryman;[e] and also, a single share for [sailors who were] naval allies, double for pilots, and four shares for ship's captains.[f] Account was frequently [64′] taken of special merit, however, as when Marcius, because of his valiant conduct, was presented by Postumius with a share of the booty acquired at Corioli.

Whatever the method of apportionment adopted, the supreme commander was permitted to receive ἐξαίρετον, a special honorary share for

a. Livy, V [xx. 5].
b. X [xvi].
c. Livy, XLV [xl].
d. *Ibid.* [xxxiv].
e. Suetonius, *Caesar,* xxxviii and Appian, *Civil Wars,* II [xv. 102].
f. Livy, XLV [xlii].

16. The insertion symbols in the MS. indicate that the slip numbered "65a" was meant to be inserted here on MS. p. 64, rather than at some point on p. 65 as one would infer from the numbering.

himself, of such worth as he might choose. Thus King Tullius [Tarquin?][17] chose for himself Ocrisia of Corniculum.[a] According to Dionysius of Halicarnassus,[b] Fabricius, in his speech before Pyrrhus, made this statement: *ἐκείνων δορυκτήτων ἐξόν μοι λαβεῖν ὁπόσα βουλοίμην*; "It was permissible for me to take as much as I wished, from the spoils that had been seized in the war." Isidore[c] alludes to that same privilege when he says, in his definition of "military law":[18] "[This phase of law] likewise [embraces] the disposition of spoils and a just apportionment thereof in accordance with the *qualifications* and *exertions* of the individuals involved, as well as the matter of *the prince's portion.*" Tarquinius Superbus (so Livy[d] relates) wished not only to be enriched in his own person, but also to soften with spoils the spirit of the common [64′a] people. Servilius,[e] in his speech on behalf of Lucius Paulus, declares that the latter could have made himself rich from the spoils available for distribution. There are some persons,[f] indeed, who prefer that the term

a. Dion. of Hal., *Roman Antiquities,* IV [i].

b. In *Frag.* [*Selections on Embassies,* p. 18].

c. *Etymologies,* V. vii, cited in *Decretum,* I. i. 10.

d. Livy, I [lvii].

e. *Ibid.* XLV [xxxvii].

f. [Pseudo-] Asconius, [*On Cicero's*] *Against Verres,* III [II. i. 59, § 154 = p. 44 verso].

17. According to the passage above cited from Dionysius of Halicarnassus, Ocrisia of Corniculum, widow of Tullius and subsequently mother of his posthumous son, Servius Tullius, was selected from the spoils *by King Tarquin* after the capture of Corniculum by the Romans and the death of her husband in that same battle. There is no indication in Dionysius' account that Ocrisia was chosen on any occasion as a share of the spoils of war by either Tullius or Servius Tullius; yet Grotius repeats this puzzling statement, citing the same source, in his treatise *On the Law of War and Peace* (III. vi. 17. 3). His memory of the account may have been confused, or he may have written "Tullius" for "Tarquin" by a slip of the pen, in the *Commentary,* copying the error inadvertently in the later work.

See also *Harper's Dictionary of Classical Literature and Antiquities* (2d ed.), under "Servius Tullius."

18. Cf. note 8, p. 208, *supra.*

manubiae should be employed to designate this portion pertaining to the supreme commander, rather than in the sense above defined.[19]

Nevertheless, the highest praise has been accorded to the abstinence of those leaders who either waived their own rights and refrained entirely from touching the spoils (the course followed by the aforementioned Fabricius, as well as by Scipio after the conquest of Carthage[a]), or else took only a small portion, as was done by Pompey, whom Cato (quoted in Lucan's work) extols for having contributed [to the state] more than he retained. [64′]

In the process of apportionment, account was sometimes taken [65] of absentees, in accordance with Hebrew custom. Fabius Ambustus ordered this to be done on the occasion of the capture of Anxur.[b] At other times, certain persons who had been present were omitted from the reckoning, as befell the army of Minucius under the dictatorship of Cincinnatus.[c]

It should also be noted that the right to distribute spoils which was invested under the old Republic in the commander-in-chief, was subsequently transferred to other officers. This fact is clearly indicated in a certain passage of the Justinian *Code,*[d] which exempts from the necessity of public registration the movable or automotive goods given to soldiers from captured enemy property, by the said officers, whether on the actual field of battle or wheresoever these soldiers may be found in residence.

[In general,] however, this practice of apportioning [spoils among the soldiers][20] rarely escaped criticism: not because anyone could say that

a. Plutarch, *On Chance* [p. 97 c].
b. Livy, IV [lix].
c. *Ibid.* III [xxix].
d. VIII. liv. 36, § 1.
19. *Supra,* p. 215.
20. At first glance, *Divisio . . . haec* (this apportionment) would seem to refer to the particular method of distribution just mentioned, i.e. distribution of spoils by subordinate officers rather than by the commander-in-chief; but the next few lines of the context clearly show that the phrase must be given a broader interpretation.

Throughout the present discussion of apportionment of spoils, the divisions of Grotius's argument are less well defined than usual, owing perhaps to the numerous deletions and insertions introduced into the MS. at this point.

such a course of conduct exceeded the authority of the supreme commander, but because it presented the appearance of an attempt to acquire private influence through the disposal of public property. Thus accusations were made against Servilius, [Marcius] Coriolanus, Camillus and others,[a] on the ground that they were bestowing largess from public sources upon their own friends and clients. Nevertheless, in some instances, donations of this kind sprang from the most equitable of motives, *ἵνα οἱ συναράμενοι τοῦ ἔργου τὸν τῶν πόνων καρπὸν κομισάμενοι προθύμως ἐπὶ τὰς ἄλλας στρατιὰς ἀπαντῶσιν,*[b][21] "the intention being, that those who had lent themselves to the enterprise in question might be rendered all the more willing, after receiving the fruit of their labours, to engage in new expeditions." Sometimes the soldiers were allowed to take booty by a process of unrestrained pillaging, after a battle or a siege, scattering for that purpose at a given signal. Such methods were rather rare in ancient times, but occasionally they were practised: by Lucius Valerius in the territory of the Aequians,[c] for example; by Quintus Fabius when the Volscians were routed and Ecetra was captured,[d] and quite frequently by other individuals of a later period. This custom, too, is condemned by some persons and defended by others. Those who condemn it maintain that hands greedy for plunder snatch away the rewards earned by valiant warriors, "since it usually comes to pass" (these are the words of Appius Claudius, as quoted by Livy[e]) "that he who is less zealous seizes the spoils, whereas he who excels in valour is wont to seek the chief share of toil and danger."[22] In reply to this contention, Appius'

a. Dion. of Hal. VI [xxx]; *ibid.* VII [lxiii]; Livy V [xxxii].

b. Dion. of Hal. VII [lxiv. 4].

c. *Ibid.* IX [lv].

d. *Ibid.* X [xxi].

e. V [xx].

21. The reference to Dionysius is inadvertently repeated after the Latin translation of this quotation.

22. Grotius deviates here more than he usually does, from the actual language of the author cited. Thus we have not so much a quotation from Livy as a paraphrase of the latter's thought, which could be literally translated as follows: ". . . since it usually comes to pass that, in proportion as a man is wont to seek a leading share in toil and danger, he is slow in seizing spoil."

opponent tells us that,[a] "in every instance, whatever a man has taken from the enemy with his own hands and carried home with him, will be a source of greater satisfaction and rejoicing than any that he might derive from something many times more valuable, received through the decision of another." An additional point to be considered, is the fact that the practice in question sometimes cannot be checked, or can be checked only by exciting the gravest ill will and indignation on the part of the soldiers. We find an early illustration of this difficulty[23] in the storming of Cortuosa:[b] for the tribunes decided too late that the spoils from that city should become the property of the state, [and were unable to take them away from the soldiers for fear of offending the latter]. Another illustration may be drawn from a later period, when the camp of the Galatians was pillaged by the troops of Gaius Helvetius, against his will.[c]

As for my assertion that spoils, or the money derived therefrom, used to be given upon occasion to persons other than soldiers, such grants generally took the form of payment of exact compensation to persons who had furnished contributions for a war. But we should also note that provision was made for public games out of the proceeds from [65′] the spoil, even in the early days when the kings ruled [Rome].[d]

Nor is it only where different wars are involved, that diverse methods of dealing with prize and booty have found favour. On the contrary, it has frequently happened that the spoils taken on a single occasion have been put to a number of uses, distinct from one another with respect both to apportionment and to the classification of the captured property itself. An example relative to apportionment may be drawn from the conduct of Camillus, who devoted a tenth part of the spoils to the ful-

a. *Ibid.* [Dion. of Hal. V. xx]
b. *Ibid.* VI [iv. 9–11].
c. Livy, XXXVIII [xxiii].
d. *Ibid.* I [xxxv].

23. Reading *e*[*ius*] (of this) for the broken word at the end of the collotype line (p. 65, l. 8 from bottom). On this page, as on many others, small portions of various words have been lost where the collotype page is worn away at the margin, although in most cases there is no doubt as to the letter or letters which should be supplied.

filment of his vow to Apollo,[a] in imitation of the Greek custom. [As for the question of classification,] the various kinds of spoil were grouped, as a rule, in the following manner: captured persons; herds and flocks, properly designated in Greek as λεία, ["pillageable property," especially cattle as contrasted with human captives]; money, and, finally, other movable goods, whether valuable or of comparatively little worth. Examples [of varying procedure based upon this system of classification] are easily found in the records of every historical period. Quintus Fabius, after defeating the Volscians, ordered that the cattle and [other saleable] spoils should be sold through the quaestor, while he himself delivered to the public treasury the money that had been seized;[b] but that same Fabius, when the Volscians and Aequians had been completely subdued, gave the captives (with the exception of the Tusculans)[c] to the soldiery, and allowed human beings and cattle to be seized as booty in the territory of Ecetra. On the occasion of the capture of Antium, Lucius Cornelius handed over the gold, silver, and copper to the treasury,[d] sold the captives and various other spoils through the agency of the quaestor, and gave to the soldiers those articles which were in the form of food or clothing. Similar to this was the plan adopted by Cincinnatus,[e] when he took Corbio, a town of the Aequians; for he sent the more valuable portion of the booty to Rome and divided what was left among the different companies. Camillus, when the Faliscans and Capenates had been routed,[f] brought back the greater part of the spoils to the quaestor and granted a much smaller share to the soldiers. That same dictator, after the conquest of Veii, gave nothing into the possession of the state save the money from the sale of captives. When the Etruscans had been vanquished and the captives taken on that occasion had been sold, he repaid the matrons out of the proceeds for the gold that they had contributed; and he also set up in the Capitoline temple three golden libation saucers.

a. *Ibid.* V [xxiii]. [Livy]
b. Dion. of Hal. VIII [lxxxii].
c. *Ibid.* X [xxi].
d. *Ibid.*
e. *Ibid.* [xxv].
f. Livy, V [xix, xxii].

Fabricius, after subduing the Lucanians, Bruttians, and Samnites,[a] enriched the soldiers, compensated the citizens for their contributions and turned four hundred talents in to the treasury. Quintus Fulvius[b] and Appius Claudius, on the occasion when Hanno's camp was captured, sold and divided the spoils, bestowing rewards upon those whose services had been outstanding. When Lamia was taken, Acilius apportioned a part of the booty, and sold a part.[c] After the Galatians had been conquered and the arms of the enemy burned in accordance with a Roman superstition, Gnaeus Manlius ordered that all should join in bringing together the remainder of the spoils:[d] a part of what was thus collected (the part destined for the public treasury) he sold, and the rest he divided among the soldiers, taking care that the division should be as equitable as possible. When Perseus was defeated, Paulus[e] gave the spoils of the conquered army to the infantry, and those taken from the surrounding country-side to the cavalry. Subsequently, when the entire war had been brought to a conclusion and immediately after the triumphal procession, he handed over to the treasury the money of the fallen king.

In view of the facts above set forth, it is apparent that spoils of war were public property according to Roman law, and that persons in high command were allowed to apportion such spoils, subject always to the understanding that they would be held liable under the laws if it should be said that they had fraudulently turned to their own advantage the authority with which they had been entrusted. This interpretation is clearly confirmed by the case of Lucius Scipio, who was tried for [66] "peculation," and convicted (so Valerius Maximus[f] tells us) of having received in silver four hundred and eighty pounds more than he turned in to the treasury. Similar confirmation is afforded by the above-mentioned instances in which certain persons were charged with distri-

a. Dion. of Hal., *Frag.* [*Selections on Embassies,* p. 18].
b. Livy, XXV [xiv].
c. *Ibid.* XXXVII [v].
d. *Ibid.* XXXVIII [xxiii].
e. *Ibid.* XLIV [xlv].
f. V. iii [2] and Livy, XLV [XXXVIII. lv. 5].

bution of largess for ambitious ends. According to Aulus Gellius,[a] Marcus Cato, in his oration *On Division of Spoils among Soldiers,* also complained vehemently and with eloquence of unpunished "peculation" and lawlessness. From that oration, Gellius[b] quotes the following statement: "Those who are guilty of private thefts pass their lives in fetters and shackles; *public thieves* pass theirs garbed in purple and gold." On another occasion, the same orator spoke of himself as marvelling "that any person should dare to set up among his household furnishings, statues which had been taken in war." Cicero[c] likewise added fuel to the ill will aroused by Verres' peculation, when he charged that Verres had carried off a statue, and one, moreover, which had been taken from the spoils of the enemy.

Soldiers who had failed to turn in their booty were also held for peculation, in precisely the same manner as their commanders. For all alike were bound (as Polybius[d] testifies) by an oath to the following effect: *περὶ τοῦ μηδένα νοσφίζεσθαι μηδὲν τῶν ἐκ τῆς διαρπαγῆς, ἀλλὰ τηρεῖν τὴν πίστιν κατὰ τὸν ὅρκον*; "that no one would purloin any part of the spoils, but each would keep faith in scrupulous observance of the oath." Perhaps we have here the source of the formal oath recorded by Gellius,[e] whereby soldiers are prohibited, while within the territory occupied by the army or lying within a range of ten miles from the army, from carrying off anything worth more than one sesterce; and whereby, in the event that they do carry off any such article, they are commanded to bring it to the consul or make public confession regarding the matter within the next three days.[24]

The foregoing formula enables us to understand the words of Modestinus:[f] "He who has pilfered spoils from the enemy, is liable to a

a. XI. xviii.
b. Priscian [*Institutiones Grammaticae*], VII [xix. 95], citing Gellius.
c. *Against Verres,* VI [IV. xli. 88].
d. X [xvi. 6].
e. XVI. iv.
f. *Dig.* XLVIII. xiii. 13.

24. The oath also provides for a third alternative, not mentioned by Grotius: restoration of the purloined article to the person thought to be its rightful owner.

charge of peculation." Even from the evidence contained in that one statement, our teachers of law should have deduced the tenet that spoils are essentially public property; for peculation can occur only in connexion with public or sacred or religious matters.[a] Thus the Romans were in complete agreement with the Greeks and with other peoples, in regard to this point. Therefore, since all nations agree in classifying the [67′][25] seizure of spoils under the head of public rather than private rights, that very concept would deserve recognition as an accepted legal principle even if its validity had not been demonstrated on the basis of natural reason. For it has been established by the unanimous opinion of the jurists[b] that, with respect to those things which have not yet been acquired in the name of any owner but which are capable of being acquired by any person whatsoever, the state possesses unrestricted power, so that it may award the things in question to whomsoever it deems most fitting, or may even attach those things to itself. For the right of acquisition involved in such cases is in a sense a common right, and rights held in common pertain to the state. Accordingly, we find that in many localities the rights over fowling, fishing, hunting, treasure troves, abandoned possessions and similar matters have been vested in the state and transferred by the latter to its ruler. Therefore, in an absolute sense, *the state that undertakes a public war acquires the spoils derived therefrom, up to the point where satisfaction has been obtained for the state's own rights.*

Conclusion IX, Article II, Part I

But it is furthermore permissible for the state, no less than for private citizens, to transfer such captured property, whether before or after acquisition. For example, transfer takes place after acquisition when spoils are awarded by the quaestor to a purchaser; or when they are bestowed upon someone as a gift, as they were bestowed upon the priests by David, upon the soldiers by Caesar during his dictatorship, or (a frequent occurrence) upon some general by the state in recognition of valour. Thus lands captured from the enemy were allotted to the veterans through an

a. *Ibid.* 1. [*Dig.* XLVIII. xiii]

b. See Covarr., *On Sext,* rule *peccatum,* Pt. III, § 2, near end.

25. Collotype p. 66′ is entirely blank, and p. 67 contains only deleted matter. Cf. note 12, p. 215, *supra.*

ordinance of Romulus,[a] and this same practice was followed in a later age over a very long period. Before acquisition, the transfer may be made either to a specified or to an unspecified person. For example, it would have been made to a specified person if anyone had purchased the Roman shops from Hannibal [in anticipation of their acquisition by him], as Dolon was promised the horses of Achilles [in anticipation of a Trojan victory]. On the other hand, the fact that spoil may rightfully be donated to an unspecified person who is nevertheless destined to become a specific individual, is evidenced by the custom of the consuls[b] which consisted in flinging forth presents to be acquired by any person who might seize them, even though the consuls themselves did not know what the various individuals would receive, just as the master of a feast prepares food for the guests [without knowing what portion will be consumed by each guest]. Hence we arrive at the following conclusion: either the state becomes the owner of the spoils, *or he to whom the state has transferred acquisition of the spoils, becomes the owner.*

Conclusion IX, Article II, Part II

The latter effect may be produced in either of two ways: through a special concession, or through a permanent legal statute. For it cannot be doubted that the laws create ownership. The said effect arose from a special grant, for instance, whenever men scattered at a given signal [68] to engage in plunder; but a similar result may arise from a legal statute. Nor do these two methods differ in any respect other than the fact that legal precepts are governed by a certain abiding principle,[c] that is to say, the principle of equity.

New explanation

Equity consists in striking a balance between gains and losses. But there are losses of more than one kind, since some befall persons who are unwilling, while others befall persons who are willing. Loss of possessions that have been seized by enemies is suffered involuntarily. We act voluntarily when we give of our labour or riches.

a. *Dig.* VI. i. 15, § 2; *ibid.* XXI. ii. 11; *ibid.* XLI. i. 16; Lampridius, *Alex. Severus* [p. 1006 A].

b. *Institutes,* II. i. 46.

c. Matthaei, Req. 2, p. 5.

Now, it is an established fact that he who employs another to discharge a mandate is responsible to the mandatary for any subsequent loss that occurs not by mere chance but in consequence of the mandate.[a] As regards expenses incurred, there has never been any doubt but that these are recoverable through a judgement based upon the existence of a mandate. In so far as concerns reward for labour expended, it is true that such a reward cannot be exacted under Roman law[b] unless an agreement has been concluded to this effect; but it is owed, none the less, under that law of nature[c] which imposes upon us the obligation of doing good, in our turn, to those who are our benefactors. This assertion is confirmed by the fact that, in many cases where civil action does not lie, mandators are nevertheless compelled, as if by natural equity operating beyond ordinary bounds, to give recompense for work performed. This is the basis of the payments[d] designated as "factorages," *ἑρμηνευτικά* [interpreters' fees], *μήνυτρα* [rewards for information], *φιλάνθρωπα* [gratuities], and by various names. Hence we infer that in other cases, too, it is not an appropriate principle of the law of nations that is lacking for the exaction of compensation, but civil authorization for that purpose. Our inference applies, for example, to those contracts which include no stipulation [providing for recompense] under the law of the Quirites;[26] to sales transacted on a basis of good faith with respect to payment, in Plato's[e] opinion; to unproven thefts, by Spartan custom, and to loans and deposits, among the East Indians of earlier times.[f] Seneca says:[g] "There are many things which do not come under the laws,

a. *Dig.* XVII. ii. 52, § 3; *ibid.* i. 15; Innocent, *On Decretals,* II. xxiv. 29, at end; Syl. on word *bellum,* [Pt.] I. vii. 10 and xi. 2 and xiii; *id.* on word *mandatum,* vi; *Dig.* XVII. I. 12, § 9; *ibid.* 56, § 4; *ibid.* 27, § 4; Laudensis, Qq. 6 and 42; Syl. on word *bellum* [Pt. I] vii. 7 and xiv [and xiii: *Non de expensis*].

b. *Dig.* XVII. i. 1, § 4.

c. *Matthew,* x. 10; see Law VI, Chap. ii, *supra,* p. 29; Seneca, *On Benefits,* VI. xv.

d. *Dig.* L. xiv; *ibid.* XIX. v. 15; *ibid.* L. xiii.

e. *Laws,* XI [p. 915 E]; Arist., *Nic. Ethics,* IX. i.

f. Stobaeus [XLIV. 42].

g. *On Benefits,* V. xxi.

26. I.e. the *ius Quiritium,* or Roman civil law, as opposed to the *ius praetorium,* or equity.

nor do they admit of action in court; and with respect to these things, human custom, which is more forceful than any law, shows us the way." Certainly it is not to be supposed that any person will leave his own affairs in large part neglected while he takes time for the affairs of another entirely gratis, since most men make their living by their daily [68 a] labour.[a] Thus Seneca[b] declares that we owe physicians and teachers a price for their labours, that is to say, compensation for the trouble they take, because they devote their efforts to serving us and put aside their own interests in order to find time for ours. According to Quintilian,[c] similar repayment is both just and necessary in the case of orators, since the actual labour required in their profession and the fact that all their time is given to the affairs of others, are factors which cut them off from every additional means of making money. Nor is the comparison [68] of what is done and what is given, the one with the other, a concept foreign to law.

Accordingly, since friendships rest upon mutual benefits, he who looks after another person's interests binds that other person to himself, under the precepts of nature, by an obligation to make repayment in excess of mere indemnification.[d] This was one reason that moved the Romans to restore goods captured from the enemy to the possession of allies who were the former owners and who recognized such goods as their own;[e] and it was also a reason for the admission of those same allies (stipulated, for example, in the treaty with the inhabitants of Latium) to a share of the spoils that would equal the Roman share.[f] Moreover, a similar interpretation must be given to the words of Ambrose[g] in the passage above cited,[27] where he says: "To be sure, Abraham declared that a part of the spoil was to be given as a reward for labour expended, to

a. *Dig.* XIX. v. 5, §§ 2, 3.

b. *On Benefits,* VI. xv.

c. *Institutes of Oratory,* XII. vii [10].

d. Argument of *Dig.* V. iii. 25, § 11.

e. Livy, IV [xxix] and *ibid.* XXIV [xvi]; see also Chap. iv, near end, *supra,* pp. 86 f.

f. Dion. of Hal. VI [xcv].

g. *On Abraham,* I. iii [17], cited in *Decretum,* II. xxiii. 5. 25.

27. *Supra,* p. 209.

those who had accompanied and aided him, possibly in the capacity of allies." This same principle—namely, that allies and subjects should have a share in the spoils—was in force among God's chosen people at all times, that is to say, from the age of Abraham to the period covered in the Books of Maccabees.[a]

The point thus raised calls for more detailed consideration, particularly in relation to subjects. In this connexion, we maintain that the following fact must be acknowledged: both allies and subjects place the state undertaking the war under obligation to them,[b] not only for [68′] losses and expenses incurred, but also for effort expended. For even though the individual subjects are in duty bound to serve the public weal, nevertheless, the principle of proportional justice[c] decrees that whatever any person expends for the community—whether by donation or by active effort—in excess of his individual obligation, may be reclaimed from the other members of the community: a precept which holds good (so we find) in all communal matters.[d] Nevertheless, subjects differ from allies[e] in one respect, as follows: allies cannot diminish their own rights save through pacts entered into by themselves, whereas the rights of subjects are frequently altered by the laws of the state,[f] since it has been agreed once for all, and confirmed by experience, that private interests should be subordinated to public interests. For this reason, it often happens that subjects do not recover compensation from the state for losses suffered in war. Let us draw some examples illustrating this point from the field of Roman law.

Originally, in the light of the established principle that things captured in war by either belligerent should fall to the lot of the captors,[g]

a. *Genesis,* xiv, at end; *2 Maccabees,* viii. 28, 30; add proof of Art. II, Pt. I, this chap., *supra,* pp. 142–56.

b. Innocent, *On Decretals,* II. xxiv. 29, n. 4; Panormitanus, *ibid.* n. 17; Laudensis, *De Bello,* Qq. 6, 42; Ayala, I. ii. 38, 40 and proof.[28]

c. Vázquez, *Ill. Cont.* vi; *id. Cont. Post.* IV. viii [*Ill. Cont.,* Pt. II, bk. I, chap. viii].

d. *Dig.* XVII. ii. 38, § 1.

e. Syl. on word *bellum* [Pt.] I. vii. 6 and more fully in xiii.

f. See discussion of Rule V, Chap. ii, *supra,* p. 42.

g. Coroll. III, Chap. viii *supra,* p. 181.

28. Grotius inadvertently repeats the reference to Laudensis.

it was generally recognized that a Roman citizen's property, after being seized by the enemy, became the property of the latter; and that it would return *ipso iure,* if recovered from the said enemy, not to the citizen but to the state, owing undoubtedly to its inclusion among the goods of one who was in debt to the state. Thus the Roman People were placed under an apparent obligation to indemnify the despoiled citizen for his loss; but this obligation was annulled on some occasions in order to prevent the public treasury from being depleted (especially in time of war) by excessive disbursements, and on other occasions, in order that no one might be enticed by this facile means of recovery into defending his property less vigorously, thereby increasing the resources of the enemy.

Before long, special cases presented themselves in which it seemed more equitable and more expedient that the state should cede its own rights to the extent of repairing losses on the part of citizens without inflicting loss upon itself, or in other words, to the extent of permitting goods recovered from the enemy to return to their former owners. Here we have the origin of the right of postliminium, a well-known institution of Roman law, although it was not clearly understood by the earliest interpreters. Let us pause to give this concept of postliminium such attention as will suffice for our discussion of spoils. For a disquisition on the subject of postliminium among remote nations, and on human beings who either return or are recaptured in warfare, would be [69] tedious and foreign to our purpose.

The right of postliminium

The Romans maintained that, by postliminium, lands reverted to the original owners.[a] Indeed, some agreement regarding indemnification was necessary in order to encourage men to hold and cultivate their estates, since military operations could not be sustained without natural produce, and since a great many persons would be impelled by threat of danger to abandon their agricultural labours, especially if they were to be deprived of all hope of recovering their estates in the future, after being driven out not in consequence of their own negligence but by the superior force of the enemy. For that is the usual cause, where lands are

New explanation

a. *Dig.* XLIX. xv. 20, § 1.

involved. A different development is observed in connexion with movable property,[a] owing not only to the difficulty of conducting investigations concerning such property, but also to the fact that in unsettled times movable possessions are burdensome rather than useful and sometimes breed timidity and an unwarlike spirit, so that they were designated by those same Romans, not inappropriately, as *impedimenta,* [i.e. impediments, or baggage]. Nevertheless, it was necessary to make an exception regarding movables useful in warfare,[b] such as warships and transports (but not fishing-smacks and pleasure-craft), stallions and mares (but only those broken to the bit, not all stallions and mares), and pack-mules, also.[c] For nothing is more advantageous in warfare than to have close at hand an abundant supply of those articles which the sudden exigencies of war often require. Therefore, it was advisable that the citizens be encouraged to make ready such a supply, and all the more so because things of this kind are frequently lost through no one's fault, as Marcellus[d] observes in regard to horses. On the other hand, it is equally easy to understand why things which could not be lost without shame, such as the arms of a soldier, were properly excluded from the class of movables subject to postliminium.[e] Owing, moreover, to the fact that in the process of commercial exchange, articles which were classified as subject to that right frequently fell into the hands not of their former owners but of persons attached to the same side,[f] the resultant question of "onerous cause," as we term it—that is to say, the question of an equitable settlement between the former owner and the purchaser—had to be settled by providing that the said owner might recover his property by offering to reimburse the purchaser.

Nowadays, of course, not all of these principles are universally observed in precise accordance with the forms established in Roman law.

a. *Dig.* XLIX. xv. 3.

b. *Ibid.* 2; Cicero, *Topics* [viii. 36]; Festus, on word *postliminium,* citing Aelius Gallus [, *Terms which Apply to the Law,* I].

c. See *Dig.* XLIX. xv. 19, at end.

d. *Ibid.* 2.

e. *Ibid.*

f. *Ibid.* 12, § 7.

To mention one example, in most regions, ships are not subject to postliminium, since they revert to their former owners only if the vessels have been recovered immediately, or else prior to their removal into the locality occupied by the enemy, and always after a fee has been tendered to the persons who recaptured them. Thus there is now no difference at all, [in most localities,] between the law regarding ships and the law regarding merchandise, an assertion which may be confirmed by consulting the French and Italian maritime regulations.[a]

To be sure, the above-mentioned remedies were established only with a view to their application *in rem,* so to speak [i.e. to the particular object lost and recaptured]. For it was not provided by Roman law that one should furnish reparations from some other source for losses connected with possessions not restored to one's own side; and the same statement holds good with respect to the present age, save for those occasional extraordinary instances in which certain portions of the spoil yet to be taken are assigned to persons who have suffered loss, and which are in a sense instances of reprisal in the very course of warfare.

On the other hand, rewards for military services cannot be paid [69′] from any other source more expediently than from spoils. For as a result of this method of payment the state is spared all expense, and at the same time the enemy becomes poorer, because soldiers are more eager for every gain if they know that they are making conquests for themselves, also. The spoils are not all allotted in this manner, however, since such an allotment would be excessive; on the contrary, only a specific kind or portion is so assigned, and this is done in accordance with the rule that each individual shall become the owner of that which he himself has taken from the enemy. Thus the uncertain perils of war find compensation in a reward that is likewise uncertain.[b]

Praeda in the strict sense of the term

Whatever falls to the lot of individuals in consequence of such lawful assignments is called *praeda* [private spoils] in a strict sense, and with a special significance attached to a term which in other contexts has a gen-

a. Constitutions of France [in *Code de Henry III*], XX. xiii. 24; *Consolato del Mare,* Chap. 287.

b. See *Dig.* L. vi. 5, § 3.

eral connotation. Varro[a] believes that this term may be traced to a form of *manu pario,* [denoting acquisition by force,] but in my opinion it was more probably derived from [a form of] *praehendendus* [to be seized][29] with an elision of the harsher sounds. Thus the expressions *publicari,* [to be made public property] and *in praeda esse* [to be a part of the private spoils], are mutually opposed.[b]

Now, different states have established different practices in this connexion.

It is generally agreed that lands captured from the enemy are not a part of the private spoils but become, instead, public property.[c] The opposite view seems to prevail in regard to movable and automotive things, for the reason that it is too difficult to recover possession of such things from the individuals holding them.

New explanation Accordingly, the principle laid down by the interpreters of civil and pontifical law as well as by some theologians[d]—namely, that movable articles taken from the enemy become the property of the individuals who seize them—is more pertinent to the present context than to our earlier discussion. For this principle proceeds, not from what we have called the primary law of nations, but rather from positive law, which is made up in large measure of customs. Moreover, the said principle is based, not upon a unanimous agreement that gives it binding force over the various states, but rather from a chance accord, so to speak, which individual

a. *On the Latin Language,* IV [V. 178].

b. *Dig.* XLIX. xv. 20, § 1; *ibid.* 28.

c. See discussion of Art. II, Pt. I, this chap., *supra,* p. 211; and Procopius there cited; Duaren, *On Dig.* XLI. i. 3; Cujas, *Observationes,* XIV. vii [XIX. vii].

d. Glossators, *On Decretals,* II. xxiv. 29; Th. Aq., *De Regimine Principum,* III. ii; Adrian, *On the IV Sentences,* Tr. *De Rest. Aggredior Casus;* Florus, III. iv. 1; John Major, *On the IV Sentences,* Dist. 15, qu. 20; Alph. de Castro, *De Just. Pun. Haeret.* II. i. 14; Tiraqueau, *De Leg. Conn. et de Iure Marit.* I. 46; Covarr., *On Sext,* rule *peccatum,* Pt. II, § 11; Vict., *De Jure Belli,* 51.

29. Presumably from the neuter plural of the gerundive, *praehendenda* ([things] to be seized), which corresponds exactly in its termination to *praeda.* Grotius has *praehendendo* (which could be construed either as a gerund or as a gerundive form), but it is probable that he used the *-o* termination merely as an ablative after the preposition *a.*

peoples are free to repudiate[a] whenever such a step seems advisable. Furthermore, even in cases where the principle is observed, acquisition takes place not directly, but by a process of fictitious delivery.

Nor should this criterion be applied indiscriminately. Spoils are seized either during a raid or in a pitched battle. In referring to these two alternatives, respectively, Italian legal authorities speak of a *correría* [foray], and of *bottino* [plunder].[b] **Correría** **Bottino**

I am of the opinion that movables seized in the course of a raid—that is to say, not by the common valour of the whole army, but [70] by a marauding band—were granted to the individuals who seized them, save in those instances where it is clear that some other action was taken. For the infliction of losses upon the enemy is practically the only purpose of such raids, and besides, any investigation in these circumstances would be difficult. We see, then, that even under Roman law, spoils taken from the enemy in combats between individuals became the property of that individual who was the victor.

But what conclusion shall we adopt in regard to formal battles and the capture of cities by assault? Goods taken from the conquered after the victory has been won in such cases would not seem to fall under the head of "military spoils"[c] [i.e. those assigned to individual soldiers]. The Greeks, when they wished to draw a distinction, referred to these articles as *σκῦλα* [spoils stripped from the enemy]. On the other hand, I find that it is the custom of a great many nations to allot to individuals the goods wrested from the foe in the heat of battle or during assault by storm, and designated by the Greeks as *λάθυρα* [spoils seized by violence]: in other words, goods torn away while

> The fury of the unsheathed sword cannot
> With ease be tempered or restrained. . . .

a. See discussion of Rule VIII, Chap. ii, *supra,* pp. 45–46.

b. Saliceto, *On Code,* VIII. l (li). 12 and others cited by Th. Grammaticus, *Decisiones,* lxxi. 18.

c. Arias, n. 162; Belli, II. xviii. 3–4; Wesenbeck, *On Institutes,* II. i. 17; Doneau, IV. xxi; Syl. on word *bellum,* in beg., from *Summa Rosella* [, Pt. I. i: *Limita etiam*].

Apparently, however, an exception must be made of things which were formerly public rather than private enemy property. Certainly we know that when the Macedonians burst into the camp of Darius after their victory by the river Pyramus, they snatched away a vast quantity of gold and silver, and left only the tent of the king untouched, "so that the victor" (these are the words of Curtius[a]) "might be received in the tent of the vanquished king, in accordance with established custom." At Arbela there were even persons who accused certain soldiers of having conspired, in defiance of custom, to appropriate all the spoils for themselves, leaving nothing to be brought to the general's tent.[b] We note, too, that there existed among the Hebrews a practice similar to the one just mentioned: the placing of the vanquished king's crown upon the head of the victorious king.[c] Again, after the conquest of the Hungarians by Charlemagne, private riches fell to the lot of the soldiers, and royal riches to the public treasury. Under the old Roman régime, however, it was not the custom to abandon the spoils to the soldiery even when a city had been taken by storm, a point very clearly brought out in the words of Lucius Aemilius as recorded by Livy and quoted by us in an earlier part of this chapter.[d] Nevertheless, I do not question the fact that the practice, already begun by the generals as a bestowal of favours, was converted into custom[30] through the licence characteristic of civil wars, which is more indulgent to the soldiers than to their leaders. Consider,

a. III [xi. 23].

b. Plutarch, *Apothegms* [*Moralia, Sayings of Kings and Commanders,* p. 180 C].

c. *2 Samuel,* xii. 30.

d. This Chap. Art. II, Pt. I, *supra,* p. 215 [Livy, XXXVII. xxxii. 12].

30. Although the MS. clearly reads *in consuetudinem,* Hamaker expands the phrase to *in contrariam consuetudinem* (into a contrary custom) without any explanation of his reason for so doing. Possibly he interpreted the preceding *beneficii* as referring to a favour enjoyed by the generals rather than to a favour conferred by them, in which case some such word as *contrariam* would be required, to complete the meaning of the sentence as follows: ". . . the fact that whatever special favour had begun to be enjoyed by the generals, was converted into a [contrary] custom through the licence . . . which grants more to soldiers than to their leaders."

Nevertheless, if we take *beneficii* as a reference to the generals' practice of granting portions of spoil to the soldiers, it is quite unnecessary to amend Grotius's wording here.

for example, the first step taken by Caesar after the battle of Pharsalia, when he handed over Pompey's camp to be plundered by the soldiers, and added:

> Reward must yet be given for our wounds.
> On me it rests to point out this reward;
> I shall not say *"to give"* it, for each man
> Will *give* it *to himself*. . .[a]

In the course of another civil war, the Flavian troops, who had been led to Cremona, conceived the desire to take that rich settlement by assault, despite the fact that night was falling; for the darkness would afford greater licence for plundering, and they feared that otherwise the wealth of the inhabitants would find its way into the purses of the commanders and lieutenants. It is in connexion with this incident that Tacitus[b] records the famous observation that, "the booty from a city taken by storm falls to the soldiery, whereas the booty from a surrendered city falls to the officers." The custom defined in this comment gradually [70′] passed into law. Undoubtedly the transition was motivated by a justifiable fear that soldiers, if they should be denied the right to receive spoils after the battle, might disregard the enemy and burden themselves with booty in the midst of the struggle, a form of avarice which in itself alone has sufficed on many occasions to stand in the way of victory. Thus Suetonius,[c] during the conflict with the Britons, exhorted his men to devote themselves steadfastly to the work of slaughter, unmindful of booty, but appended to this admonition the promise that everything would be given over to them as soon as the victory was won. Other passages of similar import may be found, scattered about in various contexts. According to Procopius,[d] when certain soldiers were claiming for themselves the fields taken from the Vandals, Solomon, the commander of the imperial bodyguard, replied to them by drawing a distinction be-

a. Lucan [*The Civil War*], VII [738 ff.].

b. *Histories,* III [xix].

c. Tacitus, *Annals,* XIV [xxxvi].

d. *Vandalic War,* II [in *History of the Wars,* IV. xiv. 10], cited by Cujas, *Observationes,* XIX. vii.

tween real and movable property. He explained that the latter was conceded to the soldiery, whereas the former was retained by the state, which had nurtured the soldiers and bestowed upon them that title and honourable position, not to the end that they themselves might possess the estates which they had taken from the barbarian insurgents against the majesty of Rome, but rather in order that these estates might be gathered into the public treasury, whence means of subsistence would be derived for those same soldiers and for other persons, too, as the need arose. Among the statements made by Solomon, the following words may be quoted:[a] *ὡς τὰ μὲν ἀνδράποδα καὶ τὰ ἄλλα πάντα χρήματα τοῖς στρατιώταις ἐς λάφυρα ἰέναι οὐκ ἀπεικὸς εἶναι· γῆν μέντοι αὐτὴν βασιλεῖ τε καὶ τῇ ῥωμαίων ἀρχῇ προσήκειν·* "Indeed, it does not seem at all unreasonable that the captives and other [movable] goods should be given as booty to the soldiers; but the land itself belongs to the ruler and empire of the Romans." The belief that this passage points to the existence of a certain universal law to the same effect, is borne out by the very fact (to which we have already alluded) that it was not at all an unheard-of occurrence for lands, also, to be allotted to soldiers, but as an exceptional measure.

Furthermore, all of the concessions in question may be made even when definite compensation has been fixed for the soldier's labour, as if to indicate by means of such concessions that the spoils are an addition to his regular pay, or that he is paid less in cash precisely because of the profit to be derived from the spoils. For, in almost all parts of the world, soldiers' wages are so niggardly that it would be difficult to find anyone attracted to the military mode of life if that hope of extra gain were not offered as an inducement. As matters stand, this one conviction sustains the soldier in his exertions, namely, the assurance that

> . . . in one short hour,
> Comes speedy death, or joyous victory.[b]

a. [Procopius, *ibid.*]
b. Horace, *Satires,* I [i. 7–8].

At the present day, indeed, a part of the spoils is everywhere given to the fighting man who makes the seizure, while a part reverts to the state or is conferred by a grant from the latter upon the leaders in the war, whatsoever their rank, as a reward for their labours. This fact is stated in the laws of all nations, in connexion with both maritime and [71] terrestrial warfare.[a] For example, according to the Spanish Constitutions [or Royal Ordinances],[b] sometimes a fifth part of the booty that has fallen into the hands of the soldier, sometimes a third part, and again, at other times, a half, is owed to the king; and a seventh, or in some instances a tenth, is owed to the leader of the army. In certain cases, it is not merely a fraction of the spoils, but all spoil pertaining to a given class, that is withdrawn: thus, by the aforesaid Spanish laws,[c] warships become the property of the sovereign.

The practice of estimating effort expended and peril undergone, when spoils are apportioned, is matched by the equally or even more justifiable practice of taking into account the expense incurred, whenever a private individual has made expenditures for a public war; and the debt owed by the state for such expenditures cannot be discharged more suitably than by payment out of the spoils. According to Italian custom,[d] when an enemy ship has been captured, one third of the prize falls to the master of the victorious ship, another third to those persons whose goods were on the latter vessel, and yet another third to the men who participated in the battle: that is to say, compensation is given in the first instance for the expense incurred, in the second instance for the risk run, and in the third instance for the labour performed. In regions outside of Italy, moreover, it is an accepted custom that he who has lent a horse to a soldier for a given expedition shall share the booty with that soldier.[e] Among the Spaniards,[f] whatever is acquired in a naval battle becomes

a. See *Instructiones Maritimae Foederatorum Belgicarum Provinciarum,* Art. 22 [in *Groot Placaet-Boeck,* V. viii. 1].

b. *Spanish Constitutions,* IV. xxvi. 2.

c. *Ibid.* XIX. xxvi. 12; *ibid.* XX.

d. *Consolato del Mare,* Chap. 285.

e. Belli, II. v [IV. viii. 8–12].

f. [*Spanish Constitutions*], XIX. xxvi. 2; *ibid.* XIV.

the property of the king, provided that the latter has fully outfitted the ships and supplied the soldiers and sailors with provisions; so that, in such cases, no part of the prize is allotted to the admiral in command. On the other hand, in cases where a ship has not been equipped at royal expense, the victors divide among themselves all that remains after the king and the admiral have been presented with their respective portions. If, then, a given person furnishes the labour for a public war (whether indirectly or through the agency of others), if he makes expenditures from his own resources, if he takes upon himself all the losses and risks, and if he does these things without having been granted any payment from the public purse, that person (according to the unvarying and commonly accepted opinion of all the doctors of law),[a] acquires for himself whatever is taken from the enemy, and acquires it, moreover, in its entirety. In short, since it is unjust (as Paul[b] declares in his *First Epistle to the Corinthians*) στρατεύεσθαί τινα ἰδίοις ὀψωνίοις, in other words, that any person should wage war "at his own charges" (or, to follow the interpretation of [St. Ephraem] the Syrian[31] "at his own expense," that is to say, without hope of compensation, an implication clearly brought out by Paul's illustrative reference to the planter of a vineyard and the feeder of a flock), and since, conversely, it is consistent with natural equity that he who suffers the disadvantageous consequences of any action shall also enjoy its advantageous consequences in accordance with a [71′] tacit agreement, such as that which exists in connexion with a pledge of antichresis, it obviously follows that the state, content to have brought misfortune upon the enemy without cost to itself, will yield its rights over enemy property in favour of the person who for his part took upon

a. Calderinus, *Consilium,* 85; Lupus, *De Bello,* § *Si bene advertas;* Jason, *On Dig.* XXX. i. 9; Franc. a Ripa, *On Dig.* XLI. ii. 1, n. 5; Covarr., *On Sext,* rule *peccatum,* Pt. II, § 11; add Bonfini, *History of Hungary,* IV. v.

b. *1 Corinthians,* ix. 7; add *Matthew,* x. 10.

31. Simply *Syrus* in the Latin; but Grotius is almost certainly referring to the fourth-century saint, Ephraem, born at Nisibis and sometimes known as "the sun of the Syrians." The works of Ephraem include commentaries on both the Old and the New Testaments.

his own shoulders the entire burden for which the state itself should have made provision.

Now, it is unquestionably true, as our legal interpreters[a] maintain, that the common law of war accepted by the majority of nations ought always to be observed, unless some different course of action has been specifically laid down by statute or by pact. For what obstacle precludes the existence of just and lawful pacts in regard to spoil as well as in regard to other matters?[b] Thus the state has the power to take for itself or to allot to others by way of recompense, a certain portion even of those spoils which are captured at private expense and with no payment for soldiers involved, as if a kind of partnership had been established[c] with respect to the said spoils[d] in that the state furnishes the cause while the subject [who bears the expense] furnishes all the other elements required. According to the laws of France, in cases of naval warfare a tenth part is taken out and awarded to the admiral in command, while the remainder is left in the possession of those who bear the expenses; and for this particular regulation there is an additional reason,[e] namely that it is of the greatest importance to the state that as many persons as possible be found to defend the public cause and fit out ships for use against the enemy, with their own resources. Among the Dutch,[f] a fifth part is owed to the state and a tenth part to the admiral, except that nowadays this rule of apportionment holds good only within the circle of the summer solstice, whereas beyond that circle the proportion specified is a thirtieth.

In preceding passages of the present chapter,[g] we have shown that acquisition may be effected either directly or through agents, and we have applied this principle both to private and to public warfare. In sup-

a. Baldus, *On Code,* VIII. xlviii. 4; add Socinus, *On Dig.* XLI. ii. 1; Calderinus, *On Decretals,* I. xxxiv; Th. Grammaticus, *Decisiones,* lxxi. 11; Syl. on word *bellum,* beg. [Pt. I. i: *et secundo bona*].

b. Baldus, *Consilia,* II. 358; argument of *Code,* II. iii. 19.

c. Covarr., *ibid.*

d. Constitutions of France [in *Code de Henry III*], XX. xiv. 1.

e. *Ibid.,* Art. 30.

f. *Instructiones Rei Maritimae,* Art. 22 [in *Groot Placaet-Boeck,* V. viii. 1].

g. In discussion of Art. I, Pt. I, this chap. *supra,* pp. 200–205; Art. II, Pt. I, *supra,* pp. 207–26.

port of our thesis, moreover, we have advanced irrefutable arguments that lead to the following conclusion: if any private individual shall conduct a public war at his own expense, to his own loss, and at the risk of damage to his personal interests,[32] while nevertheless employing for that enterprise the labour of other persons whom he has hired either at a fixed price or by entering into an agreement regarding a portion of the spoils which properly belong to him, the said individual will acquire immediately the goods captured from the enemy through the efforts of those hired assistants. For he has possession through the agents whom he was able to substitute for himself, to be sure, in the actual waging of the war;[a] and cause is supplied to him by the state. In most cases, of course, it is customary to grant certain comparatively trifling articles of spoil to agents: for example, in maritime warfare, to the sailors. The Constitutions [or Imperial Ordinances] of France[b] refer to this procedure as *des-*
Pillage *pouille* [spoliation] or *pillage* [pillage], and make it applicable to clothing as well as to gold and silver of a value not exceeding ten crowns. In some instances, a larger amount is given as a result of custom or on the basis of an agreement with the persons actually engaged in battle.

Corollary Therefore, in accordance with an absolutely indisputable right, *to him who wages a public war at his own expense, to his own loss, and* [*at the*] *risk* [*of damage to his personal interests*],[33] *through the efforts of his own agents, and in the absence of any agreement regarding recompense, all the spoil so taken properly pertains, save in so far as some part thereof is excepted in consequence of a special law or agreement.*

a. Arias, N. 180; Innocent, *On Decretals,* II. xxvii. 18; Belli, II. vi.

b. [In *Code de Henry III*] XX. xiii. 10, 16.

32. *Suarum rerum periculo;* cf. notes 1, p. 190, *supra,* and 33, this page.

33. Simply *periculo;* cf. notes 1, p. 190, *supra,* and 32, this page.

[*Here follows the historical account.*] [72]

CHAPTER XI[1]

Part I. A General Discussion, Which Deals with the Following Items:

Article I. The causes of the war waged by the Dutch against Alba, the Spaniards, Philip, &c.

Article II. The courtesies extended by the Dutch in the course of that war.

Article III. The causes of the war waged by the Dutch against the Portuguese.

Article IV. The courtesies extended by the Dutch to the Portuguese.

Article V. The injuries inflicted by the Portuguese upon the Dutch, throughout Portugal.

Article VI. The injuries inflicted by the Portuguese upon the Dutch, in other, widely distributed localities.

Article VII. The injuries inflicted by the Portuguese upon the Dutch, on the pretext that the latter were entering, for commercial purposes, regions subject to the former.

Article VIII. The same pretext, with special reference to the East Indies.

1. The original heading for this chapter was deleted and replaced by a more detailed arrangement. In the process of emendation, Grotius apparently forgot to restore the transitional phrase *Sequuntur Historica* corresponding to similar phrases marking off certain large divisions of the discussion (at the end of Chapter I and at the beginning of Chapters XII, XIV, and XV), and the main chapter head, *Caput XI.*

Part II. A Discussion of Events in the East Indies, Which Deals with the Following Items:

Article I. False accusations made by the Portuguese against the Dutch.

Article II. Enemies suborned by the Portuguese against the Dutch.

Article III. Fraudulent and perfidious conduct of the Portuguese toward the Dutch.

Article IV. The war was first undertaken by the Portuguese against the Dutch.

Article V. The war waged by the Portuguese against the friends of the Dutch.

Part I, Article I Now that we have set forth in general terms the principles of law involved, let us turn our attention to the facts of the particular case under discussion in order to facilitate consideration of the following questions: Are these facts in conformity with the said legal principles? And, are all the factors required by those principles present in the case?

We do not feel, however, that it is necessary to give an account of every event leading up in one way or another to the seizure in question. That would be an endless task, suitable only in connexion with a strictly historical work. Besides, who is ignorant of the fact that the Dutch have now been at war with the Spanish nation for thirty long years, and more?
In the year 1567 And who does not know that this conflict was begun when Fernando, Duke of Alba, penetrated with a Spanish army into the then peaceful territory of the Low Countries,[2] after he had been sent out as governor

2. *Terram Belgicam,* which might be rendered more literally here as "the Belgian territory." Grotius's conception of the terms *Belgium* and *Belgicis,* however, is quite broad and certainly includes both the Dutch and the Belgian provinces of the Low Countries in most of the passages where these terms appear throughout the *Commentary.* This broad interpretation finds further confirmation in the title of another work by Grotius, the *De Rebus Belgicis,* which consists of "The Annals, and History of the Low-Countrey-Warrs," and is so entitled in the English translation (London, 1665). Consequently, the translator of the *Commentary* has considered it advisable to render the terms in question consistently as "Low Countries," "Lowlanders," &c., despite the fact that a few of Grotius's statements could be applied specifically to the Belgian Provinces and their inhabitants.

of that region by Philip the Second, King of the Spanish realms and sovereign of the said countries?

Relying confidently upon his armed force, and with no pretext other than the occurrence, prior to his arrival, of a disturbance connected with religious questions (a disturbance for which only a very small number of individuals were to blame, as is acknowledged even by those persons who wish to establish the fact that guilt did exist, since the incident took place against the will of the majority of both magistrates and citizens), Alba proceeded to alter the laws, judicial provisions, and system of taxation. He took these measures in contravention of the statutes which the various princes had sworn to observe and which, by striking a rare balance between princely power and liberty, were preserving both the due measure of imperial sovereignty and the foundations of the local state.

The exigencies created by Alba's conduct drove private citizens, first of all, to set in motion a force whereby they might repel force: for their bodies were being dragged away to punishment, their goods were being seized either for the imperial treasury or for payment of tribute in defiance of the domestic laws above mentioned, and they were cut off from every other means of defence. Next, separate municipalities adopted a similar course of action. Shortly thereafter, the States Assembly[3] of Holland (which has been a true commonwealth for all of seven centuries) added its authority to the movement. For it is, of course, a well-known fact that this body was set up in addition to the princes and [72′] governing officials, as a guardian of the rights of the people. Gathered in public assembly, it decreed war against Alba and the Spaniards; and this war, in which other peoples of the Low Countries joined, was continued against the successors of Alba, also, since those successors de- In the year 1572

3. *Ordinum.* The term *Ordines* is variously used in the *Commentary* to refer to the States Assembly of Holland, the States-General of the United Provinces, internal governmental divisions of a larger political community, &c. In most instances, the exact connotation is clearly established by the context, and in such cases expanded translations are introduced into the English version without recourse to brackets or to explanatory footnotes.

manded all that Alba had demanded and penalties for the defensive activities, as well.

It would be too long a story, if we attempted to tell what quantities of blood have been shed from that time on; what plundering on the part of the Spaniards and what expenditures on the opposite side have drained the resources of the Low Countries (expenses so heavy, in fact, that an accurate reckoning would show them to be in excess of those borne by any other people in any age); or, finally, what perfidy characterized the Spaniards whether in the conduct of war or in the simulation of peace. These things can be inferred well enough from the following facts: the Spanish designate as "heretics" all persons who dissent from the See of Rome in regard to any interpretation of Holy Writ or any accepted religious rite, and as "rebels" all persons whatsoever not of the opinion that princes should invariably and without exception be obeyed; and at the same time, rejecting every argument in favour of conciliation or clemency, they openly declare that there is no fellowship of good faith[a] to be observed with heretics or rebels.

King Philip not only failed to defend the peoples commended to his care and refrained from punishing the authors of such injuries in accordance with their deserts, after they returned to Spain, but even rewarded the latter with honours while exerting all the strength at his disposal to crush the former, so that no one could doubt (nor did he himself dissemble the fact) that the war against the Dutch was being waged at his command, under his auspices, and at his expense, wherefore it was evident that he sought to obtain by force of arms a power greater than was legitimate. In view of all these circumstances, that last weapon of downtrodden liberty, expressly provided by the laws of the Low Countries for the purpose of escape from domestic snares, was finally and of necessity put to use. Thus Philip the Second was deprived of his princely power over the countries in question, by a decree of the States-General representative of the more powerful part of that region and comprising peoples excelled by none in their unswerving obedience to princes

In the year 1581

a. See Ayala, I. vi. 11.

throughout the whole period during which it was possible for them to preserve that attitude, or in other words, for many centuries past. This was the beginning of the movement in which oaths were taken in support of the sovereignty of the States-General as against Philip.

In consequence of the fact that the latter not only pursued his warlike course far more vehemently and bitterly than ever, but also sent [73] hired assassins (mingled with the armed forces of the state) against the champions of the laws, the defensive struggle undertaken against him has been carried forward into present times, owing to a justifiable fear of a false peace, against Philip the Third, King of the Spanish realms as son and successor of Philip the Second, and also against Isabella, sister of the present Spanish king, together with her husband, Albert of Austria (for power over the Low Countries was transferred to these two, apparently through a solemn pledge), as well as against all those who are partisans either of Philip or of Isabella and Albert.

Throughout this war, the singularly humane qualities of the Dutch, like their extraordinary fortitude, have been apparent at all times. For, with the most long-suffering patience, they have been content to ward off the violence directed against their very existence and to restore an equal degree of freedom to neighbouring cities, without undertaking any graver action against the enemy. They have also been exceedingly scrupulous in the observance of all war-time commercial rights (if this is an acceptable term) that can exist without endangering the state. Moreover, if at times the implacable ferocity of the enemy compelled the Dutch themselves to be rather severe, in defiance of their natural inclinations, they nevertheless showed themselves ready to make concessions equal to or even surpassing those made by the enemy. The latter, indeed, have invariably set an example of perfidy and cruelty; the Dutch, an example of clemency and good faith. **Article II**

To mention one particular point among others, everyone knows that the situation of the Dutch coast and the assiduity of the natives are such that merchandise is very conveniently transported from all parts of the said coast to all other localities whatsoever, since a natural bent (so to speak) for maritime enterprise characterizes our people, who regard it as the most agreeable of all occupations to aid humanity, while finding a ready means of self-support, through an international exchange of benefits from which no one suffers loss. Not even wars, though they have been waged spiritedly enough in other respects, have destroyed this notably peaceable characteristic. Up to the present time, the conduct of business has evidently been the most important consideration for the Dutch; armed force has been employed only to the extent demanded by necessity. Moreover, pursuing a course similar to that followed in earlier times (so we read)[a] by Timotheus of Athens when he was waging war against the Samians, the Dutch have aided with their supplies not only those persons who were numbered among their adversaries in the Low Countries, but also the very authors of the war, the Spaniards, in their own land of Spain, a practice which was advantageous to our merchants and which at the same time served as a means of saving the Spaniards, on various occasions, from grievous famine. For there is no prohibition against conducting armed conflicts in such a way that certain humane obligations are respected, in accordance with the examples set also in an earlier age by the Corinthians and by the inhabitants of Megara. [73′] Thus Spanish writers,[b] too, have stated that business transactions may be carried on even with enemies, that is to say, on the basis of a compact or a tacit agreement.

Article III In the year 1580 Shortly before the proclamation that deprived Philip the Second of his sovereignty over the Low Countries, he was made King of Lusitania, otherwise known as Portugal. By what right, or on what unjust grounds, this was done is a question of no importance to us; for, once he had been allowed to ascend the throne, the whole Portuguese state acknowledged him as its ruler, just as it now also acknowledges the sovereignty of his son Philip and renders to the latter the honour, tribute, and obedience customarily rendered to kings. From that time forth, the Portuguese be-

a. Arist., *Economics,* II [p. 1350 B].
b. Ayala, I. vii. 2.

gan to adopt toward the Dutch the attitude already taken by the Castilians, Leonese, Aragonese, and all other peoples of Spain, with whom they themselves had become incorporated. Accordingly, since war was being waged between the Dutch, on the one hand, and the King of Spain together with his subjects and all the allies of the Spaniards, on the other hand, it was impossible for the Dutch not to be at war against the Portuguese. This was inevitable, above all, because the taxes contributed by so rich a people had furnished considerable additional support for the war. But it was not merely the money of the Portuguese that was harmful to the Dutch. That dread fleet [the Spanish Armada] which sailed out upon the ocean under the command of the Duke of Medina Sidonia, threatening destruction not only to our own nation but also to our British allies, was made up for the most part of Portuguese ships and Portuguese sailors. Since it would have been unseemly for the Dutch to yield in any way to the enemy, they determined to avenge this affront by dispatching a hostile fleet to make a counter-attack upon Portugal and upon the regions subject to the Portuguese, either in conjunction with the British or independently. Among other measures indicative of this decision, a fleet was sent out under the command of Pieter van der Does, which attacked the island of Santo Tomás and the territory of Brazil in open warfare.

In the year 1588

In the year 1599

Thus the Portuguese conducted themselves as enemies, on the one side, and on the other, the Dutch did likewise; but it still remains for us to ascertain which belligerent has been superior in good faith and humane conduct.

Article IV

Certainly the point made just above—namely, that commerce is not necessarily abolished between enemies—could not be based in any case upon grounds more just than those existing in regard to these peoples, whose chief interests on both sides depend upon [commercial] sailing expeditions, and between whom the practice of commerce had long served as a bond. Let us pause, then, to compare the services which each nation has rendered to the other. [74]

The connexion between these nations is said to be very old. For we are told that the people of the Low Countries already enjoyed great

In the year 1150, approximately[4]

maritime power at a time when a large part of Spain was still subject to the Moors; and that, in consequence of this fact, when certain [Flemish] Crusaders bound for Syria were driven to Iberian shores by a tempest, they attacked Lisbon (a royal stronghold of the Saracens) with their fleet, in compliance with the entreaties of the Portuguese, and handed over that city, after its capture, to Portugal. In recognition of this service, many privileges and immunities, dating back to ancient times, have been accorded to the Lowlanders in Portuguese territory.

In the year 1577, on October 22. Given at Brussels

For their own part, the rulers of the Low Countries, acting in accordance with a widely accepted custom whose purpose was the strengthening of commercial ties, extended their protection to all Portuguese merchants engaged in business with Lowlanders, in order that such merchants might by this authoritative patronage be rendered more secure from every injury. When the situation at home grew unsettled, the States-General of the Low Countries provided documentary ratification of the arrangement in behalf of the Portuguese merchants, with the specific purpose of safeguarding the latter from the adverse treatment that might be accorded them under the pretext of war-time licence. Thus the Portuguese, with their wives, their children, and the other members of their household, were taken under the guardianship of the state, as were their domestic furnishings, merchandise, other possessions and all rights properly pertaining to them, regardless of whether or not they were present in person. For they were empowered to enter, depart from, or remain within the territory of the Low Countries, and to import or export their merchandise, by land or by sea. Orders were even given to all of the military commanders and soldiers, instructing them to safeguard the personal welfare and the goods of Portuguese dwelling in the said territory.

In the year 1581, on June 19, at Amsterdam

Moreover, after the Lowlanders had repudiated the rule of Philip, and the Portuguese, on the other hand, had acknowledged his sovereignty, with the result that the two peoples became enemies, that

4. In reality, the incident to which this note refers (i.e. the expulsion of the Moors from Lisbon) took place in 1145. The band of Crusaders that assisted the Portuguese in the capture of Lisbon was composed of Englishmen, Normans, and Flemings, not of Flemings exclusively.

same States-General (acting at the request of the Portuguese who were residing or doing business in the Low Countries, and moved by the consideration that it was to the interest of the natives that commerce should be cherished in security rather than impeded by war), nevertheless confirmed its earlier rescript and exempted the Portuguese from the laws of war to the extent indicated in the following provision: that all Portuguese who might wish to do so, should without danger to life or property enjoy safe passage to and fro, residence, and the practice of commerce, among the people of the Low Countries. Yet again, when the Portuguese, influenced by their consciousness of the wrongs that their own people were inflicting upon the Dutch, once more grew mistrustful of the rescripts already issued, further confirmation of these orders was obtained, not only by the Portuguese who were living in the Low Countries, but also by those in residence elsewhere. This confirmation was of such a nature that the Portuguese were enabled to carry on trade with the Lowlanders, subject to the authority of the States-General, in safety and even from within Portugal itself, with licence to pass to and fro. The privileges thus granted were to be enjoyed until an interdiction should be issued and for four months following the date of the interdiction. Next, a more liberal interpretation resulted in the inclusion under the rescripts even of those Portuguese who had established a permanent abode in [74′] Antwerp or in some other city of the Low Countries held by the enemy, although such individuals were included subject to the stipulation that persons coming from the said cities into the territory of the States-General for commercial purposes, and similarly those who, in their turn, were conveying merchandise out of this territory into that of the enemy, would be obliged to obtain special permission for transit. In a still later rescript, it was also expressly stated that merchandise could be transported to the Dutch from Brazil. By these measures, provision was made for all Portuguese who wished access to the Dutch from any region whatsoever.

In the year 1588, on February 11, at The Hague

In the year 1592, on July 30, at The Hague

In the year 1600, on October 2, at The Hague

Article V

Quite reasonably and in accordance with their rightful due, so to speak, the Dutch hoped to receive from the Portuguese treatment similar to that accorded the latter by the Dutch themselves, especially in view of the fact that the earliest trial voyages to Portugal had implanted in the voyagers a confident expectation of the same equitable conduct. No one supposed that Philip as ruler of the Portuguese would obstruct the activities of the Dutch any more than, as the enemy of the Dutch, he had obstructed the activities of the Portuguese. While a trustful sense of security was thus attracting a vast number of ships, and while men who had several times been kindly received were not warned away by any recently issued interdiction, nevertheless—in scornful disregard for that consciousness of past benefactions which not even public enmity destroys among men of moderate virtue, as well as for the sacred obligations attached to a tacit covenant—when the abundance of merchandise accumulated was adjudged sufficient to make despoliation worth while, every one of those ships (the property of entirely unsuspecting persons) was seized, in all Iberian ports and particularly in those of Portugal. Subsequently, the Dutch were compelled to pay the highest conceivable prices in order to redeem the vessels seized.

In 1582 and in following years

In view of such costly losses, absolutely ruinous to many of the most firmly established houses, what course could be followed by a populous nation accustomed to supporting itself solely through commercial exchange, other than an attempt to repair those losses by new profits from trade? After a little while, spurred on afresh by the long-suffering disposition already noted and by the hope of recompense, as well as by their confident reliance upon their own recent kindnesses to the [75] Portuguese, the Dutch fell into the old trap. Time after time this pattern of events recurred, owing to the perfidy of the one nation and the candour of the other. Eventually, the Portuguese added new brilliance to their successes by adopting the method of setting snares and committing robberies in alternate years.

Even when the Dutch state had been completely drained of resources in this manner (for there was hardly anyone who did not impute our impoverishment to these acts of violence more than to all the losses suffered through shipwreck), Iberian greed and cruelty remained unsatisfied. For, after a long series of deeds of despoliation, when Philip the Third had finally succeeded to the throne and an incredible multitude of persons was being drawn anew to the practice of commerce, when a

In the year 1598

public promise of free transit had been received from the Archduke Albert and had not yet been revoked (or, in any case, had been revoked too late for notification of the change in intention to be given to the men already approaching by sea), suddenly, by a barbarous edict quite worthy of Mithridates, ships and merchandise were confiscated, the accounts of all agents were examined, and the men themselves (so grave is the crime of extending either kindly services or trust to Spaniards!) were imprisoned and dragged off to punishment, many thousands of them being delivered to the galleys. Indeed, even now Dutchmen would be held on Spanish ships, bound with the same fetters as assassins and robbers, Christians amid Turks and Moors, merchants themselves amid pirates, if that day—so auspicious for the cause of liberty!—which witnessed the battle of Nieuwpoort, had not delivered into our hands Francisco Mendoza, the Aragonese admiral, who was at the time in command of the war. For our citizens, redeemed in exchange for this hostage, returned to the shores of their countrymen, their strength wasted by starvation, chains, and lashes. Some have been released from a miserable servitude by the recent capture of Sluis and of Spinola's ships. For who has not seen that pitiable throng, either when its members were thanking the most honourable States-General for the great kindness that enabled the exhausted victims of so many ills to breathe their last in their own native land rather than under the cruel hands of torturers, or else [75′] when they were pleading, each with his own kinsmen and others bound to him by family ties, that such a crime should under no circumstances be left unavenged? And who has not been affected in some degree by this misery and by these losses? Who does not suffer, in consequence of this barbarous episode, some deprivation either of possessions or of friends? The loss could be estimated accurately at many millions, were it not for the fact that such an estimate would be too low to cover the torture, punishments, and mortal anguish inflicted upon the bodies of free men, injuries which transcend all reckoning.

Some persons will assume that the Portuguese at least conduct themselves less savagely in the colonies and on the islands scattered far and wide among their possessions. For in their native land the commands of **Article VI** a ruler who is close at hand, and the wanton caprice of the magistrates, are perhaps influential factors. But even so, how can a people be guiltless that looks on at and allows such deeds? And whom may we justly punish, if an excuse of this kind is acceptable? To be sure, in foreign parts (that is to say, in regions where one may act with comparative safety), inborn character not totally devoid of humane qualities will manifest itself, giving rise to mutual courtesies and, in short, causing us to do as we would be done by, whenever possible. [In so far as the Portuguese are concerned, however, negative] testimony on this point will be furnished by all Dutchmen who have approached the shores of Portuguese colonies either because they were borne there by violent tempests, or because they sought to do business with the Portuguese in their ignorance of the exceedingly savage conduct characteristic of the latter. For men do not readily believe in the existence of practices which they themselves are incapable of following. I shall mention only a few recent instances of this kind. [75′a]

In the year 1598 On the Ilha do Príncipe, when several of the chief personages from the fleet of Olivier [Van Noort] of Rotterdam (a fleet which has circumnavigated the globe four times) had been sent ashore and were being received with a display of flags of truce on both sides, the Portuguese, after striving unsuccessfully to entice a larger number to the shore, slew three of the men immediately, pursued the others as they fled to the sea, and killed two of these by shooting at the skiff. In the course of the same voyage and in the vicinity of Rio de Janeiro (in Brazil), two men who had been instructed to land were spirited away by means of an ambush which the Portuguese had prepared in advance. Moreover, cannon shots were fired at the ships, severing the ropes and also resulting in the death of one man. At the Doce River, indeed, the Dutch were prevented from even approaching the shore or making use of the fresh water. Nor did a happier fate await those persons who, having set forth under the command of Laurent Becker, fell into Portuguese hands (more to be dreaded than the very rocks that rose on either side), after long tossing on the open sea. For their ship was finally driven into the harbour known as All-Saints' Bay, and was confiscated as prize together with its cargo of

In the year 1599

merchandise, while the men were thrown into chains, a disaster all the more terrifying in view of the fact that several Frenchmen were said to have been hanged on the gallows, four years previously, at that very spot. Neither do the diaries of Van Spielbergen indicate that any gentler treatment at the hands of the Portuguese and their emissaries is to be expected by persons landing, through whatsoever chance, on a certain part [75′] of the African coast. I shall refrain, however, from repeating here the account of these events [in Africa] which are described already in each man's records, inasmuch as I must resume the discussion of matters particularly pertinent to our own subject.

In the year 1601

Article VII

No one is ignorant of the fact that, just as the Castilians claim the greater part of America for themselves, so the Portuguese maintain that the commerce of the Ethiopian, Indian, and Brazilian oceans is peculiarly their own, and that all other persons should be excluded from any share therein. Although in addition to the British, both the French and [76] the Italians, as well as all the peoples most closely connected with these nations, had refrained from making any concession to the Portuguese on this point, the Dutch (who are their enemies and who possess, moreover, tremendous maritime power) did not oppose the claim. To be sure, the injustice of the Portuguese demands was no less evident to the Dutch than to others; but our gentle disposition, which was always concerned with the question of how much we must necessarily do in warfare rather than with how much we might permissibly do, was influenced to a considerable extent, even in favour of our enemies, by memories of the early principate here and of the former fellowship in Portugal. Accordingly, as long as our people were able to derive support from the commerce with Iberian countries, even though this commerce had been attended by grave injuries, we felt that on the whole endurance of such injuries was the course to be followed before, and in preference to, venturing upon some other course that seemed likely to render more difficult the eventual conduct of negotiations for peace.

During ten years and more, this policy of patience was observed. After that period, indeed, when it became apparent that the enemy had entered upon a systematic attempt to subjugate through hunger and want the nation which it had been unable to subjugate by armed force—that is to say, when the Iberian trade that had hitherto constituted our people's principal means of subsistence was cut off—we ourselves gradually began to turn our attention to lengthy voyages, and to distant nations which were known to the Portuguese but not subject to them. In adopting this course of action, however, the Dutch displayed so proper a blend of modesty and goodwill that, to any person examining each of their actions, one by one, it would be sufficiently evident that every step had been determined solely by regard for necessity.

In so far as the Dutch were concerned, meetings upon land and sea were amicable; and the Portuguese were even granted admittance to our ships and banquets. It pleased us to commit none of those acts which are held to be permissible among enemies: colonies were not attacked, ships were not set on fire, and the Portuguese were not even forbidden to come to the same marts of trade. But they were in no sense appeased either by the consideration that necessity was the cause of our voyages, or by the exceedingly peaceful manner in which we conducted our [76′] business. For our chief crime lay in the fact that, instead of being crushed by want, we vied with the Portuguese in seeking those benefits to which nature has given all men free access. Yet, under this sole pretext, the Portuguese madness (for no other term will describe their attitude) flamed out with incredible force against the Dutch, whose inoffensiveness was such that, content to act only in self-defence, they could scarcely be impelled by the most shameful crimes to exact vengeance. This assertion will be borne out by the following account of events, which is admittedly incomplete since it embraces only the principal facts, from which the rest are to be inferred.

In the year 1594

The Dutch, with Bernard of Medemblik as their guide, first undertook to approach that part of Ethiopia, bordering upon the ocean, which we call Guinea. The Portuguese, unwilling to rely upon their own unaided savagery, then persuaded the Africans (who shortly afterwards made a full confession) that robbers had arrived who would carry off the natives into captivity under the pretext of trading. Nor was it by words alone that the Portuguese created a spirit of hostility. They also offered a reward (for the African peoples, too, are open to corruption by this means) amounting to as much as a hundred florins for every person who had slain a Dutchman. Moreover, they taught the natives the trick of adulterating gold, which is a product sought from that locality. Again, when a voyage was made to Cape Corso in the same region, under the leadership of Simon Taye, and a report was circulated to the effect that the local chieftain had come to inspect the ship, the Portuguese bribed [77] other persons to surround and slay certain Dutchmen who had sailed away some distance in a light boat; and this project was carried out. A similar misfortune befell a group of men from Delft who had come to that coast, when an African trader named Votiaeo [?],[5] who enjoyed considerable influence among the Dutch because of frequent commercial dealings with them, was bought over to betray them. Some members of the group were slain; and some were taken as captives to the Portuguese citadel of São Jorge da Mina, a fate rather worse than death, so grievous is the menace of rackings and torments implicit therein. For it is a well-known fact that a Frenchman who had been brought to that same place and subsequently caught in the act of escaping, was placed inside a bronze cannon to be catapulted from it, so that the Portuguese might not fail to imitate Phalaris even in the very instrument of cruelty employed![6]

It also happened at a considerably later date that a small Dutch vessel, betrayed by the winds at a point not far from the same citadel, was unexpectedly attacked and seized by the Portuguese. After the Dutchmen, In the year 1599

5. This reading is based solely upon the appearance of the characters on collotype p. 77, end of l. 3, where the fifth letter is evidently one of the "e"s with a break between the upper and lower parts, so common throughout the MS. The same letter might possibly be interpreted as a "c," on the assumption that the upper stroke was meant as a deletion mark through the following character, which would give us the reading "Votico." Both Hamaker and Damsté interpret the name as "Votica," an interpretation certainly more pleasing to the ear than "Votieao," and possibly based upon historical records not available to the present translator, although it is not borne out by the collotype.

6. A reference to the bronze bull constructed by order of Phalaris, in which condemned persons were roasted alive.

taken by suprise, had leaped into the sea, they were dragged along by means of ropes, although they had been pierced through and through with darts and were already dead; and furthermore, in order that the governor of the citadel might be convinced that this fine deed had really been perpetrated, the heads of some victims were impaled upon stakes, while other heads were given to the barbarians serving as privileged soldiers[7] of the Portuguese, in the hope that these barbaric warriors might thereby be rendered more ferocious in spirit. It is said that they cooked the heads over a fire to draw out the juices, and that they used the skulls for drinking vessels.

But hired hatred did not long avail against the candour of the Dutch; nor did the snares prepared for them avail for long against their foresight. Unwearied by the struggle amid so many perils, even to-day they frequent that coast, bringing no accusation against the Portuguese save by the example of their own good faith.

Nevertheless, to whatsoever land we turn our eyes, in all regions we behold this same savagery on the part of the Portuguese; for a trait that far exceeds the bounds customarily observed between enemies, [77′] does not deserve to be called "enmity." It is clear from the logs kept by the men who made the voyages, that many experiences of the kind just described befell the Dutch in Brazil. We shall refrain from recounting all of those experiences, especially in view of the fact that events in the Orient (that is to say, in the East Indies) will furnish us with a wealth of material for such narrations, of a nature particularly appropriate to our argument.

Article VIII
In the year 1595

Finally, the Dutch undertook to investigate the East Indian regions, a plan as unquestionably just as it was obviously advantageous. For what, pray, are we to think of that attitude which I shall no longer characterize as insane greed for gain, but as envy pure and simple: the fierce insistence that so vast a portion of the world (extending along an immense coastline even from the Arabian Gulf—or rather, if we also take into account other

7. *Beneficiariis,* soldiers exempted from menial duties by the favour of their commanders.

regions, from the Strait of Gibraltar—to the utmost limits of the north, and spreading out to include islands so numerous that no man can reckon them or tell their names), should be dedicated exclusively to promoting the wealth, not to say the luxury, of a single people, while lying in great part neglected and useless, although this same territory would suffice to keep many nations engaged in commerce and supplied with sustenance? What of the fact that, long before the present day, the Venetians carried on trade with the East Indian peoples? What of the fact that even now the Arabs on the one hand, and on the other, the Chinese, are competing for the same trade? Will the Portuguese still dare to refuse to others any share in that which they themselves do not and cannot possess in its entirety?

Another point, too, must be considered in this connexion. At the time in question many East Indian tribes were averse not only to trade with the Portuguese, but even to contact with them and to the very sight of that people. Indeed, the Portuguese are regarded in those regions not as merchants but as foreign robbers, destructive of human liberty and aflame no less with avarice than with lust for dominion, so that no [78] one associates with them any more than is absolutely unavoidable. For when they first came to that part of the world, they established colonies and strongholds, and then (the natives having been insufficiently perceptive as to the ultimate objective of these enterprises), they reduced all nearby territories to a state of slavery. Presently, by participating in the civil wars of the East Indians, wars to a great extent instigated by the Portuguese themselves, the latter acquired a share in the victories; whereupon they turned the power that had been increased through these wiles against the very persons by whose aid they had been rendered victorious. In this manner, stationing their garrisons far and wide, and relying upon their maritime might, they taught the entire region to fear them.

But I prefer to have the reader draw information from the writings of Spaniards, rather than from my own words, regarding the instances of unparalleled treachery, the mangling of women and children belonging to the households of native potentates, the disturbance of [East Indian] kingdoms through the poisonous activities of the Portuguese and the abominable cruelty displayed toward both subject and allied peoples. For I desire testimony to the fact that my purpose in entering upon a discussion of this matter is not the abusive reviling of any nation, but the disclosure of crimes whose cause ought to be publicly revealed. By this means, moreover, I shall acquire the right to claim the indulgence customarily accorded to litigants, when it is held that they are not inflicting an injury in their refutation of testimony advanced against them by an adversary or by other witnesses.

Certainly a great many writers are of the opinion that a comparison of Spanish conduct in America with Portuguese conduct among the East Indians, will show the Spaniards to be much more notable for violence and the Portuguese for perfidy; that is to say, the latter are no less malicious than the former, but the Spaniards are endowed with greater courage and strength. This perfidy, then, was the cause of the hatred felt by the East Indians, and of the voyages undertaken by the Dutch.

From the time of those early voyages until the present day, no deed has been so impious and abominable that these exceedingly avaricious men have not attempted or even accomplished it, with the purpose of driving the Dutch away from the regions in question. For, in that quarter of the globe, the crimes of the Portuguese are more noxious than those committed elsewhere, owing to the fact that they knew themselves to be inferior there in strength and consequently donned the mask of peace and friendship, whereby they were enabled not only to enjoy greater security for themselves, but also to make unexpected attacks, with more severe effects, upon entirely inoffensive persons.

We shall touch briefly upon all of the most serious crimes, dividing them not so much chronologically (although the factor of time will also be taken into account) as according to kind, under certain specific [78′] heads. We maintain that the Portuguese, acting both as a nation and as individuals, defamed the Dutch with false charges and stirred up enmity against them, conduct which resulted in the most hideous disasters; that, in addition, they themselves slew many of our men in cruel and perfidious fashion; and that they also took the lead in resorting to war, both publicly and privately, attacking even the East Indian peoples and ravaging them with fire and sword, because the latter had engaged in negotiations with the Dutch. Furthermore, I solemnly declare that I will not record anything in this connexion that I myself have not found to be confirmed by the clearest testimony.

At first, then, as long as the East Indian tribes were unfamiliar with the character of the Dutch, and as long as the Dutch were unfamiliar with the language of the East Indians, it was assumed, reasonably enough, that nothing would be easier than to block by malicious lies the approach of our people to the Orient. Although these calumnies were very far removed not merely from the truth but even from any resemblance to the truth, it had nevertheless been possible to find credence for them among ignorant peoples who were justifiably timid and distrustful after the advent of the Portuguese to those regions. For it would have been the simplest possible task to bring all Europeans alike into ill repute among men who had seen and endured so much wickedness. The Portuguese—telling their lies in comparative safety before experience intervened, so that they disseminated the report among all the native rulers and kingdoms—made a practice of declaring that pirates had come, whose home was the sea, whose trade was robbery, and who had no peaceful dwelling-place. By way of proof, they would point to the simple garb of the Dutch, whose every adornment consisted of arms or warlike engines. For the Portuguese, partly because foolish baubles are held in high esteem among barbarians and partly because they themselves are naturally vain, affect a luxurious style in dress and furnishings, whereas they take a rather indifferent attitude toward arms, as toward something uncouth. Part II, Article I.

When their calumnies were refuted by the first actual arrival of the Dutch, other lies began to circulate; that is to say, reports that the [79] new-comers were Englishmen, treacherous and thieving persons, of a character as evil as any nurtured upon the earth. Moreover, with the purpose of aggravating the ill will felt by the East Indians and mindful of the fact that many of the coast-dwellers subject to Arabian rulers had joined the ranks of the Mohammedans, the Portuguese attributed to a band of men who were in fact entirely dissimilar from the Chinese, such traits of the latter as are most displeasing to the East Indians [of Mohammedan faith]. For it was charged that the Dutch were a people who revered no sacrosanct authority, being bound neither by religion nor by law, and that they squandered their ill-gotten wealth in a manner by no means less evil than the manner of its acquisition, since they wasted their resources in drunkenness, a vice regarded in those parts as no trifling disgrace. Another charge, odious even to the East Indians and unheard of among the Dutch, was that of perverted lust. In support of this accusation, attention was called to the fact that the Dutch were not accompanied by a train of women, as was customary with the Portuguese, whence it was inferred that the Dutch among themselves regarded nothing as illicit.

After these slanderous statements had also been disproved by direct contact with our men, another accusation was hurled against them, namely, that the country of their origin possessed a very powerful fleet, and that the object underlying their pretended interest in trade was nothing more nor less than the expulsion of the natives (once the territory had been explored) and the establishment of their own sovereignty. It was asserted that the native rulers and peoples would shortly perceive the truth of this charge, unless they appealed in time for an alliance with the Portuguese.

The facts above set forth were revealed in part by documents that were intercepted or voluntarily shown; in part, by the testimony of the nations and rulers who had been deceived.

First Episode in the year 1596

Such was the course that was being pursued by three Portuguese—Francisco de Marez, Batalha, and Pessoa—at the courts of the Rajah of Demak (the sovereign ruler of Java, according to the Portuguese) and of the King of Damma, at the time when the Dutch first came to that region with a fleet of four ships commanded by as many captains. A similar method was being followed even among the inhabitants of Bantam, who were the first of all those peoples to conclude contracts with the Dutch. For in that vicinity, the Portuguese caught at every breath of suspicion. If the exhaustion consequent upon a long voyage, and a climate to which the Dutch were unaccustomed, had thinned the ranks of the sailors, the Portuguese would report that the missing men had been lost in battle while engaged in piracy at sea; or, if purchasing was deferred for seasonal reasons, they declared that even in such circumstances there could be no doubt but that the Dutch had come to plunder and were lying in wait for a favourable opportunity. With this same hope of creating suspicion, Portuguese representatives were sent to all of the Javanese ports—Pessoa to Sidajoe and to Tuban, Batalha to Panaroekan, and others to Japara, Jacatra, and Tandjong-Java—for the purpose of [79′] bringing the Dutch into disrepute and purchasing hostility toward them. Moreover, not content with this one-sided deception, while they were retailing these stories about the Dutch to the Javanese, the Portuguese were also engaged in an unceasing attempt to frighten away the Dutch themselves from commercial undertakings (for access to our men was readily obtainable, and the Portuguese were even received at Dutch banquets) by expatiating upon the treacherous nature of the Javanese peoples.

Second Episode In the year 1599

The merchants held back until reports should have been made regarding the initial ventures; but after the return of the first voyagers from Java, the Dutch began to go to Taprobane (an island famous in very ancient times, which is now called Sumatra),[8] in ships commanded by Cornelis Houtman and dispatched under the auspices of a company established in Zeeland. In the region of Sumatra, Affonso Vicente, a Portuguese, was whispering to the King of Achin lies similar to those already fabricated for the Javanese.

Third Episode In the same year

At the same time, the first voyage of Jacob Van Neck to the Moluccas took place. Nor did the governing authorities of Amboyna (the prefect and other principal personages) conceal the fact that the Portuguese had spread abroad identical lies in that locality. It was during this period, too, that the Portuguese were troubling the mind of the King of Ternate with calumnies of the same sort. The inhabitants of the Island of Great Banda were also being incited, by means of similar accusations, to drive out those Dutchmen who had remained after the departure of the ships. Indeed, this evil practice spread so far in its stealthy course that it reached

8. See note 4, p. 14, *supra*.

and inflamed even the people of Borneo, a fact revealed by the report of the men who accompanied Olivier [Van Noort].

Fourth Episode In the year 1600

Neither were the Portuguese content to lie only once; on the contrary, resort was continually had to the same wiles. For it became evident to the Dutchmen who subsequently remained behind at Achin, in Sumatra, by order of Admiral Wilkens, that the great courtesy and the friendship of the King had been converted by these insulting calumnies into contempt and hatred, so that they found themselves not merely cut off from trade but also in peril of losing their very lives.

Fifth Episode In the same year

Shortly afterwards, when Achin was visited by ships under the command of Pieter Both (an emissary of the later Dutch company), the same stratagems were employed anew at the same Court; that is to say, a Franciscan monk was sent as a so-called legate, together with a captain named Rodrigo da Costa Motamorio, to Malacca, which is a Portuguese colony situated on the mainland opposite Sumatra. [80]

Sixth Episode In the year 1601

Again, letters written to the King of Ternate in the Malaccan language on the occasion of Van Neck's second trip, as well as the instructions given to the messenger and translated by an interpreter, contained similar accusations. Nevertheless, the King—though stricken with sudden fear and looking about, so to speak, for lurking plotters against his realm—was finally and with difficulty placated by entreaties, and dissuaded from handing over the Dutch in their innocence to the ferocity of their enemies.

Among the Chinese, too, what unrestrained and numerous attempts were made, in order to induce that people to turn against the Dutch! But the Chinese, who as a race possess quite acute powers of judgement, even now prefer to rely upon those faculties rather than to believe the Portuguese.

Seventh Episode In the year 1602

No less vainly, at the time of the arrival of Jacob Heemskerck, did the Portuguese strive at the courts of the Queen of Patani and the King of Johore (these are kingdoms on a portion of the mainland which now belongs to Siam but which, in the opinion of some authorities, was formerly part of the Golden Chersonese),[9] to cast suspicion by means of their accusations upon the friendship of the Dutch, which those rulers had most eagerly embraced. The lies of the Portuguese had by now lost their force and had been sufficiently refuted by Time itself, whose daughter (as the ancients quite rightly declared) is Truth.

Moreover, in the light of these facts which by some fortunate chance resisted concealment, may we not assume the existence of any number of similar facts not yet made public?

Article II

Accordingly, no one should think it strange, in view of the added weight lent to these calumnies by bribery, that it was possible to stir up enemies and assassins against the Dutch from a multitude of persons who were deceived or even venal. By this means, the Portuguese succeeded not only in securing peace for themselves and hardships for our men, but also in producing everywhere and simultaneously a state of agitation based upon blind suspicion; so that the Dutch, as a result of the wickedness of a few individuals, sought to avoid whole peoples whom they had esteemed, and were on the point of giving up their East Indian trade permanently because of these difficulties.

First Episode In the year 1596

Indeed, it will be worth our while to give a detailed account of the treachery and snares which the Portuguese were devising on the occasion of the first Dutch landing in Java, at the very time when they were openly professing friendly sentiments toward our people (thus committing the worst sort of injury), were frequently boarding our ships, where they met with a kind reception, and were extending invitations in turn to the Dutch.

The Rajah of Demak, whom I mentioned above, was the ruler of all Java; or, at least, he was proclaimed as its ruler by the Portuguese at that time. Nevertheless, it was reported that he had lost not only supremacy over his domain but also the greater part of his fortune, while wag-

9. *Chersonesus Aurea,* "the Golden Peninsula," was the name used by the ancients for Malacca. In Chapter XII, however (*infra,* p. 335), Grotius remarks that "many persons identify" this region with Japan. Cf. also note 11, p. 335.

ing war against certain petty kings who were withholding their [80′] allegiance. Poverty in a man of noble rank is a fertile source of audacity. Accordingly, the Rajah had provided himself, in compensation for all his losses, with these two things alone: extraordinary skill in the use of arms, in the highest degree possible to a man of that race; and (what is now regarded in that region as the last refuge of desperation) an alliance with the Portuguese, who were then honouring him with the title of Emperor. After bribing him to work for the destruction of the Dutch, the Portuguese had brought him to Bantam, where at the time in question some of our vessels lay. Moreover, they had plotted that the officers of those vessels should be invited to a banquet, so that the Rajah, under pretext of escorting the officers on their way back, might make a sudden attack upon the ships. The chief magistrate, or Regent, of Bantam (for he governs that kingdom in the name of a ward who is his kinsman), whose aid in this undertaking had been requested by the Portuguese, revealed the plot, first of all through a messenger and later in person, to envoys sent from the ships. Nor did the event belie his warnings.

Our men were invited to the entertainment. They excused themselves from attendance. A certain Portuguese named Pedro de Tayde, bound to the Dutch by the ties of honourable and intimate friendship, had withheld his assent from so villainous a deed; and therefore the others, fearing that the stratagem might be divulged through him, sent five of their number to butcher him while he lay unsuspecting at home and in bed. Their wicked plan was not frustrated.

In the meantime, seeing that the plot against the Dutch had failed, they urged the Rajah of Demak to maintain a ready force at his disposal and to fit out a fleet at the town of Jacatra; but the entire outline of this plot, too, was reported through an assistant of the slain de Tayde. This assistant was forcibly seized in Bantam by the Portuguese and cruelly tortured, because he had aided our cause.

The Portuguese were becoming convinced that they would accomplish nothing as long as the Regent of Bantam favoured us, and therefore they approached him with guile and with gifts. Nor was he averse [81] to profit of any sort, an attitude strengthened especially by the hope of acquiring spoils from the Dutch and a reward from the Portuguese through one and the same act.

In the first place, he persuasively solicited Dutch merchandise, carried it off for himself, and postponed until some future time his part in the process of exchange. While the Dutch were hesitating after being commanded to deliver more goods, the Regent summoned to his presence three ship's captains—Houtman, Willem Lodewycksz, and Gilles Valckenier—together with ten other men, and suddenly ordered them to be bound with chains. Not even then did he make a secret of the fact that these things were being done at the request of the Portuguese, who pretended to be afraid that we might intercept their ship in the harbour when she sought to depart. Under this pretext, the Portuguese had entreated that the men above mentioned be detained as hostages, although the Regent also intimated to the captives that the former, by paying a bribe of four thousand *reaes,* were striving to influence him so that they might get those captives into their own hands. Meanwhile, fear of the most horrible torments was daily instilled into the poor wretches. At this very time, however, it so happened that the Javanese, at the instigation of the Portuguese, approached to attack certain light boats and skiffs belonging to the Dutch which had sailed out rather far; and when our men bravely repelled their assailants, the Regent of Bantam, warned by this achievement that the good qualities of such men were not to be despised, undertook to negotiate peace with them. Although the conditions imposed in this connexion were very unjust and involved payment of a ransom of two thousand *reaes* for captives taken without even any shadow of a lawful pretext, they were nevertheless accepted.

But wherever the state of affairs began to improve for us, the Portuguese on that very account increased the rewards offered for treachery. An envoy came from Malacca, bringing to the Regent and other chief personages of Bantam numerous gifts, among which were included six thousand *reaes* intended to purchase the slaughter of the Dutch. A reversal of sentiment immediately resulted: trade with our people was suspended; even the Chinese merchants dwelling in Bantam were forbidden to sell anything to the Hollanders. These signs of enmity were in themselves unmistakable; and at the same time, it was reported by the host of the Dutch in Bantam as well as by other friends that the lives of all our leaders had been sold to the Portuguese. Consequently, when the Regent of Bantam asked the chief men from the ships to visit him, with the pretended purpose of instructing them personally in regard to commercial regulations, not one of them complied with his request. As a result, dissension arose between the Portuguese and the people of Bantam, since the Portuguese demanded the return of the donations [81′] made for a purpose that had not been executed, whereas the Bantamese would not renounce what they had received, regardless of the reasons for which it had been given. Accordingly, a new and different agreement was made, to the following effect: the Regent was to seize the Dutch ships forcibly, with the aid of the Portuguese, and these ships together with their cargoes of merchandise would be allotted to him, while the men would be handed over to the Portuguese; or, in the event that the ships should be destroyed, the Regent would receive, in addition to the six thousand *reaes* paid in advance, an additional two thousand by way of compensation.

As chance would have it, while these conferences concerning the lives of the Dutch were being held, the latter were in the process of withdrawing to another locality (not far from Bantam, to be sure), owing to their need of fresh water; and lo! there came a messenger from their host, reporting that a fleet was being made ready against their ships. Indeed, the Dutch themselves, prior to their departure, had witnessed certain preparations for the construction of such a fleet.[10] Not only was danger thus averted through a stroke of good fortune, but the affair also gave rise to renewed dissension between the Portuguese and the Regent, who was of the opinion that the terms of their agreement did not make it obligatory for him to follow in pursuit of the Dutch after their withdrawal.

When the Hollanders had reached a point near Jacatra, the Portuguese secretly incited Toemenggoeng (a man of Bantam and their close friend) to entice some of the sailors to a place called Tandjong-Java, quite close to Jacatra, under pretence of an intention to sell them provisions; but Chinese merchants had forewarned our men that there were Por-

10. Reading *cuius* for *quarum,* which must have been written inadvertently, since the context calls for the singular antecedent (fleet) rather than the plural ([the Dutch] ships).

tuguese stationed in that locality for the purpose of capturing or slaughtering the sailors. Toemenggoeng himself admitted the truth of this accusation when the Dutch, returning on a second voyage, found the Javanese hostile to the Portuguese and more friendly toward our own people. He excused the attempt, however, on the basis of those earlier disorders.

At Sidajoe, the most atrocious plots were fabricated under the direction of Francisco Pessoa, in the following manner. When the ships had arrived at that point and plans had been drawn up in collaboration with the Shabandar of Sidajoe (the title given to the chief local magistrate),[11] Rasalala [the Rajah of Lalang?][12]—a Portuguese by origin, born in Aveiro, but an apostate from the Christian faith and by no means unrenowned as the leader of the pirates in those regions—issued a report to the effect that spices were ready for purposes of trade and that the King of Sidajoe was disposed to be friendly. The men who were [82] sent to investigate the situation brought back the same account, since the evidence confirmed Rasalala's statement. It was also reported that the King greatly desired to inspect the ships that had sailed to his shores over so vast an expanse of sea. This, too, was a most welcome announcement. Everything was decked out in a manner befitting both the delight felt by the Dutch and the majesty of the King. Sixty proas (that is to say, ships of a special kind) made their appearance, each of them bearing at least sixty men, a spectacle which the Dutch at the moment regarded as a display of royal pomp although, as the outcome proved, it was really a hostile army. Rasalala was sent ahead to ascertain whether

11. More specifically, the Shabandar, or Shabunder, was a harbour master and official in charge of dealings with foreign traders.

12. The uncrossed "t"s in the MS. are practically indistinguishable from the "l"s, and the reading in Hamaker's edition of the *Commentary, Rasalata,* may be correct. Damsté's Dutch translation follows the latter reading, but expands it parenthetically into *Radja Lela.* Some such interpretation is certainly suggested by the similarity between this word and the title *Rasadauma,* used several times in earlier portions of Chapter XI (in the Latin text) to refer to the Rajah of Demak. The present translator, however, is unable to find any other trace of an appropriate locality named *Lela.* Hence the very tentative suggestion that Grotius may be referring here to the Rajah of the island of Lalang, which is situated near the north-eastern coast of Sumatra.

or not our men had detected any hint of hostility, and found that everything was as he wished. He was invited to remain, but refused to do so. Hardly had Rasalala departed, when the Shabandar of Sidajoe boarded one of the ships: the *Amsterdam* by name. As the ship's captain, Reinier Verhell, extended his right hand in welcome, the Shabandar, under cover of a pretended salute (for Egypt is not alone in nourishing Septimii) thrust his dagger into the captain; and at the same time the other conspirators privy to the crime, butchered the unsuspecting and incautious men upon the decks of the ship. Among the slain were Jan Schellinger (a sailor), Gilles Valckenier and nine others, aside from those who were merely wounded because the blows were badly aimed. The ship would have been captured, too, but for the fact that thirteen men (the majority of them only recently recovered from illness) had blocked the way into the lower parts of the vessel and, discharging the artillery, had caused wounds and panic whereby both those assailants who held the upper decks and those who were surrounding the ship's sides were driven into the sea. This, for the time being, saved the situation; and the Portuguese heaped futile reproaches upon the imprudence of the untutored natives whose excessive haste had brought to naught the plans so cunningly laid. Nevertheless, the losses suffered by the Dutch had been so severe that lack of manpower compelled the sailors to abandon the ship, leaving it defenceless.

Second Episode In the year 1599, on September 11

Let us turn now from the Hollanders to the Zeelanders, and from Java to Sumatra, where two ships commanded by the aforementioned Houtman came to port.

The notorious Affonso Vicente, a man whose cunning was [82′] outstandingly malignant even among the Portuguese, was present at the court of Achin. Vicente, as well as certain other Portuguese, gradually insinuated himself into a position of intimacy with Houtman and with Houtman's companions; for he made a show before them of enjoying great favour with the King and of being in a position to promote their interests among the people of Achin by his services as a friendly go-between. So zealously did he simulate this helpful attitude that on several occasions he conducted the Zeelanders to the palace, and even imparted information to them regarding certain plans entertained by the King, presenting it as secret knowledge which he had nevertheless been able to acquire from important personages who had been bribed. In the meantime, he stirred up the merchants who were residing in that region by suggesting, forsooth, that their business was being ruined as a result of the newly increased number of bidders! Vicente also excited the Shabandar Abdullah, the royal scribe Corco, and the King himself by calling attention to the fine ships and the prize so easily to be obtained. He had even devised the following pretext [for seizure of the prize]: the Dutch had decided to seek out the markets of Johore if the prices asked for merchandise [in Sumatra] should prove excessive; but a bitter and violent war was being waged at that time between the King of Johore and the people of Achin; and therefore (so Vicente urged), the ships should be seized before they could serve the enemy's cause. When both avarice and hatred had thus been set aflame, a piece of trickery was arranged.

A small quantity of pepper was delivered to the Zeelanders, and the hope was held out that larger quantities would be provided from day to day. Having asserted that this supply was approaching on their ships of war, the Shabandar and Corco, accompanied by a huge body of men from Achin, and armed without exception, as was the custom among that people, boarded the Dutch vessels under a pretence of engaging in barter. They had brought food and drink mixed with a drug which induces insanity and which the natives call *dutroa.* [13] When the sailors had gorged somewhat greedily on this drug, they suddenly began to run about the gangways and decks, tossing their heads like persons deprived of sense and even like madmen. This seemed to be the moment for carrying out the deeds that had recently been plotted. The Zeelanders, crazed and separated from one another, were slaughtered as if they were cattle. The affair was not a battle, but mere butchery. Overcome simultaneously by dizziness and by wounds, the men breathed their last amid faltering words. For they were surrounded on all sides, too, by the East Indian proas, which had been equipped with arms through Portuguese

13. Evidently a drug taken from the dutra, or *Datura metel,* a narcotic plant of the potato family.

assistance. Finally, the capture was complete, save that a very few Zeelanders, not yet overcome by the fatal banquet, had held out in an attempt both to defend their ships and to lay the savage foe low in his own bloodstained tracks with their artillery. The first ship (known as the [83]
Lion) freed itself from its assailants, assisted in liberating the second ship (named the *Lioness*), which had almost been captured, and advanced in an attack that routed the hitherto victorious men of Achin. Thus the ships were saved. Nevertheless, the sides of the vessels were dripping with the blood of innocent men, and Houtman himself, stabbed by the hand of his guest, was staining the dining-saloon with his own blood. Moreover, the poison was so potent that some of the sailors lay prostrate in a stupor during the days that followed, while others were driven by madness to inflict wounds upon one another. Nor was any gentler treatment accorded to the Dutchmen who were within the city at that time and in the power of the people of Achin, for they were slaughtered under the direction of the King's own son, who had been won over to the Portuguese by gifts and promises. No less than seventy men were lost.

Third Episode
In the year
1600, in April

Shortly afterwards, the King of Tuban, menacingly equipped with fourteen junks (a kind of boat common in the Orient) and fully fifteen hundred men, bore down upon the members of Van Neck's party (including Adriaan Veen) who had remained behind upon the island of Banda; for he had been bribed to deprive them of their arms or even put them to death. Nor is there any doubt that the party would have perished, if Divine Providence had not guided newly arrived Dutch vessels, the *Luna* and the *Lucifer,* to that very island at precisely the opportune time.

Fourth
Episode
In the same
year

In compliance with a command received from the above-mentioned ruler of Tuban and from the Portuguese, the aforesaid Rasalala, who had grown famous through his robberies, had gone to almost all of the Moluccas accompanied by soldiers from Tuban and by twenty Portuguese officers, with the purpose of driving the Dutch traders from the entire region. This was the report obtained from Sarcius Maluca and from the Regent of Bantam, by the men who had set out with Wilkens. Certainly that pirate sailed from those parts with approximately forty proas directly to Java, where (so he had been given to understand) the Dutch vessels had come into port; for he was bound by an oath to capture or destroy any such vessel [that he could find]. With this end in view, he was soliciting aid in the name of the King of Tuban from the Regent of Bantam himself. From Java, Rasalala went on to Jacatra, with the intention of seizing such opportunities as might be propitious for the setting of his snares.

Still more grave was the peril threatening those voyagers who had come to the Royal Court at Achin, accompanying Van Neck on his second trip. By taking a hasty departure, however, the men who had remained in Achin prevented the success of the deceitful Portuguese plot.

Fifth Episode In the same year

Of course, it would not have sufficed to dispatch foreigners against the Dutch without also seeking an assassin on board their own vessels! A ship from Both's fleet, under the command of Van Caerden and De Vlamingh, lay at anchor off Achin; and in the same locality there [83′] was a Portuguese ship commanded by the aforementioned Rodrigo da Costa Motamorio. The gunner of the latter vessel, a man from Hamburg called Mattys Nieu, had discussed quite frequently with the captain of the watch and with Jan, the gunner of the *Henry,* as well as with the pilot and the under-pilot, a plan to slay the officers in command of the Dutch vessel (after admitting as members of the criminal conspiracy such persons as might be found suitable) and to take the ship itself to Malacca. Nieu promised that there would be a reward of not less than two thousand ducats for each man. But the good faith characteristic of the Dutch thwarted this treacherous undertaking.

Sixth Episode In the year 1601, in January

Again, while two ships—the *Leyden* and the *Harlem* by name—under the command of Van Groesbergen (an emissary of the second Dutch Company, who had set sail at the same time as Van Neck) lay anchored in the waters of Cochin China at Sinceon, that is to say, near the Polocambares River, the inhabitants of that region and their King himself set a trap for the Dutch vessels. This was done at the instigation of a

Seventh Episode In the year 1602

Portuguese monk and because of his false accusations, as the King later confessed. The assailants seized and stabbed a score or more of Dutchmen, reduced twelve others to a state of illness and insanity with a beverage of poisoned arrack, and led six away into captivity. Moreover, the latter were not by any means men from the lowest class of sailors, and it was necessary to ransom them at the cost of two cannon and some merchandise.

Eighth Episode In the same year Yet again, upon the arrival in those parts, not long afterwards, of that Jacob Heemskerck to whose valour we owe the vengeance and the prize now under discussion, the King of Damma, a friend and ally of the Portuguese nation (as was evident from the outset), voluntarily offered the new-comer his services and an opportunity to trade in his kingdom, where a great quantity of rice is produced. He did so, however, in the hope of seizing the ships by a surprise attack. When this hope failed, the King detained as captives twenty men who had been sent on a commercial mission. Eight of them were ransomed. The others were not favoured even with this fate, but were set aside as creatures of little value, destined for use in the wars which were being waged at that time between the King of Damma and his neighbours. The latter group included the son of that Van der Does who was no less illustrious for learning than for noble lineage.

Article III But the Portuguese were not satisfied with having caused hatred [84] [of the Dutch among the natives]. For the fury characteristic of the Iberian peoples is not so phlegmatic that it will always await action by others, once the enemy has been sighted and the hope of doing injury has been conceived; and they are particularly disinclined to wait, in cases where confident expectation of success with impunity invites treachery and abominable deceit.

First Episode In the year 1596 For example, when the Dutch first came to the islands of the Orient, the Portuguese urged Toemenggoeng of Bantam (through whose agency, at a later date, the snares at Tandjong-Java were laid) to invite the leaders of the expedition and the ship's captains to dine at his villa, situated near the shore. Toemenggoeng himself afterwards revealed that the Portuguese planned to land at that very time from a ship lying near the same part of the coast, whereupon they meant to capture the guests and the host, release the latter immediately and carry the Dutch off to Malacca. He had refused to lend his assistance to the scheme, however, because he feared the Regent of Bantam. But the Portuguese—after corrupting the Regent himself (as we have already related), and after the seizure by Portuguese request of the captains Houtman and Valckenier together with some other men—became indignant because the Regent was mindful of his own profit rather than of their hatred. Consequently, they mixed poison with the food of both captives. The Shabandar of Bantam, when he perceived that the heads of the victims were swelling, that their abdomens were distended, and that they were at death's door, averted their doom by means of a well-known curative concretion called "bezoar," thus comporting himself more piously than those who boasted of being Christians. Cornelis Heemskerck, too, whom the captains had dispatched on a mission to the chief magistrate of the city, was sought and pursued everywhere by the Portuguese, with such fury that he was compelled to beg for refuge in the home of a Chinese named Lakmoy, where he hid among sacks filled with rice. When a search was made for him even there, he barely succeeded in escaping by disguising himself in Chinese attire and by allowing himself to be carried out, moreover, with the fishing equipment of his host, who pretended that he was taking a fishing trip.

Second Episode In the year 1600

Similarly, when two vessels from the fleet of Van Neck were returning from the latter's second voyage to the East Indies and had arrived at the island of Saint Helena, where four Portuguese ships were at that time assembled, the Dutch found it necessary to traverse quite a distance in search of water, and in doing so detected a fairly large number of armed Portuguese who had been stationed in ambush, doubtless for the purpose of intercepting our men as they approached. [84′]

Third Episode In the early part of the year 1601

Again, what stronger proof of uncontrollable hatred could be offered, than the hostile acts repeatedly directed against the ships left by that same Van Neck at the island of Amboyna? For the Portuguese had publicly proclaimed that to every person who slew a Dutch seaman a reward of ten *reaes* would be given, and so on, with proportionately larger rewards for other victims according to their rank and dignity. Thus whoever should bring back the head of the commander of the expedition, Cornelis Heemskerck, would receive a thousand silver coins [or *reaes?*]. We know, of course, that bidding for heads is an Iberian custom.

Fourth Episode In the same year

But even these measures did not suffice. You shall learn now of a deed more infamous than any crime that was ever committed by the Carthaginians. Forming part of the fleet commanded by Mahu, who was under orders to proceed to the Strait of Magellan, there was a ship called the *Good Faith,* a quality which that vessel was not destined to encounter. For, as she was sailing unaccompanied from the southern ocean to Tidor (which is one of the Moluccas and is included among the Portuguese colonies), the Portuguese approached her with the formal query: "Whence, whither and with what purpose do you come?" Balthasar de Cordes (who was acting as commanding officer because of the death of Jurriaen Boekholt) replied that the ship was bringing merchandise for purposes of barter. The Portuguese answered, in their turn, that they had cloves, and that some plan of exchange could easily be agreed upon if this should seem desirable. They voluntarily lent assistance to the Dutch sailors as the latter laboured to bring the ship closer to shore. Gifts were brought by the Dutch to the chief Portuguese officials. Trade agreements were formally concluded. De Cordes was told to come ashore with such sailors as were most readily available, in order to take back a gazelle that had been put aside to feed the Dutch; and in the meantime, other provisions were conveyed to the ship by the Portuguese, under the guise of gifts. These provisions, however, had been dipped in exceedingly swift poisons, undoubtedly as an additional precaution in view of the possibility that the bolder attempt which was under preparation at the same time might result in failure. The Dutch, menaced by two forms of death, were overtaken by the more evil fate; that is to say, they fell into the hands of the Portuguese. For the latter, admitted on board the ship because of the faith placed in the pacts, and bearing weapons which were concealed in their clothing, scattered in various directions so that they might seize each Dutchman individually, in the course of conversation. Thereupon, they stabbed their hosts. Like victors in a battle, they took [85] possession of the vessel (now bereft of defenders), together with all that it bore. Meanwhile, de Cordes had first been struck down in the skiff in which he chanced to be returning, and was then beheaded. The body was cast into the sea. A like fate befell the other men whom the Portuguese had summoned from the ship under pretence of inviting them to partake of an afternoon repast, except that the hosts, sated with slaughter, spared several guests out of regard for their extreme youth; or possibly these youths were spared because Divine Providence so willed, lest no witness be left to so monstrous a crime, although the perpetrators themselves, for that matter, were not ashamed to boast of the deed.

I know that the reader is astounded. I know it to be scarcely credible that a nation which is, in the first place, Christian, and which also prides itself not a little on its cultured customs and way of life, should have dared such deeds and dared them, too, in violation of its own pledged and accepted word. What, then, shall I say? In what terms shall I continue the narrative? Where can I find language that will be neither grossly inadequate to describe the vile facts, nor yet completely beyond the limits of credibility despite its perfect truth? For more—yes, even more!—remains to be told: something crueller and more characteristically Iberian. The incidents just related were merely a prelude to the Portuguese fury.

Six men, beholding the disaster that had overtaken their comrades and the blood that had been shed on land and sea, took flight in a small boat, not with any fixed hope (for the Portuguese were threatening their bark on every side), but because they resolved to make trial of the waves, of the rocks, of any other peril whatsoever, rather than of Iberian cruelty. The Portuguese, however, called out to these men that they should give themselves up, that the revenge was complete, that their lives and bodies would be safe. An oath was sworn; but an oath is for the Portuguese an instrument of deception as truly as it is for other men a bond of security. When the Dutchmen had been transferred to a small caracore (which is a kind of boat quite common in those regions), a Portuguese officer ordered that they should be drawn up in a row; then, addressing a subordinate who was holding an unsheathed sword in his hand, this officer said: "Cut off the right arm of the man who is first in line," to which he added, "Now cut off his left arm." The commands were obeyed, and in such a manner, indeed, that one might have doubted which was the more barbarous, the person issuing the orders or the person who obeyed them. Moreover, the officer next ordered that the victim's feet [85′] should be severed with separate strokes. The other captives, whom the same torments awaited, were standing by, more eager at that moment for death than they had ever been for life. Yet, as these examples were set before them, one after another, their emotion changed from fear to a mutual compassion. The trunks could be seen surviving their own mutilation and—worst of ills!—deprived of human likeness. Nevertheless, the perpetrators of the deed were much further removed from every semblance of humanity! Lastly, the heads were cut off. Two of the captives, however, were so spirited that they leaped still unharmed into the sea before their turn came at the hands of the swordsman. One of these two was drowned; the other escaped, and bore witness to that most abominable spectacle. In the following year, moreover, all of the details were revealed, when Wolphert Harmensz[14] captured several Portuguese and undertook negotiations for an exchange that would liberate the men left in Tidor as captives. Although he was not successful in this enterprise, the military equipment and the remainder of the spoils taken from the ill-fated ship were recognized on board a Portuguese vessel by the Dutch, and were recovered.

Fifth Episode **In the same year, in September**

We have yet to speak of another crime, committed at approximately the same time, but even more execrable in that the sacred cloak of law was flung about an impious act despite the fact that the deed in question was permissible neither on the basis of any just cause nor in virtue of either local or Portuguese law.

Macao is the market town of the Chinese territory extending toward the Indian Ocean. At the request of the Portuguese, a concession in Macao had been set apart for them, where they might carry on trade, and also administer justice for their own people exclusively. Even with

14. Perhaps better known under the anglicized form of his name, "Wolfert Hermann."

respect to Portuguese subjects, however, this judicial authority[15] is not unrestricted. For, in accordance with their own customs, punishments of the gravest degree may be imposed upon freeborn persons only by the Governor of Goa, unless (as frequently occurs) the accused are sent all the way back to Portugal.

The second fleet, placed under the command of Van Neck, had been driven close to that very shore by the winds. Van Neck decided that men should be sent to investigate the lay of the land and to give an explanation of the arrival of the Dutch, while procuring fresh provisions. In compliance with these instructions, Martinus Ape (who was [86] discharging the duties of finance officer for the fleet) set forth with ten other men in a light boat and perceived, as he approached the land, that the usual tokens of peace were being displayed by the inhabitants. Trusting in this display, he advanced and was met by Dom Paulo, the chief official of the Portuguese in that locality, who was accompanied by an armed band which he had kept hidden till then in a monastery, or temple, situated upon the shore. After a few questions had been asked of the Dutch, they were hurried into the temple, where certain Mandarins (that is to say, Chinese senators) presented themselves with the purpose of ascertaining what manner of men had come to visit their land. Ape explained that the visitors were Dutch merchants and that they came to engage in trade, a claim which could be thoroughly verified by examining the ships themselves, laden with merchandise, if anyone wished to make such an examination. He added that these merchants brought letters from their Prince to the ruler of the Chinese. While he was making his explanation, the crowd of Portuguese that thronged about him was raising on all sides a clamour of abuse and slander, with the result that the Mandarins took their departure, although it is uncertain whether they did so only because of an insufficient understanding of

15. *Ne* [*hoc*] *quidem* (literally: "not even this"). The word *hoc* does not appear in the collotype, but it is clearly visible in other reproductions of the MS. On this page of the collotype, as on many others, letters are missing at the ends of several lines, probably because of a fold in the margin of the MS. page. Such instances are not noted in the translation unless there is doubt as to the exact letters which must be supplied.

the situation, or also because they had been corrupted by the gifts of the Portuguese. The latter pursued the investigation with the aid of torture. Nothing was discovered. All of the Dutchmen were dragged off together from the temple, placed under guard and bound with the heaviest of fetters. They were then cast into a hideously dark and filthy cave. In the meantime, Van Neck, doubtful and apprehensive as to what was delaying the return of his men, gave orders that a second and larger skiff should take soundings so that, once the depth of the waters had been ascertained, the ships might be brought nearer to the city. This skiff, however, was unable to cope satisfactorily with the winds, and all of the nine persons aboard it, including one of the pilots, were intercepted by the Portuguese. An inquisitor, called by the Portuguese an "auditor," was in attendance. Recourse was had to the rack.

While these events were taking place, a rumour reached the neighbouring Chinese city of Canton, to the effect that, "foreigners sent ashore from their ships, had been seized by the Portuguese." In consequence of this report, the chief magistrate of Canton, whose name was Capado, ordered that a large band of men should be sent out and that the captives should be brought before him. When the Portuguese found themselves caught in this predicament and dared not oppose the demands thus made, they resorted to fraud and to their usual wiles. From the whole throng of Dutchmen, they selected six men unacquainted with any language other than that of their native land, inasmuch as they were chosen from among the common sailors. As to the other captives (for now [86′] that the rumour had spread, it was impossible to conceal the fact that there were more), the Portuguese falsely asserted that all the rest had died of diarrhoea during the last few days. Now, when the six Dutchmen above mentioned, prostrate at the feet of the Cantonese envoy, were plied with numerous questions through an interpreter who spoke in Portuguese, they lay like men without tongues, owing to their ignorance of that language and perhaps also to fear. The envoy demanded an answer to the accusations of the Portuguese, who were charging these poor sailors with piratical savagery, and when the latter could make no response even to these charges, the Portuguese insisted that their silence should be regarded as a confession. It is quite likely that a bribe was also given for the purpose of persuading the delegation to return while the business was yet unfinished, so to speak, leaving the captives in the power of the Portuguese. The Cantonese chief magistrate, however, was indignant at having been tricked through the inefficiency of his envoy, and was already drawing the inference, in agreement with the actual facts (for the Chinese are an extraordinarily shrewd race), that the purpose of the Portuguese actions was to turn other nations away from trade with the Chinese.

Seeing that a new delegation was about to be dispatched with a demand for the surrender of every one of the captives without exception, the Portuguese agents in Canton sent notice in advance regarding this intention to their men at Macao, in order that the latter might take counsel betimes for their own interests, since otherwise their fraudulent conduct would be exposed. Never before had such consternation arisen among the Portuguese. For they perceived the utter impossibility of refusing to surrender the Dutchmen, yet there could be no doubt as to the suspicions and infamy which they would stir up against themselves if the surrender took place. Confronted with this dilemma, they sought refuge in crime and audacity, mindful undoubtedly of the fact that it is foolish to observe moderation in wrongdoing. It was their plan to slay all of the prisoners, under the pretence of executing a judicial sentence, so that it would not be possible to give them up. But their own magistrate, Paulo (for we must not suppress testimony to the innocence of any person whatsoever), delayed action for a long while. Indeed, what kind of judicial sentence would that be, imposed in a city not his own, against foreigners and the lives of freeborn persons? Should the accused not be sent to Lisbon, or at least, to the Governor? With the greatest difficulty, the inquisitor finally prevailed upon Paulo to permit that his name be affixed to the sentence.

Thus it came to pass that six men of Holland—O fatherland! [87] O justice and law, and liberty vainly defended at home!—were subjected to the cruellest and most hideous punishment, suited to robbers and pirates, by Portuguese sojourners in that Kingdom of China which the Hollanders had sought amid so many hardships and perils, and where their presence was in turn desired. The Chinese looked on pityingly at this spectacle and afterwards prayed, with averted faces, that these men might not be left unavenged, whatsoever race and whatsoever region of the earth had sent them as guests to Chinese waters and shores, if they worshipped any divinity or had any native land.

But the deed which I am now about to recount was perhaps even more cruel. The eleven men who remained, and whose death of course would have to be kept secret, lest the Portuguese be convicted of the lie previously told to the envoy, were led in bonds, at midnight (so that they might be defrauded even of human witnesses and human pity), to that very shore which they had approached after sighting the signals of peace; and there, weighted with rocks, they were rolled into the sea. But even while treading the last bit of earth, even while tossed about only half-alive on the waves, they cried out (so we may well believe) not that life, which is rightly very dear to all, should be spared to them; not that they might at least be buried in their own blessed land by the hands of their wives and children; but rather, with their final faltering breath, for this one boon—that a crime so wicked might not long remain unrevealed.

God has heard their cry. Men, too, have heard it.

In the first place, four Chinese who came to Bantam gave an account of all these events, just as they had occurred, to the aforesaid Lakmoy (a very powerful personage) and to many others as well. Lakmoy transmitted the information to the Dutch; and at the same time the report was spread far and wide throughout Java and the entire region of the East Indies. In those islands it was a matter of common knowledge that certain Hollanders, after the Portuguese in defiance of plighted faith had condemned them to death by hanging, had entreated in a language which could be understood (that is to say, in Portuguese) that their [87′] fate should be remembered by their fellow countrymen. Consequently, when Wijbrandt Van Warwijck arrived in the Indies, all of the natives, aroused by the atrocity of the crime, were saying that the Dutch would be unworthy to look upon the light of day if they failed to exact fitting vengeance for such perfidy.

But the matter did not rest there. God sent the Dutch a witness to the whole series of events, one who had himself beheld a part of them, and had heard of them in part from incontrovertible authorities, including the very Portuguese who had committed the deeds as well as other persons who had been eyewitnesses. I refer to that Martinus Ape whom we mentioned just above. Out of that pitiable throng, he alone, save for two seventeen-year-old boys, was granted a respite, though not actually saved, through the entreaties of the Portuguese priests, even after he had been condemned and led forth for execution. In other respects, these priests have been exceedingly hostile toward the Dutch, so that in this circumstance, too, one may recognize the intervention of Divine Providence. Ape was sent from Macao to Malacca, and from Malacca to Goa, whence—his life having been spared by the Governor, despite the fruitless protests of the magistrates—he set out for Portugal. But he was detained again in Bayona, a town of Galicia, where once more his customary good fortune protected him. For after a long interval during which a letter from the King was awaited, Ape was finally released. He departed, and two days later the letter arrived, summoning him to the Royal Court and, beyond any shadow of doubt, to what would have been his death.

Sixth Episode
In the year 1602, in October

In the light of such a remarkable example, hardly any other incident will seem worthy of narration. Nevertheless, we find that there was another, more recent and no less illustrative of perfidy, which befell the companions of Van Warwijck at the island of Annobon, two degrees distant from the Equator. At this spot, quite shortly before, while some Frenchmen were on their way to attend Mass, many of them had been slaughtered almost at the very altar, and the rest had been captured. First of all, then, in this same place, when the Portuguese saw the Dutch heralds coming towards them and displaying the insignia of peace, they loosed their weapons against persons who by the law of nations should have been regarded as inviolable. One man fell. Not long afterwards, eight more Dutchmen were intercepted by means of an ambuscade and were put to death; others were wounded. Furthermore, even after a parley had been requested and granted, and in the very midst of the solemn conference, the Portuguese tore down the flag of truce that had been raised on their own side and, conducting themselves as if the bonds of good faith had also been loosed, attacked with weapons the incautious and entirely unsuspecting Dutchmen; nor did they fail to inflict injury in so doing. [88]

Article IV Thus we maintain that the Portuguese are men of bad faith, assassins, poisoners, and betrayers. We have taken note of the crimes which are recorded above, and because of which (as no moderately rational person will deny) war could and should have been undertaken against the Portuguese quite apart from any connexion between those crimes and the King of Spain. But I shall not press even this point. On the contrary, if I do not succeed in proving, by the clearest possible narration of various episodes, that the Portuguese, before they had been harmed by the Dutch in any way whatsoever, treated the Dutch nation and Dutchmen as enemies, waging public war against them in the Orient, and that armed force was first employed by the Portuguese themselves, then it will not be my wish that other considerations should avail the cause which I plead.

First Episode In the year 1596 When the Dutch ships that first set sail for the East Indies had been following that course for a month, they encountered four Portuguese vessels, or caracks, which appeared not all at one time, but separately. Subsequent events served to indicate that these caracks, isolated as they were, could have been captured; and one of them came so close that it undoubtedly would have been seized and held, if the Dutch had so desired. But our men made no attempt of this kind. In fact, after offering every sort of kindly service, they sailed past without inflicting any injury. Moreover, when they had reached Java and the atrocious crimes of the Portuguese were presently revealed, these same men nevertheless refrained from taking vengeance, although it would have been easy to seize the ship that was bearing the Malaccan envoy, who even at that time was a wholesale vendor of Dutch blood.

The Portuguese, on the other hand, had already associated themselves with the plans of the Rajah of Demak to the extent of agreeing to combine their own maritime forces with his fleet for the purpose of making war upon the Dutch and intercepting the ships that passed between Java and the islands of Panjang. Soon afterwards, when some of the Dutch were attempting to return to their ships at Bantam, they found the port blockaded by the Portuguese. In regard to this matter, the Shabandar advised the Dutch that considerations of good faith made their security within the city the concern of the Regent, but that they would have need of their own foresight and valour to prevent any untoward incident outside the city limits. The Portuguese also lent their assistance in the plots woven by Toemenggoeng, which we have already described, and in the treachery devised at Sidajoe. [88′]

Second Episode In the year 1597

As the Dutch prolonged their stay at Bantam, the Portuguese and the Regent of Bantam himself became allies in certain warlike enterprises whose basic pacts have been outlined in an earlier part of this chapter. Moreover, a band of men appeared under the leadership of Manoel, brother of the Governor of Goa, a band sent out by the state and sworn to the task of destroying the Dutch. There were four very large battleships, three ships of war of the kind known to us as galleys, and almost thirty brigantines. This force had been prepared by the Portuguese for use against the Hollanders, whom they were seeking. Enraged by the discovery that the Hollanders had departed, the Portuguese even turned the weapons taken up against us upon the inhabitants of Bantam (to such extremes is Portuguese hatred carried!), alleging as a pretext either the failure of the Bantamese to prohibit the departure of the Hollanders, or their failure to participate equally with the Portuguese in the subsequent pursuit.

Ask yourselves then, O fellow citizens, whether forbearance should be shown to men who from the outset were so disposed that they considered themselves injured if they were unable to inflict injury, and who regard as enemies not only the Dutch themselves but also all persons who do not seem sufficiently hostile toward the Dutch! Their purposes, their inclinations, and their plans were such as we have described; the outcome alone was of a contrary nature. The Portuguese were defeated by the Javanese, a defeat which constituted an added reason for a more yielding attitude in regard to the Dutch.

Third Episode In the year 1599, on September 13

Even under these circumstances, however, the fury of the foe and his mad lust for battle were not abated. For when Houtman came to Achin, in Sumatra (as we have already related), under the auspices of the Zeelanders, a temporary pretence on the part of the Portuguese gave the impression that the laws of friendship had been re-established there, in contrast with the earlier policy of offence; but in reality the Portuguese spirit of hostility remained unappeased, despite the terrific disaster it had succeeded in bringing upon our naval force when the latter was torn to pieces through the agency of the inhabitants of Achin and in defiance of every dictate of divine law and good faith. Savagely persisting in their molestations, and with the aim of completing the work begun through others, the Portuguese themselves rushed upon the wretched remnants of Dutch ships and sailors, with battle standards unfurled and in a hostile fleet that included approximately twelve ships of war. Force was repelled only by force.

Fourth Episode In the same year

The first voyage of Van Neck took place at almost the same time. Van Neck (as the Bishop of Malacca himself testifies, in a letter [89] addressed to the King of the Spanish realms) had caused no injury or loss whatsoever to the Portuguese or to any man. Now, it was by his order that a ship called the *Utrecht* sailed to Amboyna and thence to the [other] Moluccas, where the voyagers suffered truly grievous injuries at the hands of a hostile people (for Tidor, one of the Moluccas, is held by the Portuguese), and where they presently learned that men had also been sent to Malacca and to the Philippines in order to procure assistance in driving the Dutch out of the entire region and preventing their appearance there in the future. But the peril thus threatened was forestalled by the withdrawal of the Dutch.

Fifth Episode In the early part of the year 1601

Nevertheless, owing to the fact that Cornelis Heemskerck (who had been left behind by Van Neck) remained at Amboyna with two ships, the Portuguese persevered night and day in their threats against our light boats and skiffs; and after an interval marked by ventures of little importance, they completed the task of equipping twenty-two caracores and three brigantines. Not daring to make an assault, however, even in such circumstances, they devoted themselves to arranging—under cover of the dark, or by secretly ascending various promontories—snares and conflagrations which the prudent and ever-watchful Dutchmen easily avoided.

Shortly afterwards, it so happened that Adriaan Veen sent three men, in an East Indian proa, across the sea to Cornelis Heemskerck, that is to say, from Banda to Amboyna. One of these three was Jacob (surnamed Waterman), a surgeon by profession. The Portuguese fell upon them unexpectedly, in vastly superior numbers and strength, so that no recourse against the assailants remained other than flight. Two of the three Dutchmen hurled themselves into the sea and after strenuous efforts reached a nearby island where, dwelling in solitude among wild beasts, they nevertheless found all their surroundings to be more gentle than the Portuguese. The third man, Jacob, who did not know how to swim, fell into cruel hands. It is certain that he was slain. According to a persistent rumour that spread through all the East Indies, he was torn asunder and the pieces of his body were scattered about by means of [89′] four ships of war violently rowed in different directions. Nor is there any less reason for crediting this report than there is for believing the account (recorded in an earlier part of this chapter) of what was done to the Frenchmen[16] who were placed in bronze cannon and shot out as missiles. It is at least an established fact that many persons saw Jacob's head after it had been severed from his body and hoisted high above the caracore, as if on a frame for the display of spoils.

Sixth Episode
In May of the same year

In the meantime, the fleet previously mentioned, which was intended to drive the Dutch from the Moluccas and from Banda, was being fitted out more fully. Furthermore, letters and messengers were being dispatched to all the ruling personages of Java and other islands, intimating that the activities in question had been undertaken by the Portuguese in order to protect the natives from despoliation by the Hollanders, and

Seventh Episode
In the same year

16. Undoubtedly a reference to the episode recounted on p. 257, although Grotius there mentions only one victim of this form of punishment.

that the forces of all those rulers and peoples ought therefore to unite with the Portuguese, as with the true liberators of the Orient. Van Neck had already paid a second visit to the regions involved, but when he was warned in advance by the Regent of Bantam regarding this matter, he made his way to Ternate with two ships, trusting in the worth of his cause and in his own valour. There he ascertained that what he had heard was entirely true. For the King of that island was being incited to lend aid against the Dutch; and furthermore, the Portuguese—with two carracks, the same number of galleys, and one warship—were hugging the shore and awaiting a favourable time and occasion for setting fire to the Dutch ships. In that same spot, a battle took place in which artillery was employed.

Article V

Assuredly, all of these facts furnish such clear and palpable proof of a hostility transcending the bounds of human hatred, that any person who craves more certain evidence must be blind even to the light of noonday. For what fuller proof could be desired than the fact that the Portuguese, in pursuing their noxious course, spared neither the reputation nor the property nor the lives of the Dutch, just as they spared themselves neither expense nor danger nor even violation of good faith? [90]

Nevertheless, there is one additional point which stirs me still more deeply, and by which the noble spirits of those who cherish the fatherland and its fair fame will, I believe, be yet more keenly affected. For I shall show that the Portuguese raged no less savagely against all the peoples who permitted the entry of the Dutch for purposes of trade, than they did against the Dutch themselves—or indeed, even more savagely, in proportion to the more warlike qualifications and greater power of those peoples—with the result, naturally, that throughout the whole Orient the very name of Holland grew to be utterly abhorrent as the symbol of a loathsome curse, the fount and origin of every calamity for the natives.

First Episode
In the early part of the year 1601

Thus we find (without pausing to repeat here any of the details relative to the war against the people of Bantam which has been described above) that at the time of the appearance in Amboyna of Cornelis Heemskerck, whom we have already mentioned more than once, the Portuguese had publicly outlawed under pain of death not only the Dutch but likewise the chief men of that locality, and had set a price of one hundred *reaes* on the head of each man affected by the order. They had also provided an inducement for the assassination of the governor of the citadel located at that point, by promising the same reward as in the case of the commander of the Dutch fleet, thus informing the inhabitants of the island that they must share a common fate with the Dutch. During the same period, finding themselves quite unable to prevail against our ships, the Portuguese made a vigorous attack upon Lusitello, a walled town on the island of Amboyna. After being driven back, they abandoned the assault in favour of a siege. The situation had become critical for the defenders of the town, owing to a lack of provisions, when the leaders of the islanders formally approached our men as suppliants, begging for protection and material aid. The arrival of Dutch ships resulted in the delivery of the besieged, and brought glory to the Dutch themselves.

The Portuguese, however, renewed all their threats immediately afterwards. For they boasted far and wide, not only that they would prevent the name of Hollander from ever again being heard in those [90′] regions, but also that they would lay waste every city and every island where our compatriots had set foot.

Second Episode Toward the close of the year 1601, and in the early part of the year 1602

The Spanish royal fleet which, as a favour to the King of Calicut, had subdued Cunala (the pirate chief of the Malabar Indians, notorious for his fifty years of freebootery and his usurpation of the royal insignia), was dispatched upon the completion of that war, from Goa all the way to the Strait of Sunda, which lies between Java and Sumatra, with instructions that the force of the said fleet should be turned in this direction. Simultaneously, ships from other Portuguese colonies were assembling. The combined forces now numbered almost thirty vessels: five galleons from Goa, including one commanded by Andrés Hurtado de Mendoza (Admiral of the fleet), another commanded by Thomaz Souza de Rocha, a third under the command of Francisco Silva Meneses, a fourth under Antonio Souza, and a fifth under Lopes Dalmeyda; two caracks from Malacca, commanded by Trajano Rodrigues Castelbranco and Jorge Pinto; one from Cochin China, under the command of Sebastião Suares, and, for the rest, brigantines or galleys entrusted to the orders of André Rodrigues Palota.

The city of Bantam, which had previously been the first to receive the Dutch, was likewise the first to be hailed to punishment. According to information obtained later from Francisco Souza (the son of João Teves, an accountant in Lisbon) as well as from other captives, the Portuguese plan involved, first, an assault upon the market-place (known as the Bazaar) outside of the city, toward which the leaders of the attacking party and those persons from among the populace who had been bought over by the Portuguese were to converge suddenly at a given signal; and from there, after breaking through the defence of the Chinese guards, the assailants would rush upon the city itself. Success was felt to be so certain that bitter contention arose between the monks and the Jesuits over the prospective allotment of sees. Moreover, orders had been given that, once Bantam was stripped of its defences, Banda, [91] Amboyna, and Ternate should be compelled to submit to Spanish rule. With these ends in view, the Portuguese had brought not only instruments of warfare, but also money and spices, as rewards to be given the barbarians in exchange for treachery.

God shattered their monstrous arrogance, abruptly and unexpectedly, as He is wont to do in extraordinary manifestations of His power. Precisely at the moment when the Portuguese were intent on the destruction of Bantam, the Dutch, ignorant of these plans, arrived with the purpose of trading, in several ships commanded by Wolphert Harmensz, a man especially entitled to honourable mention, since not merely the East India Company but the very reputation of the Dutch (so I venture to say) has scarcely ever been more deeply indebted to any individual. A small Chinese vessel came to meet Harmensz, at the Strait of Sunda itself. A [Chinese] sailor gave warning that the open sea was beset by the Portuguese [and Spanish] fleet, so that, being aware of the Portuguese desire for the destruction of the Dutch, he was taking anticipatory measures in order that the latter might have an opportunity to flee unharmed. For no one supposed that a battle would take place, inasmuch as the opponents were in every respect far from evenly matched. From a numerical standpoint, what could be accomplished by Wolphert's four ships and one cutter, as against thirty enemy vessels? From the standpoint of bulk, the total tonnage of all the Dutch vessels was not equal even to that of the single ship that bore Andrés Hurtado. As for the men available on the respective sides, the entire number attached to the Dutch fleet amounted to three hundred and fifteen, whereas the Spanish fleet carried eight hundred Portuguese and, in addition, at least fifteen hundred East Indian soldiers, not to mention the throng comprised in the crews. The Dutch were inferior in everything save their spirit and their cause. Nevertheless, when they visualized the baseness of flight, the disgrace to their nation and the harm[17] that would be suffered by each man's household if the East Indian trade of the Dutch should be lost to posterity, they sailed through the strait and advanced until they were within sight [91′] of the enemy. The Portuguese growled in indignation. Sounding the war-trumpet and unfurling their battle flags, they roused the echoes with the din of artillery and, as they neared each of the opposing ships, called continually upon the Dutch to lower their sails and announce their surrender. But our men, who had by no means been taught in their native land to conduct themselves in the manner suggested, deliberately spread their sails in order to check with deeds this verbal insolence; and, borne toward the foe by the winds, they proceeded to defend themselves by discharging their weapons. Fortune favoured the brave, even though one of the Dutch guns blew up during the initial stages of the battle, causing great consternation. The Dutch recovered their courage, however, and resumed the struggle, capturing first one Portuguese ship and then another. Several of the captured vessels were so thoroughly riddled with shots that they could be of no further use, and therefore they were sunk, after the men had been taken off. The Portuguese, instantly subdued by this defeat (a reaction typical of persons who are excessively bold while circumstances are auspicious), did not dare to engage in battle during the days that followed, despite the fact that the winds favoured them. On the other hand, after the manner of wild beasts that do not lay aside

17. Reading *exitium* (harm, destruction, *or* mischief) for *exsilium* (exile), which must have been written inadvertently.

their wrath even when stripped of their strength, the enemy set fire to a number of their own ships, which were then launched against the Dutch in an attempt to satisfy the demands of hatred without disregarding the voice of fear. All in vain! For the fires burned themselves out within those very ships.

While the Dutch were pressing forward with an eagerness born of the conviction that the doors of trade would not be thrown open to them unless the enemy was routed, the Portuguese abandoned Bantam in cowardly fashion, and fled to the Moluccas. The victors, refraining from pursuit, approached the city thus liberated by them, in order that they might first accomplish the purpose for which they had come. A marvellous tale could be told regarding the congratulations and rejoicings with which they were received as conquerors by the Javanese, and the great fame which attached itself to the Hollanders and spread throughout the islands, so that this occasion may truly be described as the dawn of a supremely happy day for both the Dutch and the Oriental peoples.

But the Portuguese were cruel even in their flight. For, keeping [92] at a distance and believing themselves to be far removed from the avenger, they proceeded to indulge in unpunished acts of robbery; nor had the turn for the worse in their fortunes wrought any change of heart in these men who were bewitched by hatred, aside from the fact that they were desirous of greater security while they sinned. Accordingly, they hastened first to Amboyna, where at that time no Dutch ships were stationed. Itys, as well as the other inadequately fortified towns of Amboyna, and subsequently all of the surrounding country-side, were attacked and devastated by them. The inhabitants were subjected to the same savage treatment that the people of the Low Countries had often suffered at the hands of the Spaniards. Slaughter was practised without distinction of age or sex; little children and women were slain indiscriminately. Nor were they merely slain; for some of the Portuguese cut off the limbs of young children before the very eyes of the parents, and others searched with their swords both the wombs of pregnant women and bodies that were unquestionably innocent. A number of natives, whom time had favoured with an opportunity for flight, abandoned

Third Episode
In the same year (1602)

their ancestral homes and property after being warned by these examples, and betook themselves to deserted regions, full of bristling forests or precipitous mountains. Another group crossed over to the neighbouring island of Ceram.

It so happened that a Dutch cutter had been sent to that locality by Wolphert [Harmensz.], who was staying in Banda at the time. A deputation from Amboyna encountered the cutter and accompanied it to Banda, rejoicing in the midst of so many sorrows. Admitted to the presence of the commander, displaying in their very aspect the stamp of their current misfortunes, and even interrupted by tears, the men from Amboyna related the experiences which they had undergone. They added (though the fact was sufficiently self-evident) that these disasters had befallen them because they had cultivated commercial relations with the Dutch. Accordingly, they argued amid entreaties—in the name of God, who was granting the Dutch such felicitous voyages upon the ocean and such brilliant victories over the Spaniards; in the name of the justice characteristic of Hollanders and famous as a result of their commercial activities; and in the name of that good faith which the suppliants, following the dictates of their judgement, now regarded as the last source of aid in their desperate straits—that the Dutch should not suffer them, exiled as they were from their native land and utterly destitute, to become in addition the playthings of an enemy unsurpassed in cruelty.

Any human being whatsoever, and most of all any Dutchman [92′] (for the Dutch are by nature gentle and compassionate), might well have been moved by this plea. The commander, indeed, had been more than a little troubled by it, but he realized that the business entrusted to him as his chief care could not be neglected for the sake of these unfortunates. The time of year, too, was one that called for diligence in the conduct of trade. He therefore excused himself, while expressing the hope that the Dutch Prince and State would take to heart the cause of vengeance in behalf of the people of Amboyna. As the one measure permitted by circumstances, he released the captives whom he had taken in the battle of the Strait of Sunda (including Francisco Souza himself), freeing them without ransom and sending them to the Portuguese in Amboyna. He also supplied them with arms and provisions, so that this kindly deed would be in no respect incomplete. His hope was that the spirit of the Portuguese, howsoever savage, might be elevated and softened by the example he was setting, and that they might be induced to adopt a gentler attitude in their own turn toward the inhabitants of Amboyna, by this merciful forbearance toward the Portuguese themselves on the part of the victorious Dutch. But the outcome belied his hope. The deed of goodwill was worse than wasted upon men completely lacking in justice, men who were wont to interpret ingenuousness as folly and moderation as cowardice: not only was nothing gained by the generous gesture, but the Portuguese even persisted in their crimes all the more boldly because of it, rendered confident by so notable an example of clemency that there was no act of brigandage which they could not commit with impunity.

Fourth Episode In the same year

At last, however, when opportunities for plunder and cruelty had begun to fail them in Amboyna, they pressed on to Makian (one of the Moluccas), with seven warships, four galleons, and several caracores. There they loosed their rage, torturing the inhabitants, laying waste the fields and burning down the houses. Moreover, the chief city of the island (Tabosos [?][18] by name) was set on fire by the Portuguese, and sank in ashes. Makian, to be sure, and also the adjacent islands, are under the rule of the King of Ternate, who was showing the Dutch people a great deal of kindness at that time, an attitude which was a source of anger to the Portuguese and of misfortune to the natives. In fact, at that very moment a ship called the *Utrecht* from the fleet of Wolphert [93] [Harmenszoon] (the smallest ship of all) had stopped at Ternate for purposes of trade, in company with a cutter. The inhabitants of Makian, apparently remembering that regal rank goes hand in hand with the duty of defending subjects, came to Ternate and sought out their ruler with the plea that he should either restore the dwellings of which they had been forcibly deprived, or else provide his wretched people with some safer shelter. The King made ready to go to the aid of his subjects, and

18. Damsté, in his Dutch version of the *Commentary,* suggests "Tafasoho" as the translation of the Latin *Tabosos,* but queries the suggestion. The present translator has not found any other reference to a town of either name on the island of Makian.

also prevailed upon the Dutch to stand by him, although two ships scarcely worthy to be reckoned as such would furnish very little assistance against a whole fleet.

As [the King and his party] sailed nearer, they beheld the ill-fated island alight with flames and, shortly thereafter, the Portuguese, rushing to attack them in the most ferocious manner. For the courage of the Portuguese had increased when they saw themselves matched against East Indians, a hundred of whom they customarily regard as scarcely comparable to one individual from among their own men. Nevertheless, partly in consequence of advice offered by the Dutch, partly owing to the indignation felt by the victims of such grievous injuries, and also because the good fortune of the Dutch had by now created a belief in the possibility of vanquishing the Portuguese, an equal conflict was waged throughout the entire day between opponents unequal in skill and in strength.

A month later, the King of Ternate again set forth accompanied by the Dutch. Sailing past the island of Tidor, and encountering fifteen Portuguese caracores, he paused—motionless and with weapons held in check—waiting until the foe should call down upon himself the vengeance of God and man by being the first to enter upon the task of slaughter. As soon as this had occurred, the King rose up in all his courage and just desire for revenge. After capturing one of the Portuguese ships, he returned triumphantly to his kingdom.

In the meantime, the Portuguese had desolated Makian so thoroughly that the island was stripped of practically everything save the bare and lifeless soil. Moreover, just as a devouring flame spreads to new objects with a force that increases in proportion to its earlier inroads, so the Portuguese, coveting richer spoils in consequence of those already acquired, approached Ternate itself, with five [war]ships and four galleons. There the Dutch (who hitherto had remained close to the shore), [93′] seeing themselves surrounded by a multitude of enemies, first weighed anchor and then laid for themselves a more open course. Next, mindful of the fact that their mission was commercial and not martial, and of the further fact that they had already incurred rather grave losses in wasted time and scarcity of cargo, they departed with the King's permission, leaving behind some of their own men who were to cultivate his friendship and through whose aid and advice he might better prepare himself against the enemy. For the Portuguese, restored to even greater arrogance by the withdrawal of the Dutch, had attacked the island and were ravaging and burning certain nearby districts which had been abandoned by the terrified inhabitants.

Even now, the Portuguese continue to wage war against the King of Ternate, although it has been reported that at a later date their audacity in that contest most fortunately diminished.

Nor should we omit to mention the considerable care taken by them lest any distinction whatsoever be made between themselves and the Castilians, who are old enemies of the Dutch. Indeed, in this war centring about Ternate and directed primarily against us, the Portuguese made use of auxiliary troops and of ships sent from Manila (for the Castilians have found their way to that city, too), just as they sought aid from the Philippines on other occasions which we have already noted. Thus the two peoples in question, who in other respects are sufficiently lacking in mutual concord, nevertheless make it quite clear that they have banded together for the purpose of destroying the Dutch.

Fifth Episode
In the same year

We come now to the last part of our narrative, which has to do with the King of Johore. When I think of this monarch, I sincerely feel as if I were gazing upon the supreme and true reward of our voyages to the East Indies, and as if I were justly giving thanks to the tutelar deity of a fortunate fatherland.

For when Jacob Heemskerck came to the East Indian lands and while he was staying at Patani, whence he directed his attempts to gain access to the ruler of Johore, the King responded not only by letter but [94] also through his brother, the Prince of Siak, saying that he would be most happy to welcome Heemskerck, that his kingdom and its commerce were freely accessible, and that Heemskerck had only to behold them in order to assure himself both that the territory of Johore was richer than the other regions in those goods which the Dutch were seeking, and that the sovereign of Johore himself differed greatly from the other East Indian rulers in his inclinations and sentiments. He added that the good faith of the Hollanders was clearly evident to him, and that he would esteem nothing more highly than the friendship of those whom he knew to be as faithful to their allies as they were invincible to their enemies.

When the Portuguese learned of these negotiations, they dispatched a deputation from Malacca which was under orders not only to discourage the King, by means of slanderous lies, from engaging in trade with the Dutch, but also to threaten that implacable war would be waged against him if he did not desist from his purpose. But even these measures did not induce him to break his promises. He answered the Portuguese in a spirited yet equitable manner, to the following effect: he himself had never found the Hollanders to be as the Portuguese depicted them; to be sure, he had heard that injuries inflicted were valiantly avenged by them, and he really did not see how such vengeance could be censured; in any case, since he entertained no desire to inflict injury, he placed full confidence in the Hollanders; if any enmity existed between them and the Portuguese, that was a matter which in no wise concerned him; nor, indeed, was it right that the Portuguese should issue orders to him as to what his conduct ought to be within his own kingdom; on the contrary, it would be more fitting if the Portuguese, as occupants of Malacca (for the King of Johore claimed that region, too, as his own by ancestral right, even though he had been forced to relinquish possession), should obey his laws. These observations proved so offensive to ears impatient of the truth, that three warships and five brigantines were straightway sent to the mouth of the river flowing through the Kingdom of Johore, for the twofold purpose of blocking the approach of the Dutch, and harassing the inhabitants of the territory near that same shore with slaughter, with pillage, and, in short, in the [94′] true Portuguese manner. The King wrote to Heemskerck (who at that time was near the island of Tiuman, engaged in preparing vengeance for the injuries suffered by himself and by his allies), giving a full and careful account of all these matters, and entreating Heemskerck to prevent the benefactions conferred by the said monarch upon the Hollanders from bringing destruction upon the benefactor.

In the year 1603

The outcome clearly revealed how holy and how pleasing, in the eyes of our Heavenly Father, is the defence of those who have been unjustly oppressed. For the door to Johore was thrown open, commercial agreements were concluded, and—in the very locality where the Portuguese had practised their policy of rapine against the King of Johore because of their hatred for the Dutch, and while that ruler himself witnessed the capture from on board a Dutch vessel—a conquered Portuguese ship fell into Dutch hands.

In the light of the foregoing account, it is evident that the men who sailed to the East Indies as emissaries of the various Dutch companies (now united in a single organization) did not regard the Portuguese as enemies, even though the latter were enemies in actual fact. On the contrary, we see that these emissaries, in an attempt to establish amicable relations, waived the right to make war as long as it was at all possible for them to do so. Thus the first ship's captains to be sent out were not even given the official papers, or mandates, conferring martial powers, which as a general rule are not denied to any Dutchman. Furthermore, although such papers were indeed received by the captains dispatched at a later date, they were used very sparingly. For the recipients availed themselves of these mandates either in order to defend against actual attacks their own lives and the fortunes entrusted to them, a course of action rendered obligatory by the precepts of nature and the principle of good faith, or else on their own initiative, as an aggressive measure against the perils that threatened them, lest they should continually be, or seem to be, beset by fear. These were the motives that inspired the conduct of Van Neck at Tidor, and of Wolphert [Harmenszoon] at Bantam.

Finally, after a long series of crimes that made a mockery of Dutch candour in the manner already noted by us, the laws of war, which had remained inactive and in a more or less dormant state, were revived and openly put into practice. Even then, the Dutch did not choose to squander human life recklessly in the Portuguese fashion. On the contrary, the war was waged with almost excessive clemency. Thus nothing beyond repayment of the vast expenditures required for the protection of men, ships, and property was exacted by the armed force of the Dutch from the very persons whose armed violence had necessitated those expenditures.

In the year 1602, on March 16

First of all, a carack was seized by the Zeelanders, who took this step (near the island of Saint Helena) very tardily and only after displaying great patience. The seizure did not occur, moreover, until the Zeelanders had been provoked by a hostile response to their overtures and by previous recourse to armed attack on the part of the Portuguese. Furthermore, even though the Zeelanders had learned that those same Portuguese were under orders to make war upon them, and even though they were acquainted with the plans for the execution of the orders, nevertheless, being mindful in victory of their own humanity rather than of the injuries for which others were responsible, they not only saved those of their enemies who were in immediate danger of drowning, but actually transported the latter overseas to an island lying off the coast of Brazil. There the Zeelanders provided additional assistance in the form of supplies of every kind, and built a small boat for the Portuguese (not without expenditure of time and toil) to facilitate contact with the mainland.

The Hollanders were somewhat slower even in resorting to such action. Not a single seizure was made by them prior to the capture of the carack by Heemskerck, which took place when they were particularly stirred by the disasters visited upon their friends, and after they [95] themselves had endured seven years of injuries and losses in the East Indies, resulting from the violence or the perfidy of a hostile people. Not without reason, then, do we marvel that any doubt should be entertained as to whether that seizure was a rightful act.

Here follows an analytical discussion. [96][1]

CHAPTER XII

Wherein It Is Shown That Even If the War Were a Private War, It Would Be Just, and the Prize Would Be Justly Acquired by the Dutch East India Company; and Wherein, Too, the Following Theses Are Presented:

1. Access to all nations is open to all, not merely by the permission but by the command of the law of nations.

2. Infidels cannot be divested of public or private rights of ownership merely because they are infidels, whether on the ground of discovery, or in virtue of a papal grant, or on grounds of war.

3. Neither the sea itself nor the right of navigation thereon can become the exclusive possession of a particular party, whether through seizure, through a papal grant, or through prescription (that is to say, custom).

1. Collotype p. 95′ contains only a deleted heading, restored at the bottom of p. 96 and reading as follows: "The Freedom of the Seas, or a Dissertation on the Right of the Dutch to Carry on Trade in the East Indies." This is the full title of Grotius's celebrated treatise on the freedom of the seas (the *Mare Liberum*), now known to be simply a revised version of Chapter XII of the *Commentary on the Law of Prize and Booty.*

Owing to the deletions and insertions introduced into the original manuscript in the course of this revision, the text of pp. 96–128 (Chapter XII) in its present state is no longer that of the *Commentary.* Consequently, in order to reconstruct as accurately as possible the original contents of this chapter, the translator has retained some of the matter stricken out in the collotype, while omitting several undeleted passages obviously inserted when the above-mentioned revision took place. For example, the deleted material forming almost the entire content of p. 96 has been restored in the translation; and conversely, the undeleted insertion at the bottom of the page (the title of the *Mare Liberum*) has been omitted. Similarly, the thirteen

4. The right to carry on trade with another nation cannot become the exclusive possession of a particular party, whether through seizure, or through a papal grant, or through prescription (that is to say, custom).

For if the seizure of the carack is carefully considered in the light of the doctrines above set forth concerning justice in relation to war and to spoils, we shall find that there is absolutely no respect in which the said seizure fails to accord perfectly with those doctrines.

First of all, then, with a view to covering all of the points included in that discussion of justice, let us treat of the incident as if we were dealing not with an act of public warfare (as is really the case) but with an act of private warfare. In other words, I suggest the following procedure: consider the cause of the East India Company as something apart from the public cause of the Dutch nation; imagine that the Company consists, not of Dutchmen who have long been at war with the Portuguese, but rather of any other [people][2] whatsoever, such as Frenchmen, Germans, Englishmen, or Venetians; and reflect carefully as to whether, in these circumstances, [any reason would exist to prevent us from] regarding the prize as justly and blamelessly acquired. After weighing the private cause involved, examine the public cause. Furthermore, in regard to both these phases of the subject, ask yourselves what was permissible [with respect to] the authors of the war who were

chapter headings now appearing at various points within Chapter XII (sometimes as insertions in the old text and at other times at the head of entirely new passages) do not form part of the *Commentary* and are omitted from the translation, whereas certain deleted marginal annotations, still appropriate for the original text, are retained. In these instances, as in all others relative to the process of reconstruction, the evidence implicit in the context (from the standpoint of both substance and grammatical construction) and in the appearance of the manuscript (position of insertions, handwriting, etc.) leaves little or no doubt as to the original text.

2. The bracketed material in this paragraph corresponds to the fragment of text now missing from manuscript p. 96, which is mutilated along the margin. For purposes of translation, the missing text has been supplied from Hamaker's edition of the *Commentary,* evidently prepared before the mutilation occurred, since Hamaker does not indicate in any way that the Latin has been conjecturally restored at this point. According to his reading, the broken lines originally terminated as follows: (1) *quavi*[*s gente*]; (2) *nu*[*m quid obstet*]; (3) *cense*[*ri posset*]; (4) *auctor*[*ibus*]; (5) *a*[*utem pro*].

acting on their own behalf, [and] what, [on the other hand,] was permissible [with respect to] allies. Turn your attention next to the question of the subjects, and weigh all the classifications and definitions of cause from the standpoint of the individuals involved.

Deduction from Article I, Conclusion V Initial passage and part relative to demonstration or explanation of same; Chap. vi, *supra,* pp. 92 ff.

Now, in regard to the first phase of this examination, and in so far as it relates to the persons concerned, we find that Nature—the mistress and sovereign authority in this matter—withholds from no human being the right to carry on private wars; and therefore, no one will maintain that the East India Company is excluded from the exercise of that privilege, since whatever is right for single individuals is likewise right for a number of individuals acting as a group.

Accordingly, let us pass on to an investigation of the next point to be considered: the cause from which the war arises. We have already observed[a] that those same causes which render war just for the aggressor when they themselves are just, transfer this quality to the party defending itself[b] if that justice is wrongfully claimed for them. Therefore, let us ask of the Portuguese themselves, what it is that they require of the East India Company. Undoubtedly they will reply that their sole demand is this: that no one save themselves shall approach the East Indies for purposes of trade. Such a request, even if it were justly made, would still not serve automatically as an excuse for the stratagems and perfidious crimes above described. Nevertheless, since this pretext is pertinent [96′] to many of the points under discussion, it should be given consideration at the very outset.

Now, in the first place, we hold that, by the authority of that primary law of nations whose essential principles are universal and immutable, it is permissible for the Dutch to carry on trade with any nation whatsoever.

Thesis I

For God has not willed that nature shall supply every region with all the necessities of life; and furthermore, He has granted pre-eminence in dif-

a. Chap. vii, not far from the beginning, *supra,* p. 106.
b. See Law VII, *supra,* p. 37.

ferent arts to different nations. Why are these things so, if not because it was His Will that human friendships should be fostered by mutual needs and resources, lest individuals, in deeming themselves self-sufficient, might thereby be rendered unsociable? In the existing state of affairs, it has come to pass, in accordance with the design of Divine Justice, that one nation supplies the needs of another, so that in this way (as Pliny[a] observes) whatever has been produced in any region is regarded as a product native to all regions. Thus we hear the poets sing,

> Nor yet can ev'ry soil bear ev'ry fruit;[b]

and again,

> Others [the seething bronze] will mould [in lines
> More fair. . . .][c]

together with the remainder of the same passage.[3]

Consequently, anyone who abolishes this system of exchange, abolishes also the highly prized fellowship[4] in which humanity is united. He destroys the opportunities for mutual benefactions. In short, he does violence to nature herself. Consider the ocean, with which God has encircled the different lands, and which is navigable from boundary to boundary; consider the breath of the winds in their regular courses and in their special deviations, blowing not always from one and the same region but from every region at one time or another: are these things not sufficient indications that nature has granted every nation access to every other nation? In Seneca's[d] opinion, the supreme blessing conferred by

a. *Panegyric* [xxix. 7].

b. [Virgil, *Georgics,* II. 109.]

c. [Virgil, *Aeneid,* VI. 847 f.]

d. *Natural Questions,* III. iv [V. xviii].

3. I.e. the passage in which Anchises foretells Rome's destiny as a leader in the arts of war and government.

4. In the collotype, the right-hand margin of manuscript p. 96′ is imperfectly reproduced. For the benefit of the reader who wishes to follow the Latin word by word, it should be noted that other reproductions, in which the margin is not defective, complete the broken words as follows: *so*[*cie*]*tatem; O*[*ce*]*anus; sta*[*ti*]; *n*[*on*]; *concessum* [*a*]; *summ*[*um*]; *dissipata*[*s*]; *necess*[*a*]*rium; iu*[*s*]; *Iurisc*[*on*]*sulti; Princi*[*pem*]; *al*[*ii*]; *sa*[*nc*]*tissimum.*

nature resides in these facts: that by means of the winds she brings together peoples who are scattered in different localities, and that she distributes the sum of her gifts throughout various regions in such a way as to make reciprocal commerce a necessity for the members of the human race.

Therefore, the right to engage in commerce pertains equally to all peoples; and jurisconsults[a] of the greatest renown extend the application of this principle to the point where they deny that any state or prince has the power to issue a general prohibition forbidding others to enjoy access to or trade with the subjects of that state or prince. This doctrine is the source of the sacrosanct law of hospitality. It is the basis of the Trojan complaints: [97]

> What kind of men are these? What land allows
> So barbarous a custom? We are barred
> From welcome to its shores. . . .[b]

This other passage, too, is pertinent:

> A harmless landing-place we crave, and air
> And water, which are free to all. . . .[c]

Moreover, we know that certain wars have been undertaken precisely on such grounds. This was true, for example, of the Megarean war against the Athenians,[d] and of the Bolognese war against the Venetians.[e] Similarly, Victoria[f] holds that, if the Spaniards should be prohibited by the American Indians from travelling or residing among the latter, or if they should be prevented from sharing in those things which are common property under the law of nations or by custom—if, in short, they should be debarred from the practice of commerce—these causes might serve them as just grounds for war against the Indians; and, indeed, as

a. *Institutes,* II. i. 1; *Dig.* I. viii. 4; see Gentili, *De Iure Belli,* I. xix; *Code,* IV. lxiii. 4.
b. Virgil, *Aeneid,* I [539 f.].
c. *Ibid.* VII [229 f.].
d. Dio. Sic. XI [XII. xxxix]; Plutarch, *Pericles* [xxix, p. 168 B].
e. Sigonio, *Hist. de Regno Italiae,* last book.
f. *De Indis,* II. 1–7; add Covarr., *On Sext,* rule *peccatum,* § 9, n. 4: word *Quinta.*

grounds more plausible than others [discussed by Victoria in an earlier section of the same work]. A like example is recorded in the story of Moses[a] and in a passage from Augustine[b] based upon that story. I allude to the fact that the Israelites waged war justly against the Amorites because the right of inoffensive transit through the Amorite territory was denied them, even though such transit ought to be freely permitted according to the absolutely just *law of human fellowship.* Hercules, too, made war upon the King of the Orchomenians,[c] and the Greeks (under the leadership of Agamemnon) upon the King of the Mysians, on this same ground, namely, that highways are (so to speak) free and open by natural disposition, as Baldus[d] has declared. Yet again, according to Tacitus,[e] the Germans accused the Romans of preventing conferences and assemblages among the various tribes, and of blocking off lands, rivers, and, in a sense, the very skies. Nor did the Christians in earlier times find any more acceptable justification for their crusades against the Saracens than the charge that the latter were barring the Christians from access to the land of Palestine.[f]

From the doctrine above set forth, it follows that the Portuguese, even if they were the owners of the regions sought by the Dutch, would nevertheless be inflicting an injury if they prevented the Dutch from entering those regions and engaging in commerce therein. How much more unjust, then, is the existing situation, in which persons desirous of commerce with peoples who share that desire, are cut off from the latter by the intervention of men who are not invested with power either over the said peoples or over the route to be followed! For there is no stronger reason underlying our abhorrence even of robbers and pirates than [97′] the fact that they besiege and render unsafe the thoroughfares of human intercourse.

a. *Numbers,* xx [14–22].

b. *Qu. on Heptateuch,* IV, qu. 44, *On Numbers,* cited in *Decretum,* II. xxiii. 2. 3.

c. Sophocles, *Trachinian Women* [found in Apollodorus, *Library,* II. vii. 7].

d. *Consilia,* III. 293.

e. *Histories,* IV [lxiv].

f. Alciati, *Consilia,* VII. 130; Covarr., *On Sext,* rule *peccatum,* Pt. II, § 9 [§ 10]; Bartolus, *On Code,* I. xi. 1.

In any case, we hold that the Portuguese are not the owners of the regions visited by the Dutch (that is to say, Java, Sumatra, and most of the Moluccas), on the basis of the incontrovertible argument that no one is owner of a thing which has never been taken into his possession either by his own direct action or by another party acting in his name. The islands in question now have, and always have had, their own rulers, governments, statutes, and legal systems. The Portuguese, like other peoples, are permitted to carry on trade there. Indeed, by paying the tributes levied and also by the very act of petitioning the rulers for the right of trade, the Portuguese themselves testify clearly enough to the fact that they are not the owners of those lands, but foreign visitors. Their very residence in the islands is allowed as a favour.

Moreover, aside from the fact that title does not suffice to constitute ownership, since possession is also a requisite (for possession of a thing is different from the right to seek possession thereof), I go so far as to assert that the Portuguese do not even have any title to ownership of the said regions which has not been taken from them by the pronouncements of learned men, among whom certain Spanish authorities are included.

In the first place, if the Portuguese maintain that those territories have passed into their hands as a reward for discovery, their contention will find support neither in law nor in fact.

Discovery For discovery consists, not in perceiving a thing with the eye, but in actual seizure, as is intimated by the Emperor Gordian in one of his letters.[a] Thus the philologists[b] treat the expressions "to discover" (*invenire*) and "to take possession of" (*occupare*) as synonymous terms; and, according to all Latin usage,[c] we have "discovered" only that which we have acquired (*adepti*), the opposite process being that of "loss" (*perdere*). Furthermore, natural reason itself, the express statements of the

a. *Code,* VIII. xli. 13.

b. Nonius Marcellus [*De Compendiosa Doctrina*], IV, on word *occupare.*

c. See Connan, *Commentaria Juris Civilis,* III. iii, at end.

law, and their interpretation by men of considerable learning,[a] all clearly indicate that discovery suffices to create a title to ownership only when possession is an accompanying factor;[b] that is to say, only in cases where movable articles are seized, or immovable property is marked off by boundaries and placed under guard.[c] In the particular case under discussion, it is in nowise possible to maintain that this requisite has [98] been met; for the Portuguese have no garrisons stationed in those East Indian lands.

Besides, what answer can be made to the objection that the Portuguese cannot in any sense at all be said to have found the East Indies, a region exceedingly well known for so many centuries past, even as early as the time of Horace? [For we find these lines in his *Epistles:*][d]

> The busy trader flees from poverty,
> Across the seas to India's farthest isle.

And what of the fact that the Romans[e] have described for us with the utmost exactitude the greater part of Taprobane?[5] The other islands, too,

a. See Doneau, *Commentaries,* IV. x.
b. *Institutes,* II. i. 13.
c. *Dig.* XLI. ii. 3, § 3.
d. I. i [45 f.].
e. Pliny, *Nat. Hist.* VI. xxii [xxiv].

5. The name applied by Grotius to Sumatra, and so translated in most passages of the present volume (cf. note 4, p. 14, *supra*). This use of the Latin name *Taprobane* was not uncommon at the time when Grotius wrote. Expert Latinists now agree, however, in rendering *Taprobane* as "Ceylon" when it appears in the works of Pliny (above cited) or any other Classical Latin author. In fact, it is commonly held that Sumatra was not even known to the western world until long after the age of Pliny.

On the other hand, certain details in the classical descriptions of Taprobane apply less accurately to Ceylon than to Sumatra; and it should be remembered that the early conception of the East Indian region embraced a vast and little-known territory, so that different voyages may have resulted in accounts of two or more islands mistakenly identified as the single island of Taprobane. If Columbus was able to confuse the Antilles with the East Indies, surely travellers of a still less enlightened epoch could have confused Sumatra with Ceylon.

Since any explanation of the discrepancy between Grotius's use of the term *Taprobane* and the proper interpretation of the same term as employed in Classical Latin must be hypothetical, it has seemed advisable to retain the Latin form here, while

were already known not only to the neighbouring Persians and Arabs but also to some European peoples, and in particular to the Venetians—before the Portuguese came to know them.

Thesis II In addition to the foregoing arguments, however, it should be noted that even discovery imparts no legal right save in the case of those things which were ownerless prior to the act of discovery.[a] But at the time when the Portuguese first came to the East Indies, the natives of that region—though they were in part idolaters, in part Mohammedans, and sunk in grievous sin[b]—nevertheless enjoyed public and private ownership of their own property and possessions, an attribute which could not be taken from them without just cause. This is the conclusion expounded by the Spaniard Victoria with irrefutable logic and in agreement with other authorities of the greatest renown.

Victoria[c] declares that "Christians, whether laymen or clerics, may not deprive infidels of their civil power and sovereignty merely on the ground that the latter are infidels, unless they have been guilty of some other wrong." For the factor of religious faith, as Saint Thomas[d] rightly observes, does not cancel the natural or human law from which ownership has been derived. On the contrary, it is heretical to hold that infidels are not the owners of the property that belongs to them.[e] And the act of snatching from them, on the sole ground of their lack of faith, those goods which have been taken into their possession, is an act of thievery and rapine no less than it would be if perpetrated against Christians. Thus Victoria correctly maintains that the Spaniards acquired no greater right over the American Indians in consequence of that defect of faith, than the Indians would have possessed over the Spaniards if any of the former had been the first foreigners to come to Spain.

---

reminding the reader that Grotius himself was primarily interested in Sumatra and neighbouring localities.

a. *Dig.* XLI. i. 3.

b. Covarr., *On Sext,* rule *peccatum,* Pt. II, § 10, nn. 2, 4, 5.

c. *De Potestate Civili,* I. 9.

d. II–II, qu. 10, art. 12.

e. Vict., *De Indis,* I. 4–7 and 19.

Furthermore, the Indians of the Orient are neither insane nor irrational, but clever and sagacious, so that not even in this respect can a pretext for their subjugation be found. For that matter, any such pretext is in itself clearly unjust. Long ago, Plutarch[a] pointed out [98′] that ἡμερῶσαι τὰ βαρβαρικά [the civilizing of barbarians] served as πρόφασις πλεονεξίας [a cloak for greed], or in other words, that shameless lust for another's property was wont to take cover under the excuse of introducing civilization into barbaric regions. Nowadays, even this pretext of bringing reluctant peoples to an acceptance of more refined customs—an explanation to which recourse was had in earlier times by the Greeks and by Alexander—is regarded in the judgement of all the theologians,[b] and particularly in that of the Spaniards, as unjust and impious.

Secondly,[6] if the Portuguese are basing their claim upon the apportionment made by Pope Alexander the Sixth, it will be necessary to take under consideration before everything else the question of whether or not the Pope was interested exclusively in settling the disputes between the Portuguese and the Castilians. This task he was of course empowered to discharge in his capacity as chosen arbiter between the two peoples,[c] since the respective rulers themselves had previously concluded certain treaties on that very point. If we assume that the settlement of those disputes was the Pope's sole aim, we must infer that the apportionment was drawn up only with reference to the Spaniards and the Portuguese and therefore will not affect the other peoples of the world. Or was it, instead, his intention to bestow almost a third of the whole earth upon each of the two nations above mentioned? Even in such circumstances—that is to say, if he had intended and had been empowered to make such a donation—nevertheless, it would not necessarily follow that the Portuguese had become the owners of the Orient, since it is not the act of

a. [*Pompey,* lxx. 3.]

b. See Vázquez, *Ill. Cont.* in Pref. n. 5[–6].

c. See Osorio [*History of Emmanuel*].

6. The first suggested basis for the Portuguese claim was "reward for discovery" (*supra,* p. 306).

donation but the subsequent delivery that creates ownership.[a] Therefore, in order to give validity to such a claim, it would be necessary to add the title of actual possession to the title of donation.

Furthermore, anyone who chooses to make a thorough examination of the question of law, whether divine or human, weighing the matter independently of his personal interests, will readily discern that a donation of this kind, concerning as it does the property of others, is without effect. I shall not enter here into any dispute as to the power pertaining to the Pope (in other words, to the Bishop of the Church of Rome); nor shall I make any assertion save on the basis of a hypothesis accepted by the most erudite of those persons who attribute the highest possible degree of authority to the papal office, and among whom the Spaniards in particular are included. The latter have boldly asserted (and I use their own words), that the Pope is not the civil or temporal lord of the whole earth;[b] for, with their characteristic acuteness, they have readily grasped these facts: that Christ the Lord renounced all earthly sovereignty;[c] that in His human form He certainly did not possess dominion over the entire world; and that if He had possessed such dominion, this sovereign right could not by any series of arguments be attributed to the Pope or transferred on a vicarious basis to the Church of Rome, inasmuch as it is indubitably true that in other respects, also, Christ possessed many things to which the Pope did not fall heir.[d] Certain other admissions should also be noted, namely: that even if the Pope did have worldly power of this kind, he would still not be right in exercising it, since he ought to be content with his spiritual jurisdiction;[e] that, in any case, he would in nowise be able to cede such power to secular [99] princes; that, moreover, if he does possess any temporal power, he pos-

a. See *Institutes,* II. i. 40.

b. See Vázquez, *Ill. Cont.* xxi; Torquemada [*Summa de Ecclesia*], II. cxiii; Hugo of Pisa [*Summa on Decretum*], I. lxix [xcvi] 6; Bernard of Clairvaux, *De Consideratione ad Eugenium,* II [vi. 9–11]; Vict., *De Indis,* I. 27 [II. 3]; Covarr., *On Sext,* rule *peccatum,* Pt. II, § 9, n. 7.

c. *Luke,* xii. 14; *St. John,* xviii. 36; Vict., *De Indis,* I. 25 [II. 1].

d. Vict., *ibid.* 27 [II. 3].

e. *Matthew,* xx. 26; *St. John,* vi. 15; *Matthew,* xvii. 27 [25–7].

sesses it, as the phrase goes, for spiritual ends;[a] and that, consequently, he has no power at all over infidel peoples, since they are not members of the Church.

Thus it follows from the opinions laid down by Cajetan and by Victoria as well as from the preponderant authority of both theologians and canonists,[b] that there is no sound claim to be urged against the East Indians, either on the ground that the Pope as lord of the East Indian lands gave away this territory by an unrestricted act of donation, or on the ground that the inhabitants fail to acknowledge the papal dominion; and indeed, it is also clear that even the Saracens were never despoiled on such grounds.

Now that we have disposed of the pretexts just discussed, having plainly shown that (as Victoria[c] himself declares) the Hispanic peoples did not carry with them to still more distant regions any right to take possession of the lands to which they sailed, there remains for consideration only one possible title, based upon war. Such a title, even if it were in itself just, still could not create ownership save through the right attaching to captured property, that is to say, only after seizure. But the Portuguese, far from seizing the lands in question, were not engaged at the time in any war with the majority of the peoples visited by the Dutch. Consequently, there was no legal right that they could claim; for even if they had suffered injuries of any sort at the hands of the East Indians, it could reasonably be assumed that those injuries had been forgiven, in view of the long period of peace and the friendly commercial relations that had been established.

As a matter of fact, there was no pretext that the Portuguese could offer for going to war, since anyone who makes war upon barbarians (as the Spaniards did upon the American Indians) is wont to advance one of two pretexts: either that he is prevented by the said barbarians from

a. Vict., *ibid.* 28 [II. 4]; Covarr., *ibid.; 1 Corinthians,* v, at end.

b. Th. Aq. II–II, qu. 12, art. 2; Ayala, I. ii. 29; Vict., *ibid.* 30 [II. 6]; Covarr., *ibid.* Cajetan, *On II–II,* qu. 66, art. 8; Th. Aq. II–II, qu. 66, art. 8; Sylvester, on words [*infidelitate, et*] *infidelibus,* vii [viii]; Innocent, *On Decretals,* III. xxxiv. 8; Vict., *ibid.* 31 [II. 7].

c. Vict., *De Indis,* 31 [II. 7].

engaging in trade, or else that the latter refuse to accept the doctrines of the true faith.

The Portuguese certainly did obtain rights of trade from the East Indians, so that they have no cause for complaint in this respect.

As for the other excuse, it would be quite as unjust[a] as the argument advanced by the Greeks against the barbarians, to which Boethius[b] refers in these terms: [99′]

> Do they wage savage frays and unjust wars,
> Seeking to perish by each other's swords,
> Because they dwell apart, with unlike ways?
> This is no just sufficient cause for rage.

Moreover, St. Thomas, the Council of Toledo, Gregory, and practically all of the theologians, canonists, and jurists[c] arrive at the following conclusion: howsoever convincingly and fully the true faith may have been preached to barbarians (it is understood, of course, that quite a different question arises in the case of peoples previously subject to Christian princes, and likewise in the case of apostates), and even though the said barbarians may have refused to accept that faith, it is still not permissible to make war upon them or to deprive them of their goods merely on these grounds. It will be worth our while to quote in this connexion the exact words of Cajetan:

> Some infidels (says Cajetan)[d] do not fall under the temporal jurisdiction of Christian princes either in law or in fact. Take as an example the case of pagans who were never subjects of the Roman Empire, and who dwell in lands where the term "Christian" was never heard. For surely the rulers of such persons are legitimate rulers, despite the fact that they are infidels and regardless of whether the government in question is a monarchical régime or a commonwealth; nor are they to be

a. See Vázquez, *Ill. Cont.* xxiv; Vict., *De Indis,* II. 10.

b. *The Consolation of Philosophy,* IV. iv [7 ff.].

c. *Matthew,* x. 23; Th. Aq. II–II, qu. 10, art. 8; *Decretum,* I. xlv. 5; *ibid.* 3; Innocent thereon; Bartolus, *On Code,* I. xi. 1; Covarr., *On Sext,* rule *peccatum,* Pt. II, §§ 9–10; Ayala, I. ii. 28.

d. *On II–II,* qu. 66, art. 8.

deprived of dominion over their own peoples on the ground of lack of faith, since dominion falls within the realm of positive law[7] while lack of faith is a matter subject to divine law, and since the latter form of law does not abrogate the positive form, a point already established in the discussion of this question. Indeed, I do not know of any legal precept relative to such persons, in so far as temporal matters are concerned. No king, no emperor, not even the Church of Rome, is empowered to undertake war against them for the purpose of seizing their lands or reducing them to temporal subjection. Such an attempt would be based upon no just cause of war; for the emissaries sent forth to take possession of the world, by Jesus Christ the King of Kings, unto Whom power was given in heaven and on earth [*Matthew,* xxviii. 18], were not armed professional soldiers, but holy preachers, sheep in the midst of wolves [*Matthew,* x. 16; *Luke,* x. 3]. Thus I do not read in the Old [100] Testament, in connection with the occasions on which it was necessary to seize possession by armed force, that war was ever declared against any nation of infidels on the ground that the latter did not profess the true faith. I find, instead, that the reason for such declarations of war was the unwillingness of the infidels to concede the right of passage, or the fact that they had attacked the faithful (as the Midianites did, for example), or a desire on the part of the believers to recover their own property, bestowed upon them by divine bounty. Hence it follows that *we should be committing a very grave sin,* if we strove to extend by such means the realm of the faith of Jesus Christ. Moreover, this course of action would not make us *the legitimate masters* of the infidels; we should merely be committing *robbery on a large scale* and placing ourselves under an obligation to make restitution as *unjust conquerors or captors.* Men of integrity ought to be sent as preachers to these infidels, in order that unbelievers may be induced by teaching and by example to seek God; but men ought not to be sent with the purpose of crushing, despoiling and tempting unbelievers, bringing them into subjection, and making them twofold more the children of hell [than the emissaries themselves],[8] after the fashion of the Pharisees.

7. I.e. human positive law.

8. The bracketed phrase is inserted because Cajetan obviously had in mind the Biblical verse, "Woe unto you, scribes and Pharisees, hypocrites! for ye compass sea

We are told, too,[a] that pronouncements to precisely the same effect have frequently been issued by the Senate in Spain and by the theologians (especially the Dominicans), ruling that the American Indians should be converted to the faith not through war but solely through the preaching of the Word, and that the liberty taken from them on the pretext of conversion should be restored to them. This policy is said to have been approved by Pope Paul III and by the Emperor Charles V, King of the Spanish realms. For the rest, we shall not dwell here upon the fact that in most regions the Portuguese are in no sense advancing the cause of religion, nor even making any effort to do so, since they are intent only upon gain. Nor shall we pause to comment upon the further fact that one might truthfully apply to the Portuguese in the East Indies the observation made by the Spanish writer Victoria[b] regarding the Spaniards in America, namely: that no reports are received of miracles, portents, or examples of pious conduct, such as might impel others to embrace the same faith, whereas, on the contrary, there are numerous reports of inducements to sin, criminal acts, and impiety.

Therefore, since the Portuguese lack both possession and title to possession, since the property and sovereign powers of the East Indians ought not to be regarded as things that had no owner prior to the advent of the Portuguese, and since that property and those powers—belonging as they did to the peoples of the Indies—could not rightly be acquired by other persons, it follows that the said peoples are not Portuguese chattels, but free men possessed of full social and civil rights [*sui iuris*]. On this point there is no doubt, even among Spanish authorities.[c] [100′]

Thesis III Granting, then, that the Portuguese have not acquired any legal right over the East Indian peoples, lands or governments, let us ascertain

---

and land to make one proselyte, and when he is made, ye make him twofold more the child of hell than yourselves" (*Matthew,* xxiii. 15).

a. John Metal [Matal] in Osorio, *History of Emmanuel,* Pref.

b. [*De Indis,*] I. 38 [II. 14].

c. Vict., *De Indis,* at end of Pt. II [I. 24].

whether or not the former have been able to bring the sea and matters of navigation, or the conduct of trade, under their own jurisdiction.

We shall consider first the question of the sea. Although the sea is variously described in the phraseology of the law of nations as *res nullius,* as common property and as public property, the significance of these different terms will be very easily explained if, in imitation of the method employed by all the poets since the days of Hesiod as well as by the ancient philosophers and jurists, we draw a chronological distinction between things which are perhaps not differentiated from one another by any considerable interval of time, but which do indeed differ in certain underlying principles and by their very nature. Moreover, we ought not to be censured if, in our explanation of a right derived from nature, we avail ourselves of the authority and express statements of persons generally regarded as pre-eminent in natural powers of judgement.

New explanation Ownership and common possession

Accordingly, it must be understood that, during the earliest epoch of man's history, ownership [*dominium*] and common possession [*communio*] were concepts whose significance differed from that now ascribed to them.[a] For in the present age, the term "ownership" connotes possession of something peculiarly one's own, that is to say, something belonging to a given party in such a way that it cannot be similarly possessed by any other party; whereas the expression "common property" is applied to that which has been assigned to several parties, to be possessed by them in partnership (so to speak) and in mutual concord, to the exclusion of other parties. Owing to the poverty of human speech, however, it has become necessary to employ identical terms for concepts which are not identical. Consequently, because of a certain degree of similitude and by analogy, the above-mentioned expressions descriptive of our modern customs are applied to another right, which existed in early times. Thus with reference to that early age, the term "common" is nothing more nor less than the simple antonym of "private" [*proprium*]; and the word "ownership" denotes the power to make use rightfully of common [i.e. public] property. This attribute the Scholastics

a. Glossators and Castrensis, *On Dig.* I. i. 5 and Glossators, *On Decretum,* I. i. 7.

choose to describe as a concept of fact but not of law. For the legal right now connoted by the term "use" [*usus*] is of a private nature; or, in other words (if I may borrow from the phraseology of the Scholastics),[a] "use" carries with it a privative force with respect to all extraneous parties.

There was no private property under the primary law of nations, to which we also give the name of "natural law," from time to time, and which the poets represent in some passages as prevailing in the Golden Age while in other passages they assign it to the reign of Saturn or of Justice. In fact, we find this statement in the works of Cicero:[b] "There is, however, no such thing as private property in the natural order." Horace,[c] too, wrote as follows:

> Nor he, nor I, nor any man, is made
> By Nature private owner of the soil.

For in the eyes of nature no distinctions of ownership were discernible. In this sense, then, we say that all things were common property in those distant days, meaning just what the poets do when they declare that the men of earliest times made acquisitions on behalf of the community, and that the communal character of goods was maintained by justice in accordance with a sacred pact. In order to clarify this point, they explain that fields were not divided by boundary lines in that age, and that [101] there were no commercial transactions.

> The mingled farms throughout the countryside
> Showed that all things *seemed common* to all men.[d]

The word "seemed" was properly included in these lines, in recognition of the changed meaning of the term "common," to which we alluded above. This concept of common ownership had reference, of course, to the use of the things involved.

a. Vázquez, *Ill. Cont.* i. 10; *Sext,* V. xii. 3; *Constitutions of Clement,* V. xi. 1.
b. [*On Duties,* I. viii. 21.]
c. [*Satires,* II. ii. 129 f.]
d. Avienus, *On Aratus, Phaenomena* [302 f.].

. . . To all the way was open;
The *use* of all things was a *common* right.[a]

Thus a certain form of ownership did exist, but it was ownership in a universal and indefinite sense. For God had given all things, not to this or that individual, but to the human race; and there was nothing to prevent a number of persons from being joint owners, in this fashion, of one and the same possession. But such a concept would be completely irrational if we were giving to the term "ownership" its modern significance, involving private possession [*proprietas*], an attribute which did not reside in any person during that epoch. In fact, it has been most aptly observed that,

. . . All things belonged to him
Who put them to his use. . . .[b]

It is evident, however, that the present-day concept of distinctions in ownership was the result, not of any sudden transition, but of a gradual process whose initial steps were taken under the guidance of nature herself. For there are some things which are consumed by use, either in the sense that they are converted into the very substance of the user and therefore admit of no further use,[c] or else in the sense that they are rendered less fit for additional service by the fact that they have once been made to serve. Accordingly, it very soon became apparent, in regard to articles of the first class (for example, food and drink), that a certain form of private ownership was inseparable from use. For the essential characteristic of private property is the fact that it belongs to a given individual in such a way as to be incapable of belonging to any other individual. This basic concept was later extended by a logical process to include articles of the second class, such as clothing and various other things capable of being moved or of moving themselves. Because of these developments, it was not even possible for all immovable things (fields, for instance) to remain unapportioned, since the use of such

a. Seneca, *Octavia* [402 f.].
b. Avienus [*ibid.* 301 f.].
c. *Dig.* VII. v; *Extravagantes,* XIV. iii and v; Th. Aq. II–II, qu. 78, art. 1.

things, while it does not consist directly in their consumption, is nevertheless bound up [in some cases] with purposes of consumption (as it is when arable lands and orchards are used with a view to obtaining food, or pastures for [animals intended to provide] clothing), and since there are not enough immovable goods to suffice for indiscriminate use by all persons. [101′]

The recognition of the existence of private property led to the establishment of a law on the matter, and this law was patterned after nature's plan. For just as the right to use the goods in question was originally acquired through a physical act of attachment, the very source (as we have observed) of the institution of private property, so it was deemed desirable that each individual's private possessions should be acquired, as such, through similar acts of attachment. This is the process known as "occupation" [*occupatio*], a particularly appropriate term in connexion with those goods which were formerly at the disposal of the community. Seneca[a] has in mind that very process, when he says, in one of his tragedies:

> *A common opportunity* for crime
> Awaits the one who first shall *grasp* the chance [*occupanti*].

Again, speaking as a philosopher, he[b] makes this statement: "[. . . there are several kinds of common ownership.] The equestrian rows of seats belong to *all* the Roman knights; yet the place that I have *occupied* in those rows becomes my *own*." Similarly, Quintilian[c] notes that certain things created for all, become the reward of the industrious. Cicero,[d] too, declares that some goods are acquired, in consequence of long occupancy, as the property of those who came upon them before they had been taken into anyone's possession. This occupancy, [or tenure,] must be continuous, however, in the case of things that resist possession, such as wild beasts. In other cases, the only requisite is that the status of pos-

a. Seneca, *Thyestes* [203–4].
b. Seneca, *On Benefits,* VII. xii.
c. *Declamations,* xiii [8].
d. *On Duties,* I [vii. 21].

session initiated by a physical act shall be continued mentally. With respect to movables, moreover, occupancy implies physical seizure [*apprehensio*]; with respect to immovables, it implies some activity involving construction or the definition of boundaries. It is for this reason that Hermogenianus,[a] [in listing certain effects of the law of nations,] mentions immediately after "determination of property rights," these two items: "establishment of boundaries for lands" and "erection of buildings." The same stage in the development of private property is described by the poets. Virgil[b] wrote:

> 'Twas then men learned to capture beasts with snares,
> To practise trickery with birdlime, too.

In the works of Ovid,[c] we find the following passage:

> Then first were *houses* sought by humankind.
> . . . .
> Surveyors marked with careful, long-drawn lines,
> *The bound'ries* for the soil which *hitherto*
> Had been a *common* good like sun and air.

At a subsequent stage in the evolution of property, as Hermogenianus indicates [in the above-mentioned list], commerce began to be widely practised; and for the sake of commerce, so Ovid[d] tells us,[9]

> The keels of ships leapt over unknown waves.

During the same period, moreover, the establishment of states was first undertaken.

Accordingly, we find that those things which were wrested from the original domain of common ownership have been divided into two cate-

a. *Dig.* I. i. 5.

b. *Georgics,* I [139–40].

c. *Metamorphoses,* I [121, 135 f.].

d. [*Metamorphoses,* I. 134.]

9. It should be noted that the order of events as depicted by Ovid differs slightly from that indicated above. According to the author of the *Metamorphoses,* houses were first used in the Silver, or Second Age, whereas the navigation of unknown waters and the marking of boundaries were both activities of the Fourth or Iron Age.

gories. For some are now public property, or in other words, they are owned by the people, which is the true meaning of the expression [102] "public property"; and others are strictly private property, that is to say, they belong to individuals.

Nevertheless, occupancy of public possessions is achieved by the same method as occupancy of private possessions. Seneca[a] makes this observation: "We designate as 'territory of the Athenians,' or 'territory of the Campanians,' lands which the inhabitants in their turn divide among themselves by fixing private boundaries." For every individual nation

> Established kingdoms *marked with bound'ry lines*
> And *built* new cities. . . .[b]

In like manner, Cicero[c] notes that the territory of Arpinum is said to belong to the people of Arpinum, and that of Tusculum to the Tusculans. To this he adds the following comment: ". . . and the apportionment of private property is similar. Accordingly, since each individual's part of those things which nature gave as *common property* becomes his own, let each person retain possession of that which has fallen to his lot." On the other hand, lands that did not fall into the possession of any nation in the process of apportionment, are called by Thucydides[d] *ἀόριστον*, that is to say, "undefined" regions, marked by no fixed limits.

From the foregoing discussion, two inferences may be drawn. The first runs as follows: those things which are incapable of being occupied, or which never have been occupied, cannot be the private property of any owner,[e] since all property has its origin as such in occupancy. The second inference may be stated thus: all those things which have been so constituted by nature that, even when used by a specific individual, they nevertheless suffice for general use by other persons without discrimination, retain to-day and should retain for all time that status which

a. *On Benefits,* VII. iv.
b. Seneca, *Octavia* [420 f.].
c. *On Duties,* I [vii. 21].
d. I [cxxxix].
e. Duaren, *On Dig.* I. viii.

characterized them when first they sprang from nature. Cicero[a] upheld this principle, when he wrote: "Herein, to be sure, lies the most comprehensive of the bonds uniting men to men and all to all; and in observance thereof, our common participation in all things produced by nature for mankind's common use should be maintained."

Now, the category thus defined includes everything capable of serving the convenience of a given person without detriment to the interests of any other person; and this concept (according to Cicero[b]) is the source of the maxim, "Deny to no one the water that flows by." For running water, considered as such and not as a stream, is classed by the jurists among the things that are common to all. Ovid[c] adopts the same classification in the following lines:

> Why would you withhold *water* from my lips?
> *The use* of water is a *common* right.
> Nor sun nor air nor water's gentle *flow*
> Are *private* things by *natural* design.
> The gifts I seek are *public* property. [102′]

Thus Ovid contends that the goods above mentioned are not private possessions according to nature's plan; just as Ulpian[d] declares that by the said plan they are free to all. For, in the first place, they proceeded originally from nature and have not yet been placed under the ownership of anyone (as Neratius[e] points out); and in the second place, it is evident (as Cicero[f] observes) that nature produced them for our common use. Ovid employs the term "public" in its old sense,[g] moreover, applying it to things that are the property not of a particular nation but of human society in general. In the precepts of the law of nations, too, such things are described as "public," that is to say, as the common possession of all

a. *On Duties,* I [xvi. 51].
b. [*Ibid.* 52.]
c. *Metamorphoses,* VI [349 ff.].
d. *Dig.* VIII. iv. 13.
e. *Dig.* XLI. i. 14.
f. *Loc. cit.* [*On Duties,* I. xvi. 51].
g. See Connan, *Comm. Juris Civilis,* III. ii; Doneau, *Comm.* IV. ii.

men and the private possession of none.[a] Air falls into this class for two reasons: first, because it is not possible for air to be made subject to occupancy; secondly, because all men have a common right to the use of air. For the same reasons, the sea is an element common to all, since it is so vast that no one could possibly take possession of it, and since it is fitted for use by all, "with reference to purposes of navigation and to purposes of fishing, as well."[b] Furthermore, the right that exists in regard to the sea exists likewise in regard to anything that the latter has diverted from other uses and made its own, such as the sands of the sea, of which the portion merging into the land is called the shore. Therefore, Cicero[c] is justified in asking, "What is so *common* . . . as is the sea to those who are tossed by the waves, or the *shore* to castaways?" Similarly, Virgil[d] asserts that the air, the water, and the shore are freely accessible to everyone.

These, then, are the things described by the Romans[e] as common to all under natural law, or as public under the law of nations, which (according to the foregoing discussion) is another way of expressing the same concept. In like manner, the Romans sometimes describe the use of such things as common, while at other times they refer to it as public.

Nevertheless, even though the said things are correctly called *res nullius* in so far as private ownership is concerned, they are very different from those which are also *res nullius* but which have not been assigned for common use: e.g. wild beasts, fish, and birds. Items belonging to the latter class can be made subject to private ownership, provided that someone does take possession of them; whereas items falling within the former class have been rendered forever exempt from such ownership by the unanimous agreement of mankind, in view of the fact that the right to use them, pertaining as it does to all men, can no more be taken from humanity as a whole by one individual than my property can be taken

a. *Dig.* XLI. iii. 49 [45].

b. *Dig.* I. viii. 10 [2].

c. *Loc. cit.* [*In Defence of Sextus Roscius,* xxvi. 72].

d. [*Aeneid,* VII. 230.]

e. *Institutes,* II. i, §§ 1, 5; *Dig.* I. viii. 1, 2, 10; *ibid.* XLI. i. 14 and 50; *ibid.* XLVII. x. 13, § 7; *ibid.* XLIII. viii. 3, 4.

from me by you. Among the prime functions of justice Cicero[a] lists this very task of leading men to make use of common possessions for common interests. The Scholastics would say that the one class is common in a positive sense, and the other, in a privative sense. This distinction is not only familiar to the jurists, but also representative of the popular belief.

Thus Athenaeus depicts the master of the feast as maintaining that the sea is common property, whereas fish become the property of the persons who catch them. And again, in Plautus' play entitled *The* [103] *Rope,*[b] the fisherman assents when the young slave says,

> The sea's most certainly common to all;

but when the slave adds,

> 'Tis common property, found in the sea,

the fisherman justly objects,

> Whatever is caught by my net and hook
> Is mine in the truest sense. . . .

It is, then, quite impossible for the sea to be made the private property of any individual; for nature does not merely permit, but rather commands, that the sea shall be held in common.[c] Furthermore, not even the shore can become private property.

These statements should be qualified, however, by the addition of an interpretative comment, to the following effect: if any part of the things in question is susceptible of occupancy in accordance with nature's plan, that part may become the property of the person occupying it, in so far as is possible without impeding its common use. This principle is rightly accepted. For, under such circumstances, there is no longer any occasion to apply either of the two restrictive norms above-mentioned, which prohibit the transfer of certain things to the realm of private rights. Con-

a. *On Duties,* I [vii. 20].
b. IV. iii [975, 977, 985].
c. See Doneau, IV. ii.

sequently, since the erection of buildings upon a given site constitutes a form of occupancy, it will be permissible to erect buildings upon the shore[a] subject to the condition (expressly laid down by Pomponius[b]) that one must be able to do so without inconveniencing other persons. Following Scaevola,[c] we shall interpret this condition as meaning that the public use (that is to say, the common use) of the shore may not be impeded. Moreover, the person who constructs the building will become the owner of the site, since the latter was not previously the private property of any individual, nor was it needed for the common use. Accordingly, it belongs to the person who occupies it, but only for the duration of such occupancy.[d] For the sea would seem to resist possession, after the fashion of a wild beast which is no longer the property of its captor once it has regained its natural liberty. In precisely this fashion, the shore returns to the sea, under the principle of postliminium.

We have also shown that anything capable of becoming private property through the process of occupancy, is likewise capable of becoming public property [in the modern sense], or in other words, the possession of a particular nation.

Thus Celsus[e] held that the shore included within the limits of the Roman Empire belonged to the Roman nation; and if this contention was correct, it was not at all strange that the said nation, acting through its prince or praetor, was able to allow its subjects a certain form of occupancy in regard to the shore.[f] This kind of occupancy, however, no less than the private form, should be subject to the restriction that it must not extend to a point where it will infringe upon the uses for which the law of nations provides. Accordingly, no one could be prevented by the Roman People from approaching the shore of the sea,[g] spreading his

a. *Institutes,* II. i, § 5; *Dig.* I. viii. 5, § 1; *ibid.* XXXIX. ii. 24.
b. *Dig.* XLI. i. 50.
c. *Dig.* XLIII. viii. 4.
d. *Dig.* I. viii. 10; *ibid.* XLI. i. 14.
e. *Dig.* XLIII. viii. 3; Doneau, IV. ii, ix.
f. *Dig.* XLI. i. 50; *ibid.* XLIII. viii. 2, §§ 10 and 16.
g. *Dig.* I. viii. 4.

nets there to dry, and performing other acts which—as mankind [103′] had willed once and for all—were to be forever permissible to all men.[a]

The sea, on the other hand, differs by nature from the shore, in that the former (save for a very small portion thereof) cannot easily be built upon nor enclosed; and furthermore, even if this were not the case, the sea could hardly be so employed without hindrance to its common use. Nevertheless, if some tiny part of it does prove susceptible of such occupancy, that part is conceded to the occupant. Thus Horace[b] was exaggerating when he wrote:

> The fishes note the sea's diminished breadth
> When piers are laid that jut into the deep.

Certainly Celsus[c] maintains that piles driven into the sea are the property of him who placed them there, although the same authority adds that no such concession should be made if the structure in question is an impediment to the subsequent use of the sea. Ulpian[d] likewise declares that this protection must be extended to the rights of the person who has constructed a foundation in the sea provided that no damage to anyone else results therefrom, whereas the interdict prohibiting the erection of a building in any public place will undoubtedly be applicable if the structure is likely to conflict with the interests of another person. Similarly, Labeo[e] holds that if any structure of this kind is erected in the sea, recourse may properly be had to the interdict forbidding the construction therein of "anything whereby a harbour, a roadstead, or the course of navigation might be rendered less satisfactory."

The principle applicable in regard to navigation—namely, that the activity in question shall remain open to all—should also be applied in connexion with fishing. No transgression will have been committed, however, if someone fences in a fishing-pool for himself in some small portion of the sea, surrounding it with stakes and thus turning the spot

a. *Dig.* XLIII. viii. 3.
b. *Odes,* III [i. 33 f.].
c. *Dig.* XLIII. viii. 3.
d. *Ibid.* 2, § 8.
e. *Ibid.* xii. 1, § 17.

into private property, just as Lucullus brought the sea to his own villa by cutting through a mountain near Naples.[a] I suppose, indeed, that the marine fish-ponds mentioned by Varro[b] and by Columella[c] were of this nature. Martial,[d] too, in his description of Apollinaris' villa at Formiae, referred to the same device as follows:

> Whene'er the deep doth feel the Wind God's sway,
> Apollinaris' table mocks the storm,
> Securely stocked with produce of its own.

Yet again, we find this comment in the works of Ambrose:[e] "You bring the very sea into your estates, so that there may be no lack of fish."

New explanation

The foregoing remarks will serve to clarify the meaning of Paulus in the passage where he says that if a given individual possesses a private right to any part of the sea, he will be entitled to apply the interdict *Uti possidetis* [in the event that he is hindered from exercising the said right]. Paulus[f] adds that this device was of course intended for use in private suits, and not in those of a public nature (among which are included the suits that may be brought in accordance with the common law of nations); but he holds that the case which he describes would relate to the enjoyment of a right based on a private—rather than on a public, or common—title. For (as the testimony of Marcianus[g] indicates) whatever has been subjected to occupancy and was properly susceptible of such subjection, no longer comes under the law of nations as the sea does. For example, if any person had prevented Lucullus or Apollinaris from fishing in one of the private preserves that they had constructed by enclosing a small portion of the sea, then, in the opinion of [104] Paulus, the owner of the preserve would have been entitled to avail him-

a. Pliny, *Nat. Hist.* X. liv [X. lxxx. 170].
b. [*On Farming,* III. xvii. 9.]
c. [*Ibid.* VIII. xvi and xvii.]
d. *Epigrams,* X. xxx [19–20].
e. *On Naboth,* iii [12].
f. *Dig.* XLVII. x. 14.
g. *Dig.* I. viii. 4.

self of an interdict—based, that is to say, on grounds of private possession—and not merely to bring an action for damages. Indeed, even in the case of a small inlet of the sea, just as in the case of a river-fork,[a] if I have taken over the locality as an occupant, if I have fished there, and above all if by pursuing this course over a period of many years I have formally proclaimed my intention of establishing private possession of the inlet, then I may prohibit other persons from enjoying the same rights (a conclusion drawn from the statement of Marcianus[b]), precisely as I might do so with respect to a lake forming part of my own domain. This rule holds good for the duration of my occupancy, even as we have already shown that it does in regard to the shore.

If the region involved exceeds the limits proper to a small inlet, the said rule will not be applicable, for it might interfere with the common use of that region. Thus it has been assumed that I may prohibit fishing by any other person in front of my dwelling or country-seat, but the assumption lacks any legal basis. In fact, it is so gravely lacking in this respect that Ulpian,[c] in rejecting it, declares that anyone who is made the object of such a prohibition may bring an action for damages. The Emperor Leo[d] (whose laws we do not observe) changed this ruling, in defiance of the underlying legal principles, and maintained that *πρόθυρα*, or coastal waters "opening out upon" the sea, were the private property of the persons dwelling along the shore, to whom he also assigned the fishing rights attached to such waters. He laid down one condition, however, for the applicability of his own ruling, namely, that the site in question should be brought under occupancy by means of certain structures which would block it off and which the Greeks called *ἐποχαί*[e] [checks, i.e. breakwaters]. Leo[f] doubtless assumed that no person would begrudge another a tiny portion of the sea as long as he himself had access to [practically] all of its waters for fishing. Certainly it

a. *Dig.* XLIV. iii. 7.
b. *Dig.* XLVII. x. 13, § 7; *ibid.* XLI. iii. 45.
c. *Dig.* XLVII. x. 13, § 7.
d. Constitution lvi.
e. [*Ibid.* lvii.]
f. Constitution, cii, ciii, civ; see also Cujas, *Observationes,* XIV. i.

would be intolerably wicked for any individual to cut off a large part of the sea from public use, even if he were able to do so. Such wickedness is deservedly assailed by Saint Ambrose,[a] in the following terms: "They claim *whole tracts of the sea* for themselves *by right of formal acquisition;* and they remind us that rights over fishing, in precisely the same fashion as those over homeborn slaves, are subject to their will under conditions of servitude. 'This *curve* of the sea,' says one, 'is mine; that curve belongs to someone else.' The mighty divide the very elements among themselves."

In short, the sea is included among those things which are not articles of commerce, that is to say, the things that cannot become part of anyone's private domain.[b] Hence it follows—in the opinion of the more erudite authorities, and in the correct and strict sense—that no part of the sea may be regarded as pertaining to the domain of any given nation. Placentinus would seem to have been aware of this fact when he said that the sea was common to all in such a degree that no being save God alone could possess ownership over it. Apparently, too, Johannes Faber[c] was sensible of the same fact when he asserted that the sea had been left *sui iuris,* and still remained in that primeval state in which all things had been held in common.

If this were not the case, there would be no difference between [104′] things common to all, such as the sea, and things designated as public in the strict sense of the term, such as rivers. It was possible for a particular nation to take possession of a river, as of something enclosed within its own boundaries, but it was not possible to take possession of the sea in the same way. The dominion of a nation over its territories, however, must be the result of occupancy by that nation, just as private ownership results from occupation by individuals. This truth was perceived by Celsus,[d] who drew a very clear distinction between the shores of the sea, which the Roman nation was empowered to occupy (though

a. *Hexaemeron,* V. x [27].

b. Doneau, *Commentaries,* IV. vi.

c. *On Institutes,* II. i. 5; add Doctors, *On Dig.* XIV. ii. 9.

d. *Dig.* XLIII. viii. 3.

only subject to the condition that the common use of the shores should not be impeded by that act), and the sea itself, which retained its pristine nature unimpaired. Nor is there any law that points to a contrary doctrine. The laws cited by writers who have held a contrary view,[a] relate in point of fact either to islands, which are clearly susceptible of occupation, or to harbours, which (properly speaking) are not common, but public. Furthermore, those authorities[b] who maintained that the sea was a part of the Roman Empire, interpreted their own statement in such a way as to restrict that Roman right over the sea to functions of protection and jurisdiction, distinguishing it from the right of ownership. Perhaps, too, the said authorities paid insufficient heed to the fact that it was not in virtue of a private right, but through a common maritime right possessed by other free nations also, that the Roman People were authorized to distribute fleets for the protection of sailors, and to punish pirates captured at sea.

On the other hand, we admit that it was possible for agreements to be drawn up between specific nations, stipulating that persons captured upon the sea in this or that particular region should be subject to judgement by this or that particular state; and we furthermore admit that, in this sense, boundaries upon the seas were indeed defined, for convenience in distinguishing the different areas of jurisdiction. Such an arrangement is binding, to be sure, upon the parties who have imposed a legal agreement of this kind upon themselves; but it is not binding in like manner upon other peoples, nor does it convert an area thus delimited into the private property of any possessor, for it merely establishes a right that has force between the contracting parties.[c]

This distinction, which is in conformity with natural reason, derives further confirmation from a reply made on a certain occasion by Ulpian,[d] when the jurist was asked whether the owner of two maritime

a. *Dig.* V. i. 9; *ibid.* XXXIX. iv. 15.

b. Glossators, *On Dig.* I. viii. 2; Baldus and Glossators, *On Institutes,* II. i. 1 and 5.

c. Baldus, *On Feuds* [p. 19]; add *Code,* XI. xiii (xii); Angelus de Ubaldis, *On Dig.* XLVII. x. 14.

d. *Dig.* VIII. iv. 13; add *ibid.* 4.

estates had possessed the power to impose upon one of them, which he was selling, a servitude involving a prohibition against fishing from that estate in a certain part of the sea. Ulpian answered that the actual object concerned—namely, the sea—could not be subjected to a [105] servitude, since it was by natural dispensation open to all; but he added that the factor of good faith implicit in a contract, demanded the observance of the conditions attaching to the sale, so that the parties actually in possession and those succeeding to the right of possession were personally bound by the said conditions. It is true that Ulpian was referring to private sales and to private law; but the same principle is equally applicable to the present discussion concerning the territories and laws of nations, since nations in their relation to the whole of mankind occupy the position of private individuals.[a]

Similarly,[b] the revenues levied on maritime fisheries and regarded as belonging to the Crown, constitute a binding obligation, not in their effect upon the object of the levies (namely, the sea or the particular fishery in question) but in their effect upon the persons concerned. Accordingly, it was perhaps permissible to make such levies compulsory in regard to subjects, over whom the state or prince exercises a legislative power that is valid by common consent; whereas, in so far as foreigners are concerned, fishing rights should everywhere be exempt from public charges, lest a servitude be imposed upon the sea, which cannot properly be subjected to any servitude. For, in the case of the sea, the basic principle involved is not the same as it would be in the case of a river, since the latter has a public character (that is to say, it is the property of the nation), so that even the right to fish therein may be conceded or leased by the nation or by the prince.[c] In fact, the ancients[d] interpreted this right in such a way as to grant the lessee recourse to the interdict "Regarding the use of a public place," subject to the following condition: "provided that the privilege of using that place, shall have been leased

a. See *supra,* pp. 319–24 and 327–28.

b. *Feuds,* II. lvi.

c. Balbus, *De Praescriptionibus,* Princ. 5, pt. 4, qu. 6, n. 4.

d. *Dig.* XLVII. x. 13, § 7.

to the party in question by one who has the right of leasing it." This condition could not be met in cases involving the sea.[a] For the rest, those persons who include fishing itself among the perquisites of the Crown have paid insufficient attention to the very passage which they themselves cite, an error that has not escaped the notice of Andrea d'Isernia and Jacopo Alvarotto.[b]

We have shown it to be impossible that any private right over the sea itself (for we made an exception in regard to small forks of the sea), should pertain to any nation or private individual, since occupation of the sea is impermissible both in the natural order and for reasons of public utility. Our examination of this question was undertaken, moreover, for the purpose of making it clear that the Portuguese have not established a private right over that part of the sea which one traverses in sailing to the East Indies. For both of the factors impeding private ownership are infinitely more cogent in this particular case than in any of the others mentioned. What constitutes merely a difficulty in those other cases is in the present instance an absolute impossibility; and [105′] what we condemned as an injustice in a different connexion is in this instance utterly barbarous and even inhuman.

We are not treating here of an inner sea which washes against the land on all sides and is in some places no wider than a mere river; but it is quite certain that the Roman jurists were referring to just such a concept in the above-mentioned[c] celebrated opinions opposing private avarice. The subject of our discussion is the Ocean, which was described in olden times as immense, infinite, the father of created things, and bounded only by the heavens; the Ocean, whose never-failing waters fed not only upon the springs and rivers and seas, according to the ancient belief, but upon the clouds, also, and in a certain measure upon the stars themselves; in fine, that Ocean which encompasses the terrestrial home of mankind with the ebb and flow of its tides, and which cannot be held nor enclosed, being itself the possessor rather than the possessed.

a. *Dig.* XLIII. ix.

b. *On Feuds,* Rubric: *Quae sunt Regalia,* n. 72.

c. Cited above, *supra,* this chap., *passim.*

Moreover, the question at issue is not limited to some bay or strait located in the Ocean, nor even to the entire expanse of its waters visible from the shore. On the contrary, the Portuguese claim for themselves the whole tract lying between two parts of the world which are separated by spaces so vast that in the course of many centuries those two regions were not able to make themselves known to each other. Indeed, if the share of the Spaniards (who join in the same claim) is added to the share demanded by the Portuguese, very nearly the entire Ocean will have been delivered into the hands of two peoples, while all the remaining nations will find themselves restricted to the narrow waters of the north. Thus nature will have been sorely deceived; for when she encompassed all peoples with this watery element, she believed that it would likewise suffice for all. If anyone should cut off from the common domain, and reserve to himself, nothing more than sovereignty and dominion over so vast a body of water, he would nevertheless be regarded as a seeker after immoderate power; if he should forbid others to fish therein, he would not escape the stigma of monstrous cupidity; but what shall we say of one who obstructs even navigation upon those waters, despite the fact that he himself would suffer no loss in consequence of such navigation?

If the sole owner of a fire forbade another to take fire therefrom, [106] or to take light from his light, I should prosecute him to the bitter end as a criminal under the law of human fellowship. For the very force and essence of that law are indicated in the words of Ennius:[a]

> His own light shines no less when he hath lit
> Another's lamp therefrom. . . .

Why, then, since it is possible to do so without injury to oneself, should one not bestow upon another a share in those things which will be useful to the recipient and whose bestowal will not harm the giver?[b] It is to goods of this kind that the philosophers[c] refer, when they maintain that

a. [In Cicero, *On Duties,* I. xvi. 52.]
b. *Ibid.* [xvi. 51–2].
c. Seneca, *On Benefits,* III. xxviii [IV. xxviii].

certain benefits should be accorded not merely to foreigners but even to ingrates.

Furthermore, that attitude which comes under the head of jealousy when it relates to private possessions, must be characterized as savagery when common property is involved. For it is the height of wickedness that a thing which is no less mine than yours by natural dispensation and by the common consent of nations, should be appropriated by you in such exclusive fashion that you deny me even its use, although that concession would render the property appropriated in nowise less your own than it was, previously.

Then, too, it should be noted that even those persons who fasten upon the possessions of others, or take for themselves exclusively property that is common to all, defend themselves on the ground that a certain form of possession has been established by them. For the institution of private property arose from original occupancy, as we have already indicated; and consequently, detention of a given thing, even though it be unjust detention, produces in a sense a semblance of ownership.

But have the Portuguese people encompassed that expanse of ocean with fortifications erected on all sides, as we are wont to do when tracts of land are seized, in such fashion that they have acquired the power to exclude whomsoever they will? Or is this so far from being the case that the Portuguese, in apportioning the world to the disadvantage of other peoples, have failed even to defend their claim by marking out boundaries (whether natural or artificial), relying instead upon an imaginary line? If this claim is to be recognized, and if such a method of measurement suffices to constitute valid possession, the geometers must have taken the earth from us long since, just as the astronomers must also have taken the heavens. Where, then, in the present case, do we encounter that factor of corporeal attachment without which ownership has never been established? Surely it must be obvious that no conceivable case could better illustrate the truth of the doctrine propounded by our own learned authorities,[a] namely: that the sea, since it is as incapable of

a. Joh. Faber, *On Institutes,* II. i. 5.

being seized as the air, cannot have been attached to the possessions of any particular nation.

If, on the other hand, the Portuguese describe as "occupancy" the acts of navigating at an earlier date than other peoples and of more or less opening the way, what contention could be more absurd? For [106′] there is no part of the sea upon which someone has not been the first to enter, so that it would necessarily follow from such a contention that every navigable region had been "occupied" by some voyager. Thus we should be excluded from all parts of the sea. Indeed, it would even be necessary to admit that the [earliest] circumnavigators of the globe had acquired for themselves the whole Ocean! But no one is ignorant of the fact that a ship sailing over the sea no more leaves behind itself a legal right than it leaves a permanent track. In any case, the claim put forward by the Portuguese—namely, that no one had sailed over the aforesaid tracts of the Ocean before they themselves did so—is by no means true. For a large part of the waters in question, in the neighbourhood of Mauritania, was navigated in quite ancient times;[a] and a more distant portion of those same waters, lying toward the East, was traversed as far as the Arabian Gulf in the course of the victories won by Alexander the Great. There are, moreover, many indications that the people of Cadiz were formerly well acquainted with this navigable area: for example, the traces of ships recognized as remnants of wrecked Spanish vessels by Gaius Caesar, the [adopted] son of Augustus, when the former was in command over the Arabian Gulf; and the statement made by Caelius Antipater to the effect that he had seen a man who had voyaged from Spain to Ethiopia on a commercial mission. These very waters were known to the Arabs, also, if we may accept as true the account given by Cornelius Nepos, in which it is related that one of his contemporaries, a certain Eudoxus, sailed from the Arabian Gulf as far as Cadiz while fleeing from Lathyrus the King of Alexandria. Again, it is absolutely certain that the Carthaginians, who enjoyed great maritime power, did not long remain in ignorance regarding that part of the Ocean. For Hanno, in the days when Carthage was mighty, made the voyage from Cadiz to the borders

a. Pliny, *Nat. Hist.* II. lxix [lxvii]; *ibid.* VI. xxxi; Mela, III [ix].

of Arabia (that is to say, by sailing around the promontory that is now known as the Cape of Good Hope, although the ancient name appears to have been Hesperion Ceras); and he included in his record a description of the entire route, specifying the position of the coast and of the various islands, and stating that at the farthest point reached the sea had not ended but his supplies were indeed coming to an end. [107] Furthermore, the route described by Pliny,[a] the embassies dispatched by the East Indians to Augustus as well as those sent from the island of Taprobane[10] to Claudius, and subsequently the recorded deeds of Trajan and the writings of Ptolemy, have made it sufficiently evident that [106′] navigation was customary at the height of Rome's power also, from the Gulf of Arabia to India, to the islands of the Indian Ocean, and even to the Golden Chersonese, which many persons identify with [107] Japan.[11] Indeed, as early as the age of Strabo,[b] according to his own testimony, a fleet belonging to Alexandrian merchants set sail from the Arabian Gulf in search of the farthest regions both of Ethiopia and of India, although few ships dared to attempt that voyage in ancient times. The Roman people derived rich revenue from these sources. Pliny[c] adds that companies of archers were attached to the ships, owing to fear of pirates; that every year India alone drew from the Roman Empire fifty million sesterces, or—if Arabia and China were also to be taken into account—that the sum received from the Empire amounted to one hundred million sesterces; and that the merchandise from those regions was sold for a hundred times as much. These examples recorded by antiquity certainly afford sufficient proof that the Portuguese were not the first [navigators of the waters above mentioned].

a. *Ibid.* VI. xxiii [xxiv].

b. Strabo [*Geography*], II [v. 12] and XVII.

c. *Loc. cit.* [VI. xxiii] and XII. xix [xviii].[12]

10. Probably Ceylon. Cf. note 4, p. 14, *supra.*

11. *Chersonesus Aurea,* "the Golden Peninsula," is usually regarded as the ancient name for Malacca (cf. note 9, p. 265, *supra*). It should be noted, moreover, that Grotius himself does not expressly approve the identification of this region with Japan.

12. Book XII of Pliny has not yet appeared in the Loeb series. This reference has, therefore, been checked in the edition of Gronovius (Leyden, 1669).

For that matter, each separate part of this oceanic tract was known before the Portuguese entered upon it; nor was there ever a time when those parts were unknown. For surely the Moors, the Ethiopians, the Arabs, the Persians, and the East Indians could not have been unacquainted with the seas near which they themselves dwelt. Therefore, those persons are lying who now boast of having discovered the seas in question.

Well, then (someone will ask), does it seem a trifling matter that the Portuguese were the first to restore to use a navigable area which had lain neglected for perhaps many centuries, and that they undeniably brought this region—at the cost of tremendous labour, expense, and peril on their own part—to the attention of the European nations not acquainted with it? By no means! If this was the purpose they cherished—namely, to point out to all the tract which they had rediscovered by their own unaided efforts—who will be so insensate as to withhold acknowledgement of the great debt that he owes to them? For in that event the Portuguese will have earned the same gratitude, praise, and undying glory with which all great discoverers have been content, whenever their discoveries were made in a zealous attempt to benefit not themselves but humanity.

If, on the other hand, the Portuguese acted with a view to their own enrichment, they should have been satisfied with the profits acquired; for in enterprises of this kind the greatest gain always falls to the earliest entrants. In fact, we know that the first Portuguese voyage yielded profits amounting in some instances to forty times the sum invested or even to larger returns; and we also know that, in consequence of these returns, a people who had long dwelt in poverty, suddenly burst into unlooked-for wealth and into such lavish pomp and luxury as had hardly been attained by the most prosperous nations at the very peak of ever-increasing good fortune.

Finally, if the Portuguese led the way into this enterprise with the intention of preventing all others from following in their [107′] footsteps, they deserve no gratitude, since they were mindful of their own profit [exclusively].

Yet they cannot properly speak of such profit as their "own," inasmuch as they are snatching away something that belongs to others. For it has not been proven that no one else would have sought out the regions in question if the Portuguese had failed to do so. Indeed, the time was drawing on apace when the location of lands and seas, as well as almost every other aspect of art and science, was to become better known, day by day. The above-mentioned examples set in ancient times would in any case have excited interest; and even if those distant shores had not been laid open at a single stroke, at least they would have been revealed gradually in the course of different voyages, with each succeeding discovery pointing the way to another. In short, the achievement whose feasibility was demonstrated by the Portuguese would have been accomplished even without that people, since there were in existence many nations no less aflame with zeal for commerce and for enterprise in foreign lands. The Venetians, who had already learned a great deal about India, were eagerly disposed to seek after further knowledge. The unflagging assiduity of the Breton French, and the audacity of the English, would not have left the task unfinished. The Dutch themselves have undertaken ventures far more desperate.

Thus the contention of the Portuguese is supported neither by any argument based upon justice nor by any convincing citation of authorities. For every authority[a] who does hold that the sea can be made subject to individual sovereignty, attributes such sovereignty to him who has dominion over the closest ports and neighbouring shores. But on all the vast extent of coast to which we have referred, the Portuguese can point to no possession, aside from a few fortified posts, which they may call their own.

Furthermore, even if a given person did possess sovereignty over the sea, he would still lack authority to diminish its common usefulness, just as the Roman People lacked authority to prevent the commission, on shores belonging to the Roman Empire, of any act whatsoever that was

a. Glossators, *On Sext,* I. vi. 3. 2 and canonists thereon; Glossators, *On Decretals,* II. ix. 3.[13]

13. Reading "tit." for a reference to the *Decretals* in place of "ff" for *Digest.*

permissible under the law of nations.[a] Yet again, even if it were possible to prohibit some particular act of this kind, such as fishing (for it [108] may be maintained that the supply of fish is, in a sense, exhaustible), it would in any case be impossible to prohibit navigation, through which the sea loses nothing. By far the most conclusive evidence in support of this point is the opinion already cited[b] by us from learned authorities, as follows: even in the case of land that has been assigned as private property, whether to nations or to single individuals, it is nevertheless unjust to deny the right of passage (that is to say, of course, unarmed and innocent passage) to men of any nation, precisely as it is unjust to deny them the right of drinking from a stream. The reason underlying this opinion is clear. For it would seem that, because nature has designed a given thing for more than one use, the nations have apportioned among themselves those rights to its use which cannot properly be exercised apart from private ownership, while retaining [for the whole of mankind], on the other hand, the rights of use whose exercise would not lead to impairment of the owner's status.

It is, then, a universally recognized fact, that he who prohibits navigation on the part of another is supported by no law. In fact, Ulpian[c] declares that the person who issues such a prohibition is even liable for damages, and other authorities have furthermore held that an interdict against interference with [common] utilities would be admissible in such circumstances. Thus the Dutch plea rests upon a universal right, since it is admitted by all that navigation of the seas is open to any person whatsoever, even when permission to navigate them has not been obtained from any ruler.[d] Indeed, this principle is expressly set forth in the laws of Spain.[e]

a. *Dig.* I. viii. 4; and Gentili, I. xix, at end.

b. This chap., *supra,* pp. 303–4, and p. 320–21.

c. *Dig.* XLIII. viii. 2, § 9; Glossators,[14] *On Dig.* XLIII. xiv. 1.

d. Baldus, *On Dig.* I. viii. 3; Rod. Suárez, *De Usu Maris,* Consil. 1.

e. [*Las Siete Partidas,*] Pt. III, tit. xxviii, laws 10 and 12 [law 3].

14. The margin of the manuscript is torn at this point. The missing parts of this marginal note and the two following, have been supplied from Grotius's *Mare Liberum.*

The donation of Pope Alexander, which may be adduced by the Portuguese as a second argument in defence of their attempt to claim the sea or the right of navigation for themselves alone (since their claim on the ground of discovery fails them), is quite clearly revealed, in the light of the foregoing observations, as a vain and empty pretext. For a donation has no weight in regard to things that do not fall within the sphere of commerce; and therefore, since neither the sea nor the right of navigation thereon can be the private property of any man, it follows that such gifts could not have been bestowed by the Pope nor received by the Portuguese.

Moreover, in view of our earlier assertion (based upon the expressed opinion of particularly sagacious authorities) that the Pope is not the temporal lord of the whole earth, it will be quite readily understood that, similarly, he is not the temporal lord of the sea. But even if this form of dominion were conceded to him, it would still not be proper that part of a right attaching to the Pontificate should be transferred to any [108′] king or nation; just as the Emperor could not convert the provinces of the Empire to his own uses, nor transfer them by sale in accordance with some whim of his own.[a] In any case, only an utterly shameless person will deny the validity of the following argument: since no one concedes to the Pope the right to make rulings in temporal matters, save perhaps in so far as such intervention is required by some necessity derived from his spiritual functions, and since, moreover, the matters now under discussion—that is to say, the sea and the right of navigation—are being considered solely from the standpoint of profit and gain, not in connexion with any pious enterprise, it follows that in regard to the present question the papal power was null and void.

Then, too, what answer is there to the objection that even princes—in other words, temporal lords—are in no sense empowered to prohibit any person from navigation? For if such princes possess a right over the sea, it is merely a right of jurisdiction and protection.

Furthermore, it is a universally recognized principle, that the Pope

a. Vict., *De Indis,* 26 [II. 2].

has no authority to commit acts repugnant to the law of nature;[a] and we have already demonstrated quite clearly that it is repugnant to the law of nature for any person to possess the sea, or the use thereof, as private property.

Finally, since the Pope has no power whatsoever to deprive any man of his rights, what defence can be offered for his conduct, if we assume that he intended to exclude by a mere word a multitude of nations—undeserving of such treatment, not condemned for any fault, harmful to no one—from a right which belonged to them no less than to the Iberian peoples?

Therefore, we must conclude either that the proclamation, interpreted in the manner suggested, was without force, or else (and this alternative is no less credible) that the Pope's intention was based upon a desire to intervene in the dispute between the Spaniards and the Portuguese without diminishing in the least degree the rights of other persons.

As a last resort, injustice is frequently defended on grounds of prescription or of custom. Accordingly, the Portuguese seek also to defend themselves upon these grounds; but irrefutable legal arguments prevent them from finding support in either concept.

For prescription is rooted in civil law. Therefore, it is not applicable between kings or between free peoples,[b] and far less can it have [109] force in opposition to the law of nature, or [primary] law of nations, which is always stronger than civil law.

Furthermore, civil law[c] itself presents an obstacle to prescription in the case under discussion. For this body of law prohibits acquisition by usucapion or by prescription,[d] in regard to those things which cannot be included under the head of property, and also in regard to those which are not susceptible of possession nor of quasi possession,[e] or which can-

a. Syl., on word *Papa,* xvi.
b. Vázquez, li [23].
c. See Doneau, *Comm.* V. xxii f.
d. *Dig.* XVIII. i. 6; *ibid.* XLI. iii. 9.
e. *Ibid.* 25; *Sext,* V. xii, ult., reg. 3.

not be alienated;[a] and all of these characteristics are correctly ascribed to the sea and to the use thereof.

Again, since it is maintained that public property (in other words, the property of a given nation) cannot be [privately] acquired[b] as a result of possession over any period of time, howsoever long, either because of the nature of the property involved or because of some prerogative pertaining to those persons who would be unfavourably affected by such a prescriptive process, how much more truly must it have been a requirement of justice that this same [permanent] right should have been granted to the whole human race, in preference to any single nation, in the case of common possessions! In fact, this is precisely the principle laid down in the writings of Papinian,[c] in the following terms: "Prescription based upon long possession is not usually conceded to have force for the acquisition of places that are public [i.e. common] by the law of nations." Papinian mentions the seashore by way of illustration, referring to a hypothetical case in which a part of the shore has been occupied through the construction of a building on that spot; for if, in such a case, the said building should be demolished and another, belonging to a different person, should afterwards be erected on the same site, no exception could be taken to its erection [on the ground of previous occupancy]. He adds another illustration, based upon analogy with public [i.e. national] possessions, as follows: if a given person has fished for years in some small river fork [and has been the only one to do so], even then (assuming, of course, that there has been a subsequent interruption of this activity), he will not be empowered to prohibit another person from enjoying the same right.

Thus it seems that Angelus,[d] and those who have agreed with Angelus in saying that the Venetians and the Genoese were able to acquire through prescription a certain right over the maritime gulf adjacent to their shores, are either mistaken or guilty of deliberate deceit, as is all

a. *Dig.* L. xvi. 28; *ibid.* XXIII. v. 16.
b. *Code,* VIII. xi (xii). 6; *ibid.* XI. xlii. 9; *Dig.* XLIII. xi. 2.
c. *Ibid.* XLI. iii. 49 [45].
d. Consilium 289. This is the theme in the other chaps. on peace.

too often the case with jurists when they exercise the authority of their sacred profession, not in the interests of law and reason, but for the gratification of persons more powerful than themselves. For the reply of Marcianus[a] (to which we have referred in a previous context, [109′] also), if duly coupled with the words of Papinian, is certainly susceptible of no other interpretation than the one approved by Johannes and by Bartolus, and accepted now by all learned authorities.[b] This interpretation runs as follows: the right to impose the prohibition in question is valid while the occupation continues, but not if it has ceased; for (as Castrensis[c] correctly observes) once such an interruption occurs, occupation loses its force, though it may have continued previously throughout a thousand years. Moreover, even if Marcianus had meant to say that a prescriptive title is conceded wherever occupation is conceded (although one can scarcely believe that he entertained such an opinion), it would still be absurd to apply a statement regarding a public river to the common sea, or one regarding a small river fork to a gulf; for prescription affecting the sea or a gulf would impede the use of something that is common property by the law of nations, whereas in the other cases mentioned prescription would result in no great impediment to public use. Yet another argument drawn from Angelus[d] and concerned with aqueducts, is rightly rejected by all on the ground that it is (as that same Castrensis points out) entirely extraneous to the question.

Therefore, it is not true that prescription of the kind suggested had its origin in a remote period whose beginning lies beyond every record of memory. For that matter, in cases where the law absolutely does away with all prescription, not even such a tremendous lapse of time is accepted as a pertinent factor; that is to say (if we may borrow the explanation of Felinus[e]), an object which is imprescriptible does not become prescriptible merely because of the passage of time immemorial. Balbus[f]

a. *Dig.* XLIV. iii. 7.
b. Duaren, *On Dig.* XLI, iii; Cujas, *ibid.* 49 [45]; Doneau, *Commentaries,* V. xxii.
c. *On Dig.* XLI. i. 14, n. 4.
d. *On Code,* XI. xliii (xlii). 4; cf. *ibid.* 9; *Dig.* XLIII. xx. 3, § 4.
e. *On Decretals,* II. xxvi. 11.
f. *De Praescriptionibus,* Princ. 5, pt. 4, qu. 6, n. 8.

grants the truth of these observations, but explains that the opinion of Angelus has been accepted, for the reason that a lapse of time extending beyond the limits of memory is regarded as having the same force as a legal grant of special privilege, in that a thoroughly satisfactory title is to be inferred therefrom.

On the basis of the foregoing comments, it is apparent that the opinion of the authorities cited was nothing more nor less than this: if any part of a state (for example, some part of the Roman Empire) had exercised a right of the kind in question, at a time antedating all the annals of memory, a prescriptive title would have been conceded to the said part on that pretext, just as it would have been conceded if a similar grant had previously been made by the prince. By the same token, [110] since no person is the master of all mankind and therefore capable of having granted such a right to any particular man or nation as opposed to the whole human race, and since the said pretext is thus destroyed, it necessarily follows that the corresponding prescriptive title is also destroyed. Therefore, even according to the opinion held by those same authorities, the lapse of unmeasured time cannot avail to establish such a title in the relations between kings or free peoples.

Furthermore, Angelus propounded a thoroughly foolish doctrine when he maintained that even if prescription could not serve to produce ownership, nevertheless, an exception should be made in favour of possessors. For Papinian[a] distinctly denies the existence of such exceptions; nor would it have been possible for him to take a different stand, since prescription itself, in his day, was nothing more nor less than an exception.

Thus we have demonstrated the truth of the following conclusion, which is expressly confirmed by the very laws of Spain:[b] prescription, upon whatsoever interval of time it may be based, is not applicable in regard to those things which have been assigned to all mankind for its common use. One argument among others which support this assertion

a. *Dig.* XLI. iii. 45.

b. Pt. III, tit. xxix, law 7, in chap. *Placa;* Rod. Suárez, *De Usu Maris,* Consil. 1, n. 4.

may be set forth as follows: he who makes use of common property is obviously exercising a common and not a private right, so that, because of imperfect possession, he has no more power than a usufructuary for the establishment of a prescriptive claim. This second argument, too, is worthy of consideration: even though there may be a [general] presumption favouring the existence of a title and of good faith in connexion with prescription based upon a lapse of time extending beyond the limits of memory,[a] nevertheless, if the facts of a particular case clearly show that absolutely no title can be granted and if the existence of bad faith is correspondingly evident (bad faith being regarded as a permanent factor in the case of a nation just as in that of an individual), the prescriptive claim is invalid because of this twofold defect.[b] Yet again, a third argument lies in the fact that the question under consideration relates to a simple facultative right, a form of right which (as we shall presently show) does not allow of prescription.

There is, however, no end to the subtleties advanced in disputing this point. Some persons have been known to draw a distinction in this connexion between prescription and custom, with a view, of course, to taking refuge in the latter concept if they are cut off from the former. But the distinction set up by them is indeed absurd. They assert that a right previously pertaining to one individual and subsequently taken from him is assigned to another person by the process of prescription,[c] whereas the process involved in assigning a certain right to a given individual without first taking it from another person is called custom. But this is equivalent to saying that when the right of navigation (originally bestowed upon all men in common) is usurped by one claimant to the exclusion of the rest, it does not necessarily follow that whatever is gained by that one is lost to mankind as a whole![d]

The way was prepared for this error by a misinterpretation of the

a. Fachineus, *Controversiarum Juris Libri Tredecim,* VIII. xxvi and xxxiii; Covarr., *On Sext,* rule *De Praesc.* [*possessor*], Pt. II, § 2, n. 8; *ibid.,* § 8 [7], nn. 5 and 6.

b. Fachineus, *ibid.* VIII. xxviii.

c. [Angelus] Aretinus, *On Dig.* I. viii [*On Institutes,* II. i. 2]; Balbus, *De Praescriptionibus,* Princ. 5, pt. 4, qu. 6, n. 2.

d. See Vázquez, xxix. 38 [xx. 38].

words of Paulus. Although Paulus was discussing a private maritime right pertaining to a specific person, Accursius[a] claimed that the situation discussed in that passage could be brought about through [110′] privilege or through custom. This addition to the text of the jurist is in no sense concordant with it, and would seem to have been contributed by a poor guesser rather than by a good interpreter. We have already explained[15] what Paulus had in mind. Moreover, if those persons who misinterpret his statement had even considered with sufficient care nothing more than the words of Ulpian[b] in the passage placed just before the one in question, they would have dealt with the matter in an entirely different fashion. For Ulpian[c] admits that anyone who has been forbidden to fish in front of my dwelling is indeed the victim of an act of usurpation, an act which has been encouraged by custom without being authorized by any law, so that the person on whom the prohibition was imposed should be allowed to bring an action for injury.

Thus Ulpian rejects the practice of imposing such prohibitions, describing it as "usurpation"; and, among the Christian authorities, Ambrose[d] does likewise. Are they not right in so doing? For what could be clearer than the fact that a custom diametrically opposed to the law of nature, or to the law of nations, is not valid?[e] Custom is a form of positive law, and positive law cannot invalidate universal precepts; but it is a universal precept that the use of the sea should be common to all. Furthermore, what we have said in discussing prescription is likewise true with respect to custom: any inquiry into the opinions of those authorities who hold an opposing view will certainly show that they place custom on the same level as privilege; yet no one has the power to grant a privilege unfavourable to the interests of the human race; and therefore, the custom above mentioned has no force where the relations between different states are involved.

a. *On Dig.* XLVII. x. 14.
b. *Dig.* XLVII. x. 13, § 7.
c. See Glossators, *On Dig.* XLVII. x. 13, § 7.
d. *On Duties,* I. xxviii [132]; *Gentili,* I. xix, near end.
e. *Authentica on Code,* IX. xlviii. 1 [= *Novels,* ix]; *Decretals,* I. iv. 11.
15. *Supra,* pp. 326–27.

As a matter of fact, this entire question has been quite thoroughly discussed by Vázquez,[a] the pride of Spain, a jurist who in no instance leaves anything to be desired in the keenness of his investigation of law nor in the candour with which he expounds it. Vázquez, then, having laid down a thesis which he confirms by citing many authorities—namely, the thesis that public places which are common by the law of nations cannot be made the objects of prescription—appends to this statement certain exceptions formulated by Angelus and by others, which we have already mentioned. Before undertaking an examination of these exceptions, however, he rightly observes that the truth in regard to such matters rests upon a true conception of both the law of nature and the law of nations. For Vázquez argues that the law of nature, since it proceeds from Divine Providence, is immutable; and that the primary law of nations (which is regarded as different from the secondary [111] or positive law of nations, the latter being susceptible to change whereas the former is immutable) constitutes a part of that natural law. For if there are certain customs incompatible with the primary law of nations, they are customs proper not to human beings (in the opinion of that same jurist) but to *wild beasts;* neither do they represent law and usage, but rather, corruption and abuse; and therefore, they cannot have assumed the form of prescriptions as the result of any interval of time whatsoever, they cannot have been justified by the establishment of any law, nor can they have been definitively confirmed by agreement, acceptance, and practice even on the part of many nations. Vázquez strengthens this argument by citing several examples together with the testimony of the Spanish theologian, Alfonso de Castro.[b]

> In the light of these observations (says Vázquez),[c] we clearly perceive the questionable nature of the opinion held by the above-mentioned persons who believe that the Genoese or even the Venetians can, with-

a. *Ill. Cont.* lxxxix. 12 ff.

b. *De Potestate Legis Poenalis,* II. xiv, p. 572.

c. [*Ill. Cont.,*] p. 752, n. 30 [lxxxix. 30–5].[16]

16. The marginal references found in this and the following quotations from Vázquez are his own.

out inflicting injury, prohibit others from navigating the gulf or the open spaces of their respective seas, as if to claim by prescription the very surface of the waters. Such conduct would be contrary not only to the precepts of positive law[a] but even to the law of nature itself, or primary law of nations, which we have already characterized as immutable. The fact that it would conflict with the latter, is perfectly evident: for not only the seas and the surface thereof, but also all other immovable objects, were common property according to the said law. Moreover, even though that law was in later times partially abrogated—for example, in so far as ownership and property rights over land were concerned, since ownership over lands, though common under the law of nature, was subjected to a process of differentiation and division which removed it from that communal sphere[b]—nevertheless, ownership of the seas was and still is a different matter. For the seas, from the beginning of the world down to the present day, are and have always been common property, unvaryingly and without exception, as is well known. To be sure, I have often heard that a great many *Portuguese* hold the opinion that their King has established a prescriptive right over navigation upon the seas of the West (perhaps [an error for] "East")[17] *Indies* as well as upon that same *vast Ocean,* with the result that other peoples are not permitted to sail across those waters; [111′] and apparently *the common people* of our own country, Spain, cherish much the same belief—namely, that navigation upon *the vast and boundless deep* to the East Indian regions subjugated by our mighty rulers, the sovereigns of the Spanish realms, constitutes a right by no means open to any mortal other than the Spaniards, a contention equivalent to saying that this right was acquired by the latter through prescription. But the opinions of all these persons are no less *wildly erroneous* than the opinions of those who are wont to embrace a very similar *delusion* in regard to the Genoese and the Venetians. The *absurdity* of all such beliefs is rendered still more manifest by the fact that the individual nations involved are not able to set up prescriptions against themselves: that is to say, the Republic of Venice cannot set up

a. As stated in *Dig.* XLI. i. 14; *ibid.* iii. 49 [45]; *Institutes,* II. i. 2; *Dig.* XLIV. iii. 7; *ibid.* XLVII. x. 14.

b. As stated in *Dig.* I. i. 5; *Institutes,* I. ii, at beg.; *ibid.* I. ii. 1.

17. This parenthetical phrase was added by Grotius.

a prescription against itself, the Republic of Genoa labours under a like disability as regards its own case, and the same is true of the Kingdoms of Spain and Portugal, respectively.[a] For the agent and the passive party must be different entities.[b] On the other hand, these nations are far less able to employ prescription against other peoples, inasmuch as the right to employ this device is strictly a civil right, a point fully brought out by us in an earlier passage.[c] Thus the said right ceases to exist when the interested parties are all princes or peoples who recognize no superior in temporal matters. For the strictly civil laws of a given region have no more bearing on the issue in so far as foreign peoples, states, or even individuals are concerned, than they would if those laws did not actually exist or had never existed. In dealing with such foreign entities, the common law of nations, either in its primary or in its secondary phase, must be consulted and applied; and it is a sufficiently well-established fact that the said law has not authorized such maritime prescription and usurpation. [In this respect,] the law of nations has precisely the same effect that it has always had, since the beginning of the world; for even today the use of waters constitutes a common right. Accordingly, in cases involving the sea or other waters, men do not and cannot possess any right other than that which relates to common use. Moreover, both natural law and divine law uphold that famous precept: "Do ye not unto others what ye would not have others do unto you." Therefore, since navigation cannot prove injurious save perhaps to the navigator himself, it is fitting that the power and right to impede this activity should be denied to all persons, so that no one, by intervening in a matter whose very nature implies free participation and which is in no sense harmful to himself, shall obstruct the liberty of [112] navigators, transgressing the aforesaid precept and the established rule.[d] Our argument is strengthened by the fact that all activities against which no express prohibition is found to exist, are understood to be

a. *Dig.* XLI. iii. 4, § 27; *Institutes,* IV. vi. 14.

b. As in the aforesaid laws of the Civil Law and *Dig.* XXX. i. 11; and in Bartolus and Jason, *On Dig.* XXX. i, discussed there at length by commentators.

c. Pt. I, at beg. of Qq. 3 and 4 [of Vázquez].

d. *Dig.* I. v. 4; *Institutes,* I. iii. 1; *Dig.* XLIII. xxix. 1–2; *ibid.* XLIV. v. 1, § 5; *Code,* III. xxviii. 35, § 1.

permitted.[a] Indeed, it is not enough to say that an attempt to prevent such navigation by resorting to prescription, would be contrary to natural law, since that act of prevention would result in no advantage whatsoever to the agent [while it would result in injury to the party affected by the prohibition];[18] for we are also under a positive obligation to pursue the opposite course, that is to say, an obligation to benefit all persons whom we can benefit without consequent injury to ourselves.

After citing numerous authorities, both divine and human, in support of the foregoing argument, Vázquez[b] adds this statement:

> Thus we also clearly perceive the questionable nature of the opinion held by certain persons already cited, namely, Joannes Faber, Angelus, Baldus and [Joannes] Franciscus Balbus. For these authorities believe that places which are common property under the law of nations can be acquired through custom, even if they cannot be acquired through prescription. This contention is altogether *false;* and the doctrine implicit therein is *vague, obscure, completely cut off from the light of reason* and aimed at the establishment of a law upon a foundation of words, not facts.[c] For examples relating to the seas of the Spaniards, *Portuguese,* Venetians, Genoese, and other peoples clearly indicate that such a right to navigate and to prohibit navigation by others, can no more be acquired through custom than it can through prescription. For obviously, the principles involved are the same in both cases:[d] the laws and arguments adduced above show that acquisition of this right would be contrary to natural equity, and would produce no benefit but only injury, so that, just as such acquisition could not be expressly authorized by any precept of positive law,[e] it would likewise be impossible to authorize that same development on the basis of any tacit law, such as custom; and furthermore, the said development would not be justified

a. *Dig.* IV. vi. 28 § 2; *Code,* III. xliv. 7.
b. [*Code,* III. lxxxix.] 36.
c. Contra *Code,* VI. xliv. 2.
d. *Dig.* IX. ii. 32.
e. *Decretum,* I. iv. 2; *Dig.* I. iii. 1–2; *ibid.* I. iii. 32 f.

18. The phrase *et impedito noceat,* inserted at this point in Hamaker's edition of the *Commentary* without any editorial explanation, certainly serves to clarify the argument.

by the passage of time, but would on the contrary grow daily less valid and more unjust.[a]

Vázquez then proceeds to demonstrate that, from the time when lands first began to be occupied, it was possible for a particular people to possess the right of fishing in their own streams just as they possessed the right of hunting [in their own territory]; and he also shows that, after these rights had once been separated from the ancient community of rights in such a way as to admit of their assignment to specific [112′] individuals, it was possible for them to be acquired by the said individuals through prescription based upon the lapse of time immemorial, as if through a tacit concession on the part of the nation. In addition, however, Vázquez stresses the point that such a result would be brought about through prescription and not through custom, inasmuch as only the status of the party making the acquisition is improved, while the status of the remaining parties is impaired. Again, after enumerating the three requisites for establishment by prescription of a private right over the fishing in a given stream, the same writer[b] adds:

> And what shall we say in regard to the sea? In this connexion, indeed, the requirements are more stringent, for even the conjunction of the three requisites above mentioned would not suffice for the acquisition of such a maritime right. The reason for the distinction made between the sea, on the one hand, and lands or streams, on the other hand, is this: in cases involving the sea, today and for all time just as in earlier epochs, the right conferred by the primary law of nations in regard both to fishing and to navigation remains intact, nor has it ever been separated from the common body of human rights and attached to one or more specific individuals; whereas in cases coming under the latter head (that is to say, in those which relate to lands or streams), the course of events was different, as we have already explained. But why did the secondary law of nations cease to operate when the sea was involved, failing to produce that separation [of parts privately controlled] which it produced with respect to lands and streams? This question may be

a. *Decretals,* II. xxvi. 20.
b. *Ibid.* 39[–41].

answered as follows: "Because, in the case of lands or streams, it was expedient that the law should operate thus, whereas it was not expedient in regard to the sea." For it is generally agreed that, if a great many persons hunt or fish upon some wooded tract of land or in some stream, that wood or stream will probably be emptied of wild animals or fish, an objection which is not applicable to the sea. Similarly, the erection of edifices may easily impede or prevent the navigation of streams,[a] but not the navigation of the sea. Yet again, it is quite likely that the presence of aqueducts will leave a stream drained of its waters, but no such possibility exists where the sea is concerned. Therefore, the same line of reasoning cannot be followed in the two kinds of cases. Moreover, our preceding statement to the effect that the use of waters (including even springs and streams) constitutes a common right, is not pertinent to the question under consideration, inasmuch as the [113] said statement is understood to refer to drinking and similar acts, by which ownership of the stream or rights possessed over it are impaired very slightly or not at all. For we are not concerned with points of trifling significance.[b] Our opinion is furthermore confirmed by the fact that unjust claims are not validated by prescription, regardless of the lapse of time involved, and that, consequently, an unjust law does not result in prescription, nor is it justified, because of the passage of time.[c]

A little farther on, Vázquez[d] observes that "those things which are imprescriptible will not become the objects of prescription in consequence of legal measures, nor on the basis of lapse of time even after the passage of a thousand years." This observation is supported by the testimony of innumerable learned authorities.[e]

It will now be clear to every reader that usurpation, no matter how long continued, does not avail to prevent the use of a common possession. We must add that the opinion of those who dissent from this gen-

a. *Dig.* XLIII. xiii, whole title.

b. *Dig.* IV. i. 4; Vázquez, *De Successionum Resolutione,* I. vii.

c. Balbus, *De Praescriptionibus,* Princ. 5, pt. 5, qu. 11 and elsewhere in Princ. 5; Glossators, *On Decretum,* II. x. 3. 8; Alph. de Castro, *De Potestate Legis Poenalis,* II. xiv.

d. [*Ill. Cont.* lxxxix.] 44.

e. Baldus and Angelus de Ubaldis, *On Code,* VII. xxxix. 4.

eral conclusion cannot in any event be applied to the particular question under discussion. For the said dissenters are referring to a Mediterranean sea, whereas we are referring to the Ocean; they are discussing a mere gulf, whereas we are discussing a vast maritime tract, two concepts which differ very widely in so far as occupation is concerned. Moreover, the peoples to whom the right of prescription is conceded by such authorities[a] (for example, the Venetians and the Genoese) are the possessors of uninterrupted coast-lines along the waters in question; but the same cannot be said of the Portuguese, as we have just clearly demonstrated.

Indeed, even if (as some persons believe) the passage of time could avail to establish prescriptive rights over the public possessions of a given nation, certain necessary requisites would still be lacking in the present case. For, first of all, according to the doctrine universally upheld,[b] anyone who claims a prescriptive right over a particular act must have practised that act, not merely for a long period of time, but for a period stretching back beyond the limits of memory. A second requirement runs as follows: during all of this period, no other person shall have practised the said act, save by permission of the claimant to the prescriptive right, or else clandestinely. It is furthermore required that the claimant shall have prohibited all other persons who wished to use the possession in question, from so doing; and that he shall have issued this prohibition with the knowledge and consent of the parties concerned. For even if he had always practised the act in question and had always prohibited its practice by some, but not all, of the persons desirous of engaging in that activity, the requirements would still not be fulfilled (according to the opinion of learned authorities), since some individuals would have practised the act freely while others would have been forbidden to do so. Then, too, it is apparent that all of the conditions above mentioned must be satisfied concurrently, partly because the law is inclined to oppose the prescription of public possessions, and partly in order to make it clear that the claimant has exercised a right that is truly his own, not a common right, and that he has exercised it in virtue of

a. See Angelus de Ubaldis, *On Institutes,* II. i. 5 and others noted above.
b. Angelus de Ubaldis, *On Institutes,* II. i. 38.

uninterrupted possession. Furthermore, since one requirement is the lapse of a period extending back beyond the limits of memory, it does not always suffice (a point brought out by the leading interpreters of the laws)[a] to prove that a century has elapsed; rather, there must be a well-established tradition, handed down to us from our forebears and of such sort that no surviving person has seen or heard any evidence conflicting with it. [113′]

The Portuguese first began to investigate the more remote regions of the Ocean during the reign of King John, in the year of Our Lord 1477,[b] and in connexion with their African interests. Twenty years later, after Emmanuel had ascended the throne, they voyaged past the Cape of Good Hope. Much later still, they came to Malacca and the more distant islands, whither the Dutch also directed their ships, in 1595, certainly less than a century after the advent of the Portuguese. Moreover, even during that interval, the use made of the maritime tract in question by certain parties in opposition to others, had created an impediment to prescription by any one of the parties involved. As early as the year 1519, Portuguese possession of the sea in the vicinity of the Moluccas was rendered doubtful by the Castilians. The French and the English also pushed their way into that part of the world, not clandestinely but by employing open force. Then, too, the inhabitants of all these regions, both in Africa and in Asia, continually used the part of the sea nearest each of these peoples respectively for fishing and navigation; nor did the Portuguese at any time prohibit that practice.

Therefore, we must conclude that the Portuguese do not possess any right in virtue whereof they may forbid any other nation whatsoever to navigate the oceanic tract extending to the East Indies.

Furthermore, if the Portuguese maintain that they are the possessors of a certain exclusive right to engage in trade with the East Indians, their contention will be refuted by all of the arguments already advanced, in practically the same form. We shall review those arguments briefly, adapting them to this particular phase of the discussion.

a. Covarr., *On Sext,* rule *possessor,* Pt. II, § 3. n. 6.
b. Osorio [*History of King Emmanuel*], I [pp. 15 ff.].

Thesis IV

New explanation

Under the law of nations, the following principle was established: that all men should be privileged to trade freely with one another,[a] nor might they be deprived of that privilege by any person. Since the need for this principle existed as soon as distinctions of ownership had been drawn, it is clearly quite ancient in origin. For, as Aristotle[b] has acutely observed: *μεταβλητικὴ ἀναπλήρωσις τῆς κατὰ φύσιν αὐταρκείας*; in other words, barter supplies what nature lacks in order to meet properly the needs of all men. Therefore, according to the law of nations, the privilege of barter must be common to all, not only in a negative [i.e. non-exclusive] sense, but also positively (as the experts say)[c] or, to use another term, affirmatively. Now, the negative dispositions of the law of nations are subject to change, whereas its affirmative dispositions are immutable.

This statement of the case may be clarified as follows. Nature [114] had given all things to all men. Nevertheless, owing to the fact that the distances separating different regions prevented men from using many of the goods desirable for human life (since not all things are produced in all localities, as we have pointed out in another context), passage to and fro was found to be a necessity. Barter in the true sense was not practised as yet in that early epoch, but men followed their own judgement in using what they discovered in one another's territory, very much after the fashion in which commerce is said to be conducted among the Chinese, who leave their goods in some lonely place and rely entirely upon the scrupulousness of the persons with whom the exchange is made.[d] But as soon as movables had passed into the domain of private property rights (under pressure of necessity, as we have just explained), the process of barter was devised,[e] in order that one person's lack might be remedied by means of another person's surplus. Thus (as Pliny[f] shows, citing Homer) the practice of commerce was developed for the sake of the necessities of life. Moreover, after immovables also began to

a. *Dig.* I. i. 5 and Bartolus thereon [n. 8].
b. *Politics,* I. ix [iii].
c. See Covarr., *On Sext,* rule *peccatum,* Pt. II § 8.
d. Pomponius Mela, III [vii].
e. *Dig.* XVIII. i. 1.
f. [*Nat. Hist.*] XXXIII. i.

be divided among different owners, the general abolition of communal ownership made commerce necessary not only among men separated from one another by geographical distance but also among residents of the same vicinity. Subsequently, with a view to facilitating this commercial activity, money was invented[a] and was given its [Latin] name, [*nummus,*] ἀπὸ τοῦ νόμου, "from the Greek term νόμος[b] [custom *or* law]," because money was a civil institution.[c]

We find, then, that the general principle underlying all contracts, ἡ μεταβλητική [the principle of exchange], is in itself derived from nature;[d] whereas various specific forms of exchange, and the actual payment of a price, ἡ χρηματιστική [the money-making process], are derived from law or tradition,[20] a distinction which the older interpreters of the law have not made sufficiently clear. Nevertheless, it is universally agreed that private ownership—in the case of movable possessions, at least—has its origin in the primary law of nations,[e] and that the same is true of all contracts not involving the payment of a price.

The philosophers[f] distinguish between two kinds of μεταβλητική, a term which may be translated as "exchange," namely: ἡ ἐμπορικὴ καὶ ἡ καπηλική [wholesale commerce and retail trade]. Of these, the former—which is practised between widely separated nations, as the term itself indicates—takes precedence in the natural order, and is so ranked by Plato.[g] The latter form of exchange would seem to be identical with Aristotle's παράστασις,[h] "shopkeeping," or trade practised on a station-

a. *Dig.* XVIII. i. 1.
b. Arist., *Nic. Ethics,* V. viii [V. v. 10]; *id., Politics,* I. ix [I. iii. 15].
c. See Law VIII, Chap. ii, *supra,* p. 37.[19]
d. *Decretum,* I. i. 7; Arist., *Politics,* I. ix [I. iii].
e. Castrensis citing Cynus and others, *On Dig.* I. i. 5, nn. 20, 28.
f. Plato, *Sophist* [p. 223 D].
g. Plato, *Republic,* II [xi–xii], which is cited in *Dig.* L. xi. 2.
h. *Politics,* I. xi [I. iii. 16].

19. This marginal reference was probably intended to be deleted together with the passage which was crossed out in the text.

20. The Latin term *institutum* may refer to law or to tradition. Since the context indicates that Grotius had in mind both connotations, *ab instituto* is rendered here by the expanded English phrase.

ary basis among fellow citizens. That same author makes a division of ἡ ἐμπορικὴ [wholesale commerce] into ναυκληρία [ship-owning] and φορτηγία [hauling],[21] referring in the latter case to merchandise transported by land and in the former case to merchandise transported overseas. Retail trade is of course a comparatively humble pursuit;[a] [114′] but wholesale commerce is more creditable, and especially so when maritime transportation is involved, since this phase of commerce enables many people to enjoy a share in many things. Herein lies the reason for Ulpian's[b] assertion that the management of ships is a matter of the greatest concern to the commonwealth, whereas the services of [petty] agents[22] have not the same value. In fact, the former pursuit is absolutely necessary according to nature's plan. Thus Aristotle[c] has said: ἔστι γὰρ ἡ μεταβλητικὴ πάντων ἀρξαμένη τὸ μὲν πρῶτον ἐκ τοῦ κατὰ φύσιν τῷ τὰ μὲν πλείω, τὰ δὲ ἐλάττω τῶν ἱκανῶν ἔχειν τοὺς ἀνθρώπους; "For there exists in connexion with all things a process of exchange that originated in the first instance from the natural order, because men had more than enough of some things and less than enough of others." Seneca,[d] too, lays down this rule: "The law of nations decrees that you may sell what you have bought."

Freedom of trade, then, springs from the primary law of nations, which has a natural and permanent cause, so that it cannot be abrogated. Moreover, even if its abrogation were possible, such a result could be achieved only with the consent of all nations. Accordingly, it is not remotely conceivable that one nation may justly impose any hindrance

a. Cicero, *On Duties,* I [.xlii. 150] and Arist. *Politics,* I. ix [I. iii].

b. *Dig.* XIV. i. 1, § 20.

c. *Ibid.* [*Politics,* I. iii. 12].

d. *On Benefits,* I. ix.

21. Strictly speaking, the Aristotelian passage cited contains a *threefold* division of *commerce* in general: ship-owning, hauling, and retail trade. Thus Grotius's twofold division of all commerce exclusive of retail trade, is implied, but not expressed, in that passage.

22. *institorum,* used by Ulpian in the primary sense of the term, "an agent who sells goods for another"; but Grotius's argument suggests that he himself had in mind the secondary meaning of "huckster," or "peddler."

whatsoever upon two other nations that wish to enter into a contract with each other.

Now, in the first place, neither discovery nor occupation can have any bearing upon freedom of trade. For the right to trade freely is not a corporeal object, susceptible of seizure. Nor would the Portuguese position be strengthened even if the Portuguese people had been the first to engage in trade with the East Indians, although such a claim on their part could be regarded only as an absolute falsehood. Owing to the fact that, in the very beginning, different peoples proceeded in different directions, there must be some who were the first traders [in each of the various regions]; yet it is certain beyond all possibility of doubt that those earliest traders did not thereby acquire special rights.

Therefore, if the Portuguese do possess any right that gives them an exclusive privilege of trade with the East Indians, that right must have arisen, after the fashion of other servitudes, from an express grant, or from a tacit concession (that is to say, from prescription); for under no other circumstances could it exist.

But no one made such an express grant, unless perchance the Pope did so; and he was not properly empowered to act thus. For there is no person who has the power to bestow by grant that which is not his own; and the Pope—unless he is the temporal master of the whole world, an assumption which wise men reject—cannot maintain that even the universal right of trade falls within his jurisdiction. This objection is particularly forceful when the case in question relates solely to material gain and has no bearing whatsoever upon spiritual administration; for the papal power loses its force (as is universally admitted) beyond the limits of that spiritual sphere. Furthermore, if the Pope wished to bestow the said right upon the Portuguese alone, while taking it away from other men, he would be inflicting a twofold injury. First, he would be injuring the East Indians, who (as we have observed) are in no sense subject to the Pope, inasmuch as they were placed outside the fold of the Church. Thus the Pope has no power to deprive the latter people of anything that belongs to them; and therefore he cannot have had the power to take from them the right (which they do possess) to carry on trade with whomsoever they please. Secondly, the Pope would be injuring all other men, both Christians and non-Christians; for he has not been [115] empowered to deprive those others of the right in question, without cause and a public hearing of that cause. Indeed, how can such a papal claim be sustained, in view of the fact (which we have already demonstrated both on a logical basis and by citation of authorities) that not even temporal lords have the power to prohibit freedom of trade within their own domains? By the same token, it must also be acknowledged that no papal authority is effective against the eternal law of nature and of nations, the source of that very freedom which is destined to endure for all time.

There remains for consideration the question of prescription, or custom, if the reader prefers the latter term. But we have shown, in agreement with Vázquez, that neither custom nor prescription has any force in the relations between free nations or between the rulers of different peoples; and again, that these two factors are likewise without force when opposed to the principles introduced by the earliest form of law. Accordingly, in this connexion, too, we find that no lapse of time avails to make a private possession of the right to trade, a right which is in itself incapable of assuming the character of private property. Consequently, in the case under discussion, neither a title nor good faith can have been present; and according to the canonists, when these elements are clearly lacking, prescription will be regarded not as a right but as a wrong.

Furthermore, the very concept of quasi-possession of trade would seem to be based, not upon a private right, but upon a common right which pertains to all men alike; so that, conversely, it should not be supposed, merely because non-Portuguese peoples may have neglected to engage in commerce with the East Indies, that they refrained from so doing out of deference to the Portuguese, since one ought rather to assume that they considered the omission expedient for themselves. This attitude on their part will by no means prevent them from undertaking, at any time when such a course shall seem advantageous, the commercial activity from which they previously abstained. In fact, learned authorities[a] have laid down an infallible rule regarding these matters which in-

a. Glossators and Bartolus, *On Dig.* XLIII. xi. 2; Balbus, *De Praescriptionibus,*

volve free judgement or a simple optional faculty, to the effect that acts falling within this sphere represent merely the exercise of that power or faculty and do not constitute any new right, nor will the passage of so much as a thousand years avail in such cases to create a title based upon prescription or upon custom. This principle operates (as Vázquez[a] maintains) both affirmatively and negatively. For I am not compelled to continue doing what I have done voluntarily, nor am I compelled to refrain from doing that which hitherto I have voluntarily left undone. What could be more absurd than the conclusion which would necessarily follow upon any other line of reasoning, namely, that in consequence of our inability as individuals to enter at all times into contracts with [115′] other individuals, the right to conclude such contracts at some future time, if occasion should arise, will not be preserved to us? Moreover, that same Vázquez[b] quite rightly declares that not even the passage of immeasurable time will cause a given course of conduct to be regarded as compulsory rather than voluntary.

Therefore, in order to establish any claim of this kind, the Portuguese will have to prove that an element of coercion was involved. But coercion—since it would in the present case be contrary to the law of nature and injurious to mankind as a whole—could not of itself create the right claimed. It would also be necessary for that coercion to have persisted throughout a period extending back beyond the limits of memory;[c] and this is so far from being a fact, that not even a hundred years have passed since the time when almost the entire trade with the East Indies was in the hands of the Venetians, who conducted it by way of Alexandria.[d] Another requisite would be the absence of resistance to such coercion; but the French, the English, and others did resist it.[e] Neither will the requirements be met by the fact that some persons were coerced. On the

---

Princ. 5, pt. 4, qu. 1; Panormitanus, *On Decretals,* III. viii. 10; Doctors, *On Dig.* XLI. ii. 41 and as stated by Covarr., *On Sext,* rule *possessor,* Pt. II, § 4, n. 6.

a. *Ill. Cont.* iv. 10 and 12.

b. *Ibid.* 12.

c. *Ibid.* 11.

d. Guicciardini, *History of Italy,* XIX.

e. See *supra,* p. 337.

contrary, all persons must have been subjected to the coercion, since the claim to possession of freedom is maintained on behalf of all by failure to coerce a single individual. But the Arabs and the Chinese have traded continuously with the East Indians throughout several centuries, and are still trading with them at the present day. Consequently, the claim based upon usurpation is not valid.

The foregoing comments reveal clearly enough the blind covetousness of those who, in an attempt to prevent admittance of any other person to a share of the gains, are striving to placate their consciences with arguments which are indisputably worthless, as is convincingly demonstrated by the very Spanish authorities[a] who are their partisans. For the said authorities intimate, as plainly as they are permitted to do so, that all of the pretexts advanced in connexion with the Indian[23] questions are seized upon unjustly; and they add that the matter has never been seriously examined and approved by the theologians.

Indeed, what could be more unjust than the complaint of the Portuguese that their own profits are drained away by the multitude of persons bidding against them? For among the most incontrovertible principles of law we find the following presumption:[b] he who is availing himself of his own right is not engaged in deceitful wrongdoing, nor in contriving a fraud, nor even in the infliction of loss upon another. This presumption holds good particularly for cases wherein an act is committed, not for the purpose of causing harm to another person, but rather with the intention of advancing the interests of the agent [116] himself.[c] For attention should be fixed upon the basic purpose of the act, not upon its extrinsic consequences.[d] As a matter of fact, according

a. Vázquez, x. 10; Vict., *De Indis,* I [III]. 3.

b. *Dig.* VI. i. 27, § 4; *ibid.* L. xvii. 55; *ibid.* XLII. viii. 13; *ibid.* XXXIX. ii. 24, § 12; *ibid.* L. xvii. 151; Bartolus, *On Dig.* XLIII. xii. 1[2], n. 5; Castrensis, *On Code,* III. xxxiv. 10.

c. *Dig.* XXXIX. iii. 1, § 23.

d. See Vázquez, iv. 3 f.

23. *Indicis,* evidently used here with reference both to the East Indian questions in which Grotius was particularly interested, and to the questions concerning American Indians which are treated in the works of the Spanish authorities above cited.

to the strict interpretation placed upon such cases by Ulpian,[a] the agent does not inflict a loss, but merely prevents another person from continuing to enjoy a benefit which the latter was enjoying hitherto. Furthermore, it is natural,[b] and compatible with the highest form of law as well as with the principle of equity, that every individual should prefer to have for himself a commonly accessible source of profit, rather than to see it in the hands of another, even though it may previously have been seized by that other.[c] Who would have patience with any artisan given over to complaining that his profits are being cut off by another artisan's practice of the same craft? Yet the cause of the Dutch is more just than that of such a competitor, inasmuch as their own profit in this case is bound up with profit to the entire human race, a universal benefit which the Portuguese are attempting to destroy.

Nor can it fairly be said that the activities of the Dutch are motivated by the spirit of rivalry, a point also brought out by Vázquez[d] in connexion with a similar case. For such an assertion must be roundly denied, unless it is taken as referring to a kind of rivalry that is not merely good but even excellent in the highest degree: the kind described by Hesiod[e] when he declares that, *ἀγαθὴ δ' ἔρις ἥδε βροτοῖσι*, "Such strife is wholesome for mankind." Thus Vázquez says that any man who may be moved by compassion to sell grain at a comparatively low price during a time of extreme scarcity, will meet with opposition from the shamelessly hardhearted individuals who had intended to sell their own grain at a higher price than usual because of the cruel lack. It is true that such charitable measures lessen the proceeds accruing to other persons. "Nor do we deny this," Vázquez[f] adds. "But the diminution of those proceeds is advantageous for the human race as a whole. *Would that* the profits accruing to all *the princes and tyrants of this world* might be lessened in like manner!"

a. *Dig.* XXXIX. ii. 26.
b. See discussion of Law II, chap. ii, *supra,* p. 23.
c. Vázquez, *ibid.*
d. *Ibid.* 5.
e. [*Works and Days,* 24.]
f. [*Ibid.*]

What, then, can be so manifestly unjust as a situation in which the Iberian peoples would hold the entire world tributary, in such fashion that neither buying nor selling would be permissible save in accordance with their pleasure? In every state, hatred and even punishment are loosed upon speculators in grain;[a] nor is any other way of life held to be so abominable as this practice of whipping up the market-price of produce. Assuredly, that hatred is justified. For such speculators are committing an offence against Nature, who is fruitful for all in common.[b] Moreover, it is not to be supposed that the institution of trade was devised for the benefit of a few persons. On the contrary, it was established in order that one person's lack might be compensated by recourse to the abundance enjoyed by another, though not without a just profit for all individuals taking upon themselves the labour and peril involved [116′] in the process of transfer.[c] Shall we say, then, that the above-mentioned practice, which is regarded as gravely pernicious when carried on within a single state (that is to say, within a comparatively small unit of humanity), should be tolerated within that great community made up of the human race, thus enabling the Iberian nations to establish a monopoly over the whole earth?[24]

a. *Code,* IV. lix. 1.

b. Cajetan, *On II–II,* qu. 77, art. 1, ad 3.

c. Arist., *Politics* I. ix [I. iii].

24. The marginal passage inserted at this point on manuscript p. 116′ is one of those omitted from the present translation, as part of the emended *Mare Liberum* text but not part of the original *Commentary* (cf. note 1, p. 300–301, *supra*). On the other hand, certain phrases deleted from the upper portion of this manuscript page, together with the entire lower portion of the same page (which was also deleted), are retained in the English because they seem to have been rejected only in connexion with the revision of the text for the *Mare Liberum.* For the same reasons, pp. 117–18′ (text and notes for Chapter XIII of the *Mare Liberum*) are omitted from the translation, which passes from the bottom of p. 116′ to the top of p. 119, and includes all of the deleted material extending from that point to the bottom of p. 121′.

This reconstruction of the original Latin text is based primarily upon the substance and syntax of the passages involved, although certain physical peculiarities of the manuscript also tend to justify it: for example, the handwriting is on the whole smaller and rounder in the *Mare Liberum* insertions than in the *Commentary;* and traces of an older pagination show that pp. 116–16′ were originally numbered sheet

In short, let the Portuguese cry out, as loud and as long as they will: "You are cutting off our profits!" The Dutch will answer: "Not at all! We are looking out for our own profit!" ["You are cutting off our profits!"] "Are you indignant because we are acquiring a share in the winds and the sea?" ["You are cutting off our profits!"] "Besides, who promised that you would retain those profits of yours?" ["You are cutting off our profits!"] "You still possess unimpaired the same benefits with which we are content. [We trade at fair prices." "You are cutting off our profits!" "You maintain, then, that one should not yield to another's claim in anything that is a possible source of profit to oneself!"]

Accordingly, since it has been demonstrated above[a] (with authoritative confirmation drawn from Victoria and with the aid of examples) that a just cause of war exists when the freedom of trade is being defended against those who would obstruct it, we arrive at the conclusion that the Dutch had a just cause for war against the Portuguese. Further proof of this conclusion may be derived from the following detailed arguments.

Ded. from Art. I, Conclusion VI, and inferences supported thereby. Analysis I

The defence or recovery of possessions, and the exaction of a debt or of penalties due, all constitute just causes of war. Under the head of "possessions," even rights should be included. Thus Baldus[b] declares that it is proper for me to attack the person who prohibits me from exercising my right. But the concept of "rights" embraces both that which is due to us in our capacity as private individuals, and that which is our due by

---

112, pp. 119–19′ were marked 113, &c., while the inserted sheets (117–18′) bore the numbers 112.3 and 112.5.

The only phase of the reconstruction open to reasonable doubt is the retention of the separately deleted phrases at the top of p. 116′. These are found in the fanciful dialogue between the Dutch and the Portuguese following immediately after the point where the present note is inserted. The translator has enclosed them in brackets in order that the reader may draw his own conclusion. Hamaker retains the phrases in question, but it is quite possible that Grotius struck them from the *Commentary* itself, primarily for stylistic reasons.

a. Beg. of this chap.

b. *On Code,* VIII. iv. 1, n. 38 [35].

the law of human fellowship (a point noted by Augustine[a] in connexion with the cause for war against the Amorites): that is to say, the use of whatever is common—e.g. the sea and commercial opportunities—forms a part of the said concept. Therefore, if any person has quasi-possession of such a right, it will be proper for him to defend that claim.[b] Similarly, Pomponius[c] asserts that he who appropriates for himself to the detriment of others a thing that is the common property of all, *should be forcibly restrained.* For in all cases to which prohibitory interdicts are properly applicable in court procedure, armed opposition is [119][25] proper outside the courts. The Praetor[d] says: "I forbid the use of force to prevent a boat or raft from sailing over a public stream, or to prevent the unloading of such a vessel along the bank of that stream." The interpreters[e] of this prohibition, following the example set by Labeo,[f] maintain that an interdict should be laid down in the same form with respect to the sea. For Labeo,[g] in commenting upon the Praetor's interdict which runs, "It is decreed that nothing shall be done in a public stream nor on the bank thereof, that may be detrimental either to the anchorage or to the transit of boats," makes the observation that a similar interdict will lie when applied to the sea in these terms: "Nothing shall be done in the sea nor on the seashore, that may be detrimental to the use of ports by boats or to anchorage or to the transit of boats." In short, unjust force of the kind described is to be repelled by just force. Other writers,[h] too, whose subject is war, have upheld this same principle, asserting that war, since it may be undertaken for the defence of possessions, may likewise and above all[26] be undertaken to defend the use of

a. Cited *supra* [Augustine, *Qu. on Heptateuch, On Numbers,* IV. 44].
b. Cf. Laws II and IV, Chap. ii, *supra,* pp. 23 and 27.
c. *Dig.* XLI. i. 50.
d. *Dig.* XLIII. xiv. 1.
e. Glossators thereon.
f. *Dig.* XLIII. xii. 1.
g. *Ibid.* 1. § 17.
h. Henry of Gorkum, *De Bello Iusto,* Prop. 9.
25. *Vide* note 24, p. 362.
26. Interpreting the largely illegible phrase or word interlineated in the manuscript at this point, as *in primo* or *imprimis.*

those things which, according to natural law, should be commonly enjoyed; and therefore (so the said writers maintain), those who block the routes along which necessities are transported to and fro may be *actively* resisted, even without authorization from the ruler [of the resisting parties]. This resistance is justified, moreover, by the very imposition of a prohibition [against common use of a common possession].

Furthermore, after the prohibition has been imposed, recourse can properly be had to an action for injuries (in lieu of a restorative interdict), in cases where a given person has been forbidden to sail upon the sea, to sell his own property, or to make use thereof. This is the decision formulated by Ulpian[a] in numerous passages. Therefore such a prohibition must constitute an injury; and injury received from another provides one with a just cause of war.[b] Besides, even as it would be permissible for us to recover property that had been snatched from us, just so we may properly recover the right in question when it has been forcibly diverted from us.

Let us consider next the cause afforded by the existence of a debt.[c] For any person who has impeded another in the exercise of the said right, is bound by natural law, also, to make reparation for the loss inflicted. Sylvester[d] says: "He who prevents a fisherman, or a fowler, from catching the fish or birds (for these are things included within the sphere of *common rights*)[e] that he probably would have caught, has placed himself under an obligation in the opinion of righteous men, because the private use of the said fish or birds, which was attached to them as a free and independent right, has been cut off, together with the potential profit implicit (so to speak) in that right." The same authority adds: "Those persons who obstruct the *importation* of grain or other *merchandise* to any land, in order that they themselves may make sales at higher prices,

a. *Dig.* XLIII. viii. 2, § 9; *ibid.* XLVII. x. 13 [§ 7]; *ibid.* 24.

b. *Decretum,* II. xxiii. 2. 2.

c. Cf. Law VI.

d. On word *restitutio,* Pt. III, at end [xii. 4].

e. As stated by Gerardus, Oldradus, and Archiepiscopus.

are in debt to the purchasers who have paid the increased prices, to the extent of that increase; and they are also in debt to the persons who expected to convey the goods, to the extent of the loss suffered by the latter. For the parties creating the obstruction have acted unjustly in placing their private and personal interests above the public and *common* welfare. The same conclusion holds true in regard to persons who conspire to buy up the entire supply of some merchandise in order to sell it according to their own pleasure, inasmuch as such persons are under an obligation to make restitution for *all of the loss* involved."

Aside from that loss, however, their very guilt of itself creates an obligation,[a] a point which we have discussed elsewhere.[b] For it is contrary to natural reason that wickedness should go unpunished.[c] Civil [119′] law punishes the infliction of injuries, for the most part, with fines;[d] violence directed against liberty, with the loss of part of the offender's goods;[e] and the creation of monopolies, with public confiscation of all goods belonging to the guilty party.[f] In the present case, all of these offences are combined.

It is of course true that the severity of punishments for wrongdoing is increased or abated in accordance with considerations of public welfare. But in the case of those offences which are evil by nature rather than by law or tradition,[27] and essentially impermissible from the standpoint of due proportion, punishment may be exacted even apart from the measures provided in the laws. Accordingly, since nature rules that we ought not to convert into personal property any part of that which belongs to another, it follows that those persons who attempt to convert

a. As stated in *Dig.* XLVIII. xii. 2; *ibid.* XLVII. xi. 6 and Glossators thereon.

b. Cf. Law V, *supra,* p. 29; see Chap. iv, at beg., *supra,* pp. 74 ff.; and Chap. x, *supra,* pp. 195 f.

c. *Dig.* XLVII. x, whole title and Doctors thereon.

d. *Dig.* XLVIII. vi and vii.

e. Add *Dig.* XLIII. xvi. 11.

f. *Code,* IV. lix.

27. *non ab instituto;* for this rather full translation of the Latin phrase, *vide* note 20, p. 355, *supra.*

the common right of all mankind into a private possession of their own, sin all the more gravely in proportion to the greater number of individuals injured by such an undertaking. Moreover, that sin is particularly grave whereby harm is inflicted upon the whole of human society, to which we are bound and made answerable by the oldest of ties. It is this consideration that impels Ambrose[a] to cry out against persons who block entry to the seas; Augustine,[b] against those who obstruct the highways; and Saint Gregory Nazianzen,[c] against those who buy up and keep back commodities, hoping to reap profit for themselves alone from the universal need and, as he himself puts it, employing want as a means to an end (*καταπραγματεύονται τῆς ἐνδείας*). Indeed, in the opinion of this holy sage, [Saint Gregory,] *ὁ συνέχων σῖτον δημοκατάρατος*; in other words, that person is marked out for public execration and is held to be accursed, who juggles with the market-price of grain by holding back supplies. All of these practices, then, are wholly and unreservedly bad; and they merit punishment for the sake of the example involved, if for no other reason. But such punishment is inflicted upon no one more justly than upon those who have reserved for themselves the exercise of a common right. Baldus,[d] moreover, has said that both by canon law and by the law of conscience (which is the same as natural law) all the goods of the offender are tacitly rendered liable for the purpose of giving satisfaction. Therefore, in their war against the Portuguese, the Dutch were justified on this ground, too, as well as on those previously mentioned.

All of the foregoing arguments are based upon the bare fact that commerce was prohibited; but others no less forceful may be derived from the mode of prohibition, under which head we should place the calumnies recorded in an earlier passage.[e]

a. *Hexaemeron,* V. x.
b. Cited in *Decretum,* II. xxiii. 2. 3.
c. *In Funus Basilii* [Oration xliii, § 34, p. 797 D].
d. *On Code,* VI. ii. 15.
e. Pt. II, Art. I, Chap. xi, *supra,* pp. 261 ff.

Ded. from Article I, Conclusion VI Analysis II

Assuming that it is proper for us to defend our own possessions and that they ought not to be taken from us by anyone, we may ask, "What is so much a personal possession as the good name of the virtuous man, an asset certainly more precious to persons distinguished for nobility of spirit than any material profit, and almost more precious than life [120] itself?"[a] So truly does defamation of character constitute an injury, that the general term for injurious acts as a class has come to connote specifically this defamatory act; for we can find no more expressive word than "injury"[b] to describe contumelious conduct,[28] or what the Greeks called ὕβρις [wanton outrage]. Nor are we dealing in the present instance with contumely of a trifling sort, pleasurable to those who inflict it and not very harmful to those upon whom it is inflicted. On the contrary, we refer to that contumely which left an infamous brand upon Hollanders throughout the whole world, and which brought down upon them, by means of accusations no less false than horrible, the hatred of mankind; that contumely which caused numerous kings and peoples to abominate even contact with the Hollanders as an impious and execrable experience. In earlier times, infamy was attached to certain peoples: to the Cilicians, because of their piracy; to the Cecropians,[29] because of their thieving ways; to the Persians, because of their unspeakable love affairs, and to the Nomads because of their lawless and unsociable manner of life. But every charge that can be brought is exceeded by the abominable wickedness ascribed to those men who acknowledge no god and no religion; for such an attitude is so abhorrent to human nature that one may truthfully deny the existence of any nation that does not cherish some innate conception of divinity and practise some form of

a. *Ecclesiasticus,* xxvi. 7; Ancharano, *Consilium,* 325.

b. *Dig.* XLVII. x. 1.

28. The passage cited above from the *Digest* contains the following statement: *specialiter autem iniuria dicitur contumelia* (but specifically, the term "injury" denotes "contumely").

29. Reading *Cercopes* for *Cecropes* (perhaps written by confusion with *Cecropii,* "people of Athens *or* Attica"). According to Ovid (*Metamorphoses,* xiv. 91–100), the Cercopes, or Cecropians, were a race much given to fraud and treachery, and were changed into monkeys by Jupiter because of their crimes.

divine worship.[a] Yet all of these charges have been heaped upon the Hollanders by the Portuguese, who were so blinded by their lust for slander that it is impossible to point out a single accusation on their part which would not be more appropriate to any other nation than to our people, against whom it was brought. Indeed, the foreign scholars[b] who have devoted rather more than ordinary care to the study of questions pertaining to the Low Countries (for we shall not involve ourselves in an examination of all historical records) offer a wealth of testimony to the fact that the people of these countries are extremely zealous in the cultivation not of piracy but of commerce, being moreover free from every rapacious inclination, superior to all others in sexual temperance and in their whole way of life, and characterized by the most profound reverence for the laws, for the magistrates, and above all for religion.

Therefore, when the Hollanders found that they were being dishonoured in this fashion, they acted justly in vindicating their good name; and they rightly showed, by their very deeds, against whom they [120′] were bearing arms, so that all suspicion might be cleared from the minds of the East Indians. For how can that which is permitted in defence of other things be less permissible in defence of one's reputation?[c] In other words, how can it be impermissible to employ arms in order to preserve the integrity of one's reputation, and in order to restore its integrity after injury? This is what occurs when he who has unjustly besmirched the fair fame of the innocent, is rightfully vanquished and by his own dishonour purges the name that was defiled.[d] Nor can it be doubted that a detractor, like a thief, is under an obligation to make amends[e] which will even assume the form of pecuniary fines if due reparation cannot be provided in any other manner. Moreover, it is possible to take not

a. Cicero, *On the Nature of the Gods,* I [xvi. 43].

b. See Chasseneus, *Consuetudines Burgundiae,* Pref. word *Hollande;* [Lodovico] Guicciardini, *De Rebus Belgicis,* Chaps. *De Moribus et Consuetudinibus, De Hollandia* and *De Regimine.*

c. See Law II, Chap. ii, *supra,* p. 23.

d. Doctors, *On Dig.* XLVIII. viii. 9 and *ibid.* xix. 1; Vict., *De Jure Belli,* 4; Panormitanus, *On Decretals,* II. xiii. 12, n. 17.

e. Cf. Law VI.

only civil[a] but also criminal action for injuries inflicted;[b] and it was on this ground that the Turpilian Decree of the Senate imposed a penalty upon slanderers.[c] Accordingly, it is right to take up arms for the same causes. In the works of Virgil,[d] we find these lines:

> "Ah, Jupiter!" she cries, "Shall he depart—
> The stranger who *has mocked* at these our realms?
> Throughout the city will not *arms* be seized
> In swift pursuit? Will not the ships be torn
> From out the docks? Go hence, and bring with speed
> Bright torches; spread the sails; bend to the oars!"

Indeed, we frequently find that even in time of war persons who have assailed the enemy with excessively bitter abuse are punished by the victor,[e] a practice which seems to indicate that war itself does not excuse such virulence.

Ded. from Article I, Conclusion VI Analysis III

The causes above set forth certainly constituted just grounds for undertaking a war. In addition, however, we have observed[f] that not every right [justifying belligerent measures] exists prior to the outbreak of war. There is a form of right which arises in the midst of armed conflict and in defence whereof warfare is properly continued.

Defence of one's own life is included under this head.[g] For when we are defending or attempting to recover our property, or seeking to obtain that which is our right, while our adversary offers armed opposition to such attempts on our part, it is evident that we, though innocent, are thus brought into peril of our lives. This situation constitutes the oldest and most just of the causes of war. Moreover, it is certain that [121] belligerent activities were not even initiated on the part of the Dutch

a. Cf. Law V.
b. *Institutes,* IV. iv. 10.
c. *Dig.* XLVIII. xvi, whole title.
d. [*Aeneid,* IV. 590 ff.]
e. Plutarch, *Timoleon* [xxxii–xxxiii]; see also Gentili, II. xviii.
f. See discussion of Art. I, Chap. vii, *supra,* p. 106.
g. Cf. Law I.

prior to the existence of such a cause, a fact already brought out in our account of the order of events.[a]

Let us consider next another of these causes, namely: defence of possessions[b] [threatened in war], recovery of the actual possessions lost through war, or attainment of what may be regarded as the equivalent of property so lost. For he who wages war unjustly is liable to the just belligerent for all the losses that befall the latter by reason of the conflict. Now, it is a well-established fact that certain vessels, together with the merchandise they carried, were violently snatched from the Dutch by the Portuguese;[c] and also that many other losses were suffered, such as those resulting from the various occasions when the Dutch themselves, after undergoing disastrous defeats, were compelled to abandon and burn their own ships.

Another point to be considered is the process of exacting the debt owed by one hostile party to the other.[d] Under this head, we must include a reckoning of the costs involved. For he who was the author of an unjust war is in debt to the innocent party, to the full extent of the expenses incurred through that conflict. The whole record of events surely affords sufficient proof of the fact that it was not possible to resist the Portuguese in such a remote region of the earth without expending tremendous sums.[e] Items properly falling under this classification are: the outfitting of the ships, a process as costly as it was necessary; the employment of a larger number of sailors; the increase in the rate of pay because of the dangers involved, and the expenditures necessitated in connexion with treatment of wounds or with rewards for zeal in active service.

Furthermore, our comments regarding losses and expenses should be extended to apply also to those losses and expenses which the Dutch

a. Cf. Historical Analysis, Pt. II, Arts. II, IV, Chap. xi, *supra,* pp. 265 ff., 284 ff.

b. Cf. Law II, *supra,* p. 23; add what is stated in General Exposition in Chap. iv, *supra,* p. 68.

c. Cf. Hist. Anal. [Chap. xi], articles above cited.

d. Cf. Law VI, *supra,* p. 29, and add what is stated in General Exposition in Chap. iv, *supra,* p. 68.

e. Cf. Hist. Anal., Pt. II, in entirety, Chap. xi, *supra,* pp. 261 ff.

suffered or may have been fearful of suffering at the hands of persons who were suborned by the Portuguese. For he who gives the command [for an injurious act], as well [as the person who commits the act], is under an obligation to make reparation.[a] Under this head, a claim may be entered for the payments made to barbarians as ransom for captives.

The execution of punishment is the last item on our list of reasons justifying warfare.

For any person who knowingly wages an unjust war commits a very serious offence; and therefore, he ought properly to be punished, since the magnitude of the sin should not serve as protection for the sinner.[b] The injuries brought about by the Portuguese—partly through the medium of others, partly by direct action—are indeed grave.[c] Moreover, there is no difference, according to the jurists,[d] between the direct infliction of injuries and the infliction of the same injuries through an agent. Nor is the person who issues an injurious command any less guilty—on the contrary, he is even more guilty!—than the person who has lent his services in response to the command. It has been ruled,[e] and rightly so, that he who causes an assault by giving the command to attack or by persuasion, is justly attacked in return. For human beings should not imitate the behaviour of dogs, who rush at the stone that struck them (so the old saying goes) and not at the person who aimed the blow. [121′] To cases of this kind one may appropriately apply the moral brought out in the well-known story about the trumpeter, namely, that those individuals who incite others to war while they themselves venture nothing are especially deserving of punishment. Indeed, according to Seneca,[f] "The man who practises violence, and the man who employs for his own gain the things supplied through [the violence of][30] another,

a. Th. Aq. II–II, qu. 62, art. 7, in concl.

b. Cf. Law V, *supra,* p. 29; and Chap. iv as cited, *supra,* pp. 74 ff.

c. Cf. Hist. Anal. [Chap. xi], articles above cited.

d. See Angelus [Aretinus] and his statements in *De Maleficiis,* § *Et Sempronium.*

e. Baldus, *On Code,* VIII. iv. 1, n. 56 [35], statements of Innocent.

f. Seneca (?).

30. In the preparation of the present translation, this passage was not located in the works of Seneca. Consequently, the bracketed phrase represents merely a conjecture regarding the context of the passage.

deserve equally to be *punished.*" The same author,[a] in one of his tragedies, acutely observes:

> He is the doer of the crime,
> Who takes his profit from it.

The events narrated above also exemplify the different classes of crime.

The slaughter of a human being is the gravest of criminal offences, a fact that accounts for the laws against assassins.[b] Now, the Portuguese slaughtered many Hollanders in the vilest and most brutal fashion, and therefore, the East India Company could not conscientiously have neglected to avenge its servants. Homer[c] represents Thetis as saying:

> *ναὶ δὴ ταῦτά γε τέκνον, ἐτήτυμον οὐ κακόν ἐστι*
> *τειρομένοις ἑτάροισιν ἀμυνέμεν αἰπὺν ὄλεθρον.*

> *In truth, my child, 'tis virtuous to seek*
> *Vengeance for comrades slain by vilest means.*[31]

Again, since slavery is comparable to death, liberty must needs be placed almost on an equality with life. From this comparison, one may easily deduce the gravity of the offence involved in dragging a free-born man into unmerited captivity,[d] and in subjecting him to chains and torture, as the Portuguese have done and are still doing to many Hollanders. In fact, so stubbornly do the Portuguese cling to this course of conduct, that they have in no instance allowed such captives to be ransomed, in exchange either for a much larger number offered from among their own captive comrades or for an adequate sum of money. They have chosen, instead, to deliver into perpetual slavery the men whom they themselves

a. Seneca, *Medea* [500 f.].
b. *Dig.* XLVIII. viii; *Code,* IX. xvi.
c. [*Iliad,* XVIII. 128–9.]
d. *Dig.* XLVIII. xv, whole tit. and XLIII. xxix [whole tit.].

31. There is an unusually noteworthy discrepancy here between the Latin of Grotius (which is followed in the English translation) and the original Greek. The former refers to vengeance for comrades already slain, thus bearing out Grotius's argument at this point; the latter, however, merely commends the act of warding off destruction from living comrades.

have captured, a practice denounced by all the jurists[a] as impermissible even in a legitimate war between Christians, since it is contrary to established law.

Yet again, what is more abominable than perjury, or perfidy of any kind?[b] For other evil deeds affect, as a rule, the particular individual against whom they are directed; but those persons who are guilty of perfidy offend against God Himself, calling upon Him as a witness (perhaps in a set verbal formula, or at least by invoking His testimony in some other way), as well as against the whole of human society, [122] thus severing the bond which alone gives us security when we are among men entirely unknown to us. In earlier times, the Romans were wont to issue a statement breaking off friendly relations before they would declare war even upon those peoples against whom they had just cause to take up arms.[c] The Portuguese, on the contrary, while engaged in devising acts of exceeding cruelty against the Dutch, and with the very purpose of facilitating the success of their cruel plans, were taking advantage of the disguise afforded by a pretence of friendship.[d] But this manifestation of bad faith did not suffice them! Their outrageous conduct toward the Dutch reached the point of open defiance against the sacred insignia of peace, against pacts allowing of no ambiguity, against the holy obligations imposed by a sworn oath: in short, nothing was so sacrosanct that it could restrain the Portuguese from shedding the blood of Hollanders.

Similar to these deeds of perfidy was the Portuguese practice of resorting to poisons, and to assassins dispatched under the guise of friendship.[e] The comment formulated long ago in regard to King Perseus is

a. Bartolus, and Doctors, *On Dig.* XLIX. xv. 24 [nn. 11–12]; Covarr., *On Sext,* rule *peccatum,* Pt. II, § 11, n. 6.

b. See Doctors, *On Dig.* XII. ii. 13, § 6; add *Dig.* XLVII. xx. 4; *Code,* II. iv. 41. See Gellius [*Attic Nights*], VII [VI]. xviii and what was said in Concl. VII, Art. III, Pt. II, *supra,* pp. 172 f.

c. Livy, XXXVI [iii] and other books *passim.*

d. Cf. Hist. Anal. Pt. II, pp. 261 ff., esp. Art. III, *supra,* pp. 274 ff.

e. See *supra,* pp. 172 ff., aforesaid, Concl. VII, Art. III, Pt. II.

applicable in the present connexion: the Portuguese were not making ready for a just war; rather, they were "perpetrating crimes of robbery and violence, with the aid of every clandestine means."[a] The words addressed by Alexander to Darius could also be applied here: "You engage in impious wars; and though you have weapons at your disposal, you bid for the heads of your enemies."[b] Assuredly, according to that same Alexander, the person who commits such deeds "should be pursued, not as a just enemy but as an assassin and poisoner, until he is utterly destroyed."[c]

Certain additional offences (of a trifling nature as compared with those discussed above, but nevertheless notable if considered in themselves) still remain to be mentioned: for example, violence (public, private, or armed violence, or forceful seizure of property),[d] and other forms of crime that can hardly fail to develop in the course of an unjust war. The fact that they did develop among the Portuguese has been brought out in our narrative.

Nor should punishment even of attempted crime[e] (in the more atrocious cases, at least) be omitted. Thus the Portuguese ought not to escape punishment for the fact that they were deterred from burning whole fleets together with the men aboard, as well as from the performance of many similar misdeeds, by lack of fortune's favour but not by any lack of malicious intent. This principle is admirably expounded by Seneca, in the following statements: "He who intends to do an injury is already doing it";[f] "A man becomes a brigand even before he has stained his hands with blood, by virtue of the fact that he has already armed himself for slaughter and entertains the will to rob and slay";[g] and, "In so far as

a. Livy, XLII [xviii].

b. Curtius, IV [i. 12].

c. *Ibid.* [xi. 18].

d. See *Dig.* and *Code,* whole titles [*Dig.* XLVIII. vi and vii; *ibid.* XLIII. xvi and *Code,* IX. xii].

e. *Dig.* XLVII. x. 15, § 1, and Doctors thereon; *Code,* IX. xvi. 7.

f. Seneca, *On Anger,* I. iii [1–2].

g. Seneca, *On Benefits,* V. xiv.

a sufficient degree of guilt is concerned, all crimes are completed even before the actual deed is accomplished."[a] [122′]

Yet another principle is generally accepted, namely: if an offence is committed against any man, even though he be a free man, and an affront to a third party is involved in that act, not only the person directly injured but also the party attacked through his association (so to speak) with the direct object of the attack, will have a right to bring action for injury.[b] Thus the Hollanders are entitled to bring action against the Portuguese on the ground of wrongs inflicted upon the East Indians,[c] just as if they were bringing it in their own name.

Lastly, bearing in mind the fact that a state and its magistrates incur guilt when they fail to curb the openly shameful conduct of their own people,[d] we shall list as the final cause the offence committed by the Portuguese nation as a whole, since that nation connived at the evil deeds recorded above.[e]

Inasmuch as all of the offences listed are of a grave nature, the punishments imposed for them must by any proper reckoning be correspondingly severe. According to the precepts of civil law[f] a very few of the punishments in question are limited to fines, a great number involve the confiscation of goods in conjunction with banishment or disgrace, and many carry with them the death penalty. Therefore, it was permissible to exact such penalties as these by force of arms, since (as we shall presently explain) they could not be exacted through judicial procedure.[g] For we have certainly shown that it is right to attack in war, with the purpose of inflicting punishment for the sins committed against us, even those persons who are not subject to our power in any other sense; and we have also shown that he who justly wages war is invested with all the powers of a judge.

a. Seneca, *On the Firmness of the Wise Man,* vii [4].
b. See Bartolus, *On Dig.* XLVII. i. 3; Doctors, *On Institutes,* IV. iv. 6.
c. Cf. Hist. Anal. [Chap. xi], Pt. II Art. V, *supra,* pp. 288 ff.
d. *Decretum,* II. xxiii. 2. 2.
e. See Hist. Anal., Chap. xi, whole chap.
f. Shown by passages cited, *supra,* pp. 366 ff.
g. See discussion of Rule IX, Chap. ii, *supra,* p. 47; Vict., *De Jure Belli,* 13 and 19.

Up to this point, we have been discussing causes. Let us consider next that phase of the question which relates directly to the enemies themselves. Now, we have already concluded that war is justly waged against individuals, and against a state, when those individuals or that state or its magistrates have committed an injurious act; that a war is also just when waged against a state defending a citizen who is the author of an injurious act; and that the same is true in regard to the allies and subjects of all who commit such an act.

Ded. from Article II, Conclusion VI

In the first place, then, it was permissible for the Dutch East India Company to attack in war the individual Portuguese who committed the crimes described above.

In the second place, such an attack was also permissible against the state in question, that is to say, against the Portuguese people. For there is nothing to prevent a war from being private for one side, public for the other, and at the same time just for the former. The war waged by Abraham against the kings was of this nature, and another instance [123] is perhaps afforded by the war of David against Saul. Furthermore, the Portuguese people deserved to be attacked in war, for two reasons.

The first reason consists in the fact that the said people injured traders in the East Indies, either by their own direct action or through their magistrates. It is universally admitted[a] that acts which have taken place because of the state's decision, and even those which have been decreed by a major part of the whole state or by the magistrates, are acts of the whole community.[32] This point has been established in another part of the present treatise. Now, it was a decision of the state that caused Manoel, brother of the Governor of Goa, to be dispatched with some

a. Panormitanus, *Super Conc. Basileense;* Alex. of Imola, *Consilia,* VI. 13; Jason, *On Dig.* XII. i. 27.

32. Originally, Grotius wrote: *Omnes fatentur teneri universitatem ex iis factis quae* (It is universally agreed that the whole community is bound by those acts which . . .). In altering this sentence to read as it now stands, he introduced a new verb, *esse* (are), without deleting *teneri* (is bound). Even though, by a rather forced interpretation, the latter term might be retained in the sense of "are regarded [as acts of the whole community]," it is omitted from the English translation on the far more likely assumption that Grotius merely forgot to strike it out when he made the other alterations.

ships, under instructions to make a warlike attack upon the Hollanders at their very first approach, and even to inflict punishment upon those who might be unwilling to join him in the attack.[a] It is by decision of the state that more and still more vessels (Spanish aid also having been invoked) are being equipped against the Dutch.[b] By state decision was that dread fleet assembled, under the command of Andrés Hurtado, which was to bring utter destruction upon all the Hollanders and upon those who had granted admittance to the Hollanders.[c] Furthermore, this same Hurtado, who even now remains close to Malacca with a large fleet, is under orders to rid the entire region of all foreign merchants. Lastly, it is by decision of the state that Dutchmen are being detained as captives and sent to Portugal.

The second reason for making war upon the Portuguese people lies in the failure of the Portuguese state to take steps for the punishment of Portuguese individuals because of the crimes perpetrated by the latter against the Dutch. As a matter of fact, the state protects these malefactors, and impedes the infliction of punishment. The jurists[d] are unanimous in condemning not only states that expressly deny justice, but also those which are negligent of justice, provided that the case in question involves openly and persistently injurious conduct which the state has power to prevent or punish. To what situation will such a description apply, if not to the present case? How often, pray, have the Dutch suffered the gravest injuries at the hands of the Portuguese? Once? That would be comparatively nothing! Ten times? A scanty estimate! A hundred times? That does not approach the true number! Let us say, rather, "as often as there was any opportunity to do harm." Moreover, [123′] these injuries were inflicted not in secret but openly, in the sight of all India, on land and on sea. What obstacle, then, prevented the imposition of punishment upon the authors of such evil deeds, or at least the re-

a. Cf. Hist. Anal., Pt. II, Art. IV, Second Episode, *supra,* p. 285.

b. Same Art., Fourth Episode, and ff. [Chap. xi], *supra,* pp. 286 ff.

c. See Art. V, Second Episode [Chap. xi], *supra,* pp. 289 ff.

d. Ferrettus, *Consilia,* II; Alciati, *Consilia,* V. xxiii; Jason, *On Dig.* XII. i. 27; Doctors, *On Dig.* L. xvii. 50; Decio, *Consilium,* 486; see Gentili, *De Iure Belli,* I. xxi.

moval of their power to injure, other than this fact: that the thought shared by all alike, the resolution entertained by the whole nation, the sentiment supported by every individual Portuguese, is that no foreigner shall be suffered to approach the lands in question?

In the third place,[33] the subjects of a state that is shown to have inflicted an injury are liable, as such, to warlike attack; that is to say, every Portuguese person without exception is thus liable. This is true partly because subjects are compelled to defend their state, and partly because the act of a state is the concern of its individual members. The words of Augustine[a] may well be adapted to the present case, as follows: "The sin privately committed by any individual from among a given people, is one thing; that which is done in common, as the expression of one mind and one will, when an act is performed by a united multitude, is a different thing. Where the whole body of citizens is present, there the individual citizens are also present; but where individuals are present, it does not necessarily follow that there the whole body of the citizens is also to be found. For individuals may exist apart from the whole; but the whole must contain the various individuals, since it consists in the said individuals, gathered together or reckoned as a sum total." Of this all-inclusive nature is the extreme and headstrong obstinacy of the Portuguese, with which they strive—both as a body and individually, uniting their fortunes and their corporeal strength for the attainment of their purpose—to prevent any Dutchman from being safe in India.

We find, then, not only that there were underlying causes to justify the war, but also that the Portuguese deserved to be numbered [124] among the enemy. The difficult part of our problem lies in the fact that the power to begin a war would not seem to be granted readily to private parties.

a. [*Qu. on Heptateuch,* III,] qu. 26, *On Leviticus.*

33. This is the third main conclusion relative to the enemies who may properly be attacked, considered as a question apart from the proper causes of the war. Grotius's numbering in this connexion should not be confused with his numbering of the reasons for attacking the Portuguese people as a whole, which constitute the two immediately preceding subdivisions under the main conclusion introduced by the phrase, "In the second place . . ." (*supra,* p. 377).

Ded. from Article I, Conclusion VII

Nevertheless, we have demonstrated that in so far as judicial recourse is lacking, private individuals are not prohibited from undertaking a war. Accordingly, when the lack of judicial recourse is of continued duration, everything that is permissible by the law of nature is permissible for private individuals. Thus it is universally acknowledged that a debt may be exacted by [private] force of arms. To this thesis we have added a contention based upon the opinion of particularly judicious authorities, namely, that in such cases of necessity even the power to inflict punishment concordant with the rule of justice should not be denied.

Now, the continued lack of judicial recourse in the affair under consideration is certainly a self-evident fact. Almost all of the events that gave rise to this war took place upon the ocean; but we have maintained[a] (and rightly, I believe) that no one can claim special jurisdiction over the ocean with respect to locality. Furthermore, if any such special jurisdiction did exist [in the present instance], it would be that of the East Indian rulers, who do not wish to become involved in the case and who are not recognized by the Portuguese as judges thereof. From the standpoint of locality, therefore, judicial recourse is lacking both in law and in fact. From the standpoint of the persons involved, there could have been no judge other than the Portuguese State or ruler, or the Dutch State, since the matter is one which concerns the Portuguese and the Dutch. The Portuguese State and its ruler were the very parties who took the first step, not only in the public infliction of injury upon the Dutch, but also in initiating the war. This fact clearly deprived them of the power to serve as judges, not to mention the further consideration that, after numerous instances of perfidy, when the Portuguese (in defiance even of a formal agreement) were extending merciless treatment to the Dutch envoys, any recourse to the former might justifiably have been shunned. Consequently, the proper procedure would have consisted in resorting to the Dutch State as judge, and such action was impossible because of the vast distances between the localities involved. Thus the lack [124′] of judicial recourse was not momentary, but continuous and of long duration. The validity of this conclusion is especially evident if we bear

a. *Supra,* this chap., pp. 315 ff.

in mind the sequence and interrelationship of the events that occurred in the East Indies, viewed as forming a coherent pattern of time and place.

Granting that the war was just, we have yet to consider the question of how much was permissible in the course of that war.

We have already made it clear that one may not exceed the limits proper for the right contested and for the persons liable under the said right. The nature of the particular rights upheld by the Dutch against the Portuguese has been discussed in connexion with the causes of the war. But let us put aside every claim to vengeance which would have justified the Dutch in punishing the Portuguese for violating the law of nations by their restraint of commerce, for false and savage calumny, for homicide, perfidy, and rapine. No loss suffered by the Portuguese can ever afford satisfaction for these claims.

Ded. from Part I, Article III, Conclusion VII

Let us turn our attention rather to the following contention, whose validity has been proved beyond any possibility of dispute: the Portuguese have prevented the Dutch from trading freely with whatsoever East Indian nations the latter might choose for their trade, and are therefore under an obligation to make reparation for all of the profits lost to the Dutch by reason of that interference. The losses so caused amount to a truly enormous sum, since the first voyages were rendered practically futile and fruitless in consequence of the snares set by the Portuguese. Let us also take into consideration the fact that these same Portuguese are responsible for the damages resulting from a war unjustly initiated (including even damages incurred under the head of expenses), whose principal categories we have already indicated briefly. If an accurate reckoning were made of all such items—the interruption of profitable enterprises, and the infliction of losses and expenses—and if, on the other hand, the value of the captured carack and its cargo of merchandise should be estimated, there is no doubt but that the total cost borne by the Dutch would prove to be considerably greater than the total amount taken by them, or that the sum charged on their account against the Portuguese would be greater than the sum charged against the Dutch themselves because of their victory. In any case, it is just that an amount should have been taken from the Portuguese, sufficient to provide an additional reserve fund for future warfare, since the injury has not been wiped out, the peril has not ceased and the struggle increases in severity. Thus we find, not only that the warlike act in question did not pass beyond the limits of the right contested, but that it even stopped far short of those limits.

Neither will anyone contend that the persons from whom the goods were taken were not liable to such action. For the Portuguese State, [125] or Portuguese people, were certainly under an obligation to provide redress for all of the items that I have mentioned, since the said people impeded the practice of commerce, initiated a war, and neglected to punish the guilty. Now, we have already shown that the debt owed by a state may be exacted from individual members of that state (not, indeed, under civil law, but under the law of nations); and in this connexion we adduced, in addition to sound arguments and authoritative citations, the specific example provided by the institution of reprisals, through which any person injured by the citizen of a state that fails to enforce justice, or (still more emphatically) any person injured directly by a given state, justly recovers his due from any other person whatsoever who is a citizen of the state in question. Thus we arrive at the very conclusion supported by the testimony of the Spaniards themselves, a conclusion which runs as follows: harm may not be inflicted upon the persons of subjects in excess of that which the subjects themselves merit because of their own transgressions or because they are hindering the execution of justice; whereas spoils may justly be taken from all subjects, at any time, until the entire sum of the debt [owed by their state] has been recovered, without any exception in favour of merchants or other classes, howsoever innocent such classes may be. Therefore, it was clearly permissible to wage war upon the merchants who were the owners of the said carack and merchandise, to the extent necessary in order to bring about the surrender of those goods as prize. In this particular case, indeed, special note should also be made of the fact that the captured carack and the owners of merchandise who were on board had set sail from Macao,[a] that is to say, from the place where approximately a score of

Ded. from Corollary I, Chapter VIII

a. See Hist. Anal., Pt. II, Art. III, Fifth Episode, *supra,* pp. 178 ff.

Hollanders had been gibbeted or drowned as victims of Portuguese fury. Who would describe those owners as innocent persons? Moreover, I have another and more conclusive point to make: on the ship itself, clothing and pitiful belongings stripped from the slain were found, articles which the Portuguese were taking to their native land as spoils of a glorious victory (so to speak), doubtless in the fear that without proofs of this kind people would be insufficiently convinced that anyone had actually practised such extreme cruelty. Will pity be felt, then, for any of those men aboard the carack? Or is it not more likely that even the [125′] Portuguese will scoff at the kindliness of the Dutch, who have been content to instil fear through property losses while sparing the lives of the persons capable of perpetrating such acts as are described above?

Ded. from Part II, Article III, Conclusion VII

We have laid down another restriction for warfare, however, in addition to those turning upon the right contested. I refer to the restriction imposed by good faith. In the present instance, no promise has been made to the enemy that has not been more than amply fulfilled. To that same people who had butchered the Dutch in time of peace, life was promised and granted when they themselves had been conquered in war [by the Dutch]; and not only life but liberty, too, was freely conceded, although it would have been permissible to extort a considerable price. Furthermore, lest any part of these benefactions should have been conferred in vain, a Dutch guard was given to the Portuguese, to take them back to Malacca after their release. In short, the kindnesses extended by the victorious people to the vanquished were so considerable that the Portuguese, who marvel all the more at these virtues because they themselves are strangers to such qualities, offered the Dutch a notable testimony to their benevolence, with express mention of their *good faith,* as is evidenced by the letters (appended to this treatise)[34] from the Senate of Malacca, the Governor of Malacca, and the Commander of the cap-

34. The last page of the MS. of the *Commentary* (p. 163) contains a list of certain documents, including the letters above mentioned, which Grotius meant to append to his own text; *vide infra,* p. 497 of the present translation. The documents in question were not found with Grotius's papers, but all of them were subsequently located by Professor Fruin in the original Dutch or German texts.

August 1603 tured ship. Finally, it is a fact that the Portuguese, some time after their defeat by the ships of Van Warwijck, proclaimed in Macao their intention not to deal so gently with the Dutch if they themselves should gain the upper hand.

As for the aims of war, every individual is answerable to himself on that point. Nor is this matter subject to human judgements save in so far as the spirit of any nation has a quality common to all its people. In that sense, to be sure, individual actions form a basis for conjectural inference. We have said that the true end of war is the attainment of one's right. If the seizure of spoil serves this end, the spoil should be regarded as something justly and equitably acquired; but it should not be so regarded when a warrior is merely eager for personal gain. Let us see whether the latter supposition is more credible in the case of the Portuguese, or in the case of the Dutch.

Ded. from Article I, Conclusion VIII

Writers of ancient times[a] tell us that even long ago the Portuguese people were accustomed to live by robbery and plundering; and persons of the better class among the Portuguese themselves[b] are by no means unaware of the vileness and avarice of the blood that has been [126] intermingled with their race since those bygone times, nor have they failed to note the vast number of Portuguese who are not seriously regarded, among Christians, as Christians.

I shall not reproduce here the exceedingly honourable records which are available, by way of contrast, with reference to the Dutch. Let us be satisfied with the statement made in an earlier passage but pertinent also in the present context, to the effect that among all the peoples of these [Germanic] territories there has never been one more free from greed for spoils. Thus, when Tacitus[c] describes the war of Civilis, he depicts the Germans as fighting for plunder, and the Dutch as fighting for glory. Foreign writers[d] belonging approximately to our own period have likewise declared that the Hollanders are conspicuous among Germanic

a. Strabo [III. iii. 6]; Diodorus Siculus [V. 34]; Servius, *On the Georgics,* III [408].
b. See Osorio [*Hist. of Emmanuel*], I.
c. *Histories,* IV [lxxiii].
d. Chasseneus, *Consult. Ducatus Burg. ac Fere totius Galliae,* in Pref. word *Holande.*

peoples for their freedom from covetousness in regard to the property of others. The sentiments which the Portuguese in India itself are even now compelled to entertain with respect to the Dutch are quite adequately indicated in the letter written by the Bishop of Malacca to the King. The Bishop says: *"They have done no harm to the natives, much less to the Portuguese. In short, they have caused no trouble for any nation."* Farther on, he adds: *"Among the natives, they were most welcome and well liked, because they practised commerce justly, without resorting to violence or injury."* It is clear that the Dutch were pursuing commercial aims only, and that they would have been content with the attainment of such aims, had they not been forced into war. This fact is brought out by the whole series of events from the very beginning of their voyages, and by their patience in maintaining the peace for so long a period. For example (as we have already pointed out),[a] although they encountered four Portuguese vessels on their first trip, each of which was sailing singly, an easy prey for the covetous, the vessels were sent on their way unharmed. Furthermore, there were even occasions when things that had been captured from the Portuguese were voluntarily returned to them. That was the course of conduct adopted, for example, by Wolphert Harmensz, in connexion with a ship (belonging to the class known as "caravels") which had been dispatched to Pernambuco and had come to this side of the Equator. But when experience showed that the Portuguese would rage all the more boldly against the Dutch as the fear of retaliation grew less, the latter bestirred themselves in the mildest possible way, attempting to discover whether men no less avaricious than cruel might not at least be induced through loss of their goods to show respect for justice and peace. [126′]

A recital of the various instances of self-restraint on the part of the Dutch would constitute, in reality, an affront to the worth and reputation of that people; but there is one episode which I shall not pass over in silence, an event whose history is bound up with the very time at which the prize in question was seized. When the ruler of Damma was detaining as captives the twenty men who had been sent to him in the capacity

a. Hist. Anal., Pt. II, Art. IV, First Episode, *supra,* pp. 284 f.

of agents (an incident which we have mentioned elsewhere),[a] and when he had extorted a price for the lives of eight of them but was refusing to release the others on any condition, Heemskerck—who held that no Dutchman's freedom should be treacherously surrendered, and that this was especially true when such perfidy would plunge the victim into a condition of wretchedness—decided that vengeance should be exacted from pledges held as security. It so happened that, among other vessels from Johore, one of the type called "junks" was sailing to Damma; and Heemskerck, regarding it as property that belonged to that state, simply detained it. He sent messengers to the King in Damma, promising that, if the twelve Dutch agents who remained there should be released, he himself would in return restore the vessel and extend his friendship to Damma thereafter. But the King, entirely unmoved by Heemskerck's offer, even attempted to snatch from its guards by armed force the vessel that was being detained. In view of this reaction, it seemed that the best plan was to remove the merchandise and send the shipmaster, together with the vessel itself and seventy men, to Damma, adding a promise to the effect that, if the shipmaster should succeed in obtaining the release of the Dutchmen, either the merchandise or its equivalent in value (which had been estimated at five catties in gold) would be returned to him. Later, when seasonal considerations and the lack of fresh water made a change of anchorage necessary, Heemskerck sent all the East Indians who were in his power back to their own homes. Two he dispatched as legates to Johore, that he might make his excuses through them, asking that some authorized person be sent him, to whom he could pay the aforementioned five gold catties. The King, however, replied that he perceived nothing that called for excuses in what Heemskerck had done, since it had been made sufficiently clear that the Hollanders were so inoffensive as to wish no harm to any peace-loving [127] person, and since, for the rest, it was not only a blameless act but an act praiseworthy in the eyes of all nations, to avenge oneself upon those who had previously inflicted an injury. He added that, if the fortunes of war had caused such vengeance to be exacted at his expense or at the

a. Hist. Anal., Pt. II, Art. II, Eighth Episode, *supra,* pp. 274 f.

expense of one of his subjects, this circumstance did not constitute a reason for less equanimity on his part in enduring the outcome. As far as he himself was concerned, the friendship of the Hollanders would alone suffice by way of complete and abundant indemnification. Subsequently, when Heemskerck came to Johore for business purposes, it was only with difficulty and through entreaties that he obtained the royal permission to make reparation to the master of the ship that had been detained, a man named Rasaduta. Accordingly, in lieu of the five gold catties, he paid the willing Rasaduta twelve hundred *reaes,* even though the merchandise was worth scarcely seven hundred.

What feature of this episode is best calculated to arouse wonder? The fact that a price was paid in exchange for men who had been captured by no lawful right and in defiance of good faith? The act of releasing the East Indians while men of that race were still holding Dutchmen in captivity? Heemskerck's self-accusation before the ruler of Johore? The fact that he even pleaded [with that ruler for the privilege of making reparation]? Heemskerck's payment of more than he owed, when it was possible to refrain from making any payment whatsoever? Certainly no plunderer is so generous!

Therefore, since the more favourable interpretation should be applied in doubtful cases, even when proofs of the kind above listed do not exist, it is proper to suppose that the intentions and inclinations of the men who defeated the Portuguese consisted in the purpose of at least compelling the persons they had been unable to pacify through kindness to adopt a different course of action in view of their own losses. As Ambrose[a] has said, those whom we have been unable to deprive of the will to rob should be deprived of the power to rob.

Would that the Portuguese might lay aside their savagery, even now, acknowledging the fellowship of mankind and contending only as competitors in the prices bid! The Dutch are ready to dispense with enmity, and to forget all the crimes that we have mentioned as well as their own

a. *On Psalms,* CXVIII, sermon viii, verse 2 [verse 58, n. 25] and also in *Decretum,* II. xxiii. 4. 33.

excellent opportunities for waging a successful war. The profits derived from willing sources are sufficient for them. [127′]

Accordingly, whether we choose to interpret the aim of this war as reparation for losses and expenses, or whether we maintain that it includes also the overthrow of unjust malice, either aim suffices, and both are unquestionably just. After examining all of the causes involved, we arrive at the following verdict: the war which is being waged by the Dutch East India Company against the Portuguese, the former owners of the captured vessel, is a just war; and the seizure of the prize in question was therefore entirely just, a deduction clearly indicated by the basic principles which we have already laid down. Furthermore, since the spoils acquired through private warfare become first of all and in their entirety the property of him who is the author of a just war, up to the point where the debt owed him is satisfactorily discharged (as we have demonstrated by means of incontrovertible arguments), it will readily be granted that the carack and captured merchandise of which we are speaking, and which (as we have shown) were in any case insufficient to meet the debt that was owed, have become possessions of the East India Company, at whose private expense this war has been conducted. For we have made it clear that acquisition of spoils plays a part in private warfare no less than in public warfare. With respect to this point, indeed, even those persons who disagree on the terms to be employed, are in agreement on the essential fact. For it is universally conceded[a] that in the absence of any judge, even though this defect be temporary, the possessions of adversaries may be seized for the purpose of recovering property and collecting compensation for debts due (including costs), except that in certain cases some authorities require subsequent settlement by a judicial decree. When, in these circumstances, the seizure of spoil has been followed by the issuance of such a decree, no doubt remains.[b] The Scholastics,[c] moreover, lay down a doctrine of still broader scope, as

Ded. from Conclusion IV

Ded. from Conclusion III

Ded. from Part I, Article I, Conclusion IX

a. See what is said at beg. of Chap. x and add Bartolus, *On Reprisals,* Qu. 9, ad 4, near end.

b. See end of Pt. II in next Chap., *infra,* pp. 431–32.

c. Sylvester, on word *bellum,* [Pt.] I. x [1].

follows: Even when a war is unjust from the standpoints of cause, intent, persons concerned, and authorization, nevertheless, if some question of property is involved—for example, as a result of the fact that the war was undertaken for the purpose of reclaiming property, always assuming that an interval of time has been allowed to elapse—the party who began the war is not in conscience bound to make restitution, unless he has taken an amount, or caused losses, in excess of what has been unjustly retained from his own property by his adversary.

The foregoing observations should be applied to the cause of the Dutch East India Company, in so far as its recourse to arms on its own behalf is concerned.

Similarly, in view of what has been said above,[a] there should be no doubt but that the said Company was empowered to take up arms on the ground of injuries inflicted upon its allies and friends (such as the Zeeland Company), and to reckon whatever might be acquired in consequence as compensation, first of all, for the expenses thus incurred by the Dutch East India Company itself. In this sense, it is possible to hold that the Hollanders themselves did not begin the armed conflict [128] but merely joined the forces of the Zeelanders, or the East Indians, who were initiating that conflict; in which case, the spoils taken would become the property of the Hollanders to the extent of the allotment made to them by the authors of the war. However, since the alliance of private individuals with East Indian princes or peoples constitutes a public rather than a private war, the question just raised will be postponed for discussion in a later and more appropriate context.

Ded. from Article I, Conclusion V (in the middle) and subsequent conclusions up to and including Part II, Article I, Conclusion IX

As for the problems relating to subjects engaged in private warfare—or more specifically, to the sailors and to the individuals serving the said Company in positions of greater or less importance—discussion is practically superfluous: partly because our investigations were not undertaken primarily with reference to such persons, and partly because, in the light of the observations made above, and after evaluating them on the bases of the dogmas laid down at the outset, we cannot doubt but

Ded. from Article I, Conclusion V (at end); Articles III & IV, Conclusion VI; Article IV, Conclusion

a. See what precedes Concl. VIII, Art. I, Chap. ix, *supra,* pp. 184 ff. and discussion before Concl. IX, Art. I, Pt. I, *supra,* Chap. x, pp. 194 f. and 200 ff.

VII, with following Corollaries; Article II, Conclusion VIII, & Part II, Article I, Conclusion IX

that, in a cause so palpably just, these subject persons conducted themselves aright in rendering obedience to the Company and in carrying out its orders in its war against the Portuguese. Accordingly, if the said persons have also been assigned some part of the prize by the Company, their retention of that part will be a blameless and upright act.

CHAPTER XIII [128]

Wherein It Is Shown That the War Is Just, and That the Prize in Question Was Justly Acquired by the Company, in the Public Cause of the Fatherland

Part I. This Assertion Is True with Respect to the Governmental Assemblies[1] [of Holland and of the United Provinces], in Their Character as Voluntary Agents.

Part II. It Is True with Respect to the East India Company, in Its Character as a Subject of the Said Assemblies.

Part III. [The War and the Afore-mentioned Acquisition Are] Also [Just] on the Basis of the Public Cause of Our Allies.

In this same chapter the following theses are presented: [128 a]

1. A politically organized community, or its various internal states, even when they are ruled by a prince, nevertheless possess authority to enter publicly into a war.

2. A just ground for war against a prince is the defence of long-established hereditary laws by which the principate is bound.

3. War against the prince does not require a declaration of war.

4. It is the part of a good citizen to obey the magistrates currently in office.

5. A citizen fights in good faith against the prince, when fighting in defence of the state and the laws.

1. *Ordinum.* See note 3, p. 245, *supra.*

6. The war of a state against a prince who was formerly its own ruler is a foreign war.

7. It is sometimes right for Christians to enter into an alliance of war with infidels who are fighting against Christians. [128]

Part I of Chapter XIII Ded. from Article II, Conclusion V

Although, in the sense already indicated, this conflict could have been waged as a private war, and a just one, too, it is nevertheless more accurate to say that in actual fact it is a public war and that the prize in question was acquired in accordance with public law, the author of the conflict being, in reality, the States Assembly of Holland, now allied with the other Provinces of the Low Countries.

We have declared that the primary and supreme power to make war resides within the state, and that any perfect community is (so to speak) a true state. Thus (as Victoria[a] observes) the Kingdom of Aragon forms a state that is distinct from the Kingdom of Castile, notwithstanding the fact that both kingdoms are subject to one and the same prince. So, too, the domain of Holland in itself constitutes a whole state. Moreover, just as he who speaks of troops and cohorts is speaking of an army, so he who refers to the internal states [that make up a given political community] wishes to be understood as referring to nothing more nor less than the said community, since all the parts of an entity, when taken together, are exactly equivalent in point of fact to the whole. [128′]

Thesis I

It is a familiar observation in the learned discussions of the philosophers, that a thing which constitutes in itself the cause of a certain quality in some other thing, likewise possesses that same quality, and in a far greater degree, provided only that it is essentially capable of possessing such an attribute at all. Now, both by natural and by divine law (according to the thoroughly sound conclusion which we borrow from the aforementioned Victoria),[b] all civil power resides in the state, which is by its very nature competent to govern itself, administer its own affairs and

a. *De Jure Belli,* 7.

b. *De Potestate Civili,* 7; also discussed by Covarr., *Practicae Quaestiones,* i, concl. 1; see in discussion of Law X, Chap. ii, *supra,* p. 44.

order all its faculties for the common good. Princes, on the other hand, are invested with no just power that has not been derived from the power of the state through election either of individual rulers or of dynasties,[a] so that the right to undertake a war pertains to the prince only in the sense that he is acting for the state and has received a mandate from it.[b] Therefore, the greater and prior power to declare war lies within the state itself,[c] which is regarded as having set up the prince as its substitute for those purposes which the state could not conveniently realize by its own direct action. Thus the power of the state remains intact even after the establishment of a principate:[d] so truly intact, indeed, that the Spanish theologian[e] above cited proves that the state may change one prince for another or transfer the principate from one dynasty to another. In this connexion, Victoria mentions as an example [the deposition of Childeric by] the Franks.

In the light of these arguments, it is clear that the state of Holland, even if it was subject to a prince, did not lack authority to undertake a public war independently of that ruler; for otherwise the said state would not have been self-sufficient. Victoria,[f] too, employs this very argument of self-sufficiency to prove that kings, even when subject to an emperor, are not forbidden to undertake war independently.

Furthermore, even if those entities which we call "internal states" were not equivalent [in the aggregate] to the state itself, but had instead the character of magistracies established by the latter and inferior in rank to the prince, the conflict in question would still be a public war. For we have maintained, in agreement with Victoria[g] and with other authorities, that in cases where the prince is inactive, inferior magistrates are empowered not only to repel injuries but also to initiate a public war

a. Covarr., *ibid.* concl. 4; Vázquez, xx. 24 ff.; *ibid.* xlvii. 5; Durandus, *De Origine Jurisdictionum.*

b. Vict., *De Jure Belli,* 6.

c. Henry of Gorkum, in Pref. and in Prop. 12, ans. to last arg.

d. So asserts Vázquez, xlvii. 11.

e. Vict., *De Indis,* Pt. I [Sect. III], 16.

f. *De Jure Belli,* 8.

g. *Ibid.* 9.

for the purpose of punishing foreign malefactors. According to [129] Covarruvias,[a] even one part of a given nation may elect magistrates for itself because of such a defect in princely government, although the appointment of those magistrates might otherwise be possible only through the king. For (as Covarruvias observes) the people have retained the power conferred upon them by natural law, and may avail themselves thereof on occasions when the king himself is not making use of his own power. "Otherwise," [Covarruvias continues,] "the people themselves, and the state itself, would be exposed to an exceedingly grave and critical danger to which they could offer no opposition, a hypothesis that is absurd in the extreme." From the standpoint of law, nonexistence and existence without effect are mutually equivalent concepts. Castrensis[b] says: "It is one and the same thing to have no superior, and to have a negligent superior."

If the absence or negligence of the prince makes it permissible for inferior magistrates to undertake a war, how much more surely is this permissible when the prince himself does the state an injury that can be checked only by resort to arms? Not only those theologians[c] who regard the Pope as subject to the Council but even the members of the opposite faction, which sets the papal authority above that of the Council, concede (despite the latter doctrine) that in cases where the Pope is following a course destructive to the Church, the Council may be convoked in defiance of his will; and that, by the authority of the said Council, he may be resisted and the execution of his commands impeded, even forcibly, should such action prove necessary. Now, what is the Council, other than an ecclesiastical States Assembly? And what is a [political] States Assembly, other than a civic Council? Indeed, on the basis of this analogy, even greater licence should be conceded to the political assembly for opposing the prince than to the Council for opposing the Pope, since the very persons who declare that the Pope has received his power di-

a. *Pract. Quaes.,* iv. 3.

b. *On Dig.* I. i. 5, n. 18.

c. Sylvester, on word *Papa,* iv; Torquemada, III. x; Vict., *De Potestate Papae et Concilii,* 23–4.

rectly from Christ and not from the Church, nevertheless admit that the prince possesses no authority save that derived from the state.[a]

Therefore, the States Assembly of Holland had a right to declare war.

This same fact is brought out even far more clearly by the sanctity invariably accorded the authority of that Assembly[b] since the earliest days of the political entity of Holland, and by the confirmation of the said authority through long-continued usage, as well as by our hereditary laws, established originally at Brabant and subsequently introduced into the rest of the Low Countries. For these hereditary precepts expressly provide that the Assembly shall have full power to refuse all fealty and respect to a prince who violates the law of the land.[c] [129′]

We should, of course, be exceeding the scope of the task undertaken if we attempted to discuss the causes underlying the war waged by the Hollanders in conjunction with the other peoples of the Low Countries,[d] first against Alba and the Spaniards who accompanied him, and later against King Philip, who was also Count of Holland. Certainly, in view of all the treatises long ago made available to the public on this matter, it does not behove me to tamper with the admirable account already provided by other writers. I shall not refrain, however, from making a statement in passing, to cover such points as will suffice for present purposes.

It is well known that Alba and the Spaniards publicly declared, and even formally decreed, that all the statutes and ancestral laws of the Low Countries had been committed (so to speak) to the discretion of the prince. Yet the only pretext that could be offered in defence of this proclamation was the fact that certain disorders had arisen, caused by a few individuals in accordance with their private designs, and taking the form

Madrid, Feb. 16, 1568

a. Vict., *De Potestate Ecclesiae, Qu. 3,* n. 2; Covarr., *Pract. Quaes.* i. 2; and in c. *peccatum,* § 9, n. 6; stated by Cajetan, *On II–II,* qu. 1, art. 10 and *id., De Pot. Papae et Concl.* [*De Comparatione Auctoritatis Papae et Concilii*], II. i.

b. See Hist. Anal., Pt. I, First Episode [First Art.], *supra,* p. 245.

c. See at end of Introd. to Laetus and Guicciardini [*De Rebus Belgicis*] c. *De Privilegiis Brabantorum.*

d. See Hist. Anal. Pt. I, Art. I, *supra,* pp. 244 ff.

of a sudden uprising that was suppressed by the magistrates as quickly as possible. All legal authorities[a] unanimously and most consistently maintain that the community is not to be held liable for such offences; and therefore, any step taken under the aforementioned pretext and impermissible apart from that pretext, was certainly unjust, and called for resistance.[b]

Ded. from Article I (First Analysis), Conclusion VI

Accordingly, since the members of the States General, in their capacity of supreme magistrates, were charged with the function of watching over the rights of both state and citizenry,[c] it was their duty to defend the former against the violence imposed upon a peaceful situation by foreign arms illegally introduced.[d] Secondly, it was their duty to protect the lives and possessions of the citizens against the illegal judgements, incompatible with the forms of commonly accepted law and with our native customs, which were being carried into effect by meddling foreigners. Yet again, it was incumbent upon them to release the state and the individual citizens from requisitions of a nature not only directly contrary to the laws[e] but inimical also to the common liberty of mankind, since (as the Spanish authority Vázquez[f] observes) such requisitions open the way to immediate pillage and to future servitude. As one of their chief functions, moreover, it behoved these supreme magistrates to take pains to ensure the careful observance of the covenants handed down by our forebears[g] and consecrated by the oaths of princes, covenants which gave continuity to our sovereign form of government, lest, through the violation of those sacred pacts which had served for many centuries as the basic safeguard of our state, the latter should be made

a. Bartolus, *On Dig.* XLVIII. xix. 16, § 10; Baldus, *On Feuds* [p. 19]; Jason, *On Dig.* XII. i. 27; Andreas Gail, *De Pace Publica,* II. ix.

b. *Code,* X. i. 5; *Code,* XII. xl. 5; elsewhere, in Bartolus, Tract. *On Guelfs and Ghibellines,* 8. See also Law I, Chap. ii, *supra,* p. 23.

c. Vázquez, xli. 20 ff. and xviii. 7.

d. See Laws I and II, *supra,* p. 23.

e. See Law II, *supra,* p. 23.

f. Vázquez, viii; vii in entirety, and xliii. 6.

g. See Law VI together with Rule III, *supra,* pp. 29 and 34.

subject, after the fashion of a province, to the greedy caprice of the Spaniards. And lastly, it was also obligatory that punitive measures be [130] taken to restrain the persons who were heaping injury and abuse upon the fatherland or upon its citizens.[a]

In the circumstances described, it was undoubtedly incumbent upon Philip himself—to whom so many entreaties had been addressed—to defend the Dutch and the other peoples of the Low Countries who were being crushed by armed force, and to bring the offenders to justice. For such are the two sole functions motivating the establishment of any principate. Furthermore, leading authorities[b] on law declare that a nation may break away from its prince on the ground that he has neglected to defend them; and, according to the same authorities, not even the power to choose another ruler should be denied to such a nation. The abovementioned learned Spaniard,[c] who was also (still more significantly) a Senator of the Supreme Council of that same Philip, maintains that superiors, when they refuse justice to their subjects, are not only deprived *ipso iure* of supreme jurisdiction, but also become forever incapacitated from recovering that jurisdiction. "Therefore," [Vázquez adds,] "princes ought to observe the greatest caution lest, while they *wrongfully* and hastily deny justice, the subjects themselves in their turn should rush *rightfully* into disobedience and *rebellion.*" What, then, must be said in regard to that prince who not only fails to exact justice of persons responsible for wrongdoing but even exalts those very persons by conferring honours upon them? What must be said of a prince who does not merely fail to defend his oppressed people but personally contributes toward their oppression his counsels, money, fleets, and army, with the purpose, moreover, of imposing upon them, as upon a conquered people, in defiance of an ancient form of government, such laws as he may

Thesis II

a. See Law V, *supra,* p. 29.

b. Vázquez, v. 10; Castrensis, *On Dig.* I. i. 5, nn. 17 and 18; Doctors, *On Dig.* XLVIII. xix. 19.

c. Vázquez, Pref., nn. 16 and 17.

arbitrarily choose? Surely, in these circumstances, there is much more justification for renunciation of allegiance.

New explanation A sentence pronounced contrary to the rights of any party is said to be unjust; a sentence pronounced contrary to judicial forms is not even a true sentence. The same criteria may be applied to laws. According to divine law, a marriage is dissolved only in consequence of that sin which is contrary to the very nature of marriage and which is known as adultery. In like manner, he who is guilty of any crime other than an attack upon the state, is a citizen as long as he has not been convicted; but he who attacks the state ceases forthwith to be a citizen.[a] A similar principle prevails in regard to magistrates, including even those of the highest rank. It was on this ground that the Romans refused to recognize Antony as Consul.[b] To take another example, the statements selected by Plutarch[c] from the speech of Tiberius Gracchus are absolutely true, even though they were perhaps inaccurately applied by Plutarch. In [130′] [a translation based upon] the Latin text of these statements, they will read as follows:

> The tribune is sacrosanct because he has been consecrated to the cause of the common people and because he is their defender. But if he changes his character, wrongfully harasses the people, destroys their power and abolishes the right of suffrage, then by his own conduct he will have deprived himself of his magisterial office through the commission of every act that deviates from the purposes for which he was invested with the said office. For, in any other circumstances, even if he should proceed to demolish the Capitol and should set fire to the public dockyards, would he not[2] still be permitted to discharge his functions as tribune? Indeed, even if he conducted himself thus, he would

a. Cicero, *Against Catiline,* I [xi. 28].

b. Cicero, *Philippics,* IV [iii. 6 ff.], and *passim.*

c. *Tiberius Gracchus* [xv. 2–3].

2. Although Grotius uses the interrogative *-ne* here, simply asking for information, *nonne,* calling for an affirmative answer, would have reproduced more accurately the thought in the passage cited, which states specifically that “there would be no interference with a tribune even if he should attempt to demolish the Capitol,” &c.

nevertheless be a tribune, though a bad one; but when he overthrows the rights of the common people, he is not a tribune at all.

Again, what power could be more exalted, or more sacred, than that which some persons[a] now attribute to the Pope of Rome, when they deny that he is subject to any human judge, basing their denial on the ground that his supreme power is received not from men but from God alone? Yet these same persons admit that the Pope deposes himself by his own act if he turns away from the faith; and that, furthermore, the Council may in such a case declare him to have been deposed, since heresy is of course in direct conflict with the very institution of the papacy. For the Pope must function as a head, instilling life into the body, and therefore (so the said persons hold) he cannot be retained in the papal office after he has suffered spiritual death. Howsoever the head may be affected by illness, and even though it may be reduced to inactivity, it is still the head; but when it has been cut off, it is no longer the head. By the same token, when the Pope conducts himself in a manner contrary to the underlying pattern of the papal institution, he loses *ipso facto* all his rights and powers.[b] Moreover, if such a pontiff seeks to regain by armed force the papal power lost in the manner described, there is not the least doubt but that he ought to be restrained by armed force.[c]

Now, these same conclusions may be applied—and far more readily—to cases involving a principate, which carries with it no right other than that derived from the state. Thus (according to a doctrine which finds its chief support among the Spaniards[d] themselves), the power that has been bestowed upon a prince can be revoked, particularly when that prince exceeds the bounds defining his office, since in such circumstances he ceases *ipso facto* to be regarded as a prince.[e] For he who abuses sovereign power renders himself unworthy of sovereignty, and ceases to be a prince, in consequence of the very act by which he converts himself

a. Syl. on word *Papa,* iv; Torquemada, *Summa,* IV, pt. ii, chap. xix–xx.
b. *Decretum,* II. xxiv. I. I. 3, 4, 31.
c. See *supra,* pp. 309 ff. (?), discussion of Concl. V, Art. [Thesis?] II.
d. Vázquez, i. 8, third case, citing Isernia, St. Thomas, and Hostiensis.
e. Vázquez, viii. 19.

into a tyrant.[a] The status that will be accorded him even in the estimation of those persons who regard the state as subject to the prince, becomes clear if we consider an analogous case, relative to vassals, who are released by law from the obligation of obedience to savagely cruel masters.[b]

Argument based upon Article I, (Analysis II), Conclusion VI See discussion in Chap. VII on art. cited.

But that which has rightly been lost cannot be reclaimed without [131] wrongdoing. Therefore, when Philip strove to regain through war the sovereign status from which he had fallen, and when he sought to have punishment inflicted even for righteous deeds, the Dutch were provided with an exceedingly just motive for war, namely, the defence of their lives, property, and lawful liberty.[c]

Subsequently, the very course of the war gave rise to additional rights,[d] one after another: first, as a consequence of the tremendous losses which the Spanish inflicted unjustly upon the Hollanders[e] (in the early period of the war, by laying waste the fields or by destroying and ravaging the cities, and later, throughout many years, by the seizure of spoils); secondly, as a consequence of the expenses of the war itself, which (as we quite truthfully pointed out)[f] have been and still are so heavy from day to day that they practically defy comparison with any ever before incurred, a fact that is understandable if one considers the long duration of the conflict and the wealth of the enemy whom the Dutch were obliged to resist; and thirdly, on the ground of offences committed,[g] under which head I include not only the slaughter of the innocent, rapine, and all other violent deeds of this kind, which are sinful

a. Vázquez, i. 8, first case; *ibid.* viii. 11; *ibid.* xviii. 10; Covarr., *Pract. Quaes.* i. 6, near end; arg. of *Decretum,* II. ii. 7. 29.

b. Baldus, *On Feuds* [p. 51], at end; add *Institutes,* I. viii, at end; see *Feuds,* II. xxvi and xlvii; and Baldus thereon [p. 80 verso].

c. See Laws I and II. See text of *Dig.* I. ii. 2, § 3 and Bartolus, *De Tyrannia,* 3, at end.

d. See discussion of Art. I, Chap. vii, *supra,* p. 106, and Chap. iv, after beg., *supra,* pp. 74 ff.

e. See Law II.

f. See Law VI and Hist. Anal. [Chap. xi], Pt. I, Art. I, *supra,* pp. 244 ff.

g. See Law V.

in warfare to the extent that a given war is unjust, but also other acts which would not be permissible even for one who was waging a just war. The countless examples of offences belonging to this latter group—examples of cruelty, perfidy, and lust—so far exceed our own ability to enumerate them, that they could not be adequately described even in an historical work. If the three heads listed above are combined as one, they will form an almost immeasurable aggregation of rights, or at least an aggregation that exceeds the possibility of full recovery at any time, through whatsoever victories.

Argument based upon Article I (Analysis III), Conclusion VI

Against the Portuguese themselves, since they took the initiative in warlike attack (as they did, for example, when their forces formed part of the Spanish fleet), these same considerations[a]—self-defence against the infliction of losses, recovery for expenditures, and just punishment—constituted proper grounds for war. We should also list as justificatory grounds,[b] recovery and punishment in connexion with all that befell the Dutch ships and sailors in Portugal, where they were detained on so many occasions. And indeed, the same comment is no less applicable in connexion with everything suffered by despoiled and slaughtered Hollanders[c] throughout the whole world, wherever Portuguese power (innately designed, so it would seem, for injurious uses) has penetrated. In India itself, however, special causes existed to justify the course taken by the Dutch State. Some of these causes concerned the welfare of the state as such; and others, the welfare of its citizens.

Under the first head, we may place the injuries through which the entire Dutch people has been debarred from commerce and brought into ill repute among foreign nations.[d] Both heads have been discussed in an earlier passage, relative to the causes of private war,[e] but one point merits

a. See Laws I, II, V, VI. Also Hist. Anal., Pt. I, Art. III, *supra,* pp. 248 f.

b. See Laws II and VI, and Hist. Anal., Pt. I, Art. V, *supra.*

c. See Laws II and VI and Hist. Anal., Pt. [I], Arts. VI and VII, *supra,* pp. 253 ff.

d. See Concl. VI, Art. I, Analyses I and II, Chap. xii, *supra,* pp. 363–70 and the examples there cited which apply.

e. See Chap. vi, shortly after Art. I, *supra,* p. 96, and Chap. ix, discussion of Concl. VIII, Art. I, *supra,* pp. 182 ff., esp. p. 185.

specific mention in the present context, as follows: even if the right to carry on trade with the East Indians had belonged to the Portuguese so exclusively that the latter were empowered to prevent other nations from participating in that trade, nevertheless, owing to the fact that Holland was engaged in a just war against the ruler of the Portuguese, it would still have been permissible for the Dutch to seize for themselves this right which the Portuguese could have claimed as a unique privilege in other circumstances, just as it was permissible for the Dutch to appropriate the property of the enemy's subjects.

With respect to the second group of causes, [those relative to the welfare of Dutch citizens,] it is sufficiently evident that the state ought to have at heart the protection, the rights, and the avenging of its citizens, inasmuch as civil society was established chiefly in order that whole groups might be able to accomplish what could not be [131′] accomplished by individuals.[a] If (as Cicero[b] tells us) the Romans frequently engaged in wars because their [merchants or] shipowners[3] had suffered excessively injurious treatment, what should the Dutch not have done for the sake of that East India Company through which the lives of so many of our citizens are sustained? Certainly the Dutch were empowered—more than that, in so far as considerations of state permitted, they were in duty bound—to defend their fellow citizens before death,[c] and to avenge them after death; and in like manner, they could and should have protected or reclaimed by armed force the property of those citizens. Is there any ground for war more sacred than that which has been established both in Holy Writ and in the most ancient law of nations, as well as in civil law:[d] namely, violation of the sanctity of embassies? In what, moreover, does instigation to war consist? In failure to grant admission to the sea and to ports? The Portuguese [did not merely fail to grant admission; they] furthermore took every measure within

a. See Chap. ii, discussion of Laws VII and VIII, *supra.*

b. *On the Manilian Law* [v. 11].

c. See Laws I, V, II, and VI.

d. *2 Samuel,* x, and according to all historians. *Dig.,* L. vii. 18 (17).

3. *Mercatoribus aut naviculariis* in Cicero's text; hence the bracketed phrase in the translation.

their power to drive others away! Does it consist in the capture of human beings? But the Portuguese did not even permit the ransoming of captives! In the slaying of human beings? The Portuguese were not satisfied with slaughter unless they had first mangled their victims with torture! In martial attack? Are such attacks not far exceeded in savagery by the infliction of ills more cruel than any known to war, upon persons attracted by a pretence of peace? But I shall not overload these pages with a repetition of statements that can be found either in the portion of this work devoted to narrative or in our discussion of private war.[a] For the state must have possessed in defence of its citizens the same rights, without exception, that were possessed by the citizens themselves.

Ded. from Article II, Conclusion VI

The Dutch are justified, then, in regarding Philip and the Spaniards and the Portuguese as enemies, one and all, in view of the injuries inflicted upon our people by those three parties; and this conclusion may be based in each case upon the particular causes afforded by each of the said parties. We have already pointed out, however, that even if there were no special grounds for war against the Portuguese, the allies or subjects of enemies would in any case have the status of enemies. Now, the Portuguese were formerly subjects of King Philip the Second; and they are at present subjects of Philip the Third,[b] who succeeded his father not only on the throne but also in the war with the Dutch. This war, moreover, is deriving support from Portuguese tribute. At the same time, the Portuguese are allies of the Spaniards, and alternately offer or ask for mutual assistance against the Dutch, a point clearly brought out[c] in [the composition and activities of] the Spanish fleet, and generally indicated in our narration of events in the East Indies. Furthermore, certain arguments already presented[d] so often as to preclude their repetition here,

a. See Hist. Anal., Pt. II, in entirety, *supra,* pp. 261 ff. See Chap. ii and Concl. VI, Art. I, Analysis III, *supra,* pp. 370 ff.

b. See Hist. Anal., Pt. I, Art. III, *supra,* p. 248.

c. See Hist. Anal., Pt. II, Art. V, Fourth Episode at end, *supra,* p. 296.

d. See Hist. Anal. Pt. II, Art. II, *supra,* pp. 265 ff., and see Chap. xii, discussion of same art. [Concl. VI, Art. II], *supra,* pp. 377 ff. See discussion of Concl. VII, Art. III, with Corollary, *infra,* pp. 406 ff.

show that our classification of the Portuguese as enemies should be understood as referring to individuals no less than to the state.

Ded. from Article II, Conclusion VII

The manner in which the Dutch entered into war against the Duke of Alba and his Spaniards, then against Philip, and finally against the [132] Portuguese, was also just: that is to say, it conformed to the law of necessity. For we have shown that no formal demand for "redress as an alternative to hostilities" [*clarigatio*], nor any decree of war, is required of him who is first attacked in war. Now, it is perfectly clear that Alba and his utterly unbridled army interfered in what was at the time a peaceful situation,[a] and that Philip took up arms against the Dutch while they were still honouring him under the title of Prince.[b] The very course of events, too, has made it plain that the Portuguese were the first to engage in war.[c] Moreover, safe access to the Duke of Alba was not allowed, for he was observing in his conduct toward his enemies none of their lawful rights; and as for Philip, who would not fear to seek a meeting with him in Spain, after the deaths of the envoys, the Marquis van den Berg and the Lord of Montigny? Yet again, what security existed for any person mingling with the Portuguese in India, where not even pacts availed to protect those who came bearing flags of truce? Besides, as we have already stated, whenever the laws relative to embassies and the commercial rights of nations have been violated, no declaration of war is required.

Thesis III

It is furthermore worthy of note that, up until the time of the proclamation rejecting Philip's sovereignty, the struggle in defence of the Dutch was a civil war in so far as the principal combatants were concerned. For both the chief regional official as such, and the prince as a prince, are regarded as parts of the state, just as (according to the teachings of the theologians),[d] in the case of an abjudication against the Pope, the latter is regarded for the purposes of the judicial decree, not as the

a. Hist. Anal., Pt. I, Art. I, *supra,* pp. 244 ff.

b. *Ibid.*

c. Hist. Anal., Pt. II, Art. IV, *supra,* pp. 284 ff.

d. Syl. on word *Papa,* iv.

head of the Church but as a member thereof. Consequently, even if the enemy had not first resorted to armed force nor violated the law of nations, a declaration of hostilities, which is a formality proper to war with foreign enemies, would still have been unnecessary. Thus (as we observed in an earlier context) Cicero very aptly concluded that such a declaration, through envoys, was not obligatory against Antony, even though Antony was a consul, or in other words, a supreme magistrate of the Roman People. For the Tarquins themselves were condemned by a public decree unaccompanied by any declaration of war against the king, yet no one held the war to be less just for that reason. A vote of war, then, would suffice [in any such case of civil revolt]; and a vote of this kind was indeed passed, both against the Duke of Alba by the States Assembly of Holland, and against Philip not only by this same Assembly but also by those of other nations (including almost every nation of the Low Countries), legally convoked in council.[a]

In regard to the Portuguese, moreover, our point is still more readily proved on the basis of the following principle, already laid down by us and rejected by none of the authorities on the subject: when a war has been undertaken against a given party, it is held that an adequate declaration of war has been communicated *ipso facto* to all allies and subjects of that party, since persons who have attached themselves to the enemy must also be enemies. Nor is this argument impaired in any way by that peaceful *modus vivendi* adopted with respect to India, to which the Dutch conformed while they were allowed to do so, but which was broken off by the Portuguese. For it is quite generally agreed that,[b] when a truce has been terminated or violated, the ensuing hostilities are to be considered as constituting not a new war but part of the war previously initiated, so that there is no need for a formal declaration. As a matter of fact, however, even from the standpoint of the Portuguese, [132′] the edict issued by the States General of the United Provinces,[c] which

a. See Hist. Anal., Pt. I, Art. I, *supra,* pp. 245 f.

b. Laudensis, *De Bello,* 29; see also Gentili, II. ii.

c. See Pt. II, this chap., *infra,* pp. 419 f.

orders that the goods of all persons subject to the King of Spain shall be regarded as spoils, is equivalent to a decree of war.

Argument based upon Article III (Part I), Conclusion VII See also Chap. XII; discussion based upon same art.

It is also clear, in the light of the observations made above with reference to private wars, that the particular act of war in question did not exceed the bounds of the right contested. For we have demonstrated that the prize which is under consideration cannot even compensate for the bare losses inflicted upon the Hollanders by the Portuguese. How much greater, then, is the right which should have been ascribed to the States Assembly! For the Assembly was empowered to exact compensation not only for those particular losses, but also for all others suffered by its citizens in all parts of the world and especially in Portugal, through the seizure of ships; its members were also empowered, in their capacity as judges of the war, to impose well-deserved penalties upon the authors of so many ills; and furthermore, they were authorized to exact payment from the Portuguese, no less than from others, for the vast expenditures involved in the entire war against the Spaniards.

Argument based upon Corollary I, Chapter VIII

Nor does any cause for doubt remain in regard to the persons concerned [in the seizure of the prize]. For that opinion is absolutely true and universally approved which was set forth by the Spanish theologian, Victoria,[a] in the following terms: if the enemy is unwilling to make due restitution, and if there is no other source from which the injured party can properly recover compensation, he may obtain satisfaction from any source whatsoever, whether from the guilty or from the innocent. "For example," Victoria continues, "if French brigands shall have seized booty upon Spanish soil and the French King is unwilling, though able, to compel those brigands to make restitution, the Spaniards, with the authorization of their own sovereign, are entitled to despoil French *merchants* or farmers, *howsoever innocent* those Frenchmen may be. For though the French State or Prince may perhaps have been blameless at the outset, that state or ruler is now deserving of blame, on the ground

a. *De Jure Belli,* 41.

(as Augustine[a] declares) of neglecting to make amends for the wrongful acts committed by subjects; and the injured prince may obtain satisfaction from any member or part of the said state."

Argument based upon Article III (Part II), Conclusion VII

Neither is it possible to impugn the good faith of the Dutch from any standpoint. For no promise was made to the Portuguese in the name of the Dutch State, unless one chooses to place in this category the papers ensuring free transit which were granted to the Portuguese and which we have mentioned in another context[b] as testimonials to the [133] candour of the Dutch. Those papers, however, concede nothing more than permission to make journeys from hostile localities to Dutch territory and back again. They do not concede additional permission to pass to and fro between hostile localities and any other place whatsoever, much less between one hostile locality and another. Quite obviously, the reason for this restricted concession was the fact that our exceedingly benevolent leaders wished to advance the commercial interests of their fellow citizens, an objective advantageous also to the public treasury, but did not wish to provide our enemies with an opportunity to enrich themselves, since such a course of action would be not only profitless but even dangerous for those very leaders. Moreover, even though the most liberal interpretation may [ordinarily] be given to benefits conferred by the state, it is generally recognized[c] that this principle of liberality is not applicable in the interpretation of the privileges and dispensations of which we are speaking. For such privileges and dispensations, since they are incompatible with universal law, must not be extended to accord with their most far-reaching implications. For the moment, I shall not dwell upon the fact that a rather narrow construction should be placed upon certain other benefits,[d] too (principally upon those granted at the request of the party concerned), if they involve any new and unusual element or, in particular, any lurking threat to the public welfare. But how much

a. [*Questions on Heptateuch,* VI, qu. 10.]
b. Hist. Anal., Pt. I, Art. IV, *supra,* pp. 249 f.
c. Jason, *On Dig.* I. iv. 3, nn. 33 and 37.
d. *Ibid.,* n. 32.

more surely does this warning apply to privileges conceded to enemies, who as individuals are by no means to be favoured, and with respect to whom, moreover, the underlying motive is not only different from the motive usual in such cases, but even of a contrary nature! Nor do I need to point out that, even if the grant in question could be interpreted in the extremely broad sense suggested, anyone who has read the account of the deeds committed by the Portuguese after the grant was made will in any case not entertain the least doubt but that they have shown themselves to be unworthy of such generosity.

Argument based upon Article I, Conclusion VIII

In regard to the aims sought in the present war, whether we refer to the war as a whole or specifically to the struggle against the Portuguese, it is likewise evident that the States General has aimed solely at the attainment of rights due either to the state or to its citizens, namely: the establishment of a peace devoid of snares when the malice of the enemy has eventually been exhausted, and the maintenance meanwhile, under conditions as tranquil as possible, of a commercial interchange which is not only open to all by nature's plan but also especially well adapted to the inclinations of our people.

Ded. from Conclusions IV & III

By every criterion, then, including the criterion of conscience, the war against the Portuguese is absolutely just; and therefore, the seizure of the prize in question was also just.

Ded. from Article II (Part I), Conclusion IX[4]

This prize must be regarded as having constituted first of all an acquisition of the state (even though it may have been acquired through the services of some member of the state), up to the point where full sat-

4. This cross-reference at the bottom of collotype p. 133 (EX CONCL. IX. ART. II. PARTE I.), is followed at the top of p. 133′ by a deleted phrase, "PARTE II.," which evidently complements the reference to Part II of Article II, Conclusion IX. Since both parts of the article in question are exceedingly pertinent to Grotius's argument at this point, it seems probable that the deleted reference to the second part was stricken out inadvertently as an apparent duplication of the immediately following reference to Part II of Chapter XIII, and should have been retained. In that case, the cross-reference would read: "Deduction from Art. II (Parts I and II), Conclusion IX."

isfaction could be provided for the right defended, which in the present case greatly outweighs the value of the prize taken. Nevertheless, [133′] it was possible for the same prize to become the property of the Dutch East India Company in consequence of a grant made by the state. In a later and more appropriate context, we shall show that such a grant was actually bestowed upon the Company.

Accordingly, the truth of the foregoing assertions, already demonstrated by us with respect to the authors of the war (that is to say, the States General), will be revealed on a much more certain basis if we turn our attention to the subjects engaged in that conflict, such as the East India Company, which obeys the orders of the States General. For it will suffice, in so far as subjects are concerned, if those things are shown to be probable which must be proven as inescapably true when we are considering the authors of a war. Let us pause to develop this point, however, by applying here the principles relative to subjects which have been introduced into the laws of prize and booty from both the primary and the secondary law of nations.

Part II of Chapter XIII

In the first place, then, it is a generally accepted fact that the individuals who compose the East India Company are subject to the said States General. For all persons within the territory in question have pledged allegiance by oath to that assembly, or else tacitly give adequate assurance, by making themselves a part of the political community governed by the latter, of their intention to live in accordance with the customs of this community and to obey the magistrates recognized by it. Such an assurance (as we have pointed out in another passage)[a] is no less binding than the spoken word. It was Euripides[b] who said:

Argument based upon Article II (at close of discussion), Conclusion V, Thesis IV

a. A little after Rule III, Chap. ii, *supra,* p. 19 and before Law VII, *supra,* p. 36. See also Chap. viii, before Concl. VII, Art. III, Pt. II, *supra,* pp. 172 f.

b. [Euripides.][5]

5. The Editor has not been able to locate this quotation in the Loeb editions of Euripides' works. Since Grotius himself gives us only a blind reference, it may be suggested that the line is either inaccurately quoted or else mistakenly ascribed to Euripides. Possibly, Grotius was confusing a similar passage from some other author

> σέβειν δὲ τοὺς κρατοῦντας ἀρχαῖος νόμος·
>
> *By long-established custom, reverence*
> *Is due to those who rule. . . .*

Another tragedian[a] expressed a similar thought in these lines:

> τοιγὰρ τὸ λοιπὸν εἰσόμεσθα μὲν θεοῖς
> εἴκειν, μαθησόμεσθα δ' Ἀτρείδας σέβειν.
> ἄρχοντές εἰσιν, ὥσθ' ὑπεικτέον. τί μὴ μήν;
>
> *Henceforward, as is fitting, let us be*
> *Subservient to the gods, and reverent*
> *To both the Atridae; for 'tis a sin*
> *To yield not unto them, since they are kings.*

For, as Alcibiades declared, it is most just, *ὅπερ ἐδέξατό τις σχῆμα τῆς πολιτείας τοῦτο ξυνδιασώζειν*, "that we should strive to preserve that form of government which has been handed down to us."[b] Augustus, no less truly than wisely, defined such conduct as the duty of a [134] good man and good citizen.[c] Indeed, even He who is the Way and the Truth did not command the Jews to inquire into the right by which the Romans had taken possession of Palestine; on the contrary, because they were dwelling within the Roman Empire He bade them render obedience to the Caesars, who were at that time the lords of the Empire, as was indicated by the coin stamped with Caesar's image.[d]

Moreover, the States General should be obeyed by its subjects not only because the rule of this assembly is at present the accepted form of government, but also because its sovereignty is supported by common law. For the Dutch, and those who have formed a federation with the

---

with the Euripidean verse from *The Phoenician Maidens* (l. 393) which he quotes in a similar connexion in the *De Jure Belli ac Pacis* (Bk. I, chap. iv, sec. 2, subsec. 2), and which runs as follows in the Loeb translation:

> The unwisdom of his rulers must one bear.

a. Sophocles, *Ajax* [666 ff.].

b. Thucydides [*History of the Peloponnesian War*], VI [lxxxix. 6].

c. Macrobius, *Saturnalia,* II. iv.

d. *Matthew,* xxii. 21; *Mark,* xii. 17; *Luke,* xx. 25.

Dutch, owe no allegiance nowadays to any prince whatsoever. Among these peoples, it is customary for all princely power to originate in a mutually binding oath, and since the death of Philip the Second there has been no prince to whom they have sworn the prescribed oath. In fact, Philip the Third, who wishes to have it believed that he completely and voluntarily renounced his sovereignty over the Flemish peoples, has retained no right at all over them. Nor is it possible for Albert and his wife[6] to possess powers in excess of those received in accordance with the will of the States General, since it is perfectly clear that not even any part of a people can be transferred against its will to the domain of another people.[a] Now, in every case of any kind where there is no prince, nothing is more certain than the fact that all sovereign power is given over to the commonwealth, which is divided into various internal states, or (as Covarruvias[b] tells us) to the aristocrats and chief personages who represent the whole commonwealth and are correctly designated as a body by the title "States General," or "States Assembly."[7] "For it makes very little difference," says Paulus the jurist,[c] "whether a given act has been performed by *the entire body,*[8] or by the person to whom that *body* has entrusted the undertaking."

Therefore, since the persons of whom we are speaking are subjects of the States General, they are sufficiently absolved from responsibility if they do not regard as unjust the war waged by that assembly, always provided that no inexcusable error is involved in such an estimate. The fact that all dutiful and conscientious citizens (for it is on their behalf that the present discourse has been undertaken, the rest of the citizens

Ded. from Article III, Conclusion VI

a. Vázquez, v, whole chap.; Ayala, I. vi. 9.

b. *Pract. Quaes.* i. 4.

c. *Dig.* III. iv. 6 [§ 1]; add Joh. Faber, *On Institutes,* IV. xvi. 3, and *On Dig.* I. ii. 2, § 6.

6. Isabella, the daughter of Philip the Second.

7. These two titles are a translation of the single Latin term, *Ordines.* Cf. note 3, p. 245, *supra.*

8. *Ordo.* In the passage cited above from the *Digest,* this term (the singular of *Ordines*) refers to corporations and associations of various kinds.

being unworthy of consideration) are free from the belief that the war in question is unjust, may be proved by means of a very convincing argument, as follows: no one can with a clear conscience take part in, and support with all his might, a war which he considers to be unjust; and the above-mentioned citizens, by playing such a part (not unwillingly, moreover) bear witness to their own favourable opinion of [134′] the war. Furthermore, in the light of the statements made by us a little earlier[a] regarding the cause of this conflict, the quite unimpeachable reasoning on which that opinion is based will be readily perceived by all. Besides, even if the matter were open to question, it would still be obligatory to yield to the authority of magistrates in a doubtful case, and especially to the authority acknowledged to be supreme at the time and place involved; and the Dutch, as we have already pointed out, now recognize no supreme magisterial power other than that of the States General. For these reasons, not only the persons who are at present fighting against the Portuguese, but also those who formerly took up arms against the Duke of Alba and even against Philip himself, with the public authorization of the States General, must be regarded as combatants acting in good faith.

Thesis V The very nature of the case under consideration necessitates the avoidance here of that detestable practice of adulation which is unworthy of freeborn men and characteristic of persons who seem to have been created for the express purpose of corrupting the finest princely spirits. For such flatterers maintain that there is no such thing as a just cause for rebellion. If they are in earnest, and if they mean to say that no just cause can possibly arise for revolting or taking up arms against him who is or has been the prince, they are threatening every established throne, since at the present day hardly any sovereign power is vested in the same source as in early times. On the other hand, in the case of those rulers who cannot have claimed any valid cause at all, not even the exceptional conditions attending an extremely long interval of power will result in se-

a. See what was said in discussion of Art. III, Chap. vii, *supra,* pp. 114 f.; *Decretum,* II. xi. 3. 94.

curity of conscience. I shall not dwell upon the famous example set by David, who defended himself against Saul, nor upon that offered by the city of Libnah, which withdrew from the rule of Jehoram.[a] But what will our opponents say in regard to Abraham? Sacred history clearly bears witness to the fact that when the kingdom composed of Sodom and neighbouring cities had been for twelve years subject to Chedorlaomer, King of the Elamites, that kingdom revolted against his rule, an event which in turn caused Elam to move against Sodom. Shall we believe, then, that Abraham, a man of the most saintly character, gave aid to rebels;[9] that he placed obstacles in the path of a king who was rightfully punishing his own subjects; in short, that he involved himself in a war against the said king for which there was absolutely no justification? Or is there more truth in the words of Saint Thomas Aquinas?[b] According to the Angelic Doctor, the rule of a tyrant is unjust, because it is directed to private advantage instead of to the public good, and therefore those persons who stir up strife against his régime are falsely charged with sedition; for it would be more accurate to say that the tyrant is [135] seditious, since he feeds his subject people upon discord and civil dissension in order that he himself may rule in greater security. Nor is there any need of arguments to prove that the name of tyrant befits not only those individuals who usurp through violence a sovereign power that is not rightfully theirs, but also those who abuse with violence their lawful sovereignty;[c] that is to say, the term is applicable in cases where the fault lies not in the title to power but in the exercise thereof. Even when the sovereign concerned is the Pope or the Emperor (so Panormitanus[d] tells us), and *even in the eyes of his own subjects,* it is not the mere fact that the Pope or Emperor is waging a war which makes that war seem just; for these potentates, too, are capable of transgressing. On the contrary, there must be an underlying cause for the war.

a. *1 Samuel,* whole book [xxiii ff.]; *2 Chronicles,* xxi [10]; *Genesis,* xiv.
b. II–II, qu. 42, art. 2, ad 3.
c. Bartolus, *De Tyrannia,* 27.
d. *On Decretals,* II. xiii. 12, n. 12; Syl. on word *bellum* [Pt.] I. iv.
9. Abraham aided the Sodomites, in particular, after Chedorlaomer and his allies had engaged in retaliatory measures.

Consequently, although we shall not say that the sovereign authority of the prince may rashly be set aside, or that injury of any kind suffices to justify so grave a measure, it must nevertheless be firmly denied that all persons who have ever rejected princely authority are guilty of the crime of rebellion. For such a sweeping conclusion is subject to a number of qualifications, two of which we shall discuss forthwith.

New explanation

In the first place, even if it were in some way possible for a whole state to sin against its prince, the state that sinned thus still could not be called rebellious.[a] For the prince exists through and for the state; the latter does not exist through or for the prince.[b] Therefore, the reason for condemning as rebels those persons who have failed to obey the prince,[c] consists in the fact that such persons are offending against authority derived from the state, and are injuring in the person of one man, not a single individual but the whole community. Our opponents themselves,[d] when they seek to demonstrate that there can be no just cause against a prince, rely solely upon the following argument: there can be no just cause against the fatherland; and the state [or fatherland] is closely identified with the prince. By the same token, it is no more correct to say that a whole state is rebellious, than it would be correct to speak of a given individual as committing an injury against himself.[e] In fact, if it were worth our while, I could cite many examples, scattered throughout all the records of history, of peoples who shook off the rule of some sovereign and set themselves free without being described as rebel peoples.[f] Furthermore, the argument drawn from pontifical law and employed by some authorities in discussing this question, to the effect that it is in nowise possible for the members of a body to separate themselves from its head, is quite unsuitable when applied to sovereignty derived

a. See Vázquez, lxxxii. 6 and 9.
b. *Ibid.* i. 10.
c. See *Dig.* XLVIII. iv. 11.
d. Ayala, I. ii. 22.
e. See Arist., *Nic. Ethics,* V. xi, at end.
f. Vázquez, viii. 21. ff.

from human sources; for (as Vázquez[a] rightly observes) such an analogy involves no obstacle that would prevent the state as a whole from serving as its own head. The state can exist apart from the prince; but the prince can be created only by the general consent of the state. As for certain additional objections, frequently included in harangues against government by the people, they are in no sense pertinent here; for not [135′] all popular governments are bad, nor is every régime devoid of a prince, a popular government.

There is another qualification to be considered, however—one which is pointed out by the very proponents of the theory that princes ought to be obeyed absolutely and at all times. For the persons[b] who support this theory explain that it is applicable only when the power of the prince is unadulterated and supreme, so that it does not hold good if his sovereignty is restricted by some other power vested in the laws or in the magistrates. It was for this reason that the Romans proceeded against the Volscians, Latins, Spaniards, and Carthaginians who attempted to withdraw from the Roman Empire, as they would have proceeded not against rebels but against lawful enemies, in warfare formally declared and proclaimed, even at a time when these peoples were tributaries of the Romans, were paying taxes, and were under an obligation to respect the majesty of the Roman People. Take as examples also, on the one hand, the Spartan Ephors, and the Roman and Venetian Senates; on the other hand, the rulers Pausanias, Nero, and Falieri.[10] Will not everyone agree that the members of the latter group were more truly rebels than those of the former group? Moreover, Cajetan[c] declares that the statutes governing many localities are of such a nature that kings are kings only

a. *Ibid.* lxxxii. 9.

b. Ayala, I. ii. 26, at end.

c. *On II–II,* qu. 40, art. 1.

10. The Spartan general Pausanias legitimately exercised certain royal powers in the name of his cousin and ward, but the Ephors ordered his arrest because of his treasonable overtures to the King of Persia. Nero was condemned to death by the Roman Senate for his crimes. Marino Falieri (or "Faliero"), Doge of Venice, was beheaded by order of the Venetian Council of Ten (not by order of the Senate, as Grotius implies) because he had incited the plebeians to conspire against the nobles.

in name. Again, according to Proculus,[a] not every nation that acknowledges the supremacy of another nation, ceases to be free. Many other authorities[b] express similar views.

To be sure, we do not deny that for all good citizens the authority of the prince must take precedence over the authority of any inferior magistrate in cases that are at all doubtful; but, according to the same line of reasoning, the common decision of the state as a whole should have more force among those citizens than the will of the prince alone, since the power of the latter is derived from the power of the state.[c] In like manner, it is right that the authority of the laws handed down by our forefathers should take precedence over the authority of the prince, to the same extent that the commands of law are characterized by more sanctity and less corruption than the commands of individuals.[d]

Furthermore, if the principate has already been abolished, and a republican form of government set up, the course properly to be followed by citizens in doubtful cases will be indicated by the laws that [136] favour the claims of liberty:[e] and rightly so, since liberty is derived from nature while the power to command is derived from human acts, and since those things which have a natural origin are preferred and given the benefit of a favourable presumption[f] wherever doubt exists. Later authorities,[g] too, have laid down the following doctrine: no preceding judgement adverse to liberty shall be brought forward against subjects who are engaged in litigation regarding their own status. This principle holds good, above all, with reference to that form of liberty which is neither immoderate nor unbridled (for liberty attended by these attributes is more accurately called "licence"), or in other words, with reference to that free status which is confirmed by the princely power of the gov-

a. *Dig.* XLIX. xv. 7.

b. Vázquez, iii. 3; *ibid.* xxiii. 3; *ibid.* xlvii. 9 ff.

c. *Ibid.* i. 11.

d. *Ibid.* xli. 26 and 27; Vict. *De Potestate Papae et Concilii,* 23, at end.

e. *Code,* VII. xvi. 14; Livy, III [xliv ff.], story of Virginia; *Institutes,* I. ii. 2; words: *iure enim.*

f. See Chap. vii, before Concl. VI, Art. III, *supra,* pp. 113–14.

g. Baldus, *On Code,* VI. xxx. 21, towards the end.

erning officials, by the authority of the country's most important men and by the goodwill of the citizens. The foregoing statements, although they are formulated in general terms, can without any difficulty be specifically applied to our own thesis.

For the rest, the cause of our governing body should be rendered still more acceptable to good citizens by the fact that it has been defended, both in writing and in action, by almost all neighbouring princes.[a] For one can scarcely believe that those princes would have encouraged a war of the kind in question if it had not been based upon an absolutely clear right. Where there is no such basis, indeed, it is above all needful,

For kings to guard with zeal the life of kings.[b]

The tacit admission made by our enemies themselves has some force in regard to this same point. To be sure, when the disturbances mentioned first arose, the said enemies raged against their captives, imposing sentences for high treason and exacting capital punishment; but as soon as our state had acquired unquestionable strength and was able to oppose the foe with a well-ordered martial force, that same foe turned to the practice of ransoming captives, to the laws governing the acquisition of spoils, and to other institutions affecting reciprocal relations in time of war. Now, all of these institutions are instruments brought into use only in connexion with a just enemy: that is to say (according to the interpretation of the term adopted by us in another context),[c] an enemy supported by magisterial authority which is at least acceptable after the probabilities have been weighed. Moreover, such an interpretation is correct, if Cicero[d] does not mislead us by describing a lawful enemy as [136′] follows: one who is possessed of a state, [a senate,][11] a treasury, general support and concord among the citizens, and some rational basis on which—if the occasion permits—peace and a treaty may be founded.

a. See *Declaratio Reginae Angliae, de Causis Susceptae Defensionis Belgarum.*

b. Seneca, *Oedipus* [242].

c. See Chap. vii, near end, *supra,* p. 126.

d. *Philippics,* IV [vi. 14].

11. Cicero's description includes the specification *curiam* (a senate), which is omitted in Grotius's otherwise almost literal paraphrase.

There is, then, no motive that might impel our citizens to adopt an unfavourable opinion regarding the war against Philip, and far less, regarding the war against the Portuguese. The validity of our conclusion is confirmed, in particular, by the fact that ordinary reason deduces from incontrovertible natural principles, these two dictates: freedom of commerce must not be impeded, and good faith must not be violated. For everyone is aware of the reports indicating that the Portuguese indulge daily in both of these forbidden practices.

Having established the good faith of the said citizens, we find that we have disposed of all the other points which remained to be settled.

Argument based upon Article IV, Conclusion VI

For, from the standpoint of subjects acting in good faith, a war is just when it is waged against those whom the magistrates regard as enemies; and the Portuguese, both collectively and individually, are regarded as enemies by the States General. The truth of this last assertion is clearly indicated by the fleet dispatched under the command of Pieter van der Does to the island of Santo Tomás and to Brazil,[a] as well as by the many ships and great quantity of merchandise that the warships of the States General took from the Portuguese; and it is, moreover, self-evident that whenever a prince is an enemy, his subjects are also enemies.

On the other hand, I shall not categorically deny the possibility of good faith on the part of the Portuguese. For they may perhaps be of the opinion that Philip, their prince, probably has just grounds for his war against the Dutch, although it would be difficult for them to arrive at such a conclusion, and especially difficult for the persons dwelling among the East Indians, in view of the injuries openly committed.

Ded. from Article II, Corollary, Chapter VII

Argument based upon Article IV, Conclusion VII

In this sense, indeed (with reference to the citizens, whether Dutch or Portuguese), the war may have been just and waged with a clear conscience, on both sides. In such a war, however, that is licit which is permitted by the respective magistrates; and the States General does concede that it is permissible to despoil the Portuguese individuals who owned the carack in question.

a. Hist. Anal., Pt. I, Art. III, *supra,* pp. 248–49.

Proof of this concession is contained in the edict promulgated by the aforesaid States General of the United Provinces, after the Spaniards furnished the ultimate evidence of their own perfidy by violently seizing the vessels which had approached under assurance of public protection, and by delivering the men on board into imprisonment and the [137] most bitter kind of slavery.[a] On the basis of this evidence, the States General was able to show[12] that the Spaniards and all persons *favouring* the Spaniards or *adhering to their cause,* had been rendered so savage by insatiable lust for dominion (a lust from which no nation was safe) that, moved by their failure thus far to subjugate the Dutch and their allies through any violent or fraudulent means, they were now employing the same violence and trickery, even in contravention of their own plighted faith, in an effort to exclude those other peoples from trade with any part of the world. Accordingly, since it was the purpose of the States General to curb such savage endeavours *by taking the offensive against the Spaniards in the kingdoms and provinces which the latter had occupied, and by exacting reimbursement and reparations for the losses inflicted,* with the aid not only of vessels belonging to the state *but also of the individuals whose interests were concerned,* an order to this effect was issued by the said assembly, and it was deemed absolutely necessary to bar all transportation to and fro among the Spaniards as well as among the partisans and adherents of the Spanish cause, prohibiting the conveyance of ships or merchandise of any kind to such persons, whether by land or by sea, in any manner whatsoever. This plan of action was in conformity not only with the public law of nations,[b] Roman law, and accepted usage among belligerents, but also with the edicts published earlier by the States General itself and by the Queen of England. Accordingly, the aforementioned Edict of 1599 declares that *all men and all goods subject to the dominion of the King of the Spanish realms, in whatsoever place the said men and goods may eventually be located, are to be regarded as just spoils.* More-

Dated April 2, 1599

a. Hist. Anal., Pt. I, Art. V, *supra,* pp. 252 f.

b. See Chap. viii, before Coroll. I, *supra,* pp. 164 ff.

12. I.e., in the above-mentioned Edict. The remainder of this paragraph is in large measure a paraphrase, and in some instances a literal reproduction, of the Edict.

over, in the same document, a strict prohibition and interdict is once more laid upon the conveyance, carrying, or transportation *of ships or goods or any merchandise,* by land or by water, directly or by a roundabout route, under any pretext or excuse whatsoever, by any or all persons without exception, of whatsoever condition, realm, or region, to any port, town, or place belonging to the enemy (whether it be situated in the Kingdom of Spain, in that of *Portugal,* or in some other European kingdom) and *subject to the power of the present King of the Spanish realms* or to the rule of the Archduke [Albert] and his wife [Isabella]; and this prohibition is imposed under pain of *loss of the said ships, goods, and merchandise,* together with other penalties set forth in the edict. The States General furthermore orders that the officials in charge of maritime affairs (known collectively as the Admiralty Board), who ordinarily take cognizance of cases of this kind, shall pass judgement, in accordance with the prescriptions laid down in the said edict, concerning intercepted goods originally destined for the enemy. [137′]

[Interpretation of letters of free transit] dated September 12, 1603

The interpretation placed by this same assembly upon the letters of free transit granted to the Portuguese people conforms to the Edict of 1599.[a] For, in view of the fact that some persons were making use of those letters in a manner foreign to their intent and for forbidden purposes, the States General issued the following pronouncements: the documents in question were to be interpreted in such a way as to assure complete security, under public guaranty, for Portuguese persons and goods found within the territory of the United Provinces of the Low Countries, as well as for those goods which the same Portuguese persons were merely transporting from that territory to other lands, after obtaining special permission in accordance with the custom of the Low Countries; but if the Portuguese should be found moving merchandise either *from hostile localities to other hostile localities* (for example, from the Island of Santo Tomás or from Brazil to Lisbon, or vice versa), or else *from hostile localities to others not hostile, or from the latter to hostile destinations,* such Portuguese men, ships, or goods as might be taken in the course of that trans-

a. See Hist. Anal., Pt. I, Art. IV, *supra,* pp. 249 ff.

action would enjoy no publicly pledged security, for on the contrary, once captured either by ships belonging to the state or *by other means, they would be treated as spoils of war.*

Consequently, it is clear that the carack *Catharine* and its cargo of merchandise fell by a threefold right into the possession of the captors: first, because that vessel and cargo belonged to the Portuguese, subjects of the King of Spain; secondly, because the said vessel and cargo were coming from Macao, which is a Portuguese colony and should therefore be regarded as a hostile locality; thirdly, because their destination was Lisbon, a city of Portugal.

As for the closely related question of whether or not the persons who captured the carack had orders to do so, it is obvious that any discussion of this point would be superfluous. For in war every duty incumbent upon subjects concerns either the foe or the magistrates of the subjects themselves; but the question of whether or not an order was given is plainly a matter which in nowise concerns the foe, for whom it should suffice that cause for attack existed; and therefore, since the Portuguese occupy the status of a foe in their relation to the Dutch and since they were indeed liable to despoliation, the problem of whether they were despoiled by command or independently of any command is no concern of theirs. This distinction was quite pertinently brought into play [138] by the Carthaginian Senate in reply to the Roman inquiries regarding an act committed by Hannibal, when one of the Carthaginian nobles (so we are told) answered [in part] as follows:[a] "In my opinion, however, you should ask, not whether Saguntum was besieged as a result of private or of public policy, but *whether it was besieged justly or unjustly. For inquiry as to whether our fellow citizen has acted on our authority or on his own, and the infliction of punishment upon him in that connexion, are matters which concern us alone. We have only one question to discuss with you, namely: was his act permissible* under the treaty?"

Accordingly, from the Portuguese standpoint, there is no doubt but that it was permissible to do what was actually done [in regard to the carack *Catharine*]. In any case, both the States General of the United

a. Livy, XXI [xviii. 6–7].

Provinces and the States Assembly of Holland (the entities properly concerned with this secondary question) were so far from condemning the action of the East India Company and its servants, that they sanctioned it not only by intervening in the apportionment of the prize but also by the bestowal of rewards and honours. Thus, even if no order had been given, the lack of such authorization would nevertheless have been counterbalanced by the execution of a publicly advantageous enterprise, and by retroactive approval,[a] so to speak.

However, it is not true that no order was given in advance of the act; for it is a well-known fact—and one confirmed, moreover, by a decree of the States Assembly of Holland—that long before Heemskerck set out on his voyage, the Directors of the East India Company were warned by the said Assembly that the Company must make preparations for the protection of its business and must arm itself with that end in view, in such a way that it would be in a position not merely to ward off hostile attempts on the part of the Portuguese but also to take the initiative in making war upon the latter. Here, then, we have an order issued by a supreme magisterial body, a point which should settle the matter beyond all doubt.

Dated September 1, 1604

Furthermore, nothing would have been easier, if such a measure had seemed necessary, than to obtain from our most illustrious Prince Maurice of Nassau, in addition to the above-mentioned order, letters granting the fullest authority to wage war, such as are customarily denied to no one. The Dutch, however (as we pointed out in another [138′] passage,[b] also), have been so consistently mild-tempered that they disregarded the grounds for public war, in so far as was possible, seeking only to be safe from injury by the Portuguese and resolving to have recourse to armed violence solely in case of absolute necessity. Nevertheless, it may be argued that the act in question was authorized by such letters as were received, even if other authorizations were lacking. For certain letters were indeed granted to Heemskerck, the admiral of the fleet, and certain others to the commanders of individual ships, by the

a. *Sext,* V, ult., reg. 10.

b. At end of Chap. xi, *supra,* pp. 298 f.

aforesaid Prince Maurice, whose supremacy is derived both from his lineage and from his personal exploits, and who undoubtedly possessed the right to command that war be waged, according to the arguments elsewhere propounded by us,[a] since by order of the States General he is invested with supreme powers for warfare on land or sea. The letters addressed to Heemskerck forbid him to join battle with anyone, unless he is compelled to do so by injuries essayed against himself, his men, or his ships; but in the event that such an attempt is made, he is not merely permitted but even commanded to avail himself of all means that he may consider necessary either for the defence of his person, men, and ships, or for *the reparation of injuries.* Consequently, if individuals who have thus manifested their hostility shall fall into the power of Heemskerck, he shall either bring them before the Prince, or *make such disposition of them* as he may deem expedient and suitable to the occasion. For, in view of the fact that *the law of all nations* permits the use of force to resist force, the Prince declares that he also considers this practice to be just and honourable. Moreover, the men in command of the individual vessels are invested by the letters of the Prince with the powers proper to *captains,* or centurions; and this grant of power is given in conjunction with the order that they shall select sailors and appoint officers for the respective ships in accordance with their own judgement. The same commanders are furthermore forbidden to take up arms, *unless it shall so happen that some person makes a hostile attempt to prevent* [139] them *from engaging in navigation* or *in commerce;* for, in the event of any such attempt, they are under strict orders to spare no effort for the subjugation of the persons who have conducted themselves in this hostile manner, with the additional proviso that *the goods thus captured* shall be conveyed by the said commanders to the territory of the United Provinces, to be awarded as prize by the maritime judges of the locality to which the goods are brought, or else disposed of in some other way that circumstances may render advisable. Briefly, the commander of each vessel is ordered to discharge all of the functions proper to *a naval captain.*

Dated November 20, 1600

When a prince gives his consent to everything necessary in order to

a. Before Concl. VII, Art. IV [Chap. viii], *supra,* p. 174 f.

obtain satisfaction for injuries, and when in so doing he invokes the law of nations, one must assume that he is consenting to the exaction of reparations not only from the individuals who actually inflicted the injuries but also from all persons upon whom the law of nations imposes the obligation to make such reparations. For the alternative interpretation—namely, that we are to pursue and overtake the identical persons who harmed us—is difficult to put into practice in any situation, and almost impossible to apply in the maritime case to which we refer. Nor is it correct to suppose that orders authorizing the waging of war are of narrower import than [letters of] reprisal. Therefore the effect of the orders received is as follows: whatever acts could have been committed by private individuals under the law of nations [and have been committed in the present case], those individuals shall now be held to have committed with retroactive public authorization and in circumstances equivalent to a decree of war.

Furthermore, we have shown that,[a] according to the law of nations, acts of the state or the magistrates impose an obligation upon individual subjects, while acts of the subjects—which cannot go unpunished without guilt [on the part of the state]—impose an obligation upon the state as a whole, so that one citizen is in this sense placed under an obligation by the act of another citizen. It should be remembered, too, that the expression "reparation for injury," implies not only exaction of compensation for losses and expenses, but also punitive measures, which undoubtedly come within the scope of the state's power to command. For all of the writers[b] who interpret this point are agreed that the state has a right to inflict punishment upon foreigners in their turn, according to their deserts, as well as upon its own citizens.

Let us ascertain, then, whether or not any act classifiable as one of those which the States Assembly or the Prince intended to include under

a. See before Concl. VII, Art. III, Pt. I, *supra,* pp. 114 ff., and Chap. xii, in discussion of same article [Concl. VII, Art. III], *supra,* p. 382, and in discussion of Concl. VI, Art. II, *supra,* pp. 377 ff. Also in discussion of same arts, in first part of this chap. [xiii].

b. See Vict., *De Jure Belli,* 19; Cajetan, *On II–II,* qu. 64, art. 3.

the head of "injuries" was committed against Heemskerck, or his ships, or persons properly to be numbered among Heemskerck's men.

In this connexion, I shall forbear to stimulate ill will against [139′] the Portuguese by calling to mind the pitiful spoils discovered in that very carack,[a] spoils previously stripped from Hollanders whom the Portuguese had strangled and drowned near Macao, in contravention of every precept of divine law and good faith. Nevertheless, the connexion of those Hollanders with the fatherland and the further fact that they had been sent out by the same Company that was retaining Heemskerck's services, made it impossible to regard them as strangers;[b] nor was it any less fitting for the Admiral and all his sailors to be deeply moved by the memory of that crime, than it was certain that the States General and the Prince, if they could have been summoned to witness the affair, would have decreed war because of it and would have entrusted the conduct of the war to that same Commander and to his men. I shall also refrain from describing again the manner in which the Portuguese intercepted certain companions attached to Heemskerck on his preceding voyage (when these men were being sent from Banda to Amboyna),[c] and foully butchered one of them. Yet I am not unaware of the fact that, according to the laws,[d] he who avenges injuries inflicted upon his friends is avenging not only their wrongs but also, in a sense, his own; and I realize that this principle is particularly applicable when we find ourselves in such distant regions, far from kindred and home, so that we cherish all of our fellow countrymen as if they were intimate friends, the ties of the fatherland binding us the more firmly in proportion to the distance separating us from it. Nor shall I even recall[e] how frequently the men placed in charge of earlier expeditions by this very Company were forced to join battle with the Portuguese. [In short, our discussion here will be confined strictly to the following question:] What

a. See Chap. xii, *supra,* p. 406, in discussion of Coroll. I, Chap. viii.

b. See Card. [Zabarella], *On Clementines,* I. iii. 3, § *verum.*

c. In Hist. Anal., Pt. II, Art. IV, Sixth Episode, *supra,* pp. 287 f.

d. Gail, *On Dig.* III. iii. 35; Baldus, *On Code,* IX. ii. 1; Glossators, *On Code,* XI. xlix. 2; Alexander of Imola, *On Dig.* XLVIII. i. 4; *ibid.* ii. 2.

e. In Hist. Anal., article cited [Pt. II, Art. IV], *supra,* pp. 284 ff.

injuries, of what degree, were suffered by Heemskerck himself and by his sailors and captains [during the voyage when the capture of the carack took place]?

Hardly had Heemskerck and his men sailed past the Canary Islands, when they encountered a Spanish fleet composed of thirteen armed vessels. The Spaniards, correctly deciding that those whom they saw were Dutchmen bound for the Indies, rushed headlong to attack them as enemies. The Dutch ships were pierced with shots from cannon and rifles, and were even besieged in hand-to-hand combat. Some of the sailors were killed; not a few were wounded. Moreover, the foe [140] very nearly gained possession of the ship called *The Red Lion;* but Heemskerck came to its aid in the nick of time, though some of his subordinates were slain before his very eyes, while others were mutilated. The merchandise, the ships, and the lives of Heemskerck's band were forcibly imperilled by that encounter. These evils were augmented by the fact that *The Red Lion,* in consequence of the disastrous damages inflicted, was compelled to abandon the fleet and return to the fatherland. Furthermore, on the day after the battle, this same vessel, which was second only to that of the Admiral, once more had an encounter with the Spaniards, and barely succeeded in extricating itself from the gravest peril. Nor, indeed, was it able to rejoin the Dutch fleet at a later date, a great inconvenience in the expedition that had been undertaken.

These events, to be sure, were brought about by the Spaniards. But it cannot be denied that the latter are a people who have not only the same ruler as the Portuguese but also common causes for war, and common grudges, against the Dutch; and it was Spanish aid (as we have already pointed out) that was invoked by the Portuguese to combat the Dutch even in the East Indian regions. Therefore, we are justified in imitating their own example and failing to make any distinction between the two peoples. From the works of a famous jurist[a]—and, indeed, from the law of nations itself—we derive the following maxim: just as it is permissible to defend one's own allies, so it is permissible to attack the

a. Baldus, *On Code,* VIII. iv. 1, n. 24 [20]; Legnano, *De Repraesaliis,* II. iii, qu. 2, beg. [chap. cxxxiv].

allies of the perpetrators of crime and all persons whatsoever who have a share in the criminal guilt or criminal acts of aggressors. The force of this maxim is increased in the present case by the fact that the harm done by the Spaniards to the Dutchmen who were seeking the East Indies, was undoubtedly done at the official recommendation and request of the Portuguese, or at least for their gratification.

On the other hand, with respect to those of Heemskerck's men who were captured under pretence of commercial negotiations and held in slavery by the King of Damma[a] without any antecedent cause based on war, I shall dismiss the complaint against the Portuguese as insufficiently established, even though there is not the least doubt but that the King of Damma himself placed the blame for that affair on them. In short, I shall confine my arguments exclusively to facts that I have seen clearly proved.

When the Portuguese heard that the King of Johore was disposed to allow Heemskerck to enter into commercial relations, they assured the King, through the envoys whom we have mentioned elsewhere,[b] [140′] not only that all Hollanders were men of an exceedingly rapacious character, but also that Heemskerck had been sent out as a spy to explore the territory which the said Hollanders would attack with a great naval force and take into their own possession at some future date, after expelling the present possessors. If such calumny does not constitute an injury, what conduct can be called by that name? And who is more directly affected by the calumny than Heemskerck himself and his companions, even though in a broader sense its effects are felt by our whole nation? The Portuguese furthermore threaten to resort to war in the event that anyone shall grant admittance to the Dutch. Is this threat not also a grave injury? Nor do they merely threaten. On the contrary, they actually make war, employing the same ships as a twofold means of despoiling the people of Johore and striving to cut off the Dutch from access to that region.

a. In Hist. Anal., Pt. II, Art. II, Eighth Episode, *supra,* pp. 274 f.

b. In Hist. Anal., Pt. II, Art. I, Seventh Episode, *supra,* pp. 264 f., and Pt. II, Art. V, Fifth Episode, *supra,* p. 297.

As we explained in an earlier context,[a] real injury is inflicted when one party is driven to accept calumnies against another, and when any person is debarred from that which is his right under the law of nations.

Therefore, when we approach the question from the standpoint indicated by the letters of authorization addressed to Heemskerck, we find that there is no doubt as to the existence of injuries calling for reparation; and when we consider it from the standpoint of the orders issued to the naval captains, we see plainly that certain persons were engaged in activities detrimental to commerce. Moreover, all of the Portuguese, collectively and individually, but especially the Portuguese who were situated in that particular part of the world, were responsible for the injuries in question, not merely because of their failure to punish the crimes of certain individuals,[b] but also because of the fact that an embassy and ships were dispatched by authorization of their state and in accordance with a decree issued by the officials who govern Malacca. Consequently, there can be no doubt as to the measures permissible against the Portuguese carack under the orders given, if the question is considered either in the light of the letters addressed to the Admiral, which confer (and this is the weightier argument) the right to make decisions even regarding the disposal of persons, or in the light of those addressed to the various captains, which refer expressly to prize.

Thus a mandate to wage war was entrusted both to the Admiral and to his captains; and also, through those officers, to the sailors, whom the officers were of course authorized to select, by virtue of that mandate,[c] just as truly as if they had been in command of an army on land. Moreover, the said sailors were sworn under military oath to spare neither their lives nor their persons in disregard of the needs of the captains or the orders of their superiors. We shall make no mistake, then, in [141]

a. In Chap. xii, discussion of Concl. VI, Art. I, *supra,* pp. 363 ff.; *Dig.* XLVII. x. 13; Doctors, *On Dig.* XLVII. i. 3.

b. Cf. with Chap. xii, in discussion of Concl. VI, Art. II, *supra,* pp. 376 ff.

c. See *supra,* pp. 422 f., with respect to letters on powers of centurions. And add didactic discussion preceding Concl. VII, Art. IV, *supra,* p. 174 f.

agreeing with Ulpian[a] that not only ship's captains and commanders of triremes but all the sailors and oarsmen of a fleet, too, are classed as *soldiers.*

It should also be noted, however, that even if no order specifically concerned with prize had been issued, nevertheless, owing to the fact that both the Admiral of the fleet and the captains of the individual vessels had been granted jurisdiction by the state, these commanders would have been empowered—in the absence of other judges, and in defence of the rights of subjects as well as of their own authority—to impose punishment upon Portuguese offenders against that authority, and to seize the property of such offenders. According to experts in the fields of both canon and civil law,[b] this conclusion is especially tenable in the event that it is supported by a decree issued in advance; and in the present case such a decree was issued by the Admiral and rendered duly effective by the supreme naval council which assisted him in an assessorial capacity. Gaius Pinarius[c] acted more or less on this very principle. For, despite the fact that he had been left at Henna in Sicily to govern not the city but the garrison, when he perceived that a rebellion on the part of the townsmen was impending and that neither the Roman People nor even the Consul had the power to undertake an attack, he not only inflicted capital punishment for that incipient treachery, but also handed over the entire city to be plundered by the soldiery.

Dated December 4, 1602

Accordingly, since both the cause of the Dutch and that of the Portuguese were supported by public authority, and since the Dutch cause was sanctioned by every consideration of good faith, it follows, if one assumes the existence of equal good faith on the part of the Portuguese, that the things captured by either party were not merely susceptible of retention with a clear conscience but even became in actual fact the property of the captors, in accordance with the secondary law of nations.

Ded. from Corollaries II and III, Chapter VIII

a. *Dig.* XXXVII. xiii. 1 [§ 1].

b. Bartolus, *On Dig.* XLIX. xv. 24, nn. 11 and 12; Innocent, *On Decretals,* II. xiii. 12, n. 9 and *ibid.* xxiv. 29, n. 5 and Panormitanus, thereon, n. 9.

c. From Frontinus [*Stratagems,* IV. vii. 22] and Polyaenus [*Stratagems,* VIII. xxi].

Thesis VI

For the war in question is not a civil but a foreign war, inasmuch as the Dutch State is distinct from that of the Portuguese. Indeed, even the war against Philip was not a civil war; for as a result of that conflict no part of the State of Holland remained loyal to Philip and he himself was declared to have lost his sovereignty over Holland. Cassius, in his Oration to the Rhodians (as it is quoted by Appian),[a] maintains that when a state fights for its freedom against the despotism of one individual it is engaged not in civil dissension but in open warfare. The war of the Romans against the Tarquins[b] and the allies of the Tarquins, was nothing less than civil [foreign?][13] warfare; and accordingly, we read that spoils were acquired by both parties, and that even the Etruscans (who were adherents of the Tarquins just as the Portuguese are adherents of Philip) were despoiled by the Romans. Moreover, our own Bartolus[c] (who is followed on this point by other authorities), after declaring in a closely preceding passage that the cities of Etruria were absolutely subject to the Emperor in law and also partly subject to him in fact, nevertheless added[d] that in the event of war between the Emperor and [141′] a city assuming itself to be free (such as the city state of Florence, for example, or that of Pisa), seizure of spoils would be permissible under public law.

Argument based upon Article II, Conclusion VIII

Nor will anyone imagine that, in the present case, either the East India Company or the men who commanded the ships as representatives of the Company, were inspired by any purpose other than that of lending their services and their allegiance to the States General, which was in its turn desirous of providing both for public vengeance and for the rights of the Company itself.

a. *Civil Wars,* IV. [ix. 69].

b. Livy, II [*passim*].

c. *On Dig.* XLIX. xv. 24, nn. 3 and 4; Panormitanus, *On Decretals,* II. xxiv. 29, n. 12.

d. Bartolus, *ibid.,* n. 16.

13. In view of the context, it would seem that *civile* (civil) was written inadvertently here for the antithetical term *externum* (foreign), or possibly for *apertum* (open).

In the light of all these observations, it is apparent that the war, in so far as concerns the aspects that can be considered here, is just for the subjects involved, and that the prize in question was justly acquired. The truth of both deductions is acknowledged by that exceedingly judicious man, Fernão dal Buquerque (the Governor of Malacca), in a letter addressed to Heemskerck. Dal Buquerque says: *"You have captured a valuable vessel. Enjoy her, since she was captured in just warfare."*

Ded. from Conclusions IV and III

Dated March 9, 1603

Now, we have already stated that spoils taken in a public war are acquired—in a direct sense, that is to say, and *ipso iure*—for the state; but we have also indicated that it is possible for such spoils to be converted, either in whole or in part, by special assignment or by a general law, into an acquisition of the very individuals through whom they first became an acquisition of the state. In fact, according to a very old custom of France and the Low Countries, and also under a statute expressly established by the Dutch, a fifth part of the spoils taken by command of the state but through the instrumentality of privately equipped vessels, is owed to the state; a tenth part is the due of the admiral; and the remainder is divided among the ship-masters, captains, officials, and sailors, in the proportions consonant with custom or with such agreements as may have been adopted.[a] Therefore, since the vessels employed in the capture of the *Catharine* were the property of the Dutch East India Company itself, since the ship's captains and the sailors were all paid employees of the Company, which also supplied the arms—in short, since the entire risk and expense was the concern of that Company and the latter was not promised any reward by the State—the whole of the prize, aside from the portion specifically excepted and the share due the sailors, belongs to the East India Company, not only in virtue of the above-mentioned Dutch statute, but also by universally accepted law.

Argument based upon Article II (Part II), Conclusion IX

Ded. from Corollary, Chapter X

The foregoing inference is in accord, first of all, with the Opinion handed down by the Admiralty Board, whose members declared— [142]

Dated September 9, 1604

a. See before Corollary [Chap. x], *supra,* pp. 239 ff. *Instructiones Collegii Admiralitatis,* Art. 22 [in *Groot Placaet-Boeck,* V. viii. 1].

after issuing at the request of the Company a summons to all parties concerned in the case, and after conducting a trial at which one of the parties failed to appear—that the prize in question *was held to be a just prize,* justly acquired. Secondly, that same inference is in conformity with the Decree promulgated by the States Assembly of Holland [on September 1, 1604].[a] For even though the right of the public treasury was brought into the controversy as a factor opposed to the right of the Dutch East India Company, the seizure of the prize was approved in the most laudatory terms, and the Assembly gave orders to the State Treasurer, the other Treasury officials and all the magistrates, that this prize and whatever spoils might in future be taken in the East Indian region, should be regarded *as acquisitions obtained in a public war,* and that the disposition of such spoils should be left to the discretion of the States General of the United Provinces and of *the Admiralty Board.*

Part III of Chapter XIII

The observations already set forth ought surely to suffice for our discussion of the question propounded at the outset [regarding the justice of the case under consideration, on the basis of the public cause of the fatherland]. Nevertheless, in order that no possible grounds for dispute may remain, we shall add this further assertion: even if the said case be considered apart from the cause defended by our governmental assemblies and from the orders issued by them, the war was in any event not only just but also public in character, and the prize was acquired for the East India Company.

Argument based upon Article II, Conclusion V See also discussion thereon, in Chap. vi, at end.

This assertion is confirmed by the law of those [East Indian] peoples to whom the Company lent aid in time of war, through its servants. There is in India a kingdom called Johore, which has long been considered a sovereign principality, so that its ruler clearly possessed the authority necessary to conduct a public war. This ruler asked for help in warfare, from the Hollanders who had come to his land with their ships. Now, we have shown in another passage[b] how well it accords with nature's plan and

a. See above.

b. In discussion of same Concl. [V], Art. I, *supra,* pp. 92 f.

with human brotherhood that one person should give aid to another, and therefore we readily see that the entrance of the Dutch into the war as allies of the King of Johore was permissible. One may go farther and say that, since the Hollanders were well able to assist him thus, they could hardly have remained guiltless while withholding assistance.

This is the inference to be drawn whether we consult that page of Holy Writ[a] which bids us deliver the innocent from destruction, or whether we turn to the philosophers,[b] who maintain that there are two kinds of injustice: the kind characteristic of persons who inflict injury; and the kind characteristic of those who fail to ward off injury, when they are able to do so, from the victims upon whom it is inflicted. For he who neither repels nor resists injury when such resistance lies within his power, is as gravely at fault as if he were forsaking his parents or friends or native land,[c] since (according to the aforesaid philosophers) the contention that one must have regard for one's fellow citizens but not for foreigners, is assuredly equivalent to repudiation of the universal bond of human fellowship, a bond which one cannot repudiate without being adjudged impious toward God Himself, the Author thereof. [142′] Our jurists,[d] too, are of the opinion that the person responsible for such an omission shares in the guilt attaching to the injurious act; and the Church Fathers[e] hold that he who has failed to resist injury to his fellow man is no less culpable than the individual who inflicts that injury.

According to Aristotle,[f] this principle is based upon particularly firm grounds when the very persons on whom injury is now being visited have previously bestowed some benefit upon us. What, then, shall we suppose that Aristotle would have said of a case in which one party undergoes injury from others precisely for the reason that the victim has conferred a benefit upon us? For that is exactly what has happened to

a. *Proverbs,* xxii. ii [xxxi. 8].
b. Cicero, *On Duties,* I [vii. 23]; add *Ecclesiasticus,* iv. 9.
c. Cicero, *On Duties,* III [vi. 28].
d. Baldus, *On Code,* VI. i. 1.
e. Ambrose, *On Duties,* I. xxxvi [178].
f. *Rhetoric to Alexander,* iii [ii = pp. 1424 B, 1425 A].

the East Indians. Both the King of Johore and the [East Indian] nations elsewhere mentioned by us,[a] are being ravaged by the Portuguese with slaughter and rapine on no other pretext than this, that the said ruler and nations granted admittance to the Dutch. In the light of these arguments, is there anyone who will deny that the injuries suffered by these East Indians are properly the concern of the Dutch?

Thesis VII Or do we perhaps believe that we have nothing in common with persons who have not accepted the Christian faith? Such a belief would be very far removed from the pious doctrine of Augustine,[b] who declares (in his interpretation of the precept of Our Lord whereby we are bidden to love our neighbours) that the term *"neighbours"* obviously includes *every human being.* Moreover, the famous parable of the good Samaritan which is contained in the Gospels,[c] teaches us that the obligations of humane conduct are not dispelled on grounds of religion. Accordingly, not only is it universally admitted that the protection of infidels from injury (even from injury by Christians) is never unjust, but it is furthermore maintained, by authorities[d] who have examined this particular point, that alliances and treaties with infidels may in many cases be justly contracted for the purpose of defending one's own rights, too. Such a course of action was adopted (so we are told) by Abraham, Isaac, David, Solomon, and the Maccabees.[e]

Ded. from Article I, Conclusion VI In any case, it is certain that the cause of the King of Johore was exceedingly just.[f] For what could be more inequitable than a prohibition imposed by a mercantile people upon a free king to prevent him from

a. In Hist. Anal., Pt. II, Art. V, *supra,* pp. 288 ff.

b. *On Christian Doctrine* [I. xxx. 32].

c. *Luke,* x. 29 ff.

d. Arias, *De Bello,* 192; Panormitanus, *On Decretals,* III. xxxiv. 8, n. 15; Vict., Rel. I, pt. ii, nn. 15 and 17 [*De Indis,* Sect. III, nn. 15 and 17].

e. *Genesis,* xxi, at end; *ibid.* xxvi, at end; *1 Samuel,* xxvii ff.; see Nicholas of Lyra thereon; *1 Kings,* iii and v; Syl. on word *bellum* [Pt. I] ix. 3.

f. See Hist. Anal., Pt. II, Art. V, Fifth Episode, *supra,* pp. 296 ff.

carrying on trade with another people?[a] And what would constitute interference both with the law of nations and with the distinct jurisdictions of different princes, if such a prohibition does not? [143] Therefore, since the injury in question was inflicted upon the King of Johore with official authorization, since he was also formally threatened with war as the penalty for failure to comply with the order, and since war was forthwith begun against him, he rightly regarded the Portuguese—collectively and individually—as enemies;[b] for no one will deny that those who have decreed war against us are indeed our enemies. Consequently, it was not necessary for this king to issue a declaration of war; and it was particularly unnecessary in view of the fact that the Portuguese had already besieged his ports with hostile ships and ravaged his shores. Thus there is not the slightest excuse for doubting that the Portuguese were open to despoliation under the auspices of the ruler of Johore, since they were obligated by those crimes to give compensation for costs and damages, and to pay in addition a penalty for such flagrantly injurious conduct.

Ded. from Article II, Conclusion VI

Ded. from Article II, Conclusion VII

Ded. from Article III, Conclusion VII, & Corollary I, Chapter VIII

Now, just as the King himself acted with excellent motives in striving to uphold his rights and protect his subjects, so the kindness of the Dutch in coming to his assistance was similarly laudable. In fact, there is nothing that serves the cause of the true religion better than such acts of kindness. Care must be taken to keep men safe, lest the hope of converting them (as the Church Fathers were formerly wont to say) should perish with their bodies. The Indian peoples must be shown what it means to be a Christian, in order that they may not believe all Christians to be as the Spaniards are. Let those peoples look upon religion stripped of false symbols, commerce devoid of fraud, arms unattended by injuries. Let them marvel at the faith which forbids that even infidels should be neglected. In achieving these ends, we shall be preparing men for God.

Ded. from Article I, Conclusion VIII See discussion thereon.

a. See discussion of same art. [Concl. VI, Art. I], Chap. xii, *supra,* pp. 363 ff.
b. *Dig.* L. xvi. 118.

Deds. from Conclusion IV; Conclusion III; Article II (Parts I & II) of Conclusion IX; & Corollary in Chapter X

Thus, from every standpoint, the war was just both for the King of Johore, and for the Dutch as defenders of that King. Therefore, the seizure of the prize was also just. To be sure, by natural law the right to that prize was vested in the ruler of Johore himself; but it was also capable of becoming a Dutch right, through a grant on his part. Moreover, since war was waged on his behalf by means of ships belonging to the East India Company, at the Company's expense and at its peril, too (in so far as any unfavourable turn of fortune was concerned), as well as by the exertions of the Company's servants, without any formal agreement as to compensation, the commonly accepted usages of war,[a] confirmed by natural equity, quite clearly indicate that the prize in question was acquired *ipso iure* for the said Company.

Moreover, the statements just made with reference to the part played by the East India Company in this matter, may likewise be applied to the part played by our governmental assemblies, as follows: the prize was acquired at the command of those assemblies, on the grounds furnished by the war waged in the name of Johore, at the expense of the Company, for that Company itself. Indeed, the justice of such a title to [143′] acquisition is so fully sanctioned that learned authorities[b] bestow special commendation upon the Roman Empire precisely because the Empire strengthened itself at the expense of its enemies, in the process of protecting its allies. The Spaniards, as allies of the Tlascalans, based their claims against [other] Mexican Indians on this same title;[c] and the Portuguese themselves did likewise in many East Indian regions.

Having thoroughly examined these questions, we conclude that the war in which the Portuguese carack and its cargo were captured was just in every respect, not merely for our government but much more so for the East India Company, regardless of whether that war was public or private, and of whether—assuming that it was public—it was waged on behalf of the fatherland or on behalf of allies; and we furthermore conclude that the Company itself became the owner of the abovementioned prize, from the standpoint of all law. [144′]

a. Lupus, *De Bello,* § *Si bene advertas* and others cited on same Corollary.
b. Th. Aq., *De Regimine Principum,* III [xiii].
c. Vict., *De Indis,* Sect. III, n. 17.

Here follows a discussion as to what is honourable.

ꕥ CHAPTER XIV ꕥ

Part I. The Seizure of the Prize in Question Was Honourable

In Part I the following theses are presented:

1. Everything just is honourable.

2. It is especially honourable to take vengeance, in behalf of one's allies or one's native land, upon men who are incorrigible.

3. Seizure of spoils may be especially honourable because of the purpose served thereby.

Part II. It Is Honourable to Retain Possession of the Prize in Question

In so far as the question of justice is concerned, I believe that we have satisfied those readers who seek the truth. For we have furnished abundant proof of the fact that the despoliation of the Portuguese because of the injuries inflicted by them, and the delivery of the captured goods into the possession of certain merchants, were deeds that conformed to the requirements of piety, nature, and custom.

But those persons who are deterred by preconceived false opinions from committing their judgement to the guidance of reason, are not all to be grouped under a single head or in accordance with a simple classification. So it is that we hear of some individuals who do not venture to deny the justice of the affair which we are discussing (nor would they be able to offer any defence for such a denial), while they nevertheless maintain that this same affair seems to them not entirely honourable. Part I of Chapter XIV

Thesis I Yet their contention surely involves an obvious inconsistency, inasmuch as we have always been told that whatever is just in every respect cannot fail to be honourable.[a] For everyone who frames a definition of this latter attribute would have us believe either that it is equivalent to virtue itself, or else that it is a certain quality inherent in the virtues or proceeding from them. In any case, the concept of "that which is honourable" can never be divorced from the concept of virtue, nor can anything be good unless it is also honourable. Indeed, even the more precise authorities[b] define the former concept as follows: that is honourable which is pleasing because it is good. Accordingly, of these two attributes, the one is necessarily bound up with the other.

Nor is it possible for anything to be base, or shameful in the eyes of wise and good men, if it is in conformity with true justice. The foregoing statement may be confirmed either by arguing that no one virtue is inconsistent with virtue in general, or by referring to the dictum correctly laid down by the ancients[c] in regard to justice, namely, that in the virtue of justice all other virtues are included. As a matter of fact, however, no argument is needed to prove this point to sensible persons; for long ago (according to Plato)[d] the youth Alcibiades was prompted by Socrates to acknowledge naturally and instinctively the truth of the conclusion that he who is performing a just act must also be performing an honourable act. Moreover, this same conclusion, which is sanctioned by universal acceptance, has been expounded at length in the works of the philosophers.[e]

In order that our point may be properly grasped, it must be understood that we are not employing the term "just" to denote that which is permitted by some civil law, or (more accurately) that which is connived

a. Cicero, *On Invention,* II [iv, *passim*]; *id., On Duties,* I [ix. 62]; *ibid.* III [viii. 33–5]; Cicero, *On Ends,* I [xvi. 50]; Arist., *On Virtues and Vices,* at beg. [*Eudemian Ethics,* VII. xv].

b. Arist., *Rhetoric,* I. ix [3].

c. Arist., *Nic. Ethics,* V. iii [V. i. 15], citing an ancient poet.

d. *Alcibiades* [I, p. 114 E].

e. Arist., *Rhetoric,* I. ix [3].

at by the laws.[a] For the jurists[b] themselves rule that whatever is [144′] thus exempted from punishment and to a corresponding degree described as permissible, while in point of fact it is not just, is at the same time not honourable. On the contrary, it should be understood that we are referring to what has been decreed and firmly established by the immutable law of nature. For everything that has been so decreed and established is necessarily honourable. So extensive is the force of this principle that the Stoics and, indeed, a very considerable number of the philosophers,[c] have felt that it is absolutely impossible to define the concept of "that which is honourable" more clearly than by saying that it consists of what is prescribed by nature. Consequently, a great many writers even employ the term to denote nothing more nor less than the common law which is universally acknowledged. This interpretation explains a certain saying handed down by the sages,[d] namely, that the force inherent in honourable things is such that they are sought after spontaneously, for their intrinsic merits and (as it were) by a natural impulse.

Therefore, since we have demonstrated that the law which governs spoils, like the law of war, has its origin in a natural instinct implanted by God Himself, and since the equitable character of the act under consideration is clearly apparent when viewed in the light of the principles underlying natural law and the law of nations, surely the said act involves no element that should cause any one to feel shame.

Thesis II

For my own part, moreover, I shall maintain against any person who wishes to dispute the point, that both the seizure and the possession of enemy property under the circumstances in question, are acts not merely untainted by dishonour but even glorious in the highest degree. For those writers[e] who have devoted particular attention to the concept of what is honourable, tell us that the most important components from

a. Cicero, *Tusculan Disputations,* V [ix. 26].
b. *Dig.* L. xvii. 144; Cicero, *For Balbus* [iii. 8].
c. Cicero, *Academics,* I [II. xliii. 132]; *id., On Laws,* I [xvii. 46]; *id., On Duties,* I [xiv. 42].
d. Arist., *Rhetoric,* I. ix [3]; Cicero, *On Ends,* V [III. xi. 36].
e. Arist., *Rhetoric,* I. ix [5–6].

which this concept derives its high position among the virtues are fortitude and justice, inasmuch as these two attributes are undoubtedly the qualities most beneficial [to others],[1] both in private and in public life.

The works of the poets certainly abound in references to fortitude. How impressive are the well-known lines from the *Elegies* of Tyrtaeus:[a]

Τιμῆεν τε γάρ ἐστι καὶ ἀγλαὸν ἀνδρὶ μαχέσθαι
Γῆς πέρι, καὶ παίδων, κουριδίης τ' ἀλόχου
Δυσμένεσι.

It is a glorious and manly thing,
To risk one's life in battle with the foe,
Defending loved ones, wife and native land.

Fortitude is the virtue celebrated in triumphal processions, in the garlands that bedeck the brave, in inscriptions, and in acclamations like the one that follows:

οὗτος ἐν ἀνθρώποις νικηφόρος, οὗτος ἄριστος.

To this man is the name of "Victor" giv'n,
The title "Most illustrious of men."

It is the virtue in whose name kings rejoice to be praised, and by which men are raised to the rank of gods.

Relying on this merit, Pollux gained
A place among the stars; and Hercules,
The wand'rer, did the same. . . .[b]

Yet again, may we not say (since the case with which we are at present concerned turns also upon a naval incident), that Themistocles, who broke the power of Persia in battles waged upon the sea, achieved [145] a fame almost more illustrious [than that of Pollux or of Hercules] in the eyes of Athens and his native Greece? Cynaegirus, though he was

a. [10, lines 1 ff.]

b. Horace [*Odes,* III. iii. 9–10].

1. The bracketed phrase is introduced into the English sentence in order to preserve an essential element of Aristotle's argument, since Aristotle is the only writer specifically cited by Grotius in regard to this point.

merely a private citizen, won for himself an undying name. Among the Romans, Duilius, after conquering the Carthaginians in naval conflict, was rewarded by what may be described as an unending triumphal celebration, with torches borne before him as he walked. In short, just as cowards and ῥιψάσπιδες ["deserters," "those who throw away their shields in battle"] are everywhere crushed with contempt and in some regions severely punished, so there is no people, nor is there any state, that fails to bestow the highest honours upon those persons who have exalted their own fair fame and that of their native land by courageous deeds. The established institutions of all nations in general, as well as the special institutions which have won superlative acclaim (such as those of the Spartans and the Romans), testify so clearly to the truth of this assertion that it would surely be a waste of effort to dwell at length upon the matter here.

As for the attribute of justice, the ancients[a] have rightly declared that neither the Morning nor the Evening Star can compete with it in lustre. In fact, they have even asserted (as Cicero does, for example, [in his treatise *On the Laws*])[b] that nothing devoid of this attribute can be honourable. For in a sense the very foundation of enduring worth and fame, [so that same writer tells us in his work *On Duties,*][c] is justice, without which nothing can be deserving of praise.

What other kind of deed, then, will shine so brightly and with such splendour as one that is illumined alike by both of these virtues: fortitude and justice? Yet this combination is never more apparent than on the occasions when we are granted the opportunity, in just and open warfare,

> ἄνδρ' ἀπαμύνεσθαι ὅς τις πρότερος χαλεπήνῃ,
>
> *To seek in battle vengeance on the man*
> *Who first has done us wrong. . . .*[d]

a. Arist., *Nic. Ethics,* V. iii [V. i. 15].
b. I [*passim*].
c. I [II. xx. 71].
d. Homer [*Iliad,* XXIV. 369].

As we have observed in another passage,[a] where we quoted from Ambrose,[b] *the fortitude*[2] that defends one's native land or one's allies or the weak, is *just* in the fullest sense of the term. Aristotle,[c] too, the most sagacious of philosophers, tells us[3] that it is *honourable to take vengeance* upon one's enemies, "since the repayment of like with like is *just* and that which is just is assuredly honourable, and since, moreover, it is the duty of a man *of fortitude* to refuse to yield"; wherefore, "victory and the honours accorded to victory are also numbered among those things which are honourable" in the highest degree, so much so, indeed, that "they are desirable even when they bear no fruit," because they testify to the pre-eminence of virtue. These, I repeat, are the teachings of Aristotle.

Nor is there any valid basis for the objection that we shall be making a more noble gesture and at the same time one not inconsistent with the precepts laid down by Christ and by the philosophers, if we refrain from inflicting any harm upon those whom we have the power to harm, in order to prove by this very restraint our superiority to our enemies; for certainly such restraint, under such a pretext, is opposed to [145′] honour in precisely the same degree in which it is opposed to justice and public welfare.

We have already explained[d] that the persons who censure [certain types of] revenge are of the opinion, first, that it is not proper for private

a. See Chap. iii, at end, *supra,* p. 67.

b. *On Duties,* I. xxvii [129].

c. Arist., *Rhetoric,* I. ix [24–5].

d. In discussion of Law V, Chap. ii, *supra,* p. 32, and discussion of Concl. VII, Art. I, Chap. viii, *supra,* pp. 127 ff.

2. *Fortitudo,* which in the Latin has the twofold connotation of "fortitude" and "courage," and must be translated according to the context. In the preceding passages where this statement from Ambrose was cited, the English term "courage" was employed, as representing more accurately Ambrose's meaning; in this particular context, however, the double connotation must be brought out in order to preserve the force of Grotius's argument as well as the thought of Ambrose.

3. In the Latin, these statements drawn from *The "Art" of Rhetoric* are all reproduced in the form of a direct quotation; but parts of the Latin passage are in reality a rather loose paraphrase, as is indicated by the distribution of the quotation marks in the present translation.

individuals to seek by direct action that vengeance which they are able to seek through recourse to a judge; and secondly, that [cases where direct action is justified] must be characterized both by the existence of due cause[4] and by the observance of just limits to revenge (which must not be exceeded), as well as by a pure heart and righteous intent on the part of the avenger. These requirements, however, in nowise preclude the possibility that occasions may arise on which vengeance is both right and necessary. Seneca[a] makes this point in a concise statement: "It is as cruel to pardon *all,* as it is to pardon none." And in the works of Augustine[b] we find the following learned exposition of the same sentiment:

> To return good for good, and to return *evil for evil:* these are the two moderately virtuous forms of retribution. The first of these two courses of conduct, while it is especially characteristic of good persons, is acceptable also to the wicked. Thus Christ does not censure it, but He does say that more is required, since even the heathen make such repayment. The second course is especially characteristic of wicked persons, yet *it is acceptable* also to *the virtuous;* wherefore [divine[5]] law itself has prescribed *a due measure for revenge.*

Further on, Augustine[c] explains the foregoing statement by interpreting it thus: in acts of *just vengeance,* which is inflicted owing to *love of justice* and not because of delight in another's distress, evil is not [really] returned for evil, but rather, *justice is returned for injustice;* or in other words (still according to that same Augustine), *good is returned for evil,* a course followed by God Himself when He acts as Judge.

Therefore, in order that we may clearly understand when vengeance is honourable and when, on the other hand, mercy should be shown, it

a. *On Mercy,* I. ii [2].

b. *On Psalms,* CVIII [4], and cited in *Decretum,* II. xxiii. 3. 1.

c. [Augustine, *ibid.* 7.]

4. A reference to the *Digest* appears in the margin of the MS. at this point. No doubt Grotius intended to delete it when he crossed out the corresponding passage in the text.

5. The passage cited here from the *Decretum* refers specifically to the verse from *Exodus* (xxi. 24) which runs as follows: "Eye for eye, tooth for tooth, hand for hand, foot for foot."

seems advisable for us to draw certain distinctions both among the persons who inflict injury and among those who suffer injury.

With reference to the latter, and to cases in which the injury is suffered in common with one's allies or one's native land, it is clear that we may not forgive public wrongs, or those inflicted upon other persons, as readily as we may forgive those directed against ourselves. There is a maxim frequently reiterated by the jurists,[a] to the effect that he who fails to defend the victim of an injury, is lending support to the perpetrator of the injury. To quote Augustine[b] once more: "It has been proven that individuals who have permitted the commission of a crime *are not guiltless* of that crime. He who is able to prevent a given act and fails to [146] do so, *consents* to it." For, as this authority[c] elsewhere observes, "it is not the part of innocence to allow, *by forbearance,* too grave a lapse into wickedness. Thus it is properly *the duty of innocence,* not only to refrain from inflicting evil upon any person, but also to check the commission of sins, or even *to punish the sin that has been committed,* so that he who previously was an object of hatred *may be reformed through experience,* or others *may be deterred by dread example."* Ambrose,[d] too, severely censures that misdirected mercifulness which delivers up the innocent to destruction while *it frees from restraint the very individual who is plotting the destruction of numerous individuals.* "The guiding principle of virtue," declares Ambrose,[e] "consists not in *tolerating* but rather in *repelling* injury. For he who fails to ward off injury *from an ally* is as much *at fault* as he who inflicts the injury." Moreover, just as the foregoing tenet relative to allies is most admirable, so also is the sentiment relative to one's native land expressed by Cicero[f] (in one of his Orations against Catiline) in these terms: "If we adopt *the sternest possible attitude* toward those men who have attempted to destroy the homes of each and every one of us together with our common home, the state, we shall be considered

a. *Decretum,* I. lxxxiii. 5; Arias, *De Bello,* 37–8.
b. *On Psalms,* LXXXI.
c. *On the City of God.*
d. *On Psalms,* CXVIII, sermon viii [vs. 58, § 25].
e. Ambrose, *On Duties,* I. xxxvi [178].
f. *Against Catiline,* IV [vi. 12].

merciful; but if we choose to be *too indulgent,* we shall be obliged to suffer a reputation for *cruelty* disastrous *to the fatherland* and to our fellow citizens." In the opinion of Augustine,[a] too, the man who shows such indulgence is guilty of *betrayal* and contempt *of sovereign authority.* To this assertion Augustine appends the following comment: "Thus [a soldier][6] will be punished for failing to perform, when bidden to do so, the very act that he is punished for performing unbidden."

Secondly, as I have already pointed out, we must consider the question in its bearing upon the persons who first inflicted injury. For if it is evident that such persons are not reformed by leniency, if their stubbornness is such as to corroborate the warning found in the farce,—

> By tolerating wrongs already done,
> We ask to suffer injury anew,—

vengeance against them is undoubtedly honourable, since it is a necessity. In the works of Thucydides,[b] there are a great many brilliant observations which support this view, including the wise pronouncement quoted from the oration of Cleon, namely: that it is right to be merciful and lenient when dealing with persons who are guided in their turn by merciful sentiments, or whom one may hope to draw into a friendly relationship as a result of such conduct, whereas it is not right to deal thus with persons who cherish an enduring motive for hatred and who, even if they themselves are spared, will not for that reason be more inclined to renounce their enmity. In another passage, Thucydides[c] insists that no concession should be made to the enemy, lest he grow more insolently vainglorious, rejoicing in the opportunity offered him for abuse of another's kindness. There is, too, this additional consideration: that when we have shown mercy to men actuated by inflexible enmity, the act is ascribed to consciousness of our own weakness rather [146′]

a. *On the City of God,* I. xxvi.

b. III [xl].

c. The colloquy between Athenians and Melians in Thucydides, V [xcv, xcvii].

6. Augustine was discussing the difference between slaughter committed by a soldier in obedience to orders received, and voluntary homicide on the part of the same soldier. Cf. the longer excerpt from this same passage, *supra,* p. 123.

than to voluntary leniency, and the reputation for clemency sought in this manner is turned against us in the form of contempt. Thus Severus is quoted by Herodian[a] as saying: *ὥσπερ δὲ ἄδικον τὸ ἄρχειν ἔργων πονηρῶν, οὕτως ἄνανδρον τὸ μὴ ἀμύνασθαι πρὸς ἀδικούμενον*; "even as it is unjust to have been the first to engage in injurious acts, so it is weak to refrain from avenging injuries already inflicted."

Again, is vengeance not beneficial to the culpable parties themselves? The Platonists[b] speak the truth when they maintain that, "although the infliction of injury upon another is the worst of all evils, such evil becomes still more grave if the perpetrator of the injurious act goes unpunished; and if the impunity of the wrongdoer is protracted, and he is not chastised meanwhile by the censure of his fellow man, this situation itself will be more grievous and painful than any punishment." In a certain sense, indeed (according to our own theological writers, and also according to Augustine,[c] that greatest of theologians), we bestow a favour upon the very individuals whom we deter from wrongdoing by filling them with dread. Other statements made by Augustine may be cited to the same effect. In the *Letter to Lotharius*[d] we find these words: "He who fosters vice by extending to it indulgence and protection, in order to avoid saddening the hearts of sinners, is even less merciful than the person who refuses to snatch a knife from a child lest he hear the child crying for it, and nevertheless does not fear to see that same child wounded or killed." It is Augustine,[e] too, who offers this admonition: "Moreover, those persons who decree that for so grave a crime you should be thus gently restrained and corrected *by punishment in the form of fines depriving you of* estates or goods or *money*, are to be regarded as exceedingly careful guides and *kindly counsellors*, since they are pondering the means by which you may endure these [consequences of wrongdoing], may escape from your own acknowledged sacrilege and may be delivered

a. [*Histories*, VI. iii. 4.]
b. Apuleius, *On Plato* [II, p. 615].
c. *Letters*, cliv [xlvii. 5], *To Publicola*.
d. *Letters*, *To Lotharius*.
e. *Against Petilianus*, II.

from eternal damnation." Jerome[a] expressed a similar sentiment in his commentary on Sophonias, when he wrote as follows: "If the strength of a bandit or pirate is diminished and he is rendered feeble, he will be benefited by his own weakened condition, since the disabled members which were formerly ill employed, will cease from evil works."

Finally, that good judgement in civic matters which takes careful account of all the different parts of a war, shows us clearly enough that leniency is appropriate either at the outset or at the conclusion of wars (at the outset, of course, with a view to influencing favourably the disposition of the enemy by establishing a reputation for clemency, and at the conclusion, with the object of holding the vanquished in check more easily once security has been attained), whereas during the intervening period, while the peril is still at its height, nothing is more judicious than the dissemination of fear. [147]

Let us now examine the question with special reference to the seizure of spoils, ascertaining what kind of seizure is to be considered as honourable, and what kind, on the other hand, as base and infamous. For confusion on this point is the source of widespread and exceedingly harmful errors, which either enable evil to lie hid under the guise of the good that it resembles, or else besmirch what is righteous with the stigma befitting a closely related form of infamy. Yet nothing could be easier **Thesis III** than the drawing of the necessary distinction, provided that we bear in mind the rules above set forth in regard to what is just, which coincide with the rules relative to what is honourable.

For, in the first place, that gain is dishonourable which is acquired by individuals who despoil others through privately exercised force and without urgent reasons for so doing. To such individuals we give the name of "pirates" when their activities take place upon the sea. Secondly, the same criticism applies to acquisitions made by persons who without any legitimate cause usurp authority to wage public war. For example, it is recorded that in earlier times whole peoples—such as the Cretans, the Cilicians, and even the Greeks themselves (according to the testimony of Homer), as well as the Germans and the Normans—engaged

a. [*On Sophonias,* i.]

openly and publicly in the practice of despoliation without so much as an appropriate pretext. To despoilers of this kind we refer (and not unjustly) as "freebooters." Yet again, those persons are deserving of blame who snatch away property prior to the execution of the measures required in order that war may be lawfully undertaken. Such attacks upon property are severely censured by writers on the subject as acts of "robbery."

But these three types of dishonourable seizure are of so obvious a character as to be easily and directly identifiable. Therefore, we shall devote our attention chiefly to a fourth type, which can scarcely be detected save through conjectural inferences. It is the type of seizure that occurs when, in the course of a just war or a war believed to be just, someone grasps at profit in a way which indicates that he has been mindful only of profit for its own sake and not of the true objective of war, namely, the attainment of rights.

New explanation

The signs betokening the fact that such seizure is taking place are bound up, generally speaking, with a situation in which a given person (particularly one who has charged up no losses against the enemy), with very little force at his command, attacks and despoils the unarmed and the weak unexpectedly and at random, though he has not the strength that would embolden him to claim in battle open possession of the regions despoiled. For such a person, since he neither weakens the enemy to any appreciable extent nor advances the interests of his own side, is very liable to be suspected of engaging in war with no other motive than that of private profit. Under this head we may place the despoilers of fishermen or of ship-masters who have been caught by chance upon a sea where the assailants themselves fear to be seen. [147′]

Assuredly, that true warrior who

> Prevails not by stealth but by strength of arms,[a]

is far removed from this uncouth class. Consequently, with reference both to warfare on land and to maritime warfare, those individuals who

a. Virgil [*Aeneid,* X. 735].

steal into possession of enemy property by making clandestine raids, so to speak, have always been assigned to one category,[a] while a different estimate has been applied to whole armies or fleets which show themselves openly with their insignia on display and which either enter into battle on their own account or challenge the enemy to do so. For persons belonging to the latter class, who are motivated by an eager desire to win the war by any means whatsoever, deserve indulgence if they are in error, and glory if they are supporting a just cause; whereas persons of the former class incur universal detestation, since by audacious but unwarlike devices they turn public loss into private gain, a course of conduct clearly incompatible not only with justice but also with fortitude,[7] the virtue wherein legitimate enemies vie with one another.

If we apply the foregoing observations to our present purpose, recalling at the same time the events that have already been narrated, we shall plainly perceive that the Portuguese, though they assume the guise of merchants, are not very different from pirates. For if the name of "pirate" is appropriately bestowed upon men who blockade the seas and impede the progress of international commerce, shall we not include under the same head those persons who forcibly bar all European nations (even nations that have given them no cause for war) from the ocean and from access to India, although they are not able to find among the exceedingly diverse and mutually contradictory pretexts that they adduce in defence of their savage behaviour, so much as one excuse that can be rendered acceptable to their own relatively fair-minded compatriots? Therefore, since it was invariably held in ancient times that persons of this kind were worthy objects of universal hatred in that they were harmful to all mankind, and since even now there is no one, or at the most perhaps a very few individuals, who would absolve the Portuguese from the charge of belonging to this class, why should anyone fear that he might incur ill will by inflicting punishment upon them?

Thus we conclude that it cannot be dishonourable for merchants to

a. See on this distinction, Alphonso Guerrero *In Speculum Principum,* xlvi.

7. I.e. incompatible with the two most important virtues included in the concept of what is honourable; see pp. 439–40, *supra.*

take well-deserved vengeance upon the violators of a public right, with the purpose of ensuring greater security for themselves in the enjoyment of that right, just as there can be no one who will censure the conduct of a traveller assaulted in the course of his journey by a highwayman, if that traveller bravely and quite justifiably takes his assailant captive. Nor is the mercantile manner of life incompatible with such vengeance, any more than agricultural life is incompatible with the practice frequently followed (so we understand) by farmers in dangerous localities, when they wear the sword while guiding the plough. For Cicero[a] assures [148] us that, "There is no prohibition derived either from the natural order or from any legal precept or custom, that forbids acquaintance with more than one art on the part of one individual." How much more acceptable, then, is this versatility, when one of the arts involved is adopted by choice, the other as a result of necessity; and when the latter is combined with the former as the servant of the chosen art, because without that servant the other art could not continue to be practised! Moreover, history teaches us, not only that the Athenians, the Carthaginians, and the Portuguese themselves (both the present-day Portuguese and those of early times) have frequently employed arms for the protection of commerce, but also that the people of ancient Holland (who were men of the most saintly and blameless character, so that the ability to imitate them is a mark of surpassing virtue) have bequeathed to posterity shining examples of just such conduct. From the vast number of these examples, I shall choose one for special mention here.

In the year 1438

Many years ago, the maritime states of the Germans (Lübeck, Hamburg, Danzig, Lüneburg, Wismar, Rostock, Lunden, &c.), in alliance with the Prussians, and with the Spaniards and Venetians as well (for at that time these two peoples were likewise in the habit of navigating northern waters), had been lying in wait for those excuses to inaugurate a quarrel which are never lacking among commercial rivals. Finally, they began not only to despoil the Dutch, who were roaming the seas quite unprepared for war, but also to slay our men or else carry them off into the

a. *On the Orator,* I [l. 216].

harshest kind of captivity. The Dutch, for their part, choosing to have recourse to every other device before employing force, despite the fact that they were being harassed with the most grievous injuries, sought to reclaim their property through duly appointed embassies. They commanded the above-mentioned states to desist from private despoliation (unless the latter wished to pay assessments for damages), and to contend with the Dutch thenceforth in open warfare. Since it proved absolutely impossible, however, to elicit voluntary respect for Dutch rights from the Germans, our people undertook, with the consent of their reigning Prince (Philip the First of Burgundy), to equip and man ships in all their cities. Shortly thereafter, using these vessels to attack the enemy (in most cases after a formal declaration of intention to open battle), they entered wholeheartedly into a struggle as successful as it was valiant, with the result that in a little while no other ships than those of the Dutch were to be seen upon the ocean.

These Dutch ships, moreover, displayed drag-nets commemorating numerous victories and symbolizing a sea swept clean. In one [148′] engagement, twenty large German vessels and three Prussian vessels were captured, as well as a richly laden Venetian carack which was accompanying them. The latter was borne off to Zeeland. In a subsequent battle, three more ships, massive in size, were taken by the Dutch. The captives were accorded the most honourable treatment, even though such Dutchmen as had previously fallen into the hands of the enemy were wasting away at that very time in the vilest confinement. The victors apportioned the prize by casting lots; and this prize proved to be so valuable that it sufficed not only to provide compensation for the earlier losses but also, in a moderate degree, to defray the expenses of the war.

The Germanic states, overwhelmed by these disasters, reached the point where they begged for peace, since they feared that there was truth in the prediction made by a certain man who enjoyed considerable authority among them, to the effect that they were provoking a lion whom they would not easily lull to rest once he had been aroused. Their request was readily granted by a nation which had always kept its heart open for the admission of peace, even in the process of executing just vengeance and waging a brilliantly successful war.

Let us not trouble ourselves unduly in a search for examples from foreign sources. Many lessons can be learned from this single domestic example, which serves us as an illustration of justice in undertaking war, fortitude in actual warfare and equity in desisting from hostilities. Thus we find that the same persons who were merciful in victory, were temperate in the seizure of spoils. Moreover, anyone who compares the incident just described with the events in the East Indies narrated in an earlier chapter[a] of this discussion, will certainly admit that those early characteristics of Dutch conduct remain unchanged after the lapse of a hundred and sixty years.

We conclude, then, that vengeance of this kind, undertaken for the purpose of obtaining one's rightful due, is honourable. The Dutch merchants are justified in resorting to such vengeance against the Portuguese.

The present case, however, involves not merely the private cause of the aforesaid merchants, but the cause of the state, too, and that of its allies. The cause of the state is involved not only in consequence of the need for some great business enterprise that will provide support for the common people and resources for the treasury, but also because the interests of one and all demand that the Iberian races—who seek to erect a tyrant's throne for themselves upon the ruins of the shattered fatherland—shall be crushed and overthrown in every part of the world. [149] Otherwise, the time may come when even the farthest regions of the earth will be forced to pay tribute in order to assist in the subjugation of the Dutch. The cause of our allies is likewise involved: in other words, that of the East Indian kings and peoples, whom the Portuguese are assailing with fire and sword on the sole ground that these kings and peoples are not hostile to the Dutch. The imperilment of Bantam, the ashes of Makian, the devastation of Bachian, all bear witness to this attitude on the part of the Portuguese. Therefore, no one can pardon these injuries [against both the state and its allies] without sinking into the deepest infamy. For what could be more disgraceful than the betrayal either of that native land which shares our perils with us or of the allied peoples who are endangered for our sake?

a. [*Supra,* chap. xi, *passim.*]

We know that, in an earlier age, the Romans were admonished thus:[a] "You must seek for allies where the disaster of Saguntum is unknown."[8] You may be certain that, in like manner, the East Indians would have shuddered to see the sails of the approaching Hollanders, as one would shudder at ill-omened and deadly portents, and that [their] men would be fleeing from any contact with us or even putting our own men to flight, had it not been God's pleasure to reveal to the Asiatic nations, also, that same Dutch virtue which is renowned throughout Europe, and to demonstrate by means of a memorable object-lesson the fact that those persons are by no means deceived who prefer Dutch fortitude and good faith to the perfidy and ferocity of the Portuguese. For my part, indeed, I find that the entire history of this war, which has already been prolonged beyond its thirtieth year, contains no lesson more impressive than those relative to good faith among allies. The inhabitants of Leyden, when their city was exhausted by its misfortunes and surrounded by hostile forces, when their provisions and whatever their extreme need had converted into food was running out, still did not betray this principle of faith. Inspired by the same principle, other Dutchmen in their turn called in the ocean to cover their fields and crops. It was this good faith that defended England in our common war. It was this faith that succoured France in her distress. Good faith is a useful attribute at home and a matter of honour among neighbours, but it is a veritable necessity in those farthest corners of the world where persons previously unknown cannot very well make themselves known save through their virtues. For we have no common bond of religion with those distant peoples, nor even a bond based upon covenants; but we are linked to them by [149′] the natural and inescapable tie that unites all human beings, as well as by a special commercial relationship, a factor of fundamental importance for the support of the state and of private interests. Furthermore, any conceivable hope that the peoples in question will eventually see the

a. Livy, XXI [xix. 10].

8. This was the answer returned by the Volciani, a Spanish tribe, to the Roman ambassadors who were seeking new allies against the Carthaginians, after Rome had failed to save Saguntum from complete destruction at the hands of Hannibal.

light of reason and accept the doctrine of Christianity, must certainly be based not upon the destruction of cities nor upon the torture of the inhabitants, but rather upon conduct that will set an example of good faith, benevolence, and clemency.

On the other hand, if we turn our attention to the Portuguese character, who will be able to deny that, despite the conciliatory advances implicit in the favours extended by the Dutch even after they had suffered injury, the Portuguese were so little inclined to mitigate in any degree their ancient ferocity, that they repeatedly took advantage of this very benevolence, viewing it not merely with scorn but also as a basis for their own attempts at treachery? Thus the illustrious historian Thucydides[a] does not err when he declares that those persons who causelessly inflict injury upon another are especially unlikely to be restrained, by any benefaction whatsoever, from pursuing to his utter destruction that same victim toward whom they have once assumed a voluntary attitude of enmity. Accordingly, just as leniency in dealing with such adversaries is attended both by peril and by the shameful brand of cowardice, so the infliction of vengeance upon them is honourable because it is necessary. For we are already acquainted with the character of the Spaniards, who did not for their own part abstain from any kind of cruelty at the outset of the war now being waged in the Low Countries, although they themselves were treated with a certain measure of forbearance; nor did they swerve from their original course of conduct until it had been decided that a similar course should be followed against them.

In the East Indies, however, not even this retaliatory step was taken. Who is unaware of the fact that every bodily injury is infinitely more serious than any loss of goods?[b] Nevertheless, in those East Indian regions, while Dutchmen are being torn to pieces alive or delivered to the galleys, the life and liberty of the captives held by the Dutch are, on the contrary, preserved intact. Yet it would have been just if the said captives had been forced to undergo suffering more severe than that which they had inflicted, since they themselves, without provocation, had first set

a. III [xl. near end].
b. Doctors, *On Dig.* XLVIII. xix. 10.

the example of such savagery. In fact, this vengeance which is now being exacted is scarcely worthy of the name. It is nothing more than a species of chastisement from which hard-hearted men may learn how gravely others, too, are affected by the loss of their goods.

> 'Tis not the sons of Atreus alone
> Who feel this sorrow. . . .[a] [150]

Moreover, since honourable conduct in the seizure of spoils is a matter dependent primarily upon the end sought (as we have already observed), we must repeat at this point the statement for which proof was given in an earlier passage, as follows: the Dutch sailors have cleared themselves satisfactorily of suspicion by disregarding many opportunities for the capture of quite valuable property, and consequently no one can believe that they were motivated merely by greed for spoil in exposing themselves to such great danger; for it is clear that whatever they did, was done because they perceived the impossibility of restraining by any other means the unbounded avidity for gain characteristic of the Portuguese. Besides, the particular prize to which we refer, represents not a profit but reparation for losses, and nothing could be more honourable than such a circumstance.

Yet again, it was not by any fraudulent means, not by perfidy (though fraud and perfidy could have been regarded as exempt from the reproach of injustice when employed against the Portuguese), not even by furtive and roundabout methods, that the Dutch sought out occasions to engage in battle; on the contrary, they waged open and public warfare. Moreover, it frequently happened that a small number of Dutchmen joined battle with forces vastly larger than their own, displaying such valour of spirit and strength of body that they have a right to claim for themselves, in addition to the commendation due to justice, the glory that is awarded to fortitude.

Truly, there is no room for doubt as to what kind of deed earns censure and what kind, on the other hand, is glorious; nor is there any doubt as

a. Virgil [*Aeneid* IX. 138–39].

to the judgement that one may expect all men to render in regard to each type of conduct. Let us remember that the Hollanders were reproached by the East Indian nobles because, on the occasion of the first voyage made by our countrymen, while they were still striving zealously to preserve the peace, four [Dutch] vessels had lowered their sails before a single Portuguese carack; and let us remember that those same Hollanders were exhorted by the Chinese not to hold their own fair fame in such slight esteem as to leave unavenged (most reluctantly, to be sure) the gibbeting and drowning of their allies at the city of Macao. Now, let us imagine instead that we are listening to the joyous acclamations of the people of Bantam, who have been rescued by Dutch valour from impending disaster and who are hailing our victorious fleet as the sole author of their deliverance. How great was the fame earned throughout the islands by that act! How grave was the terror spread throughout the ranks of the enemy! How joyful was the King of Johore when he stood—secure and avenged at last—upon the thwarts of the captured [150′] carack! These are the deeds that proclaimed the glory of the Dutch nation to the uttermost ends of the earth.

For certainly it must be confessed that the reputation of the Hollanders, prior to these wars, was confined within very narrow limits of renown. Who, indeed, is unaware of this fact? Their activities and the fame of those activities were bounded by two straits: to the north, by the Sound; to the west, by the Strait of Gibraltar. The Hollanders have derived considerable benefit from the celebrity of the Spanish foe. For peoples dwelling at a great distance, along the farthest inlets of the ocean, have come to know that there is a tiny nation which has not hesitated to challenge the might of Spain and which has even succeeded in beating back that mighty force during all these years.

After the Dutch had made their appearance among the East Indians, the worth of the new-comers was carefully weighed in the Indies, as is customary in regard to merchants. Our countrymen were commended for their good faith and industry, as well as for the fact that they had traversed so vast an expanse of sea for the sake of commerce. Nevertheless, the extraordinary renown of the Spaniards [and Portuguese] remained pre-eminent, for they were believed to be the conquerors of almost every region of the earth, and the only mortals who had never been vanquished. It is true that the East Indians hated the Portuguese; but at the same time they regarded that people with fear and even with veneration, just as evil genii (so we are told) are worshipped by barbarous nations for the sole purpose of averting the injuries that might be inflicted by those evil spirits. The prestige enjoyed by the Portuguese and the fear inspired by them, enabled them to hold possession of islands and shores over which they had not been able to establish true dominion. Many persons did not even dare to set sail upon the sea without first purchasing Portuguese permission. So it was that all other peoples were looked upon as inferior and as destined to yield quite speedily before the power of the Hispanic nations. But as soon as the Dutch had been provoked to display their valour, as soon as these men who had at first been deceived by their own artlessness and by the enemy's trickery met armed force with armed force, and when the scattered flight, the disastrous defeat, and the capitulation of the Portuguese were witnessed, who among the East Indians was not struck with astonishment? Who among them did not marvel at the very existence of a nation which refrained from proving its strength until compelled to do so, although nothing was beyond its power? Everywhere the East Indians extolled the Hollanders as the most valiant of men, defenders of their allies and subduers of their enemies; and everywhere, too, they assigned to our people, with prayers and steadfast hope, the role of saviours of the Orient.

Thus the great and fearful fame of the Portuguese gave way before the Dutch, amid manifestations of affection for the latter, on the part of the peoples proclaiming this change of heart, as intense as the hatred built up by the Portuguese against themselves. Everyone wished to [151] know what land nurtured men so brave and just, what government ordered their affairs. Every East Indian state vied with the others in dispatching embassies and gifts all the way to our own part of the world. Each state strove to ally itself with the Dutch. The East Indian kings themselves hastened to meet our sailors, as if the latter were princes. Exemption was granted us from the imposts and tithes paid by other nations. In short, no act was omitted that might serve as testimony to sentiments of goodwill and even of veneration.

Furthermore, quite apart from the attitude taken in Asia, the reaction throughout Europe toward the affair in question is in no sense doubtful. For we see that the greatest princes joyfully accept the gifts sent them out of these very spoils, and that an incredibly vast throng drawn from all nations is assembling for the sale. At home, too, the States Assembly of Holland has itself indicated by the terms of its Decree that, in the opinion of that governmental body, a large part of the glory resulting from this episode sheds its lustre upon the entire state. The citizens give thanks to God; they rejoice that so signal a triumph has fallen to the lot of the fatherland; and indeed, those individuals who have played any part whatsoever in this victory are universally honoured and esteemed as persons of the highest merit.

What, then, remains to be said? It is praiseworthy to be praised, but only (as a certain famous man was wont to say), if the tribute is bestowed by those who have themselves received praise; for in so far as other critics are concerned, one is for the most part a better person in proportion to the displeasure that one has aroused in them. In fact, if there are individuals who still maintain that the crimes of the Portuguese should be encouraged with impunity, or who regard it as right that men of the most monstrous character should be exempt even from the restraint imposed by liability to seizure of goods, I for my part shall scarcely deem such individuals worthy to be called human beings and shall certainly consider them utterly unworthy of the name of "Dutchmen."

Part II of Chapter XIV

Possibly there are some critics who will admit that the Portuguese have indeed earned the penalties in question, but who will nevertheless feel that it is by no means seemly that they themselves should be found in possession of property seized from the enemy, or of any proceeds derived from that source.

But surely it is the mark of an exceedingly abject and degenerate spirit, to be fearful of incurring reproach for that form of acquisition which the greatest kings and princes, as well as all persons of outstanding worth, consider as an instrument of glory. For what other interpretation shall we place upon the memorials erected in honour of victors, the triumphal arches constructed from the spoils of the enemy, the proceeds derived from sales of captured property, and the public stages adorned [151′] (whether by the ancient Romans or by the Venetians of our own day) with the beaks of enemy ships?[9]

Certainly those fearful persons might have learned from the Holy Scriptures, not only that spoils can be acquired and held with a clear conscience, but also that these very practices are actually regarded as glorious in the highest degree, since they result at one and the same time in profit for ourselves, in terror for the enemy, and in the edification of others by means of the example set. Thus God Himself[a] adds to His promises of other gifts to be bestowed by Him upon the seed of Abraham, this further promise of a blessing which appears to be especially honourable, namely, that He will bring it to pass that Abraham's seed shall possess the gate of their enemies. Then, too, the possessions allotted by Jacob to Joseph[b] are praised by the former on the ground that they were δορύκτητοι, "taken with his sword and with his bow."[10] Yet again, we read that Joshua,[c] when he sent away the children of Manasseh, presented them with the spoil of their enemies as a mark of honour, and furthermore declared that this was a reward for services rendered. David, also, in referring to that part of the spoil which he was sending to his friends, the elders of Judah, entrusted it to them with these words:[d] "Behold a present for you of the spoil of the enemies of the LORD. . . ."

Seneca[e] lists among benefactions of prime importance, the transmission of "wealth seized by right of war" to one who is impoverished,

a. *Genesis,* xxii. 17; *ibid.* xxiv. 60.

b. *Ibid.* xlviii, at end.

c. [*Joshua*] xxii.

d. *1 Samuel,* xxx. 26.

e. *On Benefits,* III. xxxiii.

9. *Rostra,* in the present context, has implications that call for this amplified interpretation in the English. The earlier meaning of the term ("beak" of a bird, animal, or ship) eventually resulted in the connotation "public stage," "platform for public speakers," because of the beaks of captured ships that were hung about the Roman Forum. Grotius obviously wishes to call to mind by means of the single word *Rostra,* both this later connotation and the custom from which it was derived.

10. δορύκτητοι, "won by the spear," is rendered somewhat freely in order to reproduce as closely as possible the phraseology of the Biblical passage cited here by Grotius.

and the enrichment of that same impoverished person "with spoils actually taken from the enemy, the most splendid of gifts in the eyes of a military hero."[11] Moreover, if we turn to the ranks of the jurists, we find that Accursius[a] does not hesitate to say that whatever we have obtained in this manner, by our own valour, is more truly ours than that which was bequeathed to us by our ancestors.

Now, as for those persons who readily admit that spoils may be retained by the state, but who do not make the same concession with respect to private individuals, their excessive subtlety—aside from the fact that it is supported by no logical argument—will be very neatly refuted if we recall here a conclusion whose truth has been demonstrated in another passage[b] and which may be stated as follows: in a primary and direct sense, property captured in a war that is conducted in accordance with a public mandate belongs to the state; but, even as it is just to purchase this same captured property from the state, so also its acceptance as a gift is honourable. Precisely for this reason, the portion allotted to individuals from the public spoils in recognition of valour is described by Homer[c] at times as *κύδος*, [an ornament of glory,] and at other times as *γέρας*, [a gift of honour,] both being exceedingly honourable terms.

Therefore, since the States Assembly, by conceding the prize in question to the merchants, has testified to its belief that a splendid service has been rendered the state through the diligence and at the expense of the said merchants while at the same time the common enemy has found his strength diminished, and since the Assembly has also testified in this connexion that it wishes to repay the merchants out of the said prize as a token of gratitude, should not all acquisitions derived from this source be regarded as rewards for meritorious service to the fatherland? [152] And what, pray, could be more honourable than such rewards?

a. Accursius, *On Dig.* XLIX. xv. 28.

b. See Concl. IX, Art. II, Chap. x, *supra,* pp. 226 ff.

c. [e.g., *Iliad,* I. 122, 163.]

11. Seneca, in the passage above cited, is referring specifically to the spoils handed over by Scipio to the latter's father. Consequently, it would be inaccurate to present the whole of Grotius's more general statement as a direct quotation, although it appears as such in the Latin text of the *Commentary.*

Yet again, in what sense is it odious to obtain from the enemy merely enough to provide for the recovery of compensation for the losses and expenses already incurred or hereafter to be incurred in the process of fitting out and arming ships, from the very persons solely responsible for the need to make expenditures? For anyone who carefully considers the essential circumstances of the present case will find that this award differs not at all from those which are granted to us by a judicial decision covering both damages and costs, and which not infrequently have to be collected by resort even to armed force.

We may agree, then, that the following point has been established: even as acquisition of the prize was just, so there is no reason at all to hold that it is dishonourable to retain possession of the prize. [152]

Here follows a discussion as to what is beneficial.

CHAPTER XV

Part I. The Seizure of the Prize in Question Was Beneficial

In Part I the following theses are presented:

1. Everything just is beneficial.

2. Everything honourable is beneficial.

3. That which befits the circumstances in which the state is situated, is especially beneficial.

4. It is especially beneficial to do good to allies.

5. It is especially beneficial to do harm to enemies.

6. Ease of accomplishment is a beneficial factor.

Part II. Retention of Possession of the Said Prize Is Beneficial

Epilogue

Turning to the next and final phase of our discussion, let us consider the matter from the standpoint of benefit. Undoubtedly our inquiries on this subject will seem superfluous to many persons who measure benefit in terms of material gain and who will therefore assume that no one can fail to realize how beneficial it is to acquire spoil, the source of such considerable additions to private property.

Part I of Chapter XV

For my own part, however, having embraced the belief that true benefits can never be disjoined from the concepts of honour and justice,[a] so that I should regard the vaunting of benefits unattended by these two attributes as the mark of a thoroughly corrupt person, I propose to establish the existence of beneficial elements in the present case, wherein the said attributes are not lacking, precisely on the basis of its just and honourable character.

For the just man (as we have already indicated in another context)[b] benefits himself before all else. Thus Plato,[c] too, in his eulogy of justice, holds that not only glory or εὐδοξία [fair fame], but also pleasure or benefit, should be reckoned [among its effects]. Similarly, in regard to that which is honourable, whether we find that a certain perverse system of reasoning (a system undoubtedly calamitous for mankind) has violently isolated this concept which is essentially bound up with the concept [152′] of what is beneficial, or whether it is acknowledged that the attribute of honour forms an especially conspicuous and preponderant element of all things termed beneficial, assuredly everyone desirous of a reputation for virtue will readily agree that nothing base is truly advantageous, whereas nothing honourable can fail to be expedient by virtue of the very fact that it is honourable. A great many observations in support of this sentiment were made by Cicero in his treatise *On Duties.*[d] In another work by that same author,[e] the following argument is presented: "Whatever is just, is beneficial; and whatever is honourable, is also just; whence it follows that whatever is honourable is also beneficial."[1] Certainly no

Thesis I

Thesis II

a. *Supra,* Chaps. xii, xiii, xiv.
b. *Supra,* Chap. i and beg. of Chap. ii.
c. *Dialogues On Justice* [*Republic,* I. p. 352 B–D].
d. III [*passim*].
e. *On Ends,* III [xxi. 71].

1. A very loose paraphrase of Cicero's actual words: . . . *numquam aequitatem ab utilitate posse seiungi, et quidquid aequum iustumque esset id etiam honestum, vicissimque quidquid esset honestum id iustum etiam atque aequum fore* (". . . that equity can never be disjoined from expediency [i.e. benefit], and that whatever is equitable and just is also honourable, while conversely, whatever is honourable is also just and fair"). Rackham, however, in his translation of the work above cited, points out that the final *honestum* seems to have been written inadvertently for *utile,* or else employed in the sense of "held in popular esteem," and therefore, "profitable." Interpreted in

one will be able to refute this contention; for even the Epicureans, those foremost champions of personal convenience, declare that,[a] *οὐκ εἶναι ἡδέως ζῆν ἄνευ τοῦ καλῶς καὶ δικαίως ζῆν*; "it is not possible to live pleasantly unless one lives both honourably and justly." Moreover, those benefits which are of a common and public character[b] and to which the jurists[c] for the most part refer, reveal a particularly close relationship with the concept of what is honourable.

In the first place, then, since every just acquisition is beneficial and should be classified with the things described even by the strictest philosophers as *προηγμένα*, or "preferable," on the ground that riches facilitate the accomplishment of many ends, spoils come under this same head and are in nowise to be spurned, provided that they are just and honourable.

οὐ γὰρ ἀπόβλητ' ἐστὶ θεῶν ἐρικυδέα δῶρα.

God's glorious gifts are not to be despised.[d]

In fact, we have already pointed out[e] that God reckons this particular benefit as one of the blessings which He confers upon the pious.

Thus spoils are beneficial primarily because the individuals honourably enriched thereby are able to benefit many other persons, and because it is to the interest of the state that there should be a large number of wealthy citizens. Furthermore, inasmuch as a part of the prize in question has fallen to the state at no expense to the latter, a very great and special benefit is involved here, in view of the difficulties confronting the public treasury, which is exhausted in consequence of such an arduous war. Over a period of many years, the Romans were compelled to pay tribute in order to meet the needs incessantly arising from various wars, a burden which was tolerated as unavoidable, despite the fact that

---

accordance with Rackham's note, the substance of Cicero's argument is accurately reproduced by Grotius.

a. Letter of Cassius to Cicero, in Cicero, *Letters to his Friends,* XV. xix.

b. Arist., *Rhetoric,* I. vi [6–7] and *ibid.* ix [1–7].

c. *Dig.* I. iv. 2.

d. [Homer, *Iliad,* III. 65.]

e. End of Chap. xiv, *supra,* p. 459.

it was rendered onerous by the very duration of the necessity. After the conquest of Macedonia, however, the sum paid into the public treasury out of the spoils was so great as to exempt the citizens from the obligation of payment, nor were they called upon in later years for any contribution. Thus the wars that followed were conducted at the expense of the conquered peoples. I myself shall not attempt to estimate in advance the [financial] outcome for which the Dutch may hope in the future; but everyone will admit that the treasury benefits when aid is derived [153] to the greatest possible extent from the resources of the enemy rather than from those of the citizens.

The philosophers,[a] in their discussion of that which is beneficial, lay stress upon the admirable doctrine that one must take into account, in this connexion, the institutions, customs, and peculiar needs of each individual state. **Thesis III**

It is certain that in all lands the management of shipping falls within the sphere of supreme governmental power,[b] so that persons who have gone abroad for the purpose of bringing back supplies of grain and various necessities are regarded as absent practically on state business.[c] More specifically, who is so ignorant of the affairs of the Dutch as to be unaware of the fact that the sole source of support, renown, and protection for those affairs lies in navigation and trade? Among all of the Dutch enterprises in the field of trade, moreover, our business in the East Indies easily occupies first place in worth, extent, and resultant benefits.

For when the savagery of the Spaniards had interrupted our commercial activities [in other regions], God Himself by His special favour opened up that part of the world to the Dutch, whose commerce was then on the verge of ruin. It is possible, indeed, that Divine Beneficence was also making provision for the welfare of the East Indians, by willing that they should be encouraged (through the example set by the Dutch) to defy the fearful fame of the Spaniards, and at the same time given an

a. Arist., *Rhetoric,* I. viii [1–2].
b. *Dig.* XIV. i. 1, § 20.
c. *Dig.* L. vi. 5, § 3; add *ibid.* xi. 2.

opportunity to acquaint themselves with the true and unperverted faith. In any case, [it cannot be denied][2] that Providence intervened at an opportune moment in behalf of the Dutch, pointing out the regions where one might seek the very articles already long sought at far higher prices amid perils graver by land than by sea, which the ferocity of the foe would not willingly relinquish even in these new circumstances. For is it not strange and well-nigh incredible that, during ten years of voyaging to and from the Orient, in the face of uncertain and tempestuous weather, over unknown tracts of sea, to unknown ports, with Portuguese snares scattered about in every locality, it never once happened that any fleet returned entirely unladen? No doubt the purpose of this divine intervention was to prevent the consequences that must otherwise be feared, namely: dejection of spirit, and the crushing defeat of an exceedingly salutary enterprise at the very outset, the most difficult stage of any great undertaking.

Accordingly, it is my belief that the members of our States Assembly, the "Fathers of the Fatherland," were guided not merely by human wisdom, but also by what might be called a form of divine favour, when they turned their sagacious attention to this matter and ordered that the various East India companies existing under their jurisdiction (as separate and therefore mutually injurious and destructive entities) should be consolidated into a single body subject to fixed laws. The many privileges thereafter granted to the new Company by the States Assembly constituted more than sufficient testimony to the Assembly's opinion of the great public significance of this coalition. Moreover, when the task of unification had finally been accomplished (for it entailed no inconsiderable amount of trouble), there was no one who doubted that the surest possible foundations of public prosperity had been laid.

As a result of this measure, the East Indians viewed with respect the Dutch enterprises so firmly founded upon a basis of concord; [153′] the Portuguese were thrown into a state of trepidation; and other

2. Apparently some negative phrase was inadvertently omitted from the Latin at this point. Hamaker appends the words *dubitari nequit* (it is impossible to deny) at the close of the sentence.

European nations were so favourably impressed by the good faith and foresight of the Dutch that they chose to entrust their funds to a Company already established and administered in an orderly fashion, in preference to risking the perils of the sea on their own account. In this way, the business organized less than ten years previously with a fund of less than 300,000 florins, had increased its capital at the time of which we are speaking to more than 7,000,000 florins. Furthermore, the rejoicings and general expressions of delight were so lavish as to reveal an assured and prophetic hopefulness that foresaw a vast yearly increase in profits; and, in the light of the evidence already furnished by experience, that confidence was by no means unjustified.

Nevertheless, results of far greater importance remain to be achieved. Only a small number of the East Indian ports have been visited as yet. On every side inviting shores await us: here, the lands bordering upon the Arabian Sea and the Bay of Bengal; and yonder, the shores of China, so rich in new opportunities for profit that, when cargoes of merchandise are conveyed there one after another in rapid succession and distributed to the most remote regions, the prices placed on the earliest cargoes can still be maintained.

We know from what depths of poverty the Spaniards and Portuguese have risen, and to what wealth! In fact, during the earlier history of those peoples, before the days of their voyages across the seas, their rulers could scarcely scrape together enough money to fit out the first vessels; and even to-day, their custom of reckoning currency in terms of tiny copper units persists as a token of former indigence. Nowadays, however, we see that those same peoples, both at home and in their inordinately proud colonies scattered throughout the world, display in their dwellings, household furnishings, attire and retinues of servants, not merely splendour and elegance, but actual luxury, to such an extent that one may truthfully apply to them the comment made in regard to the ancient Tyrians,[a] namely, that their merchants are like princes. Indeed, when the prize from the *Catharine* was recently put up for sale, who did not marvel at the wealth revealed? Who was not struck with amazement? Who did

a. *Jeremiah* [*Isaiah*], xxiii. 8.

not feel that the auction in progress was practically a sale of royal property, rather than of a fortune privately owned?

Let the Dutch learn, even from their enemies, just methods of enriching themselves; and let them learn the proper use of riches from their own ancestors, who were honourably frugal men. Now, the finest fruits of wealth are to be found in the benefits derived from it by the community; and these benefits consist primarily in greater revenue from tributes and imposts. For even though the profitable outcome of voyages abroad emboldened the King of Spain to spread terror throughout the whole world, the success that encouraged a spirit of despotism in so far as he was concerned will serve in the case of the Dutch more justly [154] as a means of protecting life and liberty. Another aspect of the benefits to be received by the public lies in the fact that great numbers of the vast multitude comprising the common people are engaged in commerce or navigation and derive support from no other source. Thus it will come to pass, as Isaiah prophesied,[a] that all merchandise and all profit shall be consecrated to the Lord: it shall not be treasured nor laid up, but shall be for them that dwell before the Lord, that they may eat unto fullness and be clothed sufficiently.[3]

Is it desirable, then, that this commercial activity, which is so beneficial and so necessary, should be abandoned? I do not believe that there is anyone who favours the adoption of such a measure.

But that activity can be continued only if we drive away those persons who will not allow others to be secure in any locality where they themselves enjoy security, who by their words and deeds proclaim that they will not suffer any other European to approach the lands in question for purposes of trade (an attitude based, moreover, not upon some lawful right but merely upon unwillingness to forgo or share profits gained from any source whatsoever), and who leave no means untried for the acquisition of such profits, whether through treacherous guile or in open war-

a. *Isaiah,* xxiii, at end.

3. Grotius's paraphrase of the passage cited from Isaiah is so worded that the translator has thought it advisable here to adopt in part the language of the Douay version of the Bible, although the King James version is followed throughout the present translation in all direct quotations from the Scriptures.

fare. Indeed, what act for the sake of self-enrichment is incredible on the part of men who did not shrink from spreading calumny among the regional officials, or even from bribery, in an attempt to bring about the death of their own neighbours, the Castilians, subjects of the same King and practically compatriots of the calumniators themselves, not so very long after the arrival of the Castilians in China? These designs would have been successfully accomplished, too, but for the fact that among the Chinese (a people otherwise free from scruples, and justifiably hostile toward the Castilians at that time because it was reported that the Spaniards had slain ten thousand Chinese in the Philippines), the rights of suppliants and guests carried more weight than did the obligations of blood relationship among the Iberian peoples. Yet even this Portuguese treachery toward the Castilians should not cause excessive surprise, since everywhere the Portuguese, moved solely by considerations of personal profit and by jealousy, pursue to the death their own fellow countrymen when the latter are not members of the same trading company.[4] Thus it is impossible to protect oneself from persons of the kind described without resorting to vengeful measures. As the Spanish theologian Victoria has rightly observed, even war undertaken solely for defensive purposes cannot be waged without the infliction of vengeance upon the foe. "For the enemy would be emboldened to make a second attack," Victoria argues,[a] "if they were not deterred from injurious acts by the fear of punishment." Therefore, just as public interests call for the maintenance of the East Indian trade, with precisely the same urgency they call for the imposition of restraints upon the Portuguese in whatsoever manner the occasion may permit, including the infliction of ills of every kind, the least of which will be loss of property. [154′]

a. *De Jure Belli,* at beg. [n. 1, proof 5].

4. *Societatis:* this term may refer to various types of association, but it seems probable that Grotius has in mind here the fairly common connotation, "copartnership, or traders' association."

Thesis IV Although the benefits listed above are of a domestic nature, there are others, no less important, whose effects are manifested in foreign lands, in the form of advantages for allies or disadvantages for enemies.

Throughout the whole universe, there is nothing—save for immortal God—more beneficial to man than man himself, so that the most beneficial of all achievements is the winning of human goodwill. Cicero[a] treats of this point in numerous passages, where he follows Panaetius,[b] who devoted his entire discussion on the subject of expediency [i.e. that which is beneficial][5] to this same line of argument. Similarly, Aristotle[c] lists friends and friendships among those things which are most beneficial, saying that friendships are desirable both for their own sake and also because they are productive of many [beneficial] results, wherefore he holds that φιλεταιρία, "love of friends," is nobler than φιλοχρηματία, "love of money."

Thesis V

On the other hand, it also happens at times that man is exceedingly injurious to man, as is indicated in the well-known lines:

> What is the source of gravest grief to men?
> 'Tis nothing more nor less than other men;

whence it follows, by the very nature of mutually opposed factors, that what is worst for our enemies is best for us, just as, by a reverse process of reasoning, we perceive that what is pleasing to our enemies is injurious to us. Such is the implication contained in the plea:[d]

a. [*On Duties, passim.*]

b. [*Treatise on Duty.*]

c. *Rhetoric,* I. vi [I. vii. 18].

d. [Virgil, *Aeneid,* II. 105.]

5. *De Vtili,* "concerning that which is Expedient," or "Useful," or "Beneficial." For the sake of consistency, the term "beneficial" is kept throughout the translation of this chapter wherever Grotius employs *utilis* in presenting his own argument. Nevertheless, no single English term is a satisfactory equivalent for all connotations of *utilis,* and it is not always feasible to adhere to such a rigid rule of consistency in translating Grotius's references to the works of other authors.

It should also be noted that the original Greek title of Panaetius' work, *περὶ τοῦ καθήκοντος* (literally: "Concerning Those Things Which Are Meet," or "Fitting," or "Proper"), is usually rendered in English as *Treatise on Duties.*

> This would the Ithacan desire; and this
> Would Atreus' sons pay dearly to achieve.[6]

Therefore, those authors who deal with the question of what is beneficial, quite correctly attribute outstanding importance to this particular benefit, [i.e. injury to enemies,] also.

To return to our first point, however, no one is ignorant of the great force inherent in friendship; and it is because of this force that alliances not only with neighbours but even with distant communities are beneficial for persons engaged in warfare, just as they are necessary for traders. Mithridates is commended[a] because he sent envoys from the Albans all the way to Spain, to Sertorius and the generals against whom the Romans were warring at that time. For Mithridates knew the quality of the enemy with whom he had to deal: that is to say, he knew that the Romans were in possession of a large part of the world, and that they were a strong and wealthy nation. Consequently, he had arranged matters in such a way that this nation would be fighting for its supremacy while torn by a twofold struggle, in a war waged on land and sea in two entirely different and widely separated regions, against two [hostile] forces[7] acting in concert within each region.

It is not my intention either to magnify or to belittle the strength of the Iberian peoples. This I do know: that they rule over a domain more extensive than that of the Romans in the days of Mithridates, and perhaps even more extensive than any domain of our own or any other age. Furthermore, I know that the very foundations of that Iberian power lie, not in the Low Countries nor in Spain, but in transoceanic regions from which the said peoples derive their wealth and the means to [155]

a. Cicero, *On the Manilian Law* [iv. 9].

6. From the speech of Sinon, who persuaded his Trojan captors that vengeance executed upon him would be injurious to their own cause since it would be pleasing to their enemies, Ulysses (the Ithacan) and the brothers Agamemnon and Menelaus (the sons of Atreus).

7. *Binis copiis* [*hostium*]. Owing to the omission of *hostium* (hostile), Grotius's phrase is rather ambiguous, and could be translated "with twofold forces [of their own]," were it not for the fact that Cicero, in the passage cited, specifically refers to "hostile forces."

maintain their public largess and their wars. But I also know that they have gained for themselves in those distant lands as much hatred as power, and that the Dutch ought to make use of that hatred if they wish to see the war ended. The North must unite with the farthest Orient, in order that the despotism which has spread to every quarter of the world may be overthrown.

The Dutch should have sought the goodwill of the East Indian kings and peoples, long ago. But, lo and behold! the goodwill of the Dutch themselves is now voluntarily sought. For who among our chief officials has not been implored by the East Indians to lend succour and assistance against the Portuguese? What of the supplications made by the King of Ternate and by the state of Amboyna? What of the letters received from the King of Johore? Moreover, the nobles of Achin have even presented themselves in person at the palace of The Hague. Occurrences like the one regarded as an outstanding feature of the good fortune enjoyed by Augustus[a] (that is to say, the visit paid him by East Indian envoys, who came bearing precious gifts but boasting only of the length of their voyage, although the very colour of their skins showed plainly enough that they hailed from another clime), or like the event that shed special lustre on Claudius' reign[b] (his reception of an embassy from Taprobane [Ceylon]),[8] have become so ordinary among the Dutch that wonder has ceased with the cessation of novelty. And what is it that these envoys seek and entreat, other than attack against the Portuguese by a general combination of forces? So great is their confidence in our good faith, that they actually beg the Dutch to erect strongholds upon East Indian soil! They urge that the straits of Malacca and Sunda should be kept [under the control of the Dutch]. Some of them offer supplies[9] to aid

a. Florus [*Epitome of Roman History,* II. xxxiv].

b. Pliny, *Nat. Hist.* VI. xxii [VI. xxiv. 84].

8. *Taprobane,* the name employed by Grotius himself to designate Sumatra, but generally interpreted as referring to Ceylon in the passage cited here from Pliny. For the significance of *Taprobane* in other passages of the *Commentary,* see notes on pp. 14, 263, 307–8, and 335, *supra.* Cf. also, note 10, p. 473.

9. *Commeatus,* which could also be translated as "free passage," "convoys," or "transportation." Damsté's Dutch translation, which should carry special weight in passages referring to Dutch history, has *proviand* ("provisions," "supplies").

us in blockading Malacca, the very seat of slavery, and point out the ways by which this undertaking may be accomplished.

Another and more significant feature of the situation is the fact that friendship with the Dutch acts as a conciliatory force among the East Indians themselves. Already, treaties are being concluded between Sumatra and the island of Ceylon,[10] while the Kings of Kandy and Achin swear common enmity against the Portuguese. For the sake of the Hollanders, that same King of Achin is renouncing his ancient grudge against the ruler of Johore, and all rivalry between the two sovereigns is confined to one point alone, namely: which of them shall excel in the eyes of the Dutch. Many other kings, too, would have joined our cause openly long ago, if the Dutch had not seemed somewhat slack in their attitude toward the war against the Portuguese.

What, then, is the conclusion to be drawn? Should this favourable disposition be disdained? Quite aside from the fact that such indifference would be contrary to the public interest, it has been morally impossible to adopt an indifferent attitude, from the time when the Portuguese first besieged the cities of the East Indians, laid waste their fields and set aflame their rural districts, in retaliation for the friendship between [155′] the natives and the Dutch. For if it is in every sense expedient that alliances of this kind should be not merely encouraged to persist but also stimulated and expanded (and certainly there is no other alternative to the destruction of our trade itself), what pledge, what bond of good faith shall we offer to the foreign nations whose alliance we seek? Surely we must offer the sole pledge that they covet: intrepid attacks against the Portuguese (whose enemies the Dutch avow themselves to be) and treatment of the Portuguese as enemies. For even as it is just and honourable to take vengeance upon that people in accordance with their deserts, so also it is perilous to spare them; and the peril is particularly grave wher-

10. *Celonem:* apparently Grotius always uses some form of this name when he intends to refer to Ceylon. *Taprobanem,* in the same sentence, obviously refers not to Ceylon but to Sumatra, as in every other instance throughout the *Commentary* where Grotius is neither quoting from nor paraphrasing some other author. See note 8, *supra,* and other notes therein cited.

ever the suspicious disposition of the East Indians must be taken into account.

I shall describe a recent episode in support of this assertion. The King of Kandy (a country which is situated on the island of Ceylon) evinced so great an interest in the affairs of the Dutch at the time of Spilberg's arrival from Zeeland, that for whole days this ruler devoted all of his inquiries exclusively to the history of our famous war,

> About *Priam* and *Hector,* eagerly
> Seeking to learn many things. . . .[a]

Nor was he ever wearied of contemplating the likeness of Maurice, most invincible of princes, and the painting of the Battle of Nieuwpoort. Already the King himself, the Queen, and their children, had begun to learn words from our language in order that the Kingdom of Kandy might be said to have become a part of Holland. The King also declared that he wished to send his eldest child (when the latter should have reached maturity) to Prince Maurice, so that the youth might be instructed in military matters under so great a general. The same ruler entreated the Dutch to select a site wherever they pleased within his domain for the construction of a fortress, adding that he himself, aided by his wife and son and daughter, would carry the stones to that spot rather than abandon a project so dear to his own heart. Shortly afterwards, he received a visit from Sibold de Waert (second in command of the fleet that was under Wijbrandt Warwijck), and begged de Waert to grant him aid in storming the fortress of Colombo, located on the border of his kingdom and held at that time by the Portuguese. The King earnestly requested that he himself might make the assault, but asked de Waert to stand by with the ships, warding off the forces expected from Goa for the relief of the Portuguese. He offered various rewards for such assistance, and in this connexion expressed his willingness to entrust to a Dutch garrison the sites that were to be taken from the enemy. As it happened, Sibold set out from Ceylon for Achin with the purpose of acquiring allies, and captured four Portuguese vessels in the course [156] of that same voyage. Now, the King had entreated Sibold in person,

a. [Virgil, *Aeneid,* I. 750.]

and had implored him by letter after the Dutchman's departure, in the name of God, by the valour of Prince Maurice, and for the sake of their own friendship, to deliver any Portuguese whom he might seize into the hands of the ruler of Kandy himself. De Waert, however, apparently expecting no difficulty in excusing himself for his clemency, straightway freed his captives; while the King, never doubting that they would be handed over to him by de Waert, went all the way to Batticaloa (where the Dutch ships had by then arrived), as an act of courtesy, although he had promised only to come as far as the city of Vintanum to meet the Dutch commander. At Batticaloa, a deplorable event occurred, as follows: the King, amazed that men who had been captured after culpable conduct should enjoy immunity while his own request was held in contempt, ordered the execution of Sibold (who was answering him in an argumentative and rather insolent manner) together with approximately fifty other persons. In this fashion he avenged himself for the very fact that he had been left unavenged.

Moreover, that same leniency (if leniency is indeed the proper term) has given rise to mockery on the part of our enemies, suspicion on the part of our allies, and grave injury to our own people. Consequently, if the East Indian nations, which wage war more ferociously than the Europeans, can hardly be brought to accept the excuse that it is our custom to preserve our enemies even when we are able to destroy them, and if the said nations are now about to see the Portuguese ships (certainly a prize that is ready and waiting to be taken) allowed to slip from the hands of the Dutch, what can they be expected to believe, save that treachery is secretly at work, and that the Portuguese and the Dutch are working in collusion? It is necessary, therefore, to extend to them this guaranty of good faith, and to give them this cause of rejoicing in return for their friendship, this solace in compensation for the disasters suffered, namely: an opportunity for them to see the despoliation of those men who have been the despoilers of the whole world.

Let us consider next the benefits that we ourselves derive from the ills that befall our enemies.

In the Portuguese, the Dutch have just such a foe as Tacitus[a] describes

a. [*The Histories,* I. lxviii.]

in another connexion: one who is timorous when confronted by adverse circumstances, but mindful of neither divine nor human law when circumstances are propitious. Accordingly, a supremely important benefit lies in the fact that henceforth the Portuguese will tremble at the approach of the Dutch, and shaken by their earlier loss will flee from the very sight of our valiant men, nor will they dare to match their own ships, despite the considerable superiority of the latter in number and size, against the ships of the Hollanders. For the enemy will know that these are the vessels by means of which they have so often been despoiled. Consequently, since they will be afraid to approach any spot where the Dutch ships are anchored, the Dutch themselves will be not only more safe from actual danger, but also more free from anxiety. As a [156′] matter of fact, this result has already been achieved in a partial degree; for the East Indian kings declare that the Portuguese tremble and grow exceedingly pale at the sight and even at the mere mention of a Dutchman. Again, what shall we infer from the fact that the Portuguese obeyed the order to transfer the cargo of the captured ships to the Dutch ships with their own hands? Or from the further fact that already some persons have paid the Dutch for the privilege of navigating in safety? Similarly, when our enemies realize how easy it is for the Hollanders to acquire a vast horde of captives, they will be more hesitant in venting their rage upon the captives whom they in turn may have chanced to seize; and fear of retaliation will compel them to adopt the very course of conduct that they refused to follow when encouraged by kindly deeds to do so.

Moreover, in future, either they will provide us perforce with similar spoils, an alternative which obviously would result in tremendous benefits both for our state and for our private citizens, or else they will be obliged to turn from their attacks upon others to defence of themselves, keeping innumerable ships for their own protection in East Indian waters, strengthening their colonies with fortifications, and (most troublesome task of all!) maintaining a suspicious vigil over all things at one and the same time. The numerous and heavy expenses thus to be incurred will drain away not only all the private profits of the Portuguese, but also the whole of the East Indian revenue accruing to their state itself, that unwavering enemy of Dutch liberty. One can readily perceive how extremely profitable both of these consequences will be for our own state. For everyone knows that money constitutes the sinews of war and that, just as it is of the greatest importance [in war] to supply oneself with money, so the precaution of next greatest importance is to prevent the foe from being supplied with it. Accordingly, if all the produce and revenue from Philip's East Indian possessions can be encumbered with a burden of expense equal to that already laid upon certain European possessions of his, it must surely follow that the future management of the war will prove much easier for us. For no one can doubt that the aid received from Spain through Italian transactions is the chief means of prolonging that war, inasmuch as the Dutch would long since have brought the affair to a conclusion if their resources had been matched solely against the revenue derived from another part of the Low Countries. If, then, the Spanish revenues fail—and with them, the credit necessary in order to procure additional funds—what outcome is to be expected other than a military insurrection leading to a great revolution?

For it is clear to those who read the history of the events in question, that practically everything which has hitherto brought good fortune and prosperity to the Dutch, has had its cause and origin in the enemy's [157] need. The Peace of Ghent, and the union of almost the whole of the Low Countries against the name of Spain, restored our all but shattered fortunes to a state of complete well-being through the civil discord which arose among our opponents and which was the result, moreover, of the depleted condition of their treasury. What is the explanation of the fact that the Dutch, after being held in subjection for so long by the Duke of Parma, have nevertheless been victorious in their turn throughout an equal period of years under the valiant command of a magnificent leader, unless that explanation lies in the strain placed upon enemy resources (a strain so severe that their restoration has scarcely yet become possible) by the great fleet sent against Britain[11] and the crushing expenses of the war with France? It was this depletion of resources that gave rise to the frequent disturbances along the French borders, to the Italian insurrection at Sichem and to mutual slaughter among our en-

11. The famous Armada of 1588.

emies; from this starting-point sprang the defection of Saint-André, the series of fresh disturbances that left Flanders open to attack, and the opportunity to wage a famous battle;[12] this was the incentive for the rebellion of Hoogstraeten, during which the fields of the Dutch were laid waste by their own orders.

As for present events, precisely because our opponents are beginning to entertain greater hopes and are seeking even to grasp possession of those seas to which the Dutch have a special right, we should strive all the more zealously to ensure their failure in the very midst of that attempt by heaping additional expenses upon those which they have already incurred. In this connexion, it is of the utmost importance that we cause as much trouble as possible for the Iberian peoples throughout the East Indies, so that they may be thrown into confusion again and again by new defeats and losses. Such a course of action is particularly advisable in view of the fact that the expenditures which it will involve for our own side, will lay no burden upon our state but will be met instead by private citizens. Besides, who knows but that success in the East Indies might presently give us confidence to undertake some bold enterprise in the American sphere? And in such an event, surely we could regard that [Iberian] domain [in the New World], built upon the spoils of all nations, as a legitimate object of despoliation by any nation!

Thesis VI Now, if it is true (as the authorities on these matters maintain)[a] that ease of execution is a point to be borne in mind when one is estimating the benefits attached to a given project, then let the foe fit out fleets as costly as he may please, till the din of prodigious preparations resounds on all sides! If the Dutch are not entirely mistaken about that foe and about themselves, there is no danger, just as truly as no danger to the Romans was to be found in the army of King Antiochus, which (as we know) was wittily ridiculed by Hannibal. For when the King boastfully pointed

a. Arist., *Rhetoric,* I. vi [.26].

12. Probably another reference to the "Battle of the Dunes," fought in July 1600, at Nieuwpoort, a town of West Flanders. This battle resulted in a great victory for Maurice of Nassau over the Spanish forces.

out to Hannibal the vast numbers of armed men glittering with gold and silver insignia, the chariots equipped with scythes, the canopied elephants, the cavalry with its brightly shining reins, caparisons, [157′] collars and other trappings, and when he inquired whether or not the Carthaginian thought that all these things would be enough for the Romans, Hannibal (whose attention was fixed exclusively upon the weakness of the unwarlike men) declared that the things in question would indeed suffice for the Romans even if the latter were assumed to be the greediest of peoples, thus phrasing his reply as if he had been asked about spoils lying ready for seizure when in reality he had been questioned about comparative strength. We shall borrow the thought expressed by the Carthaginian general, with certain changes in wording, as follows: whatever may be the exact nature of the preparations that the Portuguese are making throughout India—preparations magnificent to behold and costly in price—these will be enough for the Dutch, even if the latter, after suffering tremendous losses, are assumed to be not unjustly desirous of proportionate compensation. As Antisthenes[a] neatly observed, long ago: *ὅ τι δεῖ τοῖς πολεμίοις εὔχεσθαι τ' ἀγαθὰ παρεῖναι χωρὶς ἀνδρείας· γίνεται οὕτως οὐ τῶν ἐχόντων, ἀλλὰ τῶν κρατούντων*; "We ought to wish that our enemies may have goods and no valour; for in such circumstances the goods become the property, not of the persons who have them [at the moment], but of those who [later] win them." Surely no one will disagree with this opinion, after judicious consideration.

In proportion as the Dutch vessels are smaller, so also they are more agile, being easily moved to meet every martial or maritime emergency and so constructed that the missiles discharged from hostile vessels fly over them harmlessly. The massive, slow-moving hulks belonging to the Portuguese, fashioned not for war but for carrying cargo, open on all sides to the enemy's fire, inadequate for strife against the winds, are in general fitted to be conquered rather than to conquer. The Dutch people—reared amid their own waters beneath a frosty, wind-swept sky, under the light of northern stars, and in an amazing number of cases accustomed even from childhood to spending more time upon the ocean

a. In Stobaeus, *Florilegium,* LII [LIV. 41].

than on land—are just as familiar with the sea as they are with the soil. They endure cold extremely well; they display the utmost patience in going without food; they are thoroughly accustomed to the hardships necessarily attendant upon extended journeys such as [the voyages to the Indies], and they have profited by the long-drawn war at home, both in boldness and in martial skill. But the weak bodies of the Portuguese, bodies enervated by warmth and accustomed to luxury, are not strong enough to endure sea-sickness or the tossing of the waves. Furthermore, the Portuguese are essentially effeminate. They are wasted with debauchery, unskilled in the use of arms, and burdened in the midst of their voyages by throngs of ailing persons who hinder the activities even of the men in good health. In short, they are unfit for war and may be described (in the well-known phrase) as "spoil for the Mysians."[13]

We find that the Dutch sailors have in consequence acquired so much self-confidence as to reject the possibility that in the event of a [158] struggle, at any time whatsoever, they themselves might be too few or the Portuguese sufficiently numerous. On many occasions, generals of exceptional sagacity, basing their opinion on the faces and bearing of their men, and observing the eagerness of the latter prior to battle, have declared that beyond any doubt victory was already theirs. In the judgement of those generals, such evidence was the best of omens and by far the surest means of prognostication. Thus the Dutch, too, should augur for themselves no slight success when they observe the courageous spirit of their men. For it is neither through recklessness nor without very good cause that these Dutchmen place confidence in their own valour and good fortune, since they have at hand the most incontrovertible proofs on this point, and pledges (so to speak) of victory.

Over a very long period of time, [to mention one proof of Spanish and Portuguese weakness,] the French[a] succeeded in disturbing [Span-

a. Joh. Metal [or Matal] in Pref. to Osorio [*History of Emmanuel,* p. 20].

13. I.e., capable of being despoiled by the weakest of nations. The inhabitants of Mysia (an ancient geographical division of Asia Minor) were held in such contempt for their effeminacy that the Greeks frequently expressed scorn for a given person by saying, "He's the lowest of the Mysians." (Cf. Cicero, *Pro Flacco,* xxvii. 65.)

ish] commerce with America to such an extent that there were few Spaniards of rank who had not fallen into French hands at one time or another; and on some of these occasions, so much spoil was taken by the victors that even every cabin-boy brought back eight hundred ducats. The French were also successful in despoiling all the islands of the New World and the American Continent itself. On the other hand, when the Spaniards in a single instance captured a French vessel—not by Spanish valour but through the timidity of the opposing commander—the event seemed to them so unusual that they celebrated the triumph in a manner suggesting that France herself rather than a French ship had been completely conquered. This situation was the result, however, not of any great superiority in maritime skill on the part of the French, but of that avarice which had induced the Spaniards to load their ships with merchandise and passengers rather than with arms of any kind. The English, too, after circumnavigating the entire globe, have left practically no part of the Spanish dominions intact. No one ever succeeded to any possession with greater impunity [than that enjoyed by the English in this matter].

What, then, may not be hoped for in regard to the Dutch, those true sons of the sea? Without wishing to make invidious comparisons, we may say that the Dutch have never been hard pressed on any field of battle where the conditions were equal, nor in any open naval combat. I shall not illustrate my point by turning to the earlier pages of our history, although glorious examples could be drawn from the records of our conflicts with the French, the Germans, and the English. Let us concentrate all our attention upon the Iberian foe—who has enjoyed some support, moreover, from the Low Countries—and let us briefly review the period extending from the very beginning of the war to the present joyful moment.

We behold the chains of the captive Bossu; the Portuguese wealth that had been seized even at that early date by the people of Zeeland; the Duke of Medinaceli fleeing in a skiff, and de Hont, dripping with Spanish blood. Furthermore, is it possible that there will ever be a more imposing fleet than the one sent forth against Britain and against the Dutch in that terrible year [of 1588]? And are not the East Indian seas much narrower in their straits and much more uncertain in their shallows than even this Gallic sea [i.e. the English Channel]? For the former are said to contain, in addition to their numerous shoals and sand-banks seventy thousand islands, against which the heavier enemy vessels will certainly be dashed. Have we forgotten the fleet near Cádiz, which was driven upon the shore and given to the flames by the Dutch and English forces? Or the ships of Spínola, so fatal to their master? Again, what braver or more illustrious leader will be granted to the enemy than Andrés Hurtado de Mendoza? Yet he was vanquished near Bantam and put to flight, although no contest could be more unequal than the one between those six comparatively small ships [on the Dutch side] and the opposing vessels, more than thirty in number, which were so [158′] large and so powerful. Since the date of Hurtado's defeat, how many Portuguese vessels have been captured, sunk, or burned? Leaving aside all the rest, let us speak only of the largest ships. In addition to the one shared as prize between Spilberg and the English, three caracks have already fallen into our hands; and these caracks, while I call them ships, might well be regarded as fortresses, or even as towns, peopled by more than seven hundred men. One of the three, taken by Cornelis Sebastiaansz near the island of Saint Helena, fell to the lot of the Zeelanders. Another is the very ship brought in by Heemskerck. Now a third carack has been captured and despoiled near Macao by the ships of Warwijck. But certain events that were even much more notable have occurred, namely: the conquest of an entire fleet; the liberation of Johore, and the release of a very friendly king from a state of siege. For Jacob Pietersz—who was taking two vessels from the above-mentioned fleet of Warwijck together with a cutter, to Patani, in the hope of enhancing the great goodwill already felt toward the Dutch by the Queen of that region—perceived in the course of this same voyage that a river belonging to the Kingdom of Johore was held by the Portuguese. The latter, with two galleons in addition to more than twenty-five brigantines and other ships of war, had filled the whole vicinity with deadly terror. Pietersz, who felt that it would not be at all right to desert an allied prince threatened by such danger, engaged in a battle that continued until late in the day, when the enemy was routed and took to the high seas. It would be a long story if we were to tell how the king himself, coming in person to the victorious ships in order to express his gratitude, extolled the good faith of his allies, which had just been proven to him anew. But not even these achievements satisfied the Dutch. On the contrary, the enemy was sought out once more and, after a long struggle, both galleons were so badly damaged that the Portuguese barely escaped by bending to their oars.

So numerous and so glorious were the victories won over the Portuguese! And are there still persons who believe that the Portuguese should be feared? By no means! Press on, press on, O nation of seafarers! Imagine that it was not to Augustus at Actium but to you yourselves that these famous words of the Oracle[a] were addressed:

> Let it not fright thee that a hundred oars
> Are plied to row each vessel of the *fleet:*
> *Unwilling* is *the sea* those vessels sail.
> Nor let it fright thee that the threat'ning prows
> Are armed with monstrous rocks, for you will find
> These are but hollow beams and painted threats.
> A soldier's strength is measured by his *cause:*
> Unless that cause be just, his shame will strike
> The weapons from the soldier's very hands. [159]

The last two lines are undeniably true, and especially pertinent to the present discussion. The Dutch sailor knows that he is fighting in defence of the law of nations while his foes are fighting against the fellowship of mankind; he knows that they fight to establish despotism, but that he himself is defending his own liberty and the liberty of others; he knows that the enemy are motivated by an inborn lust for evildoing, whereas the Dutch have been provoked repeatedly and over a long period by calumny, cruelty, and perfidy. The greatest of the Greek orators[b] spoke thus: *ὑπὲρ μὲν ὧν ἂν ἐλαττῶνται μέχρι δυνατοῦ πάντες πολεμοῦσιν· περὶ δὲ τοῦ πλεονεκτεῖν οὐχ οὕτως*. "All persons fight to the fin-

a. Propertius, *Elegies,* IV. vi [47 ff.].
b. [Demosthenes, *For the Liberty of the Rhodians,* 11, p. 193.]

ish and with all their might in a defensive action opposing the infliction of injury; but this is not the case when the motive is greed for another's property." Alexander the Great, too, expressed himself in a manner befitting his rank as commander-in-chief, when he said:[a] *τὸ μὲν ἄρχειν ἀδίκων ἔργων οὐκ ἀγνώμονα ἔχει τὴν πρόκλησιν, τὸ δὲ τοὺς ὀχλοῦντας ἀποσείεσθαι, ἔκ τε τῆς ἀγαθῆς συνειδήσεως ἔχει τὸ θαρράλεον, καὶ ἐκ τοῦ μὴ ἀδικεῖν ἀλλ' ἀμύνασθαι ὑπάρχει τὸ εὔελπι.* "He who takes the initiative in inflicting injury certainly gives provocation of the most odious kind; but when one is repelling aggressors, the purpose of the struggle is not injury but self-defence, and therefore (since a clear conscience is attended by self-confidence) the highest hopes are entertained."

The States Assembly of Holland, in its Decree [of September 1, 1604],[14] summarizes in more concise form the very observations above set forth on the subject of benefits. This Decree makes it clear that, by the grace of God, navigation and trade have been protected and expanded in the course of our struggle with the Portuguese,[b] friendly kingdoms and cities have been liberated, and outstanding victories and advantages have been won from the enemy (from whom we hope to win still greater gains), while the same document also shows clearly that every one of these advantages is heavily fraught with injury and severe loss for the enemy, but with honour, benefit, and fair repute for the United Provinces of the Low Countries and for the citizens thereof, all without any expense to the state.

Part II of Chapter XV

Now, just as the state profits quite as much as the merchants from damage done in battle to the Portuguese foe and from the despoliation of that foe, even so it is expedient for the state no less than for the merchants that the latter should become the owners of the prize in question. For, in view of the fact that the public treasury is exhausted by the multiple costs of an exceedingly long and arduous war, and particularly by the heavy naval costs, no development could be more opportune than the

a. [Plutarch, *Alexander.*]

b. Joh. Metal [or Matal] in Pref. to Osorio [*History of Emmanuel, passim*].

14. Cf. the reference to this Decree on p. 458, *supra.*

destruction of the enemy's strength at private expense. But the wise man does not incur expense unless the attendant risk is cancelled by the prospect of a fair profit. Therefore, the members of the States Assembly are making a very proper move when they not only favour the East Indian trade in all other respects but also decide that it is just, and beneficial to the state, to assign the things captured at the expense and risk of the East India Company to the members of that Company. Accordingly, in conformity with the principle expressed (for example) in Propertius'[a] verse, and furthermore implicit in natural reason itself,

> Be the spoil theirs, who won it by their toil! [159′]

We conclude, then, that he who disdains a benefit so estimable is excessively prodigal in his attitude toward opportunity and good fortune. For I should almost be justified in characterizing as a mark of senseless obstinacy the failure to seize straightway with grateful hands (so to speak) whatever becomes our own by the law of war and hence by the law of nations, as well as by grant of the States Assembly, or highest magistracy. Thus we might reasonably suppose, either that no one would persevere in a determination to resist and even fling away possession on these terms, or else, assuming the existence of persons who would do so, that such persons must be men whose example no one rightly disposed toward God and country could wish to follow. Yet there actually are Dutchmen so excessively meek that they listen patiently to sentiments befitting the foe but uttered by fellow citizens. It is indeed regrettable that [enemy] impunity has developed to a point where some Dutchmen dare to proclaim that everything is permissible for the Portuguese and nothing, for themselves! I can wish for such individuals no greater ill than that they may fall into the hands of the very foe whom they so warmly favour, though without impairment of our own sovereignty or danger to our state.

But let their idle talk—or rather, their malevolent disparagement of the public cause—be left to the punishment provided by the laws and

a. *Elegies,* III. iii [III. iv. 21].

to the diligence of the magistrates. As far as we are concerned, it is enough that we have offered enlightenment to those who are in error.

Thus, if there is any logical approach or citation of authorities capable of influencing the persons who may have rejected the profits in question on the ground that otherwise they could not have felt themselves to be complying with the demands of justice and conscience, it is possible that these persons have been rendered wiser by the arguments and corroborative examples adduced in the earlier portion of the present treatise. I myself believe that the observations already made should suffice to convince all but the very obstinate that the aforesaid profits are honourable in the highest degree.

Again, as for those critics (if such there be) who are chiefly interested in the question of benefits, let us see what objection they can offer to the acquisition of the prize. Certainly I do not think that anyone will refer in the present connexion to the well-known saying that, "Ill-gotten gains are dissipated in like fashion, and things basely acquired are not handed down to posterity." For we ourselves willingly concur in this sentiment. In fact, we go still further and deny that anything inconsistent with justice and honour can be beneficial, even if it be granted that unjust possessions might possibly enjoy the protection of fortune and the authoritative sanction derived from the passage of long periods of time. But it has already been proved by the most incontrovertible arguments that the situation under discussion is the exact opposite of that described in the saying above quoted, so that any objection whatsoever based on such grounds necessarily collapses through the removal (so to [160] speak) of its fundamental assumption. For it is, on the contrary, undeniably true that there are almost no possessions whose status dates back further than the ownership of things acquired through war, and it is equally true that the security of almost any nation depends (as Cicero indicates in his treatise *On Duties*)[a] upon possessions of this kind.

Accordingly, in the works of various writers, we frequently come across statements to the effect that whatever has been taken from enemies by armed force is justly possessed, and that such possessions are trans-

a. I [vii. 21].

mitted to one's successors by a just title and with just cause. This very point was brought out, moreover, in the reply given by the Romans to the Auruncans with reference to the territory of the Ecetrans. The Volscians, too, were told by the Romans that such martial acquisitions were no less one's own property than acquisitions obtained as gifts. Possibly these assertions were inspired by the fact that both of the parties who subject themselves to the hazards of war would seem to have entered into a species of contract which provides that captured goods shall be ceded to the captors, so that no injustice will be involved if a would-be conqueror, upon finding himself defeated instead, undergoes the [160 a] fate of the conquered. It will be worth our while to quote the exact words written by Dionysius of Halicarnassus in this connexion. In Dionysius'[a] account of the speech made by Titus Larcius, the following passage is included:

> ὅτι Ῥωμαῖοι καλλίστας ὑπολαμβάνομεν κτήσεις εἶναι καὶ δικαιοτάτας, ἃς κατάσχωμεν πολεμῷ λαβόντες, καὶ νόμῳ, καὶ οὐκ ἄν ὑπομείναιμεν μωρίᾳ τὴν ἀρετὴν ἀφανίσαι, παραδόντες αὐτὰ τοῖς ἀπολωλεκόσι· κοινωνητέον τε πᾶσι καὶ τοῖς ἐκ τούτων γενομένοις καταλιπεῖν ἀγωνιοῦμεθα. νῦν δὲ ὑπαρχόντων ἤδη στερησόμεθα, καὶ ἑαυτοὺς ὅσα πολεμίους βλάψομεν.
>
> *We Romans believe that those possessions are most honourable and most just which we have acquired by capture in accordance with the law of war, and we certainly cannot be persuaded to return the said possessions to the persons who once lost them, thus destroying with fatuous complaisance the monuments to our own valour. Since it is our belief, then, that where this public wealth is concerned we should strive to transmit a vast quantity of such possessions to our descendants, shall we allow ourselves to be despoiled of the things which we have already acquired, and shall we decree against ourselves the very measures that are wont to be decreed against enemies?*

Again, in the reply of the Roman senators to the Volscians, we find this declaration:[b]

a. VI [xxxvi].
b. [*Ibid.*] VIII [x].

ἡμεῖς δὲ κρατίστας ἡγούμεθα κτήσεις ἃς ἂν πολεμῷ κρατήσαντες λάβωμεν· οὔτε πρῶτοι καταστησάμενοι νόμον τόνδε, οὔτε αὐτὸν ἀνθρώπων ἡγούμενοι εἶναι μᾶλλον ἢ οὐχὶ θεῶν· ἅπαντάς τε [160′a] καὶ Ἕλληνας καὶ βαρβάρους εἰδότες αὐτῷ χρωμένους, οὐκ ἄν ἐνδοίημεν ὑμῖν μαλακὸν οὐδὲν, οὐδ' ἂν ἀποσταίημεν ἔτι τῶν δορυκτήτων. πολλὴ γὰρ ἂν εἴη κακότης εἴ τις ἃ μετὰ ἀρετῆς καὶ ἀνδρείας ἐκτήσατο, ταῦτα ὑπὸ δειλίας τε καὶ μωρίας ἀφαιρεθείη.

We, on the other hand, regard that which has been acquired by capture from the enemy as the most honourable kind of possession. Furthermore, since we ourselves are not the first to establish this criterion but are merely complying with it as with a law of divine rather than human origin, one confirmed by the usage of all nations, Greek and barbarian alike, we shall not be moved by cowardice to restore anything to you, nor shall we renounce the possessions acquired in warfare. For the loss, through ignorance or fear, of acquisitions made through valour and fortitude would be shameful in the extreme.

In the reply of the Samnites, too,[a] these words appear: πολέμῳ κρατησάντων ἡμῶν, ὅπερ ἐστὶ νόμος κτήσεως δικαιότατος; ". . . since we have obtained possession by force of arms, a fact which constitutes the most just title to possession." Yet again, the oration of Fabricius[b] includes the following statement: ἐκείνῃ μὲν γε κτήσει, καὶ τὸ μεθ' ἡδονῆς ποιεῖσθαι τὰς ἀπολαύσεις, πρὸς τὸ καλῶς καὶ δικαίως πόσον ἦν; "For that type of acquisition" (Fabricius is referring to acquisition through war) "was characterized not only by justice and honour, but also by the exceedingly great pleasure derived therefrom." [160]

But even if the possession of the prize in question is not in itself a matter open to doubt, we must still deal with the fears regarding some *ex post facto* development such as might occur, for example, if the case should subsequently be brought into court. We must picture the judge of that hypothetical trial, however, as being either a Spanish subject or a person of non-Spanish nationality.

Anyone who believes it possible for the Dutch ever to find themselves

a. In Frag. [Dion. of Hal., *Selections on Embassies,* p. 10.]
b. *Ibid.* [, p. 18].

under the obligation of pleading their cause even for past actions before a Spanish court, must indeed entertain the most pessimistic expectations regarding our native land. But if such a situation could and did arise—perish the ill-omened thought!—not only this particular prize but every Dutchman, too, together with all his goods, would be utterly lost. For truly,

> Should some *new judge* pass sentence on the war,
> Not one of you will find his hands unstained.[a]

Perhaps there are some who fear that as a result of such a development their own property may be held back by the enemy, in the event that commercial relations with the latter are renewed but the war continues. As if, forsooth, the foe had not adopted this very device prior to the events under discussion; or as if he needed a fresh pretext for continuing to do so! Besides, it is not sufficiently clear to me why anyone who finds the East Indian trade so lucrative and for whom it shows a daily increase in profits, should prefer that other field of trade, which is exposed to so many perils and to the malice of the enemy. In short, either we should abandon that [trade with the enemy] altogether, or else we should proceed with our activities in it only after Spain has become unable to do without Dutch merchandise. Moreover, if the foe nevertheless does revert to his former perfidious ways, the suit in question will be brought against the merchants, not[15] on the ground that they have possession of the aforementioned prize (for in those [hostile] lands no one can know who has received a share of the prize and who, on the contrary, has refused to receive any), but rather on the ground that the said [160′] merchants have engaged in trade with the East Indian peoples in defiance

a. Lucan [*The Civil War*], VII [263].

15. The Latin text at this point (line 3 from bottom of collotype p. 160) is a little confused because an alteration introduced here by Grotius was not completely carried out. The word *ex* obviously should have been deleted when *eo* was deleted, and the immediately preceding *non* has been left rather far from the phrase which it now modifies. In the English translation, the sentence is treated as if Grotius's correction had been completed; that is to say, *ex* is not translated, and the negative force of *non* is transferred to the following *quod*-clause.

of the edict issued by the King of the Spanish realms. For are we not aware of the fact that the Spanish Government has proscribed the men at the head of this commercial venture? Nor had these men yet seized the carack, at the time of their proscription. Yet the practice of trade with the East Indians was so heinous a crime in the eyes of the Spanish King, that he devised a substitute as dark and ignominious as possible for the punishment which he could not inflict upon the persons of the individuals involved. Furthermore, even with respect to charges based specifically on the acquisition of the prize, if that act be regarded as manifestly unjust (for it may perhaps be so regarded by the enemy), then the rule of restitution and the authority of legal experts will show that the responsibility lies not only with the persons who took possession, but also—and in the fullest sense—with the authors and advocates of the act.[a] Therefore, since there would be no impunity on that score if the case were submitted to a judge of Spanish nationality, there is no reason to be more fearful on this ground than on other grounds. Indeed, we ought rather to exert ourselves in order to prevent the case from ever coming before such an arbiter.

If, on the other hand, we picture the judge as being not an enemy but some friendly prince or people, then, in the first place, the fear to which we have referred is quite unfounded, since neither appropriation of pledges nor reprisals are ever allowed for acts that have passed between belligerents. Indeed, as long as a war has not been declared unjust (and no one has pronounced such a judgement against the war waged by the Dutch), the retention of captured possessions is an act so just that those possessions cannot be made the subject of controversy. Besides, recourse is had to reprisals in the interest of fellow citizens but not on behalf of foreigners, and the present case is the concern of the Portuguese [, who would not be fellow citizens of any non-Spanish subject].

Moreover, if we are to conceive of some [non-Spanish] judge who is [nevertheless] devoted to the Spanish cause and eager to surrender ev-

a. See in discussion of Concl. VII, Art. III, Pt. I, Chap. viii, *supra,* pp. 155 ff. Lupus, *De Bello,* § *Si bene advertas; Matthaei* [*De Bello*] in Req. 1, at end; [Trovamala,] *Summa Rosella,* on word *bellum,* n. 6.

erything to Spain, then surely, in the estimation of that judge, it will be not so much the acquisition of the prize, as the use of arms against the [Spanish] ruler, the practice of trade with the East Indians, and numerous other matters, that will call in part for atonement and in part for defensive pleading. For acquisition of spoils can result in an obligation equivalent to but not greater than the value of the spoils taken, so that restitution for such acquisitions merely cancels the profit derived from them without inflicting actual loss; whereas the computation of penalties for the other charges against us would be restrained by no limits.

Furthermore, in so far as reprisals are concerned, their nature is such that the act of any given citizen involves every other citizen of the same state, so that under this head nothing more is to be feared by the persons who have received a share of the prize than by those who have [161] not done so. Therefore, there is no reason [based upon the danger of reprisals] for refusing to lay claim to the prize.

As for the possibility that there may be someone who does lay claim to it in a restricted sense but nevertheless seeks to appease his scruples or timidity by some means other than [outright repudiation of his portion], such a person will be doubly in error. For that which is claimed must be either retained or transferred. It can be retained, moreover, with either of two intentions: that is to say, with the purpose of restoring it to the enemy, or with the purpose of putting it aside for one's own benefit.

Captured possessions, however, neither can nor should be returned to their former owners. For where will those owners be found? Do we perhaps expect that subjects of the enemy state will come from India, or from Lisbon, in order to reclaim their property through the legal ceremony known as an "act of joint seizure"?[16] But the owners themselves have banished from their minds all hope of reclaiming that property, as if openly acknowledging that they have merely suffered the fate decreed by the law of war; and he who takes a contrary view, questioning the

16. The Latin phrase *manum ex iure conserere* (to make a joint seizure) was used to describe the ceremony in which various litigants laid hands simultaneously upon a disputed possession, each claiming it for his own.

lawful right which not even the foe disputes, is indeed deserving of ridicule. For it is quite clear that persons waging a war in good faith are not bound, even in conscience, to make restitution. Neither is it right that spoils should be restored to the enemy, even if such restoration should be entirely possible. For deeds that aid the enemy, whether financially or in any other way, are contrary to the laws and violate the majesty of the nation.[a] If the fatherland itself were able to address the persons who attempt to give such aid, surely it would speak as follows: "All good citizens act to this end, labour in this cause and unhesitatingly pour out their blood and their riches for this purpose, namely: to ensure the greatest felicity for me by depriving the foe of every means of injury. Thus they believe it to be beneficial for me and consequently glorious for themselves to take from those who are stubbornly inimical their very lives, and from those who are in error the resources which are obviously being misused in a manner ruinous to me. As for you, do you even wish to give back to my enemies the things already snatched away from them by the fortunes of war, thereby turning my loss, forsooth, to a corresponding enrichment of those persons who—impelled not by ignorance nor by any error, but rather by their own ambition and their own avarice—have unanimously conspired to bring destruction upon me [161′] and upon each of you, individually?" In my opinion, no one after hearing this exhortation would have any choice but to acknowledge his fault, confessing that he had been led astray by false arguments rather than that he had been deliberately undutiful toward his country.

Now, granting that it is not permissible to restore captured possessions to the enemy, let us consider whether or not it is in any sense beneficial to keep those possessions apart from the rest of one's property.

If this policy is adopted in order to prevent other goods from being contaminated by the admixture of spoils, such superstitious scruples certainly call for ridicule rather than for confutation; unless, perchance, we believe that ill-got possessions are like bad eggs in that contagion creeps from coin to coin in consequence (as it were) of their mutual proximity,

a. *Dig.,* XLVIII. iv. 4.

instead of recognizing the fact that the term "patrimony" denotes a complete whole which preserves the same nature throughout, even though it may be distributed in different coffers and purses.[a] Thus, precisely as goods justly obtained (a description which includes spoils taken in a just war) serve as a righteous means of increasing and adorning that whole, so the latter cannot possibly escape contamination from goods unrighteously acquired even when they are segregated and removed to a great distance. For the only pertinent question is this: do I wish these goods to be numbered among my possessions, or not? Yet I cannot be considered to have excluded from my possessions anything that I take as my own and keep.

Again, if any person divides his property with a view to averting the necessity for a search at some future time when he may be compelled by judicial decree to make restitution [for captured goods], that person has not only become fearful of a contingency which (as we have already pointed out) need not be feared at all, or at least never in any grave degree, but he also commits a grievous error in his interpretation of the law and increases the probability of loss to himself. For one is much more easily forced to make restitution for spoils still in one's possession than for those already consumed, since it is a well-established rule that in the latter case they are ceded to the user in recognition of good faith.[b]

Nor is anything more effective accomplished by those individuals who do in actual fact lay claim to spoils, but who transfer the goods claimed to others. For, assuming that such individuals imagine some taint to be attached to the property in question, it is certainly [162] impossible to cancel by any transference of possession a responsibility that is not merely established by the laws but imposed still more forcibly by conscience.[c] Therefore, he who has assumed possession of spoils while acting in bad faith—in other words, while believing that the seizure of the spoils was unjust—is permanently bound by an obligation

a. Bartolus. *On Dig.* XXIV. iii. 2, n. 17; Doctors, *On Dig.* XII. vi. 38.
b. See in discussion of Coroll. II, Chap. viii, *supra,* p. 147; Vict. *De Jure Belli,* 33.
c. *Institutes,* II. vi. 2.

to make restitution, so that (according to the authorities[a] on the subject) he will not be released from this obligation by the act of selling or giving away the goods involved, even though they be transferred to the thousandth [subsequent] possessor. Moreover, if anyone supposes that he can be said to have shared any less in the spoils because, before touching any part of them, he transferred all right therein to another, such a person is utterly ignorant even of the ordinary aspects of jurisprudence. For whatever has fallen into another's possession by a grant from me, even though it may have been delivered to him by a process of fictitious transfer,[17] so to speak, must still be admitted to have been mine. By any other process of reasoning, nothing of all that we have received and expended through our agents will have belonged to us at all.

Furthermore, he who transfers his possessions must necessarily be distributing them among the poor, or else handing them over to some organized entity or to another individual.

When one bestows a gift upon the poor, he is to all intents and purposes making a gift to God. Such conduct is indeed praiseworthy in the highest degree. For what act is more just than the acknowledgement, when revenue has been quite unexpectedly received, of the benefaction conferred by Him to whom alone victory in war is due? Thus, not only among the Jews, but also among the Greeks, the Romans, and still other peoples, the consecration of a tithe or some such portion of the spoils became an established custom. On the other hand, this very fact indicates with sufficient clarity that it is unnecessary to give up the whole. For even Abraham,[b] who gave the priest tithes from the spoils, nevertheless did not deprive his allies nor his attendants of their portions. Again, in the history of Moses,[c] it is clearly written that, even after liberal sacrificial offerings had been made, there was still so much spoil that every man kept a great deal of it for himself. Nevertheless, the most

a. Sylvester, on word *bellum* [Pt. I] x. [3]; Lupus, § *Si bene advertas;* Matthaei, *De Bello,* in Req. 1, at end.

b. *Genesis,* xiv, at end.

c. *Numbers,* xxxi. 53.

17. *Brevi . . . manu:* more specifically, "directly from the hand [of the person preceding me as owner]."

thorough consideration must be given to the question of whether the person who sets aside a certain amount of spoil as an offering to God, makes that oblation as something of his own, or as something belonging to another. If he offers it as his own, he undoubtedly acts rightly, and we have no dispute with him; for whatever any man has acquired, he may also transfer. But if the gift is offered as the property of another, let the giver take care lest he offend God, whom he strives to placate, [162′] by the act of thrusting upon the Deity that which he believes himself unable to retain with a clear conscience. For God, who forbade that the hire of a whore should be dedicated to Him, makes it quite clear that no gift is pleasing to Him unless it be drawn from goods righteously acquired.[a] This is the import of Augustine's statement[b] that one ought not to commit thefts even for the purpose of feeding God's holy poor.

On the other hand, those persons who transfer a right either to an organized entity or to an individual, must be regarded as having sold that right, if they receive anything in exchange for it; or, even if they wish for no payment except gratitude, they still may not deny that they first considered as their own that which they are now converting into the property of another. For no one can give away what he does not possess.[c] Therefore, both before the court of conscience and in the judgement of the civil courts, the individuals who have adopted this course of action find themselves in the same position as those who have accepted ownership [of the prize]. For even the latter receive, not the actual goods involved, but the price thereof; and this, moreover, they exchange daily for other things.

Thus the persons who imagine that there is some reason which makes it imprudent to seize and hold spoil taken from the Portuguese enemy, are in numerous ways either deceivers or deceived. **Epilogue**

I therefore exhort the merchants, and the East India Company, not to allow themselves to be dissuaded on any pretext (for all of the pretexts

a. *Deuteronomy,* xxiii. 18.
b. To Claudius against Julian, V. viii [in *Letters,* ccvii].
c. Seneca, *On Benefits,* V. xii [7]; *Dig.* L. xvii. 54.

adduced are certainly false and without force) from their purpose: a purpose approved not only by accepted custom and in the eyes of mankind, but also by divine law and in the court of conscience; one which is not merely devoid of turpitude, but worthy of being regarded as especially honourable and even glorious; in fine, a purpose attended by no disadvantage whatsoever, but rather by the richest promise of benefits both from a private and from a public standpoint. Let them make frequent voyages to the most distant lands in that spirit of inviolable good faith which is characteristic of the Dutch! Let them defend the right of commerce against every possible injury! Let them win allies for the fatherland, and let them also acquire enemy property both for their country and for themselves!

Moreover, I beg and entreat of every one of our governmental assemblies (both those of our individual nations and the States General of the United Provinces), the leaders and lords of public liberty, that they will continue to promote and protect, with the favourable treatment accorded at the outset, this enterprise which is opportune in the [163] highest degree, detrimental to the foe, beneficial for our people and fraught with glory for those assemblies themselves. I beg and entreat, too, that they will not permit toil to go without rewards, valour without honour, peril without profit, and expenditures without reimbursement.

As a suppliant also before God the Eternal, sole Author of our state and its Guiding Spirit, whom we call "Most Excellent" in referring to His will and "Greatest" in referring to His power, seeing that it has pleased Him to select the Dutch in preference to all others for the purpose of manifesting through them the feebleness of any degree of human might in opposition to His strength, and seeing, too, that it has been His pleasure to reveal the glory of our race to the farthest regions of the world created by Him, I pray and reverently implore: first, that He will instil into our people such habits of conduct as befit the name of Christian, so that no fault on their part may render the true religion odious to unconsecrated nations; secondly, that He will frustrate the cruel designs of our enemies, not choosing that the innocent shall succumb to the savagery of those enemies but, on the contrary, heaping loss and disaster upon the latter, praise and honour upon the former; that

He will restrain the pestilential madness of those who are in disaccord with the fatherland; that He will impart sound understanding to those now led astray by error, and that He will bestow upon all of us a wisdom that will enable us to use and enjoy victory (which is, we acknowledge, a gift from heaven) in a spirit no less grateful than pure.

THE END

A copy of each of the following documents will be appended:[18]

The Edict of the States General of the United Provinces (April 2, 1599);

The Opinion of the Admiralty Board;

The Decree of the States Assembly of Holland (September 1, 1604);

An excerpt from the letter of the Bishop of Malacca to the King (April 30, 1600);

A letter from the Malaccan Senate (March 9, 1603);

A letter of the same date from the Governor of Malacca to Jacob Heemskerck;

Another letter from the Governor of Malacca (March 26, 1603);

A letter from the Commander of the captured vessel to Heemskerck (March 24, 1603).

18. [[Grotius failed to append the documents in question to the manuscript of *Commentary on the Law of Prize and Booty,* currently in Leiden University Library. These are reproduced in English translation in appendix I of the Liberty Fund edition—M. J. van Ittersum.]]

APPENDIX A

Table of Rules and Laws Compiled from Chapter II of the *Commentary*

Rules

RULE I. What God has shown to be His Will, that is law.

RULE II. What the common consent of mankind has shown to be the will of all, that is law.

RULE III. What each individual has indicated to be his will, that is law with respect to him.

RULE IV. What the commonwealth has indicated to be its will, that is law for the whole body of citizens.

RULE V. What the commonwealth has indicated to be its will, that is law for the individual citizens in their mutual relations.

RULE VI. What the magistrate has indicated to be his will, that is law in regard to the whole body of citizens.

RULE VII. What the magistrate has indicated to be his will, that is law in regard to the citizens as individuals.

RULE VIII. Whatever all states have indicated to be their will, that is law in regard to all of them.

RULE IX. In regard to judicial procedure, precedence shall be given to the state which is the defendant, or whose citizen is the defendant; but if the said state proves remiss in the discharge of its judicial duty, then that state shall be the judge, which is itself the plaintiff, or whose citizen is the plaintiff.

Laws

LAW I. It shall be permissible to defend [one's own] life and to shun that which threatens to prove injurious.

LAW II. It shall be permissible to acquire for oneself, and to retain, those things which are useful for life.

LAW III. Let no one inflict injury upon his fellow.

LAW IV. Let no one seize possession of that which has been taken into the possession of another.

LAW V. Evil deeds must be corrected.

LAW VI. Good deeds must be recompensed.

LAW VII. Individual citizens should not only refrain from injuring other citizens, but should furthermore protect them, both as a whole and as individuals.

LAW VIII. Citizens should not only refrain from seizing one another's possessions, whether these be held privately or in common, but should furthermore contribute individually both that which is necessary to [other] individuals and that which is necessary to the whole.

LAW IX. No citizen shall seek to enforce his own right against a fellow citizen, save by judicial procedure.

LAW X. The magistrate shall act in all matters for the good of the state.

LAW XI. The state shall uphold as valid every act of the magistrate.

LAW XII. Neither the state nor any citizen thereof shall seek to enforce his own right against another state or its citizens, save by judicial procedure.

LAW XIII. In cases where [the laws] can be observed simultaneously, let them [all] be observed; when this is impossible, the law of superior rank shall prevail.

APPENDIXES TO THE LIBERTY FUND EDITION

APPENDIX I

Documents Listed by Grotius at the End of the Manuscript

I
Edict of the Estates General of the United Provinces April 2, 1599[1]

[Front page of the pamphlet]
Proclamation of the Lords of the Generall States, of the United Provinces, whereby the Spaniards and all their goods are declared to be lawfull prize: As also containing a strickt defence or restraint of sending any goods, wares, or merchandizes to the Spaniards or their adherents, enemies to the Netherlands.

Faithfully translated out of the Dutch coppy. Printed at S. Graven Haghe by Aelbercht Heyndrickson, Printer to the Generall States.

Imprinted at London by John Wolfe, and are to be solde at his shop in Popes-head Alley, neere the Exchange. 1599.

1. The Dutch original was published in The Hague in April 1599 at the behest of the federal government of the Dutch Republic. A transcription of this document may be found in appendix B of Hugo Grotius, *De Jure Praedae Commentarius/Commentary on the Law of Prize and Booty* (Oxford: Clarendon Press, 1950), vol. 1: *A Translation of the Original Manuscript of 1604* by Gwladys L. Williams, 371–75.

The edict was quickly translated into English and appeared in print in London in 1599. The text reproduced here is a transcription of pamphlet no. 292.2 in the Goldsmiths'-Kress Library of Economic Literature, entitled *A Proclamation of the Lords of the Generall States.*

A Proclamation, of the Lordes the *generall States of the united Provinces,* whereby the Spaniards and all their goods are declared to be lawfull prize. As also containing a strict defence or restraint of sending any goods, wares, or Merchandizes to the Spaniards or their adherents, enemies to the Netherlands.

The Generall States of the United Provinces,[2] to all such as shall see or heare these presents, make knowne:

that whereas it is every day more then other most apparant and manifest, that the enterprises of the Spanish nation, with their conioyned adherents, hath not been only pretended to reduce these Netherlands by their deceitfull practises, and the uttermost violence and force, under their wilfull and superbious dominion and tyrannicall government, both over consciences, bodies, & goods: But also that in the years past, they have attempted, with their usual violent complots, to reduce the realmes of *England* and *Fraunce,* under their power.

Which they not being able (according to their desires to performe) now openly & by maine force, assault the neighbour countries of the Electors[3] and Princes, and other neutrall places of the Empire,[4] not refusing to overrun the Cities and Fortresses, with all manner of violence, barter them with peeces, ransomming them, and filling them with their souldiors, destroying the flat land, ravishing and deflowring of women and maides, pilling, rob-

2. That is, the federal government of the Dutch Republic—the modern-day Kingdom of the Netherlands has the same borders as the United Provinces after 1648.

3. The title of Holy Roman Emperor could not be inherited. Instead, three bishops and four secular princes, known collectively as the Electors, voted on the succession at the Diet of the German Estates. The Electors were mighty territorial princes in Germany in their own right.

4. The Holy Roman Empire (modern-day Germany).

bing, murdering and burning, not favouring the house or castels of Princes, Earles or Gentlemen, nor yet their persons, as sufficiently appeareth by their barbarous dealings in the bishoprick of *Collen,*[5] the Dukedomes of *Cleve* and *Bergh,* and the Bishopricke of *Munster,* and other bordering countries.

The ministers of this spanish tyrannie boasting, that according to their own pleasures they will proceede in their begunne actions, especially in these places, untill such time as they shall have reduced the whole (besides these Netherlandes) under their Spanish yoake, & wholly rooted out the exercise of the true Christian religion. To which end they have publikely in divers places of the Empire, altered the religion and pollicie of the same, by force, threats, and other undecent dealings. Moreover, vaunting to bee glad, that in the behalfe of the Princes Electors and others, the armes be taken up, for that they shall (as they say) the better attaine the purpose.

Moreover, that the new king of *Spaine,*[6] the *Infanta,*[7] and the Spanish Counsell, as well in Spaine as in the Low countries, deceitfully and forcibly, hinder and disturbe al navigations, dealings, traffique, & trade, so with inhabitants of the Netherlands, as with those of other kingdomes, countries, and citties, in most barbarous and tyrannicall sort, misusing the persons, attaching[8] their shippes, & violating their graunted promises by water and land, all under the pretence and colour, because that we have hitherto joyntly resisted their false & deceitfull dealings and have not beene mooved to yeeld and subvert the United Netherlands, and the good inhabitantes thereof, under these barbarous tyrannie, and imperious dominion.

And since that by gods mightie power, the assistance of her most excellent Majesty of England,[9] & other kings, princes, & common-weales, togither with our patience and good endevors, we have for these many yeres withstood these tyrannicall enterprises, (which they have bent against al Christendome) & hope further, with Gods helpe and assistance (as aforesaid) to withstand, & therein are resolved also to visit the Spaniards in the kingdoms & lands by

5. The German city of Cologne.

6. Philip III of Spain and Portugal (r. 1598–1621).

7. Archduchess Isabella of Austria (1566–1633) was the daughter of Philip II of Spain and Portugal. She governed the Spanish Netherlands together with her husband, Archduke Albert of Austria, from 1598 until 1621, while serving as regent for her nephew Philip IV from 1621 until her death in 1633.

8. "attacking"!

9. Queen Elizabeth I of England (r. 1559–1603).

them occupied, not onely to hinder their aforesaid tyranous pretence, but also to recover our losses & damages sustained by them, as wel with our ships of war, as by such as are allowed by our order, hoping assuredly that his divine Maiestie wil blesse our rightful & needfull enterprises, and once wholy free and deliver the Netherlands from the aforesaid tyrannie of the Spaniards and their adherents. And also will moove and incite the neighbour Kings, Princes, Electors, Earles, Barrons, and Common-wealthes, that uppon good consideration, they may take and use Armes, to assure their perrillous estate, and to that ende, to drive out the Spaniards and their complices, from the Emperours territories; and so out of the Netherlands: as also wee finde to bee most expedient and necessary for the accomplishment of so Christian lyke, rightfull, and needfull common cause, against the said Spaniards and their conioyned adherents, to be with all deepe insight looked into, that there be not any Shippes, goods or Marchandizes, sent them by water, land or otherwise, the same beeing not onely permitted by the common people, but also the emperiall rights and custome of all Kings, Princes, and Common-weales, beeing in warre or controversie, besides that the same hath beene made knowne by many firme orders and Proclaimations. As well by the above named the Queenes Maiestie of England, (with whome we are in sure alliance) as also of these countries. And we therefore intend not to permit that any person of the united lands, using trafficke or fishing at sea, or on the waters within the land, shall suffer himselfe to be deceived, seduced, and endamaged, by any deceitfull pasports, safegardes, or safe conducts of the said common enemie, as wee understand heeretofore (against our good meanings) by some hath been done.

So it is, that we uppon ripe and profound deliberation, and by the advise of the illustrious Prince and Lord Maurice,[10] borne Prince of *Orange,* Counte of *Nassou,* Marquess of *der Vere, Flushing, &c.,* Governour and Captaine Generall of *Gelderland, Holland, Zealand, Utrecht, Overysel, &c.* as Admirall generall, have declared, and declare by these presents, for good and lawfull prize, all persons and goods, under the dominion of the Spanish king, in all

10. Maurice of Nassau (1567–1625) was the second son of William the Silent, one of the instigators of the Dutch Revolt against Spain. Maurice succeeded his elder brother as Prince of Orange in 1618. After his father's assassination, he was appointed commander-in-chief of the Dutch army and navy. In addition, he held the political office of Stadtholder ("governor") of the provinces of Holland, Zeeland, Utrecht, Overijssel, and Gelderland.

places where they shall or may be got, have furthermore againe of new, stricktly defended, forbidden, and respectively notified: defend, forbid, and notifie by these presents, all and everie one, of what condition, realme, or land soever, none excepted, not to lade, ship, bring, or transport by water or land, directly or indirectly, under what colour or pretence soever, any ships, goods, wares, or merchandizes, for[11] or to any haven, cittie, or place of the enemie, in the kingdomes of *Spaine, Portugall,* or other places of *Europe,* under the dominion, subjection, or commaund of the new king of *Spaine;* the Archduke *Albertus* of Austria,[12] or the Infanta of *Spaine,* uppon paine of confiscation of the same goods, wares, or merchandizes, together with the shippes, waggons, carts, and horses, wherein, or whereon the same shall bee laden, and all such further punishment as hereafter shall be declared.

And to prevent all fraudes, subtile practises, and deceits, which might in these United Netherlands be pretended by any, of what countrie, condition, or quallitie soever, against these our orders and defences. Wee ordaine and command stricktly by these presents, all Convoy maisters,[13] Controulers, Searchers, and all other our Deputies in all Havens, Citties, and places of the same landes, uppon the oathe whereby they are bound to these countries uppon privation of their offices and arbitrall correction: We authorise likewise all others, dwelling in the aforesaide united Netherlands, or frequenting the same: dilligentlye to enquire, and to take sharpe regarde & if this our order bee by any one, of what countrie, condition or qualitie soever, violated or broken.

And if in the aforesaid Havens, Citties, or places, any goods be laden, shipped, or carred, which being found, we will and ordaine them to be ceazed & sequestrated, for summarily and without common course or traine in lawe, the saide goodes which shall bee found to have bene so laden togither with the shippes, waggons, carts, and horses, to be confiscated, the one third part to the use of the accuser, be he an officer, or otherwise in service of the land

11. "from"

12. Archduke Albert of Austria (1559–1621) governed the Spanish Netherlands from 1596 until 1621, first on behalf of his uncle, Philip II of Spain, and then in his own right. His wife, the Infanta Isabella, was made joint sovereign of the Spanish Netherlands by the king's last will and testament.

13. An employee of the Dutch Admiralty Board, charged with collecting the so-called *convoyen* and *licenten,* the import and export duties levied by the Estates General.

or no, and the other two third parts, to the use of the common causes, wherout the officer who shall follow the matter in law shall be contented. Ordaining moreover, that the proprietaries, or owners of the said goods, as also maisters of the said ships, waine men, or carmen, in whose ships, or upon whose waines or carts, they shall be found to be laden in the forbidden havens, citties, and places, to be apprehended, and stayed untill such time as they shall have paide and accomplished all such further pennalties and corrections, wherein according to the nature of their trespasse (by the arbitrements of the judge) they shall be condemned, which may not be less (for so much as toucheth the merchants) then a thousand pounds; and for each of the shippers or maisters of ships, five hundreth pounds sterling of fortie pence in the pound.[14]

And to the end that the foresaid orders may the better be followed, and all fraudes punished: We meane that within a yeare after the aforesaide trespasse, all such which shall bee found to have violated or broken the same, it shall and may be lawfull, by all officers of the saide lands, and before competent judges, to arrest and condemne them for the valew of the said goods and shippes, waggons, carts, and horses, togither with the above named penalties and corrections. The sentence whereof by provision shall be executed, all appellations & provocations notwithstanding.

And if any in the aforesaid united Provinces desired to ship or lade any goods, to transport the same to the neighbour countries or friends: the same shall not bee permitted unto him, unlesse he have leave and license thereto from us, the said Lord Admirall generall, or from those which thereunto by us shall be appointed; and that by the shippes which shall lade the same, sufficient sureties shall be set for the valew of their shippes, that the saide laden goods shall not be carried to any other place but to the havens, citties, and places of our said friends and allies; and that within a certaine prefixed reasonable time named in their pasports, according to the distance of the haven, to yeeld sufficient certification and proofe thereof; or else their bond shall be executed uppon the sureties, for the aforesaid valew, to the use of the common causes.

And further, we charge all Admirals, Vice Admirals, Captaines, and Commissioners for sea, all Chieftaines, Generals of horses, Captaines, and officers of men of war by land, to take sharpe regarde, that all such of what lande or

14. Five hundred Dutch guilders, or fifty pounds sterling.

condition soever, as shall have any goods, wares, or merchandizes in their shippes, upon their waines, cartes, horses, or otherwise laden, being bound for the saide realmes, countries and citties, held and occupied by the enemies, may be pursued, overtaken, and brought backe to the colleges of the Admiraltie,[15] and other justices aforesaid, to be punished according to the tenor of these presents.

And we being resolved to keepe a good and sure order for the defence of the ships of trade and fishing, using at sea, against all forraine invasions & robbings of the enemie, as also against the exorbitant ransomes which the common enemies use in the pilling and ransoming of the same. We have therefore forbidden and interdicted, forbid and interdicte by these present, all inhabitants of the united lands, as well Merchants Ships, Pilots, as other, using trafficke or fishing, at Sea or on the Rivers within the land, or transporting any goods beyond the seas, to take or procure any pasports or safegards of the enemies, in no manner or sort, upon confiscation of the ships and goods of such as shall be found to have taken any, with further arbitrall correction. Ordaining that the givers of the said pasports, safegardes, or safe conductes of the common enemie, shall bee for example of other,[16] punished by losse of life, and confiscation of theyr goods, as ayders of the enemy.

And if in case any of the ships or Pilots be by the enemie taken, and over and above the order by us therto established, be ransomed and endamaged, we will and ordaine that the same unreasonable ransomes and damages shall be recovered uppon the Officers, Justices, and subiects of the vilages of Brabant, Flaunders, and others, remaining under the enemies' dominion, besides what they shall pay to the commissioner for ransome, charging and authorizing the deputed counsel of the States of the respective Provinces, whose subjects against these our orders shall be by the common enemie by exorbitant and unreasonable ransomes or otherwaies endammaged, to take notice thereof, and to recover and reimburse them as before, by such proceedings and meanes of execution, as in like matter is commonly used.

And to the ende no man pretend ignorance hereof, we signifie and com-

15. The Dutch Admiralty Board consisted of five "colleges," viz. Amsterdam, South Holland (Rotterdam), the North Quarter (jointly at Hoorn and Enkhuizen), Zeeland (Middelburg), and Friesland (Dokkum).

16. "as an example to others"

maund our beloved, the States, Lieutenants,[17] and appointed Counsailors of the States, and deputed States of the respective Provinces of Gelderland, Holland, Zeeland, Utrecht, Vriesland, Overyssel, Grooning and Ommelanden,[18] and all other Justices, and Officers unto whom it doth belong to cause this our will and ordinance to be every where published and proclaimed, in the places where the publique Proclimations are usually proclaimed, we charge likewise the Chauncelor, Presidents, and provinciall Counsailours, Advocates, Fiscals, and generall Attorneys; and all other Officers, Judges, and Justices of the aforesaide Countries, together with all Chiefetaines, Coronels, Admirals, Vice-Admirals, Generals of horses, Captaines, Officers and Commaunders, to follow and ensue these our ordinances, and to cause them to be followed and ensued, proceeding and causing to be proceeded against the transgressors thereof, without grace, favour, dissimulation or delaye, as we have found the same for the Lands welfare to be most needfull.

Given in S. Graven Haghe,[19] the second of Aprill. 1599.

I. van Oldenbarnevelt v.[20]

By the order of the aforesaid
Lordes the Generall States.
C. Aerssen.[21]

II
Verdict of the Amsterdam Admiralty Board September 9, 1604[22]

Extract from the Register of Verdicts Pronounced by the Delegated Councillors of the Amsterdam College of the Admiralty Board (notarized copy).

17. Maurice of Nassau, Stadtholder of Holland, Zeeland, Utrecht, Overijssel, and Gelderland, and his cousin Count Willem Lodewijk of Nassau (1560–1620), Stadtholder of Friesland and Groningen.

18. The standing committees of the provincial Estates, which took care of day-to-day government in each of the seven provinces.

19. The Hague.

20. Johan van Oldenbarnevelt (1547–1619) served as the Advocate of Holland and political leader of the Dutch Republic from 1586 until his death. He drafted almost all the resolutions adopted by the Estates of Holland and Estates General.

21. Cornelis Aerssen (1545–1627) was the clerk of the Estates General from 1584 until 1621.

22. A notarized copy of the Dutch original may be found in the Dutch National

The Delegated Councillors of the Amsterdam Admiralty Board have reviewed the case between the Advocate-Fiscal of Holland,[23] the Company of Eight Ships,[24] and Admiral Jacob van Heemskerk—the plaintiffs, and all those contumacious persons who might otherwise have come forward for the protection of the *St. Catarina* and its cargo.[25]

In justification of the interdiction, the plaintiffs posited that the aforesaid Company had sent a fleet of eight ships to the East Indies under the command of the aforesaid Admiral in order to trade with the inhabitants in the usual fashion and with the permission of the local authorities. To that purpose, the Admiral had received a commission from His Princely Excellency,[26] which obliged the former to defend himself with all possible means against anyone who tried to attack or harm him on his voyage, while also authorizing him to obtain reparations for damages sustained.

After passing the Canaries, the fleet found itself under attack from a powerful armada of thirteen Spanish warships. The *Red Lion* bore the brunt of the Spanish cannonades and was even boarded, which caused the death of the pilot and a few other crew members and the wounding of several more. As a result, the vessel was forced to abort the voyage and return home. In his efforts to relieve it, the Admiral had been in great danger of losing his own ship—some of his crew were shot dead, while the fleet was weakened by the

---

Archives, Staten Gen. 12551.21 (Loketkas Processen nr. 21), unfoliated. My English translation is based on this notarized copy.

The verdict was published in German translation in *Achte Schiffart, oder Kurtze Beschreibung etlicher Reysen so die Holländer und Seeländer in die Ost Indien von Anno 1599 bisz Anno 1604 gethan* (Frankfurt-am-Main, 1608). This text appears as "Sententia Collegii Admiralitatis" in appendix B of Hugo Grotius, *Commentary on the Law of Prize and Booty*, 1:375–79.

23. The Advocate-Fiscal of Holland could be considered the province's public prosecutor. He was a plaintiff *nomine officii.*

24. The United Amsterdam Company.

25. The Admiralty Court imposed an interdiction on the carrack and its cargo at the request of the plaintiffs, viz. the Advocate-Fiscal of Holland, Van Heemskerck, and the United Amsterdam Company. The judges summoned all those who had a claim to the carrack and its cargo to appear in court within six weeks, on pain of being found guilty of contumacy. Since nobody presented himself, the Admiralty Court confiscated the *Santa Catarina* for the benefit of the plaintiffs.

26. Maurice of Nassau in his capacity as Lord High Admiral of Holland and Zeeland.

loss of one of its best vessels. In addition, the Vice-Admiral[27] found himself alone in the midst of the Spanish armada the following day and extricated himself with difficulty. He remained separated from the rest of the fleet for the duration of both the outward and return voyages.

Van Heemskerk continued on to Bantam, where he learned about the naval battle between the Portuguese armada commanded by André Furtado de Mendonça and the five Dutch ships, also belonging to this Company and commanded by Wolfert Hermanszoon. The Portuguese armada had been expressly authorized to destroy all Dutch ships and their crews, as well as the East Indian nations that granted the latter access to their harbors and markets. When the Portuguese were thwarted in their design to invade and subdue Bantam by the five Dutch ships, they had gone to Hitu on the island of Ambon and brutally tyrannized the poor inhabitants. In addition, they had captured and wrecked the island of Makian, which belonged to the King of Ternate, again tyrannically abusing the inhabitants. It had been their intention to do the same thing at Ternate, where two Spanish ships had arrived from Manila to assist them, for no other reason than that the King of Ternate and his subjects had traded with the Dutch. Two ships from Holland called *Utrecht* and *Guardian* had been exposed to great dangers in fighting the Iberian armada and left Ternate with less than half the cargo they were supposed to have taken in.

All this came to the notice of Van Heemskerk, along with reports of the mistreatment of twenty crew members of the fleet of Jacob van Neck, for which the Portuguese at Macao were responsible. They had shamelessly hanged and strangled seventeen crew members, while sending the other three to Goa as prisoners. When a certain Grusberghen reached Cochin China with two ships for the purpose of trading there, the local ruler, at the instigation of a Portuguese monk, slew twenty-three of his crew and imprisoned several of his officers, only to release them in exchange for two iron guns. Three men

27. The Vice-Admiral in question was Jean Grenier, commander of the *Black Lion.* Due to the naval battle off the Canaries, the *Black Lion* was separated from the rest of Van Heemskerck's fleet and continued its eastward journey all alone. Ironically, it was the only ship to reach the fleet's projected destination, the port of Aceh on the northern tip of the island of Sumatra. The journal of Reyer Cornelisz, pilot of the *Black Lion,* was recently published in Dutch in *Peper, Plancius en porselein: de reis van het schip "Swarte Leeuw" naar Atjeh en Bantam,* ed. Jan Parmentier, Karel Davids, and John Everaert (Zutphen, The Netherlands: Walburg Press, 2003).

whom Van Heemskerck had left at Banda on a previous voyage were chased relentlessly by the Portuguese when they tried to cross over to Ambon in order to trade there. Two of them escaped and saved themselves by taking refuge with the heathens on some island. Yet one of them was captured by the Portuguese and quartered alive by means of four galleys.

The Portuguese engaged in many other hostile and tyrannical procedures against us. It is notorious how gruesomely and tyrannically they treated the crew, cargo, and ships of Balthasar de Cordes at Tidore. Several of De Cordes's crew surrendered to the Portuguese in the belief that the latter would keep a promise to spare them. Yet they were shamelessly murdered by the Portuguese, who forced them to witness each other's mutilation—first hands, then feet, and finally heads were cut off. In addition, the Portuguese used fireships in an attempt to destroy two of Van Neck's vessels. At Aceh, they incited the local ruler to attack two Zeeland ships that wanted to trade there, which cost the lives of many people.

In consultation with his council of naval officers, the Admiral decided not just to resist an enemy who had subjected the Dutch to so much harm, abuse, trouble, and tyranny, but to inflict the greatest possible damage in order to prevent any repetition thereof in the future. By these means, permitted by natural law and *jus gentium* and enjoined by the commission of his Princely Excellency, the East Indian trade, so important to these Provinces, might be continued peaceably, free of violence, and without let or hindrance. With these considerations in mind, the Admiral departed from Bantam with two ships of his fleet and sailed east in search of appropriate lading.

In the vicinity of the Kingdom of Johore, he encountered the carrack in question, carrying seven hundred fighting men, most of them Portuguese and enemies of these Provinces and their commerce. Acting upon the council's aforesaid resolution and mindful of the edict of the Estates General, declaring the possessions of Philip III's subjects to be good prize, regardless of the time and place of seizure, the Admiral first attacked and captured the carrack, and then put its crew ashore safely. He took the carrack along with him to Holland, where he unloaded its cargo, including some clothes of the Dutch sailors hanged in Macao, and stored the goods in an orderly fashion for safekeeping.

The directors of the Company of Eight Ships have asked this Board to pronounce judgement in this case, which it is authorized to do according to its instructions. Since nobody has come forward for the protection of carrack and cargo, the plaintiffs have requested and obtained a citation by means of posted announcements. Following the custom of this Board, the citation has been repeated three times, with fourteen-day intervals. Since nobody has presented himself, the Board ascertains the first, second, and third defaults at the request of the plaintiffs. For the benefit of the latter, it declares all those who might have come forward for the protection of carrack and cargo guilty of contumacy, dismissing any further claims and defenses on their part. The Board sustains the claim of the plaintiffs as being supported by their documents and evidence. It concludes that the aforesaid Admiral had a sufficient cause to capture the carrack, as belonging to the Portuguese and subjects of Philip III, enemies of these United Provinces and their Indies trade, which they tried to eradicate by means of violence, intrigue, and deceit. The Admiral derived his authority not only from the written laws and *jus gentium,* but also from the edicts of the Estates General and in particular his commission, as the Portuguese admitted themselves. Even the Governor of Malacca recognized that Van Heemskerk had captured the carrack in a just war. The plaintiffs have exhibited various acts, titles, attestations, and other documents in support of the above facts and opinions. Based on these proofs, they request that the Board render a definitive verdict and impound carrack and cargo, declaring them good prize.

The aforesaid Delegated Councillors have given all of this their full consideration.

Sentencing for contumacy in the name of His Excellency as Lord High Admiral, they confiscate the aforesaid carrack, including all its cargo, and declare it to be good prize. They order the carrack to be auctioned off in its entirety and the proceeds to be divided among the plaintiffs, in accordance with the relevant instructions and ordinances of the Estates General. Drawn up and pronounced at the meeting of the aforesaid Delegated Councillors in Amsterdam on September 9, 1604.

(The Amsterdam notary H. Oosterman signed this particular copy of the verdict after collating it with the original.)

III
Decree of the Estates of Holland
September 1, 1604[28]

The Estates of Holland and West Friesland have read and examined a report submitted by the province's Audit Office and Advocate Fiscal. Citing the law and custom of Holland and West Friesland, the report argues that the County of Holland, not the East India Company,[29] should enjoy the carrack and cargo captured by Jacob van Heemskerck from the Portuguese in the East Indies.

After due deliberation the Estates of Holland and West Friesland have established that the aforesaid Van Heemskerck was appointed admiral and commander of several Indiamen by His Excellency, Lord High Admiral of the navy, and sailed to the East Indies with the approval of the Estates General. Every captain who served under Van Heemskerck received an individual commission from His Excellency as well. It is common knowledge that the Portuguese and other public enemies of these provinces attacked the fleet of Van Heemskerck with warships in order to prevent him and other inhabitants of these provinces from engaging in trade and navigation in the East Indies. Such Dutchmen as reached the East Indies were, without exception, treated as enemies by the Portuguese, who, reverting to type, murdered them cruelly. The Portuguese also besieged, attacked, and killed the inhabitants of several kingdoms, towns, and countries, which had concluded trading agreements with the Dutch. Even before Van Heemskerck's departure—for many years, in fact—the Estates General had admonished the directors of the East India Company to maintain the East Indies trade by launching well-armed fleets, sufficiently powerful not just to defend themselves against Portuguese attacks, but to go on the offensive as well.[30] Van Heemskerck and other Dutch

28. The resolution of the States Assembly of Holland was published in the *Register van Holland en Westvriesland, 1604–1606,* p. 217. It appears as "Decretum Ordinum Hollandiae" in appendix B of Grotius, *Commentary on the Law of Prize and Booty,* 1:379–80. My English translation is based on that text.

29. The United Dutch East India Company, or VOC (Verenigde Oostindische Compagnie).

30. A case in point was the resolution of the Estates General of November 1, 1603, which reminded the VOC directors that all possible damage should be done to the common enemy in the East Indies, so as to maintain and increase the company's trade "with honor." See *Resolutiën der Staten-Generaal, 1579–1609,* ed. N. Japikse and

admirals and captains fought the enemy in various places in the East Indies, facing a multitude of warships. With God's grace, they maintained and increased the East Indian navigation and trade, liberated indigenous kingdoms and towns allied to these provinces, and won notable victories over the aforesaid enemies. More advantages of this kind are expected in the future. All this has severely inconvenienced and harmed the public enemies, while increasing the honor, service, profit, and reputation of the United Provinces and its good citizens, at no expense to the commonwealth whatsoever. As a result, the Estates General has shown an even greater willingness to admonish the directors of the East India Company to maintain unity within their ranks and continue the offensive against the common enemy. To this purpose, the Estates General has incorporated the company and supported the merchants in various ways.[31]

For these and other good reasons, the Estates of Holland and West Friesland hereby resolve and decree that the *Santa Catarina* be left at the disposal of the Estates General and Admiralty Board, along with all other prizes captured in the East Indies, as a matter related to the common defense.[32] Resolution drawn up in The Hague on the first of September in the year of Our Lord and Savior, 1604.

Ha. H. P. Rijperman, vol. 12, *1602–1603* (RGP 92) (The Hague: Martinus Nijhoff, 1950), 631. See p. 422 of the present volume.

31. The United Dutch East India Company, or VOC, was a joint venture of various Holland and Zeeland trading companies. Since Oldenbarnevelt conceived of the VOC as the new military arm of the Dutch Republic, it was he who summoned the merchants to The Hague in the winter of 1601–2 and presided over their protracted negotiations. His strenuous efforts resulted in the famous VOC charter, approved by the Estates General on March 20, 1602.

32. The Union of Utrecht (1579), the constitution of the Dutch Republic, stipulated that all matters relating to the "common defense" were the exclusive preserve of the Estates General. The resolution of the Estates of Holland cleared the way for the verdict of the Amsterdam Admiralty Court of September 9, 1604.

IV
The Bishop of Malacca[33] to the King of Spain and Portugal
April 30, 1600[34]

Your Highness!

In previous years I have been in continuous correspondence with Your Majesty and informed you of anything that might affect the Lord's service, Your Majesty, and the common welfare. The present letter serves the same purpose.

In this monsoon of April 1600 I returned to Malacca in order to write to the Captain, the municipal government, the House of Mercy, and the Chapter.[35] My presence was desired by many in Malacca, where I will reside from now on, as I wrote to Your Majesty at length in December 1599. May the Almighty bestow his blessing upon me and make my presence here serviceable to His Church, as well as to Your Majesty and all the people of the South. I sent a long letter to Your Majesty with the ships that left the East Indies for Portugal this January. I mentioned whatever seemed necessary for the Lord's service and yours, as well as the common welfare of this State. I wrote a similar letter in the previous year and attached sailing directions for Aceh, Bantam, and other regions.[36] I refer you to those letters and sailing directions, which

33. Dom João Ribeiro Gaio, Bishop of Malacca (r. 1581–1601). After the Union of the Iberian Crowns, the bishop deluged Philip II with memoranda proposing the joint Luso-Spanish conquest of all of Southeast Asia. Cf. C. R. Boxer, "Portuguese and Spanish Projects for the Conquest of Southeast Asia, 1580–1600," *Journal of Asian History* 3 (1969): 118–36.

34. The Portuguese original has been lost, along with the seventeenth-century Dutch translation. Frederick Muller, an Amsterdam bookseller, bought a copy of this translation at the Martinus Nijhoff auction of Grotius's book manuscripts and personal papers in 1864. Muller's handwritten transcription is in Robert Fruin's personal papers in Leiden University Library (Ltk 1555-39) and appears as "Pars Epistolae Episcopi Malaccensis ad Regem" in appendix B of Grotius, *Commentary on the Law of Prize and Booty,* 1:380–84. My English translation is based on that text, as corrected by comparison with Muller's transcription. See p. 497 of the present volume.

35. The *capitão-mór,* or governor, was the highest-ranking Portuguese official in the town of Malacca.

Every urban center in Portugal had its House of Mercy or *misericórdia.* In Asia they served primarily as depositories for the estates of the deceased until the heirs claimed such estates and arranged for their transfer to Portugal. The Chapter of Malacca consisted of priests and other staff of the diocese.

36. The bishop's sailing directions have recently been published as *O Roteiro das Cousas do Achem de D. João Ribeiro Gaio: Um olhar português sobre o Norte de Samatra*

must have reached your private secretaries. For this reason, I will keep it short and only discuss the current state of the Southern regions.

Many letters written in March 1600 by reliable witnesses in China, Malacca, the Spice Islands, and elsewhere testify to the fact that twelve ships from Holland and Zeeland arrived in the southern region in 1599, notably ten ships at Bantam and two at Atjeh. These twelve ships must have left their country in 1598 and wintered on the eastern side of Madagascar. In total, sixteen well-armed merchantmen must have embarked on the voyage, whereof the admiral was lost and three ships were sidetracked in the Gulf of Guinea because of the weather. The letters do not say which course the ships have taken in these quarters, nor do I have any information about the three ships.

Of the ten ships that arrived at Bantam, four immediately received cargoes of pepper and spices and sailed home in January 1599, without having done any harm to the Bantamese, let alone to the Portuguese, or troubling a single other nation. They bought pepper at thirty ryals of eight per bahar and mace at eighty and ninety ryals of eight per bahar.[37] In addition, they purchased cloves, nutmeg, and other products of these regions. They were unaware of the local prices fetched by these products, but bought them nonetheless. They ended up spending a lot of money, for they paid the highest price. They were well regarded and highly esteemed by the locals, for they were honest traders who did not resort to any kind of subterfuge, harassment, or violence. They brought along many trade goods and commodities from their provinces, whereof they sold some that appealed to the locals. They also imported all kind of guns in large quantities, which found many buyers. The guns were bartered for ryals of eight, which were sold in turn to the Bantamese and Chinese. They became fast friends and allies of the King and Regents of

---

em finais do século XVI, ed. Jorge M. dos Santos Alves and Pierre-Yves Manguin (Lisbon: Comissão Nacional para as Comemoragões dos Descobrimentos Portugueses, 1997).

37. Ryals of eight, also known as Spanish dollars or pieces of eight, were Spanish silver coins used for commercial transactions in both the East and West Indies. A ryal was worth approximately two and one-half Dutch guilders. The bahar was a unit of weight common throughout the Malay Archipelago, which could be subdivided into picols and kati. They had no uniform standard in the seventeenth century, but, as a rule of thumb, the bahar was subdivided into 3 picols and the picol into 100 kati. Dutch historians usually equate 1 bahar with 364 Amsterdam pounds, approximately 180 kilos, and the kati with 1.25 Amsterdam pounds, a little more than 600 grams.

Bantam, and raised great expectations of continuing this trade and friendship on a regular basis, which God forbid.

Two other ships of this fleet of ten sailed along the north coast of Java and crossed over to the fortress at the island of Ambon, where they first loaded cloves at the island of Hitu and then departed to an unknown destination.

Two more ships of the aforesaid fleet sailed along the north coast of Java and crossed over to the Banda Islands, where they took in nutmeg and mace. After receiving their cargoes, these two ships returned to Bantam and sailed home in August 1599. I am told that serviceable winds blow over that sea every season of the year. They left ten or twelve men at the island of Banda Nera as a token of their friendship and intention to return there. Similarly, they left factors on the island of Hitu and in the Kingdoms of Bantam and Bali.

The remaining two ships of the fleet of ten awaited the new pepper harvest at Bantam in order to set out to sea in January 1600. Yet I have no confirmation of their departure or even of their destination.

The other two ships that had wintered at Madagascar reached Aceh in July 1599. They were initially well received by the King of Aceh, who sold them a small quantity of pepper. Yet a few Portuguese who were visiting Aceh warned the ruler that he risked his friendship with the Portuguese if he allowed Hollanders and Zeelanders to trade in his realm. With the King's consent, they hatched a conspiracy to set the two ships on fire. Yet some royal councillors tipped off the crews of the two vessels, which left Aceh immediately, as if they were fugitives. Of the crew members who had remained ashore [and were subsequently imprisoned], the King of Aceh sent the Captain of Malacca two men who were proficient in Spanish. One of them was a pilot born and bred in Zuricaia in Portugal, who had been aboard a Brasilman captured by the two ships and who had been forcibly taken to the East Indies against his will. Since the aforesaid men had been arrested in this city, the Captain of Malacca sent them to the Viceroy at Goa in order that he might decide on their fate. After their departure from Aceh, the two aforesaid vessels soon returned there, or to be more precise, they reached Ceylon, where the bigger ship was lost on the coast of Ceylon [near] Batticaloa. The destination of the other vessel is unknown; rumor has it that it was shipwrecked as well.

As I mentioned above, I wrote to you at length about these southern regions both this year and last. I enclosed the sailing directions for Bantam,

Aceh, Patani, Gaidela, Siam, and Cambaya, along with a proposal for resolving the situation there. It is the fruit of my discussions with people of great experience who are intimately familiar with these regions. These letters and sailing directions must currently be in the hands of the Secretaries. May Your Majesty find time to look at them for the benefit of the Lord's service as well as your own, and make such arrangements for the southern regions as will safeguard this state and commonwealth. I refer you to the aforesaid letters and sailing directions, which contain the necessary admonishments. May the Almighty grant Your Majesty a long life and good health in order to take the required measures as soon as possible.

Apart from these difficulties and new enemies in the southern regions, a junk or freighter was lost on its voyage from Japan to Macao, carrying a million in gold and over half a million in cruzados.[38] The treasure belonged to the Portuguese inhabitants of Macao, who are reduced to great poverty and despair as a result of the shipwreck.

In the kingdom of Cambodia, they killed the Portuguese, including the missionaries, and rose in rebellion against us because of some harassment or aggravation suffered by them.

In the princedom of Siam, they also murdered all the Portuguese and burned some of them alive as a result of the aggravation that we caused them.

In the islands of Solor, the blacks rebelled and captured our fortress, which they lost again after half a day.

Although we kept possession of Solor, we were not so fortunate in the kingdom of Blambangan, which was a great ally of ours and counted many churches and missionaries—the inhabitants are heathens. The ruler of Pasuruan, who is a Javanese or Muslim, attacked Blambangan with a large army and defeated the King, making himself lord and master of Blambangan. He

38. Portuguese merchantmen plied between Goa and Japan on an annual basis, the ports of call being Goa, Malacca, Macao, and Nagasaki. In the second half of the sixteenth century, the Viceroy at Goa auctioned off the Japan voyages to the highest bidder, usually high-ranking officials of the Estado da India. For the privilege of sending a ship from Goa to Nagasaki, they paid a fee of twenty-two thousand Portuguese cruzados, approximately sixty thousand Dutch guilders or six thousand pounds sterling. The fee amounted to just 3.5 percent of a voyage's actual worth, estimated at six hundred thousand Portuguese cruzados, approximately 1.5 million Dutch guilders or one hundred fifty thousand pounds sterling.

forced the heathens to convert to Islam and turned the churches into mosques, killing all the Christians.

In the Kingdom of Pegu, they killed all the Portuguese.

In the Moluccas, the inhabitants of Ternate besiege our fortress at Tidore. War is expected to break out on the island of Ambon as well.

These setbacks arise from a gross neglect of these southern regions on the part of the *Estado da India.* May Your Majesty quickly take the appropriate measures—sooner rather than later, if possible—and thus benefit these southern regions, which are the solace of the entire *Estado* and Portugal. I hope that Your Majesty will continue to give his undivided attention to these rich and excellent regions. May the Almighty reward you with many victories, which will undoubtedly result in an increased number of Christians, an expansion of the empire, and many spoils for yourself and your subjects.

The entire *Estado da India* yields one million in gold and four hundred thousand in cruzados annually in taxes, so I am told by the officers who administer the account for the auxiliary forces, conquests, and fleets of the South. As regards the current shortfall in the tax revenues, if there were a permanent southern fleet and admiral, the tax revenues of the southern regions would increase markedly. In addition to the rents that have already been allocated to the aforesaid conquests, another four hundred thousand cruzados should be used for this purpose, out of the million in gold earned in tax revenues. This should be sufficient for the fleets of the southern regions and its conquest and conservation. May the Almighty provide for what is required for His service.

In last year's correspondence I wrote at length about the state of affairs in the northern regions, to which I refer Your Majesty. In this letter, I will just discuss the events of the year 1600. Our Lord has granted us a great blessing in the assassination of Cunhale,[39] ordered by the Viceroy. Indeed, Don Fran-

39. Mahomet Kunhali Marakkar, known to Portuguese chroniclers as Cunhale Marcá, was a notorious corsair who plundered the annual Portuguese pepper shipments from the Malabar Coast to Goa in the 1580s and 1590s. When armed convoys proved insufficient to keep the corsair in check, Viceroy Francisco da Gama sent two military expeditions to the fortress of Cunhale. The first, led by Dom Luis da Gama, ended in complete failure in 1599; the second, led by André Furtado de Mendonça resulted in the corsair's surrender and execution the following year.

cisco da Gama Tralhou[40] did everything he could possibly do, as did André Furtado de Mendonça, the commander of the expedition, who acquitted himself well, along with all the other noblemen and soldiers, who gained honor by this victory, without any other claims or pretensions. May the Almighty keep and protect Your Royal Majesty, and grant you a long life for the sake of His Church. Dated Goa, April 30, 1600.

Underneath it was written and signed in a different hand:
Chaplain to Your Majesty, the Bishop of Malacca

The letter was addressed as follows: To the King our Lord
It said underneath: From the island of Malacca

Jan de Zwart, Public Notary accredited with the Provincial Court of Holland, residing in Amsterdam and proficient in Spanish, translated these articles from an authentic copy of the original letter. After completing the translation, the extract was collated with the authentic copy. Dated Amsterdam, October 23, 1604.[41]

Thus I bear witness,
(signed) Jan de Zwart, Public Notary, 1604

40. Francisco da Gama, Count Vidigueira, was Viceroy of India in 1597–1600 and 1622–28.

41. The date of the collation suggests that the letter was translated into Dutch at the request of the Amsterdam VOC directors and mailed to Grotius by Jan ten Grootenhuys. It was Grootenhuys who had sent Grotius the "book treating of the cruel, treasonous and hostile procedures of the Portuguese in the East Indies" on October 15, 1604. It consisted of fifteen notarized attestations of Dutch merchants and mariners, collected by the Amsterdam VOC directors between September 11 and October 6, 1604. Grootenhuys wrote again to Grotius on October 20, 1604, enclosing "the edict of the Estates of Holland, and the sworn statement of Mr. Apius, along with the verdict of the Amsterdam Admiralty Court." He promised to send more materials for inclusion in *De Jure Praedae* "the day after tomorrow." The letter of Dom João Ribeiro Gaio undoubtedly belonged to this third set of documents.

V
The Council of Malacca to the Four Representatives of the Dutch Ships Who Accompanied the Portuguese Prisoners to an Island near Malacca
March 9, 1603[42]

It is customary among kings and potentates that they disagree in their resolutions and opinions, while their subjects are harmed in their person and possessions. Fortune and opportunity has granted your Admiral such a big advantage that the ship from China surrendered to him.[43] Yet these are matters that are determined by the unfathomable will of God. We send Your Honors these refreshments out of gratitude, as your Admiral and you yourself have spoken the truth to the Portuguese and kept your promises to them. We will always keep this uppermost in our minds in order to behave likewise in similar circumstances. There is nothing more to be said at this time. May God Almighty keep and preserve you. Written in the [Council] Chamber by me, Paulo Mendes de Vascola, author of the same. Dated: Malacca, March 9, 1603. Signed: Ruijs Lestaomante, Andreas Fernandes, Pero de Carvalhaets, Domingos Domonte, Isaac de Gusgago.[44]

42. Although the Portuguese original has been lost, a Dutch translation of this letter is still extant in the "book treating of the cruel, treasonous and hostile procedures of the Portuguese in the East Indies." W. Ph. Coolhaas includes the translation in "Een bron van het historische gedeelte van Hugo de Groot's *De Jure Praedae,*" *Bijdragen en Mededelingen van het Historisch Genootschap* 79 (1965): 531–32. A German translation was first published in *Appendix oder Ergänzung desz achten Theils der Orientalischen Indien* (Frankfurt-am-Main: Th. de Bry, 1606), second preface, page II seqq. It appears as "Epistola Senatus Malaccensis" in Appendix B of Grotius, *Commentary on the Law of Prize and Booty,* 1:385. My English translation is based on the Dutch and German editions of this letter. See pp. 383 and 497 of the present volume.

43. Van Heemskerck captured the Portuguese carrack *Santa Catarina* on February 25, 1603. A detailed description of the seizure may be found in document IV of appendix II.

44. Malacca town councillors.

VI
The Governor of Malacca[45] to Admiral Jacob van Heemskerck March 9, 1603[46]

Wars have divers and doubtful outcomes, which, whether good or bad, arise from God's will alone—people are mere instruments in this respect. Your Honor was so lucky as to encounter a richly laden ship full of merchants, who have no stomach for fighting, along with women and other useless peoples, who are an impediment in cases of emergency. Your Honor may justly enjoy your prize, for you captured her in a public war. I am sorry for one thing, however: that Your Honor did not encounter my ship, so that you could have seen the difference in armaments and defensive capacity.

What happened to the Hollanders in China grieves me not a little, and it troubles me that such a heavy punishment was imposed with so little cause.[47] Be assured, however, that the public prosecutor of Macao, the perpetrator of

45. Fernão d'Albuquerque was a descendant of Alfonso d'Albuquerque, the conqueror of Goa (1510), Malacca (1511), and Ormuz (1515). Fernão d'Albuquerque served as *capitão-mór* (captain-major) of Malacca in 1601–3 and governor of India in 1619–22.

46. Although the Portuguese original has been lost, a Dutch translation survives in the "book treating of the cruel, treasonous and hostile procedures of the Portuguese in the East Indies." It is printed in Coolhaas, "Een bron van het historische gedeelte van Hugo de Groot's *De Jure Praedae*," 532–33. A German translation, first published in *Appendix oder Ergänzung desz achten Theils der Orientalischen Indien*, appears as "Epistola Praefecti Malaccensis ad Jacobum Hemskerckium" in appendix B of Grotius, *Commentary on the Law of Prize and Booty*, 1:385–86. My English translation is based on the Dutch and German editions of this letter. See pp. 383, 431, and 497 of the present volume.

47. Jacob van Neck, the commander of the Fourth Dutch Voyage to the East Indies, arrived off Macao with two ships on September 27, 1601. Van Neck was unaware of his location and put out first a sloop, then a longboat to take soundings in the harbor. The Portuguese officials at Macao, panic-stricken at the sight of the Dutch ships, lured the crew of the sloop ashore with white flags of truce. The longboat was captured the following day, when it came too close to the town. The Portuguese made twenty prisoners in total and secretly hanged seventeen of them in November 1601, contrary to the express wishes of the Chinese authorities. Marten Aap, the fleet's legal officer, and two cabin boys were sent to Goa, where the Portuguese viceroy released them in March 1602. See pp. 279–283, 425, and 456 of the present volume.

The Macao massacre came to Van Heemskerck's attention when his vice-admiral intercepted Portuguese correspondence in the Javanese port of Jortan in June 1602. He cited the massacre in justification of his capture of the *Santa Catarina*. Compare documents I, III, and IV in appendix II.

this misdeed, already languishes in jail, and will have to pay for it with his life. I nullified the charges against the Hollanders who arrived here from China and the Moluccas and showed myself a good friend to them. Hence Your Honor does not have sufficient reason to attack us in revenge.[48]

I dispatch a vessel in the company of the Hollanders who safely conducted the carrack's passengers and crew to Malacca at Your Honor's orders. I will kiss Your Honor's hands if it pleases Your Honor to return this vessel with the friar, brother Anthonis, the captain of the carrack, and the remaining Portuguese who are still in your protection. I should furthermore be obliged if you could negotiate the release of the passengers and crew of the Chinese junk taken by the Malayans and obtain the King [of Johore]'s promise that nothing will happen to them on their way to Malacca. It would be proof that your deeds do indeed match your words.

May the Lord preserve and keep Your Honor.

Dated: Malacca, March 9, 1603. *Signed:* Fernão d'Albuquerque.

VII
The Governor of Malacca to Admiral Jacob van Heemskerck March 26, 1603[49]

I received Your Honor's letter with great joy. It testified to the pleasure that you took in the safe arrival [at Malacca] of the crew and passengers of the captured carrack. I expected as much from an admiral like you. I will do the same for any Hollander brought into this fortress in similar circumstances.

As for the Dutchmen whom you claim to be [imprisoned] in India and Japan, the Viceroy is accustomed to treat captives well and abhors the misdeeds of the public prosecutor of Macao. He had the man arrested in order to punish him severely. Your Honor should not, therefore, take offence at the

48. The German translation omits the last sentence of this paragraph.

49. This document has had the same fate as the two previous ones: a Dutch translation in Coolhaas, "Een bron van het historische gedeelte van Hugo de Groot's *De Jure Praedae,*" 533–34, and a German translation in *Appendix oder Ergänzung desz achten Theils der Orientalischen Indien.* The latter translation appears as "Epistola Altera Ejusdem ad Eundem" in appendix B of Grotius, *Commentary on the Law of Prize and Booty,* 1:386–87. My English translation is based on the Dutch and German editions of this letter. See pp. 279–83, 383, and 497 of the present volume.

Portuguese in general. Everybody considers what was done in China an evil deed.

In the knowledge that Your Honor cares deeply for the fate of all captives and oppressed Christians, I entreat Your Honor to do me the favor of negotiating with the King of Johor and his brother. I want him to release the Portuguese and Christians whom he keeps prisoner under the pretext of peace. I do not speak of, or wish to reclaim, the cargo of the junk, which has undoubtedly been divided among the soldiers of his navy. I only desire the release of the Portuguese and Christian prisoners, who are of little importance to the Malayans. I therefore send you Philippe Lobo and Pero Mascarenhas, whom I entreat Your Honor to take into your protection, so that they may safely return with the Portuguese prisoners and not lack your favor and goodwill.

May the Lord preserve you and bring you home to Holland according to His will.

Dated: Malacca, March 26, 1603 *Signed:* Fernão d'Albuquerque

VIII
The Captain of the *Santa Catarina* to Admiral Jacob Heemskerck March 24, 1603[50]

It has pleased the Lord to bring me back to Malacca under the protection and in the favor of Your Honor. All the days of my life I will sing the praises of your steadfast promises and true friendship, which I enjoyed while I was your prisoner, along with all other people who were with me. I heartily wish that I could offer you some refreshments in order to express my gratitude for your kindness and favor. Yet I have been unable to put it into effect. I am among strangers here, with poverty as my bedfellow. Indeed, I do not even have any proper clothes to speak of. What I am currently wearing is so torn and spoiled by the hail of gunfire from Your Honor's ship that it can no longer

50. This document has had the same fate as the three previous ones: a Dutch translation in Coolhaas, "Een bron van het historische gedeelte van Hugo de Groot's *De Jure Praedae,*" 535, and a German translation in *Appendix oder Ergänzung desz achten Theils der Orientalischen Indien.* The latter translation appears as "Epistola Capitanei Captae Galeonis ad Jacobum Hemskerckium" in appendix B of Grotius, *Commentary on the Law of Prize and Booty,* 1:387. My English translation is based on the Dutch and German editions of this letter. See pp. 383–84 and 497 of the present edition.

be used as garment. For this reason I entreat Your Honor to do me a good turn and send me a piece of velvet for a new set of clothes. If Your Honor grants my request, I would consider it a great kindness and gladly receive your alms. Let Your Honor call to mind the circumstances in which you captured and released me, and in which I may find myself in the future. Whatever it pleases Your Honor to give me, you can send it to me by means of the bearer of this letter, who will deliver it to me. And I will consider myself beholden to Your Honor, since Your Honor's gifts will merit it. May God be with you and bring you back home to Holland in good health.

Dated: Malacca, March 24, 1603 *Signed:* Sebastiano Serrao

APPENDIX II

Archival Documents Relating to *De Jure Praedae*

Translated by Martine J. van Ittersum

I

Nicolas de Montalegre to André Furtado de Mendonça,[1] Capitão-Mór and General of the South Sea and His Conquests June 20, 1602[2]

Entrusted to Father Pablo de Mesquita, a Portuguese Monk Intercepted at Jortan on the island of Java between June 20 and 25, 1602, by Jan Pauwels, Vice-Admiral of the Fleet of Jacob van Heemskerck

Two ships from Holland reached Grissee on May 27 and unloaded a great quantity of trade goods. Many crew members disembarked as well.

1. The Portuguese nobleman André Furtado de Mendonça (1558–1610) served the *Estado da India* with great distinction. In March 1600, he captured Mahomet Kunhali Marakkar, a notorious pirate who had attacked Portuguese shipping all along India's west coast. Out of gratitude, the Portuguese Viceroy at Goa gave him a commission as Admiral of the Fleet of the South (1601–3), charged with ousting the Dutch interlopers from the Malay Archipelago. He became Governor of Malacca in 1603 and interim viceroy of India in May 1609.

2. This is an English translation of the second half of Montalegre's letter. The Portuguese original and Dutch translation are still extant at the Dutch National Archives. Both were published by P. A. Leupen in the appendix of his article "Kaartje van de Banda-eilanden vervaardigd door Emanoel Godinho De Eredia in 1601," *Bijdragen tot de Taal-, Land-, en Volkenkunde van Nederlandsch-Indië,* 3rd ser., 11 (1876): 386–91.

The Amsterdam VOC directors included Montalegre's letter in their "book treating of the cruel, treasonous and hostile procedures of the Portuguese in the East

They had tried to seize indigenous vessels in the port of Demak, but received their comeuppance. The Demak authorities arrested all Dutchmen who happened to be in town—there were over fifty of them—and confiscated the trade goods that had been brought ashore. The Demak authorities accepted ransom for the officers but killed the other prisoners, with the exception of twelve sailors, who are still kept in captivity.

I took father Pablo de Mesquita aboard one of the Dutch ships so that he might give you an eyewitness account of how well equipped they are in everything. The Dutch crew is particularly eager to learn whether your Armada has gun ports close to the waterline. They brag that a big fleet of warships will arrive here from their country before long and deplore the fact that they are mere merchants. Since Spanish harbors are closed to them, they have to come to the Indies in order to make money. May God Almighty provide for this and grant you many prosperous victories in defense of your holy Catholic faith.

Signed: Your Servant Nicolas de Montalegre *Dated:* Grissee, June 20, 1602

II
Jacob van Heemskerck[3]
to the Directors of the United Amsterdam Company
July 13, 1602[4]

We left the port of Grissee on the seventh of June and plotted our course north of the island of Madura in a second attempt to reach the island of Bali.

Indies," which Grotius received from Jan ten Grootenhuys on October 15, 1604. Cf. document V below and Coolhaas, "Een bron van het historische gedeelte van Hugo de Groot's *De Jure Praedae,*" 535–37. See pp. 274, 427, 531, and 543 of this volume.

3. Jacob van Heemskerck (1567–1607) participated in two of three Dutch attempts to find the Northeast Passage and served as a vice-admiral on the second Dutch voyage to the East Indies (1598–1600), in which capacity he became the first Dutch commander to visit the Banda Islands. Returning to the Malay Archipelago in February 1602, he commanded a fleet of eight ships from the United Amsterdam Company. He first sailed along the northern coast of Java and then crossed over to the Malay Peninsula, where he called at the ports of Patani and Johore. He captured the Portuguese carrack *Santa Catarina* in the Strait of Singapore in February 1603, which made him famous and rich.

The federal government of the Dutch Republic put him in charge of a Dutch navy squadron in the spring of 1607 to blockade the harbor of Lisbon and prevent

Before our departure we had increased the value of our trade goods at Grissee to two or three thousand guilders, both in coin and commodities, which were left under the supervision of Adriaen Schaeck, Hans Roef, and Gerrit van Doornick, with instructions to barter these for cloves, nutmeg, and mace. After we had struggled against the monsoon winds for seventeen or eighteen days, without any prospect of attaining our goal, we turned back and arrived at the port of Jortan on June 25.

We found our Vice-Admiral there, whom, because of three leaks in the bow of his ship and for other reasons, we had sent to Jortan eight days earlier. There was a Portuguese frigate as well, which had followed the Armada to the island of Ambon with a cargo of victuals. It had received orders from Admiral André Furtado de Mendonça to go first to the island of Solor and then to the port of Malacca, carrying 6 or 8 bahars of cloves and 150 bahars of sandal wood, each bahar worth eighty or a hundred ryals of eight.[5] The Vice-Admiral had seized the frigate with the permission of the Governess of Grissee and confiscated the cargo, giving the Portuguese a taste of their own medicine. Since they sat in the sloops and seemed to put up resistance, several of the frigate's crew and passengers were shot and killed by our men, including two monks. The bodies of the other men, six or seven in total, were recovered as well.

In reading some of the letters found aboard the frigate, we concluded that the Portuguese had Ambon at their mercy and intended to conquer Ternate, Banda, and Solor next. All of this could have been prevented, with relatively little effort, by the five Dutch ships that arrived in the East Indies in good time, had they been equipped in such a fashion as some would have liked. Yet I pray God will send some Dutch ships that will stop the Armada in its tracks and thwart its intentions. Meanwhile, I hope that Your Honors or the

---

the Portuguese from sending naval reinforcements to the East Indies. Yet the carracks scheduled for Goa that year slipped out of Lisbon before Van Heemskerck's arrival. The Dutch admiral continued to the Strait of Gibraltar, where he attacked and destroyed the mighty Spanish Armada, but lost his life in battle.

4. The original letter is available in Dutch: *De Opkomst van het Nederlandsch Gezag in Oost-Indië (1595–1610),* ed. J. K. J. de Jonge (The Hague: Martinus Nijhoff, 1864), 2:515–17.

5. Ryals of eight were Spanish silver coins used for commercial transactions in both the East and West Indies. The bahar was a unit of weight common throughout the Malay Archipelago. See footnote 37 in appendix I above.

Dutch commonwealth will take measures to remedy the situation so that we may not lose the best spice-producing regions.

Some other letters from the port of Macao revealed that two Dutch ships had arrived there in September 1601, I presume from the fleet commanded by Jacob van Neck. The Captain of Macao laid his hands on its sloop and longboat, including seventeen sailors, who were strung up in cold blood. I was so upset at the news that, if it had not been for the Dutch captives in the Sultanate of Demak and the trading post I wanted to establish at Grissee, I would have hanged our remaining prisoners from the bowsprit in full sight of the Portuguese ashore. I managed to restrain myself, however, for the reasons stated above.

On July 7, the Governess of Grissee informed us that three Portuguese ships had arrived at the port of Tuban. We raised anchor the same night and set course for Tuban in the hope of finding some means to revenge the Macao massacre. Since we lack Dutch warships to keep the enemy in check, we have to do it all ourselves. When we approached the three vessels, however, we discovered that their clove cargoes had become nutmeg loads, and that enemies had changed into friends. They informed me about the current state of the Banda Islands and Ambon, which, in their view, we may well lose if no Dutch ships go over there in the near future. I would give my life and soul for this cause, but I lack the authority and the means to do so. If fifty sailors of the fleet of Wolphert Harmenszoon had been willing to join my crew—the Admiral could easily have done without them—I would have set sail for the Spice Islands immediately in order to engage the Armada. Yet we abandoned our resolution because it did not seem feasible to enlist sailors from the fleet of Wolphert Harmenszoon against their will.

III
Jacob van Heemskerck and His Council of Naval Officers Resolve to Attack Portuguese Shipping Indiscriminately December 4, 1602[6]

After anchoring at the island of Tiuman on December 3, Admiral Jacob van Heemskerck calls a meeting of the Council and points out the fine oppor-

6. Notarized copy, dated May 24, 1605, Archives of the Estates General at the Dutch National Archives, Staten Gen. 12551.21 (Loketkas processen nr. 21), unfoliated. See p. 429 of the present volume.

tunity at hand to damage our public enemies within twenty or twenty-five days. Both the Japan carrack and the ship belonging to the Captain of Malacca, along with two other smaller vessels or junks, will come down together from Macao, situated in China, all very richly laden. We can do no greater harm or damage to our public enemy in the entire East Indies than to pull out this flight feather.

It is indeed a matter of great urgency to preserve the East Indies trade and keep the public enemy in check, lest the latter continue with his Armada as he has begun, inciting all indigenous kings against us and putting a price on our heads. The Portuguese use all possible means, however evil or godless, for our utter destruction, as shown on various occasions. For example, seventeen men of Van Neck's crew, who appeared before Macao in a sloop and barge, were captured by them and hanged in cold blood. Still not satisfied, they also seek to extirpate all native peoples who offer us trade and friendship. They would have reduced Bantam with their Armada if it had not been for the Almighty and our Dutch ships. From Bantam they sailed east to lay waste Ambon. They are determined to go to Ternate and Banda next, in order to subdue those places as well, which Heaven forbid, and deny us access to ports and trade all over the East Indies, using force against one indigenous king and threats and intimidation against another.

In view of the above, the Admiral and his Council consider it necessary and desirable to defy the enemy and show the natives that we do not fear Portuguese power. Since, as mentioned above, the Portuguese have tried to uproot us with all possible means, whether directly or indirectly, we will attack and harm them wherever we can or may. At this particular juncture we should indeed be able, God willing, to inflict the greatest damage with the least loss of time. Hence the Admiral and his Council have decided to remain anchored at the island of Tiuman for the whole month of December and await whatever victory the Almighty shall grant us against our public enemy.

Drawn up in the ship *White Lion,* lying at anchor near the aforesaid island, on December 4, 1602. Signed by Jacob van Heemskerck, Jan Pauwels, Hendrick Cornelis, and Pieter Stockmans.

IV
Jacob van Heemskerck to the Directors of the United Amsterdam Company August 27, 1603[7]

Honorable and Distinguished Sirs,

Please accept my hearty greetings and best wishes. This communication serves to update you on what has happened during our voyage. My previous letter was entrusted to Jacob van Neck, who left Patani with both his ships on August 22, 1602, sailing in the company of two Indiamen from Zeeland. After his departure, we arranged for merchant Daniel van Lecq to take over my excess trade goods as well as his, which seemed in the Company's best interest. Broadly similar commodities were to be sold en masse and their proceeds shared between the two voyages. Disparate trade goods like our lead and sandalwood and Van Neck's treasure were to be bartered for pepper first, then amalgamated with the proceeds of the aforesaid commodities and shipped home, unless Your Honors should provide for them differently.

We built a nice, big house in Patani and surrounded it with a big ditch in order to safely store our trade goods and protect them from fire. The ditch would not have been necessary if the house had been made of stone. Although preferable, this would have been difficult to achieve, however. The Portuguese sought to persuade the local authorities that our notion of a stone house was so comprehensive as to include a fortress. Yet the inhabitants of Patani did not believe them because we enjoyed greater credit and favor.

When we left Patani with both our ships and a yacht on November 16, 1602, our cargo consisted of one thousand bahars of pepper at thirty ryals per bahar, approximately eighty last of rice, textiles worth four thousand or five thousand ryals, some porcelain and copper, and ten thousand or eleven thousand ryals in cash.[8] Our intention was to sail to Banda in order to load as much nutmeg and mace as possible. We already imagined shooting the proverbial popinjay in case of success, as seemed entirely probable. Yet we

7. Received by the Amsterdam VOC directors on May 17, 1604, Archives of the Dutch Estates General at the Dutch National Archives, Staten Gen. 12551.21 (Loketkas Processen nr. 21), unfoliated.

8. The last was a unit of weight common in the Dutch Republic, but lacked a uniform standard. The United Amsterdam Company equated one last with 3,000 Amsterdam pounds, approximately 1,482 kilos. In terms of a ship's tonnage, one last was a little less than 2 tons.

anchored with our ships and yacht near the island of Tiuman, where we discussed the opportunity at hand and how best to seize it. Since we could spare a month without endangering our voyage to the Banda Islands and since we ran no risks except for the danger posed to our persons and ships by our enemies, we decided to tarry there until January 1, 1603, in the expectation of divine blessing. We had every hope of encountering a richly laden carrack from Macao according to the information we received from the Patani authorities, the Prince of Siak, brother of the King of Johore,[9] the Portuguese prisoners aboard our ships, and other people we met in Jortan and elsewhere. Every year the first of the aforesaid carracks calls on the island between December 20 and 31, and then sets course for the Strait of Singapore.

On December 18, 1602, a small Portuguese vessel, which had come from Cochin China, anchored to the windward of us near the aforesaid island. Believing it to have arrived from China proper, we did our utmost to capture the vessel in order to obtain reliable information about the Macao carrack. Since adverse winds made it impossible for us to approach it, we sent a letter demanding the vessel's surrender, in exchange for a promise not to harm its crew. They were willing to accept the ultimatum, but desired better guarantees for their safety. To that purpose they deputed Mattys D'Olivera, a man from Hamburg who had lived in Asia for fifteen years. He conveyed to us a copy of the vessel's bill of lading and a letter from its captain, requesting confirmation of our promises. After we had sent him back, we came alongside the Portuguese vessel in the evening. Since it was already dark, we decided to wait until the morning before proceeding any further. Thus it happened that, it being a dark, rainy night, almost the entire Portuguese crew gave us the slip and departed in a longboat, carrying along a jar of camphor and two or three thousand ryals of eight in both silver and gold. Their conscience must have told them that they were not worthy of our word of honor, as they had not kept faith with our men at Macao. Several hours after their departure, the blacks who had been left behind called out to our men in a sloop nearby, alerting them to the fact that the Portuguese had fled and beseeching them to take possession of the vessel, lest it be boarded by the in-

9. The "King of Johore" was 'Ala'ud-din Ri'ayat Shah III of Johore (d. 1615). His younger brother, Raja Bongsu, was the leader of a pro-Dutch faction at the Johorese court. Both in this letter and in chapter 11, Raja Bongsu is confused with Rage Syack, alias the Prince of Siak, leader of the pro-Portuguese faction and governor of Johore's territories on the east coast of Sumatra.

habitants of Tiuman. We immediately complied with their request and spent the rest of the time unloading the vessel and refurbishing it. In addition, our men held watch day and night at a certain island suitable for that purpose. We were even so vain as to assure ourselves that the coveted bird would not fly the coop.

Although our resolution had expired, we received encouraging news from the inhabitants of Tiuman and the crews of the proas that arrived daily from the port of Pahang, some of whom had been in Malacca only the week before. They informed us that no ships from Macao had passed by and that the Captain of Malacca, who was aware of our intention to intercept the carracks, had already lost his nerve, saying that his ship no longer belonged to him but to the Hollanders. The Hamburg prisoner provided us with valuable information as well. He had traveled from Goa to Malacca in the Captain's ship, which had been accompanied by a second, brand-new carrack. Both ships were expected to return soon, as it had never happened in the history of the Macao voyage that carracks bound for Goa had stayed the winter in China. Our resolution to intercept the Macao carrack was extended for another month, also because we decided against buying mace at Banda and planned to load pepper at Johore instead. Since our trading capital increased with ten thousand or twelve thousand ryals taken from the Cochin China vessel, we had ample means to obtain a cargo of pepper at Johore or Patani, where the vessel's rice, treasure, textiles, and forty bahars of aloes would be in high demand.

Meanwhile, the young King of Johore had been informed about our intention to intercept the Macao carrack—some proa had spotted our ships near Tiuman. In spite of the adverse monsoon winds, he immediately dispatched one of his noblemen in a proa or foist, who delivered the King's letter and offered me a golden dagger on his behalf. The King wrote that he had received my letters and presents sent from Jortan, along with my communications from Patani. He also acknowledged the great honors done to his brother, the Prince of Siak, when the latter paid a visit to our ships at Patani. He was disappointed that we had not called on his harbors yet, contrary to the intentions expressed in our letters, but put the blame on our pilot. He was pleased at the news that we were lying in wait for the Macao carrack near the island of Tiuman, and wished we had already captured it. Yet he argued that his river was the best place to await it, as all carracks must pass through the Strait of Singapore. Even if they should try to pass the Strait by night, which was impossible, they could never do so without being observed from the river. He added that open war had broken out between him and Malacca three months earlier due to some recent nuisance caused by the Portuguese, along with the many old and new injuries which the Portuguese had daily inflicted upon him and his subjects, regarding them as little more than dogs. When the Portuguese in Malacca became aware of our correspondence, they had positively ordered him not to befriend the Dutch, saying the Dutch were all thieves, intent upon conquering his kingdom under the pretext of friendship. If he contravened their orders, he would be considered an enemy. In reply, the King had denied ever hearing anything bad about the Dutch, who traded in the friendliest manner with the inhabitants of every place they visited. He had furthermore told the Portuguese not to meddle in the affairs of his kingdom, prescribing with whom he could or could not engage in trade. As a result, three Portuguese warships—one whereof was first captured and then released by the English—and four or five foists had been stationed near Johore Head, where they awaited the aforesaid ships from Macao in order to convoy them to Malacca. They had inflicted as much damage as they could and prevented others from navigating freely upon his river. The King assured me that I would not encounter just the Macao carracks, but vessels from every corner of the earth if I went there. In addition, I would earn myself a great reputation with the victory that he already ascribed to me, saying the Portuguese tremble at the mention of your name, while heaping many other praises on Maurice of Nassau, which would take too long to recount here.

The King's letter, along with the presents received from his ambassador, gave us food for thought. Indeed, we hardly knew what to think of it. On the one hand, we considered how near Johore was to Malacca and how detrimental it must be to the Portuguese to be at war with Johore if ships from Holland should call there year round, like at Bantam. On this assumption, the Portuguese would never break the peace with the King of Johore, but rather do everything to keep it, promising him the moon, undoubtedly. We took into account that the King of Johore might feign friendship in order to take his revenge upon us for capturing one of his subjects' junks in Japara harbor the previous year. There was also a possibility that it might all be a Portuguese plot to lure us from Tiuman to the foul ground off Johore. After our departure, the King of Pahang could easily be persuaded by Portuguese bribes to send his proas to Tiuman and instruct the Macao carracks to remain anchored there. On the other hand, we were inclined to give credence to the King of Johore because of the great grievances which the aforesaid Malay rulers nursed against the Portuguese, especially the King of Johore, not to mention the profits which he could reap from our trade and navigation. After deliberation, we decided not to turn down the ambassador's invitation to come to Johore, but explain to him that we did not dare to leave Tiuman yet. If the Macao carracks anchored at the island after our departure, its inhabitants might inform the Portuguese about our new location at Johore, which would undoubtedly induce the latter to stay there. We asked the ambassador to give us another twenty days, to which he consented, seeing he could not persuade us otherwise.

We trusted the Johorese ambassador better after he had stayed with us for a few days. I proposed to send the foist back to Johore carrying my own envoy and my letters for the King, provided he would leave one man behind as a hostage, to which he agreed immediately. While he remained aboard my ship with five or six of his attendants, I dispatched Pieter Opmeer and a sailor to Johore in order to thank the King for his presents and friendship and assure him that I believed every word he had written to us. They were to explain, however, that I could not come to Johore until I was sure that the Macao carracks would not winter at Tiuman after my departure from thence. In addition, Pieter Opmeer received instructions to discreetly inquire about the King's relations with the Portuguese, the price of rice at Johore, and the quantity of pepper marketed there. He was to send me his report promptly, borrowing a foist from the King if necessary, and include in it any information he might obtain about the Portuguese warships that blockaded Johore River.

The month of January passed without the occurrence of anything noteworthy, except for the daily reports from Malacca, arriving via Pahang, that no carracks from Macao had passed yet. This left us no choice but to extend our resolution first for ten days, then for six, and finally for four days at a time. Then, on February 18, an inhabitant of Tiuman came aboard the vice-admiral and alleged that he had seen a ship with sails made of tarpaulin, which passed the island to the seaward that morning, towing a longboat. Since the man's story was not particularly convincing and since we trusted our own sentries, we did not give him any credence. When local leaders confirmed the news two days later, we still could not believe it and considered it a ruse to lure us away from the island before the carrack's arrival. Then, on February 22, we received letters from Pieter Opmeer by means of the King's foist and learned from its crew that the first Macao carrack had passed them on their way to Tiuman. Anticipating the second ship to give the island a wide berth as well and realizing that the time had come to make our voyage, we immediately weighed anchor and set sail for Johore, where we arrived at the river mouth on the evening of the twenty-fourth. Both the King and Pieter Opmeer informed us that the first Macao carrack had safely passed the Strait of Singapore five days earlier.

At the crack of dawn on February 25, we saw with our own eyes that waking up early, keeping a close watch, and running fast availed us nothing without the blessing of the Almighty. He heard our prayers while we were asleep in order that we might not pride ourselves on our own accomplishments. Right in front of us was the second Macao carrack, a brand-new ship of 800 last. After we had carefully prepared ourselves, we hauled anchor at approximately 8 A.M. and approached the carrack, which set sail as well. All day long we pounded the carrack with both our ships, though we tried to aim for the mainsails, lest we destroy our booty by means of our own cannonades. At about 6:30 P.M., when the sun was setting and its mainsails had been shot to rags, a white flag was hoisted on the carrack. I sent over a sloop and demanded its surrender, whereupon two Portuguese came aboard my ship to negotiate terms. They had quite a few demands, in fact, none of which I granted. Finally, since fire and underwater rocks imperiled the carrack, I promised life to its crew and passengers, along with two yachts to take them to Malacca, provided they accepted my offer within one hour. If not, I would resume the battle by the light of the moon. They could figure out themselves what the consequences might be. Should the carrack hit a submerged rock, it would undoubtedly go down with all hands on board. They returned before the passing of the deadline and brought a written statement from the carrack's captain, who surrendered on the aforesaid terms.

On the morning of the 26th, six or seven Portuguese officers came aboard my ship, whereupon I approached the carrack again with both my ship and the vice-admiral. We transferred its passengers and crew to the two Portuguese yachts as best we could, making a real effort to prevent them from taking along any gold. Yet I fear that we may not have succeeded completely, since there were many people aboard the carrack, including one hundred women, who, for decency's sake, could not be searched too closely. About seven hundred and fifty souls went aboard the two yachts. According to the carrack's captain, there were seventy casualties among the passengers and crew. If half the shots that we fired at the mainsails had been aimed any lower, there would have been many more casualties, for the large number of passengers and crew made them an easy target. Indeed, the Portuguese were lucky to encounter us near the Strait and not on the open sea; otherwise we might have done an evil dance out of revenge for their misdeeds at Macao. The Portuguese used a flag of truce to lure the crew of Jacob van Neck ashore and hanged seventeen of them, while Marten Aap and one or two others were sent to Goa. Rumor has it that they are free men now. God grant that it be true. I imagine that if we pull out a flight feather, the Portuguese will change their tune and give us a better deal.

We intended to freight the carrack with pepper purchased in Johore and to unload its cargo of silk into our own ships. Since there was little pepper available in Johore, it being early in the season, and since the monsoon for Bantam was almost spent, we did our utmost to get away. Yet by the time we had freighted the carrack with 180 bahars of pepper, rewarded the King of Johore with a cargo of rice, and brought the prisoners back to Malacca—many of my men went along as guards lest the Malayans kill them—the month of March was gone.

I had agreed with Pieter Opmeer to leave behind the aloes found in the prize from Cochin China, along with thirty-five pieces of textile and several other goods. Seeing these commodities ashore, the King expressed his wish to send ambassadors to the Netherlands, which was granted him. In addition, he insisted that cape merchant Jacob Buys remain at Johore instead of Pieter Opmeer, which put me in a difficult position. I figured that Buys was wanted at Cambay in order to establish a factory there, which is essential for our trade with Southeast Asia. Since our commodities were already ashore and since I had consented to a Johorese embassy, I decided to humor the King on this point as well, also because of the kingdom's geographical location and commercial potential. It is clearly the most suitable place in all of the East Indies to load pepper and sell textiles from Cambay and San Thomé. Yet I had to use all my persuasive powers in order to convince Jacob Buys, who preferred to go home and share in the booty of the *Santa Catarina.* He will receive . . . guilders[10] for every month that he oversees the sale of the trade goods stored at Johore, to which I added more cash and commodities afterwards. Jacob Honing and the son of Jong, the burgomaster of Dordrecht, stayed with him at Johore as well, along with three sailors. If everything goes well, I expect them to collect nine hundred or a thousand bahars of pepper, weighing four picol each, not the Jambi kind, but the Andryghery, which is equal in quality to Aceh pepper.

10. The amount is unspecified in the original text, where the space is left blank.

On April 3, we set course for Bantam with our three vessels. Both the Johorese ambassador and his retinue were on board, the ambassador being a fine young man from an eminent noble family. We battled against contrary monsoon winds on our way to Bantam, which were especially dangerous for the carrack. We experienced a serious setback when we had completed two-thirds of the journey. A sloop with a complement of eleven, including Sebastiaan Hogheveer, approached some proas that we believed to be from Bantam in order to hear the latest news and obtain information about the depth of the water. Because of a navigation failure, the sloop and its crew were captured before our eyes by the proas, which were local pirates. May the Almighty have mercy on the souls of these eleven men and grant them salvation. We safely arrived at Bantam, praise be to God, with both the carrack and our two ships on June 20. We encountered Admiral Wybrandt van Warwyck at Bantam, along with six of his ships. He has supplied us with many things that we needed for the carrack, especially ropes and cordage. With God's help, we intend to tow the carrack and bring it home, drawing not more than twenty-three or twenty-four feet of water in order to navigate the ocean in a secure fashion. Since we plan to arrive in the United Provinces at the height of summer, around the month of June, we should appreciate it greatly if you could inform us where you want the carrack delivered. Here is one Van de Tissens, a pilot from the village of Huysduynen, who proposes to tow it into the Spanish Hole while drawing twenty-four feet of water. Hence it is imperative to have Your Honors' opinion on this matter sooner rather than later.

According to the Portuguese, the carrack received a cargo at Macao consisting of 2,000 picol of silk, 400 or 500 chests of silk velour, 500 pounds of aloes, 500 pounds of white granulated sugar, 500 pounds of tutenagh (an ore from which the Chinese make copper coins), lots of pockwood and radish (enough to fill a ship of 30 or 40 last), 500 pounds of red and yellow copper (both processed and unprocessed), 100 picol of camphor, a big chest filled with 300 pounds of musk balls, and 4 grosses of fine China, along with a great quantity of gilded woodwork in the shape of coaches, tables, and other things. Yet there were many other goods on board of which we have not been told yet and of which we may never have any knowledge in our lifetime. We transferred from the carrack into our ship 1,834 bales of silk, including 250 bales of raw silk, 150 barrels of camphor, 540 packs of sugar, and 74 chests of silk velour and aloes. The tutenagh, serving as ballast, was stowed both underneath and upon the dunnage and properly trimmed with bags of pepper. We also have nine or ten packs of porcelain on board. The vice-admiral took in 1,150 bales of silk, 646 packs of sugar, weighing approximately 2 picol each, 226 chests of aloes and silk velour, and 4 barrels of camphor. What still remains in the carrack is Your Honors' guess as well as mine. I laid my hands on 138 bars of gold, each weighing 0.75 pound, whereof I send Your Honors three samples, one in each ship, along with the other commodities, which are listed in the enclosed specification. I am keeping the other ingots in order to purchase pepper cargoes for our ships.

I also entrust to Captain Meerman a packet of letters and bills for Your Honors, which reveal just how important and profitable the China trade is for the Portuguese. It is imperative for us to enter this trade, in particular because the United Dutch East India Company has just been established and chartered for twenty years. It would be desirable if Your Honors sent the three best ships of the fleet of the spring of 1603 to China, carrying all the fleet's bullion, and instructed the other vessels to fetch home any remaining merchandise. However much money is imported into China, it will always go to good use if spent on trade goods. A ship of four hundred last will not be sufficient for the large amounts of pepper that we expect to be bought on our account at Johore and Patani. Indeed, it will take a ship of five hundred last to collect the merchandise and bullion that the fleets of Jacob van Neck and the Zeeland Company left at Patani. Look at how much bullion and trade goods Van Warwyck's fleet will leave behind for the purchase of pepper in Bantam and spices in the Moluccas and Banda Islands. According to the latest news from the Banda Islands, mace costs forty ryals of eight per bahar this year, and nutmeg four ryals per bahar. In sum, the twenty-year company would do better to invest its money in the China trade, lest we drown ourselves in pepper and spices.

In future, we should not use silver ryals to buy pepper, but textiles from Cambay and San Thomé, which will earn us at least one xeraphine in all the pepper marts and be much more profitable than payment in ryals.[11] The natives do not wear ryals of eight around their necks, nor can they clothe themselves with silver coins, as both the Sabandar of Patani and various officials in other ports pointed out to me, saying "bring us textiles and we will declare war on the Portuguese."

11. The xeraphine was a Portuguese currency minted at Goa and commonly used in the Malay Archipelago. One xeraphine was equivalent to one-half ryal of eight or approximately one and one-quarter Dutch guilders.

Your Honors should establish a rendezvous in these regions as well. Although Bantam is a suitable place geographically speaking, hefty tolls and the minority of its king make for a badly ordered government, creating many dangers when there are no Dutch ships anchored in its roadstead. Patani must be deemed the most secure of all the pepper marts. Silver is always at a premium in Patani, due to bullion exports to Siam and China. Siam also seems a good market for quite a few of our trade goods. We found the Patani magistrates to be much more sensible than their colleagues in other ports. In our estimation, the town's only disadvantage is its remote location. Johore would be much more suitable than the other two, certainly with respect to the trade in Indian textiles and the pepper producing regions, which are right at its doorstep. The kingdom is happily situated in the middle of the southern countries that produce diamonds and *lapus beser.* Yet Malacca surpasses them all: the purse would be safe there from enemy assaults, raging fires, and other hazards, since the Portuguese elite already lives in stone houses and the town itself is ringed by a stone wall. Indeed, it is about time that we force the Portuguese out of Malacca and transfer them to Ceylon, for which we will have the wherewithal if, with God's help, we arrive home with the carrack.

Since the Almighty has blessed our East Indies trade immeasurably, and let us become friends with so many different nations and kings in so short a time span, we should not pass up the present opportunity. Instead, we must do our utmost to settle our nation in the East Indies and establish both a spiritual and a political commonwealth, placing our hope in God, who will let it blossom and bloom. Truly, we see before our own eyes the great blessings bestowed on the East Indies trade and the progress made within just a few years, as manifested by the friendship of the natives and the astonishment of all our enemies. We are therefore obliged to contribute our mite in the place where the Lord has blessed us and continues to bless us. Oh, may God's glory be exalted among so many different nations, peoples, and countries by means of the true Protestant religion. Perhaps the Lord will use a small, despised country and nation to work his mighty miracles.

There are two things necessary for the continuation and flourishing of this trade. Our ships should first call upon the ports of Gujarat and Cambay and then visit San Thomé and the Coromandel Coast in order to buy as many textiles as possible, either for money or trade goods. By these means we could not just corner the entire pepper trade, but also obtain many other commodities produced in the southern East Indies. And as far as Dutch settlements are concerned, if we cannot establish ourselves in Malacca, we should do so at Johore, its strategic location being comparable with Malacca's. Once we control the textile trade at Johore, Malacca will be sufficiently besieged. Nor will the Portuguese dare to sail to China when our ships are stationed at the mouth of the Johore River, allowing us to take over the China and Japan trade. We should not just import the merchandise into the United Provinces, but also sell it along the coast of the northern East Indies, where the Portuguese do a brisk trade with Chinese commodities like spices and other products. Three or four big carracks, along with several small ships and junks, sail from Malacca to Goa every year. I assure Your Honors—indeed, I cannot in good conscience desist from emphasizing—that these two places are the nodal points of the entire East Indies trade: Gujarat and San Thomé to buy textiles, and Malacca or Johore to sell them and establish a rendezvous.

I left Jacob Buys there in order to make sure that Your Honors would receive further information about Johore's trade and strategic location by means of the first Dutch ships that should call there after us. A solid foundation for Your Honors' trade can best be laid in the initial stages. It is no mean feat that a United East India Company has been established in our country and that it enjoys a monopoly on the navigation between the East Indies and the Dutch Republic by the virtue of its charter. Yet the hunters who are currently locating the quarry in the East Indies do not deserve to be excluded from the trade as a reward for our hard labors. I hope, however, that you will make a special arrangement for us before the gate is closed entirely.

When I arrived in Bantam, I was pleasantly surprised to learn that our Vice Admiral Jean Grenier[12] had joined the other ships of our fleet here and that they had all left for Holland on June 10, 1602, richly laden. May the Almighty preserve them and bring them home safely. The bullion and merchandise that they left behind were lost in a fire, with the exception of five hundred ryals of eight. By adding another five hundred ryals, the amount was sufficient to pay ransom for the five prisoners still held at Demak. They are now here with us—praise be to God for their release. It would be desirable if we could also get back the eleven men who were kidnapped only recently. Since their kidnappers have no other objective than to profit by their prisoners, taking them daily to an island under the jurisdiction of the King of Johore in order to sell them there, we trust that Jacob Buys will find a way to pay a ransom for them.

12. See appendix I, note 27, above.

Two Johorese junks carried my letters for Adriaan Schaeck, our man in Grissee, authorizing him to close the factory there and join us at Bantam. When I arrived here, however, I could tell from the contents of his epistles that he had never received mine. I chartered a proa for one hundred ryals of eight and sent new letters to Jortan, ordering him to leave the place and return to Bantam aboard the flagship of Admiral Van Warwyck. In case the vessel was no longer at Jortan, he could freight one or two junks with his stock. We are still waiting for Schaeck, yet fear that he may not arrive any time soon, since we have no idea whether our last letter actually reached him, despite the one hundred ryals paid for its delivery. If the flagship of Admiral Van Warwyck had carried an express order from Your Honors to bring home as much merchandise and as many people as possible, I would have had all my men here already. For I had explicitly told Schaeck to book passage aboard the first Dutch ship that should call at Grissee and that could take home his stock as payload. Since things turned out otherwise, we will have to put up with it and bide our time. We could certainly use him and his staff aboard our ships, but, in their absence, we can only exercise patience. Schaeck's merchandise was worth approximately forty thousand guilders, which he sold for cash. He may meanwhile have invested the money in a return cargo.

We have freighted our ships with 494,635 pounds of pepper (our weight), whereof we loaded 398,115 pounds at Patani. We used the ingots to purchase 96,520 pounds of pepper at Johore, the price being thirty-nine ryals of eight per bahar of four picol. It is our intention first to load four thousand sacks of pepper here and then to return to Holland, towing the lightly laden carrack. We will leave Bantam in September or the middle of October at the latest and sail in the company of the ships *Mauritius* and *Cleyn Rotterdam.* Your Honors can expect us in the month of June or thereabouts, God willing.

The two remaining ships of Jacob van Neck's fleet were still in Cochin China last November, where a cargo of pepper was obtained for one of them. As a result of Portuguese intrigue, the local ruler assaulted them at their arrival ashore, killing twenty or twenty-two of our men and imprisoning both merchants. The latter were ransomed for one or two thousand ryals of eight and seven iron guns. Once we had reestablished amicable relations with the King, it took our men little time to discover that his friendship was feigned. Cornelis Claessen thereupon went ashore with two or three sloops and put fire to the place, killing several people. Yet we made a good peace with the King, who offered his apologies, saying that the Portuguese had fooled him into believing that the Hollanders were thieves intent upon conquering his kingdom, but that he knew better now. They managed to double the hulls of their ships there. Each vessel had a complement of about forty-five if we may believe the sailor from Hamburg, whom we found aboard the captured junk from Cochin China. The captain and merchants, including Groesberghen, Pieter Lourens, Christopher Williams, and Daen den Knecht, who sailed to China alongside Jacob van Neck, are all still alive. Just before we departed from Johore, we learnt that two Dutch ships had arrived at Patani. These must have been the two vessels from Cochin China. I hope that they will arrive home in the summer of 1604 as well.

Herewith honorable, discreet, and prudent Directors, I commend you into the grace and mercy of the Almighty. May the Lord bestow his blessing on the new company and preserve Your Honors, grant you a long and happy life, and, finally, a peaceful death. Written in the ship *White Lion* on August 27, 1603, by Your Honors' servant Jacob Heemskerck.

[In a different hand]
Received on March 17, 1604
No. 1
Letter from Jacob Heemskerck, dated August 27, 1603, in Bantam

To be put in drawer no. 11

V
Jan ten Grootenhuys[13] to Hugo Grotius
October 15, 1604[14]

At last, oh most learned of men, we send you the Indian Reports which you have been expecting for a long time. These reports were taken from the cap-

13. Jan ten Grootenhuys (1573–1646) served as a liaison between Grotius and the Amsterdam directors of the VOC in the autumn of 1604. He was the younger brother of VOC director Arent ten Grootenhuys (1570–1615), as well as a merchant and VOC shareholder in his own right. He had been Grotius's roommate in The Hague at some point between 1598 and 1602, when Grotius boarded with the Reformed minister Johannes Wtenbogaert (1557–1644). Like Grotius, Jan ten Grootenhuys was a jurist by training. He clearly shared his friend's enthusiasm for the *studia humanitatis,* however.

14. The original letter is printed in Latin in *Briefwisseling van Hugo Grotius,* ed. P. C. Molhuysen, B. L. Meulenbroek, and H. J. M. Nellen, vol. 1 (The Hague: Martinus Nijhoff, 1928), 44–45.

tains of the ships themselves, who had to confirm them under oath as well.[15] You will clearly understand from them what the Portuguese have attempted against each of the voyages for the purpose of destroying our men. In addition, you will derive from them countless proofs of perfidy, tyranny, and hostility suitable to your apology. We trust that your apology, begun so felicitously, will be completed in a short while thanks to your attentiveness. The letters of Peter Plancius, the privateering commissions, and other documents if necessary will be delivered to you at the first opportunity, as will those that your affection should subsequently demand from us, you to whom we offer every service with the greatest pleasure.[16]

Your commentary on our country's history pleased me wondrously and sparked a desire in me to read the first part as well. I beg you to grant my request, by virtue of your benevolent disposition toward me. Contact me, I beseech you, by means of your most welcome letters if you know something about the illness of our Wtenbogaard and the death of Dousa, the father of learning. Indicate as well whether you have received this book, and notify me if you hear something new from Baudius about France or England. We heard that he had given a most elaborate oration in England in defense of our country and that he was already on the way home.

My brother greets you, along with the other Amsterdam directors, who entrust to you the defense of this case, as I commend you to God Almighty. May He keep and preserve you for the sake of our fatherland and republic. Farewell, my most humane Grotius, and love your Grootenhuys as he loves you. I wrote this on October 15, 1604.

Addressee: The Honorable, Wise, and Very Prudent Hugo Grotius, lawyer accredited with the Provincial Court of Holland, boarding with Miss F. Flori on Spui street. *Enclosures:* one book.

15. The Amsterdam VOC directors took sworn statements from admirals, merchants, and sailors who had participated in the early Dutch voyages to the East Indies. The Amsterdam notary Jan Franszoon Bruyningh countersigned eight attestations between September 11 and October 4, 1604. Grotius received a set of notarized copies from Grootenhuys, entitled "book treating of the cruel, treasonous and hostile procedures of the Portuguese in the East Indies." See Coolhaas, "Een bron van het historische gedeelte van Hugo de Groot's *De Jure Praedae,*" 415–540.

16. Grootenhuys sent Grotius more materials five days later, including the placard of the Estates General of April 2, 1599, and the verdict of the Amsterdam Admiralty Court of September 9, 1604. Both documents are printed in appendix I.

Hugo Grotius noted on the reverse side of the letter:

privateering commissions
the verdict of the Admiralty Court
the edict of the Estates of Holland
obtain from Plancius the titles of such books on Portuguese trade in the East Indies as may be purchased here

VI
Jan ten Grootenhuys to Hugo Grotius
October 20, 1604[17]

We hope that you have received those documents pertaining to the Indies trade that I recently sent to you. For the present we enclose the edict of the Estates of Holland, and the sworn statement of Mr. Apius, along with the verdict of the Amsterdam Admiralty Court. The day after tomorrow, God willing, we will send you the rest, wherein I will write to you at length. Meanwhile, good-bye, written by him who is most devoted to you.

Grotius noted on the reverse side of the letter:

the placard of the Estates General
edict
the instructions mentioned by them
. . . .
of Amsterdam
. . . .
map of the East Indies
the location of the carrack's capture and a description of its seizure
placards and extracts from the instructions with regard to the prize
Plancius's memorandum
map of the East Indies

17. The original letter is printed in Latin in *Briefwisseling van Hugo Grotius,* 1:45. The safe return home of Martin Aap (here, Mr. Apius), one of the few survivors of the Macao massacre, is heralded in both *De Jure Paedae* and other documents in this appendix.

VII
Petition of the United Dutch East India Company Drafted by Hugo Grotius Submitted to the Estates General on March 4, 1606[18]

To the Right Honorable Members of the Estates General of the United Provinces

With all due respect, the directors of the United Dutch East India Company would like to remind Your Honors that you admonished them on several occasions to instruct the VOC fleets to do as much damage to the enemy as possible, including the persons, ships, and goods of his subjects. It was Your Honors' argument that the petitioners might otherwise not maintain their trade with honor or even increase it, adding that this was the principal reason for Your Honors to establish the United Dutch East India Company and authorize its offensive war against the Portuguese. Your Honors undoubtedly realized that it would greatly benefit the common cause not just to protect a trade against enemy violence, which is of great importance for the welfare of the common people, but also to deny the King of Spain his revenues from the East Indies. After all, these revenues give him the wherewithal to ruin and destroy these provinces. In addition, any damage done to the enemy in the East Indies would give Your Honors occasion to undertake many more military and naval expeditions outside of these provinces, all to the detriment of the enemy.

Since they cared deeply for the fatherland and Your Honors' government, the petitioners took this serious admonition to heart and equipped their ships for warfare, which is not customary for merchants and cost the Company a great deal of money. The officers of the VOC fleets were commanded to do all possible damage to Philip III and his subjects. When Steven van der Haghen sailed in December 1603 with his fleet of twelve ships, he carried with him secret instructions suggesting ways to inflict great harm on the common enemy, both at sea and on land, all for the benefit and honor of these provinces. The secret instructions were communicated to some representatives of Your Honors, who, we trust, read them with great satisfaction. In-

18. The Dutch original may be found in the Grotius Papers at the Dutch National Archives, Supplement I, fol. 374–79. It is a scribal copy with marginalia in Grotius's hand and contains a separate sheet with his reading notes.

deed, the secret instructions have already borne fruit in the waters around Mozambique and Goa, where Steven van der Haghen has made himself master of the sea and pushed back the Portuguese with superior ability. It impresses upon the natives that the Dutch have sufficient prowess and courage not just to protect themselves and their allies from Spanish violence, but also to attack the Portuguese in their own strongholds. Cornelis Matelief, who sailed last year in command of eleven ships, received the same instructions, which, we hope, will result in similar or greater successes.

Yet it is becoming more difficult and expensive for the Company to implement this policy. The petitioners have learned the hard way that it is nearly impossible for private merchants to wage war against such a powerful public enemy without government subsidies. Hence they will abort their offensive unless they receive special assistance from Your Honors. They consider this demand neither unreasonable nor unfair because the war in the East Indies strengthens the Republic's reputation abroad, disadvantages its enemies, and benefits the federal government by means of taxes levied on booty and imported and exported goods. Several petitions were submitted to Your Honors to this purpose, along with various other requests. Your Honors admonished the petitioners on February 26, 1605, to manfully pursue their praiseworthy policy, and to protect the East Indies trade from Iberian intimidation and harassment, while doing the King of Spain and his subjects all possible damage. Due to the departure of some provincial deputies, as well as for other reasons, Your Honors deemed it inadvisable to entertain the requests that had been submitted along with the petition. Yet Your Honors also decided that, for the purpose of implementing and furthering the aforesaid praiseworthy policy, the petitioners should enjoy the benefit of a previous resolution of the Estates General, which assigned them two ships, along with their sails, anchors, cordage, and cannons. In addition, the petitioners received assurances that the Estates General would continue to support the VOC offensive in the East Indies and show them all favor, goodwill, and accommodation. Yet the petitioners never enjoyed the full benefit of the promised assistance, au contraire. Instead of receiving two fully armed warships, they were fobbed off with an unrigged vessel.

There is another problem as well. Because of their large equipages, the previous voyages have cost the Company nearly all its capital. After the departure of the eight ships commanded by Pauwels van Caerden, which are fitted out right now, there will be only five hundred thousand guilders left in the Company's war chest, barely enough to outfit two ships and a yacht for next year.[19] As for the return cargoes that we expect in the near future, nearly all of them belong to the fleet of fourteen ships commanded by Wybrandt van Warwyck, little remaining for the ten-year Company. In any case, we probably will not be able to use the proceeds of the return cargoes in the way we did before. For the VOC directors may well decide that the fleets of Van der Haghen and Matelief, along with the third one currently under preparation, carry greater complements and more ammunition and provisions than are strictly necessary for commercial purposes. Instead of these warships, they could have fitted out ten merchantmen for next year, for example.

In consideration of these excessive costs and the great service done to the Republic, Your Honors have not bestowed any extraordinary favors on the petitioners, but been very precise in levying taxes on booty captured at no cost to the country.[20] Nor are these tax revenues earmarked for the upkeep and increase of VOC privateering, even though they could hardly be spent on anything more appropriate. This must be disconcerting to the Company's many shareholders, who consented to the VOC offensive in the East Indies in the expectation of Your Honors' support. They undoubtedly realize that, provoked by our hostile procedures, the King of Spain will not spare any costs to shore up his position in the East Indies, and that the VOC cannot hope to be victorious without some material support from Your Honors, instead of admonishments and empty promises. Failing Your Honors' assistance, the VOC shareholders may well waver in their resolution and demand easy and immediate profits, eschewing great costs and dangers by means of a strictly defensive strategy. This could mean the demise of the East Indian navigation, wherein consists the welfare, indeed, the life of so many people, which all serves to invigorate the enemy.

Since Van Caerden's fleet is ready for departure and in need of instructions, which should include something about federal assistance, the petition-

19. Modern historians estimate the VOC's military expenditures at *f*420,000 (£42,000) per annum in the first two decades of its existence, which did indeed make it very difficult for the company to achieve a net surplus. Compare Hans den Haan, *Moedernegotie en grote vaart: een studie over de expansie van het Hollandse handelskapitaal in de 16e en 17e eeuw* (Amsterdam: SUA, 1977), 114–15, 119–20, 122.

20. A federal organization supervised by the Estates General, the Admiralty Board collected taxes on booty as well as import and export duties in order to finance the Dutch navy. All this was of little use to the VOC, however, as the Dutch navy limited its operations to European waters and never seemed particularly enthusiastic about lending the company its warships and cannons.

ers have considered it necessary to remind Your Honors of their many previous requests. They entreat Your Honors not to mishandle this important affair, but to finally decide on the most suitable means for giving effect to your earlier promises. The most convenient solution would be to assign them the resources that are crucial for waging the war in the East Indies, but do not burden Your Honors financially.

With Your Honors' permission, and provided His Excellency[21] gives his approval as well, we will bring together in an *aerarium militare*[22] all the ships, commodities, ammunition, prisoners' ransoms, and other kinds of booty captured at the VOC's expense in the East Indies. We will keep separate accounts for the *aerarium militare,* and make no disbursements to anyone, nor pay import taxes on East Indian goods. The *aerarium militare* will be used exclusively for waging war in the East Indies, ransoming Dutch prisoners, and safeguarding the places seized by the Company. If approved by Your Honors, an *aerarium militare* should result in memorable conquests and put courage into your subjects, who would save no trouble to attack even the most impregnable of fortresses, such as are of great importance to the enemy and will be even more so to Your Honors. These feats will be testimony to the fact that federal funds can nowhere be spent better for the honor, reputation, and benefit of the Republic and the enemy's evident ruination than in the East Indies. The petitioners trust that Your Honors will easily see the merits of this proposal, which will be of greater benefit to the common cause than to the petitioners themselves. While Your Honors would relinquish the fifth share of all booty taken in the East Indies, and His Excellency the thirtieth part, the petitioners should be content to contribute their four-fifths share to the war against Spain, which they could otherwise have invested in trade, yielding immediate and predictable profits. There would be one condition, however. The hostilities should serve the purpose of protecting this notable navigation and trade. The petitioners are perfectly willing to give Your Honors and His Excellency the opportunity to inspect the accounts of the *aerarium militare* once in a while. In addition, the petitioners would be happy to keep Your Honors and His Excellency informed about East Indian

21. As Lord High Admiral, Maurice of Nassau was entitled to a thirtieth share of the booty captured by the VOC.

22. A humanist flourish typical for Grotius: the Roman emperor Augustus had established a pension fund for his discharged soldiers in A.D. 6 called *aerarium militare.*

affairs. If the capture of several richly laden prizes should allow for some disbursements, after subtraction of the costs involved and the contribution to the *aerarium militare,* the petitioners will immediately provide Your Honors and His Excellency with the fifth and thirtieth shares of the booty, respectively.

May it please Your Honors to respond favorably to their petition or otherwise to depute a few members to first ascertain the importance of the issue and then report back to the Estates General, so that the case may finally be disposed of for the good of the country.

Herewith . . .

Petition or request submitted in March 1606 to the Estates General by the Directors of the East Indian Company.

VIII
Hugo Grotius to G. M. Lingelsheim[23]
November 1, 1606[24]

The little treatise on Indian affairs is complete: but I do not know whether it should be published as it was written or only those parts which pertain to the universal law of war and booty. Many indeed have dealt with this subject both old and new. But I believe that new light can be thrown on the matter with a fixed order of teaching, the right proportion of divine and human law mixed together with the dictates of philosophy.

23. Grotius was introduced to George Michael Lingelsheim in late May 1603, when the latter visited The Hague as an envoy of the Elector Palatine. Grotius corresponded with the Heidelberg town councilor for the remainder of his life.

24. There are only a few sentences that deal with *De Jure Praedae* in Grotius's letter to Lingelsheim. The entire letter, written in Latin, is printed in *Briefwisseling van Hugo Grotius,* 1:72.

IX
The Directors of the United Dutch East India Company to the Sultan of Tidore[25] Drafted by Hugo Grotius Winter of 1606–7[26]

Serene Highness,

It is not unknown to Your Majesty that the inhabitants of our Provinces [who are more inclined to commerce than all other peoples] have applied themselves to the East Indian trade for the past couple of years, initially laboring under the aegis of several regional companies. Yet we considered it appropriate to combine these regional companies into a general one [while expressly forbidding our subjects to trade in the East Indies unless employed by the aforesaid united company]. There were good reasons for pooling the resources of the inhabitants of these Provinces, which are so evidently full of ships and people (God be praised). Our purpose was not just to protect ourselves against the Spanish and Portuguese [*who have unjustly sought to proscribe free trade throughout the world*], but also to be most diligent in liberating East Indian princes and nations from Iberian tyranny. The enemy tyrannized them for many years, in accordance with his nature and habit [*which is to incorporate into his empire all earthly power and authority*]. Our people have shown great zeal and courage in pursuing this aim. Their efforts have been blessed by the Almighty, who abhors all pride and injustice; witness the various feats set before the eyes of Your Majesty and neighboring nations. For example, they captured the fortress which the Portuguese were [forcibly] occupying in Your Majesty's country, [*which contributed not a little to the safety and security of Your Majesty*] [which was the only way to liberate Your Majesty] and your subjects. We are determined to fight on to the bitter end and not to desist before we have the desired result. [To this purpose, we stationed twenty-five warships off the coast of [*new*] Spain [*in order to prevent enemy ships from*

25. Grotius Papers at the Dutch National Archives, Supplement I, fol. 344–66. Draft letters in Grotius's hand, addressed to various Asian rulers, including the "Queen" of Patani, the Samorin of Malabar, the "Seigneuries" of Banda and Ambon, and the "Kings" of Johore, Siau, Bantam, Ternate, and Tidore. The letter to the Sultan of Tidore covers folios 365–66.

26. Note on the Translation: The deletions and insertions found in Grotius's draft letter are included in this translation. They are separated from the main text by square brackets. Italic type stands for deleted text, roman type for inserted text.

sailing to the East Indies] in order to prevent the enemy from sending ships to the East Indies and force him to unload the vessels which were ready for departure.] [We have already prepared a [*new*] similar fleet, which will again be stationed off the enemy's coast in the coming year.][27]

We kindly request that Your Majesty, whose first priority must be the expulsion of our common enemies, be equally steadfast in your resolution. We trust Your Majesty's wisdom and experience, it being sufficiently known that strife and discord among East Indian princes has always served to strengthen the position of the [*Spanish and*] Portuguese. But if divided we fall, united we stand. It can hardly be doubted that [*the issues*] the differences that have arisen between Your Majesty and the King of Ternate and that still continue until this day—to our regret and the enemy's glee—will hamper the execution of our plans. Since our enemies are still very strong and not very far away, they may well take advantage of the situation. In order to guard against this and prevent private quarrels from endangering public liberty, we really must seriously admonish you, as we did the King of Ternate, to settle the dispute between you and become good allies. We offer Your Majesty all possible assistance and support to this purpose.

There is something else we would like to bring to your attention, Serene Highness. We receive daily reports that several of our neighbors want to try their hand at the East Indies trade, without having the will [*or power*] to do any harm to the Spanish and Portuguese, with whom they are at peace. The United Company of these Provinces, burdened by the costs of warfare, may suffer great damage as a result of their trade, which, in turn, would allow the enemy to remain lodged in the East Indies, unless some preventive measures are taken. We entreat Your Majesty to attend to this with your customary benevolence and prefer the aforesaid United Company to all others in matters of trade. A fast friendship and military alliance deserve favors from you that are greater than mere unpredictable profits.[28] While we expect these favors

27. A Dutch navy squadron under the command of Willem de Soete had blockaded Lisbon in April and May 1606, preventing the departure of the annual fleet of the Carreira da India. At the request of the Estates General, the VOC directors had subsidized this expedition to the tune of 125,000 guilders. The directors again put 125,000 guilders at the disposal of the Dutch navy in the spring of 1607, in the expectation that a naval blockade of Lisbon would do great damage to its Portuguese rival.

28. The English East India Company was the VOC's biggest competitor in the northern European spice markets. Sir Henry Middleton, the commander of its sec-

from you, we will not fail to [*show our appreciation*] reciprocate and confer similar or greater benefactions on you at every possible occasion. Meanwhile, we wish Your Majesty a long life and prosperous reign.

X
The Zeeland Directors of the United Dutch East India Company to Hugo Grotius
November 4, 1608[29]

Honorable, Wise, Prudent, and Very Distinguished Sir and Friend,
We have always considered it appropriate for the United Company to have the right of navigation—which is competent to the Dutch nation over the whole wide world—thoroughly examined and adduced with rational as well as legal arguments. It would serve to assure the inhabitants of these provinces of the worthiness of the cause, in case some still doubt it, and, more importantly, encourage neighboring princes and monarchs to help defend the nation's rights. What we deemed opportune in the past currently seems well nigh a necessity because of the peace and truce negotiations.[30] Regardless of whether the issue be peace or truce, the talks will have to give due consideration to our trade in the East Indies, along with our conquests and alliances there, which the King of Spain seeks to destroy with all his might. It is imperative to thwart his plans and persuade both our government and neighboring princes to staunchly defend our, as well as the nation's, rights. Although we were of this opinion already, we received further encouragement from the speech that Jan Boreel, J.D., delivered at our recent meeting.[31] He

ond voyage, had reached the Moluccas in late March 1605. At his arrival, he sought and was denied permission to trade there by the sultans of Ternate and Tidore, who were under heavy pressure from the Dutch commander Cornelis Bastiaanszoon. After the latter's victory over the Portuguese at Tidore, the VOC obtained the right of preemption in Ternate and Tidore, along with their subject territories. The sultans agreed to reserve the entire clove harvest for the VOC out of gratitude for their "liberation" from the Portuguese and in repayment of the military expenses that the VOC had incurred on their behalf.

29. The Dutch original may be found in *Briefwisseling van Hugo Grotius*, 1: 128–29.

30. The negotiations that resulted in the Twelve Years' Truce between Spain and the Netherlands (1609–21).

31. Johan Boreel was the eldest son of Zeeland VOC director Jacob Boreel and a close friend of Grotius. He was one of the few people to whom Grotius showed all

also suggested to us the best means for realizing our intentions, saying that you had already prepared all the material on this topic, which gave us great pleasure.

Since we do not doubt Your Honor's concern for the welfare of the United Company, we request that Your Honor assist the Company with your labors. Indeed, we trust that Your Honor has already received a similar request from the Amsterdam VOC directors. We ask that you be prompt in order that we may enjoy the benefit during the negotiations and bask in the favor of those who preside over the talks.[32]

We, along with the directors of the other VOC Chamber in Holland, are extremely obliged to Your Honor for your services.[33] Herewith, etc. Dated Middelburg, November 4, 1608.

Addressee:
Honorable, Wise, and Prudent Mr. Hugo de Groot, J.D.
Advocate-Fiscal of Holland, Zeeland, and West Friesland

The Hague

---

or part of the manuscript of *De Jure Praedae.* A newly discovered letter of Johan Boreel reveals that it was at his instigation that the Zeeland VOC directors requested the publication of *Mare Liberum.* His letter of November 6, 1608, explicitly mentions the directors' commissioning of *Mare Liberum*—"the VOC wrote to you on the subject familiar to you"—and his own efforts to bring this about—"I exhorted these tardy men to attend to their own affairs, and wrote letters as well." Compare *Briefwisseling van Hugo Grotius,* vol. 17 (2001), 41–42.

32. The special envoys of Henry IV of France and James I of England.

33. The United Dutch East India Company consisted of several "chambers," the remnants of the Holland and Zeeland trading companies that preceded the VOC.

The Dutch original literally says "the other chamber of Holland," which, considering the balance of power within the VOC, must denote the Amsterdam directors. If they ever contacted Grotius about the publication of *Mare Liberum,* their letter has not survived.

BIBLIOGRAPHY FOR INTRODUCTION AND NOTES

Manuscript Sources

Dutch National Archives (Nationaal Archief), The Hague, The Netherlands
    12551.21 (Loketkas Processen nr. 21), unfoliated
    Hugo Grotius Papers, Supplement I, fol. 344–66, 374–79

Manuscripts Collection of Leiden University Library, Leiden, The Netherlands
    Robert Fruin Papers (Ltk 1555-39), unfoliated

Printed Sources

Appendix oder Ergänzung desz achten Theils der Orientalischen Indien. Frankfurt-am-Main: Th. de Bry, 1606.

Coolhaas, W. Ph. "Een bron van het historische gedeelte van Hugo de Groot's *De Jure Praedae.*" *Bijdragen en Mededelingen van het Historisch Genootschap* 79 (1965): 415–540.

Grotius, Hugo. *Briefwisseling van Hugo Grotius.* Edited by P. C. Molhuysen, B. L. Meulenbroek, and H. J. M. Nellen. 17 vols. Vol. 1, *1583–1618* (RGP 64, Grote Serie). Vol. 3, *1626–1628* (RGP 105, Grote Serie). Vol. 17, *1583–1645* (RGP 248, Grote Serie). The Hague: Martinus Nijhoff, 1928–2001.

———. *Commentary on the Law of Prize and Booty.* Edited by Gwladys L. Williams and W. H. Zeydel. Vol. I, *A Translation of the Original Manuscript of 1604* by Gwladys L. Williams. Vol. II, *The Collotype Reproduction.* The Classics of International Law, no. 22. Oxford: Clarendon Press, 1950.

———. *De Jure Praedae Commentarius.* Edited by H. G. Hamaker. The Hague: Martinus Nijhoff, 1868.

———. *The Free Sea, with William Welwod's Critique and Grotius's Reply.*

Translated by Richard Hakluyt. Edited by David Armitage. Indianapolis: Liberty Fund, 2004.

Hulsius, Levinus. *Achte Schiffart, oder Kurtze Beschreibung etlicher Reysen so die Holländer und Seeländer in die Ost Indien von Anno 1599 bisz Anno 1604 gethan.* Frankfurt-am-Main: Matthis Beckern, 1608.

Leupen, P. A. "Kaartje van de Banda-eilanden vervaardigd door Emanoel Godinho De Eredia in 1601." *Bijdragen tot de Taal-, Land-, en Volkenkunde van Nederlandsch-Indië.* 3rd ser., 11 (1876): 386–91.

Les Negotiations de monsieur le President Jeannin. 4 vols. Amsterdam: Andries van Hoogenhuysen, 1695.

De Opkomst van het Nederlandsch Gezag in Oost-Indië (1595–1610). Edited by J. K. J. de Jonge. 3 vols. The Hague: Martinus Nijhoff, 1862–65.

O Roteiro das Cousas do Achem de D. João Ribeiro Gaio: Um olhar português sobre o Norte de Samatra em finais do século XVI. Edited by Jorge M. dos Santos Alves and Pierre-Yves Manguin. Lisbon: Comissão Nacional para as Comemoragões dos Descobrimentos Portugueses, 1997.

A Proclamation of the Lords of the Generall States. Goldsmiths'-Kress Library of Economic Literature, no. 292.2. London: John Wolfe, 1599.

Register van Holland en Westvriesland, 1604–1609. Printed minutes of the Estates of Holland.

Resolutiën der Staten-Generaal, 1579–1609. Printed resolutions of the Estates General of the Dutch Republic. Edited by N. Japikse and H. H. P. Rijperman. 14 vols. Vol. 12, *1602–1603* (RGP 92, Grote Serie). The Hague: Martinus Nijhoff, 1915–70.

Secondary Literature

Andrews, Kenneth R. *Elizabethan Privateering: English Privateering during the Spanish War, 1585–1603.* Cambridge: Cambridge University Press, 1964.

———. *Trade, Plunder, and Settlement: Maritime Enterprise and the Genesis of the British Empire, 1480–1630.* Cambridge: Cambridge University Press, 1984.

Borschberg, Peter. "*'De Pace':* Ein unveröffentlichtes Fragment von Hugo Grotius über Krieg und Frieden." *Zeitschrift der Savigny-Stiftung für Rechtsgeschichte, Romanistische Abteilung* 115 (1996): 268–92.

———. *"De Societate Publica cum Infidelibus:* Ein Frühwerk von Hugo Grotius." *Zeitschrift der Savigny-Stiftung für Rechtsgeschichte, Romanistische Abteilung* 115 (1998): 355–93.

———. "Grotius, East India Trade and the King of Johor." *Journal for South East Asian Studies* 30 (1999): 225–48.

———. *Hugo Grotius "Commentarius in Theses XI": An Early Treatise on Sovereignty, the Just War, and the Legitimacy of the Dutch Revolt.* Berne: Peter Lang, 1994.

———. "A Luso-Dutch Naval Confrontation in the Johor River Delta in 1603." *Zeitschrift der Deutschen Morgenländischen Gesellschaft* 153 (2003): 158–75.

———. "Luso-Johor-Dutch Relations in the Straits of Malacca and Singapore, ca. 1600–1623." *Itinerario* 28 (2004): 15–33.

———. "Portuguese, Spanish and Dutch Plans to Construct a Fort in the Straits of Singapore, *ca.* 1584–1625." *Archipel* 65 (2003): 55–88.

———. "Remapping the Straits of Singapore: New Insights from Old Sources." In *Iberians in the Singapore-Melaka Area (16th to 18th Century).* Edited by Peter Borschberg. South China and Maritime Asia, 14:93–130. Wiesbaden: Harrassowitz Verlag, 2004.

Boxer, C. R. "Portuguese and Spanish Projects for the Conquest of Southeast Asia, 1580–1600." *Journal of Asian History* 3 (1969): 118–36.

Cornelisz, Reyer. Peper, *Plancius en porselein: de reis van het schip "Swarte Leeuw" naar Atjeh en Bantam.* Edited by Jan Parmentier, Karel Davids, and John Everaert. Zutphen, The Netherlands: Walburg Press, 2003.

Enthoven, Victor. *Zeeland en de opkomst van de Republiek: Handel en Strijd in de Scheldedelta, ca. 1550–1621.* Ph.D. diss., Leiden University, 1996.

Foster, Sir William. *England's Quest of Eastern Trade.* London: Black, 1933.

Fruin, Robert. "An Unpublished Work of Hugo Grotius." *Bibliotheca Visseriana* 5 (1925): 3–74.

Gaastra, Femme S. *The Dutch East India Company: Expansion and Decline.* Zutphen, The Netherlands: Walburg Press, 2003.

Goor, Jurrien van. *Prelude to Colonialism: The Dutch in Asia.* Hilversum, The Netherlands: Verloren Publishers, 2004.

Haan, Hans den. *Moedernegotie en grote vaart: een studie over de expansie van het Hollandse handelskapitaal in de 16e en 17e eeuw.* Amsterdam: SUA, 1977.

Ittersum, Martine Julia van. "Hugo Grotius in Context: Van Heemskerck's Capture of the *Santa Catarina* and Its Justification in *De Jure Praedae* (1604–1606)." *Asian Journal of Social Science* 31 (2003): 511–48.

———. *Profit and Principle: Hugo Grotius, Natural Rights Theories and the Rise of Dutch Power in the East Indies, 1595–1615.* Studies in Intellectual History. Leiden: Brill Academic Publishers, 2006.

Nellen, H. J. M. *Hugo de Groot (1583–1645): De Loopbaan van een Geleerd Staatsman.* Weesp, The Netherlands: Heureka, 1985.

Tuck, Richard. *Natural Rights Theories: Their Origin and Development.* Cambridge: Cambridge University Press, 1979.

———. *Philosophy and Government, 1572–1651.* Cambridge: Cambridge University Press, 1993.

———. *The Rights of War and Peace: Political Thought and the International Order from Grotius to Kant.* Oxford: Oxford University Press, 1999.

SUGGESTIONS FOR FURTHER READING

Armitage, David. "The Fifty Years' Rift: Intellectual History and International Relations." *Modern Intellectual History* 1 (2004): 97–109.

———. *The Ideological Origins of the British Empire.* Cambridge: Cambridge University Press, 2000.

Brett, Annabel S. "Natural Right and Civil Community: The Civil Philosophy of Hugo Grotius." *Historical Journal* 45 (2002): 31–51.

Gelderen, Martin van. "The Challenge of Colonialism: Grotius and Vitoria on Natural Law and International Relations." *Grotiana,* n.s., 14–15 (1993–94): 3–37.

Grotius, Hugo. *The Free Sea, with William Welwod's Critique and Grotius's Reply.* Translated by Richard Hakluyt. Edited by David Armitage. Indianapolis: Liberty Fund, 2004.

———. *The Rights of War and Peace.* Edited by Richard Tuck. Indianapolis: Liberty Fund, 2005.

Haakonssen, Knud. "Hugo Grotius and the History of Political Thought." *Political Theory* 13 (1985): 239–65.

Hugo Grotius and International Relations. Edited by Hedley Bull, Benedict Kingsbury, and Adam Roberts. Oxford: Clarendon Press, 1990.

Keene, Edward. *Beyond the Anarchical Society: Grotius, Colonialism and Order in World Politics.* Cambridge: Cambridge University Press, 2002.

Pagden, Anthony. "Human Rights, Natural Rights, and Europe's Imperial Legacy." *Political Theory* 31 (2003): 171–99.

Seed, Patricia. *Ceremonies of Possession in Europe's Conquest of the New World, 1492–1640.* Cambridge: Cambridge University Press, 1995.

Tully, James. *A Discourse on Property: John Locke and His Adversaries.* Cambridge: Cambridge University Press, 1980.

INDEXES

AUTHOR INDEX

SUBJECT INDEX

This book is set in Adobe Garamond, a modern adaptation by Robert Slimbach of the typeface originally cut around 1540 by the French typographer and printer Claude Garamond. The Garamond face, with its small lowercase height and restrained contrast between thick and thin strokes, is a classic "old-style" face and has long been one of the most influential and widely used typefaces.

Printed on paper that is acid-free and meets the requirements of the American National Standard for Permanence of Paper for Printed Library Materials, z39.48-1992. ♾

Book design by Louise OFarrell
Gainesville, Florida
Typography by Apex Publishing, LLC
Madison, Wisconsin
Printed and bound by Worzalla Publishing Company
Stevens Point, Wisconsin